INSTRUCTOR'S MANUAL AND TEST BANK

Give Me Liberty!

An American History

FOURTH EDITION

VOLUME 1

Give Me Liberty!

An American History

FOURTH EDITION

By
Robert M. O'Brien

LONE STAR COLLEGE–CYFAIR

Volker Janssen

CALIFORNIA STATE UNIVERSITY–FULLERTON

VOLUME 1

W • W • NORTON & COMPANY • NEW YORK • LONDON

Printed in the United States of America
Layout/Composition by Westchester Publishing Services
Project Manager: Sean Mintus
Ancillary Editor: Lorraine Klimowich

Fourth Edition

ISBN 13: 978-0-393-92283-7 (pbk.)

W. W. Norton & Company, Inc., 500 Fifth Avenue, New York, NY 10110 wwnorton.com

W. W. Norton & Company Ltd., Castle House, 75/76 Wells Street, London W1T 3QT 1234567890

CONTENTS

PREFACE

When was the last time you were pleased with the consistency and quality of the assessment supplements that come with survey texts? If you are like most professors, you probably find that these assessment packages do not always meet your needs. To address this issue, Norton has collaborated with Valerie Shute (Florida State University) and Diego Zapata-Rivera (Educational Testing Services) to develop a methodology for delivering high-quality, valid, and reliable assessment supplements through our Test Banks and extensive suite of support materials.

WHY A NEW APPROACH?

In evaluating the Test Banks that accompany introductory texts, we found four substantive problem areas associated with the questions:

1. Test questions were misclassified in terms of type and difficulty.
2. The prevalence of low-level and factual questions misrepresented the goals of the course.
3. Topics were unevenly distributed: Trivial topics were tested via multiple items, while important concepts were not tested at all.
4. Links to course topics were too general, thus preventing diagnostic use of the item information.

STUDENT COMPETENCIES AND EVIDENCE-CENTERED DESIGN

In December 2007, Norton conducted a focus group with the brightest minds in educational testing to create a new model for assessment. A good assessment tool must:

1. define what students need to know and the level of knowledge and skills that constitute competence in the concepts they are learning about;
2. include test items that provide valid and reliable evidence of competence by assessing the material to be learned at the appropriate level; and
3. enable instructors to judge accurately what students know and how well they know it, thus allowing instructors to focus on areas where students need the most help.

HOW DOES IT WORK?

The Test Bank authors develop a concept map that identifies the core concepts present in each chapter of the textbook. Once the concept maps were created, the authors developed six types of questions designed to test students' knowledge of each concept. By asking students questions that vary in both type and level of difficulty, instructors can gather different types of evidence, which will allow them to assess more effectively how well students understand specific concepts.

LEARNING OBJECTIVES

The Focus Questions found at the beginning of each chapter in *Give Me Liberty* have been reformulated into a set of Learning Objectives for the American history survey course. After reading each chapter of the textbook and attending class or lecture, students should be able to meet these learning objectives, which have been worded to emphasize action verbs like "explain," "understand," or "summarize." By tying these outcomes to test questions, instructors can easily assess and report student mastery of state-mandated learning outcomes and similar core curricula.

SIX QUESTION TYPES

1. Remembering questions—test declarative knowledge, including textbook definitions and relationships between two or more pieces of information. Can students recall or remember the information in the same form it was learned?
2. Understanding questions—pose problems in a context different from the one in which the material was learned, requiring students to draw from their declarative and/or procedural understanding of important concepts. Can students explain ideas or concepts?
3. Applying questions—ask students to draw from their prior experience and use critical thinking skills to take part in qualitative reasoning about the real world. Can students use learned information in another task or situation?
4. Analyzing questions—test students' ability to break down information and see how different elements relate to each other and to the whole. Can students distinguish among the different parts?
5. Evaluating questions—ask students to assess information as a whole and frame their own argument. Can students justify a stand or decision?
6. Creating questions—pose questions or objectives that prompt students to put elements they have learned together into a coherent whole to generate new ideas. Can students create a new product or point of view based on data?

THREE DIFFICULTY LEVELS

1. Easy questions—require a basic understanding of the concepts, definitions, and examples presented in the textbook.
2. Moderate questions—direct students to use critical thinking skills and to demonstrate an understanding of core concepts independent of specific textbook examples.

3. Difficult questions—ask students to synthesize textbook concepts with their own experience, making analytical inferences about historical topics and more.

GENERAL RULES FOR NORTON ASSESSMENT

Each question measures and links explicitly to a specific competency and is written with clear, concise, and grammatically correct language that suits the difficulty level of the specific competency being assessed. To ensure the validity of the questions, no extraneous, ambiguous, or confusing material is included, and no slang expressions are used. In developing the questions, every effort has been made to eliminate bias (e.g., race, gender, cultural, ethnic, regional, disability, age, and so on) to require specific knowledge of the material studied, not general knowledge or experience. This ensures accessibility and validity.

READING THE TEST ITEM NOTATION

Each question in the Test Bank is tagged with six pieces of information designed to help instructors create the most ideal mix of questions for their quizzes or exams. These tags are:

ANS: This is the correct answer for each question.

DIF: This is the difficulty assigned to the problem. Problems have been classified as Easy, Moderate, or Difficult.

REF: This is the number of the page in the textbook from which a question is drawn. To ensure that the Test Bank material flows in the same order as the topics covered in the textbook, the questions have been numbered in order based on the "REF" field.

TOP: This references the topic, taken from the chapter opening concept map, that is tested by the question.

MSC: This is the knowledge type (see above) that the question is designed to test.

OBJ: This is the learning objective that is tested by the question.

CHAPTER 1 | A New World

This chapter concentrates on the contact between Indians and early European explorers and settlers in the Americas. It begins by examining the first Americans—the often quite sophisticated Native American cultures in South and North America before European contact. The next major theme is the European expansion pioneered by the Portuguese and Spanish and propelled by the search for African gold and a direct sea route to Asia. Portuguese contact with African societies, the voyages of Columbus, and the Spanish conquest of Mexico and South America are discussed, with critical analysis of the demographic consequences of those contacts. Other aspects of Spanish colonization—including justifications for conquest, economic matters, and Spanish-Indian relations—are also considered. The Spanish priest Bartolomé de Las Casas gives a damning report of Spanish rule in the New World in "Voices of Freedom." The Pueblo Revolt, an Indian uprising in New Mexico, is also highlighted in "Voices of Freedom," through the account of a Spanish-speaking Indian. The next section focuses on the French and Dutch empires in North America. The relatively few French who lived in New France (French Canada) consisted mainly of fur traders, indentured servants, and Jesuit missionaries. The French drew Indians into the Atlantic economy and into conflict with European powers. The Dutch, mainly interested in trade, established friendly commercial and diplomatic relations with the Iroquois but conflicted with other Indians over land in New Netherland.

CHAPTER OUTLINE

I. Introduction: Columbian Exchange

II. The First Americans
   A. The Settling of America

1. "Indians" settled the New World between 15,000 and 60,000 years ago, before the glaciers melted and submerged the land bridge between Asia and North America.
B. Indian Societies of the Americas
   1. North and South American societies built roads, trade networks, and irrigation systems.
   2. Societies from Mexico and areas south were grander in scale and organization than those north of Mexico.
      a. Indians north of Mexico lacked literacy, wheeled vehicles, metal tools, and scientific knowledge necessary for long-distance navigation.
C. Mound Builders of the Mississippi Valley
   1. Built approximately 3,500 years ago along the Mississippi River in modern-day Louisiana, a community known today as Poverty Point was a trading center for the Mississippi and Ohio River valleys.
   2. Near present-day St. Louis, the city known as Cahokia, which flourished with a population of 10,000–30,000 around 1200 CE, featured large human-built mounds.
D. Western Indians
   1. Hopi and Zuni ancestors settled around present-day Arizona and New Mexico and built large planned towns with multiple-family dwellings, and traded with peoples as far away as Mississippi and central Mexico.
   2. Indians in the Pacific Northwest lived primarily by fishing and gathering, whereas on the Great Plains, the Indians hunted buffalo or lived in agricultural communities.
E. Indians of Eastern North America

1. Indian tribes living in the eastern part of North America sustained themselves with a diet of corn, squash, and beans and supplemented it by fishing and hunting.
2. Native Americans believed sacred spirits could be found in living and inanimate things such as animals, plants, trees, water, and wind. This idea is known as animism.
3. Tribes frequently warred with one another; however, there were also many loose alliances.
4. Indians saw themselves as one group among many; the sheer diversity seen by the Europeans upon their arrival was remarkable.

F. Native American Religion
   1. Religious ceremonies were often directly related to farming and hunting.
   2. Those who were believed to hold special spiritual powers held positions of respect and authority.
   3. Indian religion did not pose a sharp distinction between the natural and the supernatural.

G. Land and Property
   1. The idea of owning private property was foreign to Indians.
   2. Indians believed land was a common resource, not an economic commodity.
   3. Wealth mattered little in Indian societies and generosity was far more important.

H. Indian Gender Relations
   1. Women could engage in premarital sex and choose to divorce their husbands, and most Indian societies were matrilineal.
   2. Since men were often away on hunts, women attended to the agricultural duties, as well as the household duties.

I. European Views of the Indians
   1. Europeans felt that Indians lacked genuine religion.
   2. Europeans claimed that Indians did not "use" the land and thus had no claim to it.
   3. Europeans viewed Indian men as weak and Indian women as mistreated.

III. Indian Freedom, European Freedom
   A. Indian Freedom
      1. Europeans concluded that the notion of freedom was alien to Indian societies.
      2. Europeans concluded that Indians were barbaric because they were *too* free.
      3. European understanding of freedom was based on ideas of personal independence and the ownership of private property—ideas foreign to Indians.

B. Christian Liberty
   1. Europeans believed that to embrace Christ was to provide freedom from sin.
   2. "Christian liberty" had no connection to later ideas of religious tolerance.

C. Freedom and Authority
   1. Europeans claimed that obedience to law was another definition of freedom; law was liberty's salvation.
   2. Under English law, women held very few rights and were submissive to their husbands.

D. Liberty and Liberties
   1. Liberty came from knowing one's place in a hierarchical society and fulfilling duties appropriate to one's rank.
   2. Numerous modern civil liberties (such as freedom of worship and of the press) did not exist.

IV. The Expansion of Europe
   A. Chinese and Portuguese Navigation
      1. Chinese admiral Zheng He led seven naval expeditions into the Indian Ocean between 1405 and 1433, even exploring East Africa on the sixth voyage.
      2. Caravel, compass, and quadrant made travel along the African coast possible for the Portuguese in the early fifteenth century.

B. Portugal and West Africa
   1. Africa was a wealthy continent and the search for African gold drove the early explorers.
   2. The Portuguese established trading posts, "factories," along the western coast of Africa.
   3. Portugal began colonizing Atlantic islands and established sugar plantations worked by slaves.

C. Freedom and Slavery in Africa
   1. Slavery was already one form of labor in Africa before the Europeans came.
   2. Europeans traded textiles and guns for African slaves; this greatly disrupted African society.
   3. By the time Vasco da Gama sailed to India in 1498, Portugal had established a vast trading empire.

D. The Voyages of Columbus
   1. Both commercial trade and religious conversions motivated Columbus.
   2. Christopher Columbus, an Italian, got financial support from King Ferdinand and Queen Isabella of Spain.
   3. In the same year, 1492, the king and queen completed the *reconquista*, ordering all Muslims and Jews to convert to Catholicism or leave the country.

V. Contact
- A. Columbus in the New World
  1. Columbus landed on Hispaniola in 1492 and colonization began the next year.
  2. Nicolas de Ovando established a permanent base in Hispaniola in 1502.
  3. Amerigo Vespucci sailed along the coast of South America between 1498 and 1502, and the New World came to be called America.
- B. Exploration and Conquest
  1. News could now travel quickly, especially with the invention of Johann Gutenberg's movable-type printing press in the early 1400s.
  2. John Cabot had traveled to Newfoundland in 1497 and soon many Europeans were exploring the New World.
  3. Vasco Núñez de Balboa trekked across Panama and was the first European to see the Pacific Ocean. Ferdinand Magellan led an expedition to sail around the world.
  4. Two Spanish conquistadores, Hernán Cortés and Francisco Pizarro, led devastating expeditions against the Aztec and Inca civilizations, respectively, in the early 1500s.
- C. The Demographic Disaster
  1. The Columbian Exchange transferred not only plants and animals, but also diseases, such as smallpox and influenza.
  2. The native populations were significantly depleted through wars, enslavement, and disease.

VI. The Spanish Empire
- A. Governing Spanish America
  1. Spain established a stable government modeled after Spanish home rule and absolutism.
     - a. Power flowed from the king to the Council of the Indies to viceroys to local officials.
  2. The Catholic Church played a significant role in the administration of Spanish colonies.
- B. Colonists in Spanish America
  1. Gold and silver mining was the primary economy in Spanish America.
     - a. Mines were worked by Indians.
     - b. Many Spaniards came to the New World for easier social mobility.
- C. Colonists and Indians
  1. Indian inhabitants always outnumbered European colonists and their descendants in Spanish America.
  2. Spanish America evolved into a hybrid culture—part Indian, part Spanish, and, in places, part African.
     - a. Mestizos are persons of mixed Indian and Spanish origin.

- D. Justifications for Conquest
  1. To justify their claims to land that belonged to someone else, the Spanish relied on cultural superiority, missionary zeal, and violence.
- E. Spreading the Faith
  1. A missionary element existed from the church's long holy war against Islam, and was renewed with the Protestant Reformation in the sixteenth century.
  2. National glory and religious mission went hand in hand, with the primary aim of the Spaniards to transform the Indians into obedient Catholic subjects of the crown.
- F. Piety and Profit
  1. The souls to be saved could also be a labor force in the gold and silver mines.
- G. Las Casas's Complaint
  1. Bartolomé de Las Casas wrote about the injustices of Spanish rule toward the Indians.
  2. Las Casas insisted that Indians were rational beings and Spain had no grounds to deprive them of their land or liberty.
  3. He believed that "the entire human race is one," but favored African slavery.
- H. Reforming the Empire
  1. Las Casas's writings encouraged the 1542 New Laws, which forbade the enslavement of Indians.
  2. The Black Legend was an image, put forth in part by Las Casas, that Spain was a uniquely brutal and exploitive colonizer.
- I. Exploring North America
  1. Spanish explorers migrated into what is now the United States in search of gold; first was Juan Ponce de León in Florida (1513).
  2. Large Spanish expeditions traveled through Florida, the Gulf of Mexico region, and the Southwest (1520s–1540s).
  3. These expeditions, particularly Hernando de Soto's, brutalized Indians and spread deadly diseases.
- J. Spanish Florida
  1. Florida, the first present-day U.S. area colonized by Spain, had forts as early as the 1560s to protect Spanish treasure fleets from pirates.
  2. Spanish missionaries sought to convert Indians, without much success.
  3. As late as 1763, Spanish Florida had only 4,000 inhabitants of European descent.
- K. Spain in the Southwest
  1. Juan de Oñate led settlers into present-day New Mexico (1598).

2. Oñate destroyed Acoma, a centuries-old Indian city, in response to an attack.
   L. The Pueblo Revolt
   1. In 1680 Pueblo Indians, led by Popé, rebelled against the Spanish colonists in present-day New Mexico for forcing the Indians to convert to Christianity.

VII. The French and Dutch Empires
   A. French Colonization
   1. The French were hoping to find gold and the Northwest Passage to the Pacific, but found only what they considered a barrier: a large North American continent.
   2. Samuel de Champlain founded Quebec in 1608, and others explored and claimed the entire Mississippi Valley for France.
   3. Relatively few French colonists arrived in New France; most were engagés (indentured servants), who returned home when their contracts expired. The white population in 1700 was only 19,000.
   B. New France and the Indians
   1. With few settlers, friendly relations with the Indians were essential for France.
   2. The French prided themselves on adopting a more humane policy toward the Indians than Spain, yet their contact still brought disease and their fur trading depleted the native animal population.
   3. The *métis* were children of Indian women and French men.
   C. The Dutch Empire
   1. Henry Hudson sailed into New York Harbor and claimed the area for the Netherlands (1609).
   2. Dutch traders established Fort Orange (near modern Albany) (1614) and the Dutch West India Company settled colonists on Manhattan Island (1626).
   3. The Netherlands dominated international commerce in the early seventeenth century.
   D. Dutch Freedom
   1. The Dutch prided themselves on their devotion to liberty; freedoms of the press and of private religious practice were unique to the Dutch.
   2. Amsterdam was a refuge for many persecuted Protestants and Jews.
   E. Freedom in New Netherland
   1. New Netherland was a military post, not governed democratically, but the citizens possessed rights.
   2. Slaves had "half-freedom" as they were given land to support families.

3. Women had more rights and independence than other European colonies as they could go to court, borrow money, and own property.
   F. The Dutch and Religious Toleration
   1. New Netherland was a remarkably diverse colony with eighteen different languages spoken in New Amsterdam.
   2. The Dutch were more tolerant in religious matters than other European countries, but they still had an official religion, the Dutch Reformed Church.
   3. Governor Petrus Stuyvesant denied open practice of other religious faiths.
   4. No one in New Netherland was forced to attend the Dutch Reformed Church or executed for different religious beliefs.
   G. Settling New Netherland
   1. Cheap livestock and free land after six years of labor were promised in an attempt to attract settlers.
   2. A plan was adopted to offer large estates to *patroons,* shareholders who agreed to transport tenants for agricultural labor.
   H. New Netherland and the Indians
   1. The Dutch came to trade, not to conquer, and were determined to treat the Indians more humanely, although conflict was not completely avoided.

SUGGESTED DISCUSSION QUESTIONS

- Compare and contrast the following precontact societies: Aztec, Inca, Cahokia, and the ancestors of the Hopi and Zuni.
- The Europeans' understanding of freedom based on ownership of private property had little meaning to most Indian societies. What was far more important than individual autonomy to most Indian communities, and why?
- Evaluate "Gold, God, and Glory" as reasons for the European conquest of the Americas. Did one outweigh another in motivating the Europeans? How were these reasons used to justify the conquest? How genuine were they?
- The conquest of the New World by the Europeans resulted in interaction among cultures. Discuss this interaction and how it affected both the Europeans and the Indians. Be sure to discuss the demographic consequences.
- Bartolomé de Las Casas was a voice of freedom for the Indians in Spanish America. Explain what motivated him to speak out. What kind of influence did he have on the Spanish? On the Indians? On the African slaves? In what sense was his understanding of freedom limited?

- Compare the Spanish colonies with those of the French and Dutch. Think about economies, freedoms, religion, government structure, and intermarriage. How did the French and Dutch learn from the experiences of the Spanish?
- Imagine you are an attorney accusing Spain of human rights violations in a sixteenth-century world criminal court. Draw on the "Voices of Freedom" pieces in this chapter to help you prepare your closing argument. What do you imagine Spain's defense attorney would argue?

SUPPLEMENTAL WEB AND VISUAL RESOURCES

American Beginnings
http://nationalhumanitiescenter.org/tserve/divam.htm
http://nationalhumanitiescenter.org/tserve/nattrans/nattrans.htm
http://nationalhumanitiescenter.org/pds/tblibrary.htm
The National Humanities Center. Teacher Serve: An Interactive Curriculum Enrichment Service for Teachers. Two sections: one on religion and the national culture and one on the environment in American history. Toolbox Library offers a plethora of primary sources, discussion questions, additional online sources, and talking points.

www.nhc.rtp.nc.us/pds/amerbegin/amerbegin.htm
The site takes you to American Beginnings: The European Presence in North America, 1492–1690.

Caribbean Amerindians
http://indigenouscaribbean.wordpress.com/articles/issues-in-indigenous-caribbean-studies/
Issues in Indigenous Caribbean Studies is a collection of online academic papers.

Columbian Exchange
www.nhc.rtp.nc.us/tserve/nattrans/ntecoindian/essays/columbian.htm
The National Humanities Center chronicles the Columbian Exchange with help from Alfred Crosby.

Conquistadors
www.pbs.org/conquistadors
This is a two-volume PBS Home Video hosted by Michael Wood. Wood travels the routes that the Spanish conquistadores took in the sixteenth century. Cortés and the Pizarro brothers are highlighted.

Images of Pre-Columbian America
http://www.hort.purdue.edu/newcrop/hort_306/reading/Images%2014.pdf
Hosted by Purdue, this site offers over fifty photographs of ancient artifacts.

1492: An Ongoing Voyage
www.ibiblio.org/expo/1492.exhibit/Intro.html
This is an exhibit hosted by the Library of Congress, providing a variety of resources and information about Columbus and the consequences of his voyage.

The Mound Builders
www.crt.state.la.us/parks/ipvertypt.aspx
The Louisiana State Department of Culture, Recreation and Tourism, Office of State Parks, offers this website of the Poverty Point Historic Site.

www.cr.nps.gov/archeology/feature/builder.htm
The National Park Service's archaeology site features a time line, artifacts, "delta voices," and more from the mound builders.

The Pueblo Revolt of 1680
www.pbs.org/weta/thewest/resources/archives/one/pueblo.htm
This PBS site offers useful information about the Pueblo Revolt. Also linked is information on the PBS documentary *The West,* the first volume of which covers the Pueblo Revolt.

SUPPLEMENTAL PRINT RESOURCES

Axtell, James. "The Moral Dimensions of 1492." *Historian* 56, no. 1 (1993): 17–28.
Bradley, James W. *Evolution of the Onondaga Iroquois: Accommodating Change, 1500–1655.* Lincoln: University of Nebraska Press, 2005.
Crosby, Alfred. *The Columbian Exchange: Biological and Cultural Consequences of 1492.* Westport, CT: Greenwood Press, 1972.
Davis, David Brion. "Constructing Race: A Reflection." *William and Mary Quarterly* 54, no. 1 (1997): 7–18.
Greenblatt, Stephen. *Marvelous Possessions: The Wonder of the New World.* Chicago: University of Chicago Press, 1991.
Lunenfield, Marvin, ed. *1492: Discovery, Invasion, Encounter: Sources and Interpretations.* Lexington, MA: Heath/Houghton Mifflin, 1991.
Pauketat, Timothy R. *Cahokia: Ancient America's Great City on the Mississippi.* New York: Viking Press, 2009.
Townsend, Camilla. "Burying the White Gods: New Perspectives on the Conquest of Mexico." *American Historical Review* 108, no. 3 (2003): 659–687.
Wright, Ronald. *Stolen Continents: 500 Years of Conquest and Resistance in the Americas.* New York: Mariner, 2005.

TEST BANK

Matching

TEST I

____ 1. Christopher Columbus
____ 2. Hernán Cortés
____ 3. Adam Smith

___ 4. Amerigo Vespucci
___ 5. John Cabot
___ 6. Pedro Cabral
___ 7. Bartolomé de Las Casas
___ 8. Samuel de Champlain
___ 9. Juan Ponce de Léon
___ 10. Vasco da Gama
___ 11. Johannes Gutenberg
___ 12. Zheng He

a. claimed Brazil for Portugal in 1500
b. founded Quebec
c. Italian who sailed for Spain in 1492
d. Dominican priest who preached against Spanish abuses of Indians
e. British economist who wrote *The Wealth of Nations*
f. Spanish conquistador who conquered the Aztecs
g. sailed around southern Africa and into the Indian Ocean
h. America was named for him
i. first European to discover Newfoundland in 1497
j. explored Florida
k. led seven large naval expeditions in early 1400s
l. developed movable-type printing press

Answer Key: c, f, e, h, i, a, d, b, j, g, l, k

TEST 2

___ 1. Columbian Exchange
___ 2. "coverture"
___ 3. New Laws
___ 4. mestizos
___ 5. Great League of Peace
___ 6. criollos
___ 7. Black Legend
___ 8. *patroons*
___ 9. matrilineal
___ 10. haciendas
___ 11. mound builders
___ 12. Pueblo Revolt

a. society centered on the mother's family
b. Spanish brutality
c. uprising against Spanish colonists in New Spain
d. Dutch landowners of large estates
e. large-scale farm owned by a Spanish landlord
f. persons of mixed Spanish and Indian origin
g. Spanish reform measures toward Indians
h. a married woman surrendering her legal identity
i. transfer of plants, animals, and diseases between New and Old Worlds
j. confederation of five Iroquois tribes
k. person born in the Spanish colonies of European ancestry
l. ancient residents of the Mississippi Valley region

Answer Key: i, h, g, f, j, k, b, d, a, e, l, c

Learning Objectives

1. Describe the patterns of Native American life in North America before Europeans arrived.
2. Explain how Indian and European ideas of freedom differed on the eve of contact.
3. Explain the reasons for European exploration in the New World.
4. Explain what happened when the peoples of the Americas came in contact with Europeans.
5. Identify the chief features of the Spanish empire in America.
6. Identify the chief features of the French and Dutch empires in North America.

Multiple Choice

1. Adam Smith recorded in 1776 that the "two greatest and most important" events in the history of mankind were the:
   a. discovery of America and the Portuguese sea route around Africa to Asia.
   b. discovery of America and the beginning of the slave trade.
   c. birth of mercantilism and the Portuguese sea route around Africa to Asia.
   d. beginning of the slave trade and the Portuguese sea route around Africa to Asia.
   e. discovery of America and the birth of mercantilism.

   ANS: A   TOP: Global awareness | Introduction: Columbian Exchange   DIF: Easy   REF: Full pp. 5, 18 | Seagull pp. 1, 15   MSC: Remembering   OBJ: 3

2. In approximately 7000 BCE, agriculture developed in the Americas in:
   a. the Mississippi Valley.
   b. Mexico and Peru.
   c. the Yucatan Peninsula.
   d. Chesapeake Bay.
   e. Brazil.

   ANS: B   TOP: Ethnicity | The Settling of America   DIF: Easy   REF: Full p. 6 | Seagull p. 5   MSC: Remembering   OBJ: 1

3. Both the Aztec and Inca empires were:
   a. rural and poor.
   b. small in population, but sophisticated in infrastructure.
   c. large, wealthy, and sophisticated.
   d. large in geographic size, but sparsely populated.
   e. rural, with few impressive buildings.

   ANS: C   TOP: Ethnicity | Indian Societies of the Americas   DIF: Easy   REF: Full p. 8 | Seagull pp. 4–5   MSC: Remembering   OBJ: 1

4. Which one of the following statements is true of the Aztec capital, Tenochtitlán?
   a. It had a complex system of canals, bridges, and dams, with the Great Temple at the center.
   b. It was located in the dense jungle of the Yucatan Peninsula.
   c. Its defeat was due to its leader surrendering too soon to Hernán Cortés, who was in fact outnumbered and outgunned.
   d. Technologically and architecturally, it was so far behind European capitals that its defeat was certain.
   e. It had the New World's first mass transit system.

   ANS: A   TOP: Ethnicity | Indian Societies of the Americas   DIF: Moderate   REF: Full p. 9 | Seagull p. 4   MSC: Remembering   OBJ: 1

5. The city situated along the Mississippi River with between 10,000 and 30,000 residents in the year 1200 is today known as:
   a. Poverty Point.
   b. Cahokia.
   c. Pueblo Bonita.
   d. Iroquois.
   e. Tenochtitlán.

   ANS: B   TOP: Ethnicity | Mound Builders of the Mississippi Valley   DIF: Easy   REF: Full p. 9 | Seagull p. 6   MSC: Remembering   OBJ: 1

6. Pueblo Indians lived in what is now:
   a. the eastern United States.
   b. the southwestern United States.
   c. Mexico.
   d. the northeastern United States.
   e. Central America.

   ANS: B   TOP: Ethnicity | Western Indians   DIF: Easy REF: Full p. 10 | Seagull p. 6   MSC: Remembering OBJ: 1

7. The Pueblo Indians encountered by the Spanish in the sixteenth century:
   a. had engaged in settled village life only briefly before the Spanish arrived.
   b. had been almost completely isolated from any other people before the Spanish arrived.
   c. used irrigation systems to aid their agricultural production.
   d. were called mound builders for the burial mounds they created.
   e. created a vast empire that included control of the Incas.

   ANS: C   TOP: Ethnicity | Western Indians DIF: Moderate   REF: Full p. 10 | Seagull p. 6 MSC: Remembering   OBJ: 1

8. Before the arrival of Columbus, Native North Americans:
   a. had elaborate trade networks.
   b. were entirely agricultural and rural.
   c. across the continent were very similar in their political and religious beliefs.
   d. always lived in small family units.
   e. lived only in coastal areas.

   ANS: A   TOP: Ethnicity | Indians of Eastern North America   DIF: Moderate   REF: Full p. 10 | Seagull p. 7   MSC: Understanding   OBJ: 1

9. When Europeans arrived, many Native Americans:
   a. tried to use them to enhance their standing with other Native Americans.
   b. immediately opened treaty negotiations.
   c. learned their languages.
   d. hid in nearby cave dwellings.
   e. simply attacked them.

   ANS: A   TOP: Ethnicity | Indians of Eastern North America   DIF: Easy   REF: Full p. 12 | Seagull p. 7 MSC: Remembering   OBJ: 4

10. Native American religious ceremonies:
    a. had nothing to do with farming or hunting.
    b. were related to the Native American belief that sacred spirits could be found in living and inanimate things.
    c. were designed to show that supernatural forces must control man.
    d. were the same in every community.
    e. did not exist until arriving Europeans insisted on knowing about Native American customs.

    ANS: B   TOP: Ethnicity | Cultural history | Native American Religion   DIF: Moderate   REF: Full p. 12 | Seagull pp. 7–8   MSC: Remembering   OBJ: 1

11. Which statement about the Indians of North America is FALSE?
    a. Indians were very diverse.
    b. The idea of private property was foreign to Indians.
    c. Many Indian societies were matrilineal.
    d. Indians did not covet wealth and material goods as the Europeans did.
    e. Indians lacked genuine religion.

    ANS: E   TOP: Ethnicity | Native American Religion DIF: Moderate   REF: Full p. 12 | Seagull p. 7 MSC: Understanding   OBJ: 1

12. How did Native Americans conceive of property?
    a. Native Americans believed that land should never be claimed.
    b. Families might use a specific plot of land for a season.
    c. Individuals could own land outright and pass it on to family members.

d. A family could claim land forever, but an individual could not.

e. Native Americans and Europeans conceived of property in the same way, though Europeans claimed otherwise as an excuse to take Indian land.

ANS: B   TOP: Ethnicity | Land and Property
DIF: Moderate   REF: Full p. 12 | Seagull p. 9
MSC: Remembering   OBJ: 1

13. Far more important to most Indian societies than freedom as personal independence were all of the following EXCEPT:
    a. kinship ties.
    b. secure rights to owning land.
    c. the ability to follow one's spiritual values.
    d. the well-being of one's community.
    e. the security of one's community.

ANS: B   TOP: Ethnicity | Land and Property
DIF: Moderate   REF: Full pp. 12–13 | Seagull p. 9
MSC: Understanding   OBJ: 1

14. Which one of the following is true about Native Americans and material wealth?
    a. Chiefs were expected to share some of their goods rather than hoard them.
    b. Eastern Native Americans were more materialistic than those who lived west of the Mississippi.
    c. Wealth mattered less to them than to Europeans, but inherited social status was equally important to both peoples.
    d. Native Americans actually suffered more social inequality than Europeans did.
    e. Native Americans had no material wealth.

ANS: A   TOP: Ethnicity | Land and Property
DIF: Moderate   REF: Full p. 13 | Seagull p. 9
MSC: Remembering   OBJ: 1

15. Which statement about gender relations is FALSE for most Native American societies?
    a. Men and women engaged in premarital sex.
    b. It was acceptable for a woman to seek a divorce.
    c. Tribal leaders were almost always women.
    d. Women owned dwellings and tools.
    e. Societies were matrilineal.

ANS: C   TOP: Ethnicity | Indian Gender Relations
DIF: Difficult   REF: Full p. 14 | Seagull p. 10
MSC: Understanding   OBJ: 1

16. Which one of the following was NOT true of women in Native American societies?
    a. In contrast to their European counterparts, it was considered more acceptable for them to engage in premarital sexual relations.

b. Children usually became members of the mother's family, not the father's.

c. Women often participated in the administration of village affairs and in agriculture.

d. Women dressed scantily by European standards.

e. Women made all decisions about trade relations with other tribes.

ANS: E   TOP: Ethnicity | Social history | Indian Gender Relations   DIF: Moderate   REF: Full p. 14 | Seagull p. 10   MSC: Understanding   OBJ: 1

17. Europeans tended to think which one of the following about Native Americans and their cultures?
    a. All Native Americans were gentle and friendly.
    b. Native Americans worshiped the same God that Europeans did, although they called him by different names.
    c. Native Americans failed to make use of the land, so it was acceptable for Europeans to take it and use it.
    d. Because Native American men engaged in masculine pursuits such as hunting and fishing, Indian gender divisions were acceptable.
    e. Native American cultures were actually superior to those of Europeans.

ANS: C   TOP: Ethnicity | European Views of the Indians   DIF: Moderate   REF: Full p. 15 | Seagull p. 11   MSC: Understanding   OBJ: 4

18. Europeans—particularly the English, French, and Dutch—generally claimed North American Indian land as their own based on:
    a. the Treaty of Tordesillas of 1494.
    b. the biblical story of Noah's division of the world among his sons.
    c. financial transactions between Indian peoples and themselves.
    d. their view that Indians did not use the land properly.
    e. various papal decrees that privileged the claims of European Christians over those of Indian "heathens."

ANS: D   TOP: Ethnicity | European Views of the Indians   DIF: Moderate   REF: Full p. 15 | Seagull p. 11   MSC: Remembering   OBJ: 4

19. As colonization began, the European idea of freedom:
    a. was enjoyed by a large portion of the population.
    b. included the idea of abandoning sin to embrace the teachings of Jesus Christ.
    c. included a few narrowly defined rights and privileges.
    d. would be completely unrecognizable to those alive today.
    e. embraced the view that Indians deserved liberty, too.

ANS: B   TOP: Cultural history | Christian Liberty
DIF: Difficult   REF: Full p. 16 | Seagull p. 13
MSC: Remembering   OBJ: 2

20. In Europe on the eve of colonization, one conception of freedom, called "Christian liberty,"
    a. was a set of ideas today known as "religious toleration."
    b. mingled ideas of freedom with servitude to Jesus Christ—concepts that were seen as mutually reinforcing.
    c. found expression in countries dominated by Catholics but not in primarily Protestant ones.
    d. argued that all Christians should have equal political rights.
    e. referred to the policy of trying to overthrow any non-Christian regime around the world.

    ANS: B   TOP: Cultural history | Christian Liberty
    DIF: Difficult   REF: Full p. 16 | Seagull p. 13
    MSC: Remembering   OBJ: 2

21. Which one of the following is true of religion in seventeenth-century Europe?
    a. Few nations had established churches.
    b. The churches condemned dissenters, but the governments protected them.
    c. Wars were fought over the right of an individual to religious freedom.
    d. Religious uniformity was thought to be essential to public order.
    e. Religious uniformity had nothing to do with ideas about public order.

    ANS: D   TOP: Social history | Christian Liberty
    DIF: Moderate   REF: Full p. 17 | Seagull p. 14
    MSC: Remembering   OBJ: 3

22. "Coverture" refers to:
    a. a woman's responsibility to wear a scarf covering her head when in public.
    b. knowing your place in society, especially at church when sitting in the pews.
    c. a tax one pays on one's property that is assessed quarterly.
    d. a woman surrendering her legal identity when she marries.
    e. a binding legal agreement between an indentured servant and his or her master.

    ANS: D   TOP: Social history | Freedom and Authority   DIF: Easy   REF: Full p. 17 | Seagull p. 14   MSC: Remembering   OBJ: 2

23. In England, social inequality:
    a. was part of a hierarchical society.
    b. did not keep British subjects from enjoying the same degree of individual freedom.
    c. did not mean that there was economic inequality.
    d. was banned under the doctrine of coverture.
    e. prompted Henry VIII's break with the Catholic Church.

    ANS: A   TOP: Social history | Freedom and Authority   DIF: Easy   REF: Full p. 17 | Seagull p. 14   MSC: Remembering   OBJ: 2

24. Under English law in the sixteenth and seventeenth centuries, women:
    a. enjoyed far greater rights than they did in Spain and Spanish America.
    b. who outlived their husbands were entitled to one-half of the husband's property.
    c. surrendered their legal identities when they married.
    d. were expected to submit to their husbands in public, but not in private.
    e. gained a great deal of personal and political power during the reigns of Queen Mary and Queen Elizabeth.

    ANS: C   TOP: Social history | Freedom and Authority
    DIF: Easy   REF: Full p. 17 | Seagull p. 14
    MSC: Remembering   OBJ: 2

25. What motivated the Portuguese to begin exploration to find a water route to India, China, and the East Indies?
    a. To prove that the world was round.
    b. To spread the Protestant faith.
    c. To establish land empires in India and China.
    d. To eliminate the Muslim "middlemen" in the luxury goods trade.
    e. To find markets for Portugal's surplus manufactured goods.

    ANS: D   TOP: Geographic issues | The Expansion of Europe   DIF: Moderate   REF: Full p. 18 | Seagull p. 15   MSC: Understanding   OBJ: 3

26. Portuguese trading posts along the western coast of Africa were called factories because:
    a. the merchants were known as factors.
    b. the trading posts made the goods there in makeshift factories.
    c. the African slaves built factories along the coast to manufacture guns.
    d. the slave traders called their system a labor factory.
    e. that is how the Africans translated "trading post."

    ANS: A   TOP: Economic development | Portugal and West Africa   DIF: Moderate   REF: Full p. 20 | Seagull p. 17   MSC: Remembering   OBJ: 3

27. Slavery in Africa:
    a. resulted from the arrival of Europeans.
    b. included no form of rights for the slaves.
    c. was the only kind of labor on that continent.

d. involved the enslavement of criminals, debtors, and war captives.

e. accelerated with the arrival of the French in the 1520s.

ANS: D   TOP: Social history | Freedom and Slavery in Africa   DIF: Easy   REF: Full p. 20 | Seagull p. 17   MSC: Remembering   OBJ: 3

28. Before the transatlantic slave trade began, approximately 100,000 African slaves were transported between 1450 and 1500 to:
a. England and Ireland.
b. Spain and France.
c. Portugal and Spain.
d. Portugal and the Netherlands.
e. England and the Netherlands.

ANS: C   TOP: Global awareness | Freedom and Slavery in Africa   DIF: Moderate   REF: Full p. 20 | Seagull p. 17   MSC: Remembering   OBJ: 3

29. Which one of the following statements about African slavery within Africa is FALSE?
a. African slaves tended to be criminals, debtors, or captives in war.
b. Slavery was one of several forms of labor in Africa.
c. Slaves had well-defined rights and could possess property.
d. The slave trade within Africa accelerated between 1450 and 1500.
e. Only men were taken for the slave trade.

ANS: E   TOP: Social history | Freedom and Slavery in Africa   DIF: Moderate   REF: Full p. 20 | Seagull p. 17   MSC: Understanding   OBJ: 3

30. The *reconquista* was the reconquest of Spain from the:
a. Jews.
b. British.
c. Protestants.
d. Moors.
e. Aztecs.

ANS: D   TOP: Global awareness | The Voyages of Columbus   DIF: Easy   REF: Full p. 21 | Seagull p. 19   MSC: Remembering   OBJ: 3

31. What geographic error did Columbus make?
a. He grossly underestimated the size of the earth.
b. He thought the earth was not round, but flat.
c. He was certain that India was east of the Americas.
d. He expected the weather in India to be the same as in the North Atlantic.
e. He confused the Atlantic Ocean with the Indian Ocean.

ANS: A   TOP: Geographic issues | The Voyages of Columbus   DIF: Easy   REF: Full p. 21 | Seagull p. 18   MSC: Remembering   OBJ: 3

32. What role did religion play in Columbus's explorations?
a. None whatsoever.
b. Columbus was determined to convert Native Americans to Christianity.
c. Catholics in Spain and Italy supported his expeditions because they wanted to end Muslim control of the eastern trade.
d. Columbus benefited from Ferdinand and Isabella's efforts to promote tolerance in Spain.
e. Spain wanted Columbus to find a refuge for the Jews the king was driving out of the country.

ANS: C   TOP: Geographic issues | The Voyages of Columbus   DIF: Difficult   REF: Full p. 21 | Seagull p. 18   MSC: Understanding   OBJ: 3

33. The first center of the Spanish empire in America:
a. was a prosperous settlement that Columbus created.
b. was the island of Hispaniola.
c. fell to Dutch raiders in 1506.
d. resulted from Columbus's last voyage to the New World in 1502.
e. was Cuba.

ANS: B   TOP: Geographic issues | Columbus in the New World   DIF: Easy   REF: Full p. 21 | Seagull p. 19   MSC: Remembering   OBJ: 5

34. Amerigo Vespucci:
a. named the New World after himself.
b. helped to correct Columbus's theory that he had found a route to Asia.
c. agreed with Columbus that Native Americans were East Indians.
d. was funded by the English.
e. actually named the continent Vespucci, but it was changed.

ANS: B   TOP: Geographic issues | Columbus in the New World   DIF: Moderate   REF: Full p. 23 | Seagull p. 19   MSC: Remembering   OBJ: 5

35. John Cabot sailed to:
a. Newfoundland.
b. New York.
c. Jamestown.
d. Hispaniola.
e. Quebec.

ANS: A   TOP: Geographic issues | Exploration and Conquest   DIF: Easy   REF: Full p. 23 | Seagull p. 20   MSC: Remembering   OBJ: 3

36. Why did European exploration of the New World proceed so rapidly after Columbus's discoveries?
a. Gutenberg's invention of the printing press enabled the rapid dissemination of information.
b. England, France, and Spain united to fund exploration, eliminating one of the problems that Columbus had faced.

c. Spain was determined to protect the Native Americans against Protestant missionaries from rival European states, inspiring the government to fund numerous expeditions.

d. The amount of gold that Columbus brought back to Spain was so inspiring that other countries inevitably followed suit.

e. The Dutch became involved and had more money than other countries to finance expeditions, so those other countries worked together and raced against the Dutch for control.

ANS: A   TOP: Geographic issues | Cultural history | Exploration and Conquest   DIF: Easy   REF: Full p. 23 | Seagull pp. 19–20   MSC: Remembering   OBJ: 3

37. In 1519, who became the first European explorer to encounter the Aztec empire?
    a. Vasco da Gama.
    b. Ferdinand Magellan.
    c. John Cabot.
    d. Hernán Cortés.
    e. Francisco Pizarro.

ANS: D   TOP: Chronology | Exploration and Conquest   DIF: Easy   REF: Full p. 23 | Seagull p. 21   MSC: Remembering   OBJ: 3

38. The ritual sacrifices practiced by the Aztecs:
    a. occurred one at a time and therefore were minimal.
    b. prompted most Aztecs to oppose their leaders, who opposed the sacrifices.
    c. disgusted Europeans despite their own practices of publicly executing criminals and burning witches at the stake.
    d. were always held at an arena in Tenochtitlán that resembled the Roman Colosseum.
    e. cost the Spanish several hundred men before Cortés conquered the Aztecs.

ANS: C   TOP: Ethnicity | Exploration and Conquest DIF: Moderate   REF: Full p. 23 | Seagull p. 21 MSC: Understanding   OBJ: 4

39. Which of the following was NOT a technique that Spanish conquistadores used to conquer Native American empires?
    a. Kidnapping a leader and holding him for ransom.
    b. Dividing and conquering them by taking advantage of old rivalries.
    c. Relying upon the spread of diseases, even though they may not have been introduced intentionally.
    d. Negotiating treaties.
    e. Using their superior military technology.

ANS: D   TOP: Ethnicity | Exploration and Conquest DIF: Easy   REF: Full pp. 23–24 | Seagull p. 21 MSC: Remembering   OBJ: 4

40. The transatlantic flow of people and goods such as corn, potatoes, horses, and sugarcane is called:
    a. globalization.
    b. the Columbian Exchange.
    c. the Great Circuit.
    d. the Atlantic system.
    e. trade.

ANS: B   TOP: Geographic issues | The Demographic Disaster   DIF: Moderate   REF: Full p. 24 | Seagull p. 21   MSC: Remembering   OBJ: 4

41. The Columbian Exchange was:
    a. the agreement that documented what Christopher Columbus would give to Spanish leaders in return for their sponsorship of his travel to the New World.
    b. the transatlantic flow of plants, animals, and germs that began after Christopher Columbus reached the New World.
    c. John Cabot's exploration of the New World, which brought more of the goods that Columbus had found back to the Old World.
    d. responsible for introducing corn, tomatoes, and potatoes to the Americas.
    e. the first store in the New World, named for the man who founded it.

ANS: B   TOP: Geographic issues | The Demographic Disaster   DIF: Moderate   REF: Full p. 24 | Seagull p. 21   MSC: Remembering   OBJ: 4

42. In 1492, the Native American population:
    a. was at least 100 million.
    b. lived exclusively in villages of no more than 1,000 individuals.
    c. declined catastrophically due to exposure to the Black Plague.
    d. lived mostly in what is today the United States.
    e. lived mostly in Central and South America.

ANS: E   TOP: Chronology | The Demographic Disaster   DIF: Moderate   REF: Full p. 24 | Seagull p. 22   MSC: Remembering   OBJ: 4

43. The Spanish empire in America:
    a. included most of the populated part of the New World but few of its natural resources, making the empire rich in people but poor economically.
    b. paled in comparison with the ancient Roman Empire.
    c. was, unlike the French and English New World empires, a mostly urban civilization.
    d. was centered in Lima, Peru.
    e. allowed religious freedom and therefore attracted colonists from throughout Europe.

ANS: C   TOP: Social history | The Spanish Empire DIF: Moderate   REF: Full p. 25 | Seagull p. 23 MSC: Understanding   OBJ: 5

44. The government of the Spanish empire in America:
    a. established the principle of the separation of church and state by keeping the Catholic Church out of civic affairs.
    b. was dominated by the conquistadores, who had conquered lands and retained control over them.
    c. included local officials who held a great deal of control.
    d. was troubled due to constant turmoil and local divisions back in Spain.
    e. operated out of Monterey, California.

    ANS: C   TOP: Political history, changes | Governing Spanish America   DIF: Moderate   REF: Full p. 25 | Seagull p. 23   MSC: Remembering   OBJ: 5

45. Alarmed by the destructiveness of the conquistadores, the Spanish crown replaced them with a more stable system of government headed by:
    a. lawyers and bureaucrats.
    b. bishops of the Catholic Church.
    c. landed wealthy elite.
    d. elected local officials.
    e. entrepreneurs.

    ANS: A   TOP: Political history, changes | Governing Spanish America   DIF: Moderate   REF: Full p. 25 | Seagull p. 23   MSC: Remembering   OBJ: 5

46. Which one of the following is true of agriculture in Spanish America?
    a. African-American slaves performed most of the labor.
    b. The main crops were vastly different than they had been before Spain's arrival.
    c. Spain introduced wheat as a crop.
    d. Indian slaves did the work on small-scale farms.
    e. Catholic priests were forbidden to be involved in farming.

    ANS: C   TOP: Economic development | Colonists in Spanish America   DIF: Difficult   REF: Full p. 25 | Seagull pp. 23–24   MSC: Remembering   OBJ: 5

47. Which one of the following is true of Spanish emigrants to the New World?
    a. Many of the early arrivals came to direct Native American labor.
    b. From the beginning, they arrived as families.
    c. They were all at the bottom of the social hierarchy.
    d. They soon outnumbered Native Americans.
    e. Only the residents of the Malaga province migrated.

    ANS: A   TOP: Social history | Colonists in Spanish America   DIF: Moderate   REF: Full p. 26 | Seagull p. 24   MSC: Remembering   OBJ: 4 / 5

48. Which one of the following statements about Spanish America is true?
    a. Over time, Spanish America evolved into a hybrid culture—part Spanish, part Indian, and, in some areas, part African.
    b. Mestizos enjoyed much political freedom and held most of the high government positions.
    c. Spaniards outnumbered the Indian inhabitants after fifty years of settlement.
    d. The Catholic Church played only a minor role in Spanish America.
    e. Spanish America was very rural and had few urban centers.

    ANS: A   TOP: Ethnicity | Colonists and Indians   DIF: Moderate   REF: Full p. 27 | Seagull p. 24   MSC: Understanding   OBJ: 4

49. The Spanish justified their claim to land in the New World through all of the following EXCEPT:
    a. believing that their culture was superior to that of the Indians.
    b. violence.
    c. a missionary zeal.
    d. a decree from the Pope.
    e. defeating the English fleet in 1588.

    ANS: E   TOP: Social history | Justifications for Conquest   DIF: Easy   REF: Full pp. 27–28 | Seagull p. 25   MSC: Remembering   OBJ: 5

50. In 1517, the German priest _____ began the Protestant Reformation by posting his Ninety-Five Theses, which accused the Catholic Church of worldliness and corruption.
    a. Martin Buber
    b. Ulrich Zwingli
    c. Martin Luther
    d. Reinhold Niebuhr
    e. Johannes Gutenberg

    ANS: C   TOP: Chronology | Spreading the Faith   DIF: Easy   REF: Full p. 28 | Seagull p. 25   MSC: Remembering   OBJ: 3

51. How did Spain justify enslaving Native Americans?
    a. The Spanish believed that enslavement could liberate Native Americans from their backwardness and savagery and introduce them to Christian civilization.
    b. Pope Alexander VI had approved Spanish slavery but banned slavery in Portuguese holdings in the New World.
    c. The writings of Bartolomé de Las Casas explained that the Bible approved slavery and that therefore it was acceptable.
    d. If England and France were to be defeated in the quest for empire, Spain needed to take a step they

had avoided—imposing slavery upon the native population.

e. The Spanish actually never enslaved Native Americans; the charge that they did was simply part of the Black Legend spread by the English and other enemies.

ANS: A   TOP: Social history | Piety and Profit
DIF: Moderate   REF: Full p. 29 | Seagull p. 26
MSC: Remembering   OBJ: 5

52. According to Bartolomé de Las Casas:
   a. Spain needed to institute a more humane system of Native American slavery in order to avoid offending Pope Paul III.
   b. Spain had caused the deaths of millions of innocent people in the New World.
   c. despite his opposition to slavery, he needed to keep his slaves so that he would have time to devote to working for abolition and emancipation.
   d. slavery needed to be eliminated entirely from the Earth.
   e. converting Native Americans to anything but Catholicism would lead to their death.

ANS: B   TOP: Social history | Las Casas's Complaint
DIF: Moderate   REF: Full p. 30 | Seagull p. 27
MSC: Remembering   OBJ: 4

53. Bartolomé de Las Casas argued that Indians:
   a. could be enslaved because they lacked true religion.
   b. were more akin to beasts than humans.
   c. should overthrow their cruel Spanish masters and reestablish the Inca and Aztec empires.
   d. were treated well by the Spanish.
   e. should enjoy "all guarantees of liberty and justice" as subjects of Spain.

ANS: E   TOP: Political history, changes | Las Casas's Complaint   DIF: Easy   REF: Full p. 30 | Seagull p. 27   MSC: Remembering   OBJ: 2 / 4

54. The New Laws of 1542:
   a. led Protestant Europeans to create the Black Legend about Spanish rule in the Americas.
   b. introduced the *encomienda* system.
   c. were adopted at the urging of Gonzalo Pizzaro, brother of Peru's conqueror.
   d. commanded that Indians no longer be enslaved in Spanish possessions.
   e. forbade the enslavement of Africans in New Spain.

ANS: D   TOP: Political history, changes | Reforming the Empire   DIF: Moderate   REF: Full pp. 30–31 | Seagull p. 27   MSC: Remembering   OBJ: 5

55. Which one of the following lists the events in proper chronological order, from first to last?
   a. Pueblo Revolt, the Dutch settle Manhattan, Quebec founded, Spain adopts New Laws
   b. Spain adopts New Laws, Pueblo Revolt, Quebec founded, the Dutch settle Manhattan
   c. Quebec founded, the Dutch settle Manhattan, Pueblo Revolt, Spain adopts New Laws
   d. The Dutch settle Manhattan, Spain adopts New Laws, Pueblo Revolt, Quebec founded
   e. Spain adopts New Laws, Quebec founded, the Dutch settle Manhattan, Pueblo Revolt

ANS: E   TOP: Chronology | Reforming the Empire | The Pueblo Revolt | French Colonization | The Dutch Empire   DIF: Difficult   REF: Full pp. 30–31, 34–35, 38, 41 | Seagull pp. 27, 31, 35, 38
MSC: Remembering   OBJ: 5 / 6

56. The Black Legend described:
   a. the Aztecs' view of Cortés.
   b. English pirates along the African coast.
   c. Spain as a uniquely brutal colonizer.
   d. Portugal as a vast trading empire.
   e. Indians as savages.

ANS: C   TOP: Global Awareness | Reforming the Empire   DIF: Moderate   REF: Full p. 31 | Seagull p. 28   MSC: Remembering   OBJ: 5

57. The *repartimiento* system established by the Spanish in the mid-1500s:
   a. officially designated Indians in New Spain as slaves of European colonists.
   b. recognized Indians as free but required them to perform a fixed amount of labor.
   c. gave voting rights in local assemblies to mestizos but not to *peninsulares*.
   d. required all Indians to convert to Catholicism or face execution.
   e. set up a system of local courts of law that proved essential to Spanish rule in Peru.

ANS: B   TOP: Economic development | Reforming the Empire   DIF: Moderate   REF: Full p. 31 | Seagull p. 28   MSC: Remembering   OBJ: 5

58. Exploring the North American interior in the 1500s, _____ was the first European to encounter the immense herds of buffalo that roamed the Great Plains.
   a. Francisco Vásquez de Coronado
   b. Hernando de Soto
   c. Jacques Marquette
   d. Juan Ponce de León
   e. Juan Rodríguez Cabrillo

ANS: A   TOP: Geographic issues | Exploring North America   DIF: Difficult   REF: Full p. 31 | Seagull pp. 28–29   MSC: Remembering   OBJ: 5

59. Which of the following is true of Spain's explorations of the New World?
    a. Individual conquistadores always traveled alone.
    b. Members of the Spanish parties suffered greatly from disease.
    c. Florida was the first region in the present-day United States that Spain colonized.
    d. Spain sought to forestall Portuguese incursions into the New World.
    e. Spain's explorations had no impact on the size of the Native American population.

ANS: C   TOP: Geographic issues | Spanish Florida   DIF: Moderate   REF: Full p. 33 | Seagull p. 29   MSC: Remembering   OBJ: 5

60. The Spanish set up outposts from Florida to South Carolina in part because:
    a. Spanish missionaries hoped to convert local Native Americans to Christianity.
    b. English colonists from Virginia were attacking Spanish settlements.
    c. they sought to prevent the escape of African slaves to English colonies located north and east of the Savannah River.
    d. the discovery of gold mines in central Florida meant that other powers were likely to encroach on Spanish territories.
    e. they needed to protect St. Augustine, which became the capital of New Spain in 1542.

ANS: A   TOP: Social history | Spanish Florida   DIF: Moderate   REF: Full p. 33 | Seagull p. 29   MSC: Remembering   OBJ: 5

61. Spanish Florida:
    a. attracted large numbers of settlers.
    b. became a British colony in 1607.
    c. was little more than an isolated military settlement.
    d. was the site of Juan de Oñate's attack on the inhabitants of Acoma.
    e. attracted mostly elderly Spaniards.

ANS: C   TOP: Political history, changes | Spanish Florida   DIF: Easy   REF: Full p. 33 | Seagull p. 29   MSC: Remembering   OBJ: 5

62. Acoma was an Indian city in present-day _____ that the Spanish destroyed.
    a. New Mexico
    b. Florida
    c. Cuba
    d. California
    e. Puerto Rico

ANS: A   TOP: Ethnicity | Spain in the Southwest   DIF: Moderate   REF: Full p. 33 | Seagull p. 31   MSC: Remembering   OBJ: 4

63. The first permanent European settlement in the Southwest, established in 1610, was:
    a. Tucson.
    b. Albuquerque.
    c. El Paso.
    d. San Diego.
    e. Santa Fe.

ANS: E   TOP: Chronology | Spain in the Southwest   DIF: Easy   REF: Full p. 34 | Seagull p. 31   MSC: Remembering   OBJ: 5

64. Which statement about the Pueblo Revolt is FALSE?
    a. It resulted in a wholesale expulsion of the Spanish settlers.
    b. It arose in part from missionaries burning Indian religious artifacts.
    c. It resulted in a total renunciation of Catholicism by the Indians.
    d. It was successful because the Pueblo peoples cooperated with each other.
    e. It was inspired by the Pope, but he died before the actual revolt took place.

ANS: E   TOP: Cultural history | Ethnicity | The Pueblo Revolt   DIF: Moderate   REF: Full pp. 34–35 | Seagull p. 34   MSC: Understanding   OBJ: 4

65. The first French explorations of the New World:
    a. brought great riches to France.
    b. were intended to locate the Northwest Passage.
    c. led to successful colonies in Newfoundland and Nova Scotia.
    d. were in response to an intense rivalry with the Netherlands.
    e. created no permanent settlements until the eighteenth century.

ANS: B   TOP: Geographic issues | French Colonization   DIF: Moderate   REF: Full p. 35 | Seagull p. 35   MSC: Remembering   OBJ: 6

66. The Pueblo Indian uprising of 1680:
    a. followed their leader Popé's arrest for engaging in sexual relations with a non–Native American woman.
    b. helped lead to the most complete victory for Native Americans over Europeans.
    c. was based entirely on economic factors.
    d. was the work of one Native American tribe.
    e. began a long tradition of cooperation between New Mexico's tribes.

ANS: B   TOP: Ethnicity | Social history | The Pueblo Revolt   DIF: Moderate   REF: Full p. 35 | Seagull p. 34   MSC: Understanding   OBJ: 4

67. In 1608, Samuel de Champlain founded:
    a. Montreal.
    b. New York.
    c. Champlain.
    d. Quebec.
    e. Albany.

    ANS: D   TOP: Chronology | French Colonization
    DIF: Easy   REF: Full p. 38 | Seagull p. 35
    MSC: Remembering   OBJ: 6

68. French Canada:
    a. was a very democratic colony.
    b. was founded by Jesuit priests who were working as fur traders as a way to meet and convert Native Americans.
    c. consisted mainly of male colonists.
    d. had, by 1700, twice as many colonists as all the English North American colonies combined.
    e. gave the French a world monopoly on fur production.

    ANS: C   TOP: Social history | French Colonization
    DIF: Moderate   REF: Full p. 38 | Seagull pp. 36–37
    MSC: Remembering   OBJ: 6

69. Which one of the following is true of New France?
    a. It was the subject of a great deal of favorable publicity throughout Europe.
    b. Its commitment to religious toleration was a source of great embarrassment for less tolerant powers like England and Spain.
    c. Its population was limited at best, because France feared that a significant emigration would undermine its role as a great European power.
    d. The only women allowed to reside there were nuns, a reflection of the French commitment to spreading Catholicism.
    e. Seigneuries were the only democratic areas in the colony.

    ANS: C   TOP: Social history | French Colonization
    DIF: Difficult   REF: Full p. 38 | Seagull p. 37
    MSC: Understanding   OBJ: 6

70. New France was characterized by:
    a. severe conflict between French settlers and the Indians.
    b. a well-defined line between Indian society and French society.
    c. more peaceful European-Indian relations than existed in New Spain.
    d. a Protestant missionary zeal to convert the Indians.
    e. its lack of devastating epidemics.

    ANS: C   TOP: Ethnicity | New France and the Indians   DIF: Easy   REF: Full pp. 38–40 | Seagull p. 37   MSC: Remembering   OBJ: 6

71. How did French involvement in the fur trade change life for Native Americans?
    a. It didn't; Native Americans were already hunting beaver and buffalo for their skins.
    b. Native Americans benefited economically but were able to avoid getting caught in European conflicts and rivalries.
    c. The French were willing to accept Native Americans into colonial society.
    d. The English and French quests for beaver pelts prompted a surge in the Native American population.
    e. It forced Native Americans to learn new trapping techniques that were far superior to their old ways.

    ANS: C   TOP: Social history | New France and the Indians   DIF: Moderate   REF: Full p. 40 | Seagull p. 37   MSC: Understanding   OBJ: 4

72. The Jesuit religious order was particularly influential in:
    a. New Netherland.
    b. Brazil.
    c. England.
    d. New France.
    e. Cuba.

    ANS: D   TOP: Cultural history | New France and the Indians   DIF: Easy   REF: Full p. 40 | Seagull pp. 37–38   MSC: Remembering   OBJ: 6

73. As early as 1615, the _____ people of present-day southern Ontario and upper New York State forged a trading alliance with the French, and many of them converted to Catholicism.
    a. Pequot
    b. Lenni Lenape
    c. Iroquois
    d. Cherokee
    e. Huron

    ANS: E   TOP: Ethnicity | New France and the Indians
    DIF: Moderate   REF: Full p. 40 | Seagull p. 38
    MSC: Remembering   OBJ: 6

74. Which one of the following was true of French relations with Native Americans?
    a. The French appropriated significant amounts of land for fur trading.
    b. The French were proud that they were considered tougher on Indians than their English and Spanish counterparts.
    c. The French sent nuns to try to Christianize the natives, because they understood that gender relations were different among Native Americans than they were among whites.
    d. Native Americans resented that the French had no need for their help in the fur trade.

e. Jesuit missionaries tried to convert Native Americans, but gave them far more independence than did Spanish missionaries.

ANS: E TOP: Social history | New France and the Indians DIF: Moderate REF: Full p. 40 | Seagull p. 37 MSC: Remembering OBJ: 6

75. Henry Hudson:
a. set sail into the bay that bears his name as a representative of the British empire.
b. was searching for the Pacific Coast.
c. hoped to find the Northwest Passage to Asia.
d. set up a Dutch colony based on the idea of consent of the governed.
e. was the architect of the Dutch overseas empire.

ANS: C TOP: Geographic issues | The Dutch Empire DIF: Easy REF: Full p. 41 | Seagull p. 38 MSC: Remembering OBJ: 3

76. Which European city was known in the early seventeenth century as a haven for persecuted Protestants from all over Europe and even for Jews fleeing Spain?
a. Amsterdam
b. Geneva
c. Marseilles
d. London
e. Brussels

ANS: A TOP: Global awareness | Dutch Freedom DIF: Moderate REF: Full p. 41 | Seagull p. 39 MSC: Remembering OBJ: 3

77. Which European country dominated international commerce in the early seventeenth century?
a. France
b. The Netherlands
c. Britain
d. Spain
e. Portugal

ANS: B TOP: Economic development | The Dutch Empire DIF: Easy REF: Full p. 41 | Seagull p. 39 MSC: Remembering OBJ: 3

78. How did the Dutch manifest their devotion to liberty?
a. They supported tolerance in religious matters in their colony.
b. Their colony was the first in the Americas to have a bill of rights.
c. They allowed freedom of speech.
d. They issued the Edict of New Netherland, declaring the Puritans to be heathens because they refused to allow religious freedom.
e. They gave men ownership of their wives, which gave married men the property ownership and inde-

pendence they needed to participate in political activities.

ANS: A TOP: Social history | The Dutch and Religious Toleration DIF: Moderate REF: Full p. 42 | Seagull p. 39 MSC: Remembering OBJ: 6

79. Which statement about New Netherland is FALSE?
a. Some slaves possessed half-freedom.
b. No elected assembly was established.
c. The Dutch enjoyed good commercial and diplomatic relations with the Five Iroquois Nations.
d. Women had many liberties, but could not retain their legal identity after marriage.
e. Religious toleration was extended to Catholics and Jews.

ANS: D TOP: Social history | Freedom in New Netherland | The Dutch and Religious Toleration DIF: Moderate REF: Full p. 42 | Seagull pp. 39–40 MSC: Remembering OBJ: 6

80. Which of the following is true of freedom in New Netherland?
a. The colony's elected assembly enjoyed greater rights of self-government than any English colonial legislative body.
b. The Dutch commitment to liberty prompted the colony to ban slavery there.
c. Religious intolerance led the Dutch to ban all Jewish peoples from the colony.
d. Of all of the colonies in the New World, New Netherland required the longest period of service from indentured servants.
e. Married women retained a legal identity separate from that of their husbands.

ANS: E TOP: Social history | Freedom in New Netherland DIF: Moderate REF: Full p. 42 | Seagull pp. 39–40 MSC: Remembering OBJ: 2

81. As governor of New Netherland, Petrus Stuyvesant:
a. welcomed all religious faiths to the colony.
b. favored Catholics over Jews in New Amsterdam.
c. encouraged the Dutch colonists to convert the Indians.
d. saw women as equals in the Dutch Reformed Church.
e. refused the open practice of religion by Quakers and Lutherans.

ANS: E TOP: Social history | The Dutch and Religious Toleration DIF: Moderate REF: Full p. 43 | Seagull p. 41 MSC: Remembering OBJ: 2

82. What does the seal of New Netherland, adopted by the Dutch West India Company in 1630, suggest is central to the colony's economic prospects?
a. tobacco
b. fish

c. silver
d. timber
e. fur

ANS: E   TOP: Economic development | New Netherland and the Indians   DIF: Easy
REF: Full p. 43 | Seagull p. 42   MSC: Remembering
OBJ: 6

83. Patroonship in New Netherland:
   a. was a great success, bringing thousands of new settlers to the colony.
   b. meant that shareholders received large estates for transporting tenants for agricultural labor.
   c. was like a system of medieval lords.
   d. led to one democratic manor led by Kiliaen van Rensselaer.
   e. involved joint Dutch and Indian control of farmland.

   ANS: B   TOP: Economic development | Settling New Netherland   DIF: Moderate   REF: Full p. 43 | Seagull p. 41   MSC: Understanding   OBJ: 6

84. In their relations with Native Americans, the Dutch:
   a. sought to imitate the Spanish.
   b. concentrated more on economics than religious conversion.
   c. tried to drive Native Americans into the Puritan colony.
   d. avoided warfare at all costs.
   e. called them members of a deceitful race.

   ANS: B   TOP: Economic development | New Netherland and the Indians   DIF: Easy   REF: Full pp. 44–45 | Seagull p. 42   MSC: Remembering   OBJ: 6

True or False

1. Agriculture did not come to the American continents, around Mexico and Peru, until approximately 1000 CE

   ANS: F   TOP: Social history | The Settling of America   DIF: Easy   REF: Full p. 6 | Seagull p. 5   MSC: Remembering   OBJ: 1

2. The mound builders were a sophisticated ancient peoples living in the American Southwest.

   ANS: F   TOP: Ethnicity | Mound Builders of the Mississippi Valley   DIF: Moderate   REF: Full p. 9 | Seagull p. 5   MSC: Remembering   OBJ: 1

3. The Indians of North America believed that land was a common resource and the basis of economic life.

   ANS: T   TOP: Ethnicity | Land and Property DIF: Moderate   REF: Full p. 12 | Seagull p. 9 MSC: Remembering   OBJ: 1

4. The Indians, although diverse, all seemed to observe religious ceremonies centered around hunting or farming.

   ANS: T   TOP: Ethnicity | Native American Religion DIF: Easy   REF: Full p. 12 | Seagull p. 7 MSC: Remembering   OBJ: 1

5. Most, although not all, Indian societies were matrilineal.

   ANS: T   TOP: Social history | Indian Gender Relations   DIF: Moderate   REF: Full p. 14 | Seagull p. 10   MSC: Remembering   OBJ: 1

6. "Christian liberty" was the basis for religious toleration.

   ANS: F   TOP: Cultural history | Christian Liberty DIF: Difficult   REF: Full p. 17 | Seagull p. 13 MSC: Remembering   OBJ: 2

7. Under English law, women held many legal rights and privileges.

   ANS: F   TOP: Social history | Freedom and Authority DIF: Moderate   REF: Full p. 17 | Seagull p. 14 MSC: Remembering   OBJ: 2

8. Portuguese seafarers initially hoped to locate African gold.

   ANS: T   TOP: Geographic issues | Chinese and Portuguese Navigation   DIF: Easy   REF: Full p. 19 | Seagull pp. 16–17   MSC: Remembering   OBJ: 3

9. The Spanish were the first to sail down the western coast of Africa, establishing trading posts, called factories.

   ANS: F   TOP: Economic development | Portugal and West Africa   DIF: Easy   REF: Full p. 20 | Seagull p. 17   MSC: Remembering   OBJ: 3

10. African society did not practice slavery before Europeans came.

   ANS: F   TOP: Social history | Freedom and Slavery in Africa   DIF: Easy   REF: Full p. 20 | Seagull p. 17   MSC: Remembering   OBJ: 3

11. Columbus was Spanish.

   ANS: F   TOP: Ethnicity | The Voyages of Columbus DIF: Moderate   REF: Full p. 20 | Seagull p. 18 MSC: Remembering   OBJ: 3

12. The Spanish *reconquista* required that all Muslims and Jews convert to Catholicism or leave Spain immediately.

   ANS: T   TOP: Political history, changes | The Voyages of Columbus   DIF: Easy   REF: Full p. 21 | Seagull p. 19   MSC: Remembering   OBJ: 6

13. Columbus first sailed to what is now Venezuela.

    ANS: F   TOP: Geographic issues | Columbus in the
    New World   DIF: Moderate   REF: Full p. 21 |
    Seagull p. 19   MSC: Remembering   OBJ: 6

14. Columbus established the first permanent settlement on
    Hispaniola in 1502.

    ANS: F   TOP: Geographic issues | Columbus in the
    New World   DIF: Difficult   REF: Full p. 21 |
    Seagull p. 19   MSC: Remembering   OBJ: 6

15. Thanks to Martin Luther, the movable-type printing
    press is one of the most important inventions in
    modern times, helping to rapidly disseminate
    information around the world.

    ANS: F   TOP: Cultural history | Exploration and Con-
    quest   DIF: Easy   REF: Full p. 23 | Seagull
    pp. 19–20   MSC: Remembering   OBJ: 6

16. Cortés conquered the capital city of the Aztec empire
    with an army of over 1,000 men.

    ANS: F   TOP: Geographic issues | Exploration and
    Conquest   DIF: Moderate   REF: Full pp. 23–24 |
    Seagull p. 21   MSC: Remembering   OBJ: 4

17. The catastrophic decline in the native populations of
    Spanish America was mostly due to the fact that they
    were not immune to European diseases.

    ANS: T   TOP: Geographic issues | The Demographic
    Disaster   DIF: Moderate   REF: Full p. 24 | Seagull
    p. 22   MSC: Remembering   OBJ: 4

18. By 1550, the Spanish empire in the New World
    exceeded the ancient Roman Empire in size.

    ANS: T   TOP: Political history, changes | The Spanish
    Empire   DIF: Moderate   REF: Full p. 25 | Seagull
    p. 23   MSC: Remembering   OBJ: 5

19. *Peninsulares* stood atop the social hierarchy in Spanish
    America.

    ANS: T   TOP: Social history | Colonists and Indians
    DIF: Difficult   REF: Full p. 26 | Seagull p. 24
    MSC: Remembering   OBJ: 5

20. Spain insisted that the primary goal of colonization
    was to save the Indians from heathenism.

    ANS: T   TOP: Cultural history | Spreading the Faith
    DIF: Moderate   REF: Full p. 28 | Seagull p. 26
    MSC: Remembering   OBJ: 5

21. The Spanish aim was to exterminate or remove the
    Indians from the New World.

    ANS: F   TOP: Ethnicity | Spreading the Faith
    DIF: Difficult   REF: Full p. 28 | Seagull p. 26
    MSC: Remembering   OBJ: 5

22. During the Pueblo Revolt, the Indians destroyed
    symbols of Catholic culture, like crosses and statues of
    the Virgin Mary.

    ANS: T   TOP: Cultural history | The Pueblo Revolt
    DIF: Easy   REF: Full p. 37 | Seagull p. 34
    MSC: Remembering   OBJ: 4

23. When the Edict of Nantes, which had granted religious
    toleration to French Protestants (Huguenots), was
    revoked in 1685, 100,000 Huguenots fled France for
    New France.

    ANS: F   TOP: Cultural history | French Colonization
    DIF: Moderate   REF: Full p. 38 | Seagull p. 37
    MSC: Remembering   OBJ: 6

24. Like the Spanish, the French often intermarried with
    the Indians, resulting in mixed-race children.

    ANS: T   TOP: Ethnicity | New France and the Indians
    DIF: Moderate   REF: Full p. 40 | Seagull p. 38
    MSC: Remembering   OBJ: 6

25. Before helping to colonize New France, the Jesuits had
    previously established missions in Asia.

    ANS: T   TOP: Cultural history | New France and the
    Indians   DIF: Moderate   REF: Full p. 40 | Seagull
    pp. 37–38   MSC: Remembering   OBJ: 6

26. The French established the first permanent European
    settlement in what would become New York City.

    ANS: F   TOP: Geographic issues | The Dutch Empire
    DIF: Moderate   REF: Full p. 41 | Seagull p. 38
    MSC: Remembering   OBJ: 6

27. In New Netherland the Dutch were intolerant of
    diverse religious practices and issued an edict that all
    had to convert to the Dutch Reformed Church.

    ANS: F   TOP: Cultural history | The Dutch and Reli-
    gious Toleration   DIF: Moderate   REF: Full
    pp. 42–43 | Seagull p. 41   MSC: Remembering
    OBJ: 6

Short Answer

Identify and give the historical significance of each of the
following terms, events, and people in a paragraph or two.

1. conquistadores
2. Pueblo Revolt
3. private property
4. African slave trade
5. Columbian Exchange
6. Indian freedom
7. Black Legend
8. mound builders
9. Christopher Columbus

10. Zheng He
11. Bartolomé de Las Casas
12. "coverture"
13. Jesuits

Essay Questions

1. Explain as thoroughly as you can how the slave trade affected African society.

   Answers will vary   TOP: Global awareness | Geographic issues | Political history, changes | Social history | Freedom and Slavery in Africa
   DIF: Moderate   MSC: Analyzing   OBJ: 3

2. One Spanish official remarked that "the maxim of the conqueror must be to settle." Explain what you think he meant by this statement. Illustrate the various ways conquerors settled the New World, commenting on what worked, what did not work, and the consequences of those methods.

   ANS: Answers will vary   TOP: Economic development | Ethnicity | Global awareness | Geographic issues | Political history, changes | Social history | Exploration and Conquest | Colonists in Spanish America | Colonists and Indians | Las Casas's Complaint | Reforming the Empire | The Pueblo Revolt | New France and the Indians | New Netherland and the Indians
   DIF: Moderate   MSC: Analyzing   OBJ: 3 / 4

3. Explain the chapter's title: "A New World." What was new? Is "new" an appropriate term? Does perspective play a role in calling the Americas new? Be sure to comment on whether freedom was new in this New World.

   ANS: Answers will vary   TOP: Chronology | Cultural history | Economic development | Ethnicity | Global awareness | Geographic issues | Political history, changes | Social history | Indian Freedom | Exploration and Conquest | Exploring North America | French Colonization | Freedom in New Netherland | The Demographic Disaster | Native American Religion | Land and Property | Indian Gender Relations | Colonists in Spanish America   DIF: Difficult   MSC: Evaluating   OBJ: 1 / 2 / 3 / 4 / 5 / 6

4. Compare Indian society with that of the Europeans. What differences were there? Similarities? Be sure to include in your analysis ideas about religion, land, and gender roles, as well as notions of freedom.

   ANS: Answers will vary   TOP: Cultural history | Economic development | Ethnicity | Global awareness | Geographic issues | Political history, changes | Social history | Native American Religion | Land and Property | Indian Gender Relations | Indian Freedom | Christian Liberty | Freedom and Authority | Liberty and Liberties   DIF: Moderate
   MSC: Analyzing   OBJ: 1 / 2 / 4

5. The Dutch prided themselves on their devotion to liberty. Explain what kinds of liberties and freedoms the Dutch recognized that other nations, such as Spain, did not. How did these notions of freedom affect the development of their North American empire? Be sure to include the Indians and slaves in your discussion.

   ANS: Answers will vary   TOP: Cultural history | Economic development | Ethnicity | Global awareness | Geographic issues | Political history, changes | Social history | The Dutch Empire | Dutch Freedom | Freedom in New Netherland | The Dutch and Religious Toleration | Settling New Netherland | New Netherland and the Indians   DIF: Moderate
   MSC: Analyzing   OBJ: 2 / 5 / 6

6. The sophistication and diversity of the peoples in the early Americas is remarkable. Explore that diversity in an essay that discusses early Native American culture, architecture, religion, gender relations, economy, and views of freedom.

   ANS: Answers will vary   TOP: Cultural history | Economic development | Ethnicity | Global awareness | Geographic issues | Political history, changes | Social history | Mound Builders of the Mississippi Valley | Western Indians | Indians of Eastern North America | Native American Religion | Land and Property | Indian Gender Relations   DIF: Moderate
   MSC: Analyzing   OBJ: 1 / 2

7. The Spanish had a long history of conquering in the name of God. From the *reconquista* to the conquistadores to the settlement of the New World, Spain justified its conquests as a mission to save the souls of heathens, while putting them to work in subhuman conditions. Explore this paradox of conquering and killing in the name of saving. Remember to think about what else was going on in the world at that time with regard to the Protestant Reformation and the Inquisition.

   ANS: Answers will vary   TOP: Cultural history | Economic development | Ethnicity | Global awareness | Geographic issues | Political history, changes | Social history | Justifications for Conquest | Spreading the Faith | Piety and Profit | Las Casas's Complaint | Reforming the Empire   DIF: Moderate
   MSC: Evaluating   OBJ: 3 / 4

CHAPTER 2 | Beginnings of English America, 1607–1660

This chapter concentrates on the early history of the Chesapeake and New England colonies, between 1607 and 1660. The chapter begins by exploring the motives behind English colonization of the New World, then considers who was emigrating to North America, and for what reasons. Contact with the Indians and the subsequent transformation of Indian life is examined. The settlement in the Chesapeake region, where tobacco emerged as the economic engine and most early colonists cultivated that crop as indentured servants, is compared with the more family- and spiritually-oriented, more economically diverse New England settlements. There is an ironic note in the story of New England's economic development: although Puritanism's religion-based work ethic partially encouraged the region's economic growth, the wealth it created eventually weakened the power and influence of Puritan authority. Religion and freedom are common themes in this chapter, relevant to the establishment of Maryland, Massachusetts, and Rhode Island. The Puritan distinction between moral liberty and religious freedom plays a significant role in the banishment of Roger Williams and Anne Hutchinson from the Massachusetts colony. Puritanism and liberty are highlighted in "Voices of Freedom," with excerpts from The Trial of Anne Hutchinson and from a speech given by John Winthrop. The chapter concludes by looking at the history of English ideas of freedom from the Magna Carta through England's Civil War of the 1640s, which gave the English the belief that they were the world's guardians of liberty. As such, the English believed they were destined to free the Americas from the hold of the Spanish.

CHAPTER OUTLINE

I. Introduction: Jamestown

II. England and the New World

A. Unifying the English Nation
  1. England's stability in the sixteenth century was undermined by religious conflicts.
B. England and Ireland
  1. England's methods to subdue Ireland in the sixteenth and early seventeenth centuries established patterns that would be repeated in America.
C. England and North America
  1. The English crown issued charters for individuals such as Sir Humphrey Gilbert and Sir Walter Raleigh to colonize America at their own expense, but both failed.
D. Spreading Protestantism
  1. Anti-Catholicism had become deeply ingrained in English popular culture.
  2. *A Discourse Concerning Western Planting* argued that settlement would strike a blow at England's most powerful Catholic enemy: Spain.
  3. National glory, profit, and a missionary zeal motivated the English crown to settle America with the goal of rivaling Spain and France.
E. The Social Crisis
  1. A worsening economy and the enclosure movement led to an increase in the number of poor and to a social crisis.
  2. Unruly poor were encouraged to leave England for the New World.
F. Masterless Men
  1. Thomas Moore's *Utopia* (1516) describes a place where settlers could go to escape the economic inequalities of Europe—a place such as many could imagine America to be.
  2. The English increasingly viewed America as a land where a man could control his own labor

and thus gain independence, particularly through the ownership of land.

III. The Coming of the English
   A. English Emigrants
      1. Sustained immigration was vital for the settlement's survival.
      2. Between 1607 and 1700, a little over half a million people left England.
         a. They settled in Ireland, the West Indies, and North America.
         b. The majority of settlers in North America were young, single men from the bottom rungs of English society.
   B. Indentured Servants
      1. Two-thirds of English settlers came to North America as indentured servants.
      2. Indentured servants did not enjoy any liberties while under contract.
   C. Land and Liberty
      1. Land was the basis of liberty including voting rights in most colonies.
      2. Colonies were started as huge land grants to a company or proprietor.
      3. Land was also a source of wealth and power for colonial officials.
   D. Englishmen and Indians
      1. As many more settlers went to the Chesapeake and New England than New Mexico, Florida, and New France combined, the English were chiefly interested in displacing the Indians and settling on their land.
      2. The English did emphasize converting Indians like the Spanish and French did.
      3. Most colonial authorities in practice recognized the Indians' title to land based on occupancy.
      4. The seventeenth century was marked by recurrent warfare between colonists and Indians.
         a. Wars gave the English a heightened sense of superiority.
   E. Transformation of Indian Life
      1. Like other colonial empires, the English used Indians as guides, trading partners, and allies in wars.
      2. English goods were eagerly integrated into Indian life.
      3. Over time, those European goods changed Indian farming, hunting, and cooking practices.
         a. Exchanges with Europeans stimulated warfare between Indian tribes.
   F. Changes in the Land
      1. As the English sought to reshape Indian society and culture, their practices only undermined traditional Indian society.

      2. Settlers fenced in more land and introduced more crops and livestock, transforming the natural environment.

IV. Settling the Chesapeake
   A. The Jamestown Colony
      1. Settlement and survival were questionable in the colony's early history because of high death rates, frequent changes in leadership, inadequate supplies from England, and placing gold before farming.
      2. By 1616, about 80 percent of the immigrants who had arrived in the first decade were dead.
      3. John Smith's tough leadership held the early colony together.
   B. From Company to Society
      1. New policies were adopted in 1618 so that the colony could survive.
         a. Headright system
         b. A charter of grants and liberties provided an elected assembly (House of Burgesses), which first met in 1619.
      2. The first blacks arrived in 1619, the first hint of slavery in the colony.
   C. Powhatan and Pocahontas
      1. Powhatan, the leader of thirty tribes near Jamestown, eagerly traded with the English.
      2. English-Indian relations were mostly peaceful early on.
         a. Smith tried to maintain the peace, but his return to England in 1610 brought tension and sporadic conflict between the two groups.
         b. After Pocahontas was captured by the English, she married John Rolfe in 1614, symbolizing Anglo-Indian harmony.
   D. The Uprising of 1622
      1. Once the English decided on a permanent colony instead of merely a trading post, conflict was inevitable.
         a. Opechancanough, brother of Powhatan, led an attack on Virginia's settlers in 1622.
      2. The English forced the Indians to recognize their subordination to the government at Jamestown and moved them onto reservations.
      3. The Virginia Company surrendered its charter to the crown in 1624.
   E. A Tobacco Colony
      1. Tobacco was Virginia's "gold" and its production reached 30 million pounds by the 1680s.
      2. The expansion of tobacco production led to an increased demand for field labor.
   F. Women and the Family
      1. Virginia society lacked a stable family life.

2. Social conditions opened the door to roles women rarely assumed in England.

G. The Maryland Experiment
1. Like in Virginia, tobacco came to dominate the economy and tobacco planters the society.
2. Maryland was established in 1632 as a proprietary colony under Cecilius Calvert.
3. Calvert imagined Maryland as a feudal domain.

H. Religion in Maryland
1. Calvert envisioned Maryland as a refuge for persecuted Catholics.
2. Most appointed officials were initially Catholic, but Protestants always outnumbered Catholics in the colony.
3. Although it had a high death rate, Maryland offered servants greater opportunity for land ownership than Virginia.

V. The New England Way
A. The Rise of Puritanism
1. Puritanism emerged from the Protestant Reformation in England.
   a. Puritans believed that the Church of England retained too many elements of Catholicism.
2. Puritans considered religious belief a complex and demanding matter, urging believers to seek the truth by reading the Bible and listening to sermons.
   a. Puritans followed the teachings of John Calvin.
   b. God predetermined who was saved and damned.

B. Moral Liberty
1. Many Puritans immigrated to the New World in hopes of establishing a Bible Commonwealth that would eventually influence England.
2. They came to America in search of liberty and the right to worship and govern themselves.
3. Puritans were governed by a "moral liberty," "a liberty to that only which is good," which was compatible with severe restraints on speech, religion, and personal behavior.

C. The Pilgrims at Plymouth
1. Pilgrims sailed in 1620 to Cape Cod aboard the *Mayflower*.
   a. Before going ashore, the adult men signed the Mayflower Compact, the first written frame of government in what is now the United States.
   b. Pilgrims settled first in an abandoned Indian village as many tribes had been decimated by European diseases introduced by traders.

2. Squanto provided much valuable help to the Pilgrims, and the first Thanksgiving in America was celebrated in 1621.

D. The Great Migration
1. The Massachusetts Bay Company was charted in 1629 by London merchants wanting to further the Puritan cause and to turn a profit from trade with the Indians.
2. New England settlement was very different from settlement in the Chesapeake colonies.
   a. New England had a more equal balance of men and women.
   b. New England enjoyed a healthier climate.
   c. New England had more families.

E. The Puritan Family
1. Puritans reproduced the family structure of England with men at the head of the household.
2. Women were allowed full church membership and divorce was legal, but a woman was expected to obey her husband fully.
3. Puritans believed that a woman achieved genuine freedom by fulfilling her prescribed social role and embracing subjection to her husband's authority.
4. New England had a higher birth rate than the Chesapeake region so much time was spent bearing and rearing children.

F. Government and Society in Massachusetts
1. Massachusetts was organized into self-governing towns.
   a. Each town had a Congregational Church and a school.
   b. To train an educated ministry, Harvard College was established in 1636.
2. The freemen of Massachusetts elected their governor.
3. Church government was decentralized.
   a. Full church membership was required to vote in colony-wide elections.
   b. Church and colonial government were intricately linked.

G. Church and State in Puritan Massachusetts
1. Puritans defined liberties by social rank, producing a rigid hierarchal society justified by God's will.
2. The Body of Liberties affirmed the rights of free speech and assembly and equal protection for all.
3. Although ministers were forbidden to hold office in Massachusetts, church and state were closely interconnected.
4. Puritans, like other faiths, believed that religious uniformity was essential to social order.
   a. Puritans were not tolerant of other religions.
   b. Puritans wanted to complete the Reformation and spread these ideas back to England.

VI. New Englanders Divided
  A. Roger Williams
    1. A young minister, Williams preached that any citizen ought to be free to practice whatever form of religion he chose.
    2. Williams believed that it was essential to separate church and state.
  B. Rhode Island and Connecticut
    1. Banished from Massachusetts in 1636, Williams established Rhode Island.
    2. Rhode Island was a beacon of religious freedom and democratic government.
    3. Other spin-offs from Massachusetts included New Haven and Hartford, which joined to become the colony of Connecticut in 1662.
  C. The Trials of Anne Hutchinson
    1. Hutchinson was a well-educated, articulate woman who charged that nearly all the ministers in Massachusetts were guilty of faulty preaching.
    2. Puritans in Massachusetts found the idea of religious pluralism troubling and Hutchinson was placed on trial in 1637 for sedition.
       a. Authorities charged her with Antinomianism (putting one's own judgment or faith above human law and church teachings).
       b. On trial she spoke of divine revelations.
       c. She and her followers were banished; she died in what is now New York.
    3. As seen with Williams and Hutchinson, Puritan New England was a place of religious intolerance.
  D. Puritans and Indians
    1. Colonial leaders had differing opinions about the English right to claim Indian land.
    2. To New England's leaders, the Indians represented both savagery and temptation.
       a. The Connecticut General Court set a penalty for anyone who chose to live with the Indians.
       b. The Puritans made no real attempt to convert the Indians in the first two decades.
  E. The Pequot War
    1. As the white population grew, conflict with the Indians became unavoidable, and the turning point came when a fur trader was killed by Pequots.
    2. Colonists warred against the Pequots in 1637, massacring 500 at the Indian village of Mystic and exterminating or selling into slavery the tribe.
    3. Removal of the Pequot opened the Connecticut River Valley to rapid white settlement.
  F. The New England Economy
    1. Most migrants were textile craftsmen and farmers.
    2. Fishing and timber were exported, but the economy centered on family farms.
  G. The Merchant Elite
    1. Per capita wealth was more equally distributed in New England than in the Chesapeake.
    2. A powerful merchant class rose up, assuming a growing role based on trade within the British empire.
    3. Some clashed with the church and left to establish a new town, Portsmouth, in New Hampshire.
  H. The Half-Way Covenant
    1. By 1650, many Massachusetts residents, children of the Great Migration generation, had been baptized as infants but could not prove they had undergone the conversion experience necessary for full church membership.
    2. The question arose: Could the children of this second generation be baptized?
    3. In 1662, the Half-Way Covenant answered with a compromise that allowed the grandchildren of the Great Migration generation to be baptized and be granted a kind of half-way membership in the church.
    4. As church membership stagnated, ministers castigated the people for various sins.

VII. Religion, Politics, and Freedom
  A. The Rights of Englishmen
    1. By 1600, the idea that certain rights of Englishmen applied to all within the kingdom had developed alongside the traditional definition of liberties.
    2. This tradition rested on the Magna Carta, which was signed by King John in 1215.
       a. It identified a series of liberties, which barons found to be the most beneficial.
    3. The Magna Carta over time came to embody the idea of English freedom:
       a. Habeas corpus
       b. The right to face one's accuser
       c. Trial by jury
  B. The English Civil War
    1. Unrest existed between Parliament and the Stuart monarchy, leading to the beheading of Charles I.
    2. Commonwealth established under Oliver Cromwell ruled England until 1660 when the monarchy was restored under Charles II.
    3. English Civil War of the 1640s illuminated debates about liberty and what it meant to be a freeborn Englishman.

C. England's Debate over Freedom
1. John Milton called for freedom of speech and of the press in the 1640s.
2. The Levellers called for an even greater expansion of liberty, moving away from a definition based on social class.
3. The Diggers was another political group attempting to give freedom an economic underpinning through the common ownership of land.
D. English Liberty
1. After the English Civil War, there emerged a more general definition of freedom grounded in the common rights of all individuals within the English realm:
  a. A belief in freedom as the common heritage of all Englishmen
  b. A belief that England was the world's guardian of liberty
E. The Civil War and English America
1. Most New Englanders sided with Parliament in the Civil War.
2. Ironically, Puritan leaders were uncomfortable with the religious toleration for Protestants gaining favor in England, as it was Parliament that granted Williams his charter for Rhode Island.
3. A number of Hutchinson's followers became Quakers; four were hanged in Massachusetts.
F. The Crisis in Maryland
1. Virginia sided with Charles I, but in Maryland, crisis erupted into civil war.
2. In 1649, Maryland adopted an Act Concerning Religion, which institutionalized the principles of toleration that had prevailed from the colony's beginning.
G. Cromwell and the Empire
1. Oliver Cromwell, who ruled England from 1649 until his death in 1658, pursued an aggressive policy of colonial expansion, promotion of Protestantism, and commercial empowerment in the British Isles and the Western Hemisphere.
2. The next century was a time of crisis and consolidation.

SUGGESTED DISCUSSION QUESTIONS

• What motivated England to colonize the New World? How similar to or different from Spain's motives, discussed in Chapter 1, were England's?
• Why was the Jamestown Colony unstable and its survival questionable? Who settled there? What were their goals? How did they interact with the Indians?
• Explain the religious attitudes of settlers in Maryland. How did those compare to the religious attitudes in Massachusetts and in Rhode Island? How was religious freedom defined in each of these colonies?
• What were the differences between the Pilgrims and the Puritans? Were they the same? Compare the Plymouth Colony with the Massachusetts Bay Colony.
• How were Puritan women expected to achieve genuine freedom?
• Explain how Roger Williams and Anne Hutchinson showed how the Puritan belief in each individual's ability to interpret the Bible could easily lead to criticism of the religious establishment.
• Discuss the idea of the rights of Englishmen and what that meant to the settlers in the New World. How did the English Civil War affect the colonists' understanding of their rights?
• Discuss Puritan theology. How does it compare to your own theology, if you have one? How does it use the utopian ideas of America as a place to begin anew—as a place to be able to worship and govern freely—to justify its rather rigid doctrine?
• What points do you imagine John Winthrop and Roger Williams would have made in a debate about church-state relations? Explore this by creating a fictional dialogue between the two men.

SUPPLEMENTAL WEB AND VISUAL RESOURCES

American Beginnings
http://nationalhumanitiescenter.org/tserve/divam.htm
http://nationalhumanitiescenter.org/tserve/nattrans/nattrans.htm
http://nationalhumanitiescenter.org/pds/tblibrary.htm
The National Humanities Center. Teacher Serve: An Interactive Curriculum Enrichment Service for Teachers. Two sections: one on religion and the national culture and one on the environment in American history. Toolbox Library offers a plethora of primary sources, discussion questions, additional online sources, and talking points.

www.nhc.rtp.nc.us/pds/amerbegin/amerbegin.htm
The site takes you to American Beginnings: The European Presence in North America, 1492–1690.

Chesapeake Colonies
www.marinersmuseum.org/sites/micro/cbhf/colonial/col001.html
The Mariner's Museum's website contains the history of the various colonies in the Chesapeake Bay area.

Mayflower History

   www.mayflowerhistory.com

   Home page for a site that provides historical facts about the *Mayflower* and full-text primary sources of books and letters written by passengers of the *Mayflower.*

Plymouth Colony

   www.plimoth.org

   Plimoth Plantation in Massachusetts offers living history, online activities, and useful tours. This is a Smithsonian Institution Affiliations program.

Pocahontas

   http://apva.org/rediscovery/page.php?page_id=26

   This website provides helpful information to separate myth from fact about Pocahontas and her remarkable life as the Indian woman who saved John Smith's life and married Jamestown settler John Rolfe.

The 1629 Charter of Massachusetts Bay

   www.law.ou.edu/hist/massbay.html

   The University of Oklahoma Law Center has posted the charter of the Massachusetts Bay Company.

Virtual Jamestown

   jefferson.village.virginia.edu/vcdh/jamestown

   This is perfect for the classroom. It offers 3-D creations of the village, documents, interviews, maps, labor contracts, court records, and public records.

SUPPLEMENTAL PRINT RESOURCES

Banner, Stuart. *How the Indians Lost Their Land: Law and Power on the Frontier.* Cambridge, MA: Harvard University Press, 2005.

Bragdon, Kathleen J. *The Columbia Guide to the American Indians of the Northeast.* Columbia Guides to American Indian History and Culture Series. New York: Columbia University Press, 2001.

Irwin, Raymond. "Cast Out from the 'City upon a Hill': Antinomianism Exiles in Rhode Island, 1638–1650." *Rhode Island History* 52, no. 1 (1994): 2–19.

Kupperman, Karen Ordahl. *The Jamestown Project.* Cambridge, MA: Harvard University Press, 2007.

Morgan, Edmund. *The Puritan Dilemma: The Story of John Winthrop.* White Plains, NY: Pearson Longman, 1999.

Morgan, Edmund. *Roger Williams: The Church and the State.* New York: W. W. Norton & Company, 2007.

Quitt, Martin. "Trade and Accumulation at Jamestown, 1607–1609: The Limits of Understanding." *William and Mary Quarterly* 52, no. 2 (1995): 227–258.

Russell, Conrad. *The Causes of the English Civil War.* New York: Oxford University Press, 1990.

Saxton, Martha. "Bearing the Burden? Puritan Wives." *History Today* (1994): 28–33.

Townsend, Camilla. *Pocahontas and the Powhatan Dilemma.* New York: Hill and Wang, 2004.

TEST BANK

Matching

TEST 1

____ 1. Squanto
____ 2. John Smith
____ 3. Anne Hutchinson
____ 4. Powhatan
____ 5. John Calvin
____ 6. Roger Williams
____ 7. Cecilius Calvert
____ 8. John Winthrop
____ 9. William Bradford
____ 10. Pocahontas
____ 11. Walter Raleigh
____ 12. Henry Care

a. proprietor of Maryland
b. wife of John Rolfe
c. Pilgrim leader
d. leader of Indians near Jamestown
e. governor of Massachusetts
f. his settlement at Roanoke Island failed
g. was denounced for Antinomianism
h. Indian who helped the Pilgrims
i. French-born theologian who influenced the Puritans
j. established Rhode Island
k. believed a balanced constitution was essential to liberties
l. early leader of Jamestown

Answer Key: h, l, g, d, i, j, a, e, c, b, f, k

TEST 2

____ 1. Virginia Company
____ 2. an Act Concerning Religion
____ 3. Puritans
____ 4. tobacco
____ 5. Mayflower Compact
____ 6. headright system
____ 7. Quakers
____ 8. indentured servant
____ 9. House of Burgesses
____ 10. Half-Way Covenant
____ 11. Magna Carta
____ 12. Levellers

a. principles of religious toleration
b. believed the spirit of God dwelled in all persons
c. gave five to seven years of service for passage to America
d. first elected assembly in colonial America
e. charter company that established Jamestown

f. first written frame of government in British America
g. a religious compromise for the descendants of the Great Migration
h. primary crop of the Chesapeake colonies
i. argued the Church of England was still too Catholic
j. granted fifty acres to anyone who paid his own passage
k. a political movement favoring expanded liberties
l. written in 1215, this document was said to embody English freedom

Answer Key: e, a, i, h, f, j, b, c, d, g, l, k

Learning Objectives

1. Describe the main contours of English colonization in the seventeenth century.
2. Identify the obstacles the English settlers in the Chesapeake had to overcome.
3. Explain how Virginia and Maryland developed in their early years.
4. Identify what made the English settlement of New England distinctive.
5. Describe the main sources of discord in early New England.
6. Explain how the English Civil War affected the colonies in America.

Multiple Choice

1. In 1607, the colonists who sailed to Jamestown on three small ships:
   a. were funded entirely by the queen's government.
   b. chose an inland site partly to avoid the possibility of attack by Spanish warships.
   c. were officers and sailors in the British Royal Navy.
   d. built a colony at Cape Henry in the mouth of Chesapeake Bay.
   e. were members of Puritan congregations in search of religious freedom.

   ANS: B   TOP: Geographic issues | Introduction
   DIF: Moderate   REF: Full p. 49 | Seagull p. 45
   MSC: Remembering   OBJ: 3

2. The 104 settlers who remained in Virginia after the ships that brought them from England returned home:
   a. were all men, reflecting the Virginia Company's interest in searching for gold as opposed to building a functioning society.
   b. included women and children, because the Virginia Company realized that a stable society would improve the settlers' chances of success, economic and otherwise.
   c. included representatives of several other countries, part of England's effort to build a strong network of supporters in case of Spanish attack.
   d. built the second permanent British settlement in North America after Roanoke.
   e. were only half of those who originally set sail; the rest turned around and went back.

   ANS: A   TOP: Social history | Introduction
   DIF: Moderate   REF: Full p. 49 | Seagull p. 46
   MSC: Remembering   OBJ: 3

3. Which one of the following lists these colonies in the proper chronological order by the dates they were founded, from the earliest to the latest?
   a. Plymouth, Jamestown, Massachusetts Bay, Rhode Island
   b. Plymouth, Massachusetts Bay, Rhode Island, Jamestown
   c. Jamestown, Massachusetts Bay, Plymouth, Rhode Island
   d. Massachusetts Bay, Plymouth, Rhode Island, Jamestown
   e. Jamestown, Plymouth, Massachusetts Bay, Rhode Island

   ANS: E   TOP: Chronology | Introduction
   DIF: Difficult   REF: Full p. 50 | Seagull p. 48
   MSC: Remembering   OBJ: 3 / 4

4. Why did King Henry VIII break from the Catholic Church?
   a. The Pope had banned England from exploring the New World because the Church already had limited land ownership there to Spain and Portugal.
   b. He wanted a divorce, and the Pope refused to grant it.
   c. He was trying to unify Great Britain.
   d. He wanted to be pope, and the College of Cardinals refused to elect an English Catholic.
   e. He thought the Catholic Church was corrupt and he wanted to protect the English people from its abuses.

   ANS: B   TOP: Global awareness | Unifying the English Nation   DIF: Moderate   REF: Full p. 50 | Seagull p. 47   MSC: Remembering   OBJ: 1

5. Which one of the following statements is true of Queen Mary of England, who reigned from 1553 to 1558?
   a. She ascended to the throne immediately after a long period of civil war and successfully unified the nation.
   b. Her refusal to marry led to her designation as "the Virgin Queen," after whom Virginia was named.
   c. When the Pope refused to allow her to divorce her French royal husband, she founded an independent Church of England.
   d. She temporarily restored Catholicism as the state religion of England.
   e. Under her authority, colonists established the first permanent English settlement in North America.

ANS: D   TOP: Global awareness | Unifying the English Nation   DIF: Moderate   REF: Full p. 50 | Seagull p. 47   MSC: Remembering   OBJ: 1

6. Why did Sir Humphrey Gilbert and Sir Walter Raleigh fail in their attempts to colonize the New World?
   a. The government provided insufficient financial support.
   b. They were more interested in agriculture than in trade, and they chose areas without good farmland.
   c. They tried to set up colonies on the coast of Florida, and the Spanish fought off their attempts.
   d. Native Americans attacked the settlers, driving them from the land.
   e. They tried to mingle Protestants and Catholics, who were unable to get along.

   ANS: A   TOP: Economic development | England and North America   DIF: Moderate   REF: Full p. 51 | Seagull p. 49   MSC: Understanding   OBJ: 1

7. During the reign of _____, the English government turned its attention to North America by granting charters to Humphrey Gilbert and Walter Raleigh for the establishment of colonies there.
   a. Henry VIII
   b. Mary I
   c. James I
   d. James II
   e. Elizabeth I

   ANS: E   TOP: Global awareness | England and North America   DIF: Moderate   REF: Full p. 51 | Seagull p. 49   MSC: Remembering   OBJ: 1

8. Just as the reconquest of Spain from the Moors established patterns that would be repeated in Spanish New World colonization, the methods used in which one of the following countries anticipated policies England would undertake in America?
   a. Ireland
   b. India
   c. China
   d. Scotland
   e. Wales

   ANS: A   TOP: Global awareness | England and Ireland   DIF: Easy   REF: Full p. 51 | Seagull p. 48   MSC: Remembering   OBJ: 1

9. Why did England consider Spain its enemy by the late 1500s?
   a. Because of religious differences: England had officially broken with the Roman Catholic Church, while Spain was devoutly Catholic.
   b. Because of the Spanish Armada's successful invasion of Great Britain in 1588.

c. Because Spain had allied with France to invade English colonies in the New World.
d. Because one of Henry VIII's beheaded wives was a Spanish princess, and the Spanish government announced it would be at war with England until Henry apologized.
e. Because both the English and Spanish royal families laid claim to the Irish throne.

   ANS: A   TOP: Global awareness | Spreading Protestantism   DIF: Moderate   REF: Full p. 52 | Seagull p. 50   MSC: Remembering   OBJ: 1

10. How did Richard Hakluyt explain his claim that there was a connection between freedom and colonization?
    a. The English constitutional system would improve on Spain's less structured system in the New World.
    b. English colonization would save the New World from Spanish tyranny.
    c. The only way to achieve true freedom was through wealth, and the abundant gold in the New World would make all Englishmen wealthy.
    d. A person was only truly free when outside the constraints of established societies such as those in Europe.
    e. He claimed no such connection; he saw them as separate and unrelated.

    ANS: B   TOP: Global awareness | Spreading Protestantism   DIF: Difficult   REF: Full p. 52 | Seagull p. 50   MSC: Understanding   OBJ: 1

11. All of the following contributed to the English social crisis of the late sixteenth century EXCEPT:
    a. a lower birth rate, which made it difficult to find workers for new industries.
    b. the enclosure movement, which forced thousands of peasants from farms.
    c. increased prices buoyed by the influx of gold and silver from Latin America.
    d. decreased wages in the cities.
    e. the invasion of the cities by vagrants, who wandered the roads in search of work.

    ANS: A   TOP: Social history | Economic development | The Social Crisis   DIF: Difficult   REF: Full p. 53 | Seagull p. 51   MSC: Understanding   OBJ: 1

12. As a result of British landowners evicting peasants from their lands in the sixteenth and seventeenth centuries:
    a. there was an increase in the number of jobless peasants, whom the British government aided with an early form of welfare.
    b. efforts were made to persuade or even force those who had been evicted to settle in the New World, thereby easing the British population crisis.

c. mass numbers of peasants converted from Protestantism to Catholicism, because the Catholic Church took better care of the poor.
d. there was a sharp reduction in the number of sheep and other livestock.
e. the spread of the Black Plague decreased because of the elimination of cramped living quarters.

ANS: B   TOP: Social history | Economic development | The Social Crisis   DIF: Moderate   REF: Full p. 53 | Seagull p. 51   MSC: Remembering   OBJ: 1

13. Which one of the following is true of poverty in seventeenth-century Great Britain?
a. About half of the population lived at or below the poverty line by the end of the seventeenth century.
b. The problem was so bad that Henry VIII authorized judges to order the jobless to work.
c. Poverty rates were worse in British colonies than in the mother country.
d. John Winthrop solved the problem by creating the Massachusetts Bay Colony.
e. Queen Mary's failure to address the problem helped lead to her overthrow.

ANS: A   TOP: Social history | Economic development | The Social Crisis   DIF: Difficult   REF: Full p. 53 | Seagull p. 51   MSC: Remembering   OBJ: 1

14. In Great Britain, the idea of working for wages:
a. was so dishonorable that many refused to accept money for their work and instead received food and shelter.
b. was associated with servility and the loss of liberty.
c. was romanticized in ballads and tales.
d. meant true freedom.
e. grew more popular among the poor during the sixteenth century.

ANS: B   TOP: Social history | Masterless Men   DIF: Moderate   REF: Full p. 53 | Seagull p. 52   MSC: Remembering   OBJ: 1

15. What did English settlers in North America believe was the basis of liberty?
a. literacy
b. land
c. the English Bill of Rights
d. church membership
e. a wage-paying job

ANS: B   TOP: Political history, changes | Land and Liberty   DIF: Moderate   REF: Full p. 54 | Seagull p. 54   MSC: Remembering   OBJ: 1

16. Of the half million people who left England between 1607 and 1700:
a. more than half of them settled in North America.

b. more went to the West Indies than to North America.
c. Ireland was the most popular destination, far outdistancing other English colonies.
d. about half returned.
e. almost all were members of aristocratic families.

ANS: B   TOP: Geographic issues | English Emigrants   DIF: Difficult   REF: Full p. 54 | Seagull pp. 52–53   MSC: Remembering   OBJ: 2

17. Most seventeenth-century migrants to North America from England:
a. arrived with other members of their families.
b. were single, middle-class men.
c. were lower-class men.
d. had been released from debtors' prisons.
e. sought to escape the Black Death then ravaging England.

ANS: C   TOP: Social history | English Emigrants   DIF: Moderate   REF: Full p. 54 | Seagull p. 53   MSC: Remembering   OBJ: 2

18. During the seventeenth century, indentured servants:
a. made up less than one-third of English settlers in America.
b. had to surrender their freedom for a minimum of ten years to come to the colonies.
c. had a great deal of trouble acquiring land.
d. had to pay half of the fare to get them to the New World.
e. were almost entirely Irish.

ANS: C   TOP: Social history | Economic development | Indentured Servants   DIF: Moderate   REF: Full p. 55 | Seagull p. 54   MSC: Remembering   OBJ: 2

19. Which one of the following is true of indentured servants?
a. They could not be sold by their masters.
b. Their masters could determine whether they could marry.
c. Pregnant women received their freedom early.
d. They could not be physically punished because, unlike slaves, they had rights as English citizens.
e. Three-quarters of them ran away and found permanent freedom.

ANS: B   TOP: Social history | Indentured Servants   DIF: Moderate   REF: Full p. 55 | Seagull p. 53   MSC: Remembering   OBJ: 2

20. How did indentured servants display a fondness for freedom?
a. They became abolitionists, fighting to end slavery in British North America.
b. Some of them ran away or were disobedient toward their masters.

c. They sent letters home telling their fellow Englishmen that the American colonies offered special opportunities for freedom.

d. They insisted on their right to serve in the militia, because they believed in the right to bear arms.

e. They published pamphlets criticizing their masters, displaying their love of free speech.

ANS: B   TOP: Social history | Indentured Servants
DIF: Moderate   REF: Full p. 55 | Seagull p. 54
MSC: Remembering   OBJ: 2

21. Intermarriage between English colonists and Native Americans in Virginia:

a. began with the wedding of John Smith and Pocahontas.

b. was common.

c. was very rare before being outlawed by the Virginia legislature in 1691.

d. created a mixed race of Native Americans who often wound up enslaved.

e. produced a member of a British royal family who became an Indian chief.

ANS: C   TOP: Social history | Ethnicity |
    Englishmen and Indians   DIF: Moderate
REF: Full p. 56 | Seagull p. 54   MSC: Remembering
OBJ: 2

22. In regard to religion:

a. Native Americans eagerly converted to Christianity.

b. the English showed curiosity toward Native American religions.

c. Native Americans showed indifference to European religious conflict.

d. the English spent much time in Native American villages converting them.

e. the English created churches for Native Americans in most New England towns.

ANS: C   TOP: Social history | Ethnicity | Englishmen and Indians   DIF: Moderate   REF: Full pp. 56–57 | Seagull p. 55   MSC: Understanding   OBJ: 2

23. Which of the following best describes how the English viewed Native American ties to the land?

a. Although they felt the natives had no claim since they did not cultivate or improve the land, the English usually bought their land, albeit through treaties they forced on Indians.

b. They simply tried to wipe out Native Americans and then took their land.

c. They encouraged settlers to move onto Native American land and take it.

d. They totally respected those ties and let the natives stay in all rural areas, negotiating settlements to obtain the coastal lands.

e. The English offered natives the chance to remain on the land as slaves and, when this offer was declined, forced them off of it.

ANS: A   TOP: Social history | Ethnicity |
    Englishmen and Indians   DIF: Moderate   REF:
    Full p. 57 | Seagull p. 55   MSC: Understanding
OBJ: 2

24. Which of the following is true of warfare between colonists and Native Americans during the seventeenth century?

a. Colonists were surprised and disappointed in their inability to defeat Indians easily.

b. Among the colonists, it generated a strong sense of superiority.

c. New England colonists fared far better in warfare than their Virginia counterparts.

d. Treaties quickly ended each of the wars.

e. Native Americans actually had more sophisticated and dangerous weaponry than the English.

ANS: B   TOP: Social history | Ethnicity |
    Englishmen and Indians   DIF: Difficult
REF: Full p. 57 | Seagull p. 55   MSC: Understanding
OBJ: 2

25. In the economic exchanges between the English colonists and eastern Native Americans:

a. the arrival of new English goods had no impact on how Indians lived.

b. Native Americans initially welcomed the colonists' goods.

c. Native Americans sought to keep English goods from influencing their religious ceremonies.

d. Native Americans never became integrated into the Atlantic economy.

e. Native Americans soon saw that the colonists' goods were shoddier than their own.

ANS: B   TOP: Ethnicity | Economic development |
    Transformation of Indian Life   DIF: Moderate
REF: Full p. 57 | Seagull p. 55   MSC: Remembering
OBJ: 2

26. Who received most of the profits from trade between Native Americans and colonists?

a. Native Americans

b. British soldiers

c. colonial and European merchants

d. the king

e. Parliament

ANS: C   TOP: Ethnicity | Economic development |
    Transformation of Indian Life   DIF: Easy
REF: Full p. 57 | Seagull p. 56   MSC: Remembering
OBJ: 2

27. Which English group did the most to reshape Native American society and culture in the seventeenth century?
    a. traders
    b. religious missionaries
    c. colonial authorities
    d. settlers farming the land
    e. the Royal Geographical Society

    ANS: D   TOP: Social history | Changes in the Land
    DIF: Moderate   REF: Full p. 58 | Seagull p. 56
    MSC: Remembering   OBJ: 2

28. Which of the following is NOT a way that colonists undermined traditional Native American agriculture and hunting?
    a. Their freely roaming pigs and cattle trampled Native American cornfields and gardens.
    b. Their need for wood depleted the forests that Native Americans needed for hunting.
    c. Their reliance on the fur trade reduced the population of beaver and other animals important to the Native Americans.
    d. They changed the land to suit their way of life instead of adapting to their new surroundings.
    e. Their refusal to build fences and permanent structures created conflict with Native American hunting methods.

    ANS: E   TOP: Social history | Ethnicity | Changes in the Land   DIF: Moderate   REF: Full p. 58 | Seagull p. 56   MSC: Understanding   OBJ: 2

29. Which of the following statements is true about the early history of Jamestown?
    a. The colony's problems were due largely to its leadership: the same people remained in charge for the first two decades and refused to change their methods.
    b. The first settlers were farmers and laborers who were so eager to make money that they refused to work and could not be controlled.
    c. The death rate was extraordinarily high.
    d. The supplies from England were excellent, but the colonists wasted them.
    e. John Smith took the credit, but he had nothing to do with Jamestown's success.

    ANS: C   TOP: Social history | The Jamestown Colony
    DIF: Easy   REF: Full p. 58 | Seagull p. 57
    MSC: Remembering   OBJ: 3

30. Why was the death rate in early Jamestown so high?
    a. It lay beside a malarial swamp.
    b. The ample food was full of botulism.
    c. It was not high; most of the colonists survived.
    d. Constant Native American attacks decimated the population.

    e. Many of the colonists committed suicide.

    ANS: A   TOP: Social history | The Jamestown Colony   DIF: Easy   REF: Full p. 58 | Seagull p. 57
    MSC: Remembering   OBJ: 2

31. As leader of the Jamestown Colony, John Smith:
    a. was a failure and had to return to England.
    b. improved relations with Native Americans by marrying Pocahontas.
    c. used rigorous military discipline to hold the colony together.
    d. used an elaborate reward system to persuade colonists to work.
    e. set up the first representative assembly in the New World.

    ANS: C   TOP: Political history, changes | The Jamestown Colony   DIF: Moderate   REF: Full p. 59 | Seagull p. 58   MSC: Remembering   OBJ: 3

32. How did the Virginia Company reshape the colony's development?
    a. It instituted the headright system, giving fifty acres of land to each colonist who paid for his own or another's passage.
    b. It fired John Smith and brought in a more popular leader.
    c. It gave control back to the king, who straightened out its problems.
    d. It required all settlers to grow tobacco, a highly profitable crop.
    e. It created an executive committee that really ran the colony and a committee of colonists who thought they were running it.

    ANS: A   TOP: Economic development | From Company to Society   DIF: Easy   REF: Full p. 59 | Seagull p. 58   MSC: Remembering   OBJ: 3

33. The Virginia House of Burgesses:
    a. was dissolved by King James because he objected to all representative government.
    b. was created as part of the Virginia Company's effort to encourage the colony's survival.
    c. banned the importation of servants.
    d. had more power than the governor.
    e. was included in the original charter for the Jamestown Colony.

    ANS: B   TOP: Political history, changes | From Company to Society   DIF: Moderate   REF: Full p. 59 | Seagull p. 58   MSC: Remembering   OBJ: 3

34. The Native American leader Powhatan:
    a. tried to avoid trade with the colonists because he believed that it would destroy Native American culture.

b. managed to consolidate control over some thirty nearby tribes.

c. was the brother of Pocahontas.

d. invited the colonists to feasts with his tribe and then slaughtered eighty Virginia settlers.

e. won the respect of the colonists when he defeated John Smith in a wrestling match.

ANS: B   TOP: Ethnicity | Powhatan and Pocahontas DIF: Moderate   REF: Full p. 59 | Seagull p. 58 MSC: Remembering   OBJ: 3

35. To entice settlers to Virginia, the Virginia Company established the headright system, which:

a. granted religious freedom.

b. provided land to settlers who paid their own and others' passage.

c. brought slavery to the colony.

d. promised every single man a bride.

e. enslaved Indians.

ANS: B   TOP: Economic development | From Company to Society   DIF: Easy   REF: Full p. 59 | Seagull p. 58   MSC: Remembering   OBJ: 3

36. The marriage between John Rolfe and Pocahontas:

a. brought unrest and conflict between the English and the Indians.

b. split the church.

c. was seen in England as a sign of Anglo-Indian harmony and missionary success.

d. marked the beginnings of many ethnically mixed marriages between Indians and the English.

e. caused King James I to denounce John Rolfe.

ANS: C   TOP: Social history | Ethnicity | Powhatan and Pocahontas   DIF: Moderate   REF: Full p. 60 | Seagull p. 59   MSC: Understanding   OBJ: 3

37. It can be argued that conflict between the English settlers and local Indians in Virginia became inevitable when:

a. the Native Americans realized that England wanted to establish a permanent and constantly expanding colony, not just a trading post.

b. Pocahontas married John Rolfe.

c. the House of Burgesses passed a law ordering Native Americans out of the colony.

d. Powhatan led an attack against the English settlers in 1644.

e. Spain formed a military alliance with Powhatan.

ANS: A   TOP: Social history | Ethnicity | The Uprising of 1622   DIF: Moderate   REF: Full p. 60 | Seagull p. 59   MSC: Understanding   OBJ: 2

38. Opechancanough:

a. succeeded his father, Powhatan, as the leader of Virginia's Indians.

b. married Pocahontas after the death of John Rolfe.

c. was the first Native American invited to address the House of Burgesses.

d. mounted a surprise attack in 1622 that wiped out one-quarter of Virginia's settlers.

e. killed John Smith.

ANS: D   TOP: Social history | Ethnicity | The Uprising of 1622   DIF: Moderate   REF: Full p. 60 | Seagull p. 59   MSC: Remembering   OBJ: 2

39. Virginia's colonial policy of requiring Native Americans to move to reservations:

a. immediately followed the Pequot War.

b. came after the Native American population had risen to 10,000.

c. followed a precedent established by the English in Ireland.

d. led to the Trail of Tears of Native Americans from the Virginia coast to an inland area.

e. ended in failure in 1633.

ANS: C   TOP: Social history | Ethnicity | The Uprising of 1622   DIF: Moderate   REF: Full pp. 60–61 | Seagull p. 60   MSC: Remembering   OBJ: 2

40. When the Virginia Company gave control of the Virginia colony to the king in 1624:

a. it did so under pressure from the king, who was trying to consolidate his ownership of all colonies.

b. its white population had quintupled since settlement began in 1607.

c. this meant that control over the colony would rest entirely in royal hands, ending the local control that had existed under the Virginia Company.

d. Virginia became the first royal colony.

e. James wanted to change the colony's name to Jamesland, but Parliament rejected it.

ANS: D   TOP: Political history, changes | The Uprising of 1622   DIF: Moderate   REF: Full p. 61 | Seagull p. 60   MSC: Remembering   OBJ: 3

41. What was Virginia's "gold," which ensured its survival and prosperity?

a. cotton

b. fur

c. tobacco

d. indigo

e. sugar

ANS: C   TOP: Economic development | A Tobacco Colony   DIF: Easy   REF: Full p. 61 | Seagull p. 61 MSC: Remembering   OBJ: 3

42. Tobacco production in Virginia:

a. enriched an emerging class of planters and certain members of the colonial government.

b. benefited from the endorsement of King James I.

c. declined after its original success, as Europeans learned the dangers of smoking.

d. resulted in more unified settlements, thanks to tobacco's propensity to grow only in certain areas of Virginia.

e. was under the control of two planters, Walter Winston and the Earl of Kent.

ANS: A   TOP: Economic development | A Tobacco Colony   DIF: Easy   REF: Full p. 61 | Seagull p. 61   MSC: Remembering   OBJ: 3

43. Which statement about women in the early Virginia colony is FALSE?

a. Women mostly came to Virginia as indentured servants.

b. Some women took advantage of their legal status as femme sole.

c. Women consisted of about half the white population.

d. Women often married at a relatively late age—mid-twenties.

e. There was a high death rate among women.

ANS: C   TOP: Social history | Women and the Family   DIF: Moderate   REF: Full p. 62 | Seagull p. 61   MSC: Remembering   OBJ: 3

44. Maryland was similar to Virginia in that:

a. both started out as proprietary colonies.

b. tobacco proved crucial to its economy and society.

c. John Smith had to take over the colony and organize its settlers to work.

d. both offered settlers total religious freedom.

e. the king approved the creation of each colony only because of pressure from Parliament.

ANS: B   TOP: Economic development | The Maryland Experiment   DIF: Moderate   REF: Full p. 63 | Seagull p. 63   MSC: Remembering   OBJ: 3

45. Maryland's founder, Cecilius Calvert:

a. wanted Maryland to be like a feudal domain, with power limited for ordinary people.

b. supported total religious freedom for all of the colony's inhabitants.

c. gave a great deal of power to the elected assembly but not to the royal governor.

d. lost ownership of the colony and died a pauper.

e. actually hated Catholics, which is why he set up a colony for them in a swamp.

ANS: A   TOP: Political history, changes | The Maryland Experiment   DIF: Moderate   REF: Full p. 64 | Seagull p. 63   MSC: Remembering   OBJ: 3

46. Maryland was established as a refuge for which group?

a. Quakers

b. Puritans

c. Pilgrims

d. Native Americans

e. Catholics

ANS: E   TOP: Social history | Religion in Maryland   DIF: Easy   REF: Full p. 64 | Seagull p. 63   MSC: Remembering   OBJ: 3

47. Which of the following is true of the Puritans of the seventeenth century?

a. They were completely unified on all issues.

b. They agreed that the Church of England retained too many elements of Catholicism in its rituals and doctrines.

c. They differed completely with the views of the Church of England.

d. They came to the colonies because they had no hope of holding any power in England.

e. John Winthrop founded the church.

ANS: B   TOP: Cultural history | The Rise of Puritanism   DIF: Moderate   REF: Full p. 65 | Seagull p. 64   MSC: Understanding   OBJ: 4

48. Puritans followed the religious ideas of the French-born theologian:

a. John Calvin.

b. Martin Guerre.

c. Jacques Baptiste.

d. Charles LeGrand.

e. Ulrich Zwingli.

ANS: A   TOP: Cultural history | The Rise of Puritanism   DIF: Easy   REF: Full p. 65 | Seagull p. 65   MSC: Remembering   OBJ: 4

49. Why did Puritans decide to emigrate from England in the late 1620s and 1630s?

a. Because so many of them had become separatists, they had to leave England to save their church.

b. Charles I had started supporting them, creating conflicts with Catholic nobles.

c. The Church of England was firing their ministers and censoring their writings.

d. Puritan leader John Winthrop wanted a high-level position, and leaving England was the only way for him to get it.

e. The Poor Law of 1623 banned non-Catholics from receiving government aid.

ANS: C   TOP: Social history | Moral Liberty   DIF: Easy   REF: Full p. 65 | Seagull p. 65   MSC: Remembering   OBJ: 4

50. What was Puritan leader and Massachusetts Bay Governor John Winthrop's attitude toward liberty?
    a. He saw two kinds of liberty: natural liberty, the ability to do evil, and moral liberty, the ability to do good.
    b. He saw two kinds of liberty: negative liberty, the restricting of freedoms for the sake of others, and positive liberty, the assuring of rights through a constitution.
    c. He believed that individual rights took precedence over the rights of the community.
    d. He believed in a dictatorship, with only himself in charge of it.
    e. He believed "liberty" had a religious but not a political meaning.

    ANS: A   TOP: Social history | Moral Liberty
    DIF: Moderate   REF: Full p. 66 | Seagull pp. 65–66
    MSC: Remembering   OBJ: 4

51. Why did the Pilgrims flee the Netherlands?
    a. They sought new opportunities after a severe economic downturn in the Netherlands left many of them unemployed.
    b. They felt that the surrounding culture was corrupting their children.
    c. England had gone to war with the Netherlands, and the Pilgrims felt caught in the middle.
    d. The Catholic Church took over the Netherlands under a papal edict in 1617, and the Pilgrims felt that they had no choice but to go.
    e. The Dutch government ordered them to leave because of their radical religious ideas.

    ANS: B   TOP: Social history | The Pilgrims at Plymouth
    DIF: Moderate   REF: Full p. 66 | Seagull p. 66
    MSC: Remembering   OBJ: 4

52. Where in the Americas did the Pilgrims originally plan to go?
    a. New Netherland
    b. Plymouth Rock
    c. Boston
    d. Virginia
    e. Pennsylvania

    ANS: D   TOP: Social history | The Pilgrims at Plymouth   DIF: Medium   REF: Full p. 66 | Seagull p. 66   MSC: Remembering   OBJ: 4

53. The Mayflower Compact established:
    a. religious toleration and freedom in Massachusetts.
    b. the right to emigrate to America.
    c. a company chartered to settle New England.
    d. a civil government for the Plymouth Colony.
    e. peaceful relations between English colonists and Indians in Rhode Island.

ANS: D   TOP: Primary document analysis | The Pilgrims at Plymouth   DIF: Moderate   REF: Full p. 66 | Seagull p. 66   MSC: Remembering   OBJ: 4

54. What benefited the Pilgrims when they landed at Plymouth?
    a. They met a Native American, Opechancanough, who helped them.
    b. It was the late spring, so it was planting season.
    c. Native Americans, decimated by disease, left behind cleared fields for farming.
    d. The local Indian leader considered the English to be divine.
    e. John Smith arrived to help organize them.

    ANS: C   TOP: Social history | Economic development | The Pilgrims at Plymouth   DIF: Moderate
    REF: Full p. 66 | Seagull p. 66   MSC: Remembering
    OBJ: 4

55. In contrast to life in the Chesapeake region, life in New England:
    a. was more family-oriented.
    b. did not involve class-based hierarchies.
    c. was not as deeply religious.
    d. allowed for equal legal rights for women and men.
    e. centered on an economy based on one cash crop.

    ANS: A   TOP: Social history | The Great Migration
    DIF: Easy   REF: Full p. 67 | Seagull p. 67
    MSC: Remembering   OBJ: 4

56. Puritan women:
    a. could not legally divorce.
    b. were not allowed full church membership.
    c. were said to achieve freedom by embracing subjection to their husbands' authority.
    d. could become ministers if they were widows of ministers.
    e. married late in life.

    ANS: C   TOP: Social history | The Puritan Family
    DIF: Moderate   REF: Full p. 68 | Seagull p. 69
    MSC: Understanding   OBJ: 4

57. The Puritans believed that male authority in the household was:
    a. an outdated idea.
    b. to be unquestioned.
    c. so absolute that a husband could order the murder of his wife.
    d. not supposed to resemble God's authority in any way, because that would be blasphemous.
    e. limited only by the number of children—the more, the better.

    ANS: B   TOP: Social history | The Puritan Family
    DIF: Easy   REF: Full p. 68 | Seagull p. 69
    MSC: Remembering   OBJ: 4

58. In Puritan marriages:
    a. reciprocal affection and companionship were the ideal.
    b. divorce was not allowed.
    c. husbands could beat their wives without interference from the authorities.
    d. wives were banned from attending church because they might end up disagreeing with how their husbands interpreted the sermon.
    e. women could speak only when spoken to.

    ANS: A   TOP: Social history | The Puritan Family
    DIF: Moderate   REF: Full p. 68 | Seagull p. 69
    MSC: Understanding   OBJ: 4

59. How did John Winthrop view a woman's liberty?
    a. A woman was equal to her husband in the eyes of the Puritan faith.
    b. Once a woman married a man, she was his subject.
    c. A woman had no right to choose a husband; the church should choose one for her.
    d. Men and women were equal until they married, and then they were one.
    e. He never even mentioned women.

    ANS: B   TOP: Social history | The Puritan Family
    DIF: Moderate   REF: Full p. 68 | Seagull p. 69
    MSC: Remembering   OBJ: 4

60. In Puritan New England:
    a. it was illegal for a woman to have children after the age of twenty-eight, so childbearing began earlier than it did elsewhere.
    b. infant mortality rates were lower than in the Chesapeake colonies, because the environment was healthier.
    c. women married at an older age than their English counterparts.
    d. most women gave birth at least ten times.
    e. men were required by law to become fathers.

    ANS: B   TOP: Social history | The Puritan Family
    DIF: Moderate   REF: Full p. 68 | Seagull p. 69
    MSC: Remembering   OBJ: 4

61. In early seventeenth-century Massachusetts, freeman status was granted to adult males who:
    a. owned land, regardless of their church membership.
    b. had served their term as indentured servants.
    c. were freed slaves.
    d. were landowning church members.
    e. voted.

    ANS: D   TOP: Political history, changes | Government and Society in Massachusetts   DIF: Easy
    REF: Full p. 68 | Seagull p. 70   MSC: Remembering
    OBJ: 4

62. In New England towns:
    a. there was no local government because Massachusetts Bay leaders feared dissent.
    b. much of the land remained in common, for collective use or to be divided among later settlers.
    c. there were several churches.
    d. the colony divided up the land because it wanted to keep the settlers from having any role in government.
    e. ministers conducted town meetings, just as they conducted church services.

    ANS: B   TOP: Economic development | Government and Society in Massachusetts   DIF: Moderate
    REF: Full p. 69 | Seagull p. 69   MSC: Remembering
    OBJ: 4

63. The Massachusetts General Court:
    a. reflected the Puritans' desire to govern the colony without outside interference.
    b. was chosen by the king.
    c. was chosen by the governor.
    d. ruled the colony from its beginnings in 1630.
    e. by law had to consist of a majority of Puritan judges.

    ANS: A   TOP: Political history, changes | Government and Society in Massachusetts   DIF: Moderate
    REF: Full p. 69 | Seagull p. 70   MSC: Understanding
    OBJ: 4

64. In what way was Puritan church membership a restrictive status?
    a. Only those who could prove they had received formal education could be members, because the ability to read and discuss sermons was so highly valued.
    b. Although all adult male property owners elected colonial officials, only men who were full church members could vote in local elections.
    c. Only property owners could be full members of the church.
    d. Full membership required demonstrating that one had experienced divine grace.
    e. Full membership required that one's parents and grandparents had been church members.

    ANS: D   TOP: Cultural history | Government and Society in Massachusetts   DIF: Moderate
    REF: Full p. 69 | Seagull p. 70   MSC: Understanding
    OBJ: 4

65. Which one of the following is an accurate statement about the class-based society of the Massachusetts Bay Colony?
    a. Only wealthy landowners or merchants were allowed membership in Puritan churches.
    b. The Body of Liberties of 1641 stated that a debtor became the servant of his creditor if he could not repay a loan within a year.

c. The General Court banned ordinary people from wearing the garb of gentlemen.

d. A member of the upper class was known as a gentleman or lady, while a member of the lower class was simply called friend.

e. Voting was restricted by law to men who came from designated "good families" in England.

ANS: C   TOP: Social history | Church and State in Puritan Massachusetts   DIF: Moderate   REF: Full p. 70 | Seagull p. 70   MSC: Remembering   OBJ: 5

66. How did most Puritans view the separation of church and state?

a. They were so determined to keep them apart that they banned ministers from holding office, fearing that they would enact pro-religious legislation.

b. They allowed church and state to be interconnected by requiring each town to establish a church and levy a tax to support the minister.

c. The Massachusetts Bay Colony endorsed the Puritan faith but allowed anyone the freedom to practice or not practice religion.

d. They had never even heard of the concept.

e. They invented the concept but refused to indulge in it.

ANS: B   TOP: Social history | Church and State in Puritan Massachusetts   DIF: Moderate   REF: Full p. 70 | Seagull p. 71   MSC: Understanding   OBJ: 4

67. In regard to religious toleration, the Puritans:

a. ignored the Reformation.

b. encouraged religious dissent.

c. saw only their faith as the truth.

d. accepted only Christian faiths.

e. treated Native American priests as equals.

ANS: C   TOP: Social history | Church and State in Puritan Massachusetts   DIF: Moderate   REF: Full p. 70 | Seagull p. 71   MSC: Understanding   OBJ: 5

68. Puritans viewed individual and personal freedom as:

a. good, because Massachusetts Bay leaders welcomed debate over religion.

b. dangerous to social harmony and community stability.

c. important, but they banned neighbors from reporting on one another, because that would breed division that could harm the community.

d. vital, because they had been discouraged from enjoying these back in England.

e. dangerous to the individual but good for the community.

ANS: B   TOP: Social history | New Englanders Divided   DIF: Moderate   REF: Full p. 71 | Seagull p. 71   MSC: Understanding   OBJ: 5

69. Roger Williams argued that:

a. church and state must be totally separated.

b. Puritans must stay in the Church of England and reform it.

c. religious wars were necessary to protect not only religion, but also freedom.

d. Puritans were on a divine mission to spread the true faith.

e. only John Winthrop was capable of explaining the word of God.

ANS: A   TOP: Social history | Political history, changes | Roger Williams   DIF: Easy   REF: Full p. 71 | Seagull p. 72   MSC: Remembering   OBJ: 5

70. When Roger Williams established the colony of Rhode Island:

a. he required voters there to be members of a Puritan church.

b. the king refused to give it a charter, and it remained a renegade colony until Williams died.

c. he made sure that it was more democratic than Massachusetts Bay.

d. he felt that too much democracy would be bad because it might interfere with religious freedom.

e. the colony became a haven for Protestants of all kinds, but it banned Jews.

ANS: C   TOP: Political history, changes | Rhode Island and Connecticut   DIF: Moderate REF: Full p. 71 | Seagull p. 73   MSC: Understanding OBJ: 5

71. The Puritan minister Thomas Hooker:

a. founded what became part of the colony of Connecticut.

b. insisted that Massachusetts pay Indians for land the colony took from them.

c. was Anne Hutchinson's minister and thus created problems for the Puritan leadership.

d. tried to minister to Puritan women who fell victim to the big city of Boston, for which his name eventually became associated with prostitutes.

e. defended the rights of conscience in a spirited debate with Puritan leaders about church-state relations.

ANS: A   TOP: Social history | Political history, changes | Rhode Island and Connecticut   DIF: Easy REF: Full p. 72 | Seagull p. 74   MSC: Remembering OBJ: 5

72. Anne Hutchinson:

a. was no threat to the Puritan establishment because women were so clearly considered inferior.

b. angered Puritan authorities by supporting the claims of Roger Williams.

c. engaged in Antinomianism, a sexual practice that the Puritans considered threatening to traditional gender relations.

d. opposed Puritan ministers who distinguished saints from the damned through church attendance and moral behavior rather than through focusing on an inner state of grace.

e. would have been left alone if she had not also run for a seat in the General Court.

ANS: D   TOP: Social history | The Trials of Anne Hutchinson   DIF: Moderate   REF: Full p. 73 | Seagull p. 74   MSC: Remembering   OBJ: 5

73. At Anne Hutchinson's trial:
a. her argument on her own behalf swayed the jury.
b. she violated Puritan doctrine by claiming that God spoke to her directly rather than through ministers or the Bible.
c. she was acquitted, but was so displeased with her treatment that she left the colony for Rhode Island.
d. Governor John Winthrop was critical of her but admitted that she was an impressive antagonist.
e. Roger Williams served as her attorney.

ANS: B   TOP: Social history | The Trials of Anne Hutchinson   DIF: Easy   REF: Full p. 73 | Seagull p. 74   MSC: Remembering   OBJ: 5

74. For most New Englanders, Indians represented:
a. savagery.
b. teachers.
c. curiosities.
d. culture.
e. survival.

ANS: A   TOP: Social history | Ethnicity | Puritans and Indians   DIF: Easy   REF: Full p. 76 | Seagull p. 75   MSC: Remembering   OBJ: 5

75. John Winthrop followed which one of the following policies toward Native Americans?
a. He declared all Indian land to be the property of the Massachusetts Bay Colony.
b. He insisted that they agree to submit to English authority.
c. He required Puritans to pay them.
d. He urged all Puritans to work at converting Native Americans to Christianity.
e. He called for their immediate extermination.

ANS: B   TOP: Social history | Ethnicity | Puritans and Indians   DIF: Moderate   REF: Full p. 76 | Seagull p. 75   MSC: Remembering   OBJ: 5

76. In the Pequot War of 1637:
a. the Pequots defeated the Puritans in a battle that temporarily drove back the Massachusetts Bay settlers to only three coastal towns.

b. Connecticut and Massachusetts soldiers teamed with Narragansett allies to set the main Pequot village afire and kill 500 Pequots.
c. the Narragansetts joined the Pequots to fight the Puritans, leading to the elimination of both tribes.
d. the barbarity of the Native Americans surprised the colonists.
e. the Pequots took over the old Pilgrim colony and made it their own.

ANS: B   TOP: Social history | Ethnicity | The Pequot War   DIF: Moderate   REF: Full pp. 76–77 | Seagull pp. 78–79   MSC: Remembering   OBJ: 5

77. In the seventeenth century, New England's economy:
a. grew at a very slow rate because few settlers moved to the region.
b. suffered because most early settlers were poor and could not gain access to land.
c. centered on family farms and also involved the export of fish and timber.
d. boasted a significant manufacturing component that employed close to one-third of all men.
e. relied heavily on indentured servants in the labor force.

ANS: C   TOP: Economic development | The New England Economy   DIF: Moderate   REF: Full p. 77 | Seagull p. 79   MSC: Remembering   OBJ: 4

78. Boston merchants:
a. challenged the subordination of economic activity to Puritan control.
b. refused to trade with anyone outside of the Puritan faith.
c. paid for Anne Hutchinson's prosecution.
d. had enjoyed widespread freedom to trade since the establishment of the colony.
e. controlled John Winthrop.

ANS: A   TOP: Economic development | Social history | The Merchant Elite   DIF: Moderate   REF: Full p. 78 | Seagull p. 80   MSC: Understanding   OBJ: 5

79. The Half-Way Covenant of 1662:
a. set up civil government in Massachusetts.
b. allowed Baptists and Quakers to attend, but not join, Puritan churches.
c. gave women limited voting rights in Puritan congregations.
d. permitted anyone who paid a tithe to be baptized in a Puritan church.
e. did not require evidence of conversion to receive a kind of church membership.

ANS: E   TOP: Cultural history | The Half-Way Covenant   DIF: Moderate   REF: Full p. 79 | Seagull p. 81   MSC: Remembering   OBJ: 5

80. The Magna Carta:
    a. was an agreement between King Henry VIII and the Anglican Church.
    b. guaranteed religious freedom in Great Britain.
    c. granted many liberties, but mainly to lords and barons.
    d. was seen as embodying English freedom, until Parliament repealed it in 1722.
    e. was, like the English Constitution, unwritten.

    ANS: C   TOP: Political history, changes | Global awareness | The Rights of Englishmen
    DIF: Moderate   REF: Full pp. 79–80 | Seagull p. 82
    MSC: Remembering   OBJ: 6

81. A central element in the definition of English liberty was:
    a. the right to a trial by jury.
    b. the right to self-incrimination.
    c. that each English citizen owned a copy of the English Constitution.
    d. freedom of expression.
    e. what an individual king or queen said it was.

    ANS: A   TOP: Political history, changes | The Rights of Englishmen   DIF: Easy   REF: Full p. 80 | Seagull p. 82   MSC: Remembering   OBJ: 6

82. In the battles between Parliament and the Stuart kings, English freedom:
    a. played a minimal role.
    b. greatly expanded amid the debate over which of these groups should be elected.
    c. remained an important and a much-debated concept even after Charles I was beheaded.
    d. was the excuse given for restoring Charles II in 1685.
    e. led to the overthrow of James III in 1700.

    ANS: C   TOP: Political history, changes | Global awareness | The English Civil War   DIF: Moderate
    REF: Full p. 80 | Seagull pp. 82–83
    MSC: Analyzing   OBJ: 6

83. In the 1640s, leaders of the House of Commons:
    a. accused the king of imposing taxes without parliamentary consent.
    b. supported efforts to move England back to Catholicism.
    c. aided Charles I in overthrowing his father, James I.
    d. opposed Oliver Cromwell's "Commonwealth" government.
    e. refused to allow new colonists to emigrate to America.

    ANS: A   TOP: Political history, changes | The English Civil War   DIF: Moderate   REF: Full p. 80 | Seagull p. 82   MSC: Understanding   OBJ: 6

84. During the English political upheaval between 1640 and 1660:
    a. new religious sects began demanding the end of public financing and special privileges for the Anglican Church.
    b. groups began calling for the elimination of a written English constitution, on the grounds that kings merely abused its privileges.
    c. writer John Milton called for an end to freedom of speech and press, because it caused too much controversy.
    d. the execution of King Charles II led to new debates about crime and punishment.
    e. thousands of American colonists returned to England to participate in the Civil War.

    ANS: A   TOP: Political history, changes | Global awareness | England's Debate over Freedom
    DIF: Moderate   REF: Full pp. 80–81 | Seagull p. 83
    MSC: Understanding   OBJ: 6

85. The Levellers:
    a. got their name for knocking down (leveling) the Parliament building.
    b. called for the strengthening of freedom and democracy at a time when those principles were seen as possibly contributing to anarchy.
    c. opposed a written constitution on the grounds that it institutionalized social inequality.
    d. proposed to abolish Parliament.
    e. claimed the world was flat or level.

    ANS: B   TOP: Political history, changes | Global awareness | England's Debate over Freedom
    DIF: Easy   REF: Full p. 81 | Seagull p. 83
    MSC: Remembering   OBJ: 6

86. The Diggers of Great Britain:
    a. proposed building a tunnel to Rome to surprise and overpower the Catholic Church, thereby eliminating a source of controversy in English society.
    b. sought to eliminate male ownership of land as a means of promoting social equality for women.
    c. influenced the development of the American colonies, because some of their members and ideas crossed the Atlantic to the New World.
    d. executed King James I.
    e. overthrew parliamentary forces in 1642.

    ANS: C   TOP: Political history, changes | Global awareness | England's Debate over Freedom
    DIF: Moderate   REF: Full p. 81 | Seagull p. 83
    MSC: Understanding   OBJ: 6

87. A consequence of the English Civil War of the 1640s was:
    a. an English belief that England was the world's guardian of liberty.

b. an increase in the power of the Stuart kings.
c. the establishment of Plymouth Colony.
d. the signing of the Magna Carta.
e. the outbreak of war between Spain and England.

ANS: A   TOP: Political history, changes; Global
awareness | English Liberty   DIF: Easy   REF: Full
p. 81 | Seagull p. 84   MSC: Understanding   OBJ: 6

88. Which of the following is true of the Puritans' dealings
with Quakers?
a. Their officials in Massachusetts punished Quakers
financially and physically, even hanging several of
them.
b. They welcomed the Quakers and thus were happy to
help them set up the Pennsylvania colony.
c. They fought Charles II's efforts to oppress and
suppress Quakers.
d. They passed a law ordering all Quakers to leave
Massachusetts or face imminent death.
e. They resented the Quakers for their shrewd business
practices.

ANS: A   TOP: Social history | The Civil War and
English America   DIF: Moderate   REF: Full p. 82
| Seagull p. 84   MSC: Understanding   OBJ: 6

89. Which one of the following is an accurate statement
regarding the impact on Maryland of seventeenth-
century England's Protestant-Catholic conflict?
a. The conflict had no effect on far-off Maryland.
b. To win the favor of Protestant kings, Maryland gave
all authority to Protestants.
c. The English government temporarily repealed
Calvert's ownership of Maryland and the colony's
policies of religious toleration.
d. Maryland's Catholic leaders banned Protestant
worship in 1671.
e. The conflict eventually led to the Puritan
government of the 1640s taking refuge in
Maryland.

ANS: C   TOP: Political history, changes | Social history
| The Crisis in Maryland   DIF: Moderate   REF: Full
p. 83 | Seagull p. 85   MSC: Understanding   OBJ: 6

90. Which colony adopted the Act Concerning Religion in
1649, which institutionalized the principle of religious
toleration?
a. Virginia
b. Maryland
c. Massachusetts
d. Rhode Island
e. Connecticut

ANS: B   TOP: Political history, changes | Social history
| The Crisis in Maryland   DIF: Moderate   REF: Full
p. 83 | Seagull p. 85   MSC: Remembering   OBJ: 6

91. In the 1650s, who pushed England toward a policy of
expanding territory and commercialism?
a. Oliver Cromwell
b. John Smith
c. Charles I
d. Charles II
e. James I

ANS: A   TOP: Political history, changes | Cromwell
and the Empire   DIF: Easy   REF: Full p. 83 |
Seagull p. 85   MSC: Remembering   OBJ: 6

True or False

1. Jamestown was originally settled only by men.

ANS: T   TOP: Social history | Introduction
DIF: Easy   REF: Full p. 49 | Seagull p. 46
MSC: Remembering   OBJ: 3

2. *A Discourse Concerning Western Planting* argued that
English settlement of North America would strike a
blow against Spain.

ANS: T   TOP: Political history, changes | Spreading
Protestantism   DIF: Moderate   REF: Full p. 52 |
Seagull p. 50   MSC: Remembering   OBJ: 1

3. The English increasingly viewed America as a land
where a man could control his own labor and thus gain
independence.

ANS: T   TOP: Political history, changes | Land and
Liberty   DIF: Easy   REF: Full pp. 53–54 | Seagull
p. 52   MSC: Remembering   OBJ: 1

4. Disease killed many Indians, but European settlers
were not affected by disease.

ANS: F   TOP: Ethnicity | Indentured Servants
DIF: Easy   REF: Full p. 54 | Seagull p. 52
MSC: Remembering   OBJ: 2

5. Nearly two-thirds of English settlers arrived as
indentured servants.

ANS: T   TOP: Social history | Indentured Servants
DIF: Moderate   REF: Full p. 55 | Seagull p. 53
MSC: Remembering   OBJ: 2

6. English settlers believed land was the basis of liberty.

ANS: T   TOP: Political history, changes | Land and
Liberty   DIF: Moderate   REF: Full p. 55 | Seagull
p. 54   MSC: Remembering   OBJ: 2

7. Indians mostly traded furs and animal skins for European goods.

ANS: T   TOP: Economic development | Ethnicity |
Transformation of Indian Life   DIF: Easy

REF: Full p. 57 | Seagull p. 56   MSC: Remembering
OBJ: 2

8. Growing connections with Europeans lessened warfare between Indian tribes.

    ANS: F   TOP: Social history | Ethnicity | Transformation of Indian Life   DIF: Moderate   REF: Full pp. 57–58 | Seagull p. 56   MSC: Remembering   OBJ: 2

9. Early settlers of Jamestown preferred gold to farming.

    ANS: T   TOP: Economic development | The Jamestown Colony   DIF: Easy   REF: Full p. 58 | Seagull p. 57   MSC: Remembering   OBJ: 2

10. Treatment of the Indians by members of the Virginia colony was influenced in part by Las Casas's condemnation of Spanish behavior.

    ANS: T   TOP: Social history | Ethnicity | Powhatan and Pocahontas   DIF: Difficult   REF: Full pp. 59–60 | Seagull pp. 58–59   MSC: Understanding   OBJ: 2

11. The Virginia Company accomplished its goals for the company and for its settlers.

    ANS: F   TOP: Economic development | The Uprising of 1622   DIF: Moderate   REF: Full p. 61 | Seagull p. 60   MSC: Understanding   OBJ: 2

12. Believing that tobacco was harmful to one's health, King James I warned against its use.

    ANS: T   TOP: Economic development | A Tobacco Colony   DIF: Moderate   REF: Full p. 61 | Seagull p. 61   MSC: Remembering   OBJ: 3

13. Puritans believed that the Church of England was not in need of reform.

    ANS: F   TOP: Social history | The Rise of Puritanism   DIF: Easy   REF: Full pp. 64–65 | Seagull p. 64   MSC: Remembering   OBJ: 4

14. The Pilgrims intended to set sail for Cape Cod in 1620.

    ANS: F   TOP: Chronology | The Pilgrims at Plymouth   DIF: Moderate   REF: Full p. 66 | Seagull p. 66   MSC: Remembering   OBJ: 4

15. Like the first Jamestown settlers, the settlers of Massachusetts were mostly families.

    ANS: F   TOP: Social history | The Great Migration   DIF: Moderate   REF: Full p. 67 | Seagull p. 67   MSC: Remembering   OBJ: 4

16. Under English law, married women held many legal rights and privileges.

    ANS: F   TOP: Social history | The Puritan Family   DIF: Moderate   REF: Full p. 68 | Seagull p. 68   MSC: Remembering   OBJ: 4

17. Puritans relied on and deeply valued education.

    ANS: T   TOP: Social history | Government and Society in Massachusetts   DIF: Easy   REF: Full p. 69 | Seagull p. 69   MSC: Remembering   OBJ: 4

18. Religious toleration violated the Puritan understanding of moral liberty.

    ANS: T   TOP: Social history | Church and State in Puritan Massachusetts   DIF: Moderate   REF: Full p. 70 | Seagull p. 75   MSC: Remembering   OBJ: 5

19. Roger Williams imagined Rhode Island as a feudal domain.

    ANS: F   TOP: Political history, changes | Rhode Island and Connecticut   DIF: Easy   REF: Full p. 71 | Seagull p. 73   MSC: Remembering   OBJ: 5

20. In British America, unlike other New World empires, Indians performed most of the labor in the colonies.

    ANS: F   TOP: Social history | Ethnicity | The New England Economy   DIF: Easy   REF: Full p. 77 | Seagull p. 80   MSC: Remembering   OBJ: 5

21. The English Civil War was a bloodless war that restored Catholicism to England.

    ANS: F   TOP: Political history, changes | The English Civil War   DIF: Easy   REF: Full p. 80 | Seagull pp. 82–83   MSC: Remembering   OBJ: 6

22. After the English Civil War, it was generally believed that freedom was the common heritage of all Englishmen.

    ANS: T   TOP: Political history, changes | English Liberty   DIF: Moderate   REF: Full p. 81 | Seagull p. 84   MSC: Remembering   OBJ: 6

23. Henry Care believed that the English system of government was the best in the world.

    ANS: T   TOP: Political history, changes | English Liberty   DIF: Easy   REF: Full p. 81 | Seagull p. 84   MSC: Remembering   OBJ: 6

24. Oliver Cromwell's Parliament passed the first Navigation Act, aimed to wrest control of world trade from the Dutch.

    ANS: T   TOP: Political history, changes | Cromwell and the Empire   DIF: Moderate   REF: Full p. 83 | Seagull p. 86   MSC: Remembering   OBJ: 6

25. Even Jewish people enjoyed religious freedom under Maryland's Act Concerning Religion.

    ANS: F   TOP: Social history | Political history, changes | The Crisis in Maryland   DIF: Moderate   REF: Full p. 83 | Seagull p. 85   MSC: Remembering   OBJ: 6

Short Answer

Identify and give the historical significance of each of the following terms, events, and people in a paragraph or two.

1. Henry Care
2. Puritanism
3. civil versus natural liberty
4. Half-Way Covenant
5. Act Concerning Religion
6. English Civil War
7. Roger Williams
8. Virginia Company
9. tobacco
10. Anne Hutchinson
11. headright system
12. Magna Carta

Essay Questions

1. What key political, social, and religious ideas and institutions defined the English nation around 1600?

    ANS: Answers will vary   TOP: Social history | Political history, changes | Cultural history | The Rights of Englishmen | English Liberty | Unifying the English Nation | Spreading Protestantism | The Social Crisis   DIF: Moderate   MSC: Understanding   OBJ: 1

2. Once England decided to create an overseas empire, it did so with impressive speed. Explain the motives behind English expansion to the North American continent, including the Great Migration.

    ANS: Answers will vary   TOP: Political history, changes | Economic development | English Emigrants | The Great Migration | Spreading Protestantism | The Social Crisis | The Jamestown Colony | A Tobacco Colony | The Maryland Experiment | The Pilgrims at Plymouth   DIF: Moderate   MSC: Understanding   OBJ: 1 / 3 / 4

3. Many degrees of freedom coexisted in seventeenth-century North America. Discuss the various definitions of freedom. Be sure to include slaves, indentured servants, women, Indians, property owners, and Puritans in your discussion. Identify any similarities and differences among these different versions of freedom.

    ANS: Answers will vary   TOP: Economic development | Social history | Ethnicity | Indentured Servants | Transformation of Indian Life | Women and the Family | The Puritan Family | Church and State in Puritan Massachusetts | Puritans and Indians   DIF: Difficult   MSC: Analyzing   OBJ: 6

4. Explain the reasons behind the various conflicts between the English and the Indians. How do differing perceptions of land and liberty fit into the story? How does trade play a part?

    ANS: Answers will vary   TOP: Political history, changes | Social history | Ethnicity | Economic development | Puritans and Indians | The Pequot War | Powhatan and Pocahontas | The Uprising of 1622 | Englishmen and Indians | Transformation of Indian Life | Changes in the Land   DIF: Moderate   MSC: Analyzing   OBJ: 2 / 3 / 5

5. John Winthrop distinguished between natural and moral liberty. What was the difference? How did moral liberty work, and how did Puritans define liberty and freedom? Discuss the restrictions of moral liberty and the consequences as illustrated by Roger Williams and Anne Hutchinson. Be sure to address Winthrop's speech in the "Voices of Freedom" box.

    ANS: Answers will vary   TOP: Political history, changes | Social history | Moral Liberty | The Puritan Family | Church and State in Puritan Massachusetts | Roger Williams | Rhode Island and Connecticut | The Trials of Anne Hutchinson   DIF: Moderate   MSC: Analyzing   OBJ: 4 / 5

6. Compare the Chesapeake and New England colonies. Explore the various reasons for the colonists' emigrating to the New World, their economies, gender roles, demographics, religion, and relations with the Indians. Which pattern of settlement is more representative of American development after the seventeenth century?

    ANS: Answers will vary   TOP: Political history, changes | Social history | Ethnicity | Economic development | The Jamestown Colony | From Company to Society | A Tobacco Colony | Powhatan and Pocahontas | The Uprising of 1622 | Women and the Family | The Maryland Experiment | The Pilgrims at Plymouth | The Great Migration | The Puritan Family | Puritans and Indians | The Pequot War | The New England Economy   DIF: Difficult   MSC: Evaluating   OBJ: 2 / 3 / 4 / 5

7. Both religious freedom and the separation of church and state are taken for granted today. In seventeenth-century British America, freedom and religion did not necessarily go hand in hand, for many believed that the church ought to influence the state. Describe the varying degrees of religious freedom practiced in the colonies as well as differing attitudes about the relationship between church and state. Be sure to consider the following colonies, at least: Massachusetts Bay, Rhode Island, and Maryland.

ANS: Answers will vary   TOP: Political history,
changes | Social history | Church and State in
Puritan Massachusetts | Roger Williams | Rhode
Island and Connecticut | The Trials of Anne
Hutchinson | Religion in Maryland | Government
and Society in Massachusetts   DIF: Moderate
MSC: Analyzing   OBJ: 5 / 6

8. How had the concept of English freedom developed
   through the centuries before 1700? What had defined freedom, and to whom were liberties granted? How and why
   had those definitions changed over the centuries? How did
   the English Civil War help to change those definitions?

ANS: Answers will vary   TOP: Political history,
changes | Social history | Ethnicity | Economic devel-
opment | The Rights of Englishmen | The English
Civil War | England's Debate over Freedom | English
Liberty | The Civil War and English America
DIF: Moderate   MSC: Understanding   OBJ: 6

CHAPTER 3 | Creating Anglo-America, 1660–1750

Opening with the crisis of King Philip's War, this chapter concentrates on the reasons behind colonial crises as well as the unifying experience of a uniquely Anglo-American understanding of liberty. The chapter begins with a description of the growth of the English commercial empire in North America through mercantilism, slavery, and the establishment of colonies in New York, Carolina, and William Penn's Pennsylvania, whose "holy experiment" offered many liberties for all of its residents. However, many inhabitants of these new colonies were indentured servants and non-English immigrants, who had varying views on the freedoms offered in the new lands; their opinions can be gleaned from two excerpts found in "Voices of Freedom." The next section, which examines the origins of American slavery, discusses the sometimes ambiguous line between slavery and freedom in the seventeenth century. Another colonial crisis highlighted is Bacon's Rebellion, which demonstrated many poor farmers' frustration with Virginia's privileged elite. The Glorious Revolution in England, which placed the Protestant William of Orange and his wife, Mary, on the throne and gave England a constitutional monarchy, threw the colonies into crisis once again, as American colonists began to demand that they be given certain liberties. The chapter also discusses population growth in colonial America and touches on its religious and regional diversity. It concludes with a broad look at eighteenth-century colonial society, which was becoming increasingly diverse, stratified, and consumer driven.

CHAPTER OUTLINE

I. King Philip's War
   A. In 1675, King Philip and his forces attacked nearly forty-five New England towns.

B. The settlers counterattacked in 1676, breaking the Indians' power once and for all.

II. Global Competition and the Expansion of England's Empire
   A. The Mercantilist System
      1. England attempted to regulate its economy to ensure wealth and national power.
         a. Commerce, not territorial plunder, was the foundation of the English empire.
      2. The Navigation Acts required colonial products to be transported in English ships and sold at English ports.
         a. These Acts stimulated New England's shipbuilding industry.
   B. The Conquest of New Netherland
      1. The restoration of the English monarchy came in 1660, and the government chartered new trading ventures such as the Royal African Company.
      2. In 1664, during an Anglo-Dutch war, New Netherland was surrendered by the Dutch without a fight in order to retain their holdings in Africa, Asia, and South America.
   C. New York and the Rights of Englishmen and Englishwomen
      1. The terms of Dutch surrender guaranteed some freedoms and liberties but reversed others, especially for blacks.
      2. The Duke of York governed New York, and by 1700, nearly 2 million acres of land were owned by only five New York families.
   D. New York and the Indians
      1. The English briefly held an alliance with the Five Nations known as the Covenant Chain,

but by the end of the century the Five Nations adopted a policy of neutrality.

E. The Charter of Liberties
1. New York colonists demanded more liberties, especially the right to consent for taxation.
2. The English of New York got an elected assembly, which drafted a Charter of Liberties and Privileges in 1683.

F. The Founding of Carolina
1. Carolina was established as a barrier to Spanish expansion north of Florida.
2. Carolina was an offshoot of Barbados and, as such, a slave colony from the start; yet agriculture was not initially central to the economy.
3. Early settlers sought Carolina-area Indians as allies and encouraged them to attack and capture Florida Indians as slaves.
4. From 1670 until 1720, Carolina engaged in a slave trade that sold captured Indians to other mainland colonies and to the West Indies.
5. The Fundamental Constitutions of Carolina envisioned a feudal society, but it was not established as such. The colonial government did allow for religious toleration, an elected assembly, and a generous headright system.
6. The economy grew slowly until planters discovered rice, which would make them the wealthiest elite in English North America.

G. The Holy Experiment
1. Pennsylvania was the last seventeenth-century colony to be established and was given to proprietor William Penn.
2. A Quaker, Penn envisioned a colony of peaceful harmony between colonists and Indians and a haven for spiritual freedom.

H. Quaker Liberty
1. Quakers believed that liberty was a universal entitlement.
   a. Liberty extended to women, blacks, and Indians.
2. Religious freedom was a fundamental principle.
   a. Quakers upheld a strict moral code.

I. Land in Pennsylvania
1. Penn established an assembly elected by male taxpayers and "freemen," which meant that a majority of the male population could vote.
2. He owned all of the colony's land and sold it to settlers at low prices rather than granting it outright.
3. Pennsylvania prospered under Penn's policies as it attracted settlers from several European countries.

4. As Pennsylvania grew, the benevolent Indian policy would start to change.

III. Origins of American Slavery
A. Englishmen and Africans
1. The spread of tobacco led settlers to turn to slavery, which offered many advantages over indentured servants.
2. In the seventeenth century, the concepts of race and racism had not fully developed.
3. Africans were seen as alien in their color, religion, and social practices.

B. Slavery in History
1. Although slavery has a long history, slavery in North America was markedly different.
2. Slavery developed slowly in the New World because slaves were expensive and their death rate was high in the seventeenth century.
3. Slavery came to be associated with race, drawing a permanent line between whites and blacks.

C. Slavery in the West Indies
1. By 1600, huge sugar plantations worked by slaves from Africa were well-established in Brazil and in the West Indies.
2. Prior to 1600, Indians and white indentured servants had done the labor; but by the first few decades of the sixteenth century disease had killed off the Indians and white indentured servants were no longer willing to do the backbreaking work required on sugar plantations.
3. Sugar was the first New World crop to be mass marketed to Europe.
4. In contrast to Brazil and the West Indies, slavery developed slowly in North America.
   a. Cost
   b. High death rate

D. Slavery and the Law
1. On paper, slaves in Spain's American empire had more legal rights when compared with slaves in the English American empire.
2. The line between slavery and freedom was more permeable in the seventeenth century than it would become later.
   a. Some free blacks were allowed to sue and testify in court.
   b. Anthony Johnson arrived as a slave but gained his freedom and then eventually owned slaves and several hundred acres of land.

E. The Rise of Chesapeake Slavery
1. It was not until the 1660s that the laws of Virginia and Maryland explicitly referred to slavery.

2. A Virginia law of 1662 provided that in the case of a child born to one free parent and one slave parent, the status of the offspring followed that of the mother.

3. In 1667, the Virginia House of Burgesses decreed that conversion to Christianity did not release a slave from bondage.

4. By 1680, the black population was small, but notions of racial difference were well entrenched in law.

5. No mixed-race class existed as the law treated everyone with African ancestry as black.

F. Bacon's Rebellion: Land and Labor in Virginia

1. Virginia's shift from white indentured servants to African slaves as the main plantation labor force was accelerated by Bacon's Rebellion.

2. Virginia's government ran a corrupt regime under Governor Berkeley, who maintained peaceful relations with the Indians.

3. Good, free land was scarce for freed indentured servants, and taxes on tobacco were rising as the prices were falling.

4. Nathaniel Bacon, an elite planter, called for the removal of all Indians, lower taxes, and an end to rule by "grandees." His campaign gained support from small farmers, indentured servants, landless men, and even some Africans.

5. In some ways Bacon's Rebellion was a clash between two different elite groups.

G. The End of the Rebellion and Its Consequences

1. Bacon promised freedom (including access to Indian lands) to all who joined his ranks.

2. The rebellion's aftermath left Virginia's planter elite to consolidate their power and improve their image.

H. A Slave Society

1. By the end of the seventeenth century, a number of factors made slave labor very attractive to English settlers; slavery began to supplant indentured servitude between 1680 and 1700.

2. By the early eighteenth century, Virginia had transformed from a society with slaves to a slave society.

   a. In 1705, the House of Burgesses enacted strict slave codes.

I. Notions of Freedom

1. From the start of American slavery, blacks ran away and desired freedom.

2. Settlers were well aware that the desire for freedom could ignite the slaves to rebel.

IV. Colonies in Crisis

A. The Glorious Revolution in England

1. The Glorious Revolution in 1688 established parliamentary supremacy and secured the Protestant succession to the throne.

2. Rather than risk a Catholic succession through James II, a group of English aristocrats invited the Dutch Protestant William of Orange to assume the throne.

3. The overthrow of James II entrenched the notion that liberty was the birthright of all Englishmen.

   a. Parliament issued a Bill of Rights (1689) guaranteeing individual rights such as trial by jury.

   b. Parliament adopted the Toleration Act (1690), which allowed Protestant Dissenters to worship freely, although only Anglicans could hold public office.

B. The Glorious Revolution in America

1. In 1675, England established the Lords of Trade to oversee colonial affairs, but the colonies were not interested in obeying London.

2. To create wealth, between 1686 and 1685 James II created a "super-colony," the Dominion of New England.

   a. The new colony threatened liberties.

C. The Maryland Uprising

1. News in America of the Glorious Revolution in England resulted in a reestablishment of former colonial governments.

2. Lord Baltimore was overthrown in Maryland.

D. Leisler's Rebellion

1. Jacob Leisler, a Calvinist, took control of New York.

2. New York was divided along ethnic and economic lines.

3. Leisler was hanged, and New York politics remained polarized for years afterward.

E. Changes in New England

1. In New England, Plymouth was absorbed into Massachusetts, and the political structure of Massachusetts was transformed.

   a. Land ownership, not church membership, was required to vote.

   b. A governor was appointed in London rather than elected.

   c. The colony had to abide by the Toleration Act, which increased the power of some non-Puritan merchants and landowners.

   d. These events along with French and Indian raids created tension in Massachusetts.

F. The Prosecution of Witches

1. Witchcraft was widely believed in and punishable by execution.

2. Most accused were women.

G. The Salem Witch Trials
1. In 1691, several girls suffered fits and nightmares, which were attributed to witchcraft.
2. Three women, including a Caribbean slave named Tituba, were named as witches.
3. Accusations snowballed; ultimately fourteen women and six men were executed before the governor halted all prosecutions.
4. Increase Mather published *Cases of Conscience Concerning Evil Spirits*, which advised people not to take accusations of witchcraft seriously.

V. The Growth of Colonial America
A. A Diverse Population
1. In the eighteenth century, African and non-English European arrivals skyrocketed.
2. As England's economy improved, large-scale migration was draining labor from the mother country.
a. Efforts began to stop emigration.
B. Attracting Settlers
1. London believed colonial development bolstered the nation's power and wealth.
a. Fifty thousand convicts were sent to the Chesapeake to work in the tobacco fields.
2. One hundred forty-five thousand Scottish and Scotch-Irish immigrants came to North America.
C. The German Migration
1. Germans, 110,000 in all, formed the largest group of newcomers from the European continent.
2. Germans tended to travel in entire families.
3. Their migration greatly enhanced the ethnic and religious diversity of Britain's colonies.
D. Religious Diversity
1. Eighteenth-century British America was not a "melting pot" as ethnic groups lived and worshipped in homogeneous communities.
2. Eighteenth-century British America was very diverse, a host to many religions.
3. Most colonies did not adhere to separation of church and state.
a. Taxes were levied to pay for ministers.
b. Catholics and Jews could not vote or hold office in most colonies.
c. Jews, however, were able to escape the rigid religious restrictions of German-speaking parts of Europe.
4. Other liberties also attracted settlers:
a. Availability of land
b. Lack of a military draft
c. Absence of restraints on economic opportunity

E. Indian Life in Transition
1. Indian communities were well integrated into the British imperial system.
2. Traders, British officials, and farmers all viewed Indians differently.
3. The Walking Purchase of 1737 used deceit to gain more land from the Pennsylvania Indians.
F. Regional Diversity
1. The backcountry was the most rapidly growing region in North America.
2. Farmers in the older portions of the Middle Colonies enjoyed a standard of living unimaginable in Europe.
a. Pennsylvania was known as "the best poor man's country."
G. The Consumer Revolution
1. Great Britain eclipsed the Dutch in the eighteenth century as a leader in trade.
a. Colonial products like coffee and tea
b. Manufactured goods such as linen, metalware, pins, ribbons, glassware, ceramics, and clothing
2. Eighteenth-century colonial society enjoyed a multitude of consumer goods from England and Asia.
H. Colonial Cities
1. Spanish colonial cities such as Mexico City were much more populated than British North American cities.
2. Although relatively small and few in number, port cities like Philadelphia were important.
3. Cities served mainly as gathering places for agricultural goods and for imported items to be distributed to the countryside.
I. Colonial Artisans
1. The city was home to a large population of artisans.
a. Myer Myers was a Jewish silversmith from New York, whose career reflected the opportunities open to men of diverse backgrounds in colonial cities.
2. Despite the influx of British goods, American craftsmen benefited from the expanding consumer market.
J. An Atlantic World
1. Trade unified the British empire and connected it to other parts of the world.
2. Membership in the empire had many advantages for the colonists.
a. Colonists did not complain about British regulations of trade.
b. British lax enforcement led to smuggling.
c. Royal Navy protected American shipping.

VI. Social Classes in the Colonies
 A. The Colonial Elite
  1. Expanding trade created the emergence of a powerful upper class of merchants.
  2. In the Chesapeake and Lower South, planters accumulated enormous wealth.
  3. America had no titled aristocracy or established social ranks.
  4. By 1770, nearly all upper-class Virginians had inherited their wealth.
 B. Anglicization
  1. Colonial elites began to think of themselves as more and more English.
  2. Desperate to follow an aristocratic lifestyle, many planters fell into debt.
 C. The South Carolina Aristocracy
  1. The richest group of mainland colonists was South Carolina planters.
  2. The tie that held the elite together was the belief that freedom from labor was the mark of the gentleman.
 D. Poverty in the Colonies
  1. Although poverty was not as widespread in the colonies as it was in England, many colonists had to work as tenants or wage laborers because access to land diminished.
  2. Taking the colonies as a whole, half of the wealth at mid-century was concentrated in the hands of the richest 10 percent of the population.
  3. The better-off in society tended to view the poor as lazy and responsible for their own plight.
   a. Communities had policies to ward off undesirables.
 E. The Middle Ranks
  1. Many in the nonplantation South owned some land.
  2. By the eighteenth century, colonial farm families viewed land ownership almost as a right: the social precondition of freedom.
 F. Women and the Household Economy
  1. The family was the center of economic life, and all members contributed to the family's livelihood.
  2. The work of farmers' wives and daughters often spelled the difference between a family's self-sufficiency and poverty.
  3. As population grew and death rate declined, family life stabilized and marriages became lifetime commitments.
  4. With growing colonial structure, opportunities for women decreased.
   a. Division of labor along gender lines solidified.
   b. Despite more consumer products, women's work increased.
   c. As infant mortality decreased, women spent more with child care.
 G. North America at Mid-Century
  1. As compared to Europe, colonies were diverse, prosperous, and offered many liberties.

SUGGESTED DISCUSSION QUESTIONS

- Dutch and French societies in North America differed in many ways from those established by the English. Using as evidence material from Chapters 1 to 3, discuss some of those differences, particularly with regard to labor systems, attitudes toward Indians, trade, settlement, and notions of freedom.
- In the Chesapeake region during the mid-seventeenth century, how similar was the experience of an indentured servant to that of an enslaved person? Be as specific as possible in your response.
- Eric Foner writes that "the freedoms Pennsylvania offered to European immigrants contributed to the deterioration of freedom for others." What examples can you cite that prove that statement?
- Why did the English government create the Dominion of New England? How did the colonists in the region react, and why? Why did the Dominion fail?
- What commonalities were there between Bacon's Rebellion and King Philip's War? How did the two reveal strains in colonial society? How did the colonists in each case use the language of liberty?
- Describe colonial society at the midpoint of the eighteenth century. Be sure to compare the colonial elite to the middle ranks and the poor. What role was there for women?
- How did the colonists benefit from being part of the British empire? Describe the role with trade each colonial region in British North America played in the Atlantic World.
- Imagine you are an indentured servant in the Chesapeake region or a recent European immigrant to any colony. Write a letter to your family back in Europe describing your life. Keep in mind the time of your letter (are you living relatively early in the colony's history or later when things are more developed?) as well as your geographic location, social status, age, sex, and occupation. Feel free to use the letter in Chapter 3's "Voices of Freedom" as a guide.

SUPPLEMENTAL WEB AND VISUAL RESOURCES

A Midwife's Tale
www.pbs.org/wgbh/amex/mwt/filmmore/index.html
A Midwife's Tale, a PBS American Experience film, recreates the life of Martha Ballard, a midwife from colonial New

England. The documentary is based on the Pulitzer Prize-winning book by Laurel Thatcher Ulrich.

Robert "King" Carter
etext.lib.virginia.edu/users/berkeley
This website has the diary, correspondence, and papers of Robert "King" Carter, one of the wealthiest Virginians and speaker of the House of Burgesses. This is a useful site for gaining insight into eighteenth-century aristocratic, political, and economic life in the Chesapeake region.

Africans in America
www.pbs.org/wgbh/aia/home.html
Africans in America is a four-part PBS video about America's journey through slavery. Part I is "The Terrible Transformation, 1450–1750."

Bacon's Rebellion
www.virginiaplaces.org/military/bacon.html
Although this page offers only a brief overview of the rebellion, the links near the end of the page provide additional useful resources.

Indentured Servants
www.pbs.org/opb/historydetectives/investigations/212_indentured feature.html
This website is for the PBS show *History Detectives*.

www.pbs.org/wgbh/aia/part1/1narr3.html
This website is for the PBS program *Africans in America*.

www.virtualjamestown.org/indlink.html
This website, Virtual Jamestown, shows various statutes pertaining to indentured servants.

King Philip's War
www.pilgrimhall.org/philipwar.htm
This website from America's Museum of Pilgrim Possessions offers a helpful overview of the war.

Salem Witch Trials
etext.lib.virginia.edu/salem/witchcraft/
This University of Virginia site hosts the Salem Witch Trials Documentary Archive and Transcription Project.

SUPPLEMENTAL PRINT RESOURCES

Breen, T. H. "'Baubles of Britain': The American and Consumer Revolutions of the Eighteenth Century." In *Diversity and Unity in Early North America*, 227–256. Edited by Philip Morgan. London: Routledge, 1993.

Brewer, John. *The Sinews of Power: War, Money and the English State, 1688–1783*. Cambridge, MA: Harvard University Press, 1988.

Brown, Kathleen. *Good Wives, Nasty Wenches, and Anxious Patriarchs: Gender, Race and Power in Colonial Virginia*. Chapel Hill, NC: University of North Carolina Press, 1996.

Davis, David Brion. "Constructing Race: A Reflection." *William and Mary Quarterly* 54, no. 1 (1997): 7–18.

Greene, Jack. *Pursuits of Happiness: The Social Development of Early Modern British Colonies and the Formation of American Culture*. Chapel Hill, NC: University of North Carolina Press, 1988.

Harley, David. "Explaining Salem: Calvinist Psychology and the Diagnosis of Possession." *American Historical Review* 101, no. 2 (1996): 307–330.

Nash, Gary. "Urban Wealth and Poverty in Pre-Revolutionary America." In *Colonial America: Essays in Politics and Social Development*, 447–483. Edited by Stanley Katz and John Murrin. New York: McGraw-Hill, 1983.

Nicholson, Bradley. "Legal Borrowing and the Origins of Slave Law in the British Colonies." *American Journal of Legal History* 38, no. 1 (1994): 38–51.

Parent, Anthony S., Jr. *Foul Means: The Formation of a Slave Society in Virginia, 1660–1740*. Chapel Hill, NC: University of North Carolina Press, 2002.

Ulrich, Laurel Thatcher. *Good Wives: Image and Reality in the Lives of Women in Northern New England, 1650–1750*. New York: Vintage Books, 1980.

Webb, Stephen Saunders. *1676: The End of American Independence*. Syracuse, NY: Syracuse University Press, 1995.

TEST BANK

Matching

TEST I

___ 1. Nathaniel Bacon
___ 2. Robert "King" Carter
___ 3. William Penn
___ 4. William of Orange
___ 5. Anthony Johnson
___ 6. Duke of York
___ 7. Jacob Leisler
___ 8. James II
___ 9. King Philip
___ 10. William Berkeley
___ 11. Edmund Andros
___ 12. Myer Myers

a. established a Committee of Safety in New York
b. a Protestant who became King of England
c. Metacom
d. formed Covenant Chain with Iroquois
e. elite planter who called for reform in Virginia
f. governor of Virginia during Bacon's Rebellion
g. a Catholic who became King of England
h. wealthy Virginian speaker of the House of Burgesses
i. proprietor of Pennsylvania
j. successful Jewish silversmith
k. overthrown in the Glorious Revolution
l. slave who became free and owned slaves himself

Answer Key: e, h, i, b, l, g, a, k, c, f, d, j

TEST 2

___ 1. Charter of Liberties
___ 2. mercantilism
___ 3. Royal African Company
___ 4. Anglicization
___ 5. Bacon's Rebellion
___ 6. Toleration Act
___ 7. King Philip's War
___ 8. Navigation Act
___ 9. West Jersey Concessions
___ 10. Quakers
___ 11. Covenant Chain
___ 12. Glorious Revolution

a. elites in America becoming more culturally English
b. allowed Protestant Dissenters to worship freely in England
c. government regulation of the nation's economy (to assure national power)
d. placed William of Orange on the English throne
e. had a monopoly on the slave trade
f. a very liberal frame for government
g. English demanded this over their former Dutch rulers
h. agreement between New York and Iroquois
i. believed in the equality of all persons
j. law that regulated the shipping and selling of colonial products
k. the poor of Virginia demand change
l. war between New Englanders and Indians

Answer Key: g, c, e, a, k, b, l, j, f, i, h, d

Learning Objectives

1. Explain how the English empire expanded in America in the mid-seventeenth century.
2. Explain how slavery was established in the Western Atlantic world.
3. Identify the major social and political crises that rocked the colonies in the late seventeenth century.
4. Describe the directions of social and economic change in the eighteenth-century colonies.
5. Explain how the patterns of class and gender roles changed in eighteenth-century America.

Multiple Choice

1. What was the impact of King Philip's War (1675–1676)?
   a. New England's tribes united against the colonists.
   b. In the long run the war produced a broadening of freedom for whites in New England.
   c. Native Americans up and down the eastern seaboard began rebelling against colonial rule when they saw what happened to their New England counterparts.
   d. Massachusetts banned all Native Americans from living within its borders.
   e. Great Britain formed the New England Confederation to protect against Native American depredations.

   ANS: B   TOP: Ethnicity | King Philip's War
   DIF: Moderate   REF: Full p. 87 | Seagull p. 89
   MSC: Understanding   OBJ: 3

2. According to the economic theory known as mercantilism:
   a. merchants should control the government because they contributed more than others to national wealth.
   b. the government should regulate economic activity so as to promote national power.
   c. the government should encourage manufacturing and commerce by keeping its hands off of the economy.
   d. colonies existed as a place for the mother country to send raw materials to be turned into manufactured goods.
   e. England wanted the right to sell goods in France, but only to non-Catholic buyers.

   ANS: B   TOP: Economic development | The Mercantilist System   DIF: Moderate   REF: Full p. 88 | Seagull p. 89   MSC: Understanding   OBJ: 3

3. The first English Navigation Act, adopted during the rule of Oliver Cromwell:
   a. required the Royal Navy to use only Protestant navigators on its ships.
   b. aimed to wrest control of world trade from the Dutch.
   c. freed England's North American colonies from economic regulations (in order to stimulate prosperity).
   d. added New Netherland to the British empire.
   e. authorized several mapmaking expeditions to the New World.

   ANS: B   TOP: Economic development | The Mercantilist System   DIF: Moderate   REF: Full p. 88 | Seagull p. 90   MSC: Understanding   OBJ: 1

4. "Enumerated" goods:
   a. made up the bulk of items imported into the colonies from abroad.
   b. were those the English colonies could not produce under terms of the Navigation Acts.
   c. created a financial drain on the English government during the seventeenth century.

d. were colonial products, such as tobacco and sugar, that first had to be imported to England.

e. were specifically exempt from England's mercantilist regulations.

ANS: D   TOP: Economic development | The Mercantilist System   DIF: Difficult   REF: Full p. 88 | Seagull pp. 90–91   MSC: Remembering   OBJ: 1

5. What sparked a new period of colonial expansion for England in the mid-seventeenth century?
a. England's defeat of the Netherlands in the Fourth Anglo-Dutch War of 1649
b. England's victory in a 1676 religious war with Spain
c. a treaty signed with the Iroquois Confederacy
d. the incredible financial success of the British East India Company
e. the restoration of the monarchy in 1660

ANS: E   TOP: Political history, changes | The Conquest of New Netherland   DIF: Difficult
REF: Full p. 88 | Seagull p. 91   MSC: Remembering
OBJ: 1

6. When England took over the Dutch colony that became New York:
a. the English eliminated all of the religious freedoms that the Dutch had allowed.
b. the English ended the Dutch tradition of allowing married women to conduct business in their own names.
c. the English respected Dutch antislavery laws, so that New York became a center for free African-Americans in North America.
d. the local population declined because of England's new and repressive rule.
e. England tried to maintain Dutch culture but ordered residents to learn English.

ANS: B   TOP: Political history, changes | Social history | New York and the Rights of Englishmen and Englishwomen   DIF: Moderate   REF: Full p. 90 | Seagull p. 91   MSC: Understanding   OBJ: 1

7. How did English rule affect the Iroquois Confederacy?
a. After a series of complex negotiations, both groups aided each other's imperial ambitions.
b. The English destroyed the Iroquois Confederacy temporarily but revived it under Sir Edmund Andros's rule after the Glorious Revolution of 1688.
c. English oppression drove the Iroquois to the side of the French, who eagerly sought their support.
d. It enabled the Iroquois to build alliances with other tribes against a common enemy.
e. The Iroquois adopted the English constitutional system.

ANS: A   TOP: Ethnicity | New York and the Indians
DIF: Moderate   REF: Full p. 90 | Seagull p. 93
MSC: Understanding   OBJ: 1

8. What was the Covenant Chain?
a. the promise James II gave Parliament that he would marry a Protestant princess
b. an agreement between the Dutch and the Mohican Nation that led to the founding of New Netherland
c. a mythical piece of priceless gold jewelry that Europeans wished to acquire from the Iroquois
d. an important Puritan text that spelled out the doctrine of predestination
e. an alliance made by the governor of New York and the Iroquois Confederacy

ANS: E   TOP: Ethnicity | New York and the Indians
DIF: Moderate   REF: Full p. 90 | Seagull p. 93
MSC: Remembering   OBJ: 1

9. The Charter of Liberties and Privileges in New York:
a. was the work of the Dutch, who did not trust the English to protect their religious freedom.
b. resulted especially from displeasure among residents of Manhattan.
c. reflected in part an effort by the British to exert their influence and control over the Dutch.
d. affirmed religious toleration for all denominations.
e. eliminated the property requirement for voting.

ANS: C   TOP: Political history, changes | The Charter of Liberties   DIF: Moderate   REF: Full p. 91 | Seagull pp. 93–94   MSC: Understanding   OBJ: 1

10. In its early years, Carolina was the "colony of a colony" because its original settlers included many:
a. former indentured servants from Virginia.
b. supporters of Anne Hutchinson seeking refuge from Massachusetts.
c. landless sons of wealthy planters in Barbados.
d. Protestants upset over Catholic rule in Maryland.
e. planters from Cuba hoping to expand their sugarcane empires.

ANS: C   TOP: Social history | The Founding of Carolina   DIF: Moderate   REF: Full p. 92 | Seagull p. 94   MSC: Remembering   OBJ: 1

11. The Fundamental Constitutions of Carolina:
a. were modeled on the governing structure of the Iroquois Confederacy.
b. banned slavery as antithetical to their goal of creating a society based on peasants working for noblemen.
c. allowed no elected assembly.
d. permitted only members of the Church of England to worship freely.

e. proposed a feudal society in the New World, complete with hereditary nobility.

ANS: E   TOP: Constitutional history | The Founding of Carolina   DIF: Moderate   REF: Full p. 92 | Seagull p. 94   MSC: Understanding   OBJ: 1

12. What inspired the 1715 uprising by the Yamasee and Creek peoples against English colonists in Carolina?
    a. the colonists' refusal to trade with the Yamasee and Creek
    b. an alliance of the Yamasee and Creek with the Iroquois Confederacy, which had declared war against New York colonists
    c. high debts incurred by the Yamasee and Creek in trade with the English settlers
    d. the English colonists' plans to begin capturing Native Americans to sell as slaves
    e. a bloody rebellion by African slaves against their masters near Charles Town

ANS: C   TOP: Ethnicity | The Founding of Carolina DIF: Moderate   REF: Full p. 92 | Seagull p. 94 MSC: Understanding   OBJ: 1

13. The economy of the Carolina colony:
    a. was based on plantation agriculture from the beginning.
    b. immediately proved profitable because of its reliance upon rice.
    c. was exactly the same as that of Barbados.
    d. originally centered on cattle-raising and trade.
    e. had nothing to do with slavery.

ANS: D   TOP: Economic development | The Founding of Carolina   DIF: Moderate   REF: Full p. 92 | Seagull p. 95   MSC: Remembering OBJ: 1

14. Carolina grew slowly until:
    a. rice as a staple crop was discovered to be extremely profitable.
    b. slaves were brought into the colony.
    c. an alliance with the Indians was signed.
    d. cotton was introduced into the colony.
    e. the king forced the English poor to settle the area.

ANS: A   TOP: Economic development | The Founding of Carolina   DIF: Moderate   REF: Full p. 92 | Seagull p. 95   MSC: Remembering   OBJ: 1

15. Of colonists in British North America, which group was the wealthiest?
    a. Philadelphia merchants
    b. Boston political elite
    c. Virginia tobacco farmers
    d. South Carolina rice planters
    e. New York merchants

ANS: D   TOP: Economic development | The Founding of Carolina   DIF: Moderate   REF: Full p. 92 | Seagull p. 95   MSC: Remembering OBJ: 1

16. William Penn obtained the land for his Pennsylvania colony because:
    a. King Charles I wanted Quakers to have a place where they could enjoy religious toleration.
    b. he supported the crown during the Glorious Revolution.
    c. the king wanted to cancel his debt to the Penn family and bolster the English presence in North America.
    d. he conquered the Swedes and Dutch who previously had controlled the land.
    e. his invention of what was then called the "penncill" made him incredibly rich.

ANS: C   TOP: Political history, changes | The Holy Experiment   DIF: Moderate   REF: Full p. 92 | Seagull p. 95   MSC: Understanding   OBJ: 1

17. To Quakers, liberty was:
    a. limited to white, landowning men.
    b. strictly defined.
    c. a universal entitlement.
    d. extended to women but not to blacks.
    e. limited to the spiritually inclined.

ANS: C   TOP: Political history, changes | Quaker Liberty   DIF: Moderate   REF: Full p. 93 | Seagull p. 95   MSC: Remembering   OBJ: 1

18. What was William Penn's most fundamental principle?
    a. voting rights for all adult men
    b. religious freedom
    c. communally owned property
    d. economic liberty
    e. support for women's suffrage

ANS: B   TOP: Political history, changes | Quaker Liberty   DIF: Easy   REF: Full p. 93 | Seagull p. 96 MSC: Remembering   OBJ: 1

19. William Penn was a member of which religious group?
    a. Puritans
    b. Anglicans
    c. Quakers
    d. Roman Catholics
    e. Presbyterians

ANS: C   TOP: Cultural history | The Holy Experiment DIF: Easy   REF: Full p. 93 | Seagull p. 95 MSC: Remembering   OBJ: 1

20. Before founding Pennsylvania, William Penn assisted a group of English Quakers to set up a colony in what became:
    a. New Hampshire.
    b. North Carolina.
    c. Delaware.
    d. New Jersey.
    e. Ontario.

    ANS: D   TOP: Political history, changes | The Holy Experiment   DIF: Difficult   REF: Full p. 93 | Seagull p. 95   MSC: Remembering   OBJ: 1

21. Pennsylvania's treatment of Native Americans was unique in what way?
    a. Pennsylvania was the only colony in which efforts at conversion focused on turning Native Americans into Quakers.
    b. The colony bought all of the land the Native Americans occupied and moved them west of the Appalachians, meaning that Indians were relocated but not decimated.
    c. Because Quakers were pacifists, they had to bring in militias from other colonies to take over Native American lands.
    d. Despite Quaker pacifism, Pennsylvanians were determined to exterminate the natives.
    e. Pennsylvania purchased Indian land that was then resold to colonists and offered refuge to tribes driven out of other colonies.

    ANS: E   TOP: Social history | Ethnicity | Quaker Liberty   DIF: Moderate   REF: Full p. 93 | Seagull p. 95   MSC: Understanding   OBJ: 1

22. What was one of Pennsylvania's only restrictions on religious liberty?
    a. Settlers could belong to any denomination but had to sign an oath affirming that they would not oppress Quakers.
    b. Holding office required an oath affirming a belief in Jesus Christ, which eliminated Jews from serving.
    c. Atheists were welcome as long as they promised not to publicly attack religion.
    d. Church attendance was mandatory, but the state did not specify which type of church.
    e. There were no restrictions.

    ANS: B   TOP: Social history | Quaker Liberty   DIF: Moderate   REF: Full p. 93 | Seagull p. 96   MSC: Understanding   OBJ: 1

23. What form of behavior did William Penn ban in his Pennsylvania colony?
    a. swearing
    b. alcohol consumption
    c. dancing in public or in private
    d. laughing during religious services
    e. singing outside of church

    ANS: A   TOP: Cultural history | Quaker Liberty   DIF: Moderate   REF: Full p. 93 | Seagull p. 96   MSC: Remembering   OBJ: 1

24. What ironic consequence did William Penn's generous policies, such as religious toleration and inexpensive land, have?
    a. They contributed to the increasing reliance of Virginia and Maryland on African slave labor.
    b. Now that Pennsylvania attracted so many settlers, Carolina was desperate for laborers and began a vast Indian slave trade.
    c. They actually discouraged suspicious Europeans from choosing Pennsylvania as a place to settle.
    d. They led the Puritan authorities in Massachusetts to adopt religious toleration in order to compete with Pennsylvania for colonists.
    e. They encouraged poor residents of New York and New Jersey to move to Pennsylvania in such numbers that Penn repealed his policies within a decade.

    ANS: A   TOP: Social history | Land in Pennsylvania   DIF: Difficult   REF: Full p. 94 | Seagull p. 96   MSC: Understanding   OBJ: 2

25. Who in the Pennsylvania colony was eligible to vote?
    a. everyone, male and female
    b. a majority of the male population
    c. all males
    d. Quakers
    e. all people of European descent

    ANS: B   TOP: Political history, changes | Land in Pennsylvania   DIF: Moderate   REF: Full p. 94 | Seagull p. 96   MSC: Remembering   OBJ: 2

26. Which of the following was NOT a factor that made African slavery appealing to English planters in the New World?
    a. Since slaves' terms of service never expired, unlike those of indentured servants, Africans could create a permanent labor force.
    b. Europeans believed that Africans were more accustomed to hard agricultural labor than were Native Americans, and thus would be better workers.
    c. Africans had long since developed a resistance to European diseases, making epidemics less likely than among Native American laborers.
    d. Africans could not claim the protection of English common law.
    e. A long English legal tradition of discriminating against dark-skinned peoples eased the legalization of slavery.

ANS: E   TOP: Civil rights | Origins of American Slavery   DIF: Difficult   REF: Full p. 94 | Seagull p. 97   MSC: Understanding   OBJ: 2

27. Ideas of race and racism in seventeenth-century England:
   a. inspired the creation of an African slave labor force.
   b. caused many Englishmen to become abolitionists when they saw that slavery was based on these ideas.
   c. had not fully developed as modern concepts.
   d. originated in the writings of Sir Walter Raleigh.
   e. prompted Shakespeare to write *Hamlet.*

   ANS: C   TOP: Social history | Englishmen and Africans   DIF: Moderate   REF: Full pp. 94–95 | Seagull p. 97   MSC: Understanding   OBJ: 2

28. Which of the following is true of slavery?
   a. The English word "slavery" derives from "Slav," reflecting the slave trade in Slavic peoples until the fifteenth century.
   b. Christians never were enslaved.
   c. The Roman Empire outlawed it, but it revived, thanks to Columbus.
   d. It was nonexistent in Africa until the arrival of European slave traders.
   e. In every culture in which it existed, it was based on the needs of large-scale agriculture.

   ANS: A   TOP: Social history | Slavery in History   DIF: Moderate   REF: Full p. 95 | Seagull p. 98   MSC: Understanding   OBJ: 2

29. Unlike slavery in America, slavery in Africa:
   a. declined in importance during the 1600s.
   b. was more likely to be based in the household than on an agricultural plantation.
   c. led to much higher death rates.
   d. was entirely race-based.
   e. existed only for women.

   ANS: B   TOP: Social history | Slavery in History   DIF: Moderate   REF: Full p. 95 | Seagull p. 98   MSC: Understanding   OBJ: 2

30. Which commodity drove the African slave trade in Brazil and the West Indies during the seventeenth century?
   a. tobacco
   b. indigo
   c. silver
   d. cotton
   e. sugar

   ANS: E   TOP: Global awareness | Slavery in the West Indies   DIF: Easy   REF: Full p. 96 | Seagull p. 99   MSC: Remembering   OBJ: 2

31. Which one of the following is true of the English West Indies in the seventeenth century?
   a. By the end of the century, the African population far outnumbered the European population on most islands.
   b. Mixed economies with small farms worked by indentured servants dominated islands such as Barbados throughout the century.
   c. Frequent uprisings by African slaves caused the English to abandon the West Indies by the 1680s and to relocate staple crop production to mainland North America.
   d. The free labor system of the West Indies stood in stark contrast to the slave labor system of the Chesapeake.
   e. Indentured servants replaced African slaves in the West Indies once the demand for slaves in Carolina drained away the African population of the islands.

   ANS: A   TOP: Global awareness | Slavery in the West Indies   DIF: Easy   REF: Full p. 96 | Seagull p. 99   MSC: Understanding   OBJ: 2

32. Slavery developed more slowly in North America than in the English West Indies because:
   a. it was a longer trip from Africa to North America, making slavery less profitable.
   b. planters in Virginia and Maryland agreed that indentured servants were far less troublesome.
   c. the high death rate among tobacco workers made it economically unappealing to pay more for a slave likely to die within a short time.
   d. Parliament passed a law in 1643 that gave tax breaks to British West Indian planters who imported slaves but not to American colonists who imported slaves.
   e. those living in the British West Indies opposed slavery until the American colonies won their independence in the Revolutionary War.

   ANS: C   TOP: Social history | Slavery in the West Indies   DIF: Moderate   REF: Full p. 97 | Seagull p. 100   MSC: Understanding   OBJ: 2

33. Spain's *Las Siete Partidas*, a series of laws touching on slavery:
   a. strongly influenced the English as they devised their own laws about slavery.
   b. was strictly enforced in Mexico, Cuba, and other Spanish colonies until those areas achieved independence.
   c. required masters to free female slaves on their twenty-first birthdays.
   d. gave slaves some opportunities to claim rights under the law in Spain's American empire.

e. did not apply to Spanish possessions in the New World.

ANS: D   TOP: Global awareness | Slavery and the Law   DIF: Moderate   REF: Full p. 97 | Seagull p. 100   MSC: Understanding   OBJ: 2

34. According to laws in the seventeenth-century Chesapeake:
   a. black men were not permitted to marry white women, but black women could marry white men.
   b. free blacks had the right to sue and testify in court.
   c. free blacks were not permitted to serve in the militia unless they signed a loyalty oath.
   d. the sale of any married slave was prohibited.
   e. the children of enslaved women were free; the status of enslavement was not inherited.

   ANS: B   TOP: Civil rights | Slavery and the Law DIF: Difficult   REF: Full p. 98 | Seagull p. 101 MSC: Understanding   OBJ: 2

35. Which man was once a slave, only to be freed and own slaves himself?
   a. William Penn
   b. Anthony Johnson
   c. Olaudah Equiano
   d. Robert Carter
   e. Nathaniel Bacon

   ANS: B   TOP: Civil rights | Slavery and the Law DIF: Moderate   REF: Full p. 98 | Seagull p. 101 MSC: Remembering   OBJ: 2

36. What historical evidence demonstrates that blacks were being held as slaves for life by the 1640s?
   a. Property registers list white servants with the number of years they were to work, but blacks (with higher valuations) had no terms of service associated with their names.
   b. Transcripts from legislative debates in the House of Burgesses show that Virginia lawmakers were debating whether permanent slave status was a good idea.
   c. Records of declining tobacco prices show that it had become harder to keep labor, which would have forced planters to turn increasingly to Africans and away from white servants.
   d. There is none, because slavery did not fully exist in Virginia until after Bacon's Rebellion in 1676.
   e. Advertisements for slaves began appearing in newspapers regularly by 1642.

   ANS: A   TOP: Civil rights | The Rise of Chesapeake Slavery   DIF: Difficult   REF: Full p. 98 | Seagull p. 101   MSC: Understanding   OBJ: 2

37. When the Virginia House of Burgesses decreed that religious conversion did not release a slave from bondage:
   a. every other colonial assembly followed suit.
   b. Governor William Berkeley vetoed the measure, which led to Bacon's Rebellion.
   c. it meant that, under Virginia law, Christians could own other Christians.
   d. mass protests followed.
   e. slaves quit attending church.

   ANS: C   TOP: Civil rights | The Rise of Chesapeake Slavery   DIF: Easy   REF: Full p. 99 | Seagull p. 101 MSC: Understanding   OBJ: 2

38. Governor William Berkeley's regime:
   a. corrupted Penn's plans for the Pennsylvania colony, but the democratic system that Penn created made it impossible for him to do anything about it.
   b. was a corrupt alliance of the Virginia colony's wealthiest tobacco planters.
   c. offended tobacco planters, who felt that he allowed Nathaniel Bacon to exert too much influence in the House of Burgesses.
   d. greatly affected Virginia during its four years in power.
   e. extended Virginia's claims to California, thus leading to the naming of the northern California city of Berkeley.

   ANS: B   TOP: Political history, changes | Bacon's Rebellion: Land and Labor in Virginia DIF: Moderate   REF: Full p. 99 | Seagull p. 102 MSC: Understanding   OBJ: 2

39. Which of the following was true of small farmers in 1670s Virginia?
   a. The economy was doing so well that even though they made less money than large-scale planters, their problems were too small to justify their rebellion.
   b. They had access to the best land, but a glut in the tobacco market left them in poverty.
   c. Their taxes were incredibly low—the one issue with which they were pleased.
   d. They could count on the government to help them take over Native American lands and thereby expand their meager holdings.
   e. The lack of good land, high taxes on tobacco, and falling prices reduced their prospects.

   ANS: E   TOP: Social history | Bacon's Rebellion: Land and Labor in Virginia   DIF: Moderate   REF: Full p. 99 | Seagull p. 102   MSC: Understanding   OBJ: 2

40. Bacon's Rebellion was a response to:
   a. worsening economic conditions in Virginia.
   b. increased slavery in the Carolinas.

c. Indian attacks in New England.
d. the Glorious Revolution in England.
e. the Salem witch trials.

ANS: A   TOP: Social history | Bacon's Rebellion:
Land and Labor in Virginia   DIF: Easy   REF: Full
p. 99 | Seagull p. 103   MSC: Remembering
OBJ: 2

41. Nathaniel Bacon:
a. actually was socially closer to the elite than to the
indentured servants who supported him.
b. had no connection to Virginia's wealthiest planters.
c. won unanimous support for his effort to reduce
taxes, but his effort to remove all Native Americans
from the colony doomed his rebellion.
d. burned down Jamestown but never succeeded in
taking over the colony or driving out Governor
Berkeley.
e. was the first colonist to open his own
slaughterhouse.

ANS: A   TOP: Social history | Bacon's Rebellion:
Land and Labor in Virginia   DIF: Moderate
REF: Full p. 100 | Seagull p. 103   MSC: Understanding
OBJ: 2

42. Bacon's Rebellion contributed to which of the
following in Virginia?
a. a large and sustained increase in the importation of
indentured servants
b. generous payments to Native Americans to
encourage them to give up their lands to white
farmers
c. changes in the political style of Virginia's powerful
large-scale planters, who adopted a get-tough policy
with small farmers and hired their own militia to
enforce their will
d. the replacing of indentured servants with African
slaves on Virginia's plantations
e. an order from Governor Berkeley that Native
Americans could serve in the militia

ANS: D   TOP: Social history | The End of the Rebel-
lion and Its Consequences   DIF: Moderate
REF: Full p. 100 | Seagull p. 103   MSC: Understanding
OBJ: 2

43. Slave labor in the Chesapeake region increasingly
supplanted indentured servitude during the last two
decades of the seventeenth century, in part because:
a. the opening of the new colony of North Carolina
attracted enough whites to make up for the loss of
those who would have come to the New World as
indentured servants.
b. Bacon's Rebellion reminded leaders of the dangers
of allowing racial intermarriage.

c. improving conditions in England reduced the
number of transatlantic migrants.
d. a monopoly on the slave trade made it easier to
import Africans.
e. indentured servants began forming associations that
went on strike for better conditions.

ANS: C   TOP: Economic development | A Slave
Society   DIF: Moderate   REF: Full p. 100 |
Seagull p. 104   MSC: Understanding   OBJ: 2

44. The Virginia slave code of 1705:
a. simply brought together old aspects of the laws
governing slaves and slavery.
b. completely rewrote and changed the earlier slave
laws.
c. embedded the principle of white supremacy in law.
d. made clear that slaves were subject to the will of
their masters but not to anyone who could not claim
ownership of them.
e. was the work of Nathaniel Bacon.

ANS: C   TOP: Civil rights | A Slave Society
DIF: Moderate   REF: Full p. 101 | Seagull p. 104
MSC: Understanding   OBJ: 2

45. Which of the following is true of slave resistance in the
colonial period?
a. Runaways were very rare because slaves knew that
attempting to escape would be futile.
b. Some slaves were the offspring of white traders and
therefore knew enough English to turn to the legal
system, at least until Virginia lawmakers prevented
them from doing so.
c. A number of bloody rebellions prompted a
wholesale revision of slave codes.
d. It was limited because slaves at the time were too
new to the colonies to understand the concept of
freedom.
e. All runaways headed for freedom in French Canada.

ANS: B   TOP: Civil rights | Notions of Freedom
DIF: Moderate   REF: Full p. 101 | Seagull pp. 104–105
MSC: Understanding   OBJ: 2

46. The Glorious Revolution of 1688:
a. resulted mainly from the fears of English aristocrats
that the birth of James II's son would lead to a
Catholic succession.
b. ended parliamentary rule in Great Britain until
Queen Anne's War in 1702.
c. was the work of an ambitious Danish prince out to
avenge his father's murder by a British nobleman.
d. had no impact on the British colonies in America.
e. prompted Scotland's secession from Great Britain
and thus a reduction in Scotch-Irish immigration to
the colonies.

ANS: A   TOP: Political history, changes | The Glorious Revolution in England   DIF: Easy   REF: Full p. 102 | Seagull p. 105   MSC: Understanding   OBJ: 3

47. The English Bill of Rights of 1689:
   a. was unwritten, like the English Constitution on which it was based.
   b. was King William's finest writing on the importance of liberty.
   c. divided power in England between the king and Parliament.
   d. was copied word for word into the U.S. Constitution a century later.
   e. listed parliamentary powers over such individual rights as trial by jury.

ANS: E   TOP: Political history, changes | The Glorious Revolution in England   DIF: Moderate
REF: Full p. 102 | Seagull p. 106   MSC: Remembering
OBJ: 3

48. In what ways did England reduce colonial autonomy during the 1680s?
   a. Charles II revoked the charters of all colonies that had violated the Navigation Acts.
   b. It created the Dominion of New England, run by a royal appointee without benefit of an elected assembly.
   c. Because Charles II and James II were at least closet Catholics, the colonies no longer could have established churches within their borders.
   d. The king started appointing all judges.
   e. Not at all; this was the era in which colonies achieved autonomy.

ANS: B   TOP: Political history, changes | The Glorious Revolution in America   DIF: Moderate
REF: Full p. 103 | Seagull pp. 106–107
MSC: Understanding   OBJ: 3

49. The Glorious Revolution witnessed uprisings in colonial America, including ones in:
   a. New Hampshire and Pennsylvania.
   b. New York and Maryland.
   c. Virginia and New York.
   d. Pennsylvania and Maryland.
   e. New York and New Hampshire.

ANS: B   TOP: Social history | The Maryland Uprising   DIF: Difficult   REF: Full pp. 103–104 | Seagull p. 107   MSC: Remembering   OBJ: 3

50. Captain Jacob Leisler, the head of the rebel militia that took control of New York in 1689:
   a. was a close ally of Sir Edmund Andros, who was trying to regain control of the Dominion of New England.
   b. was overthrown and killed in so grisly a manner that the rivalry between his friends and foes polarized New York politics for years.
   c. was knighted for his role in supporting the Glorious Revolution.
   d. sought to impose Catholic rule but was defeated by a Protestant militia in a short but bloody civil war.
   e. slaughtered so many Native Americans that wars between whites and the remaining tribes kept New York in an uproar for the next two decades.

ANS: B   TOP: Social history | Leisler's Rebellion
DIF: Moderate   REF: Full p. 104 | Seagull p. 108
MSC: Remembering   OBJ: 3

51. How did the new Massachusetts charter of 1691 change that colony's government?
   a. Puritans were required to permit religious tolerance of all Christian denominations.
   b. It eliminated town government, which had been the heart of Puritan control of the commonwealth.
   c. It made Massachusetts a royal colony rather than under the control of Puritan "saints."
   d. It required all judges to be Anglican, greatly reducing Puritan influence over the three branches of government.
   e. It moved the seat of government to Salem, which contributed greatly to the problems involving witchcraft.

ANS: C   TOP: Political history, changes | Changes in New England   DIF: Difficult   REF: Full p. 104 | Seagull p. 108   MSC: Remembering   OBJ: 3

52. Once Massachusetts became a royal colony in 1691:
   a. it was required to abide by the English Act of Toleration, which displeased many Puritan leaders.
   b. it received the right to have its voters elect its own governor and legislative assembly.
   c. Plymouth was split off from Massachusetts to become its own independent colony.
   d. church membership became the chief legal requirement for voting.
   e. social tensions generally decreased and a relatively peaceful period ensued.

ANS: A   TOP: Political history, changes | Changes in New England   DIF: Moderate   REF: Full pp. 104–105 | Seagull p. 108
MSC: Understanding   OBJ: 3

53. According to New England Puritans, witchcraft:
   a. was perfectly acceptable when it was used for proper purposes.
   b. was punishable by hanging unless it was used to reinforce men's standing and God's will.

c. resulted from pacts that women made with the devil to obtain supernatural powers or interfere with natural processes.

d. was restricted to Salem.

e. was due entirely to exposure to Catholicism.

ANS: C   TOP: Social history | The Prosecution of Witches   DIF: Easy   REF: Full p. 105 | Seagull p. 109   MSC: Remembering   OBJ: 3

54. Which of the following fits the description of a person most likely to have been accused of witchcraft in seventeenth-century New England?

a. a single young woman whose attractiveness meant that some saw her as a threat to Puritan values

b. a married woman who normally was subservient to her husband and the community, which made her behavior seem all the more bizarre

c. a widow who presumably was too lonely or too dependent on the community to be taken seriously, but who had to be tried and convicted to keep others from thinking similarly

d. a married woman who had just lost a child

e. a woman beyond childbearing age who was outspoken, economically independent, or estranged from her husband

ANS: E   TOP: Social history | The Prosecution of Witches   DIF: Moderate   REF: Full p. 105 | Seagull p. 109   MSC: Understanding   OBJ: 3

55. Why did the accusations of witchcraft in Salem suddenly snowball in 1692?

a. The only way to avoid prosecution was to confess and name others.

b. When Tituba testified, the issue became racial and divided the town.

c. All of the accused were children, and Puritans were determined to force their young to accept their religious traditions or face death.

d. The colonial capital had just been moved to Salem, upsetting the normally staid town.

e. They did not; actually, the number of accusations was average and Salem was highly overrated as a place for charges of witchcraft.

ANS: A   TOP: Social history | The Salem Witch Trials   DIF: Moderate   REF: Full p. 106 | Seagull p. 110   MSC: Understanding   OBJ: 3

56. Who finally ended the Salem witch trials?

a. the Massachusetts governor

b. the local pastor

c. Salem's judge

d. Tituba

e. Increase Mather

ANS: A   TOP: Social history | The Salem Witch Trials   DIF: Moderate   REF: Full p. 106 | Seagull p. 110   MSC: Remembering   OBJ: 3

57. As accusations and executions multiplied in Salem, what was the long-term impact of the witchcraft trials there?

a. Puritan leader Increase Mather encouraged juries to take testimony and accusations more seriously.

b. The idea of prosecuting witches gained widespread support.

c. The number of witchcraft prosecutions in Massachusetts declined markedly.

d. Colonial leaders saw something was seriously wrong with their judicial system and outlawed witchcraft trials in 1715.

e. Witchcraft prosecutions were put under the control of the Massachusetts General Court.

ANS: C   TOP: Social history | The Salem Witch Trials   DIF: Moderate   REF: Full p. 106 | Seagull p. 110   MSC: Understanding   OBJ: 3

58. Which of the following best sums up population diversity in colonial British America?

a. From the beginning of British settlement, the colonies were highly diverse in race and religion.

b. Great Britain originally promoted emigration to the colonies as a means of ridding itself of excess population but cut back in the eighteenth century, opening the colonies to a more diverse group of settlers.

c. Men and women arrived in almost equal numbers because British officials encouraged women to leave, believing that fewer women in the mother country would equal slower population growth.

d. Great Britain urged professionals and skilled craftspeople to go to its colonies in America because it wanted to create a model society there, but eventually it began to urge vagabonds and "masterless men" to go instead.

e. Germans were the only non-British group allowed to live in the colonies.

ANS: B   TOP: Ethnicity | A Diverse Population   DIF: Moderate   REF: Full p. 107 | Seagull pp. 111–112   MSC: Understanding   OBJ: 4

59. Great Britain sought to attract which of the following to its American colonies in the eighteenth century?

a. Protestants from non-English and less prosperous parts of the British Isles

b. Catholics from France and Spain, thereby weakening England's enemies

c. professionals and skilled craftsmen from England

d. members of non-mainstream religions, particularly Quakers and Anabaptists

e. wealthy merchants who could spur economic growth in the colonies

ANS: A   TOP: Ethnicity | Attracting Settlers
DIF: Moderate   REF: Full pp. 107, 109 | Seagull p. 112   MSC: Understanding   OBJ: 4

60. The Scottish and Scotch-Irish immigrants to the colonies:
    a. were almost uniformly Catholics.
    b. usually worked in the West Indies before moving to the mainland colonies.
    c. were not only poor farmers, but physicians, merchants, and teachers, too.
    d. did little to add to the religious diversity in America.
    e. represented only a small fraction of the immigration to the colonies.

ANS: C   TOP: Ethnicity | Attracting Settlers
DIF: Moderate   REF: Full p. 109 | Seagull p. 112
MSC: Remembering   OBJ: 4

61. The German migration to the English colonies:
    a. was unusual because few Germans left their part of Europe during the American colonial era.
    b. consisted mainly of single young males, as with their counterparts who migrated from England.
    c. was mainly to Maryland, because most of the German immigrants were Catholic.
    d. led to the formation of many farming communities.
    e. led to the separation of church and state.

ANS: D   TOP: Ethnicity | The German Migration
DIF: Moderate   REF: Full p. 110 | Seagull p. 114
MSC: Understanding   OBJ: 4

62. English and Dutch merchants created a well-organized system for "redemptioners." What was this system for?
    a. for New Englanders to trade molasses for rum with the West Indies
    b. for bringing Protestant refugees to North America for a hefty fee
    c. for carrying indentured German families to America where they would work off their transportation debt
    d. for unloading the unwanted convicts of London and Amsterdam to ports such as Boston and New York
    e. for pirating against Spain and France, their Catholic archenemies

ANS: C   TOP: Ethnicity | The German Migration
DIF: Moderate   REF: Full p. 110 | Seagull p. 114
MSC: Remembering   OBJ: 4

63. The separation of church and state:
    a. existed only in the southern colonies.
    b. existed only in a few colonies.
    c. was limited in the colonies and existed only to promote all forms of Christianity.
    d. resulted in the colonies from the Glorious Revolution of 1688.
    e. was due largely to the increasing German presence in the colonies.

ANS: B   TOP: Political history, changes | Religious Diversity   DIF: Moderate   REF: Full p. 110 | Seagull p. 114   MSC: Remembering   OBJ: 4

64. All of the following were factors enticing migration to the British colonies EXCEPT:
    a. availability of land.
    b. lack of a military draft.
    c. absence of restraints on economic opportunity.
    d. religious toleration.
    e. cheap and safe transatlantic transportation.

ANS: E   TOP: Ethnicity | Religious Diversity
DIF: Easy   REF: Full p. 110 | Seagull p. 115
MSC: Understanding   OBJ: 4

65. The biggest reason Jews left Europe was:
    a. for the economic opportunities in New England.
    b. to be involved in colonial governments.
    c. to become indentured servants in North America.
    d. to escape rigid religious restrictions in German-speaking areas of Europe.
    e. to escape violence.

ANS: D   TOP: Ethnicity | Religious Diversity
DIF: Moderate   REF: Full p. 110 | Seagull pp. 114–115
MSC: Understanding   OBJ: 4

66. Indians in eighteenth-century British America:
    a. were well integrated into the British imperial system.
    b. benefited from the Walking Purchase of 1737.
    c. were viewed in the same way by traders, British officials, and farmers.
    d. never warred with the colonists.
    e. had access to the liberties guaranteed to Englishmen.

ANS: A   TOP: Ethnicity | Indian Life in Transition
DIF: Moderate   REF: Full p. 111 | Seagull p. 115
MSC: Understanding   OBJ: 4

67. What role did Native Americans play in British imperial wars during the eighteenth century?
    a. They avoided all involvement.
    b. They did much of the fighting in the wars.
    c. They fought only in Canada and in the Ohio Valley.

d. They caused some of them, because the French resented British treatment of Indians.

e. They uniformly sided with the French against the British.

ANS: B   TOP: Ethnicity | Indian Life in Transition
DIF: Moderate   REF: Full p. 111 | Seagull pp. 115–116
MSC: Remembering   OBJ: 4

68. The Walking Purchase of 1737:
    a. sparked King Philip's War.
    b. was a deceitful deal for the Lenni-Lenape Indians.
    c. was part of the West Jersey Concessions.
    d. was led by Nathaniel Bacon.
    e. was rescinded by the governor of Pennsylvania the following year.

ANS: B   TOP: Ethnicity | Indian Life in Transition
DIF: Moderate   REF: Full pp. 111, 114 | Seagull p. 118
MSC: Understanding   OBJ: 4

69. Which of the following was true of agriculture in the colonies during the eighteenth century?
    a. It was in decline in the backcountry as compared to coastal areas.
    b. Because New York's landlords had taken over so much land, agriculture grew more slowly in New York than in other colonies.
    c. New England moved away from smaller farming and increasingly toward large-scale farms and plantations.
    d. The standard of living on farms was far lower than it was in Europe.
    e. Farmers in the Middle Colonies had no interest in the market.

ANS: B   TOP: Economic development | Regional Diversity   DIF: Moderate   REF: Full p. 115 | Seagull p. 119   MSC: Understanding   OBJ: 4

70. By the eighteenth century, consumer goods such as books and ceramic plates:
    a. were found in many colonial residents' homes.
    b. were specifically banned in the colonies by the Navigation Acts.
    c. were rare in the colonies, thus demonstrating that the colonists lived in a premodern world.
    d. were manufactured in several mainland English colonies but had to be shipped to England for sale.
    e. were almost entirely Dutch-made.

ANS: A   TOP: Social history | The Consumer Revolution   DIF: Moderate   REF: Full p. 115 | Seagull p. 119   MSC: Remembering   OBJ: 4

71. During the colonial era, Philadelphia:
    a. became home to a varied population of artisans and craftsmen.

b. was one of the empire's least successful seaports.

c. was large by European standards.

d. was populated almost entirely by wealthy citizens.

e. came under the almost dictatorial control of Benjamin Franklin.

ANS: A   TOP: Social history | Colonial Artisans
DIF: Easy   REF: Full p. 116 | Seagull p. 120
MSC: Remembering   OBJ: 4

72. North American crops and products:
    a. played only a small role in the British empire.
    b. were consumed entirely overseas.
    c. were part of a commercial trade network that knitted together a far-flung empire.
    d. compared unfavorably with those throughout the rest of the empire.
    e. led to numerous complaints to the parliamentary consumer advocate.

ANS: C   TOP: Economic development | An Atlantic World   DIF: Easy   REF: Full p. 116 | Seagull p. 121   MSC: Understanding   OBJ: 4

73. Which of the following was true of the colonial elite?
    a. As with the mother country, the colonies had a titled aristocracy.
    b. They controlled colonial government.
    c. They often encountered financial trouble because they lacked connections to their counterparts back in the mother country.
    d. Most of them were as wealthy as, if not wealthier than, the British aristocracy.
    e. All of them were careful to marry outside of their families.

ANS: B   TOP: Social history | The Colonial Elite
DIF: Moderate   REF: Full p. 118 | Seagull p. 122
MSC: Understanding   OBJ: 5

74. "Anglicization" meant all of the following EXCEPT:
    a. colonists were determined to speak English as perfectly as those who lived in England.
    b. colonists imported the latest London fashions and literature.
    c. the colonial elite modeled their homes on the English gentry's estates and townhouses.
    d. those colonists who could afford to do so often sent their sons to England to be educated.
    e. the upper-class colonists often had coats of arms designed for their families, as the upper class did in England.

ANS: A   TOP: Social history | Anglicization
DIF: Moderate   REF: Full p. 119 | Seagull p. 123
MSC: Understanding   OBJ: 5

75. How did the colonial elite view their role in society?
  a. Social obligations demanded that they give everyone the same liberties that they enjoyed.
  b. It meant the power to rule—the right of those blessed with wealth and prominence to dominate others.
  c. They should enjoy their wealth but not parade it by dressing differently or by living in homes that were more elaborate than those of a lower status.
  d. They should work hard, because that is how they would make more money.
  e. They felt that they had no role and that those beneath them should just take care of themselves.

  ANS: B   TOP: Social history | The South Carolina Aristocracy   DIF: Moderate   REF: Full p. 119 | Seagull p. 124   MSC: Understanding   OBJ: 5

76. Which of the following was true of poverty in the colonial period?
  a. Poverty was greater in the colonies than it was in Great Britain, which had more economic activity.
  b. The percentage of colonists living in poverty was great because the northern colonists considered slaves poverty-stricken.
  c. Limited supplies of land, especially for inheritance, contributed to poverty.
  d. Colonists differed greatly from the British back in England in how they viewed poverty and those living in poverty.
  e. It declined in the cities because of the rise of consumer markets.

  ANS: C   TOP: Social history | Poverty in the Colonies   DIF: Moderate   REF: Full p. 120 | Seagull p. 124   MSC: Understanding   OBJ: 5

77. By the eighteenth century, colonial farm families:
  a. almost always owned at least three slaves.
  b. were in decline as bigger cities like Philadelphia expanded.
  c. saw freedom as depending on their political rights, not their ownership of property.
  d. viewed land ownership almost as a right, a precondition of freedom.
  e. engaged in arranged intermarriages.

  ANS: D   TOP: Social history | The Middle Ranks   DIF: Moderate   REF: Full p. 122 | Seagull p. 125   MSC: Understanding   OBJ: 5

78. As English colonial society became more structured in the eighteenth century, what were the effects on women?
  a. They received more legal rights, such as the right to own property in their own names.
  b. Women's work became more clearly defined as tied closely to the home.
  c. Their workloads decreased thanks to technological advances such as the spinning wheel and to declining infant mortality rates.
  d. Women were permitted to practice law.
  e. Women bore so fewer children that population levels slightly declined in the 1740s, then stabilized until the American Revolution.

  ANS: B   TOP: Social history | Women and the Household Economy   DIF: Moderate   REF: Full p. 123 | Seagull p. 126   MSC: Understanding   OBJ: 5

True or False

1. English observers of New Netherland believed religious toleration led to Dutch prosperity.

  ANS: T   TOP: Social history | New York and the Rights of Englishmen and Englishwomen   DIF: Difficult   REF: Full p. 90 | Seagull p. 91   MSC: Understanding   OBJ: 1

2. New Netherland never became an important or sizable colony in the Dutch empire.

  ANS: T   TOP: Global awareness | The Conquest of New Netherland   DIF: Moderate   REF: Full p. 90 | Seagull p. 91   MSC: Remembering   OBJ: 1

3. English settlers in New York demanded their rights over their former Dutch rulers through the Charter of Liberties.

  ANS: T   TOP: Political history, changes | The Charter of Liberties   DIF: Moderate   REF: Full p. 91 | Seagull pp. 93–94   MSC: Remembering   OBJ: 1

4. Early settlers of Carolina desired primarily deer hides and slaves from Indians.

  ANS: T   TOP: Ethnicity | The Founding of Carolina   DIF: Moderate   REF: Full p. 92 | Seagull p. 94   MSC: Remembering   OBJ: 1

5. William Penn believed in equality and liberty, but not for Indians or blacks.

  ANS: F   TOP: Political history, changes | The Holy Experiment   DIF: Easy   REF: Full p. 92 | Seagull p. 95   MSC: Remembering   OBJ: 1

6. Race and racism are modern concepts and had not been fully developed by the seventeenth century.

  ANS: T   TOP: Civil rights | Englishmen and Africans   DIF: Moderate   REF: Full pp. 94–95 | Seagull p. 97   MSC: Understanding   OBJ: 2

7. Slavery flourished in Brazil and the West Indies in the seventeenth century because of tobacco.

   ANS: F   TOP: Social history | Slavery in the West Indies   DIF: Moderate   REF: Full p. 96 | Seagull p. 99   MSC: Remembering   OBJ: 2

8. The law of slavery in English North America became far more repressive than in the Spanish empire.

   ANS: T   TOP: Civil rights | Slavery and the Law   DIF: Moderate   REF: Full p. 97 | Seagull p. 100   MSC: Understanding   OBJ: 2

9. As in the Spanish empire, British North America developed a distinctive mulatto, or mixed-race, class.

   ANS: F   TOP: Geographic issues | The Rise of Chesapeake Slavery   DIF: Moderate   REF: Full p. 99 | Seagull p. 102   MSC: Remembering   OBJ: 2

10. Bacon's Rebellion was caused by a conflict between blacks and whites in Virginia.

    ANS: F   TOP: Social history | Bacon's Rebellion: Land and Labor in Virginia   DIF: Moderate   REF: Full p. 99 | Seagull p. 103   MSC: Remembering   OBJ: 2

11. Nathaniel Bacon, who led Bacon's Rebellion against the Virginia elite, was himself a wealthy planter.

    ANS: T   TOP: Social history | Bacon's Rebellion: Land and Labor in Virginia   DIF: Moderate   REF: Full p.100 | Seagull p. 103   MSC: Remembering   OBJ: 2

12. A consequence of Bacon's Rebellion was a consolidation of power among Virginia's elite.

    ANS: T   TOP: Social history | The End of the Rebellion and Its Consequences   DIF: Moderate   REF: Full p. 100 | Seagull p. 103   MSC: Understanding   OBJ: 2

13. The Glorious Revolution in England was tragically bloody.

    ANS: F   TOP: Political history, changes | The Glorious Revolution in England   DIF: Easy   REF: Full p. 102 | Seagull p. 106   MSC: Remembering   OBJ: 3

14. Parliament enacted a bill of rights on the completion of the Glorious Revolution.

    ANS: T   TOP: Political history, changes | The Glorious Revolution in England   DIF: Moderate   REF: Full p. 102 | Seagull p. 106   MSC: Remembering   OBJ: 3

15. Following the Glorious Revolution, the Massachusetts colony had to abide by the Toleration Act.

    ANS: T   TOP: Political history, changes | Changes in New England   DIF: Moderate   REF: Full p. 104 | Seagull p. 108   MSC: Remembering   OBJ: 3

16. The Toleration Act passed by Parliament in 1690 was widely praised by the Puritans in Massachusetts.

    ANS: F   TOP: Political history, changes | Changes in New England   DIF: Easy   REF: Full p. 104 | Seagull p. 108   MSC: Remembering   OBJ: 3

17. Most of those accused of witchcraft in Salem were young children.

    ANS: F   TOP: Social history | The Salem Witch Trials   DIF: Easy   REF: Full p. 106 | Seagull p. 110   MSC: Remembering   OBJ: 3

18. The Salem witch trials revealed a serious problem of witchcraft in Massachusetts that spread throughout the colonies, until there were witch trials in all but three of the colonies.

    ANS: F   TOP: Social history | The Salem Witch Trials   DIF: Easy   REF: Full p. 106 | Seagull p. 110   MSC: Remembering   OBJ: 3

19. In the eighteenth century, efforts began to stop emigration from England, except that convicts were still sent to bolster the Chesapeake labor force.

    ANS: T   TOP: Social history | Attracting Settlers   DIF: Moderate   REF: Full p. 107 | Seagull p. 112   MSC: Understanding   OBJ: 4

20. German immigrants greatly enhanced the ethnic and religious diversity of Britain's colonies.

    ANS: T   TOP: Ethnicity | The German Migration   DIF: Easy   REF: Full p. 110 | Seagull p. 114   MSC: Remembering   OBJ: 4

21. Many perceived Pennsylvania to be "the best poor man's country."

    ANS: T   TOP: Social history | Regional Diversity   DIF: Moderate   REF: Full p. 113 | Seagull p. 119   MSC: Understanding   OBJ: 4

22. The Indians entered into the Walking Purchase in good faith, but they were taken advantage of by the Pennsylvania governor.

    ANS: T   TOP: Ethnicity | Indian Life in Transition   DIF: Moderate   REF: Full p. 114 | Seagull p. 118   MSC: Remembering   OBJ: 4

23. The cities were the most rapidly growing region in North America by the mid-eighteenth century.

    ANS: F   TOP: Social history | Colonial Cities   DIF: Moderate   REF: Full p. 115 | Seagull p. 119   MSC: Remembering   OBJ: 4

24. Anglicization meant that the colonial elites rejected all things British.

    ANS: F   TOP: Ethnicity | Anglicization   DIF: Easy
    REF: Full p. 119 | Seagull p. 123   MSC: Remembering
    OBJ: 5

25. Attitudes toward poverty in colonial America were much more progressive than in Britain.

    ANS: F   TOP: Social history | Poverty in the Colonies
    DIF: Moderate   REF: Full p. 121 | Seagull p. 125
    MSC: Understanding   OBJ: 5

26. The middle ranks of colonial America were those who lived between extreme wealth and poverty.

    ANS: T   TOP: Social history | The Middle Ranks
    DIF: Easy   REF: Full p. 121 | Seagull p. 125
    MSC: Remembering   OBJ: 5

27. The work of farmers' wives and daughters often spelled the difference between a family's self-sufficiency and poverty.

    ANS: T   TOP: Social history | Women and the
    Household Economy   DIF: Moderate   REF: Full
    p. 123 | Seagull p. 126   MSC: Remembering   OBJ: 5

Short Answer

Identify and give the historical significance of each of the following terms, events, and people in a paragraph or two.

1. Slavery
2. Duke of York
3. Mercantilism
4. Salem witch trials
5. King Philip's War
6. Toleration Act
7. Charter of Liberties and Privileges
8. Bacon's Rebellion
9. Glorious Revolution
10. Anglicization
11. Consumer revolution
12. William Penn
13. Leisler's Rebellion

Essay Questions

1. Discuss the major social and political crises that the English colonies of North America experienced in the late seventeenth century. What were the sources of these crises, and how did they affect the inhabitants of the colonies?

   ANS: Answers will vary   TOP: Political history,
   changes | Social history | Bacon's Rebellion: Land
   and Labor in Virginia | The End of the Rebellion
   and Its Consequences | The Maryland Uprising |
   Leisler's Rebellion | The Salem Witch Trials
   DIF: Moderate   MSC: Understanding   OBJ: 3

2. Various groups in this period of colonial history seized on the language of freedom to advance their goals. Analyze how these groups defined freedom and used its language. How successful were they in achieving their goals?

   ANS: Answers will vary   TOP: Political history,
   changes | Social history | Quaker Liberty | Changes in
   New England | Attracting Settlers | Religious Diversity
   | Regional Diversity | North America at Mid-Century
   DIF: Moderate   MSC: Analyzing   OBJ: 1 / 2 / 3 / 4 / 5

3. William Penn called his colony a "holy experiment." Chronicle the development of Pennsylvania, with particular attention to the advantages that the colony offered to settlers. What liberties were guaranteed and to whom?

   ANS: Answers will vary   TOP: Cultural history |
   Political history, changes | Social history | The Holy
   Experiment | Quaker Liberty | Land in Pennsylvania
   DIF: Moderate   MSC: Understanding   OBJ: 1 / 4

4. The Glorious Revolution solidified the notion that liberty was a birthright of the Englishman. Explain how the Glorious Revolution contributed to this idea and how it subsequently affected the colonies. Did all of the colonists react to the Glorious Revolution in the same way? If there were differences, what were they? How was the language of liberty used?

   ANS: Answers will vary   TOP: Political history,
   changes | Social history | Global awareness | The
   Glorious Revolution in England | The Glorious
   Revolution in America | The Maryland Uprising |
   Leisler's Rebellion | Changes in New England
   DIF: Moderate   MSC: Analyzing   OBJ: 3

5. "Liberty of conscience," wrote a German newcomer in 1739, was the "chief virtue" of British North America, "and on this score I do not repent my immigration." Explain what he meant by that remark. What did immigrants find attractive about the British colonies? What liberties and freedoms were available to the newcomers?

   ANS: Answers will vary   TOP: Political history,
   changes | Social history | Global awareness | Ethnicity
   | Primary document analysis | Religious Diversity | A
   Diverse Population | Attracting Settlers
   DIF: Moderate   MSC: Applying   OBJ: 4

6. "North America at mid-eighteenth century was home to a remarkable diversity of people and different kinds of social organization." In a thoughtful essay, defend this statement, touching on each of the colonies, the various

groups of people living in those colonies, and the freedoms and liberties extended to them.

ANS: Answers will vary   TOP: Ethnicity | Social history | Political history, changes | Religious Diversity | A Diverse Population | Attracting Settlers | Regional Diversity | The Colonial Elite | The Middle Ranks | New York and the Rights of Englishmen and Englishwomen | The Founding of Carolina | Quaker Liberty | Land in Pennsylvania | Colonial Artisans | Women and the Household Economy
DIF: Moderate   MSC: Evaluating   OBJ: 4

7. By the 1750s, North American colonists possessed a dual identity: they were both British in their attempts at Anglicization and also distinctly American. What factors contributed to this dual identity? What reinforced the British identity? What reinforced the American identity? Be sure to discuss political, cultural, social, and economic aspects of society.

ANS: Answers will vary   TOP: Ethnicity | Social history | Political history, changes | Cultural history | Economic development | Anglicization | The South Carolina Aristocracy | Poverty in the Colonies | An Atlantic World | Religious Diversity | Regional Diversity   DIF: Moderate   MSC: Analyzing
OBJ: 4 / 5

8. Explain how and why tobacco planters in the Chesapeake region came to rely on African slaves rather than European indentured servants over the course of the seventeenth century. At what point did the Chesapeake become a "slave society" rather than merely a "society with slaves"?

ANS: Answers will vary   TOP: Civil rights | Social history | Political history, changes | Cultural history | Economic development | The Rise of Chesapeake Slavery | Bacon's Rebellion: Land and Labor in Virginia | The End of the Rebellion and Its Consequences | A Slave Society   DIF: Moderate
MSC: Analyzing   OBJ: 2

9. The line between slavery and freedom was more permeable in the seventeenth century than it would become later. Explain how slavery was treated in the seventeenth century by discussing the law, customs, and liberties extended to slaves. What contributed to the hardening of the line between slavery and freedom?

ANS: Answers will vary   TOP: Civil rights | Social history | Political history, changes | Cultural history | Economic development | Slavery and the Law | Notions of Freedom | A Slave Society | The Rise of Chesapeake Slavery | Englishmen and Africans
DIF: Moderate   MSC: Understanding   OBJ: 2

CHAPTER 4 | Slavery, Freedom, and the Struggle for Empire to 1763

This chapter concerns the simultaneous growth of slavery and freedom in British North America up to the immediate aftermath of the Seven Years' War. It opens with an account of Olaudah Equiano, who experienced both freedom and slavery; "Voices of Freedom" features an excerpt from his autobiography. Following treatment of how slavery functioned as the engine of the Atlantic world's economy, the chapter considers the different slave systems of the Chesapeake, the rice kingdom of South Carolina and Georgia, and the northern colonies. African-American culture, religion, and slave resistance are also highlighted. The next section, on British freedoms, explains the rights of Englishmen, the rise of republicanism and liberalism, and the limitations of freedom of speech and the press. It also focuses on how American colonists exercised their rights as Englishmen in colonial politics. Next, two eighteenth-century movements—the intellectual Enlightenment and the religious Great Awakening—are explored, with special emphasis on how both served to expand the public sphere and to encourage colonists to use the language of liberty. Then, this chapter examines the weaker Spanish and French empires in North America and the clash of imperial interests that led to the Seven Years' (or French and Indian) War. The chapter concludes with consideration of the war's impact on Anglo-Indian relations, with special attention to Pontiac's Rebellion (the subject of another "Voices of Freedom"), as well as on the colonists' sense of identity.

CHAPTER OUTLINE

I. Introduction: Olaudah Equiano

II. Slavery and Empire
   A. Atlantic Trade
      1. A series of triangular trade routes crisscrossed the Atlantic.
      2. Colonial merchants profited from the slave trade, even in areas where slavery was a minor institution.
      3. Slavery became connected with the color black, and liberty with the color white.
         a. One historian: "The growth and prosperity of the emerging society of free colonial British America . . . were achieved as a result of slave labor."
   B. Africa and the Slave Trade
      1. With the exception of the king of Benin, most African rulers took part in the slave trade, gaining guns and textiles in exchange for their slaves.
      2. The slave trade was concentrated in western Africa, greatly disrupting its society and economy.
   C. The Middle Passage
      1. The Middle Passage was the voyage slaves took across the Atlantic from Africa.
      2. Slaves were crammed aboard ships for maximum profit.
      3. Slave traders took the vast majority of slaves to Brazil and to the West Indies, where death rates were high.
      4. Less than 5 percent of African slaves went to what became the United States, but the slave population there increased steadily through natural reproduction.
   D. Chesapeake Slavery
      1. Three distinct slave systems were well entrenched in Britain's mainland colonies:
         a. Chesapeake
         b. South Carolina and Georgia
         c. Nonplantation societies of New England and the Middle Colonies

2. Chesapeake slavery was based on tobacco.
3. After 1680, labor switched from indentured servitude to slavery.
   a. As Virginians moved westward so did slavery.
   b. The center of slavery moved from the Tidewater region to the Piedmont.
4. Slavery transformed Chesapeake society into an elaborate hierarchy of degrees of freedom:
   a. Large planters
   b. Yeomen farmers
   c. Indentured servants and tenant farmers
   d. Slaves
E. Freedom and Slavery in the Chesapeake
   1. With the consolidation of a slave society, planters enacted laws to protect their power over the slaves.
   2. Race became more important as a line of social division, and free blacks lost rights as "free" and "white" became virtually identical.
F. Indian Slavery in Early Carolina
   1. The Creek Indians initially sold the early settlers their slaves, generally war captives and the captives' families.
   2. As the Carolina plantations grew, the Creeks became more concerned.
G. The Rice Kingdom
   1. South Carolinian and Georgian slavery rested on rice.
   2. Rice and indigo required large-scale cultivation (which was done by slaves).
   3. Under the task system, individual slaves did daily jobs, the completion of which allowed time for leisure or cultivation of their own crops.
   4. By 1770, the number of South Carolina slaves had reached 100,000—well over half the colony's population.
H. The Georgia Experiment
   1. Georgia was established by a group of philanthropists led by James Oglethorpe in 1733.
   2. Oglethorpe had banned liquor and slaves, but the settlers demanded their right of self-government and repealed the bans by the early 1750s.
   3. In 1751, Georgia became a royal colony.
I. Slavery in the North
   1. Since the economies of New England and the Middle Colonies were based on small farms, slavery was far less important.
   2. Given that slaves were few and posed little threat to the white majority, laws were less harsh than in the South.

3. Slaves did represent a sizable percentage of urban laborers, particularly in New York and in Philadelphia.

III. Slave Culture and Slave Resistance
   A. Becoming African-American
      1. The common link among Africans in America was not kinship, language, or even "race," but slavery itself.
      2. For most of the eighteenth century, the majority of American slaves were African by birth.
   B. African Religion in Colonial America
      1. The experience of transitioning from traditional African religions to Christianity was difficult for the slaves.
      2. West African religions were of a great variety, but shared a belief in spiritual forces in nature.
      3. When slaves adopted Christian religious practices, many melded this new religion with their traditional beliefs.
   C. African-American Cultures
      1. In the Chesapeake, slaves learned English, participated in the Great Awakening, and were exposed to white culture.
      2. In South Carolina and Georgia, two very different black societies emerged:
         a. Communities on rice plantations retained significant African cultural elements (e.g., housing styles, child naming practices, language).
         b. Had little contact with whites
         c. Enjoyed much more autonomy when compared to slaves from other economies.
         d. Slaves in the cities of Charleston and Savannah assimilated more quickly into Euro-American culture.
      3. In the northern colonies a distinctive African-American culture developed more slowly, and African-Americans enjoyed more access to the mainstream of life.
   D. Resistance to Slavery
      1. A common thread among African-Americans was the experience of slavery and desire for freedom.
         a. Many plantation slaves in South Carolina and Georgia ran away to Florida or to cities.
      2. The first eighteenth-century slave uprising occurred in New York City in 1712.
      3. Uprisings also occurred in French Louisiana and on various Caribbean islands.
   E. The Crisis of 1739–1741
      1. The Stono Rebellion of 1739 in South Carolina led to the tightening of the slave code.

2. A panic in 1741 swept New York City after a series of fires broke out that were rumored to have been part of a slave conspiracy to attack whites.

IV. An Empire of Freedom
  A. British Patriotism
    1. Despite the centrality of slavery to its empire, eighteenth-century Great Britain prided itself on being the world's most advanced and freest nation.
    2. Most Britons shared a common law, a common language, a common devotion to Protestantism, and a common enemy in France.
    3. Britons believed that wealth, religion, and freedom went together.
  B. The British Constitution
    1. Central to this sense of British identity was the concept of liberty.
    2. British liberty was simultaneously a collection of specific rights, a national characteristic, and a state of mind.
    3. Britons believed that no man was above the law, not even the king.
    4. Britons saw other European nations, especially Catholic ones, as being "enslaved."
  C. The Language of Liberty
    1. The idea of liberty became increasingly identified with a general right to resist arbitrary government.
    2. Most white men in Britain and colonies lacked the right to vote but served on juries and protested in the streets against any oppressive authority.
  D. Republican Liberty
    1. Republicanism celebrated active participation in public life by economically independent citizens.
    2. Republicanism held virtue—meaning a willingness to subordinate self-interest to the public good—to be crucial in public life.
    3. Republicanism in Britain was associated with the Country Party, which criticized corruption (loss of virtue) in British politics.
      a. *Cato's Letters,* imbued with republican ideas, were widely read by the American colonists.
  E. Liberal Freedom
    1. Liberalism was strongly influenced by the philosopher John Locke.
    2. Lockean ideas included individual rights, the consent of the governed, and the right of rebellion against unjust or oppressive government.

3. Locke's ideas excluded many from freedom's full benefits in the eighteenth century, but they opened the door for many to challenge the limitations on their own freedom later.
4. Although republicanism and liberalism eventually came to be seen as alternative understandings of freedom, often in the eighteenth century they overlapped and reinforced each other.

V. The Public Sphere
  A. The Right to Vote
    1. Ownership of property was a common qualifier for voting in the colonies.
    2. Suffrage was much more common in the colonies than in Britain.
    3. Colonial politics was hardly democratic in a modern sense.
      a. Suffrage was almost universally limited to males.
      b. In some colonies Jews, Catholics, Baptists, and Quakers could not vote.
      c. During the eighteenth century, most blacks—even those with property—lost the franchise.
      d. Native Americans were generally prohibited from voting.
  B. Political Cultures
    1. Considerable power was held by those with appointive, not elective, offices.
    2. Property qualifications for officeholding were far higher than for voting.
    3. Deference—the notion among ordinary people that wealth, education, and social prominence carried a right to public office—limited choices in elections.
    4. In New England, most town leaders were the biggest property holders.
  C. Colonial Government
    1. During the first half of the eighteenth century the colonies were largely left to govern themselves, as British governments adopted a policy of "salutary neglect."
    2. The colonial elected assemblies used their control of finance to exercise great influence over governors and other appointed officials.
  D. The Rise of the Assemblies
    1. Elected assemblies became more assertive in colonial politics during the eighteenth century.
    2. The most powerful assembly was in Pennsylvania, followed by those in Massachusetts, New York, Virginia, and South Carolina.

3. Battles took place between assemblies and governors over land policy.
4. Leaders of the assemblies found in the writings of the English Country Party a theory that made sense of their own experience.

E. Politics in Public
   1. The American gentry were very active in the discussion of politics, particularly through clubs.
      a. The Junto was a club for mutual improvement, founded in 1727 by Benjamin Franklin.

F. The Colonial Press
   1. Widespread literacy and the proliferation of newspapers encouraged political discourse.
   2. Bookstores, circulating libraries, and weekly newspapers all contributed to the dissemination of information.
      a. In Philadelphia Ben Franklin founded the first library in colonial America.
   3. Political commentary was widespread in colonial newspapers.

G. Freedom of Expression and Its Limits
   1. Freedom of speech was a relatively new idea.
   2. Freedom of the press was generally viewed as dangerous.
   3. After 1695, the government could not censor print material, and colonial newspapers defended freedom of the press as a central component of liberty.
   4. Elected assemblies, not governors, discouraged freedom of the press.
      a. Routinely, publishers were forced to apologize for negative comments about assembly members.
      b. Colonial newspapers defended freedom of the press as a central component of liberty.

H. The Trial of Zenger
   1. Newspaper publisher John Peter Zenger went on trial in 1735 for seditious libel, due to criticism of New York's governor.
      a. He was found not guilty.
      b. The outcome promoted the idea that publishing the truth should always be permitted and demonstrated that free expression was becoming ingrained in the popular imagination.

I. The American Enlightenment
   1. Americans sought to apply to political and social life the scientific method of careful investigation based on research and experiment.
   2. One inspiration for the Enlightenment was a reaction against the bloody religious wars that wracked Europe in the seventeenth century.
   3. Belief in Deism (the notion that because God set up natural laws to govern the universe, following the act of creation, God did not intervene in the world) embodied the spirit of the American Enlightenment.
      a. Ben Franklin and Thomas Jefferson were among a small influential group of Deists.

VI. The Great Awakening
   A. Religious Revivals
      1. The Great Awakening was a series of local events united by a commitment to a more emotional and personal Christianity than that offered by existing churches.
      2. Islam and Judaism in Asia and Europe, respectively, saw a rise in fundamentalism.
      3. The Great Awakening was led by flamboyant preachers like Jonathan Edwards, whose *Sinners in the Hands of an Angry God* stressed the need for humans to seek divine grace.

   B. The Preaching of Whitefield
      1. The English minister George Whitefield is often credited with sparking the Great Awakening.
      2. The Great Awakening enlarged the boundaries of liberty as Old Lights (traditionalists) and New Lights (revivalists) defended their right to worship.
         a. New Light churches criticized colonial taxes used to support an established church.

   C. The Awakening's Impact
      1. The Great Awakening inspired criticism of many aspects of colonial society.
      2. A few preachers explicitly condemned slavery, but most slave masters managed to reconcile Christianity and slaveholding.
      3. Especially in the Chesapeake area, slaves became Christian.
      4. The Great Awakening expanded the circulation of printed material in the colonies.

VII. Imperial Rivalries
   A. Spanish North America
      1. A vast territorial empire on paper, Spanish North America (in what would become the future United States) actually consisted of a few small and isolated urban clusters.
      2. Despite establishing religious missions and *presidios*, the Spanish population in Spain's North American empire remained relatively small and sparse.

   B. The Spanish in California
      1. Spain ordered the colonization of California in response to a perceived Russian threat.
         a. Junípero Serra founded the first mission in San Diego in 1769.

2. California was a mission frontier.
   a. Heavy death toll of Native Americans existed due to forced labor and disease.
C. The French Empire
   1. France was Britain's biggest rival in Europe and North America.
   2. The French empire in the early eighteenth century expanded.
   3. Much smaller in population, the French tended to view North America as a place of cruel exile for criminals and social outcasts.

VIII. Battle for the Continent
A. The Middle Ground
   1. Indians were constantly being pushed from their homes into a "middle ground" between European empires and Indian sovereignty.
   2. The Indians of the Ohio River Valley saw the rivalry of Britain and France as a threat and an opportunity.
   3. The government of Virginia gave an immense land grant in 1749 to the Ohio Company.
B. The Seven Years' War
   1. In the first half of the eighteenth century, wars against Spain and France set the stage for England becoming the dominant power in Europe.
   2. The war began in 1754 as the British tried to dislodge the French from western Pennsylvania.
   3. The war went against the British until 1757, when William Pitt became British Secretary of State and turned the tide of battle.
   4. In 1760, the French surrendered Montreal, their last North American outpost, to the British.
C. A World Transformed
   1. The Peace of Paris in 1763 resulted in the expulsion of France from North America.
   2. Pitt declared that peace would be as hard to make as war, and the war indeed put future financial strains on all the participants.
D. Pontiac's Rebellion
   1. With the removal of the French, the balance-of-power diplomacy that had enabled groups like the Iroquois to maintain a significant degree of autonomy was eliminated.
   2. In 1763, Indians launched a revolt against British rule.
   3. Neolin championed a pan-Indian identity.
E. The Proclamation Line
   1. To avoid further Indian conflicts, London issued the Proclamation of 1763, which banned white settlement west of the Appalachian Mountains.

2. The Proclamation enraged settlers and land speculators hoping to take advantage of the expulsion of the French.
F. Pennsylvania and the Indians
   1. The war deepened the hostility of western Pennsylvanian farmers toward Indians and witnessed numerous indiscriminate assaults on Indian communities.
   2. The Paxton Boys demanded that Indians be removed from Pennsylvania.
G. Colonial Identities
   1. The colonists emerged from the Seven Years' War with a heightened sense of collective identity.
   2. The war also strengthened the colonists' pride in being members of the British empire.
   3. Britain's empire expanded with tens of thousands of French Catholics and millions of people from India as subjects.
      a. Edmund Burke wondered if British liberty could be reconciled with rule over a vast empire.

SUGGESTED DISCUSSION QUESTIONS

- One early American contemporary stated that there was a widespread "dangerous spirit of liberty" among the New World's slaves. Explore that idea by considering slave culture and forms of resistance. Be sure to discuss Olaudah Equiano's ideas expressed in "Voices of Freedom."
- How vital was slavery to the Atlantic economy in the eighteenth century? Provide specific evidence to support your response.
- Discuss republicanism and liberalism. What are the similarities and differences between the two concepts?
- Explain why property was important as a qualifier for voting in British America. How did such a policy exclude able voters? Were liberty and property ownership linked? Why or why not?
- How did the Great Awakening inspire ordinary citizens to assert their right to independent judgment? Did the movement expand freedoms? Why or why not?
- How did Indians cope with the increasing settlement of whites during the eighteenth century and the subsequent removal of the French after the French and Indian War? Discuss how the ideas of freedom and liberty expressed by the English were never intended to be extended to the Indians.
- Have the students each write a broadside to be posted in the classroom. It can be for anything they would like: an advertisement for a consumer good, a slave advertisement, a political announcement or announcement for a new club, or an advertisement for a religious

revival meeting. Use the completed broadsides to generate discussions.

SUPPLEMENTAL WEB AND VISUAL RESOURCES

Africans in America
www.pbs.org/wgbh/aia/home.html
Africans in America is a four-part PBS video about America's journey through slavery. Part I is "The Terrible Transformation, 1450–1750."

Father Serra in California
www.pbs.org/weta/thewest/people/s_z/serra.htm
This is from the PBS series on the West.

www.catholic-church.org/serra-beth/serra-4.htm
This is from the Catholic Church of America.

French and Indian War
The Price of Freedom: Americans at War
americanhistory.si.edu/militaryhistory/exhibition/flash.html
From the Smithsonian Institution's National Museum of American History, select a war (e.g., Revolutionary War, which begins at the French and Indian War) and enter an exhibit that includes a movie, learning resources, statistics, printable exhibition, maps, and time lines.

Great Awakening
www.nhc.rtp.nc.us/index.htm
The National Humanities Center. Teacher Serve: An Interactive Curriculum Enrichment Service for Teachers. Two sections: one on religion and the national culture and one on the environment in American history. Toolbox Library offers a plethora of primary sources, discussion questions, additional online sources, and talking points.

www.nhc.rtp.nc.us/tserve/eighteen/ekeyinfo/grawaken.htm
This site takes you to the section on the Great Awakening.

www.pbs.org/wgbh/pages/frontline/shows/apocalypse/explanation/puritans.html
This PBS site offers information on the Frontline video *Apocalypse*. There is a list of primary sources and other valuable information pertaining to the Great Awakening.

Pontiac's Rebellion
www.ohiohistorycentral.org/entry.php?rec=539
This website from the Ohio Historical Society has useful information on the rebellion itself, but it also has wonderful links to other related topics.

SUPPLEMENTAL PRINT RESOURCES

Aldridge, A. Owen. "Natural Religion and Deism in America before Ethan Allen and Thomas Paine." *William and Mary Quarterly* 54, no. 4 (1997): 835–838.

Anderson, Fred. *A People's Army: Massachusetts Soldiers and Society in the Seven Years' War.* New York: W. W. Norton & Company, 1985.

Breen, T. H., and Stephen Innes. *"Myne Owne Ground": Race and Freedom on Virginia's Eastern Shore, 1640–1676.* New York: Oxford University Press, 1980.

Carretta, Vincent. *Equiano, the African: Biography of a Self-Made Man.* Athens, GA: University of Georgia Press, 2005.

King, Duane H., ed. *The Memoirs of Lt. Henry Timberlake.* Chapel Hill, NC: University of North Carolina Press, 2007.

Marsden, George. *Jonathan Edwards: A Life.* New Haven, CT: Yale University Press, 2003.

Maynard, Theodore. *The Long Road of Father Serra.* New York: Appleton-Century-Crofts, 1954.

Morgan, Edmund S. *Benjamin Franklin.* New Haven, CT: Yale University Press, 2002.

Sidbury, James. *Ploughshares into Swords: Race, Rebellion, and Identity in Gabriel's Virginia, 1730–1810.* New York: Cambridge University Press, 1997.

Sobel, Mechal. *The World They Made Together: Black and White Values in Eighteenth-Century Virginia.* Princeton, NJ: Princeton University Press, 1987.

Stout, Harry S. *The Divine Dramatist: George Whitefield and the Rise of Modern Evangelicalism.* Grand Rapids, MI: William B. Eerdman's, 1991.

Wood, Peter. *Black Majority: Negroes in Colonial South Carolina from 1670 through the Stono Rebellion.* New York: W. W. Norton & Company, 1996.

TEST BANK

Matching

TEST I

____ 1. Olaudah Equiano
____ 2. James Oglethorpe
____ 3. Pontiac
____ 4. Benjamin Franklin
____ 5. William Pitt
____ 6. Jonathan Edwards
____ 7. Junípero Serra
____ 8. John Peter Zenger
____ 9. George Whitefield
____ 10. John Locke
____ 11. William Cosby
____ 12. Trenchard and Gordon

a. German-born printer of a colonial weekly journal
b. Great Awakening preacher
c. survived the Middle Passage
d. founded the first mission in San Diego
e. founder of Georgia
f. British prime minister
g. Ottawa war leader
h. wrote *Sinners in the Hands of an Angry God*
i. English Enlightenment political philosopher

j. founder of the Junto, a club for mutual improvement
k. authors of *Cato's Letters*
l. victim of Zenger's pen

Answer Key: c, e, g, j, f, h, d, a, b, i, l, k

TEST 2

___ 1. Middle Passage
___ 2. Gullah
___ 3. Evangelists
___ 4. Maroons
___ 5. deference
___ 6. Proclamation of 1763
___ 7. *asiento*
___ 8. Republicanism
___ 9. Deism
___ 10. Old Lights
___ 11. Stono Rebellion
___ 12. Junto

a. Jamaican fugitive slaves
b. bearers of the good news
c. distinct slave dialect
d. no colonial settlement west of the Appalachians
e. the ship voyage for slaves from Africa to the New World
f. right to provide slaves to Spanish America
g. religious traditionalists who did not support revivalism
h. courteous respect
i. Enlightenment religion
j. virtuous elite giving themselves to public service
k. political club
l. slaves fought in South Carolina

Answer Key: e, c, b, a, h, d, f, j, i, g, l, k

Learning Objectives

1. Explain how African slavery differed regionally in eighteenth-century North America.
2. Identify the factors that led to distinct African-American cultures in the eighteenth century.
3. Identify the various meanings of British liberty in the eighteenth century.
4. Identify the concepts and institutions that dominated colonial politics in the eighteenth century.
5. Explain how the Great Awakening challenged the religious and social structure of British North America.
6. Explain how the Spanish and French empires in America developed in the eighteenth century.
7. Describe the impact of the Seven Years' War on imperial and Indian-white relations.

Multiple Choice

1. Olaudah Equiano:
    a. wrote the eighteenth century's most widely read account by a slave of a slave's own experiences.
    b. was popular with Europeans for telling them that their culture was far superior to that of Africans like himself.
    c. demonstrated in his writings that he perfectly fit the stereotype that blacks were savages incapable of becoming civilized.
    d. led several Central American slave insurrections before his death.
    e. was one of the few children of African-American and Native American descent ever to be the chief of his Indian tribe.

ANS: A   TOP: Civil rights | Introduction
DIF: Moderate   REF: Full p. 127 | Seagull p. 130
MSC: Remembering   OBJ: 2

2. All of the following statements are true of the Atlantic trade in the eighteenth century EXCEPT:
    a. Although important, slave-grown crops actually accounted for only a small portion of the value of the trade.
    b. The profits from the slave trade in particular stimulated the rise of key English ports.
    c. New England and the Middle Colonies exported fish, grain, and lumber to the West Indies.
    d. Profits from the Atlantic trade helped finance the early Industrial Revolution.
    e. Europe was the primary market for colonial-grown products such as rice and indigo.

ANS: A   TOP: Economic development | Atlantic Trade
DIF: Moderate   REF: Full pp. 128–129 | Seagull pp. 132–133   MSC: Understanding   OBJ: 1

3. What did the British acquire from the Netherlands in the Treaty of Utrecht of 1713?
    a. sufficient gold to pay off the British national debt
    b. the right to trade at Dutch outposts in what is now South Africa
    c. the right to transport slaves from Africa to Spain's New World colonies
    d. New Netherland, which was then renamed New York
    e. New Holland, which later became known as Australia

ANS: C   TOP: Economic development | Slavery and Empire   DIF: Difficult   REF: Full p. 128 | Seagull p. 131   MSC: Remembering   OBJ: 1

4. Which of the following is a true statement about the Atlantic slave trade's effect in West Africa?
    a. It had little effect on West Africa, because more than 90 percent of enslaved people came from East Africa.
    b. It helped lead to the rise of militarized states in West Africa, whose large armies preyed upon their neighbors in order to capture slaves.

c. It encouraged the expansion of West Africa's domestic textile industry, which supplied clothing for slaves.

d. It led to an increase in West Africa's population during the 1700s as slave traders encouraged women to have more children who would then be sold into slavery.

e. It successfully united West African nations to resist European slave traders, who reluctantly ended the trade by 1763.

ANS: B   TOP: Global awareness | Africa and the Slave Trade   DIF: Moderate   REF: Full p. 130 | Seagull p. 134   MSC: Understanding   OBJ: 1

5. Which one of the following statements is NOT true of the slave trade in the eighteenth-century Atlantic world?

a. Slaves were bought and sold in the Atlantic world as part of a series of trading routes that also involved British manufactured goods and colonial products such as tobacco and sugar.

b. The Atlantic slave trade was a vital part of world commerce in the 1700s.

c. Even those in areas where slavery was only a minor institution, such as Massachusetts and Rhode Island, profited from the slave trade.

d. Slightly more than half of slaves from Africa were taken to mainland North America (what became the United States).

e. Many slaves died of diseases on board slave ships during the Middle Passage.

ANS: D   TOP: Economic development | The Middle Passage   DIF: Moderate   REF: Full p. 132 | Seagull p. 135   MSC: Understanding   OBJ: 1

6. Tobacco plantations in the Chesapeake region:

a. were so profitable that by the mid-eighteenth century their owners became the wealthiest people in British North America.

b. did not have any slaves on small farms.

c. helped make the Chesapeake colonies models of mercantilism.

d. were far less successful than tobacco plantations that developed in the lower southern colonies.

e. were known throughout the world as models of how slaves should be treated.

ANS: C   TOP: Economic development | Chesapeake Slavery   DIF: Moderate   REF: Full p. 132 | Seagull p. 136   MSC: Understanding   OBJ: 1

7. In the Chesapeake region, slavery:

a. was geographically restricted to the Tidewater area until transportation improved in the nineteenth century.

b. rapidly became the dominant labor system after 1680.

c. was the labor system preferred by planters as early as the 1620s.

d. allowed planters to make vast profits from cotton and rice as well as from tobacco.

e. was so widely practiced that nearly three-fifths of white households in 1770 included a slave owner.

ANS: B   TOP: Economic development | Chesapeake Slavery   DIF: Moderate   REF: Full p. 132 | Seagull p. 136   MSC: Understanding   OBJ: 1

8. As slave society consolidated in the Chesapeake region, what happened to free blacks?

a. They retained the same rights because they were free.

b. Their population grew rapidly through natural reproduction.

c. The British government ordered the colonies to treat them better.

d. They bought increasing numbers of plantations.

e. They lost many of their rights.

ANS: E   TOP: Civil rights | Freedom and Slavery in the Chesapeake   DIF: Easy   REF: Full p. 133 | Seagull p. 137   MSC: Understanding   OBJ: 1

9. The early South Carolina economy focused on the export of deerskins and furs to England as well as on:

a. the cultivation of cotton.

b. small-scale manufacturing of firearms for use in raids against Spanish Florida.

c. the export of Indian slaves to the Caribbean.

d. shipbuilding.

e. copper mining.

ANS: C   TOP: Economic development | Indian Slavery in Early Carolina   DIF: Moderate   REF: Full p. 133 | Seagull p. 137   MSC: Remembering   OBJ: 1

10. The development of rice plantations in South Carolina:

a. occurred only after the colony's planters unsuccessfully sought to cultivate tobacco, sugarcane, and indigo.

b. required such large capital investments that Carolina's planters never became as wealthy as those in the Chesapeake region.

c. would have proven impossible without the importation of thousands of European indentured servants to serve as a labor force.

d. led to a black majority in that colony by the 1730s.

e. is considered by most historians to be the most important cause of the Yamasee War.

ANS: D   TOP: Social history | The Rice Kingdom   DIF: Moderate   REF: Full p. 134 | Seagull p. 138   MSC: Understanding   OBJ: 1

11. The task system:
    a. was the most widely used form of labor discipline in British North America.
    b. allowed slaves to own a portion of the land they worked.
    c. meant that slaves were strictly supervised and had little autonomy.
    d. was created by the South Carolina assembly in response to the Stono Rebellion.
    e. assigned slaves daily jobs and allowed them free time upon completion of those jobs.

    ANS: E   TOP: Economic development | The Rice Kingdom   DIF: Moderate   REF: Full p. 134 | Seagull p. 138   MSC: Remembering   OBJ: 1

12. Georgia was established by James Oglethorpe, whose causes included improved conditions for imprisoned debtors and the abolition of:
    a. indentured servitude.
    b. a hereditary system.
    c. taxes.
    d. slavery.
    e. property requirements for voting.

    ANS: D   TOP: Political history, changes | The Georgia Experiment   DIF: Moderate   REF: Full p. 134 | Seagull p. 139   MSC: Remembering   OBJ: 1

13. Which of the following was true of Georgia?
    a. Colonists sought self-government to gain the right to introduce slavery.
    b. It was the only colony to maintain a ban on liquor until independence.
    c. The philanthropists who founded it expected slavery to help the lower class Englishmen they brought to the colony.
    d. Its residents invaded Florida and took it from Spain in the War of Jenkins' Ear.
    e. It was named for the most important British queen of the eighteenth century.

    ANS: A   TOP: Political history, changes | The Georgia Experiment   DIF: Moderate   REF: Full pp. 134–135 | Seagull p. 139   MSC: Remembering   OBJ: 1

14. Why was slavery less prevalent in the northern colonies?
    a. Northern whites were not as racist as southern whites.
    b. It was too expensive to transport slaves to the North.
    c. The small farms of the northern colonies did not need slaves.
    d. More reformers lived in the North.
    e. The northern colonies used Indian labor instead.

    ANS: C   TOP: Social history | Slavery in the North   DIF: Easy   REF: Full p. 135 | Seagull p. 139   MSC: Understanding   OBJ: 1

15. In the northern colonies, slaves:
    a. lived in segregated but prosperous communities.
    b. became more important in New England after the Half-Way Covenant.
    c. were far less important to New England than the Middle Colonies.
    d. were forbidden by law to display any aspect of African culture in public.
    e. faced far harsher treatment than they did in the South.

    ANS: C   TOP: Social history | Slavery in the North   DIF: Easy   REF: Full p. 135 | Seagull p. 139   MSC: Understanding   OBJ: 1

16. In the forest regions of West Africa, before being captured slaves worshipped:
    a. Protestantism.
    b. Islam.
    c. Catholicism.
    d. aspects of nature.
    e. no religion.

    ANS: D   TOP: Cultural history | African Religion in Colonial America   DIF: Moderate   REF: Full pp. 136–137 | Seagull p. 141   MSC: Remembering   OBJ: 2

17. When brought to the New World, with regard to religion, slaves:
    a. gave up practicing African beliefs.
    b. quickly converted to Christianity.
    c. mixed elements of Christianity with African beliefs.
    d. looked to convert colonists to African religions.
    e. did not see a connection between African-based spirits and Catholic saints.

    ANS: C   TOP: Cultural history | African Religion in Colonial America   DIF: Moderate   REF: Full pp. 136–137 | Seagull p. 142   MSC: Remembering   OBJ: 2

18. Which one of the following statements about slaves in the Chesapeake is FALSE?
    a. Slaves learned English.
    b. Slaves participated in the Great Awakening.
    c. Slaves were exposed to white culture.
    d. Slaves began to experience family-centered communities.
    e. Slave communities remained distinctly African in culture.

ANS: E   TOP: Cultural history | African-Ameri-
can Cultures   DIF: Moderate   REF: Full
pp. 137–138 | Seagull p. 142   MSC: Understanding
OBJ: 2

19. The language (with mixed African roots) spoken by
African-American slaves on the rice plantations of
South Carolina and Georgia during the eighteenth
century was known as:
a. Ashanti.
b. Yoruba.
c. Creole.
d. Gullah.
e. Ibo.

ANS: D   TOP: Cultural history | African-American
Cultures   DIF: Moderate   REF: Full p. 138 |
Seagull p. 142   MSC: Remembering   OBJ: 2

20. Which of the following is true of eighteenth-century
slavery in South Carolina and Georgia?
a. The laws in those colonies created a very static
institution with few differences among plantations,
small farms, and cities.
b. Plantation slaves enjoyed far more autonomy than
they did in other colonies, allowing them to
maintain more of their African culture.
c. Because of the high death rates of Africans due to
malaria, slave populations declined by 5 to 10
percent per decade during the 1700s.
d. Because the governments of South Carolina and
Georgia strictly enforced laws preventing sexual
contact between whites and blacks, a significant
population of racially mixed individuals never
developed.
e. Colonial law gave freedom to any slave who
successfully escaped to Charleston or Savannah.

ANS: B   TOP: Cultural history | African-American
Cultures   DIF: Difficult   REF: Full p. 138 |
Seagull p. 142   MSC: Understanding   OBJ: 2

21. The participants in South Carolina's Stono Rebellion:
a. surrendered without any bloodshed and agreed to
pledge loyalty to the colony.
b. were mostly former indentured servants upset over
the colony's Indian policy.
c. included some who apparently had been soldiers in
Africa.
d. laid siege to Charleston but had to retreat when the
Royal Navy brought reinforcements.
e. were unsuccessful because of divisions over
language and ethnicity.

ANS: C   TOP: Civil rights | The Crisis of 1739–1741
DIF: Moderate   REF: Full p. 139 | Seagull p. 144
MSC: Remembering   OBJ: 2

22. The 1741 panic in New York City that led to thirty-four
executions was sparked by:
a. a series of murders.
b. the seizing of the armory.
c. a rally of boisterous Irish.
d. the imprisonment of twenty free blacks.
e. a series of fires.

ANS: E   TOP: Civil rights | The Crisis of 1739–1741
DIF: Moderate   REF: Full p. 139 | Seagull
pp. 144–145   MSC: Remembering   OBJ: 2

23. Slave resistance in the eighteenth century:
a. was limited to running away, since mounting an
armed rebellion would have been impossible and
deadly.
b. included rebellions in both northern and southern
colonies that led to the deaths of several of those
involved in planning the conspiracies.
c. most famously included the War of Jenkins' Ear,
fought over the habit that masters developed of
slicing off the ears of rebellious slaves.
d. prompted southern lawmakers to cut off slave
imports from Africa and the Caribbean by
mid-century.
e. led to a strong but ultimately unsuccessful
movement to abolish slavery in Georgia in the
1760s.

ANS: B   TOP: Civil rights | The Crisis of 1739–1741
DIF: Moderate   REF: Full p. 139 | Seagull
pp. 144–145   MSC: Remembering   OBJ: 2

24. During the eighteenth century, British patriotism:
a. reflected the rise of Spain as Great Britain's
traditional enemy, in place of France.
b. emphasized England's freedom of religion.
c. celebrated individual freedom and the rule of law.
d. included the admission that slavery and freedom
were wholly contradictory.
e. was the subject of numerous satires by Benjamin
Franklin.

ANS: C   TOP: Political history, changes | British
Patriotism   DIF: Moderate   REF: Full p. 140 |
Seagull p. 145   MSC: Remembering   OBJ: 3

25. The British concept of liberty:
a. allowed for unrestrained government authority,
since restraints would contradict the very idea of
liberty.
b. meant that liberty and power could be compatible.
c. was a constant reminder to the British that their
governmental system was not the best means of
preventing absolutism.
d. had no connections to how the British viewed their
empire.

e. included both formal restraints on authority and a collection of specific rights.

ANS: E   TOP: Political history, changes | The British Constitution   DIF: Moderate   REF: Full pp. 140–141 | Seagull p. 146   MSC: Understanding   OBJ: 3

26. The language of British liberty:
    a. was Latin and Greek, reflecting the emphasis that the educated upper class put on the subject.
    b. did not include the idea that the people had the right to protest government actions.
    c. excluded those outside the "political nation" (meaning those who voted or held office).
    d. allowed those outside of office to speak openly, but not to write down their views.
    e. was used by humble members of society as well as by the elite.

    ANS: E   TOP: Political history, changes | The Language of Liberty   DIF: Moderate   REF: Full p. 141 | Seagull pp. 146–147   MSC: Understanding OBJ: 3

27. "Republicanism" in the eighteenth-century Anglo-American political world emphasized the importance of _____ as the essence of liberty.
    a. protecting the natural rights of all humans
    b. active participation in public life by property-owning citizens
    c. a strong central state
    d. supporting royal authority as opposed to parliamentary authority
    e. voting rights for all adult men

    ANS: B   TOP: Political history, changes | Republican Liberty   DIF: Moderate   REF: Full p. 141 | Seagull pp. 147–148   MSC: Understanding   OBJ: 3

28. The British Country Party:
    a. declined in popularity as England became an increasingly urbanized country.
    b. underwrote the expenses of a large number of the migrants to the American colonies.
    c. opposed the power of the landed gentry in British politics.
    d. sought to stop corruption in British politics.
    e. required its leaders to dress in work clothes to promote the idea of being "of the people."

    ANS: D   TOP: Political history, changes | Republican Liberty   DIF: Moderate   REF: Full p. 142 | Seagull p. 148   MSC: Remembering   OBJ: 3

29. John Locke's political philosophy stressed:
    a. a contract system between the people and the government.
    b. the necessity of the monarch having absolute power.

c. that mercantilism was necessary for a strong nation.
d. religious toleration for all.
e. that strong government prevented a "war of all against all."

ANS: A   TOP: Political history, changes | Liberal Freedom   DIF: Moderate   REF: Full p. 143 | Seagull p. 148   MSC: Understanding   OBJ: 3

30. The idea of liberalism in eighteenth-century British politics:
    a. had the same meaning as liberalism in twenty-first-century American politics.
    b. had mainly a civic and social quality.
    c. brought great wealth and power to its main voice, John Locke.
    d. was compatible with inequalities in wealth and well-being.
    e. prompted two eighteenth-century leaders, Joseph McCarthy and Hugh McCarran, to demand independence for Ireland.

    ANS: D   TOP: Political history, changes | Liberal Freedom   DIF: Moderate   REF: Full p. 143 | Seagull p. 149   MSC: Understanding   OBJ: 3

31. How did John Locke reconcile his belief in natural rights and his support for slavery?
    a. He did not have to, because he opposed slavery.
    b. He believed that the free individual in liberal thought was the propertied white man.
    c. His belief in democracy meant that if a majority wanted to own slaves, they should be free to do so.
    d. He explicitly argued that Africans were not truly human and therefore possessed no natural right to liberty.
    e. He suggested that natural rights only applied to the English, not to other Europeans and certainly not to Africans.

    ANS: B   TOP: Political history, changes | Liberal Freedom   DIF: Difficult   REF: Full p. 143 | Seagull p. 149   MSC: Understanding   OBJ: 3

32. It is estimated that between _____ percent of adult white men could vote in eighteenth-century colonial British America.
    a. 5 and 10
    b. 25 and 40
    c. 33 and 50
    d. 50 and 80
    e. 75 and 90

    ANS: D   TOP: Political history, changes | The Right to Vote   DIF: Difficult   REF: Full p. 144 | Seagull p. 150   MSC: Remembering   OBJ: 4

33. How did colonial politics compare with British politics?
   a. British politics were far more democratic, befitting the British belief in liberty and the number of proprietary and royal colonies.
   b. Colonists tended to agree with the British that owning property was related to having the right to vote.
   c. Most colonies, unlike Britain, at least allowed propertied women to vote.
   d. Elections throughout the colonies were more hotly contested than British ones, with many different candidates and parties represented on the ballot.
   e. Colonial politics proved far more corrupt until the Licentiousness Act of 1694.

   ANS: B   TOP: Political history, changes | The Right to Vote   DIF: Easy   REF: Full p. 144 | Seagull p. 150   MSC: Understanding   OBJ: 4

34. Property qualifications for holding office:
   a. were the same in every colony as they were for voting.
   b. meant that women served regularly in colonial legislatures.
   c. meant that the landed gentry wielded considerable power in colonial legislatures.
   d. existed for legislators but not for judges, who were esteemed for their legal ability.
   e. disappeared from Parliament before they were eliminated by colonial legislatures.

   ANS: C   TOP: Political history, changes | Political Cultures   DIF: Moderate   REF: Full pp. 144–145 | Seagull p. 151   MSC: Understanding   OBJ: 4

35. The assumption among ordinary people that wealth, education, and social prominence entitled leaders to public office was called:
   a. liberalism.
   b. Lockeanism.
   c. Deism.
   d. deference.
   e. suffrage.

   ANS: D   TOP: Political history, changes | Political Cultures   DIF: Moderate   REF: Full p. 145 | Seagull p. 151   MSC: Remembering   OBJ: 4

36. "Salutary neglect" meant:
   a. providing little oversight of slaves engaged in the task system.
   b. colonial legislatures were supposed to meet only when absolutely necessary.
   c. failing to salute British officers was a punishable offense for colonists.
   d. the same thing that "child neglect" means today.

   e. British governments left the colonies largely alone to govern themselves.

   ANS: E   TOP: Political history, changes | Colonial Government   DIF: Moderate   REF: Full p. 145 | Seagull p. 151   MSC: Remembering   OBJ: 4

37. During the eighteenth century, colonial assemblies:
   a. lost political power to colonial governors.
   b. remained purely advisory bodies to the royal governor.
   c. became more assertive.
   d. concentrated on the patronage system.
   e. rejected the theories of the English Country Party.

   ANS: C   TOP: Political history, changes | The Rise of the Assemblies   DIF: Moderate   REF: Full p. 146 | Seagull p. 152   MSC: Understanding   OBJ: 4

38. The most successful colonial governors:
   a. blocked the rising power of colonial assemblies, thereby pleasing the king and Parliament.
   b. used their appointive powers and control of land grants to win allies in colonial legislatures.
   c. abolished the colonial judicial system, whose members frequently overturned their executive orders and legislative action.
   d. were able to stay in office during the Revolutionary War and went on to enjoy political power after independence.
   e. had to leave office after twelve years, because the king and Parliament imposed term limits.

   ANS: B   TOP: Political history, changes | The Rise of the Assemblies   DIF: Moderate   REF: Full p. 146 | Seagull p. 152   MSC: Understanding   OBJ: 4

39. Which issue divided colonial governors appointed by the king and legislatures elected by colonists?
   a. Legislatures wanted universal white male suffrage, and the governors wanted to maintain the less democratic system under which British politics functioned.
   b. They were divided about how to respond to the lack of economic growth in the colonies—legislators wanted to act to help the economy, and governors preferred to let events take their course.
   c. To deal with a scarcity of gold and silver coins, legislatures supported printing paper money despite opposition from the governors.
   d. Governors wanted slavery outlawed because they considered it antithetical to the British idea of liberty, but legislators supported it.
   e. Governors wanted life terms for judges, and legislators sought elections every ten years.

   ANS: C   TOP: Political history, changes | The Rise of the Assemblies   DIF: Difficult   REF: Full p. 146 | Seagull p. 152   MSC: Understanding   OBJ: 4

40. Which one of the following did NOT contribute to the expansion of the public sphere during the eighteenth century?
    a. the establishment of literary and philosophical clubs
    b. widespread literacy
    c. the proliferation of newspapers and libraries
    d. the trial of John Peter Zenger
    e. the founding of the California missions

    ANS: E   TOP: Social history | Politics in Public | The Colonial Press | The Trial of Zenger   DIF: Easy
    REF: Full pp. 146–148 | Seagull pp. 153–154, 155–156
    MSC: Understanding   OBJ: 4

41. The American Philosophical Society in its modest beginnings was called:
    a. the Junto.
    b. Cato's Club.
    c. Common Sense.
    d. Publick Occurrences.
    e. Britannia.

    ANS: A   TOP: Social history | Politics in Public
    DIF: Difficult   REF: Full p. 147 | Seagull p. 153
    MSC: Remembering   OBJ: 4

42. John Peter Zenger's libel trial:
    a. resulted from his publication of news stories questioning the intelligence of the king.
    b. probably would not have ended in his acquittal if he had attacked someone other than the colonial governor.
    c. set back freedom of the press when it ended in his conviction and imprisonment for printing the truth.
    d. showed that the public was not yet ready to accept the idea of freedom of speech.
    e. led to the overturning of the Licentiousness Act of 1694.

    ANS: B   TOP: Political history, changes | The Trial of Zenger   DIF: Moderate   REF: Full p. 149 | Seagull p. 156   MSC: Understanding   OBJ: 4

43. The American version of the Enlightenment:
    a. produced no one who achieved world renown, unlike the English and French versions.
    b. led to the increased popularity of Arminianism but not of Deism.
    c. was exemplified by Benjamin Franklin.
    d. had no impact on religion.
    e. was sparked by Isaac Newton's colonial tour in 1739.

    ANS: C   TOP: Cultural history | The American Enlightenment   DIF: Moderate   REF: Full p. 149 | Seagull p. 156   MSC: Remembering   OBJ: 4

44. Deists shared the ideas of eighteenth-century European Enlightenment thinkers, namely that:
    a. the universe was unknowable.
    b. Christ's divinity was beyond question.
    c. science could uncover God's laws that governed the natural order.
    d. God did not exist.
    e. divine revelation was necessary for a proper understanding of truth.

    ANS: C   TOP: Cultural history | The American Enlightenment   DIF: Moderate   REF: Full p. 150 | Seagull p. 157   MSC: Understanding   OBJ: 4

45. Deists concluded that the best form of religious devotion was to:
    a. read the Bible.
    b. attend revival meetings.
    c. worship in organized churches.
    d. study the workings of nature.
    e. appeal to divine grace for salvation.

    ANS: D   TOP: Cultural history | The American Enlightenment   DIF: Moderate   REF: Full p. 150 | Seagull p. 157   MSC: Understanding   OBJ: 4

46. Which of the following is NOT true of the Great Awakening?
    a. Its more subdued style of preaching appealed to a wider audience than the older, bombastic style employed by the Puritans.
    b. It was due in part to concerns among ministers that religious devotion was in decline due to economic growth.
    c. It involved several denominations, not just Congregationalists.
    d. It increased social tensions because ministers criticized certain aspects of colonial society such as commercialism and slavery.
    e. It was a transatlantic movement and not just an American one.

    ANS: A   TOP: Cultural history | Religious Revivals | The Preaching of Whitefield | The Awakening's Impact   DIF: Moderate   REF: Full pp. 150–151 | Seagull pp. 157–160   MSC: Understanding   OBJ: 5

47. The most famous Great Awakening revivalist minister was:
    a. John Locke.
    b. George Whitefield.
    c. Cotton Mather.
    d. John Peter Zenger.
    e. James Oglethorpe.

    ANS: B   TOP: Cultural history | The Preaching of Whitefield   DIF: Easy   REF: Full p. 151 | Seagull pp. 158–159   MSC: Remembering   OBJ: 5

48. Revivalist preachers during the Great Awakening frequently:
    a. formed influential organizations dedicated to abolishing slavery.
    b. praised Deism.
    c. criticized commercial society.
    d. sought to avoid emotional styles of preaching.
    e. accepted financial support from colonial governments.

    ANS: C   TOP: Cultural history | The Awakening's Impact   DIF: Moderate   REF: Full p. 152 | Seagull p. 159   MSC: Remembering   OBJ: 5

49. In the eighteenth century, the Spanish empire in North America:
    a. consisted of a few small and isolated urban clusters until Great Britain conquered it by force.
    b. rested economically on trading with and extracting labor from surviving Native Americans.
    c. attracted thousands of settlers after Spain built a series of missions and *presidios.*
    d. helped the Native American population to grow considerably through the mission system.
    e. forced Spanish priests to choose between loyalty to the Pope and loyalty to the king.

    ANS: B   TOP: Geographic issues | Spanish North America   DIF: Moderate   REF: Full p. 153 | Seagull p. 160   MSC: Understanding   OBJ: 6

50. What did Junípero Serra hope to do in California?
    a. convert Indians to Christianity and to settled farming
    b. explore the Sacramento River basin to find gold
    c. claim the land for Spain and earn the praise of Queen Isabella
    d. stop the common practice of using Indians as forced laborers
    e. take over the Russian trading post at what is now Santa Barbara

    ANS: A   TOP: Ethnicity | The Spanish in California   DIF: Moderate   REF: Full p. 154 | Seagull p. 162   MSC: Remembering   OBJ: 6

51. The French in North America:
    a. had a rapidly expanding empire, in large part because of the strong encouragement the French government gave to citizens wanting to move to the New World.
    b. made it a point to avoid competing with the British.
    c. won control of the Ohio Valley in the Seven Years' War.
    d. were greatly outnumbered by the British on the continent.

    e. were notorious for their poor relations with Native Americans.

    ANS: D   TOP: Geographic issues | The French Empire   DIF: Moderate   REF: Full p. 155 | Seagull p. 163   MSC: Remembering   OBJ: 6

52. The French and Indian War began because some American colonists felt that:
    a. the Indians along the frontier finally had to be subdued.
    b. France was encroaching on land claimed by the Ohio Company.
    c. they had to aid the English, who were fighting Napoleon in Europe.
    d. taxes were too high, so they solicited help from both the French and the Indians.
    e. French Jesuits were converting too many Indians to Catholicism, endangering the Protestant majority on the North American continent.

    ANS: B   TOP: Geographic issues | Military history | The Seven Years' War   DIF: Moderate   REF: Full p. 158 | Seagull p. 164   MSC: Remembering   OBJ: 7

53. The English finally became successful in defeating the French in the Seven Years' War under the leadership of:
    a. George Washington.
    b. Edward Braddock.
    c. Robert Carter.
    d. John Locke.
    e. William Pitt.

    ANS: E   TOP: Global awareness | Military history | The Seven Years' War   DIF: Moderate   REF: Full p. 158 | Seagull p. 166   MSC: Remembering   OBJ: 7

54. Neolin, a Delaware Indian and religious prophet, helped inspire _____ Rebellion in 1763.
    a. Bacon's
    b. the Stono
    c. Pontiac's
    d. the Yamasee
    e. Leisler's

    ANS: C   TOP: Ethnicity | Pontiac's Rebellion   DIF: Easy   REF: Full p. 160 | Seagull p. 167   MSC: Remembering   OBJ: 7

55. What did Neolin tell his people they must reject?
    a. a pan-Indian identity
    b. European technology and material goods
    c. the enslavement of Africans
    d. an alliance with the French

e. the use of English in trade negotiations

ANS: B   TOP: Ethnicity | Pontiac's Rebellion
DIF: Moderate   REF: Full p. 160 | Seagull p. 167
MSC: Remembering   OBJ: 7

56. Pontiac's Rebellion:
   a. greatly helped the British defeat the French in the Seven Years' War.
   b. although named for an Ottawa warrior, owed its origins as much to the teachings of a religious prophet.
   c. established the Mississippi River as the western boundary of British North America.
   d. ended with surrender of all the Indian forces only six months after fighting began.
   e. led Britain to adopt the policy of salutary neglect in its American colonies.

ANS: B   TOP: Ethnicity | Pontiac's Rebellion
DIF: Moderate   REF: Full p. 160 | Seagull p. 167
MSC: Understanding   OBJ: 7

57. What was the primary purpose of the Proclamation of 1763?
   a. to end the slave trade
   b. to protect the Indians
   c. to open up more land for settlement
   d. to bring stability to the colonial frontier
   e. to prohibit Catholicism in the territory newly acquired from France

ANS: D   TOP: Geographic issues | The Proclamation Line   DIF: Moderate   REF: Full p. 161 | Seagull p. 167   MSC: Understanding   OBJ: 7

58. What did the Paxton Boys demand?
   a. that liquor not be banned in Georgia
   b. that slave codes be tightened in New York
   c. that the Indians be removed from Pennsylvania
   d. that the French be hanged in Quebec
   e. that John Peter Zenger be tried for treason

ANS: C   TOP: Ethnicity | Pennsylvania and the Indians
DIF: Moderate   REF: Full p. 161 | Seagull p. 170
MSC: Remembering   OBJ: 7

59. Who drafted the Albany Plan of Union?
   a. George Washington
   b. Benjamin Franklin
   c. William Pitt
   d. John Peter Zenger
   e. Thomas Jefferson

ANS: B   TOP: Political history, changes | Colonial Identities   DIF: Moderate   REF: Full p. 164 | Seagull p. 171   MSC: Remembering   OBJ: 7

60. Which of the following was a consequence of the Seven Years' War?
   a. strengthened pride among American colonists about being part of the British empire
   b. the founding of the new colony of Ohio in territory acquired from France
   c. a weakening of liberties as France made gains in North America
   d. the creation of a central colonial government under the Albany Plan of Union
   e. increased popularity of the Anglican Church among ordinary colonists

ANS: A   TOP: Global awareness | Military history | Colonial Identities   DIF: Easy   REF: Full p. 164 | Seagull pp. 171–172   MSC: Understanding OBJ: 7

True or False

1. Some contemporaries spoke of British America as a "rising empire" that would one day eclipse the mother country in population and wealth.

ANS: T   TOP: Global awareness | Introduction
DIF: Moderate   REF: Full p. 127 | Seagull p. 130
MSC: Understanding   OBJ: 1

2. Recent scholarship has suggested that Olaudah Equiano may have been born in the New World rather than in Africa.

ANS: T   TOP: Divergent viewpoints | Introduction
DIF: Moderate   REF: Full p. 127 | Seagull p. 130
MSC: Remembering   OBJ: 1

3. The transatlantic slave trade was not a vital part of world commerce.

ANS: F   TOP: Economic development | Slavery and Empire   DIF: Easy   REF: Full p. 128 | Seagull p. 131   MSC: Remembering   OBJ: 1

4. In the 1700s, the militarily strong West African nations of Ashanti and Dahomey refused to participate in the slave trade.

ANS: F   TOP: Global awareness | Africa and the Slave Trade   DIF: Moderate   REF: Full p. 130 | Seagull p. 134   MSC: Remembering   OBJ: 1

5. Most of the slaves carried to the New World were destined for mainland North America.

ANS: F   TOP: Social history | The Middle Passage
DIF: Moderate   REF: Full p. 132 | Seagull p. 135
MSC: Remembering   OBJ: 1

6. Creek Indians sold war captives and their families to South Carolina planters as slaves.

   ANS: T   TOP: Ethnicity | Indian Slavery in Early Carolina   DIF: Moderate   REF: Full p. 133 | Seagull p. 137   MSC: Remembering   OBJ: 1

7. In eighteenth-century Chesapeake, race took on greater importance over time, and whites increasingly considered free blacks dangerous and undesirable.

   ANS: T   TOP: Civil Rights | Freedom and Slavery in the Chesapeake   DIF: Easy   REF: Full p. 133 | Seagull p. 137   MSC: Understanding   OBJ: 1

8. Africans had experience cultivating rice in Africa and helped the English settlers grow it in the South.

   ANS: T   TOP: Social history | The Rice Kingdom DIF: Moderate   REF: Full p. 134 | Seagull p. 138 MSC: Remembering   OBJ: 1

9. Initially, the proprietors of Georgia banned the introduction of both liquor and slaves.

   ANS: T   TOP: Political history, changes | The Georgia Experiment   DIF: Moderate   REF: Full p. 134 | Seagull p. 139   MSC: Remembering   OBJ: 1

10. In the early eighteenth century, only one-quarter of the Northern urban elite owned at least one slave.

    ANS: F   TOP: Social history | Slavery in the North DIF: Difficult   REF: Full p. 135 | Seagull p. 139 MSC: Remembering   OBJ: 1

11. Most slaves in eighteenth-century British America had been born in the colonies.

    ANS: F   TOP: Social history | Becoming African-American   DIF: Moderate   REF: Full p. 136 | Seagull p. 141   MSC: Remembering   OBJ: 2

12. Evidence that slaves frequently tried to escape in the eighteenth century was the numerous advertisements in colonial newspapers for runaways.

    ANS: T   TOP: Civil rights | Resistance to Slavery DIF: Moderate   REF: Full p. 138 | Seagull p. 143 MSC: Remembering   OBJ: 2

13. Most Britons believed that the king was above the law.

    ANS: F   TOP: Constitutional history | The British Con- stitution   DIF: Moderate   REF: Full pp. 140–141 | Seagull p. 146   MSC: Remembering   OBJ: 3

14. Increasingly in the eighteenth century, liberty was being used to express a right to rebel.

    ANS: T   TOP: Political history, changes | The Lan- guage of Liberty   DIF: Moderate   REF: Full p. 141 | Seagull p. 147   MSC: Understanding   OBJ: 3

15. John Locke believed that slaves could not be considered part of civil society.

    ANS: T   TOP: Political history, changes | Liberal Freedom   DIF: Easy   REF: Full p. 143 | Seagull p. 149   MSC: Remembering   OBJ: 3

16. A higher percentage of the population in Britain enjoyed the suffrage as compared to the American colonies.

    ANS: F   TOP: Political history, changes | The Right to Vote   DIF: Moderate   REF: Full p. 144 | Seagull p. 150   MSC: Understanding   OBJ: 4

17. In the northern colonies the law did not prohibit blacks from voting but local custom did.

    ANS: T   TOP: Social history | The Right to Vote DIF: Moderate   REF: Full p. 144 | Seagull p. 150 MSC: Remembering   OBJ: 4

18. Pennsylvania had the most powerful assembly of all the colonies.

    ANS: T   TOP: Political history, changes | The Rise of the Assemblies   DIF: Difficult   REF: Full p. 146 | Seagull p. 152   MSC: Remembering OBJ: 4

19. Colonial governments generally viewed freedom of the press as dangerous.

    ANS: T   TOP: Political history, changes | Freedom of Expression and Its Limits   DIF: Moderate REF: Full p. 148 | Seagull p. 155 MSC: Remembering   OBJ: 4

20. Deists concluded that the best form of religious devotion was to devoutly worship in organized churches.

    ANS: F   TOP: Cultural history | The American Enlightenment   DIF: Easy   REF: Full p. 150 | Seagull p. 157   MSC: Remembering   OBJ: 4

21. The religious emotionalism of the Great Awakening was confined to the American colonies in the mid-eighteenth century.

    ANS: F   TOP: Cultural history | The Preaching of Whitefield   DIF: Moderate   REF: Full p. 151 | Seagull p. 158   MSC: Remembering   OBJ: 5

22. Benjamin Franklin wrote an influential essay criticizing George Whitefield's preaching tour of the colonies.

    ANS: F   TOP: Cultural history | The Preaching of Whitefield   DIF: Moderate   REF: Full p. 151 | Seagull p. 159   MSC: Remembering   OBJ: 5

23. By the 1750s, the Great Awakening had resulted in the consolidation of all American Protestant churches into three denominations: Anglican, Congregationalist, and Quaker.

    ANS: F   TOP: Cultural history | The Awakening's Impact   DIF: Moderate   REF: Full p. 152 | Seagull p. 159   MSC: Remembering   OBJ: 5

24. The Spanish and French North American empires were densely populated areas.

    ANS: F   TOP: Geographic issues | Spanish North America | The French Empire   DIF: Moderate REF: Full pp. 152, 155 | Seagull pp. 160, 162–163 MSC: Remembering   OBJ: 6

25. Father Junípero Serra established the first mission in California and converted many Indians to Christianity, but his missions also relied on forced Indian labor and brought devastating diseases.

    ANS: T   TOP: Geographic issues | The Spanish in California   DIF: Moderate   REF: Full p. 154 | Seagull p. 162   MSC: Remembering   OBJ: 6

26. The "middle ground" was an area shared by Indians and European traders.

    ANS: T   TOP: Ethnicity | The Middle Ground DIF: Moderate   REF: Full p. 156 | Seagull p. 164 MSC: Remembering   OBJ: 6

27. Pontiac's Rebellion was an Indian revolt against British rule.

    ANS: T   TOP: Ethnicity | Pontiac's Rebellion DIF: Moderate   REF: Full p. 160 | Seagull p. 167 MSC: Remembering   OBJ: 7

Short Answer

Identify and give the historical significance of each of the following terms, events, and people in a paragraph or two.

1. Seven Years' War
2. republicanism and liberalism
3. newspapers
4. European Enlightenment
5. salutary neglect
6. Georgia colony
7. Deism
8. the Great Awakening
9. Stono Rebellion
10. Benjamin Franklin
11. Pontiac's Rebellion
12. the Middle Passage
13. African religions

Essay Questions

1. Explain what one historian meant by this statement: "The growth and prosperity of the emerging society of a free colonial British America . . . were achieved as a result of slave labor."

   ANS: Answers will vary   TOP: Political history, changes | Social history | Slavery and Empire | Liberal Freedom | The American Enlightenment DIF: Moderate   MSC: Understanding   OBJ: 1 / 3 / 4

2. The slave experience was diverse in British America. Describe how slavery evolved in the various regions of British America. What role did African religions play? What liberties, if any, were extended to slaves in the northern colonies, the Chesapeake region, and the rice kingdom of South Carolina and Georgia? What was the impact of the Stono Rebellion?

   ANS: Answers will vary   TOP: Social history | Cultural history | Civil rights | Chesapeake Slavery | The Rice Kingdom | The Georgia Experiment | Slavery in the North | African-American Cultures DIF: Moderate   MSC: Understanding   OBJ: 1 / 2

3. While slavery was expanding in British America, so too was freedom. Compare the simultaneous expansion of freedom and slavery. How was the concept of race increasingly important in this process?

   ANS: Answers will vary   TOP: Political history, changes | Civil rights | Chesapeake Slavery | The Rice Kingdom | The Georgia Experiment | Slavery in the North | African-American Cultures DIF: Moderate   MSC: Analyzing   OBJ: 1 / 3 / 4

4. Britons believed that wealth, religion, and freedom went together. Explain why they believed that those three things went hand in hand. Do you agree with this statement? What evidence is there that proves the statement's validity?

   ANS: Answers will vary   TOP: Political history, changes | Cultural history | The British Constitution DIF: Moderate   MSC: Evaluating   OBJ: 3 / 4 / 5

5. The eighteenth century witnessed a considerable expansion of the public sphere. Define what is meant by "public sphere," and describe the various ways in which the colonists participated in it. Be sure to include in your discussion not only who was participating but also who was excluded.

   ANS: Answers will vary   TOP: Social history | Political Cultures | The Right to Vote | The Rise of the Assemblies | Politics in Public   DIF: Moderate MSC: Understanding   OBJ: 4

6. In *Cato's Letters,* the authors declare that "Without freedom of thought there can be no such thing as wisdom, and no such thing as public liberty, without freedom of speech." To what extent did freedom of thought and freedom of speech exist in eighteenth-century British America?

   ANS: Answers will vary   TOP: Political history, changes | Republican Liberty | Liberal Freedom | Politics in Public | The Colonial Press | The Trial of Zenger   DIF: Moderate   MSC: Applying   OBJ: 3 / 4

7. Explain the impact on colonial life of the religious revival movement known as the Great Awakening. Be sure to discuss its social as well as religious effects. What do you imagine some of the Great Awakening's "significant political consequences" alluded to by Eric Foner might have been?

   ANS: Answers will vary   TOP: Social history | Cultural history | Political history, changes | The American Enlightenment   DIF: Moderate   MSC: Evaluating   OBJ: 5

8. The Enlightenment had a profound impact on the thinking of American colonists. Explain the essential ideas associated with the Enlightenment and the implications of these new ideas on American thought and society.

   ANS: Answers will vary   TOP: Cultural history | The American Enlightenment   DIF: Moderate   MSC: Understanding   OBJ: 3 / 4

9. Explain the impact of the Seven Years' War on colonial society. Pay particular attention to how the war and its outcome shaped colonial identities as well as to the relationship between colonists and Indians.

   ANS: Answers will vary   TOP: Military history | Social History | Ethnicity | The Seven Years' War   DIF: Moderate   MSC: Understanding   OBJ: 7

10. Discuss the ways in which the colonists became increasingly integrated into the British empire from roughly 1700 to 1763.

    Answers will vary   TOP: Global awareness | Social History | The Seven Years' War | Colonial Identities   DIF: Difficult   MSC: Understanding   OBJ: 1 / 4 / 7

11. As Europeans continued to settle the North American continent during the 1700s, Indians constantly struggled to maintain their independence and identities. Illustrate the common obstacles the Indian communities faced and the ways they tried to unite to overcome their hardships during the eighteenth century. Consider the Indians in California during the Spanish missionary period, the Creeks during the early settlement of Carolina, the Indians in Pennsylvania, and the Indians during and after the French and Indian War (including Pontiac's Rebellion).

    Answers will vary   TOP: Ethnicity | The Seven Years' War | The Spanish in California | Pontiac's Rebellion | Indian Slavery in Early Carolina | Pennsylvania and the Indians   DIF: Moderate   MSC: Applying   OBJ: 6 / 7

CHAPTER 5 | The American Revolution, 1763–1783

This chapter concentrates on the events leading up to the American Revolution and on the war itself. Beginning with the 1765 rioting at the home of Massachusetts Lieutenant Governor Thomas Hutchinson by an angry mob in response to the Stamp Act, the chapter explains how a crisis in Anglo-American relations grew from taxation policies rooted in Britain's need for increased revenue as a consequence of the Seven Years' War. Believing that the Stamp Act was a direct infringement on their liberty, many colonists reacted with indignation and violence. The ensuing decade was fraught with similar calls for an end to the British "enslavement" of the colonists and the rise of opposition groups such as the Sons of Liberty. When war broke out in 1775, independence was not a clear goal of the Continental Congress. Thomas Paine's *Common Sense,* excerpted in "Voices of Freedom," was crucial in educating the common people about their natural right to freedom and liberties that Britain denied. The Declaration of Independence, signed six months after the publication of *Common Sense,* forever changed the meaning of American freedom by proclaiming "unalienable rights" that no government could ever take away. The chapter concludes with an overview of the war. It gives attention to the role of free and enslaved blacks in the conflict as well as the arguments of Loyalists, which are highlighted in a "Voices of Freedom" piece by Jonathan Boucher, a minister in Virginia who opposed the Revolution. Major battles and strategies of the war are also discussed, especially the pivotal Battle of Saratoga, which convinced France to ally with the United States, and the Battle of Yorktown, where Lord Cornwallis's surrender signaled the end for the British. The chapter concludes with a consideration of the 1783 Treaty of Paris, in which Great Britain formally recognized American independence.

CHAPTER OUTLINE

I. Introduction: Thomas Hutchinson
   A. His home was attacked by protesters of the Stamp Act in 1765.
   B. Protests in British North America launched the Age of Revolution, which lasted a half century in the Western world.
   C. Revolution is a dynamic process whose consequences no one can anticipate.

II. The Crisis Begins
   A. Consolidating the Empire
     1. Prior to the Seven Years' War, London had loosely tried to regulate some of the colonies' economy.
       a. Various acts forbade colonial manufacturing of items like hats, wool, and iron and trading for molasses with the French Caribbean.
       b. Navigation Acts
     2. After the Seven Years' War, London insisted that the colonists play a subordinate role to the mother country and help pay for the protection the British provided.
     3. Members of the British Parliament had virtual representation.
     4. The colonists argued London could not tax them because they were underrepresented in Parliament.
     5. British writs of assistance to combat smuggling alarmed many colonists.
   B. Taxing the Colonies
     1. The Sugar Act of 1764 and the Revenue Act threatened the profits of colonial merchants and aggravated an economic recession.

C. The Stamp Act Crisis
 1. The Stamp Act of 1765 was a direct tax on all sorts of printed materials.
  a. First time taxes used to raise revenue in British North American history.
 2. The act was wide-reaching and offended virtually every free colonist.
 3. Opposition to the Stamp Act was the first great drama of the Revolutionary era and the first major split between the colonists and Great Britain over the meaning of freedom.
D. Taxation and Representation
 1. American leaders viewed the British empire as an association of equals in which free settlers overseas enjoyed the same rights as Britons at home.
 2. Patrick Henry led opposition by proposing four resolutions approved by Virginia's House of Burgesses.
 3. The Stamp Act Congress met in 1765 to endorse Virginia's House of Burgesses's resolutions.
  a. Parliament had inadvertently unified the thirteen colonies.
E. Liberty and Resistance
 1. No word was more frequently invoked by critics of the Stamp Act than "liberty":
  a. Liberty Tree
  b. Liberty Hall
  c. Liberty Pole
 2. Colonial leaders prevented the Stamp Act's implementation.
 3. A Committee of Correspondence was created in Boston and other colonies to exchange ideas about resistance.
F. Politics in the Streets
 1. The Sons of Liberty were organized to resist the Stamp Act and to enforce a boycott of British goods.
 2. A stunned Parliament repealed the Stamp Act, but issued the Declaratory Act.
  a. The new act stated Parliament could pass future colonial taxes.
G. The Regulators
 1. Two groups in the Carolinas were known as Regulators in the 1760s.
 2. The South Carolina Regulators consisted of wealthy backcountry residents who protested against their underrepresentation in the colonial assembly and the lack of local governments.
 3. The North Carolina Regulators mobilized small farmers upset with corrupt local government run by elites.

 4. The North Carolina militia defeated the North Carolina Regulators at the Battle of Alamance (1771), which ended their protests.
H. The Tenant Uprising
 1. Tenants along New York's Hudson River in the mid-1760s seized land from landlords, but were suppressed by British and colonial troops.
 2. Disputed land claims between New York and New Hampshire led to the creation of the state of Vermont in the mid-1770s under Ethan Allen and his Green Mountain Boys.

III. The Road to Revolution
A. The Townshend Crisis
 1. The 1767 Townshend Act imposed taxes on imported goods.
  a. Believed colonists agreed with taxes used to regulate trade.
 2. By 1768, colonies were again boycotting British goods.
 3. *Letters from a Farmer in Pennsylvania*
  a. John Dickinson's pamphlet of essays argues for reconciliation with the mother country.
  b. Colonists deserve all traditional rights of Englishmen.
  c. It demonstrated the Enlightenment influence on the colonies as well as the assumption that political debate was for the educated elite.
B. Homespun Virtue
 1. Rather than rely on British goods, colonists relied on homespun clothing; use of American goods came to be seen as a symbol of American resistance.
  a. Women, who spun and wove at home, were Daughters of Liberty.
 2. Chesapeake planters owing money to British merchants favored the homespun goods.
 3. Urban artisans strongly supported the boycott.
C. The Boston Massacre
 1. The March 1770 conflict between Bostonians and British troops left five Bostonians, including a mixed-race sailor named Crispus Attucks, dead.
  a. John Adams defended soldiers in court. Seven were found not guilty and two were convicted of manslaughter.
  b. Paul Revere's inaccurate engraving stirred up anger throughout the colonies.
 2. The boycott ended after the Townshend duties were repealed, except for a tax on tea.
D. Wilkes and Liberty
 1. The treatment of John Wilkes and the rumors of Anglican bishops being sent to America

convinced many settlers that England was
succumbing to the same pattern of political
corruption and decline of liberty that afflicted
other countries.
E. The Tea Act
  1. The East India Company was in financial
    crisis, and the British government decided to
    market the company's Chinese tea in North
    America.
  2. The Tea Act was intended to aid the East India
    Company and to help defray the costs of
    colonial government.
  3. December 16, 1773: colonists threw more than
    300 chests of tea into Boston Harbor.
F. The Intolerable Acts
  1. London's response to the Bostonians' action
    was swift and harsh with the so-called
    Intolerable Acts.
    a. Closed port of Boston until tea was paid for
    b. Curtailed town meetings in Massachusetts
    c. Stopped elections of council members
    d. Authorized lodging of British soldiers in
      private homes
  2. The Quebec Act granted religious toleration
    for Catholics in Canada and extended southern
    boundary to the Ohio River.

IV. The Coming of Independence
  A. The Continental Congress
    1. Boston issued Suffolk Resolves, which urged
      Americans not to obey new laws, to withhold
      taxes, and to prepare for war.
    2. To resist the Intolerable Acts, a Continental
      Congress convened in Philadelphia in 1774.
  B. The Continental Association
    1. The Congress adopted the Continental
      Association, which called for an almost
      complete halt to trade with Great Britain and
      the West Indies.
    2 Committees of Safety were established to take
      over governing and enforce the boycotts.
    a. The Committees of Safety enlarged the
      "political nation."
  C. The Sweets of Liberty
    1. By 1775, talk of liberty pervaded the colonies,
      including people of German heritage.
    2. As the crisis deepened, Americans
      increasingly based their claims not simply on
      the historical rights of Englishmen but on the
      more abstract language of natural rights and
      universal freedom.
    a. John Locke's theory of natural rights
    b. Thomas Jefferson's *A Summary View of the
      Rights of British America*

D. The Outbreak of War
  1. In April 1775, war broke out at Lexington and
    Concord.
  2. The Battle of Bunker Hill was a British
    victory, but the colonists forced General Howe
    from Boston by March 1776.
    a. Cannon from Fort Ticonderoga
  3. The Second Continental Congress raised an
    army and appointed George Washington its
    commander.
E. Independence?
  1. That the goal of this war was independence
    was not clear by the end of 1775.
  2. Opinions varied in the colonies as to the
    question of independence.
F. *Common Sense*
  1. Thomas Paine published *Common Sense* in
    January 1776.
  2. Criticizing monarchy and aristocracy, Paine
    called for a democratic system based on
    frequent elections and a written constitution.
  3. Paine termed absurd a small island ruling a
    continent.
  4. Paine tied the economic hopes of the new
    nation to the idea of commercial freedom.
  5. Paine argued that America would become a
    haven for liberty, "an asylum for mankind."
G. Paine's Impact
  1. Paine dramatically expanded the public sphere
    where political discussion took place.
  2. He pioneered a new style of political writing,
    engaging a far greater audience than anyone
    before him.
    a. *Common Sense* stood in marked contrast to
      Dickinson's *Letters from a Farmer in
      Pennsylvania.*
  3. His persuasions led the Second Continental
    Congress to sever the colonies' ties with Great
    Britain.
H. The Declaration of Independence
  1. The Declaration of Independence declared that
    Britain's aim was to establish "absolute tyranny"
    over the colonies and, as such, Congress declared
    the United States an independent nation.
  2. Jefferson's preamble gave the Declaration its
    enduring impact.
I. The Declaration and American Freedom
  1. The Declaration of Independence completed
    the shift from the rights of Englishmen to the
    rights of mankind as the object of American
    independence.
    a. The "pursuit of happiness" was unique and
      became the central element of American
      freedom.

J. An Asylum for Mankind
  1. The idea of "American exceptionalism" was prevalent in the Revolution.
K. The Global Declaration of Independence
  1. Although for most Americans winning international recognition for their independence trumped concern for global human rights, Thomas Jefferson hoped the Declaration would inspire others to claim liberty and self-government.
  2. Numerous anticolonial movements—from Flanders in 1790 to Vietnam in 1945—have modeled their own declarations of independence on America's.
  3. The Declaration's principle that political authority rests on the will of "the people" has been influential around the world.

V. Securing Independence
  A. The Balance of Power
    1. Britain had the advantage of a large, professional army and navy.
    2. Patriots had the advantages of fighting on their own soil and a passionate desire for freedom.
  B. Blacks in the Revolution
    1. George Washington accepted black recruits after Lord Dunmore's proclamation offered freedom to slaves who fought for the British.
      a. Five thousand African-Americans enlisted in state militias and the Continental army and navy.
      b. Some slaves gained freedom by serving in place of an owner.
    2. Siding with the British offered slaves far more opportunities for liberty.
  C. The First Years of the War
    1. The war initially went badly for Washington; many of his troops went home.
    2. He managed a successful surprise attack on Trenton and Princeton.
      a. Inspired in part by Thomas Paine's *The American Crisis*
  D. The Battle of Saratoga
    1. The Battle of Saratoga in October 1777 gave the patriots a victory and boost to morale.
      a. The victory convinced the French to aid the Americans in 1778.
    2. Winter of 1777–1778
      a. British were quartered in Philadelphia with plenty of supplies.
      b. American troops, half of which were immigrants or African-Americans, suffered at Valley Forge.

E. The War in the South
  1. The focus of the war shifted to the South in 1778.
  2. Continental Congress was essentially bankrupt.
  3. British achieved some victories, but commanders were unable to consolidate their hold on the South.
F. Victory at Last
  1. American and French troops surrounded General Cornwallis at Yorktown, where he surrendered in October 1781.
  2. The Treaty of Paris was signed in September 1783.
    a. The American delegation was made up of John Adams, Benjamin Franklin, and John Jay.
    b. In addition to independence, America granted land in the frontier to the Mississippi River.

SUGGESTED DISCUSSION QUESTIONS

- Explain why colonists felt that the Stamp Act violated their liberty.
- How did the Stamp Act inadvertently serve to unite the colonies?
- How and why did many colonists come to believe that membership in the British empire was a threat to their freedom, rather than the foundation of their freedom?
- Discuss Paine's views on natural rights and the monarchy. What role did *Common Sense* play in American independence?
- What was the thesis or main argument of the Declaration of Independence? What evidence did it use to make its case? Why do you think so many colonists found it persuasive?
- How can Jefferson's statement that "all men are created equal" be reconciled with the reality of slavery, social hierarchy, and mistreatment of Indians?
- Might the colonists have worked things out with the British, or was rebellion inevitable? What might the British have done to appease the colonists and avoid conflict?
- Discuss how the war affected slaves, depending on whether they fought for the British or the Americans. Also discuss the war's effect on the particular states where slaves lived. How do you think the slaves could have brought themselves to fight for one side or the other?
- Have the students convene as the Continental Congress, after the publication of *Common Sense* but before the drafting of the Declaration of Independence. Have them debate what the course of action ought to be for this war. Is Paine correct that independence makes sense, or should modest requests of England be the goal of the Congress?

SUPPLEMENTAL WEB AND VISUAL SOURCES

American Revolution
revolution.h-net.msu.edu/
This site was created by H-Net Humanities and Social Sciences from the generous support of the National Endowment for the Humanities to serve as a complement to the official companion site to PBS's *Liberty!* documentary series. Helpful sub-links are "Essays" and "Resources."

Blacks in the War
http://www.seacoastnh.com/Black-History/Black-History/Colored-Patriots-of-NH/
This website from Portsmouth, New Hampshire, discusses the state's "Colored Patriots" of the Revolution.

From Revolution to Reconstruction
odur.let.rug.nl/~usa/D/index.htm#1751
This site contains documentation that was written before and after the Revolutionary War. Documents include Resolutions of the Stamp Act Congress and the Treaty of Paris.

Liberty!
www.pbs.org/ktca/liberty/
Liberty! is a PBS documentary about the American Revolution that features dramatic readings from letters and diaries of the period. The series includes: "The Reluctant Revolutionaries," "The Times That Try Men's Souls," and "Are We to Be a Nation?"

The Boston Massacre
www.bostonmassacre.net/
This high-quality website from the Boston Massacre Historical Society offers useful insight into the Boston Massacre as well as excellent pictures and time lines.

The Revolutionary War
The Price of Freedom: Americans at War
americanhistory.si.edu/militaryhistory/exhibition/flash.html
From the Smithsonian Institution's National Museum of American History, select a war (e.g., Revolutionary War) and enter an exhibit that includes a movie, learning resources, statistics, printable exhibition, maps, and time lines.

SUPPLEMENTAL PRINT RESOURCES

Bullion, John. "British Ministers and American Resistance to the Stamp Act, October–December 1765." *William and Mary Quarterly* 49, no. 1 (1992): 89–107.
Clodfelter, Mark. "Between Virtue and Necessity: Nathaniel Greene and the Conduct of Civil Military Relations in the South, 1780–1782." *Military Affairs* 52, no. 4 (1988): 169–175.
Fenn, Elizabeth A. *Pox Americana: The Great Smallpox Epidemic of 1775–82.* New York: Hill and Wang, 2001.
Horton, James Oliver, and Lois Horton. *In Hope of Liberty: Culture, Community, and Protest among Northern Free Blacks, 1700–1860.* New York: Oxford University Press, 1998.
Jayne, Allen. *Jefferson's Declaration of Independence: Origins, Philosophy and Theology.* Lexington, KY: University Press of Kentucky, 1998.
Kaplan, Sidney, and Emma Kaplan. *The Black Presence in the Era of the American Revolution.* Amherst, MA: University of Massachusetts Press, 1989.
Kaye, Harvey. *Thomas Paine: Firebrand of Revolution.* New York: Oxford University Press, 2000.
Kruman, Marc. *Between Authority and Liberty: State Constitution Making in Revolutionary America.* Chapel Hill, NC: University of North Carolina Press, 1997.
Resch, John. *Suffering Soldiers: Revolutionary War Veterans, Moral Sentiment, and Political Culture in the Early Republic.* Amherst, MA: University of Massachusetts Press, 1999.
Wheeler, Richard. *Voices of 1776: The Story of the American Revolution in the Words of Those Who Were There.* New York: Meridian Publishing, 1991.

TEST BANK

Matching

TEST I

____ 1. Thomas Hutchinson
____ 2. Thomas Paine
____ 3. George Washington
____ 4. Charles Townshend
____ 5. Crispus Attucks
____ 6. Thomas Jefferson
____ 7. Lord Dunmore
____ 8. Sir William Howe
____ 9. Patrick Henry
____ 10. Benedict Arnold
____ 11. Ethan Allen
____ 12. John Dickinson

a. offered freedom to slaves if they fought for the British
b. American traitor in command of West Point
c. *Letters from a Farmer in Pennsylvania*
d. British chancellor of the Exchequer
e. Massachusetts lieutenant governor
f. wrote *Common Sense*
g. commander of the Continental army
h. author of the Declaration of Independence
i. British commander
j. sailor who died in the Boston Massacre
k. declared "Give me liberty, or give me death!"
l. founder of Vermont

Answer Key: e, f, g, d, j, h, a, i, k, b, l, c

TEST 2

____ 1. Stamp Act
____ 2. Sons of Liberty

___ 3. *Common Sense*
___ 4. Committee of Correspondence
___ 5. Quebec Act
___ 6. virtual representation independence
___ 7. Regulators
___ 8. East India Company
___ 9. Saratoga
___ 10. Loyalists
___ 11. homespun virtue
___ 12. Ethiopian regiment residents

a. first significant American victory
b. beneficiary of the Tea Act
c. religious tolerance for Catholics
d. colonists who were loyal to Britain
e. black loyalist forces
f. pamphlet that argued for American independence
g. each member of Parliament represented the entire empire
h. exchanged ideas about resistance
i. street protesters
j. wealthy South Carolina backcountry
k. refusal to buy British goods
l. viewed by colonists as a major violation of liberty

Answer Key: l, i, f, h, c, g, j, b, a, d, k, e

Learning Objectives

1. Describe the roots and significance of the Stamp Act controversy.
2. Identify the key events that sharpened the divisions between Britain and the colonists in the late 1760s and early 1770s.
3. Identify the key events that marked the move toward American independence.
4. Explain how American forces were able to prevail in the Revolutionary War.

Multiple Choice

1. The attack by Massachusetts colonists on the home of lieutenant governor and chief justice Thomas Hutchinson:
   a. convinced him that the Stamp Act, which he had previously supported, was unwise.
   b. physically assaulted Hutchinson's family, an act that prompted Great Britain to clamp down on colonial liberties.
   c. led Hutchinson to believe that effective British rule would require the loss of some liberties for the colonists.
   d. led Parliament to repeal the Townshend Acts immediately.
   e. included Samuel and John Adams.

ANS: C   TOP: Political history, changes | Introduction: Thomas Hutchinson   DIF: Moderate   REF: Full p. 171 | Seagull p. 175   MSC: Understanding OBJ: 1

2. Which major event first led the British government to seek ways to make the colonies bear part of the cost of the empire?
   a. the Declaration of Independence
   b. King Philip's War
   c. the Seven Years' War
   d. the Boston Tea Party
   e. the appointment of William Pitt as British prime minister

ANS: C   TOP: Global awareness | Military history | The Crisis Begins   DIF: Easy   REF: Full pp. 171–172 | Seagull p. 175   MSC: Remembering   OBJ: 1

3. All of the following were attempts to regulate colonial trade before the Seven Years' War EXCEPT for the:
   a. Molasses Act.
   b. Proclamation Line.
   c. Hat Act.
   d. Iron Act.
   e. Wool Act.

ANS: B   TOP: Chronology | Consolidating the Empire   DIF: Moderate   REF: Full p. 172 | Seagull p. 176   MSC: Remembering   OBJ: 1

4. Virtual representation was the idea:
   a. that only those who were elected by a given population could represent that population in a legislative body.
   b. about representation that most politically active American colonists in the 1760s and 1770s embraced.
   c. endorsed by the Stamp Act Congress in 1765.
   d. that each member of Britain's House of Commons represented the entire empire, not just his own district.
   e. that the king should appoint delegates to represent the colonies in the British House of Commons.

ANS: D   TOP: Political history, changes | Consolidating the Empire   DIF: Moderate   REF: Full p. 173 | Seagull p. 177   MSC: Understanding   OBJ: 1

5. The Sugar Act alarmed colonists, in part because it:
   a. increased the tax on molasses and made rum more expensive to produce.
   b. made sugar, a key consumer good, too expensive.
   c. mandated that violators of the act be tried in a court with a jury.
   d. eliminated the admiralty courts, which colonists had long favored.

e. threatened the profits of colonial merchants already in economic trouble.

ANS: E   TOP: Economic development | Taxing the Colonies   DIF: Difficult   REF: Full p. 173 | Seagull p. 178   MSC: Understanding   OBJ: 1

6. The Stamp Act created such a stir in the colonies because:
   a. it raised prices on printed products so much that most colonists no longer could afford to buy books and newspapers.
   b. lawyers were offended that they could be jailed for not using the correct stamp on legal documents.
   c. it was the first direct tax Parliament imposed on the colonies.
   d. none of the revenue raised would be spent within the colonies themselves.
   e. Benjamin Franklin went public with his opposition to it.

ANS: C   TOP: Political history, changes | The Stamp Act Crisis   DIF: Moderate   REF: Full pp. 173–174 | Seagull p. 179   MSC: Understanding   OBJ: 1

7. What contribution did the Stamp Act episode make to the colonists' concept of liberty?
   a. The elite became more aware of liberty, but the lower classes remained unconcerned, choosing instead just to follow leaders who encouraged them to riot.
   b. The Stamp Act Congress insisted that the right to consent to taxation was essential to people's freedom.
   c. It led the Stamp Act Congress to adopt the Declaratory Act, which defined American liberties.
   d. It convinced colonists that revolting against Great Britain was the only way to secure their liberties.
   e. Requiring everyone freed from jail to wear a stamp reminded colonists that they were prisoners of the British empire.

ANS: B   TOP: Political history, changes | Taxation and Representation   DIF: Moderate   REF: Full p. 175 | Seagull p. 180   MSC: Understanding   OBJ: 1

8. The Sons of Liberty:
   a. enjoyed support from New York craftsmen and laborers.
   b. won widespread support from New York's upper classes.
   c. opposed any violent response to the Stamp Act.
   d. prompted founder Samuel Adams and his cousin John Adams to break off relations.
   e. caused the Boston Massacre in 1765.

ANS: A   TOP: Social history | Politics in the Streets DIF: Moderate   REF: Full p. 176 | Seagull p. 181 MSC: Remembering   OBJ: 1

9. The Declaratory Act:
   a. imposed a boycott on all manufactured goods produced in the colonies.
   b. declared that colonists had to house British soldiers in their homes.
   c. closed the Port of Boston on account of the Boston Tea Party.
   d. rejected American claims that only their elected representatives could levy taxes.
   e. proclaimed the colonies' independence from Great Britain.

ANS: D   TOP: Political history, changes | Politics in the Streets   DIF: Moderate   REF: Full p. 176 | Seagull p. 182   MSC: Remembering   OBJ: 1

10. Violent social turmoil in rural areas during the 1760s:
    a. was due entirely to Great Britain's Proclamation of 1763, banning western settlement.
    b. ended when the British army drove out Native Americans beyond the line of settlement.
    c. flourished because the British army had no interest in going beyond coastal cities.
    d. led to the creation of the Sons of Liberty.
    e. involved events in both northern and southern colonies.

ANS: E   TOP: Social history | The Regulators DIF: Moderate   REF: Full p. 176 | Seagull pp. 182–183 MSC: Remembering   OBJ: 1

11. Which one of the following did NOT specifically provide for direct or indirect taxes on the colonies?
    a. the Sugar Act
    b. the Tea Act
    c. the Townshend Act
    d. the Stamp Act
    e. the Declaratory Act

ANS: E   TOP: Political history, changes | Politics in the Streets   DIF: Easy   REF: Full p. 176 | Seagull p. 182   MSC: Understanding   OBJ: 1

12. Which armed group, motivated by deep frustrations with the corruption of North Carolina's county officials, was defeated by the colony's militia at the 1771 Battle of Alamance?
    a. the Sons of Liberty
    b. the Regulators
    c. the Blue Ridge Boys
    d. the Association
    e. the Rangers

ANS: B   TOP: Political history, changes | The Regulators   DIF: Moderate   REF: Full p. 177 | Seagull p. 183   MSC: Remembering   OBJ: 1

13. Ethan Allen and the Green Mountain Boys:
    a. started the colony of New Hampshire.
    b. forced the British army to retreat at Concord.
    c. were spies working for the Sons of Liberty.
    d. put down the revolt of the Regulators in North Carolina.
    e. fought intrusions by New York landlords into what became Vermont.

    ANS: E   TOP: Social history | The Tenant Uprising
    DIF: Moderate   REF: Full p. 178 | Seagull p. 183
    MSC: Remembering   OBJ: 1

14. The Townshend Acts did all of the following EXCEPT:
    a. impose new import duties on glass and tea.
    b. encourage some colonies to boycott British goods.
    c. reaffirm Boston's decision to abide by the Quartering Act.
    d. create a Board of Customs Commissioners to catch smugglers.
    e. raise revenue to pay the salaries of American governors and judges.

    ANS: C   TOP: Political history, changes | The Townshend Crisis   DIF: Easy   REF: Full p. 178 |
    Seagull p. 184   MSC: Understanding   OBJ: 2

15. In *Letters from a Farmer in Pennsylvania*, John Dickinson:
    a. denied the ideas of the Enlightenment.
    b. reached out to working-class Americans.
    c. stated independence from Great Britain was the best course of action.
    d. argued for reconciliation with Great Britain along with the same rights as Englishmen.
    e. set the stage a year later for Thomas Jefferson's Declaration of Independence.

    D   TOP: Political history, changes | The Townshend Crisis   DIF: Moderate   REF: Full pp. 178–179 |
    Seagull p. 184   MSC: Understanding   OBJ: 2

16. The "Daughters of Liberty" was the name given to:
    a. the female children of the Founding Fathers, especially the daughters of Washington, Adams, and Jefferson.
    b. New England women who won voting rights in the 1770s.
    c. the brave women who cared for wounded soldiers during the early battles of the Revolution.
    d. women who spun and wove to create their own clothing rather than buy British goods.
    e. the first national women's patriotic organization, which raised money to provide supplies for the Continental army after Saratoga.

    ANS: D   TOP: Social history | Homespun Virtue
    DIF: Moderate   REF: Full p. 179 | Seagull p. 184
    MSC: Remembering   OBJ: 2

17. The Boston Massacre occurred when British soldiers:
    a. killed Indians who were raiding frontier towns.
    b. fired into a mob and killed a number of Boston residents.
    c. captured members of the Sons of Liberty involved in the Boston Tea Party.
    d. fired on local minutemen guarding an arsenal.
    e. tried to defend Thomas Hutchinson from an angry mob.

    ANS: B   TOP: Social history | The Boston Massacre
    DIF: Moderate   REF: Full pp. 179–180 | Seagull p. 185
    MSC: Remembering   OBJ: 2

18. Crispus Attucks:
    a. defended in court the British soldiers who participated in the Boston Massacre.
    b. organized the boycott of British imports following the Townshend Act.
    c. was the first person of mixed race to serve in the Continental Congress.
    d. has been called the first martyr of the American Revolution.
    e. died bravely at the Battle of Concord.

    ANS: D   TOP: Social history | The Boston Massacre
    DIF: Moderate   REF: Full p. 180 | Seagull p. 185
    MSC: Remembering   OBJ: 2

19. The expulsion of the journalist John Wilkes from his seat in Parliament:
    a. symbolized the threat to liberty for many in both Britain and America.
    b. pleased most American colonists because of Wilkes's pro-Stamp-Act editorials.
    c. resulted from a column Wilkes wrote that was sympathetic toward those killed in the Boston Massacre.
    d. came after a London jury convicted him of colluding with pro-independence colonists.
    e. was reversed by the king, which led to a British constitutional crisis that diverted attention from the colonies.

    ANS: A   TOP: Global awareness | Wilkes and Liberty
    DIF: Moderate   REF: Full p. 181 | Seagull
    pp. 186–187   MSC: Understanding   OBJ: 2

20. Why did colonists object to the Tea Act?
    a. Because it would aid a different part of the empire than their own, colonists felt that this was the kind of discriminatory action that violated the concept of liberty.
    b. By paying it, they would be acknowledging Great Britain's right to tax the colonists.
    c. It granted a monopoly, and the colonists opposed all forms of monopoly.

d. The British East India Company made inferior tea, and colonists preferred not to drink it.

e. It raised the tax on tea so much as to make tea prohibitively expensive.

ANS: B   TOP: Political history, changes | The Tea Act   DIF: Moderate   REF: Full p. 181 | Seagull p. 187   MSC: Understanding   OBJ: 2

21. Britain responded to the Boston Tea Party with:
    a. the Townshend Act.
    b. the Intolerable Acts.
    c. a declaration of war.
    d. the Suffolk Resolves.
    e. the Boston Massacre.

    ANS: B   TOP: Political history, changes | The Intolerable Acts   DIF: Moderate   REF: Full pp. 181–182 | Seagull pp. 187–188   MSC: Remembering   OBJ: 3

22. Which of the following was associated with the Intolerable Acts?
    a. For the first time British authorities stationed soldiers in Boston.
    b. Parliament closed all American ports to all trade until the tea destroyed by the Boston Tea Party was paid for.
    c. The Massachusetts Charter of 1691 was changed to curtail town meetings.
    d. The office of governor of Massachusetts became an elected position.
    e. Colonists were prevented from producing items made from glass, paper, or lead.

    ANS: C   TOP: Political history, changes | The Intolerable Acts   DIF: Moderate   REF: Full pp. 181–182 | Seagull pp. 187–188   MSC: Remembering   OBJ: 2

23. The Quebec Act:
    a. granted religious toleration to Catholics in Canada.
    b. placed a tax on all imported goods from Canada.
    c. removed the Ohio River Valley from the province of Quebec.
    d. called for Canada to join America in the struggle for independence.
    e. created Quebec out of the preexisting provinces of Ontario and New Brunswick.

    ANS: A   TOP: Political history, changes | The Intolerable Acts   DIF: Moderate   REF: Full p. 182 | Seagull p. 188   MSC: Remembering   OBJ: 3

24. What were the Suffolk Resolves?
    a. the peace treaty that ended the Regulator movement in North Carolina
    b. a list of demands addressed to landlords, made in 1772 by New York tenant farmers

c. a group of anti-Tea Act petitions from Boston merchants to the Massachusetts royal governor

d. the resolutions pledging the Continental Congress's loyalty to King George III in 1775

e. a set of resolutions made in 1774, urging Massachusetts citizens to prepare for war

ANS: E   TOP: Political history, changes | The Continental Congress   DIF: Difficult   REF: Full p. 182 | Seagull p. 188   MSC: Remembering   OBJ: 3

25. The Committees of Safety:
    a. served to warn colonists if the Royal Navy was approaching.
    b. were part of a series of efforts by the Continental Congress to promote unity and to take action against enemies of liberty.
    c. killed twenty-eight Loyalists before the Revolutionary War began.
    d. took action against Catholics trying to spread Quebec's influence.
    e. were designed to protect British officials like Thomas Hutchinson, but attracted too small a number of members to succeed.

    ANS: B   TOP: Political history, changes | The Continental Association   DIF: Moderate   REF: Full p. 183 | Seagull p. 189   MSC: Understanding   OBJ: 3

26. In the years immediately before the American Revolution, the concept of natural rights:
    a. greatly influenced Thomas Jefferson's early writings.
    b. prompted Thomas Jefferson to support independence before the war even began.
    c. caused many American colonists to call for the abolition of the monarchy.
    d. contradicted the argument for colonial resistance.
    e. led to Parliament's passage of the Declaratory Act of 1766.

    ANS: A   TOP: Political history, changes | The Sweets of Liberty   DIF: Difficult   REF: Full p. 184 | Seagull p. 190   MSC: Understanding   OBJ: 3

27. Which of the following was NOT a significant battle during the first year of the Revolutionary War?
    a. Lexington and Concord, which included "the shot heard 'round the world'"
    b. Fort Ticonderoga, where soldiers commanded by Ethan Allen and Benedict Arnold forced a British surrender
    c. Breed's Hill, where the British suffered heavy casualties trying to dislodge colonial militiamen
    d. the Siege of Boston, which culminated in Sir William Howe's troops abandoning the city
    e. Cowpens, which helped turn the tide of war in the South

ANS: E   TOP: Chronology | Military history | The
Outbreak of War   DIF: Difficult   REF: Full
pp. 184–185 | Seagull pp. 190–191
MSC: Remembering   OBJ: 3

28. John Adams recommended George Washington as
commander of the Continental army because:
a. he knew that Washington was weighing an offer
from Britain to lead its North American forces.
b. he shared Washington's view of the importance of
natural rights.
c. the fact that Washington was from Virginia could
help unify the colonists.
d. he knew Washington had opposed General Howe's
forces cutting down the Liberty Tree.
e. they had an agreement that Adams would then be
put in charge of administering the army in the New
England colonies.

ANS: C   TOP: Political history, changes | The Outbreak
of War   DIF: Moderate   REF: Full p. 185 | Seagull
pp. 191–192   MSC: Understanding   OBJ: 3

29. What did Lord Dunmore do that horrified many
southerners?
a. He encouraged Indians to conduct raids against
backcountry settlements in the Carolinas.
b. He issued a proclamation freeing all slaves south of
the Ohio River.
c. He promised freedom to slaves who joined the
British cause.
d. He confiscated property of Loyalists.
e. He circulated germ-ridden blankets among frontier
towns to spread disease.

ANS: C   TOP: Social history | Independence?
DIF: Moderate   REF: Full pp. 185–186 | Seagull
p. 192   MSC: Remembering   OBJ: 3

30. Who argued that "true liberty" could only be achieved
by remaining in the British Empire?
a. Ben Franklin
b. Sam Adams
c. Ethan Allen
d. George Washington
e. Joseph Galloway

ANS: E   TOP: Political history, changes |
Independence?   DIF: Moderate   REF: Full p. 186 |
Seagull p. 192   MSC: Remembering   OBJ: 3

31. The Olive Branch Petition:
a. was meant to ease tensions among the organized
political parties within the Continental Congress.
b. enabled northern and southern colonies to work
together.
c. convinced Thomas Paine that he had enough
support to write *Common Sense*.

d. was Parliament's final attempt to explain virtual
representation to the colonists.
e. was addressed to King George III and reaffirmed
American loyalty to the crown.

ANS: E   TOP: Political history, changes | *Common
Sense*   DIF: Moderate   REF: Full p. 186 | Seagull
p. 192   MSC: Remembering   OBJ: 3

32. Thomas Paine's *Common Sense:*
a. argued that the British governmental system was
perfectly good, but that current officials had
corrupted it.
b. made highly original arguments in favor of
independence.
c. sold well among the elite, who in turn were able to
convey its ideas to the lower classes.
d. argued that America would become the home of
freedom and "an asylum for mankind."
e. led to his arrest on charges of treason, but he saved
himself by writing another pamphlet taking the
opposite position.

ANS: D   TOP: Primary document analysis | *Common
Sense*   DIF: Moderate   REF: Full p. 187 | Seagull
p. 193   MSC: Understanding   OBJ: 3

33. Which statement about Thomas Paine's *Common
Sense* is FALSE?
a. It was published in 1776.
b. It called for a democratic system based on frequent
elections and a written constitution.
c. It tied the economic hopes of the new nation to the
idea of commercial freedom.
d. It dramatically expanded the public sphere.
e. It was breathtakingly original in its ideas.

ANS: E   TOP: Primary document analysis | Paine's
Impact   DIF: Moderate   REF: Full p. 187 | Seagull
p. 193   MSC: Understanding   OBJ: 3

34. Most of the text of the Declaration of Independence:
a. was originally drafted by Benjamin Franklin and
then brilliantly edited by Thomas Jefferson.
b. consists of a list of grievances against King
George III.
c. is an updated version of John Locke's classic, *The
Rights of Man.*
d. specifically attacks the idea that Parliament has a
right to enact any laws for the colonies.
e. is an irrefutable argument for the notion of virtual
representation.

ANS: B   TOP: Primary document analysis | The
Declaration of Independence   DIF: Moderate
REF: Full pp. 189–190 | Seagull p. 196
MSC: Understanding   OBJ: 3

35. In the Declaration of Independence, Jefferson's biggest influence with regard to natural rights came from?
    a. John Adams
    b. Thomas Paine
    c. Joseph Galloway
    d. John Locke
    e. Lord Dunmore

    ANS: D   TOP: Primary document analysis | The Declaration and American Freedom   DIF: Easy
    REF: Full p. 190 | Seagull p. 197   MSC: Remembering
    OBJ: 3

36. All of the following are true of the Declaration of Independence EXCEPT:
    a. ultimately, it is an assertion of the right of revolution.
    b. its arguments made it a uniquely American document with little relevance to other nations.
    c. it celebrated individual self-fulfillment as a central element of American freedom.
    d. it completed the shift of Americans' focus from their rights as Englishmen to their rights as human beings.
    e. it deemphasized tradition as a force in shaping American society.

    ANS: B   TOP: Primary document analysis | An Asylum for Mankind   DIF: Easy   REF: Full p. 191 | Seagull pp. 197–198   MSC: Understanding
    OBJ: 3

37. By the time of Thomas Jefferson's death in 1826 about _____ other declarations of independence had been issued in Europe and the Western Hemisphere.
    a. 5
    b. 10
    c. 15
    d. 20
    e. 25

    ANS: D   TOP: Global awareness | The Global Declaration of Independence   DIF: Difficult   REF: Full p. 192 | Seagull p. 198   MSC: Remembering   OBJ: 3

38. All of the following were advantages enjoyed by the British during the American Revolution EXCEPT:
    a. the world's best navy.
    b. a professionally trained army.
    c. the ability to recruit German soldiers to fight for the British.
    d. an intimate knowledge of the terrain.
    e. the ability to lure slaves to fight for the British in exchange for their freedom.

    ANS: D   TOP: Military history | The Balance of Power | Blacks in the Revolution   DIF: Moderate
    REF: Full p. 193 | Seagull pp. 199–200
    MSC: Understanding   OBJ: 4

39. Which of the following is true of the soldiers who fought for American independence?
    a. During the war's later years, the Continental army relied increasingly on young men with limited economic prospects.
    b. Relatively few—only one in sixty—lost their lives in the war.
    c. Nearly one-third of all American soldiers were slaves fighting as substitutes for their masters.
    d. Because they had the most to gain, men of substantial property served in disproportionately high numbers throughout the war.
    e. Lacking any military experience and unsure of their cause, the soldiers performed so poorly that it took the addition of 25,000 French ground troops to prevent a British victory.

    ANS: A   TOP: Military history | Social history | The Balance of Power   DIF: Moderate   REF: Full p. 193 | Seagull p. 199   MSC: Understanding   OBJ: 4

40. During the eight years of war, approximately how many Americans bore arms in the Continental army and state militias?
    a. 80,000
    b. 125,000
    c. 200,000
    d. 350,000
    e. 500,000

    ANS: C   TOP: Military history | The Balance of Power   DIF: Difficult   REF: Full p. 193 | Seagull p. 199   MSC: Remembering   OBJ: 4

41. Which of the following statements regarding black soldiers during the American Revolution is FALSE?
    a. No southern state allowed blacks to serve in its militia.
    b. A total of approximately 5,000 African Americans served in state militias and in the Continental army and navy.
    c. Rhode Island, which had a relatively high black population for New England, formed a black regiment.
    d. George Washington initially refused to allow black recruits, but later changed his mind.
    e. Blacks and whites served together in racially integrated Continental army units.

    ANS: A   TOP: Civil rights | Military history | Blacks in the Revolution   DIF: Moderate   REF: Full pp. 193–194 | Seagull p. 201   MSC: Understanding   OBJ: 4

42. The main point of *The American Crisis* is:
    a. that the Continental Congress should agree to peaceful reunification with Britain.
    b. to inspire American soldiers to continue to fight despite demoralizing military losses.
    c. that independence was too costly a goal for the colonies.
    d. to encourage European powers to provide military assistance to the cause of American independence.
    e. a prediction that the war would end unhappily for supporters of independence.

    ANS: B   TOP: Military history | Primary document analysis | The First Years of the War   DIF: Moderate
    REF: Full p. 195 | Seagull p. 202
    MSC: Understanding   OBJ: 4

43. In the winter of 1776–1777, Washington won important victories that improved American morale. These battles were at:
    a. Saratoga and Albany, New York.
    b. Morristown and East Orange, New Jersey.
    c. Long Island and White Plains, New York.
    d. Lexington and Concord, Massachusetts.
    e. Trenton and Princeton, New Jersey.

    ANS: E   TOP: Military history | The First Years of the War   DIF: Difficult   REF: Full p. 195 | Seagull p. 202   MSC: Remembering   OBJ: 4

44. A key consequence of the Battle of Saratoga in October 1777 was:
    a. France became an ally to the United States.
    b. the adoption of the Declaration of Independence by the Continental Congress.
    c. the immediate surrender of all British troops to the Continental army.
    d. British commanders taking the war into the heart of New England for the first time.
    e. General Washington's decision to retreat to Valley Forge for the winter.

    ANS: A   TOP: Global awareness | Military history | The Battle of Saratoga   DIF: Moderate   REF: Full p. 197 | Seagull p. 204   MSC: Remembering   OBJ: 4

45. In 1778, the focus of the war shifted:
    a. from minor skirmishes of fewer than 100 men to major battles, each involving thousands of soldiers.
    b. from fighting in the southern states to fighting in New York and New England.
    c. to an emphasis on the Continental army's trying to capture British strongholds in the Ohio Valley.
    d. to the South, where the British captured Savannah that year.
    e. to emancipation, when General Washington declared all slaves who fought for American independence should be free.

    ANS: D   TOP: Military history | The War in the South   DIF: Moderate   REF: Full p. 197 | Seagull p. 204   MSC: Understanding   OBJ: 4

46. During the Revolutionary War, tensions between backcountry farmers and wealthy planters:
    a. enabled the British to turn around their previously unsuccessful performance during the war.
    b. prompted several mutinies within colonial ranks.
    c. gave the British hope that they might be able to enlist the support of southern Loyalists.
    d. led Benedict Arnold to defect to the British.
    e. caused Francis Marion's eventual defeat at the Battle of Cowpens.

    ANS: C   TOP: Military history | Social history | The War in the South   DIF: Difficult   REF: Full p. 197 | Seagull p. 204   MSC: Understanding   OBJ: 4

47. Cornwallis was defeated at Yorktown because:
    a. he had no land or water escape route.
    b. he was overwhelmed by Washington's much larger and better trained army.
    c. General Clinton had withdrawn from Yorktown, leaving Cornwallis vulnerable.
    d. most of his troops were cold, starving, and ready to surrender.
    e. King George III ordered an end to the war.

    ANS: A   TOP: Military history | Victory at Last   DIF: Moderate   REF: Full pp. 199–200 | Seagull p. 206   MSC: Understanding   OBJ: 4

48. Washington's defeat of Cornwallis at Yorktown:
    a. allowed Washington to march his men unmolested through the Lower South where he achieved ultimate victory at Camden.
    b. would have been impossible without Benedict Arnold's poor generalship on behalf of the British.
    c. angered the French, whose fleet had yet to arrive and who wanted credit for the victory.
    d. destroyed British public support for the war.
    e. made up for Washington's failure to support General Nathanael Greene at the Battle of Guilford Courthouse.

    ANS: D   TOP: Global awareness | Military history | Victory at Last   DIF: Moderate   REF: Full p. 200 | Seagull p. 206   MSC: Understanding   OBJ: 4

49. The negotiation of the Treaty of Paris of 1783:
    a. ignored those who had been loyal to the British empire.

b. was a masterful bit of diplomacy by Thomas Jefferson.

c. gave the new American nation control of Florida.

d. led to the British government receiving compensation for anything the Continental Congress had taken from British citizens.

e. began only after the Battle of Yorktown.

ANS: E   TOP: Global awareness | Military history | Victory at Last   DIF: Moderate   REF: Full p. 200 | Seagull p. 206   MSC: Remembering   OBJ: 4

50. British possessions in the West Indies:

a. were handed over to the new United States in the Treaty of Paris.

b. issued their own declarations of independence in the late 1770s.

c. remained loyal to the crown during the American Revolution because their leaders feared slave uprisings.

d. all fell into the hands of the French, either through conquest or treaty, as a result of the American Revolution.

e. were divided during the American Revolution: some islands sent regiments to the Continental army, while others proudly fought for the king.

ANS: C   TOP: Global awareness | Victory at Last
DIF: Difficult   REF: Full p. 200 | Seagull p. 208
MSC: Remembering   OBJ: 4

51. The Treaty of Paris did NOT:

a. recognize American independence.

b. sever the alliance between the United States and France.

c. give the United States territory between Canada and Florida east of the Mississippi River.

d. give Americans the right to fish in Atlantic waters off of Canada.

e. require the restoration of Loyalist property seized by local and state governments.

ANS: B   TOP: Global awareness | Victory at Last
DIF: Moderate   REF: Full p. 200 | Seagull pp. 207–208
MSC: Understanding   OBJ: 4

True or False

1. Prior to the Seven Years' War, Britain had not tried to regulate the colonies' economy.

ANS: F   TOP: Political history, changes | Consolidating the Empire   DIF: Moderate   REF: Full p. 172 | Seagull p. 176   MSC: Remembering   OBJ: 1

2. Although a few were outraged by the Stamp Act, most politically active colonists actually supported it.

ANS: F   TOP: Political history, changes | The Stamp Act Crisis   DIF: Easy   REF: Full p. 174 | Seagull p. 179   MSC: Remembering   OBJ: 1

3. American colonists widely believed that Britain had no authority to tax the colonists since the colonists had no elected representative in Parliament.

ANS: T   TOP: Political history, changes | Taxation and Representation   DIF: Easy   REF: Full p. 173 | Seagull p. 180   MSC: Understanding   OBJ: 1

4. American leaders viewed the British empire as an association of equals.

ANS: T   TOP: Political history, changes | Taxation and Representation   DIF: Moderate   REF: Full p. 174 | Seagull p. 179   MSC: Understanding   OBJ: 1

5. The Sons of Liberty enforced a boycott of British goods.

ANS: T   TOP: Social history | Politics in the Streets
DIF: Easy   REF: Full p. 176 | Seagull p. 181
MSC: Remembering   OBJ: 1

6. Ethan Allen led the Hudson Bay Boys in New York to protect the liberties of small farmers.

ANS: F   TOP: Social history | The Tenant Uprising
DIF: Moderate   REF: Full p. 178 | Seagull p. 183
MSC: Remembering   OBJ: 1

7. Homespun clothing became a symbol of American resistance during the American boycott on British goods.

ANS: T   TOP: Social history | Homespun Virtue
DIF: Easy   REF: Full p. 179 | Seagull p. 184
MSC: Remembering   OBJ: 2

8. Samuel Adams defended the British soldiers involved in the Boston Massacre in a court of law.

ANS: F   TOP: Political history, changes | The Boston Massacre   DIF: Moderate   REF: Full p. 180 | Seagull p. 185   MSC: Remembering   OBJ: 2

9. Paul Revere created an engraving that distorted the Boston Massacre.

ANS: T   TOP: Social history | The Boston Massacre
DIF: Moderate   REF: Full p. 180 | Seagull p. 185
MSC: Remembering   OBJ: 2

10. John Wilkes was expelled from his seat in Parliament for his scandalous writings about the king; this caused many colonists to rally to his side with the call "Wilkes and Liberty."

ANS: T   TOP: Global awareness | Wilkes and Liberty   DIF: Moderate   REF: Full p. 181 | Seagull pp. 186–187   MSC: Remembering   OBJ: 2

11. To resist the Intolerable Acts, a Continental Congress convened in Philadelphia.

    ANS: T   TOP: Political history, changes | The Continental Congress   DIF: Moderate   REF: Full p. 182 | Seagull p. 188   MSC: Remembering   OBJ: 3

12. The First Continental Congress raised an army and appointed George Washington as its commander.

    ANS: F   TOP: Military history | Political history, changes | The Outbreak of War   DIF: Moderate REF: Full p. 185 | Seagull p. 191   MSC: Remembering OBJ: 3

13. Thomas Paine wrote *Common Sense* as a response to Thomas Jefferson's Declaration of Independence.

    ANS: F   TOP: Primary document analysis | *Common Sense*   DIF: Easy   REF: Full p. 186 | Seagull pp. 192–193   MSC: Understanding   OBJ: 3

14. Thomas Paine's *Common Sense* was written specifically for the educated elite.

    ANS: F   TOP: Primary document analysis | Paine's Impact   DIF: Moderate   REF: Full p. 187 | Seagull p. 196   MSC: Understanding   OBJ: 3

15. The idea of American exceptionalism was prevalent in the Revolution.

    ANS: T   TOP: Social history | An Asylum for Mankind   DIF: Moderate   REF: Full p. 191 | Seagull p. 197   MSC: Understanding   OBJ: 3

16. Today, more than half of the countries in the world have some sort of declaration of independence.

    ANS: T   TOP: Global awareness | The Global Declaration of Independence   DIF: Moderate REF: Full p. 192 | Seagull p. 198   MSC: Remembering OBJ: 3

17. British soldiers alienated many Americans, while citizen-soldiers displayed great valor.

    ANS: T   TOP: Military history | Social history | The Balance of Power   DIF: Easy   REF: Full p. 193 | Seagull p. 200   MSC: Understanding   OBJ: 4

18. Blacks who fought under George Washington did so in segregated units.

    ANS: F   TOP: Civil rights | Military history | Blacks in the Revolution   DIF: Moderate   REF: Full p. 194 | Seagull p. 201   MSC: Remembering OBJ: 4

19. Siding with the British offered slaves far more opportunities for liberty than did siding with the pro-independence Americans.

    ANS: T   TOP: Civil rights | Blacks in the Revolution DIF: Moderate   REF: Full p. 194 | Seagull pp. 200–201   MSC: Remembering   OBJ: 4

20. Washington's army was demoralized by repeated failures early in the war, and many soldiers simply went home.

    ANS: T   TOP: Military history | The First Years of the War   DIF: Moderate   REF: Full pp. 194–195 | Seagull p. 202   MSC: Remembering   OBJ: 4

21. The American victory at Trenton convinced the French to join the American cause.

    ANS: F   TOP: Global awareness | The Battle of Saratoga   DIF: Moderate   REF: Full p. 197 | Seagull p. 204   MSC: Remembering   OBJ: 4

22. Benedict Arnold almost succeeded in turning over to the British the important Fort Ticonderoga on Lake Champlain.

    ANS: F   TOP: Military history | The War in the South DIF: Difficult   REF: Full p. 197 | Seagull p. 206 MSC: Remembering   OBJ: 4

23. British commanders were never able to consolidate their hold on the South.

    ANS: T   TOP: Military history | The War in the South   DIF: Moderate   REF: Full p. 199 | Seagull p. 206   MSC: Remembering   OBJ: 4

24. The French played a significant role in the surrender of Cornwallis at Yorktown.

    ANS: T   TOP: Global awareness | Military history | Victory at Last   DIF: Easy   REF: Full p. 199 | Seagull p. 206   MSC: Remembering   OBJ: 4

25. The Treaty of Paris was negotiated within six months after Cornwallis's surrender.

    ANS: F   TOP: Global awareness | Victory at Last DIF: Moderate   REF: Full p. 200 | Seagull p. 207 MSC: Remembering   OBJ: 4

26. Americans did not gain much more than independence from the Treaty of Paris.

    ANS: F   TOP: Global awareness | Victory at Last DIF: Easy   REF: Full p. 200 | Seagull pp. 207–208 MSC: Remembering   OBJ: 4

Short Answer

Identify and give the historical significance of each of the following terms, events, and people in a paragraph or two.

1. Stamp Act
2. Sons of Liberty
3. *Common Sense*

4. Declaratory Act
5. Treaty of Paris (1783)
6. Dunmore's Proclamation
7. Continental Association
8. East India Company
9. virtual representation
10. Battle of Saratoga
11. Declaration of Independence
12. Daughters of Liberty
13. *Letters from a Farmer in Pennsylvania*

Essay Questions

1. What problems did the British government face after the Seven Years' War and what solutions did it propose? How reasonable were London's solutions, and in what ways did the colonists view them as an attack on their liberty?

   ANS: Answers will vary   TOP: Political history, changes | Consolidating the Empire | Taxing the Colonies | The Stamp Act Crisis   DIF: Moderate   MSC: Evaluating   OBJ: 1

2. Discuss the debates that occurred over virtual representation. How did the leaders in London and the leaders in America view participation in governing the empire differently?

   ANS: Answers will vary   TOP: Political history, changes | Taxation and Representation | Liberty and Resistance | Politics in the Streets   DIF: Moderate   MSC: Analyzing   OBJ: 1

3. Describe how *Letters from a Farmer in Pennsylvania*, *Common Sense,* and the Declaration of Independence dealt with the concept of liberty.

   ANS: Answers will vary   TOP: Political history, changes | Primary document analysis | The Townshend Crisis | *Common Sense* | Paine's Impact | The Declaration of Independence | The Declaration and American Freedom   DIF: Moderate   MSC: Understanding   OBJ: 2 / 3

4. Revolution is a dynamic process with consequences no one can anticipate. Explain the initial goals of the colonists in 1765 at the time of the Stamp Act and the evolution of their ultimate decision to declare independence in 1776. What were the political and social consequences of the Revolution that had emerged by 1783?

   ANS: Answers will vary   TOP: Political history, changes | Social history | Taxation and Representation | The Continental Congress | The Sweets of Liberty | The Outbreak of War | Independence? | *Common Sense* | The Declaration of Independence | The Declaration and American Freedom | An Asy-
lum for Mankind | The Global Declaration of Independence   DIF: Difficult   REF: | MSC: Understanding   OBJ: 1 / 2 / 3

5. Many students commonly believe that the Revolutionary War was a short and relatively painless war. However, for Americans, only the Vietnam War lasted longer than the Revolutionary War. In a thoughtful essay, describe why the war was so lengthy and what the costs involved were for the British and for the Americans.

   ANS: Answers will vary   TOP: Military history | Global awareness | The First Years of the War | The Battle of Saratoga | The War in the South | Victory at Last   DIF: Moderate   MSC: Understanding   OBJ: 4

6. Compare the relative advantages of the American and the British militaries. How was George Washington able to secure a victory over the most powerful nation in the world?

   ANS: Answers will vary   TOP: Military history | The Balance of Power | The First Years of the War | The Battle of Saratoga | The War in the South | Victory at Last   DIF: Difficult   MSC: Analyzing   OBJ: 4

7. Discuss the ways in which both supporters and opponents of independence used the concepts of "freedom" and "slavery" during the American Revolution. Be sure to consider the perspectives of Thomas Paine and Jonathan Boucher (both in "Voices of Freedom"), the slaves who fought for both sides, and others whose ideas you consider significant.

   ANS: Answers will vary   TOP: Political history, changes | Primary document analysis | Liberty and Resistance | Wilkes and Liberty | The Sweets of Liberty | *Common Sense* | Voices of Freedom | The Declaration and American Freedom | An Asylum for Mankind | Blacks in the Revolution   DIF: Difficult   MSC: Analyzing   OBJ: 3 / 4

8. How did the colonists justify their protests and ultimate rebellion? What sources did they call on? What philosophies were influential? How was the language of freedom and liberty used?

   ANS: Answers will vary   TOP: Political history, changes | Primary document analysis | The Stamp Act Crisis | Taxation and Representation | Liberty and Resistance | The Intolerable Acts | The Continental Congress | The Continental Association | The Sweets of Liberty | *Common Sense* | The Declaration of Independence | The Declaration and American Freedom | An Asylum for Mankind   DIF: Moderate   MSC: Applying   OBJ: 1 / 2 / 3

9. As the imperial crisis deepened in the late 1760s and into the 1770s, Americans increasingly based their claims not simply on the historical rights of Englishmen but on the more abstract language of natural rights and universal freedom. Thinking back to previous chapters, chronicle this evolution from the English Civil War and the Glorious Revolution to the Great Awakening and Enlightenment and finally to the events of the 1760s and 1770s. Your essay should demonstrate the various definitions of freedom and liberty from the mid-seventeenth century until the Revolutionary era.

ANS: Answers will vary   TOP: Political history, changes | Global awareness | Taxation and Representation | Liberty and Resistance | The Sweets of Liberty | *Common Sense* | The Declaration of Independence | The Declaration and American Freedom

DIF: Difficult   MSC: Analyzing   OBJ: 6 / 3 / 4 / 5 / 1

CHAPTER 6 | The Revolution Within

This chapter concentrates on the political and social changes resulting from the American Revolution. It focuses on how the concepts of liberty and freedom continued to evolve during the Revolution and how they transformed society and politics in the 1770s and 1780s. The chapter begins with a look at a remarkable American woman, Abigail Adams. Her memorable plea to her husband to "Remember the Ladies" can be heard in "Voices of Freedom." The democratization of freedom in the public sphere is explored through an examination of how new state constitutions dealt with suffrage requirements. The chapter also explores how the Revolution affected religious liberty, religious toleration, and the separation of church and state. The next topic is economic freedom. Here the text contrasts the idea that government should regulate for the public good with a newer idea, which gained support from Adam Smith's *The Wealth of Nations,* that individual self-interest acting in a free market should be the rule. Limitations on freedom—with emphasis on the experiences of Loyalists, Indians, slaves, and women—are then discussed. Those who remained loyal to the British found some of their liberties stripped away, but mostly they were able to reintegrate into society. Indians lost much of their land and freedom as a result of the war. Slaves believed that they could rely on the American rhetoric of freedom and liberty to press for emancipation. Some slaves presented petitions for freedom to New England courts; "Voices of Freedom" includes excerpts from two such petitions from Massachusetts. The Revolution did result in gradual emancipation in the North and some voluntary manumissions in the Upper South, but not in the complete elimination of slavery. The chapter concludes with a look at women and their various roles in the war and its aftermath, including serving as soldiers and as "republican mothers," charged with the serious task of raising the next generation of republican leaders.

CHAPTER OUTLINE

I. Introduction: Abigail Adams
   A. Wife of John Adams
      1. Gave political views in letters to him.
         a. Resented "absolute power" husbands exercised over their wives.

II. Democratizing Freedom
   A. The Dream of Equality
      1. The Revolution unleashed public debates and political and social struggles that enlarged the scope of freedom and challenged inherited structures of power within America.
         a. The principle of hereditary aristocracy was rejected.
      2. The Declaration of Independence's assertion that "all men are created equal" announced a radical principle whose full implications could not be anticipated.
         a. American freedom became linked with equality, which challenged the fundamental inequality inherent in the colonial social order.
   B. Expanding the Political Nation
      1. The leaders of the Revolution had not intended this disruption of social order.
      2. The democratization of freedom was dramatic for free men.
      3. In the eighteenth century, democracy had multiple meanings.
      4. Artisans, small farmers, laborers, and the militia all emerged as self-conscious elements in politics.
   C. The Revolution in Pennsylvania

1. The prewar elite of Pennsylvania opposed independence.
   a. This left a vacuum of political leadership filled by Paine, Rush, Matlack, and Young.
2. Pennsylvania's 1776 constitution sought to institutionalize democracy in a number of ways, including: establishing an annually elected, one-house legislature; allowing tax-paying (not just property-owning) men to vote; and abolishing the office of governor.

D. The New Constitutions
1. Each state wrote a new constitution and all agreed that their governments must be republics.
2. States disagreed as to how the government should be structured:
   a. One-house legislatures were adopted only by Pennsylvania, Georgia, and Vermont.
   b. John Adams's "balanced governments" included two-house legislatures.

E. The Right to Vote
1. The property qualification for suffrage was hotly debated.
2. The least democratization occurred in the southern states, where highly deferential political traditions enabled the landed gentry to retain their control of political affairs.
3. Most democratic new constitutions moved toward voting as an entitlement rather than a privilege.
   a. Vermont was only state not to have financial considerations for suffrage.

F. Democratizing Government
1. By the 1780s, with the exceptions of Virginia, Maryland, and New York, a large majority of the adult white male population could meet voting requirements.
   a. Until 1807, property-owning women in New Jersey could vote.
2. Freedom and an individual's right to vote had become interchangeable.

III. Toward Religious Toleration
A. Catholic Americans
1. Joining forces with France and inviting Quebec to join in the struggle against Britain had weakened anti-Catholicism.

B. The Founders and Religion
1. The end of British rule led to questioning the privilege of the Anglican Church in many colonies.
2. Many believed that religion was necessary as a foundation of public morality, but were skeptical of religious doctrine.
   a. Enlightenment influenced this skepticism.

C. Separating Church and State
1. The drive to separate church and state brought together Deists with members of evangelical sects.
2. States disestablished established churches depriving them of specific public funding and legal privileges.
3. The seven state constitutions that began with declarations of rights all included a commitment to "the free exercise of religion."
4. Many states still limited religious freedoms (e.g., barring Jews from voting and holding office, except in New York; or publicly financing religious institutions, such as in Massachusetts).
5. Catholics gained the right to worship without persecution throughout the states.

D. Jefferson and Religious Liberty
1. Thomas Jefferson's "Bill for Establishing Religious Freedom" separated church and state in Virginia.
2. James Madison insisted that one reason for the complete separation of church and state was to reinforce the principle that the new nation offered "asylum to the persecuted and oppressed of every nation and religion."

E. The Revolution and the Churches
1. As religious liberty expanded, some church authority was undermined.
2. Thanks to religious freedom, the early republic witnessed an amazing proliferation of religious denominations.
   a. Today more than 1,300 religions are practiced.

F. Christian Republicanism
1. Religious and secular language merged in the struggle for independence, creating what scholars call Christian Republicanism.
   a. Both religious and political leaders feared moral corruption so personal virtue needed to be emphasized.
2. Despite a separation of church and state, public authority (Christians and Deists) continued to support religious values.
3. Leaders wished to encourage virtue—the ability to sacrifice self-interest for the public good.

IV. Defining Economic Freedom
A. Toward Free Labor
1. The lack of freedom inherent in apprenticeship and servitude increasingly came to be seen as incompatible with republican citizenship.

2. By 1800, indentured servitude had all but disappeared from the United States.
   a. The distinction between freedom and slavery sharpened.

B. The Soul of a Republic
   1. To most free Americans, equality meant equal opportunity rather than equality of condition.
   2. Thomas Jefferson and others equated land and economic resources with freedom.

C. The Politics of Inflation
   1. Some Americans responded to wartime inflation by accusing merchants of hoarding goods and by seizing stocks of food to be sold at the traditional "just price."
      a. From 1776–1779, more than thirty incidents occurred where crowds confronted merchants.

D. The Debate over Free Trade
   1. Congress urged states to adopt measures to fix wages and prices.
   2. Adam Smith's argument that the "invisible hand" of the free market directed economic life more effectively and fairly than governmental intervention offered intellectual justification for those who believed that the economy should be left to regulate itself.

V. The Limits of Liberty
   A. Colonial Loyalists
      1. An estimated 20 to 25 percent of Americans were Loyalists (those who retained their allegiance to the crown).
      2. Loyalists included:
         a. Wealthy men with close working relationships with Britain
         b. Ethnic minorities fearful of losing to local majorities their freedom to enjoy cultural autonomy
         c. Many southern backcountry farmers and New York tenants who opposed wealthy planter patriots and landlord patriots, respectively

   B. The Loyalists' Plight
      1. The War for Independence was in some respects a civil war among Americans.
      2. War brought a deprivation of basic rights to many Americans.
         a. Many states required residents to take oaths of allegiance to the new nation.
      3. When the war ended, as many as 60,000 Loyalists were banished from the United States or emigrated voluntarily.
         a. Ten thousand of them were slaves.

C. The Indians' Revolution
   1. American independence meant the loss of freedom for Indians.
   2. Indians were divided in allegiance during the War of Independence.
   3. Both the British and Americans were guilty of savagery toward the Indians during the war.

D. White Freedom, Indian Freedom
   1. To many patriots, access to Indian land was one of the fruits of American victory.
      a. But liberty for whites meant loss of liberty for Indians.
   2. The Treaty of Paris marked the culmination of a century in which the balance of power in eastern North America shifted away from the Indians and toward white Americans.
   3. "Freedom" had not played a major part in Indians' vocabulary before the Revolution, but now freedom meant defending their own independence and retaining possession of their land.

VI. Slavery and the Revolution
   A. The Language of Slavery and Freedom
      1. During the debates over British rule, "slavery" was invoked as a political category.
         a. Britain was a "kingdom of slaves," whereas America was a "country of free men."
      2. James Otis wrote of universal freedom, even for blacks.
      3. The irony that America cried for liberty while enslaving Africans was recognized by some (e.g., the British statesman Edmund Burke and the British writer Dr. Samuel Johnson).

   B. Obstacles to Abolition
      1. Most founders owned slaves at one point in their respective lives.
         a. John Adams and Thomas Paine were exceptions.
      2. Some patriots argued that slavery for blacks made freedom possible for whites.
      3. According to a reading of Locke, for government to seize property (including slaves) would be an infringement on liberty.

   C. The Cause of General Liberty
      1. By defining freedom as a universal entitlement rather than as a set of rights specific to a particular place or people, the Revolution inevitably raised questions about the status of slavery in the new nation.
      2. Samuel Sewall's *The Selling of Joseph* (1700) was the first antislavery tract in America.
      3. Benjamin Rush warned (1773) that slavery was a "national crime" that would bring "national punishment."

D. Petitions for Freedom
1. Slaves in the North and in the South appropriated the language of liberty for their own purposes.
2. Slaves presented "freedom petitions" in New England in the early 1770s.
3. Many blacks were surprised that white America did not realize their rhetoric of revolution demanded emancipation.
4. The poems of Phillis Wheatley, a slave in Boston, often spoke of freedom.
E. British Emancipators
1. Nearly 100,000 slaves deserted their owners and fled to British lines.
2. At the end of the war, over 15,000 blacks accompanied the British out of the country.
   a. Many ended up in Nova Scotia, England, and Sierra Leone, a West African settlement established by Britain for former U.S. slaves.
   b. Some were re-enslaved in the West Indies.
F. Voluntary Emancipations
1. For a brief moment, the revolutionary upheaval appeared to threaten the continued existence of slavery as some slaveholders, primarily in the Upper South, provided for the emancipation of their slaves.
2. In the Lower South the emancipation process never started.
G. Abolition in the North
1. Between 1777 and 1804, every state north of Maryland took steps toward emancipation.
2. Abolition in the North was a slow process and typically applied only to future children of current slave women.
H. Free Black Communities
1. After the war, free black communities with their own churches, schools, and leaders came into existence.
2. In all states except Virginia, South Carolina, and Georgia, free black men who met taxpaying or property qualifications were "citizens of color" who could vote.
3. Despite the rhetoric of freedom, the war did not end slavery for blacks.

VII. Daughters of Liberty
A. Revolutionary Women
1. Many women participated in the war in various capacities.
   a. Deborah Sampson, for example, dressed as a man and enlisted in the Continental army.
   b. The Ladies' Association raised funds to assist American soldiers.
2. Within American households, women participated in the political discussions unleashed by independence.
B. Gender and Politics
1. "Coverture" (which meant a husband held legal authority over his wife) remained intact in the new nation.
2. In both law and social reality, women lacked the opportunity for autonomy (based on ownership of property or control of one's own person) and hence lacked the essential qualification of political participation.
3. Many women who entered public debate felt the need to apologize for their forthrightness.
4. Most men considered women to be naturally submissive and irrational and therefore unfit for citizenship.
C. Republican Motherhood
1. Women played a key role in the new republic by training future citizens.
2. The idea of republican motherhood reinforced the trend toward the idea of "companionate" marriage.
3. The Revolution altered the structure of family life.
   a. In North, hired workers were not considered part of the family like indentured servants and slaves had been.
D. The Arduous Struggle for Liberty
1. The Revolution changed the life of virtually every American.
2. America became a beacon of hope to those chafing under Old World tyrannies.
   a. The idea that "the people" possessed rights was quickly internationalized.

SUGGESTED DISCUSSION QUESTIONS

- What did Abigail Adams mean when she wrote to her husband, "Remember the ladies"? Did she believe in the modern notion of equality of the sexes?
- Discuss how the struggle for American liberty emboldened various groups of colonists to demand more liberty for themselves.
- How fully did Revolutionary-era Americans embrace the concept of religious freedom? What evidence can you cite that indicates the young republic was committed to religious freedom? What evidence is there that there were limitations to religious freedom?
- Discuss the irony in the American call for freedom at a time when America was a slave society.
- The Revolutionary War was empowering for some women. Discuss the various ways that women were able

to express greater freedoms and liberties. How did the idea of "republican motherhood" elevate a woman's position? What limitations on freedom did women in the new nation encounter?

- Comment on the title of the chapter: The Revolution Within.
- Discuss the Indians' Revolution, comparing white freedom to Indian freedom. How did the removal of the British and the newly formed United States affect the Indians?
- Discuss the ideas of economic freedom brought about by the American Revolution. What influence did Adam Smith's *The Wealth of Nations* have on American leaders and society? Compare Smith's ideas on the free market to the economy in today's United States and the globalizing world.
- Discuss how the Revolution affected the Loyalists and the various circumstances that led to them leaving the United States. What country or other colony seems like the best place to escape for a Loyalist?

SUPPLEMENTAL WEB AND VISUAL RESOURCES

Abolition
www.loc.gov/exhibits/african/afam005.html
Numerous antislavery newspaper articles and other publications from the Revolutionary era are available on this site.

Indians in the War
http://www.nps.gov/revwar/about_the_revolution/american _indians.html

http://www.americanrevolution.org/ind1.html
Links to two essays by historians on Indians in the American Revolution. The first essay is by Colin Calloway. The second essay by Wilcomb E. Washburn is longer and more detailed, but is older.

Religion and the American Revolution
http://nationalhumanitiescenter.org/tserve/index.htm
The National Humanities Center. Teacher Serve: An Interactive Curriculum Enrichment Service for Teachers. Two sections: one on religion and the national culture and one on the environment in American history.

http://americainclass.org/primary-sources/
Toolbox Library offers a plethora of primary sources, discussion questions, additional online sources, and talking points.

Revolutionary War
www.pbs.org/georgewashington/timeline/revolutionary_war .html
George Washington is emphasized in this PBS website pertaining to the Revolutionary War. Multimedia options are available as well as letters Washington wrote to family and to commanders.

Women in the Revolutionary War
http://userpages.aug.com/captbarb/femvets.html
This site contains information on specific women, such as Deborah Samson and Nancy Hart, who made considerable contributions to the Revolutionary War.

SUPPLEMENTAL PRINT RESOURCES

Andrews, Dee. *The Methodists and Revolutionary America, 1760–1800: The Shaping of an Evangelical Culture.* Princeton, NJ: Princeton University Press, 2000.

Fitz, Caitlin A. "'Suspected on Both Sides': Little Abraham, Iroquois Neutrality, and the American Revolution." *Journal of the Early Republic* 28, no. 3 (2008): 299–335.

Glatthaar, Joseph, and James Martin. *Forgotten Allies: The Oneida Indians and the American Revolution.* New York: Hill and Wang, 2006.

Kerber, Linda. *Women of the Republic: Intellect and Ideology in Revolutionary America.* Chapel Hill, NC: University of North Carolina Press, 1985.

Kulikoff, Allan. "Revolutionary Violence and the Origins of American Democracy." *Journal of the Historical Society* 2, no. 2 (2002): 229–260.

Mason, Keith. "Localism, Evangelicalism, and Loyalism: The Sources of Discontent in the Revolutionary Chesapeake." *Journal of Southern History* 56, no. 1 (1990): 23–54.

Nash, Gary. *Race and Revolution.* Madison, WI: Madison House Publishers, 1990.

Purcell, Sarah. *Sealed with Blood: War, Sacrifice, and Memory in Revolutionary America.* Philadelphia, PA: University of Pennsylvania Press, 2002.

Sobel, Mechal. *Teach Me Dreams: The Search for Self in the Revolutionary Era.* Princeton, NJ: Princeton University Press, 2000.

TEST BANK

Matching

TEST I

___ 1. Thomas Jefferson
___ 2. Adam Smith
___ 3. Samuel Sewall
___ 4. Benjamin Rush
___ 5. Phillis Wheatley
___ 6. Abigail Adams
___ 7. James Otis
___ 8. John Adams
___ 9. John Sullivan
___ 10. Robert Morris
___ 11. Joseph Brant
___ 12. James Carroll

a. black poet
b. Pennsylvania radical

c. *Thoughts on Government* author
d. burned forty Indian towns
e. America's first Roman Catholic bishop
f. director of congressional fiscal policy
g. *The Selling of Joseph* author
h. wrote of universal freedom, even for blacks
i. drafted Virginia's "Bill for Establishing Religious Freedom"
j. "Remember the ladies"
k. *The Wealth of Nations* author
l. Mohawk Indian

Answer Key: i, k, g, b, a, j, h, c, d, f, l, e

TEST 2

___ 1. virtue
___ 2. freedom petitions
___ 3. Loyalists
___ 4. Ladies' Association
___ 5. republican motherhood
___ 6. suffrage
___ 7. free labor
___ 8. patriots
___ 9. militia
___ 10. Moravian Brethren
___ 11. Sierra Leone
___ 12. Popery

a. raised funds to assist American soldiers
b. working for wages, or owning a farm or shop
c. an offensive term for the rituals of the Catholic Church
d. "School of political democracy"
e. retained their allegiance to the crown
f. fighting for the American cause
g. Revolution undermined church authority among this group
h. responsible for raising the next generation of leaders
i. the right to vote
j. action slaves took for their immediate release
k. ability to sacrifice self-interest for the public good
l. settlement in Africa for freed slaves

Answer Key: k, j, e, a, h, i, b, f, d, g, l, c

Learning Objectives

1. Explain how equality became a stronger component of American freedom after the Revolution.
2. Describe how the expansion of religious liberty after the Revolution reflected the new American ideal of freedom.
3. Explain how the definition of economic freedom changed after the Revolution and identify who benefited from the changes.
4. Explain how the Revolution diminished the freedoms of both Loyalists and Native Americans.

5. Describe the impact the Revolution had on slavery.
6. Explain how the Revolution affected the status of women.

Multiple Choice

1. As a result of the American Revolution, Americans rejected:
   a. obedience to the male heads of household.
   b. the principle of hereditary aristocracy.
   c. the establishment of a republic.
   d. the definition of liberty as a universal entitlement.
   e. all kinds of organized religion.

   ANS: B   TOP: Social history | The Dream of Equality
   DIF: Easy   REF: Full p. 206 | Seagull p. 212
   MSC: Remembering   OBJ: 1

2. How did the Revolutionary War change the meaning of freedom?
   a. It meant that all men now had a legal claim to an equal distribution of property.
   b. It challenged the inequality that had been fundamental to the colonial social order.
   c. It ended colonial society's legally established hereditary aristocracy.
   d. It ended coverture, under which husbands exercised full legal authority over their wives.
   e. It meant that, for the first time, men were free to pursue whatever occupations they wished.

   ANS: B   TOP: Political history, changes | The Dream of Equality   DIF: Moderate   REF: Full p. 206 | Seagull p. 213   MSC: Understanding   OBJ: 1

3. What served as a sort of "school of political democracy" for the members of the "lower orders" in the colonies-turned-states?
   a. the Protestant Church
   b. the lower house of the state legislatures
   c. the taverns
   d. the militia
   e. the first public schools

   ANS: D   TOP: Political history, changes | Expanding the Political Nation   DIF: Moderate   REF: Full p. 207 | Seagull p. 213   MSC: Remembering   OBJ: 1

4. How did Pennsylvania display the Revolutionary War's radical potential?
   a. Benjamin Franklin's departure for France left control of the state up for grabs, and the lower classes took over.
   b. The prewar elite had supported independence, then tried to negotiate with Great Britain, costing themselves the respect of the lower classes, who took power from them.

c. Philadelphia's artisan and lower-class communities took control and put a new emphasis on freedom and on more democratic politics.
d. The Second Continental Congress had to take over the state when the people voted to abolish the position of governor, thereby showing how the new nation's power dynamic would differ greatly from the old system.
e. Just through the population retaining the old style of government, they demonstrated that major change was possible without uprooting the whole system.

ANS: C   TOP: Social history | The Revolution in Pennsylvania   DIF: Moderate   REF: Full p. 207 | Seagull p. 214   MSC: Understanding   OBJ: 1

5. Which statement about Revolutionary Pennsylvania is FALSE?
a. Nearly all of its prewar elites opposed independence.
b. The radical leadership that emerged included Thomas Paine and Benjamin Rush.
c. The radical leadership attacked property qualifications for voting.
d. The state's new constitution gave only limited power to the state's governor.
e. Its new constitution centralized political power in a one-house legislature.

ANS: D   TOP: Constitutional history | The Revolution in Pennsylvania   DIF: Difficult   REF: Full p. 208 | Seagull p. 214   MSC: Remembering   OBJ: 1

6. In his *Thoughts on Government* (1776), John Adams advocated state constitutions that provided for:
a. a powerful governor and a two-house legislature that reflected the division of society between wealthy and ordinary men.
b. a legislature elected and controlled entirely by the wealthy, with a weak governor elected by the people so that they would feel that they had a role.
c. voting rights for all men at least twenty-one years old.
d. centralizing political power in a one-house legislature and dispensing with the office of governor.
e. allowing women who owned a certain amount of property to vote, but preventing them from holding political office.

ANS: A   TOP: Constitutional history | The New Constitutions   DIF: Moderate   REF: Full p. 208 | Seagull p. 215   MSC: Remembering   OBJ: 1

7. In regards to voting for the states, what was a contentious issue?
a. being a Native American
b. being an Anglican
c. owning property
d. not owning slaves
e. being a woman

ANS: C   TOP: Constitutional history | The Right to Vote   DIF: Moderate   REF: Full p. 209 | Seagull p. 215   MSC: Understanding   OBJ: 1

8. The constitution of which state eliminated all property and tax qualifications for voting in 1777?
a. Vermont
b. New York
c. Maryland
d. Virginia
e. Massachusetts

ANS: A   TOP: Constitutional history | The Right to Vote   DIF: Difficult   REF: Full p. 209 | Seagull p. 216   MSC: Remembering   OBJ: 1

9. Which state's constitution granted suffrage to all "inhabitants" who met a property qualification, allowing property-owning women to vote until an 1807 amendment limited suffrage to males?
a. New York
b. Virginia
c. New Jersey
d. Massachusetts
e. Pennsylvania

ANS: C   TOP: Constitutional history | The Right to Vote   DIF: Difficult   REF: Full pp. 209–210 | Seagull p. 216   MSC: Remembering   OBJ: 1

10. The new state constitutions created during the Revolutionary War:
a. completely eliminated property qualifications for voting.
b. became far more democratic in the southern states than in the northern states.
c. greatly expanded the right to vote in almost every state.
d. did nothing to change the composition of elite-dominated state legislatures.
e. all retained tax-supported churches as a way of ensuring a virtuous citizenry.

ANS: C   TOP: Constitutional history | Democratizing Government   DIF: Moderate   REF: Full pp. 209–210 | Seagull p. 216   MSC: Remembering   OBJ: 1

11. An example of anti-Catholicism during the 1770s was the:
a. barring of Catholics from southern state militias.
b. Second Continental Congress's refusal to accept aid from Catholic France.
c. widespread arrests of Catholics as potential British spies by Pennsylvania authorities.

d. famous attack on a Boston convent by Massachusetts minutemen.

e. First Continental Congress's denunciation of the Quebec Act.

ANS: E   TOP: Social history | Catholic Americans
DIF: Moderate   REF: Full p. 211 | Seagull p. 218
MSC: Remembering   OBJ: 2

12. How did the War for Independence affect anti-Catholicism in America?

a. Anti-Catholicism increased when Quebec Catholics volunteered in large numbers for the British army.

b. Because Americans resented Catholic France negotiating a separate peace with Great Britain, anti-Catholicism became more prevalent.

c. Independence led the states to impose anti-Catholic laws that they had been unable to adopt when they were under British control.

d. The alliance with France, a predominantly Catholic country, helped diminish American anti-Catholicism.

e. Spain's wartime aid to Britain led Georgian colonists to attack Catholic missions in Florida.

ANS: D   TOP: Social history | Catholic Americans
DIF: Moderate   REF: Full p. 211 | Seagull p. 218
MSC: Understanding   OBJ: 2

13. Benedict Arnold offered which justification for his treason?

a. He believed George Washington treated his soldiers poorly.

b. America's new alliance with France, a Catholic state, was too much for him to bear.

c. He was a distant cousin of King George III through marriage.

d. He believed that until the United States abolished slavery, its cause to liberty was hypocritical.

e. He considered the cause of independence already lost.

ANS: B   TOP: Global awareness | Catholic Americans   DIF: Moderate   REF: Full p. 211 | Seagull p. 218   MSC: Remembering   OBJ: 2

14. Thomas Jefferson's views on religion and Christian doctrines:

a. were very similar to those expressed by Isaac Backus, a Baptist leader.

b. show that he actively sought to stamp out religious worship.

c. indicate he did not believe in a benevolent Creator.

d. demonstrated his rejection of the divinity of Jesus.

e. found widespread acceptance among evangelicals in the new nation.

ANS: D   TOP: Cultural history | The Founders and Religion   DIF: Moderate   REF: Full p. 212 | Seagull p. 219   MSC: Remembering   OBJ: 2

15. Which of the following is true of how the new state constitutions in the Revolutionary era dealt with the issue of religious liberty?

a. Several states finally allowed Jews to vote and to hold public office.

b. States increased public funding of religion because they no longer had to win British approval to do so.

c. Seven state constitutions began with a declaration of rights that included a commitment to "the free exercise of religion."

d. Thomas Jefferson wrote a "Bill for Establishing Religious Freedom" in Virginia, but the House of Burgesses never adopted it.

e. Deists and evangelicals fought with one another over whether church and state should be separate.

ANS: C   TOP: Constitutional history | Separating Church and State   DIF: Moderate   REF: Full pp. 212–213 | Seagull p. 219   MSC: Remembering OBJ: 2

16. Thomas Jefferson's Virginia "Bill for Establishing Religious Freedom" did the following EXCEPT:

a. eliminated religious qualifications for voting.

b. removed religious qualifications for holding political office.

c. allowed a second set of standards for Catholics.

d. removed government financial support for churches.

e. people could not be forced to pick a religion.

ANS: C   TOP: Political history, changes | Jefferson and Religious Liberty   DIF: Difficult   REF: Full pp. 213–214 | Seagull p. 220   MSC: Understanding OBJ: 2

17. For which three accomplishments did Thomas Jefferson wish to be remembered?

a. presidency, the Declaration of Independence, the Constitution

b. louisiana Purchase, presidency, the Declaration of Independence

c. the Constitution, the University of Virginia, presidency

d. the "Bill for Establishing Religious Freedom," the Declaration of Independence, Louisiana Purchase

e. the Declaration of Independence, the University of Virginia, the "Bill for Establishing Religious Freedom"

ANS: E   TOP: Political history, changes | Jefferson and Religious Liberty   DIF: Difficult   REF: Full p. 214 | Seagull p. 220   MSC: Remembering   OBJ: 2

18. As a result of the religious freedom created by the Revolution:
    a. organized religion became less important in American life over the next thirty years.
    b. upstart churches began challenging the well-established churches.
    c. the number of religious denominations in the United States declined.
    d. violent struggles between religious groups were not uncommon in the backcountry.
    e. tax-supported churches flourished in every state in the new nation.

    ANS: B   TOP: Social history | The Revolution and the Churches   DIF: Easy   REF: Full p. 214 | Seagull p. 221   MSC: Understanding   OBJ: 2

19. In order to encourage virtue in future citizens, Thomas Jefferson and John Adams:
    a. asked for the Declaration of Independence to be read every month at the town square.
    b. proposed free public education.
    c. wanted church attendance to be mandatory.
    d. proposed that ministers become teachers in public schools.
    e. wanted a second revolution.

    ANS: B   TOP: Social history | Christian Republicanism   DIF: Moderate   REF: Full p. 215 | Seagull p. 222   MSC: Remembering   OBJ: 2

20. Christian republicanism is a scholarly idea that was characteristic of all of the following EXCEPT it:
    a. was supported by some ministers.
    b. was encouraged by Revolutionary leaders.
    c. was motivated by a fear of corruption and vices.
    d. was fearful of a lack of moral restraint.
    e. was promoting free trade and markets.

    ANS: B   TOP: Social history | Christian Republicanism   DIF: Moderate   REF: Full p. 215 | Seagull p. 221   MSC: Understanding   OBJ: 2

21. Why did apprenticeship and indentured servitude decline after the Revolution?
    a. King George III had supported them, and anything associated with the king was unpopular in the United States.
    b. Many apprentices and indentures had refused to fight in the Revolution, and their bosses, resenting them for it, got rid of them.
    c. Thomas Paine's criticism of them in *Common Sense* greatly influenced the many who had read his pamphlet.
    d. Northerners were outlawing slavery in their state constitutions and began to eliminate apprenticeship

and indentured servitude as well amid southern charges of hypocrisy.
    e. The lack of freedom inherent in apprenticeship and indentured servitude struck growing numbers of Americans as incompatible with republican citizenship.

    ANS: E   TOP: Social history | Toward Free Labor   DIF: Moderate   REF: Full pp. 215–216 | Seagull p. 222   MSC: Understanding   OBJ: 3

22. According to Noah Webster, what was the very soul of a republic?
    a. equality
    b. diversity
    c. democracy
    d. freedom
    e. industry

    ANS: A   TOP: Social history | The Soul of a Republic   DIF: Moderate   REF: Full p. 217 | Seagull p. 223   MSC: Remembering   OBJ: 3

23. Why did John Adams believe that land ownership was vital to society?
    a. He opposed slavery and felt that if small farmers owned land, they would have the power to outvote slaveowners.
    b. If more people owned land, it would be less likely that fixed and unequal social classes would emerge.
    c. Land ownership would make people more conservative, and that would counteract any democratic impulses.
    d. Government would have to encourage it, and Adams believed in an activist federal government.
    e. Adams had lost his land when he took the unpopular position of representing British soldiers who participated in the Boston Massacre, and he knew how important the issue was.

    ANS: B   TOP: Social history | The Soul of a Republic   DIF: Moderate   REF: Full p. 217 | Seagull p. 223   MSC: Understanding   OBJ: 3

24. What role did rising prices play during the Revolution?
    a. They encouraged more men to enlist in the Continental army because military pay increased with inflation.
    b. Angry Americans voted out congressmen who had approved the paper money that caused the inflation.
    c. They prompted protests by Americans, especially women, who took goods from merchants whom they accused of hoarding.
    d. They led the Continental Congress to obtain huge loans from Catherine the Great of Russia.

e. They prompted the writers of the Constitution to ban paper money—a provision that later was repealed.

ANS: C   TOP: Social history | The Politics of Inflation
DIF: Moderate   REF: Full p. 217 | Seagull p. 224
MSC: Understanding   OBJ: 3

25. In order to deal with a wartime economic crisis in 1779, Congress urged states to:
    a. allow the free market to operate without regulation.
    b. adopt measures to fix wages and prices.
    c. establish food banks to distribute food to the needy.
    d. raise taxes on the wealthy.
    e. seek loans from friendly European governments.

ANS: B   TOP: Economic development | The Debate over Free Trade   DIF: Difficult   REF: Full p. 218 | Seagull p. 224   MSC: Remembering   OBJ: 3

26. Which of the following contributed to the success of free trade advocates during the Revolutionary War?
    a. the publication of Adam Smith's *The Wealth of Nations*
    b. Isaac Newton's explanation of the law of gravity as applied to economics
    c. the failure of wartime tariffs to solve the problem of the national debt
    d. riots over inflation in the streets of Boston
    e. memories of the despised Intolerable Acts

ANS: A   TOP: Economic development | The Debate over Free Trade   DIF: Moderate   REF: Full p. 218 | Seagull p. 225   MSC: Remembering   OBJ: 3

27. What did the "invisible hand" refer to?
    a. gradual emancipation laws
    b. republican motherhood
    c. royal authority
    d. pro-British loyalties
    e. the free market

ANS: E   TOP: Economic development | The Debate over Free Trade   DIF: Easy   REF: Full p. 218 | Seagull p. 225   MSC: Remembering   OBJ: 3

28. Approximately how many free Americans remained loyal to the British during the war?
    a. 5 to 10 percent
    b. 10 to 15 percent
    c. 20 to 25 percent
    d. 30 to 35 percent
    e. 45 to 50 percent

ANS: C   TOP: Social history | Colonial Loyalists
DIF: Difficult   REF: Full p. 219 | Seagull p. 226
MSC: Remembering   OBJ: 4

29. Which of the following groups did NOT include a significant proportion of Loyalists during the Revolutionary War?
    a. Anglican ministers and imperial officials
    b. Highland Scots in North Carolina
    c. southern backcountry farmers
    d. wealthy New York families
    e. slaves hoping for freedom with a British victory

ANS: D   TOP: Social history | Colonial Loyalists
DIF: Moderate   REF: Full p. 219 | Seagull p. 226
MSC: Remembering   OBJ: 4

30. Which of the following was NOT an example of Loyalists being deprived of their freedom by patriots?
    a. New state governments suppressed newspapers thought to be loyal to Britain.
    b. Pennsylvania's government seized property from members of pacifist religious groups.
    c. Many states required oaths of allegiance to the new nation.
    d. Several states denied Loyalists the right to vote and forced them into exile.
    e. The New England states forced Loyalists into militias against their will.

ANS: E   TOP: Social history | The Loyalists' Plight
DIF: Difficult   REF: Full p. 219 | Seagull pp. 226, 228
MSC: Remembering   OBJ: 4

31. Which statement about Loyalists is FALSE?
    a. Confiscated property was not returned to them after the war.
    b. Fewer than 10,000 Loyalists left America after the war.
    c. Hostility toward Loyalists after the war proved to be short-lived.
    d. Loyalists were quickly reintegrated into American society.
    e. Soon after the war, states repealed test oaths that discriminated against Loyalists.

ANS: B   TOP: Social history | The Loyalists' Plight
DIF: Moderate   REF: Full p. 221 | Seagull p. 228
MSC: Understanding   OBJ: 4

32. What role did Native Americans play in the Revolutionary War?
    a. They all allied themselves with the British, who promised to protect them against American encroachment.
    b. They all allied themselves with the Americans, since the British had failed to protect them against American encroachment.
    c. Most tribes officially maintained neutrality but secretly aided one side or the other.
    d. They divided in allegiance, just as white Americans did.

e. They volunteered to fight in the Continental army, but George Washington rejected them.

ANS: D   TOP: Ethnicity | The Indians' Revolution
DIF: Easy   REF: Full p. 221 | Seagull p. 229
MSC: Remembering   OBJ: 4

33. General John Sullivan:
a. led pro-American Cherokee troops in campaigns against Lord Cornwallis in North Carolina.
b. surrendered his forces to the Stockbridge Indians in a humiliating defeat.
c. destroyed forty Indian towns in a campaign against the Iroquois.
d. encouraged American forces to treat Indians and their lands "truly well and gently."
e. was a British spy whom pro-American Creek Indians unmasked.

ANS: C   TOP: Ethnicity | The Indians' Revolution
DIF: Difficult   REF: Full p. 222 | Seagull p. 229
MSC: Remembering   OBJ: 4

34. What policy did the new United States pursue in its dealings with Native Americans?
a. The U.S. government generally left them alone because it was busy trying to restore order after the war.
b. The U.S. government tried to protect them from encroachment by backcountry farmers, as required by the Treaty of Paris.
c. The U.S. government set out to dispossess the Native Americans of their remaining rich lands and drive them westward.
d. The U.S. government pursued a policy of outright extermination.
e. The U.S. government recognized Indian claims to their traditional lands from the Appalachians to the Mississippi River.

ANS: C   TOP: Ethnicity | White Freedom, Indian Freedom   DIF: Moderate   REF: Full p. 222 | Seagull pp. 229–230   MSC: Remembering OBJ: 4

35. Joseph Brant, a young Mohawk:
a. wanted to create an Indian confederacy between Canada and the United States.
b. allied with the Continental Congress and led troops against the British in the Great Lakes region.
c. represented Indian interests at the negotiations of the Treaty of Paris.
d. urged all Indians to move west of the Mississippi River to preserve their cultures from "contamination" by whites.
e. was appointed first governor-general of Upper Canada in 1781.

ANS: A   TOP: Ethnicity | White Freedom, Indian Freedom   DIF: Moderate   REF: Full p. 222 | Seagull p. 230   MSC: Remembering   OBJ: 4

36. Apart from "liberty," _____ was the word most used in the late eighteenth century in legal and political literature.
a. voting
b. tolerance
c. slavery
d. equality
e. suffrage

ANS: C   TOP: Civil rights | The Language of Slavery and Freedom   DIF: Moderate   REF: Full p. 223 | Seagull p. 231   MSC: Remembering   OBJ: 5

37. In a famous speech to Parliament, the British statesman Edmund Burke said what regarding a link between slavery and liberty for American colonists?
a. He argued that the colonists were sensitive to threats to their liberties because they were so familiar with slavery.
b. He said the colonists were hypocrites for claiming to be pro-liberty while they themselves owned slaves.
c. He said John Locke's ideas about property rights meant colonists were justified in claiming that their liberty included slave ownership rights.
d. He praised liberty-loving Pennsylvanians for organizing the world's first antislavery society.
e. He stated that a threat to liberty anywhere is a threat to liberty everywhere, so American slavery threatened British freedom.

ANS: A   TOP: Civil rights | The Language of Slavery and Freedom   DIF: Moderate   REF: Full p. 224 | Seagull p. 232   MSC: Remembering   OBJ: 5

38. Virtually every founding father owned at least one slave at some point in his life. Who was a notable exception?
a. George Washington
b. John Adams
c. Thomas Jefferson
d. Benjamin Franklin
e. James Madison

ANS: B   TOP: Social history | Obstacles to Abolition
DIF: Moderate   REF: Full p. 224 | Seagull p. 233
MSC: Remembering   OBJ: 5

39. What did South Carolina promise every white volunteer at the war's end?
a. a musket of his own
b. two acres of land
c. the right to vote

d. one hundred shillings
e. a slave

ANS: E   TOP: Social history | Obstacles to Abolition
DIF: Moderate   REF: Full p. 224 | Seagull p. 233
MSC: Remembering   OBJ: 5

40. Which of the following was NOT a key obstacle to the abolition of slavery in the Revolutionary era and new nation?
a. the Lockean belief in protecting property against outside interference
b. the idea that slavery for blacks made freedom possible for whites
c. the fact that slavery was an old institution in America
d. the widespread fear that freed slaves would move west and unite with Indians
e. the reality that a high percentage of some states' populations consisted of slaves

ANS: D   TOP: Social history | Obstacles to Abolition
DIF: Easy   REF: Full pp. 224–225 | Seagull pp. 232–233   MSC: Understanding   OBJ: 5

41. Who publically referred to slavery as a "national crime" that would one day bring "national punishment"?
a. Thomas Jefferson
b. Joseph Brant
c. Lord Dunmore
d. George Washington
e. Benjamin Rush

ANS: E   TOP: Social history | The Cause of General Liberty   DIF: Moderate   REF: Full p. 225 | Seagull p. 234   MSC: Remembering   OBJ: 5

42. Who was Phillis Wheatley?
a. a poet who wrote about how African-Americans felt about freedom
b. a fund-raiser for the Ladies' Association, whose efforts fed nearly starving men at Valley Forge
c. a pamphleteer whose ringing protests reminded Bostonians that women, too, cared about liberty
d. a woman who, disguised as a man, died while fighting during the Yorktown campaign
e. a slave who helped dozens of other slaves escape to freedom behind British lines

ANS: A   TOP: Cultural history | Petitions for Freedom   DIF: Moderate   REF: Full p. 226 | Seagull p. 235   MSC: Remembering   OBJ: 5

43. Which settlement in Africa did the British establish for former slaves from the United States?
a. Liberia
b. Sierra Leone
c. Monrovia
d. Ghana
e. Benin

ANS: B   TOP: Global awareness | British Emancipators   DIF: Difficult   REF: Full p. 228 | Seagull p. 236   MSC: Remembering   OBJ: 5

44. The efforts to emancipate slaves in the 1770s and 1780s:
a. occurred only in the New England states.
b. resulted entirely from the voluntary work by slaveholders.
c. included all slaves north of South Carolina.
d. reflected the importance of property rights.
e. were reversed in 1792 by the U.S. Supreme Court in the *Dred Scott* case.

ANS: D   TOP: Civil rights | Abolition in the North
DIF: Moderate   REF: Full p. 228 | Seagull p. 237
MSC: Understanding   OBJ: 5

45. Which statement about blacks and freedom in the Revolutionary era is FALSE?
a. The language of liberty echoed in slave communities, North and South.
b. "Freedom petitions" were presented by slaves in New England beginning in the early 1770s.
c. Many blacks were surprised that white America did not realize their rhetoric of revolution demanded emancipation.
d. After the Revolution, emancipation in the North was swift and all-encompassing.
e. The number of runaway slaves, as measured by newspaper advertisements, rose dramatically.

ANS: D   TOP: Civil rights | Abolition in the North
DIF: Moderate   REF: Full p. 229 | Seagull p. 237
MSC: Remembering   OBJ: 5

46. After the Revolution, African-Americans in the North:
a. often wound up in a state similar to that of indentured servitude.
b. began fleeing to the South when they saw that the new states would not approve emancipation.
c. benefited greatly from the popularity of manumission (or voluntary emancipation of slaves by whites).
d. were happy that the process of abolition under the new state constitutions meant that all current slaves would be free during their lifetimes.
e. were unable to establish their own institutions because their numbers were too low.

ANS: A   TOP: Civil rights | Abolition in the North
DIF: Moderate   REF: Full p. 229 | Seagull p. 237
MSC: Understanding   OBJ: 5

47. The free black population after the Revolution:
    a. declined in number as newly freed slaves left the country whenever possible.
    b. often enjoyed the right to vote if its male members met taxpaying or property qualifications.
    c. all took the last names of their former masters.
    d. refused to provide havens for fugitive slaves because doing so would have led to the revocation of their own emancipation.
    e. avoided supporting the abolitionist cause out of fear of reprisals.

    ANS: B   TOP: Civil rights | Free Black Communities
    DIF: Moderate   REF: Full p. 229 | Seagull p. 240
    MSC: Remembering   OBJ: 5

48. Which of the following was NOT a way in which women contributed to the Revolutionary cause?
    a. participating in crowd actions against merchants accused of hoarding goods
    b. contributing homemade goods to the army
    c. replacing their husbands in political offices
    d. spying on the British army
    e. fighting in the war

    ANS: C   TOP: Social history | Revolutionary Women
    DIF: Easy   REF: Full p. 232 | Seagull p. 241
    MSC: Understanding   OBJ: 6

49. Which statement about gender and politics in the Revolutionary era is FALSE?
    a. The winning of independence did not alter the law of family inherited from Britain.
    b. In both law and social reality, women lacked the essential qualification of political participation.
    c. In appreciation for their invaluable contribution to the war effort, women were allowed universal suffrage.
    d. Many women who entered public debate felt the need to apologize for their forthrightness.
    e. Most men considered women to be naturally submissive and irrational and therefore unfit for citizenship.

    ANS: C   TOP: Social history | Gender and Politics
    DIF: Easy   REF: Full pp. 233–234 | Seagull p. 242
    MSC: Understanding   OBJ: 6

50. Republican motherhood encouraged:
    a. greater educational opportunities for women.
    b. a radical change in the patriarchal structure of the family.
    c. women to become public speakers for various social causes in the 1780s.
    d. widespread resentment among women.
    e. a significant increase in women's direct involvement in politics in the 1780s.

    ANS: A   TOP: Social history | Republican Motherhood   DIF: Easy   REF: Full p. 234 | Seagull p. 243   MSC: Remembering   OBJ: 6

51. "Republican motherhood" was an ideology that held:
    a. women should be granted suffrage rights.
    b. women played an indispensable role in the new nation by training future citizens.
    c. Thomas Jefferson's Republican Party represented maternal interests better than its opponents did.
    d. education was wasted on women, who should only worry about having many children to populate the republic.
    e. political equality of the sexes fit a republican society.

    ANS: B   TOP: Social history | Republican Motherhood   DIF: Moderate   REF: Full p. 234 | Seagull p. 243   MSC: Remembering   OBJ: 6

True or False

1. Part of the philosophy of the Revolution was embracing the principle of hereditary aristocracy.

   ANS: F   TOP: Social history | The Dream of Equality   DIF: Easy   REF: Full p. 206 | Seagull p. 213   MSC: Remembering   OBJ: 1

2. The men who led the Revolution from start to finish were, by and large, members of the American elite.

   ANS: T   TOP: Social history | The Dream of Equality   DIF: Easy   REF: Full p. 206 | Seagull p. 212   MSC: Remembering   OBJ: 1

3. Thomas Jefferson's declaration that "all men are created equal" did not radically alter society.

   ANS: F   TOP: Social history | The Dream of Equality   DIF: Moderate   REF: Full p. 206 | Seagull p. 212   MSC: Remembering   OBJ: 1

4. The men who served in the Revolution through militias were empowered and demanded certain rights, thereby establishing the tradition that service in the army enabled excluded groups to stake a claim to full citizenship.

   ANS: T   TOP: Social history | Expanding the Political Nation   DIF: Moderate   REF: Full p. 207 | Seagull p. 214   MSC: Understanding   OBJ: 1

5. In Pennsylvania nearly the entire pre-Revolutionary elite opposed the American independence movement.

   ANS: T   TOP: Social history | The Revolution in Pennsylvania   DIF: Moderate   REF: Full p. 207 | Seagull p. 214   MSC: Remembering   OBJ: 1

6. In their Revolutionary era constitutions, all states adopted John Adams's idea of a "balanced" government.

   ANS: F   TOP: Constitutional history | The New Constitutions   DIF: Moderate   REF: Full pp. 208–209 | Seagull p. 215   MSC: Remembering   OBJ: 1

7. The property qualification for voting was hotly debated during the 1770s and 1780s.

   ANS: T   TOP: Political history, changes | The Right to Vote   DIF: Easy   REF: Full p. 209 | Seagull pp. 215–216   MSC: Remembering   OBJ: 1

8. Until New Jersey added the word "male" to its constitutional definition of a voter in 1807, some of the state's women enjoyed suffrage rights.

   ANS: T   TOP: Constitutional history | Democratizing Government   DIF: Moderate   REF: Full pp. 209–210 | Seagull p. 216   MSC: Remembering   OBJ: 1

9. Freedom and an individual's right to vote had become interchangeable by the war's end.

   ANS: T   TOP: Constitutional history | Democratizing Government   DIF: Moderate   REF: Full p. 210 | Seagull p. 216   MSC: Remembering   OBJ: 1

10. The War of Independence weakened the deep tradition of American anti-Catholicism.

    ANS: T   TOP: Social history | Catholic Americans   DIF: Moderate   REF: Full p. 211 | Seagull p. 218   MSC: Remembering   OBJ: 2

11. When America's first Roman Catholic bishop, James Carroll of Maryland, visited Boston in 1791, he was greeted by an angry mob chanting anti-Catholic slurs.

    ANS: F   TOP: Social history | Catholic Americans   DIF: Difficult   REF: Full p. 211 | Seagull p. 218   MSC: Remembering   OBJ: 2

12. Despite the rhetoric of religious freedom, many states had limitations on religious freedom, such as limiting office holding to Protestants.

    ANS: T   TOP: Social history | Separating Church and State   DIF: Easy   REF: Full p. 213 | Seagull p. 219   MSC: Remembering   OBJ: 2

13. Nearly every state constitution adopted in the 1770s and 1780s allowed Jews to vote and hold public office.

    ANS: F   TOP: Constitutional history | Separating Church and State   DIF: Moderate   REF: Full p. 213 | Seagull p. 219   MSC: Remembering   OBJ: 2

14. Because Americans were preoccupied with war, religious liberty was a rather peripheral issue in the 1770s and 1780s.

    ANS: F   TOP: Social history | Jefferson and Religious Liberty   DIF: Moderate   REF: Full p. 214 | Seagull p. 220   MSC: Understanding   OBJ: 2

15. There were very few religious denominations created after the Revolutionary War.

    ANS: F   TOP: Social history | The Revolution and the Churches   DIF: Moderate   REF: Full p. 214 | Seagull pp. 220–221   MSC: Remembering   OBJ: 2

16. In spite of the revolutionary rhetoric of freedom, indentured servitude was still widely practiced in the northern states by 1800.

    ANS: F   TOP: Social history | Toward Free Labor   DIF: Moderate   REF: Full p. 216 | Seagull p. 222   MSC: Remembering   OBJ: 3

17. Adam Smith's argument that the "invisible hand" of the free market directed economic life more effectively and fairly than governmental intervention offered intellectual justification for those who believed that the economy should be left to regulate itself.

    ANS: T   TOP: Economic development | The Debate over Free Trade   DIF: Easy   REF: Full p. 218 | Seagull p. 225   MSC: Remembering   OBJ: 3

18. For those Loyalists who remained in the United States after the war, hostility toward them proved to be long and intense.

    ANS: F   TOP: Social history | The Loyalists' Plight   DIF: Moderate   REF: Full pp. 219–220 | Seagull p. 228   MSC: Remembering   OBJ: 4

19. The American victory in the Revolution marked a new era of expanding freedom for Indians living east of the Mississippi River.

    ANS: F   TOP: Ethnicity | White Freedom, Indian Freedom   DIF: Easy   REF: Full pp. 222–223 | Seagull p. 230   MSC: Remembering   OBJ: 4

20. "Freedom" had not played a major part in Indians' vocabulary before the Revolution, but after the war, freedom meant defending their own independence and retaining possession of their land.

    ANS: T   TOP: Ethnicity | White Freedom, Indian Freedom   DIF: Moderate   REF: Full p. 223 | Seagull p. 230   MSC: Remembering   OBJ: 4

21. During the American Revolutionary War, the buying and selling of slaves was temporarily halted.

    ANS: F   TOP: Social history | The Language of Slavery and Freedom   DIF: Moderate   REF: Full p. 223 | Seagull p. 232   MSC: Remembering   OBJ: 5

22. The irony that America cried for liberty while enslaving Africans was not lost on some British observers like Dr. Samuel Johnson.

ANS: T   TOP: Social history | The Language of Slavery and Freedom   DIF: Easy   REF: Full p. 224 | Seagull p. 232   MSC: Remembering OBJ: 5

23. As one of the few southern white elite men who did not own slaves, Thomas Jefferson was able to honestly declare that all men had inalienable rights.

ANS: F   TOP: Social history | Obstacles to Abolition DIF: Easy   REF: Full p. 224 | Seagull p. 233 MSC: Remembering   OBJ: 5

24. During the American Revolutionary period, slavery for the first time became a focus of public debate.

ANS: T   TOP: Social history | The Cause of General Liberty   DIF: Moderate   REF: Full p. 225 | Seagull p. 234   MSC: Remembering OBJ: 5

25. In the Upper South, a considerable number of slaveholders emancipated their slaves.

ANS: T   TOP: Civil rights | Voluntary Emancipations DIF: Moderate   REF: Full p. 228 | Seagull p. 237 MSC: Remembering   OBJ: 5

26. Britain eventually paid compensation to some Americans after the war who claimed they had been improperly deprived of their slave property.

ANS: T   TOP: Social history | British Emancipators DIF: Difficult   REF: Full p. 228 | Seagull p. 236 MSC: Remembering   OBJ: 5

27. After the war, abolition of slavery in the North was swift and applied to all slaves.

ANS: F   TOP: Civil rights | Abolition in the North DIF: Easy   REF: Full p. 229 | Seagull p. 237 MSC: Remembering   OBJ: 5

28. The idea of republican motherhood encouraged direct female involvement in politics.

ANS: F   TOP: Social history | Republican Motherhood DIF: Easy   REF: Full p. 234 | Seagull p. 243 MSC: Remembering   OBJ: 6

29. The ideas of the American Revolution took decades to spread across the globe and effect change.

ANS: F   TOP: Global awareness | The Arduous Struggle for Liberty   DIF: Easy   REF: Full pp. 235–236 | Seagull p. 244   MSC: Remembering OBJ: 6

Short Answer

Identify and give the historical significance of each of the following terms, events, and people in a paragraph or two.

1. suffrage
2. virtuous citizenry
3. "Bill for Establishing Religious Freedom"
4. Ladies' Association
5. freedom petitions
6. free trade
7. "wall of separation"
8. republican motherhood
9. Phillis Wheatley
10. Treaty of Paris
11. Joseph Brant
12. Loyalists

Essay Questions

1. Freedom and an individual's right to vote became interchangeable in the wake of the Revolution. Describe how that transformation came about and how the various state constitutions dealt with voting qualifications.

ANS: Answers will vary   TOP: Constitutional history | Political history, changes | Democratizing Government | The Dream of Equality | Expanding the Political Nation | The Right to Vote   DIF: Moderate MSC: Understanding   OBJ: 1

2. Thomas Paine wrote that the essence of a republic was not the "particular form" of government, but its object: the "public good." Discuss how the various states structured their governments and how they believed those governments provided for the public good.

ANS: Answers will vary   TOP: Constitutional history | Economic development | Ethnicity | Political history, changes | The New Constitutions   DIF: Moderate MSC: Understanding   OBJ: 1

3. Thomas Jefferson claimed that no nation could expect to be ignorant and free. Explain what he meant by this. How did he define virtue and how was that important to his vision?

ANS: Answers will vary   TOP: Social history | Political history, changes | Jefferson and Religious Liberty | Christian Republicanism   DIF: Moderate MSC: Understanding   OBJ: 1

4. To what extent did Revolutionary-era Americans agree with Noah Webster's statement that equality was the very soul of a republic? Your response should define what Americans meant by equality and should consider groups that seemed to enjoy equality as well as those groups that did not.

ANS: Answers will vary   TOP: Civil rights | Social history | Political history, changes | Democratizing Government | The Dream of Equality | The Right to Vote | The Soul of a Republic   DIF: Moderate   MSC: Applying   OBJ: 1

5. How did Loyalists view liberty? How were they treated after the war? Why?

ANS: Answers will vary   TOP: Social history | Colonial Loyalists | The Loyalists' Plight   DIF: Moderate   MSC: Applying   OBJ: 4

6. When Dr. Samuel Johnson, the British writer, asked how it was "that we hear the loudest yelps for liberty from the drivers of negroes," he was pointing to a key irony of the American independence movement. What arguments did supporters of American independence use to justify retaining the institution of slavery? Did any of their contemporaries in America counter their arguments? How?

ANS: Answers will vary   TOP: Civil rights | Social history | Political history, changes | The Language of Slavery and Freedom | Obstacles to Abolition | Petitions for Freedom | The Cause of General Liberty   DIF: Moderate   MSC: Analyzing   OBJ: 5

7. How did the Revolution's language of liberty affect slaves and slavery in the 1770s and 1780s? Be sure to include in your response information from "Voices of Freedom."

ANS: Answers will vary   TOP: Civil rights | Social history | Political history, changes | Primary document analysis | The Language of Slavery and Freedom | Voices of Freedom   DIF: Moderate   MSC: Applying   OBJ: 5

8. How did women react to the language of freedom and liberty? Be sure to include in your response Abigail Adams's opinions that appear in "Voices of Freedom."

ANS: Answers will vary   TOP: Social history | Political history, changes | Primary document analysis | Revolutionary Women | Gender and Politics | Voices of Freedom   DIF: Moderate   MSC: Applying   OBJ: 6

9. Not everyone supported the independence movement within the colonies. Explain who supported independence and who did not. Be sure to include a discussion about how socioeconomic standing, race, religion, and gender affected an individual's support for or opposition to independence. Also consider why the other regions of the British Empire, such as Canada, the Caribbean islands, and Florida, did not also rebel and seek independence.

ANS: Answers will vary   TOP: Civil rights | Social history | Political history, changes | Colonial Loyalists   DIF: Moderate   MSC: Analyzing   OBJ: 4

10. How did the Revolution transform religion in the new nation? Consider especially issues related to religious toleration, religious liberty, and church-state relations.

ANS: Answers will vary   TOP: Social history | Political history, changes | The Revolution and the Churches | The Founders and Religion | Separating Church and State | Catholic Americans | Jefferson and Religious Liberty   DIF: Difficult   MSC: Analyzing   OBJ: 2 / 3 / 4 / 5 / 6

CHAPTER 7 | Founding a Nation, 1783–1791

This chapter concentrates on the making of the U.S. Constitution and begins with a description of some of the colorful celebrations held in cities to honor the ratification of the Constitution. The chapter explains the strengths and weaknesses of the first written constitution, the Articles of Confederation. A key success of the Confederation Congress was its western land policy, including the Northwest Ordinance, while its inability to deal with financial and economic problems weakened the government. Those weaknesses as well as Shays's Rebellion convinced many leading Americans of the need for a stronger central government. Their push for greater national authority resulted in the meeting of the Constitutional Convention (May–September 1787). The chapter covers the Convention's debates on separation of powers, division of powers, and slavery. Ratification of the document was not a foregone conclusion. Federalists such as James Madison, Alexander Hamilton, and John Jay worked hard at promoting support for ratification by writing a series of essays called *The Federalist*. The Anti-Federalists, concerned that the Constitution endangered liberty since it contained no Bill of Rights, opposed them. The "Voices of Freedom" for this chapter highlights the Anti-Federalist James Winthrop and includes David Ramsey's piece praising American constitutions, state and federal. The chapter concludes with a discussion about who was included in "We the People." Whites clearly did not consider Indians and enslaved blacks to be part of "the people," and the liberties and freedoms guaranteed in the Constitution were not extended to those groups. As the nation consolidated and enlarged the meaning of freedom, a widening gap emerged between "free whites" and "enslaved blacks."

CHAPTER OUTLINE

I. Introduction: Ratification Celebrations

II. America under the Confederation
   A. The Articles of Confederation
      1. The first written constitution of the United States
         a. One-house Congress
         b. No president
         c. No judiciary
      2. The only powers granted to the national government were those for declaring war, conducting foreign affairs, and making treaties.
         a. Amending required unanimous state approval.
         b. No proposed amendment ever passed.
      3. Congress established national control over land to the west of the thirteen states and devised rules for its settlement.
   B. Congress and the West
      1. In the immediate aftermath of independence, Congress took the position that by aiding the British, Indians had forfeited the right to their lands.
      2. Congress faced conflicting pressures from settlers and land speculators regarding western development.
   C. Settlers and the West
      1. Peace brought rapid settlement into frontier areas.
         a. Taking possession of land was seen as an essential element of American freedom.
         b. Ignored Indian titles to land and urged low prices for land.

2. Leaders feared unregulated flow of settlement across the Appalachian Mountains could provoke constant warfare with the Indians.
D. The Land Ordinances
   1. The Ordinance of 1784 established stages of self-government for the West.
   2. The Ordinance of 1785 regulated land sales in the region north of the Ohio River and established the township system there.
      a. One section set aside to provide funds for education.
   3. Like the British before them, American officials found it difficult to regulate the thirst for new land.
      a. Private companies and speculators benefited most from the land sales.
   4. The Northwest Ordinance of 1787 established policy that admitted the area's population as equal members of the political system.
      a. Prohibited slavery
E. The Confederation's Weaknesses
   1. The war created an economic crisis that the Confederation government could not adequately address.
   2. With Congress unable to act, the states adopted their own economic policies.
F. Shays's Rebellion
   1. Facing seizure of their land, debt-ridden farmers closed the courts in western Massachusetts in 1786.
      a. They modeled their protests on those of the Revolutionary era, using liberty trees and liberty poles.
   2. Rebellion put down by Massachusetts governor in 1787 with more than 1,000 arrested.
   3. Shays's Rebellion convinced many of the need for a stronger central government to protect property rights (a form of private liberty) from too much power in the hands of the people.
G. Nationalists of the 1780s
   1. Nation builders like James Madison and Alexander Hamilton called for increased national authority.
   2. The concerns voiced by critics of the Articles found a sympathetic hearing among men who had developed a national consciousness during the Revolution.
   3. Economic concerns played a part, too, as bondholders feared not being paid by the national government, artisans wanted tariff protection, and merchants desired access to British markets.
   4. At a meeting in Annapolis (September 1786), delegates called for a convention to amend the

Articles of Confederation in order to avoid anarchy and monarchy.

III. A New Constitution
A. The Structure of Government
   1. Prominent wealthy and well-educated men took part in the Constitutional Convention.
   2. Delegates quickly agreed the Constitution would create a legislature, an executive, and a national judiciary.
   3. The key to stable, effective republican government was finding a way to balance the competing claims of liberty and power.
   4. A compromise about the shape of Congress emerged from debates over the Virginia and New Jersey Plans.
      a. Virginia Plan (favored by more populous states): two-house legislature where state's population determined representation in both houses
      b. New Jersey Plan (favored by smaller states): one-house legislature in which each state cast one vote
      c. Compromise: two-house Congress consisting of Senate (each state had two members) and House of Representatives (apportioned according to states' populations)
B. The Limits of Democracy
   1. The Constitution left the determination of voter qualifications to the states.
   2. The new government was based on a limited democracy and the assumption that only prominent men would hold office.
   3. Federal judges would be appointed by the president.
   4. The president would be elected by an electoral college, or, in the case of a tie in that body, by the House of Representatives.
      a. Delegates wanted indirect election because they did not trust ordinary voters.
C. The Division and Separation of Powers
   1. The Constitution embodies federalism and a system of checks and balances.
      a. Federalism refers to the relationship between the national government and the states.
   2. States could not issue money, impair contracts, interfere with interstate commerce, or levy import or export duties, but dealt with most other daily affairs such as education and law enforcement.
      a. The separation of powers, or the system of checks and balances, refers to the way the Constitution seeks to prevent any branch of

the national government from dominating
the other two.
D. The Debate over Slavery
1. Slavery divided the delegates.
2. The words "slave" and "slavery" did not appear
in the Constitution, but it did protect slavery.
3. The South Carolinian delegates proved very
influential in preserving slavery within the
Constitution.
a. It threatened disunion if Atlantic slave trade
was banned immediately.
E. Slavery in the Constitution
1. The Constitution prevented Congress from
prohibiting the slave trade until 1808.
2. The fugitive slave clause made clear that the
condition of bondage remained attached to a
person even if he or she escaped to a free area,
and it required all states to help police the
institution of slavery.
3. The federal government could not interfere
with slavery in the states.
a. Slave states had more power due to the
three-fifths clause.
4. Twelve of the first sixteen presidents were
southern slaveholders.
F. The Final Document
1. Gouverneur Morris put finishing touches on
the final draft, adding in the preamble that the
new national government would "establish
justice," promote "general welfare," and
"secure the blessings of liberty."
2. Delegates signed the final draft on September
17, 1787.
3. The Constitution created a new framework for
American development.

IV. The Ratification Debate and the Origin of the Bill of
Rights
A. *The Federalist*
1. Nine of the thirteen states had to ratify the
document.
a. Not a given that ratification would occur.
b. Each state elected delegates to special
convention.
2. *The Federalist* was published to generate
support for ratification.
a. Hamilton argued that government was an
expression of freedom, not its enemy.
B. "Extend the Sphere"
1. Madison had a new vision of the relationship
between government and society in *Federalist*
no. 10 and no. 51.
2. Madison argued that the large size of the United
States was a source of stability, not weakness.

3. Madison helped to popularize the liberal idea
that men are generally motivated by self-
interest and that the good of society arises
from the clash of these private interests.
C. The Anti-Federalists
1. Anti-Federalists, who opposed ratification,
argued that the republic had to be small and
warned that the Constitution would result in an
oppressive government.
2. Liberty was the Anti-Federalists' watchword.
a. They argued for a Bill of Rights.
3. Federalists tended to be men of substantial
property, urban dwellers seeking prosperity,
and rural residents tied to the commercial
marketplace.
4. Anti-Federalists drew support from small
farmers in more isolated rural areas (e.g., New
York's Hudson Valley, western Massachusetts,
the southern backcountry).
5. Federalists dominated the press, which helped
them carry the day.
6. Madison won support for the Constitution by
promising a bill of rights later.
7. By mid-1788, the required nine states had
ratified.
8. Only Rhode Island and North Carolina voted
against ratification, but they eventually joined
the new government.
D. The Bill of Rights
1. Madison believed the Constitution would protect
liberty without the addition of a bill of rights.
2. Still, to satisfy the Constitution's critics,
Madison introduced a bill of rights to the first
Congress.
a. In a sense, the Bill of Rights defined the
"unalienable rights" of the Declaration of
Independence.
3. Some rights, such as the prohibiting of
excessive bail and cruel and unusual
punishments, reflected English roots, while
others, such as the recognition of religious
freedom, were uniquely American.
4. Not until the twentieth century would the Bill
of Rights be revered.
5. Among the most important rights were
freedom of speech and of the press, vital
building blocks of a democratic public sphere.

V. We the People
A. National Identity
1. The Constitution identifies three populations
inhabiting the United States:
a. Indians
b. "Other persons," which meant slaves

c. "People," who were the only ones entitled to American freedom

2. American nationality combined aspects of both civic and ethnic nationalisms.

   a. The political principles of the Revolution held Americans together.

   b. For most of U.S. history, citizenship has been defined by blood as well as political allegiance.

B. Indians in the New Nation

1. Indian tribes, seen by most white Americans as savages, had no representation in the new government.

2. The treaty system was used with Indians, and Congress forbade the transfer of Indian land without federal approval.

3. The U.S. victory at the Battle of Fallen Timbers led to the Treaty of Greenville in 1795.

   a. Under this treaty, twelve Indian tribes ceded most of Ohio and Indiana to the United States.

   b. The treaty established the annuity system— yearly grants of federal money to Indian tribes that led to continuing U.S. government influence in tribal affairs.

4. Some prominent Americans believed that Indians could assimilate into society.

   a. Assimilation meant transforming traditional Indian life with tools and changing gender roles.

   b. Most Indians rejected these changes.

C. Blacks and the Republic

1. The status of citizenship for free blacks was left to individual states.

2. Crèvecoeur's *Letters from an American Farmer* described America as a melting pot of Europeans.

3. Like Crèvecoeur, many white Americans excluded blacks from their conception of the American people.

   a. The Naturalization Act of 1790 limited naturalization (the process by which immigrants become citizens) to "free white persons."

D. Jefferson, Slavery, and Race

1. John Locke and others maintained that reason was essential to having liberty.

   a. Many white Americans did not consider blacks to be rational beings.

   b. Jefferson's *Notes on the State of Virginia* claimed blacks lacked self-control, reason, and devotion to the larger community.

2. Jefferson did not think any group was fixed permanently in a status of inferiority.

3. He did not believe black Americans should stay in America.

   a. Freeing the slaves without removing them from the country would endanger the nation's freedom.

4. Jefferson saw slave trade as immoral and tried to avoid selling his own slaves.

   a. Ironically upon his death, more than 200 of his slaves were sold to pay his large debts.

E. Principles of Freedom

1. The Revolution widened the divide between free Americans and those who remained in slavery.

2. "We the people" increasingly meant white Americans.

SUGGESTED DISCUSSION QUESTIONS

- What were the primary weaknesses and strengths of the Articles of Confederation?

- Why was ratification of the Constitution not a foregone conclusion? What were the basic arguments for and against ratification put forth by Federalists and Anti-Federalists?

- Were the fears of the Anti-Federalists realistic? How did the Federalists deal with the Anti-Federalists' concerns?

- What does "republicanism" mean? Why was America a republic and not a democracy?

- How did blacks and Indians fit into the new political order created by the Constitution of 1787? What liberties were extended or denied them?

- What was the Naturalization Act of 1790 and how did it shape the future America?

- Have the students write a constitution for the classroom, school, or university. On the basis of the ideas put forth by the Federalists and Anti-Federalists and drawing on who "the people" are, have the students defend their document while the class analyzes its strengths and weaknesses.

SUPPLEMENTAL WEB AND VISUAL RESOURCES

Articles of Confederation
http://avalon.law.yale.edu/18th_century/artconf.asp
This site is produced by Yale University and contains the Articles of Confederation as well as the discussions and debates surrounding it.

Shays's Rebellion
www.calliope.org/shays/shays2.html
With an abundance of material pertaining to Shays's Rebellion, this site offers a film resource and a bibliography.

The Bill of Rights
http://ffh.films.com/ItemDetails.aspx?TitleId=10062
Films for the Humanities & Sciences offers a video series covering Amendments 1 to 10.

The Constitution
http://constitution.org/c5/index.php
The Constitution Society has a useful website that covers the concepts behind the Constitution and includes images and other resources.

The Federalists and Anti-Federalists
www.usconstitution.net/consttop_faf.html
This site lists the conflicts between the Federalists and the Anti-Federalists during debates before the Constitution was ratified. It lists the events that occurred in each state.

http://www.constitution.org/fed/federa00.htm
Here is a page with links to all 85 Federalist essays.

The Founding Fathers
The popular *Founding Fathers* (2000) and *Founding Brothers (2002)* documentaries are available on DVD from A&E on *Amazon.com* and at many libraries.

SUPPLEMENTAL PRINT RESOURCES

Amar, Akhil Reed. *America's Constitution: A Biography.* New York: Random House, 2005.

Beeman, Richard. *Plain, Honest Men: The Making of the American Constitution.* New York: Random House, 2009.

Brandon, Mark. *Free in the World: American Slavery and Constitutional Failure.* Princeton, NJ: Princeton University Press, 1998.

Eisgruber, Christopher, and Lawrence Sager. *Religious Freedom and the Constitution.* Cambridge, MA: Harvard University Press, 2006.

Gibson, Alan. *Understanding the Founding: The Crucial Questions.* Lawrence, KS: University Press of Kansas, 2007.

Hunt, Lynn. *Inventing Human Rights: A History.* New York: W. W. Norton & Company, 2007.

McCormick, Richard. "The 'Ordinance' of 1784." *William and Mary Quarterly* 50, no. 1 (1993): 112–122.

Newman, Simon. *Parades and Politics of the Streets: Festive Culture in the Early American Republic.* Philadelphia: University of Pennsylvania Press, 1997.

Rakove, Jack. "Smoking Pistols and the Origins of the Constitution." *Reviews in American History* 22, no. 1 (1994): 39–44.

TEST BANK

Matching

TEST I

____ 1. Alexander Hamilton
____ 2. Daniel Shays
____ 3. Henry Knox
____ 4. John Adams
____ 5. Hector Crèvecoeur
____ 6. George Washington
____ 7. Thomas Jefferson
____ 8. Little Turtle
____ 9. Patrick Henry
____ 10. James Madison
____ 11. Arthur St. Clair
____ 12. James Winthrop

a. an Anti-Federalist
b. Treaty of Greenville
c. *Notes on the State of Virginia*
d. *Letters from an American Farmer*
e. led uprising of Massachusetts farmers
f. Agrippa
g. willed his slaves to be freed upon the death of his wife
h. defeated by Little Turtle
i. served as a diplomat to England and was unable to attend the Constitutional Convention
j. author of most of *The Federalist* essays
k. father of the Constitution
l. Secretary of War

Answer Key: j, e, l, i, d, g, c, b, a, k, h, f

TEST 2

____ 1. Articles of Confederation
____ 2. Federalism
____ 3. Virginia Plan
____ 4. checks and balances
____ 5. *The Federalist*
____ 6. New Jersey Plan
____ 7. three-fifths clause
____ 8. Treaty of Greenville
____ 9. Naturalization Act of 1790
____ 10. Bill of Rights
____ 11. slave trade
____ 12. *Somerset* case

a. annuity system
b. unicameral system
c. first written American constitution
d. abolished in 1808
e. two houses based on proportional representation
f. separation of powers
g. division of powers
h. essays that generated support for Constitutional ratification
i. amendments
j. citizenship limited to whites only
k. slave compromise
l. ruled slavery unlawful in England

Answer Key: c, g, e, f, h, b, k, a, j, i, d, l

Learning Objectives

1. Identify the achievements and problems of the Confederation government.
2. Explain how the major disagreements and compromises molded the final content of the Constitution.
3. Explain how the Anti-Federalist concerns raised during the ratification process led to the creation of the Bill of Rights.
4. Explain how the definition of citizenship in the new republic excluded Native Americans and African Americans.

Multiple Choice

1. Which of the following was a characteristic of the federal government under the Articles of Confederation?
   a. Congress was a two-chambered body, with a House of Delegates and a Council.
   b. Congress could not levy taxes or regulate commerce.
   c. Congress could amend the Articles by a two-thirds vote.
   d. There were two branches of government—judicial and legislative—but no executive.
   e. The more populous a state, the more votes it cast in Congress.

   ANS: B   TOP: Constitutional history | The Articles of Confederation   DIF: Moderate   REF: Full p. 240 | Seagull p. 249   MSC: Remembering   OBJ: 1

2. Under the Articles of Confederation, Congress was able to:
   a. establish national control over land to the west of the thirteen states.
   b. sign major treaties with France and Spain.
   c. create a new tax policy that would better fund the government.
   d. eliminate a provision giving judges power to reject congressional acts.
   e. block the passage of numerous constitutional amendments.

   ANS: A   TOP: Constitutional history | The Articles of Confederation   DIF: Difficult   REF: Full p. 240 | Seagull p. 249   MSC: Remembering   OBJ: 1

3. What was Congress able to accomplish with its Native American policy under the Articles of Confederation?
   a. Nothing; Congress was so powerless under the Articles that nothing happened in this area.
   b. It negotiated treaties for the tribes to keep their lands, but Congress was so lacking in power that the treaties proved useless.
   c. Congress demanded and received surrenders of large amounts of Indian land north of the Ohio River and in the South.
   d. Congress backed away from any involvement when land companies requested that the government step aside and leave the West's economic development in private hands.
   e. Congress recruited enough state militias to force the Native Americans off of their land.

   ANS: C   TOP: Ethnicity | Congress and the West   DIF: Moderate   REF: Full p. 242 | Seagull p. 250   MSC: Remembering   OBJ: 1

4. Why did Congress claim that some Indians had forfeited their land rights in the aftermath of independence?
   a. Because they did not farm it.
   b. Because they had never believed that the Indians owned the land.
   c. Because they were racially inferior.
   d. Because they had no written title to the land.
   e. Because they had aided the British during the war.

   ANS: E   TOP: Ethnicity | Congress and the West   DIF: Moderate   REF: Full p. 242 | Seagull p. 250   MSC: Remembering   OBJ: 1

5. In the 1780s, settlers in western areas such as Tennessee and Kentucky:
   a. were especially attentive to what land belonged to Indians and purchased Indian land legally.
   b. found that the soil was poor for growing cash crops such as tobacco or cotton and moved westward.
   c. believed they had a right to take possession of western lands and use them as they saw fit.
   d. were largely wealthy plantation owners who helped settle thriving trading towns along the rivers.
   e. threatened civil war because they considered the Confederation Congress to be too powerful.

   ANS: C   TOP: Geographic issues | Settlers and the West   DIF: Moderate   REF: Full p. 242 | Seagull p. 252   MSC: Remembering   OBJ: 4

6. Which of the following is true of how the leaders of the new nation viewed settlers moving west across the Appalachians in the 1780s?
   a. They shared their British predecessors' fears that frontier settlers would fight constantly with Native Americans.
   b. They viewed them as the start of a brigade that was going to spread American values and virtues across the continent.
   c. They hated them enough to pass laws banning their movement—much like the British Proclamation of 1763—but the settlers ignored them.

d. Benjamin Franklin advocated movement westward, but Thomas Jefferson fought him on it.
e. They expressed no views that historians have been able to find.

ANS: A TOP: Geographic issues | Settlers and the West DIF: Moderate REF: Full pp. 242–243 | Seagull p. 252 MSC: Remembering OBJ: 4

7. The Northwest Ordinance of 1787:
   a. established the policy to admit the area's population as equal members of the political system.
   b. regulated western land sales through a policy that was amicable to the Indians.
   c. abolished the Articles of Confederation and called for a second Constitutional Convention.
   d. was the first step in Alexander Hamilton's plan for economic growth.
   e. declared all Indian land to be the possession of the U.S. government.

ANS: A TOP: Geographic issues | The Land Ordinances DIF: Moderate REF: Full p. 245 | Seagull p. 254 MSC: Remembering OBJ: 1

8. With regard to slavery, the Northwest Ordinance of 1787:
   a. allowed for new territorial governments to ban or permit the institution as they saw fit.
   b. allowed the importation of slaves into the Old Northwest for at least another twenty years.
   c. banned slavery in the area north of the Ohio River and east of the Mississippi River.
   d. made no difference, because the U.S. Supreme Court declared it unconstitutional the following year.
   e. gave slaveholders the right to recover slaves who escaped into the area north of the Ohio River.

ANS: C TOP: Geographic issues | The Land Ordinances DIF: Moderate REF: Full p. 245 | Seagull p. 254 MSC: Remembering OBJ: 1

9. Under the Articles of Confederation, the states did what with regard to economics?
   a. They collected money from the Confederation government.
   b. They sold land under various land ordinances.
   c. They refused to print money.
   d. They signed trade agreements with England.
   e. They created a variety of economic policies.

ANS: E TOP: Constitutional history | The Confederation's Weaknesses DIF: Moderate REF: Full p. 245 | Seagull p. 254 MSC: Understanding OBJ: 1

10. Which of the following did states NOT do during the period when the Articles of Confederation governed the United States?
    a. They imposed their own tariffs.
    b. They printed their own money.
    c. They postponed debt collection.
    d. They called out militias to stop foreclosures on the homes of debtors.
    e. They held legislative elections in which candidates attacked creditors.

ANS: D TOP: Constitutional history | The Confederation's Weaknesses DIF: Moderate REF: Full pp. 245–246 | Seagull pp. 254–255 MSC: Understanding OBJ: 1

11. Shays's Rebellion was significant because it demonstrated:
    a. that land distribution policies were out of date.
    b. that controversies over the emancipation of slaves could turn violent.
    c. that Congress's attempts to pass pro-debtor laws were unpopular with farmers.
    d. the need for a stronger central government.
    e. the chaotic nature of Indian policy after the Battle of Fallen Timbers.

ANS: D TOP: Social history | Shays's Rebellion DIF: Moderate REF: Full p. 246 | Seagull p. 255 MSC: Understanding OBJ: 1

12. Shays's Rebellion:
    a. drew on the terminology of revolution and liberty.
    b. was aimed at the Vermont government, which was especially hard on debtors.
    c. ended only because the Confederation government used force to put it down.
    d. had the support of George Washington, but not of Thomas Jefferson.
    e. arose from the struggle to ratify the Constitution in 1787–1788.

ANS: A TOP: Social history | Shays's Rebellion DIF: Moderate REF: Full p. 246 | Seagull p. 255 MSC: Understanding OBJ: 1

13. James Madison:
    a. urged an expansion of public liberty.
    b. played no role at the Constitutional Convention.
    c. was Thomas Jefferson's ally and disciple.
    d. opposed the idea of a strong national government.
    e. distinguished himself as the presiding officer at the Constitutional Convention.

ANS: C TOP: Social history | Nationalities of the 1780s DIF: Moderate REF: Full p. 246 | Seagull p. 256 MSC: Remembering OBJ: 2

14. Which of the following people would have been the most likely supporter of the Articles of Confederation?
    a. a merchant desiring access to British markets
    b. a Continental army officer from the Revolutionary War
    c. an urban artisan
    d. a person who owned a bond issued by the Congress
    e. an indebted farmer in western Massachusetts

    ANS: E   TOP: Social history | Nationalists of the 1780s   DIF: Easy   REF: Full p. 247 | Seagull p. 256   MSC: Understanding   OBJ: 1

15. Which two prominent men were not at the Constitutional Convention?
    a. Benjamin Franklin and John Adams
    b. Thomas Jefferson and George Washington
    c. John Adams and George Mason
    d. Thomas Jefferson and John Adams
    e. Benjamin Franklin and George Washington

    ANS: D   TOP: Constitutional history | A New Constitution   DIF: Difficult   REF: Full p. 247 | Seagull p. 257   MSC: Remembering   OBJ: 2

16. Which of the following does NOT describe those who attended the Constitutional Convention?
    a. Most were better educated than the average American of the time.
    b. Most were prosperous by the standards of the day.
    c. A significant percentage had served in the army during the Revolutionary War.
    d. Most had earned their wealth after rising from humble origins.
    e. A majority had participated in interstate conventions during the 1760s and 1770s.

    ANS: D   TOP: Constitutional history | A New Constitution   DIF: Easy   REF: Full p. 248 | Seagull p. 257   MSC: Understanding   OBJ: 2

17. What proposal by Alexander Hamilton found little support in the Constitutional Convention?
    a. a democratically elected Congress, president, and judiciary
    b. life terms for president and senators
    c. a strengthened Congress, but no executive or judiciary
    d. granting states the right to create their own tariffs
    e. the inclusion of a Bill of Rights

    ANS: B   TOP: Constitutional history | The Structure of Government   DIF: Difficult   REF: Full p. 248 | Seagull p. 258   MSC: Remembering   OBJ: 2

18. Which of the following is true of the Virginia Plan?
    a. James Madison opposed it, but the other delegates from Virginia supported it.
    b. It proposed a one-house legislature, with population determining representation.
    c. It proposed a two-house legislature, with population determining representation in each house.
    d. It called for each state to have one vote in Congress.
    e. It was strongly opposed by the larger, more populated states.

    ANS: C   TOP: Constitutional history | The Structure of Government   DIF: Moderate   REF: Full p. 248 | Seagull p. 258   MSC: Remembering   OBJ: 2

19. The New Jersey Plan:
    a. was mainly supported by the smaller, less populated states.
    b. contained a gradual emancipation requirement that proved quite controversial.
    c. was a thinly disguised attempt to resurrect monarchy in America.
    d. found its greatest support from the Pennsylvania and Massachusetts delegations.
    e. called for a radical departure from the Articles of Confederation in every way.

    ANS: A   TOP: Constitutional history | The Structure of Government   DIF: Moderate   REF: Full pp. 248–249 | Seagull p. 258   MSC: Remembering   OBJ: 2

20. What qualifications did the Constitution, ratified in 1787, impose for voting?
    a. None; it left voting rules to the states.
    b. It allowed all white males over twenty-one to vote but expressly banned women.
    c. It allowed all white males over twenty-one to vote and said nothing about women.
    d. It imposed a property requirement.
    e. It specifically banned African-Americans from voting.

    ANS: A   TOP: Constitutional history | The Limits of Democracy   DIF: Difficult   REF: Full p. 249 | Seagull p. 258   MSC: Remembering   OBJ: 2

21. Why was the original House of Representatives so small, with only 65 members?
    a. It was not; it had the 435 members it has now.
    b. The founders assumed that only prominent individuals could win elections in large districts, and that is what the founders wanted.
    c. The founders thought that only five people per state were enough.
    d. Since each state had one vote in the House, the founders thought that this would make debate more cordial.
    e. There was a housing shortage in Philadelphia, so there was nowhere for more members to stay.

ANS: B   TOP: Constitutional history | The Limits of Democracy   DIF: Moderate   REF: Full p. 249 | Seagull p. 259   MSC: Remembering   OBJ: 2

22. Why did the founding fathers create the electoral college?
    a. They did not; it was added to the Constitution after the disputed election of 1796.
    b. Small states insisted that they have a chance to play a role in choosing the president, and that wouldn't have been possible with direct elections.
    c. Alexander Hamilton wanted a king, James Madison wanted no president, and the result was this compromise so that there could be a president.
    d. They did not trust ordinary voters to choose the president and vice president directly.
    e. They knew the Constitution would make them unpopular, so they wanted to create a way to avoid letting voters choose the president, thereby giving themselves a chance to be elected.

    ANS: D   TOP: Constitutional history | The Limits of Democracy   DIF: Easy   REF: Full pp. 249–250 | Seagull p. 259   MSC: Understanding   OBJ: 2

23. As designed by the Constitution:
    a. the president was elected by popular vote.
    b. senators were to serve two-year terms.
    c. federal judges were appointed by the president, not elected by the people.
    d. the congressional representatives were to be appointed by state legislatures.
    e. the Supreme Court justices were to serve ten-year terms.

    ANS: C   TOP: Constitutional history | The Limits of Democracy   DIF: Moderate   REF: Full pp. 249–250 | Seagull p. 259   MSC: Remembering   OBJ: 2

24. The relationship between the national government and the states is called:
    a. the separation of powers.
    b. the New Jersey Plan.
    c. Federalism.
    d. the Virginia Plan.
    e. the Constitution.

    ANS: C   TOP: Constitutional history | The Division and Separation of Powers   DIF: Moderate   REF: Full p. 250 | Seagull p. 259   MSC: Remembering   OBJ: 2

25. Which of the following is NOT a check against presidential power in the Constitution?
    a. Congress can override a president's veto with a two-thirds vote.
    b. The House can impeach the president for "high crimes and misdemeanors."

c. The House can remove the president from office after impeaching him.
    d. Congress has the authority to accept or reject some presidential appointments.
    e. Although the president appoints judges, they serve for life to ensure their independence.

ANS: C   TOP: Constitutional history | The Division and Separation of Powers   DIF: Difficult
REF: Full pp. 250–251 | Seagull p. 260
MSC: Understanding   OBJ: 2

26. Which of the following is true of the Constitution of 1787 and slavery?
    a. Despite protests from southern delegates, the document permanently freed runaway slaves who made it to the "free air" of the North.
    b. The Constitution declared that all territories of the United States would be "free soil" where slavery would not be permitted.
    c. The Constitution explicitly protected the security of property in slaves in any state of the Union, so that a slave owner could move permanently with his slaves from South to North.
    d. The Constitution provided for half of a state's slave population to be counted in determining its membership in the House of Representatives.
    e. Although never using the word "slavery," the document protected several aspects of the institution.

ANS: E   TOP: Constitutional history | The Debate over Slavery   DIF: Moderate   REF: Full p. 251 | Seagull pp. 260–261   MSC: Understanding   OBJ: 2

27. Which of the following is true regarding Congress and the African slave trade in the United States under the Constitution?
    a. Congress never prohibited this slave trade.
    b. The First Congress under the Constitution prohibited the importation of slaves into the United States.
    c. Congress always let individual states make their own decisions with regard to importing slaves.
    d. Congress prohibited the African slave trade ten years after ratification of the Constitution.
    e. Congress prohibited the African slave trade twenty years after ratification of the Constitution.

ANS: E   TOP: Civil rights | Constitutional history | The Debate over Slavery   DIF: Moderate   REF: Full p. 251 | Seagull p. 260   MSC: Remembering   OBJ: 2

28. How did southern states react to the Constitution's provisions regarding slavery?
    a. South Carolina and Georgia immediately began importing increased numbers of Africans, because

in twenty years, the international slave trade could be constitutionally prohibited.

b. They refused to ratify the Constitution without assurances that a bill of rights would be added to protect their right to slave property.

c. The personal opposition of Jefferson and Madison to slavery prompted Virginia to oppose ratification at first.

d. They objected to the electoral college on the grounds that it ignored the number of slaves in their states and thereby reduced their power.

e. They were critical of the provision in Article I allowing African-Americans to be armed during wartime.

ANS: A   TOP: Civil rights | Constitutional history | Slavery in the Constitution   DIF: Moderate
REF: Full p. 252 | Seagull p. 261
MSC: Understanding   OBJ: 2

29. The three-fifths clause in the U.S. Constitution:
a. requires that all revenue bills receive a three-fifths affirmative vote in the U.S. House.
b. gave the white South greater power in national affairs than the size of its free population warranted.
c. explicitly declared that slaves were not fully human and were therefore undeserving of legal rights.
d. made it easier to amend the Constitution than it had been to amend the Articles of Confederation.
e. expired in the year 1808 because of a key sectional compromise at the Constitutional Convention.

ANS: B   TOP: Constitutional history | Slavery in the Constitution   DIF: Moderate   REF: Full p. 252 | Seagull p. 262   MSC: Understanding   OBJ: 2

30. The Constitution explicitly granted Congress the power to do all of the following EXCEPT:
a. pass tariffs.
b. coin money.
c. regulate interstate commerce.
d. issue patents.
e. emancipate slaves.

ANS: E   TOP: Civil rights | Constitutional history | Slavery in the Constitution   DIF: Easy   REF: Full p. 252 | Seagull p. 261   MSC: Remembering OBJ: 2

31. The *Somerset* case:
a. ended the importation of slaves into the United States.
b. ruled that slavery was unlawful in England.
c. freed slaves from the ship *Amistad*.
d. used the language of liberty to rule that free blacks could own property.

e. set the precedent that fugitive slaves had to be returned to their masters.

ANS: B   TOP: Global awareness | Slavery in the Constitution   DIF: Moderate   REF: Full p. 252 | Seagull pp. 261–262   MSC: Remembering   OBJ: 2

32. Who wrote the preamble and put the final written touches on the Constitution?
a. Gouverneur Morris
b. James Madison
c. Ben Franklin
d. Alexander Hamilton
e. John Jay

ANS: A   TOP: Constitutional history | The Final Document   DIF: Moderate   REF: Full p. 253 | Seagull p. 262   MSC: Remembering   OBJ: 2

33. The eighty-five essays written in support of ratification of the Constitution are called:
a. *Wealth of Nations.*
b. the Articles of Confederation.
c. *The Federalist.*
d. "Agrippa."
e. *The History of the American Revolution.*

ANS: C   TOP: Constitutional history | *The Federalist*
DIF: Easy   REF: Full p. 254 | Seagull p. 263
MSC: Remembering   OBJ: 3

34. Who wrote the majority of the eighty-five essays in *The Federalist*?
a. Alexander Hamilton
b. James Madison
c. Benjamin Franklin
d. John Jay
e. John Adams

ANS: A   TOP: Constitutional history | *The Federalist*
DIF: Moderate   REF: Full p. 254 | Seagull p. 263
MSC: Remembering   OBJ: 3

35. In *The Federalist*, James Madison argued that:
a. the large size of the United States was a source of political stability.
b. to be a republic, a country must be geographically small.
c. church and state must be linked in order to encourage republican virtue.
d. it was essential that slavery be abolished for liberty to flourish.
e. presidential power must be stronger than that of Congress and the courts.

ANS: A   TOP: Constitutional history | "Extend the Sphere"   DIF: Moderate   REF: Full p. 255 | Seagull p. 265   MSC: Remembering   OBJ: 3

36. What was "the first object of government," according to James Madison?
    a. Feed the poor.
    b. Protect free speech.
    c. Guarantee voting rights.
    d. Protect property rights.
    e. Secure freedom.

    ANS: D   TOP: Constitutional history | "Extend the Sphere"   DIF: Difficult   REF: Full p. 255 | Seagull p. 264   MSC: Remembering   OBJ: 3

37. Which of the following groups tended to be Anti-Federalist during the ratification debates?
    a. wealthier citizens
    b. rural residents closely tied to the commercial marketplace
    c. merchants engaged in foreign commerce
    d. state politicians fearful of a strong central government
    e. urban artisans, laborers, and sailors

    ANS: D   TOP: Constitutional history | The Anti-Federalists   DIF: Moderate   REF: Full p. 256 | Seagull p. 265   MSC: Understanding   OBJ: 3

38. Anti-Federalists included:
    a. Patrick Henry and John Adams.
    b. George Washington and John Hancock.
    c. Samuel Adams and James Madison.
    d. Benjamin Franklin and John Jay.
    e. Samuel Adams and Patrick Henry.

    ANS: E   TOP: Constitutional history | The Anti-Federalists   DIF: Difficult   REF: Full p. 256 | Seagull p. 265   MSC: Remembering   OBJ: 3

39. During the process of ratifying the Constitution:
    a. two states, Rhode Island and North Carolina, voted against ratification.
    b. Alexander Hamilton reversed himself and argued against ratification.
    c. propertied men and urban dwellers formed the chief support for the Anti-Federalists.
    d. northern state conventions unanimously supported ratification while southern ones were deeply divided.
    e. Thomas Jefferson sent numerous letters from Paris opposing passage, but he was too far away to be really influential.

    ANS: A   TOP: Constitutional history | The Anti-Federalists   DIF: Moderate   REF: Full p. 257 | Seagull p. 266   MSC: Remembering   OBJ: 3

40. All of the following statements are true of the Bill of Rights EXCEPT:
    a. English law strongly influenced some of its provisions.
    b. It defined, in part, the "unalienable rights" of the Declaration of Independence.
    c. James Madison considered it unnecessary, but proposed it anyway.
    d. Reflecting a change in American life caused by the Revolution, it protected religious freedom.
    e. It explicitly granted states the right of secession.

    ANS: E   TOP: Constitutional history | The Bill of Rights   DIF: Easy   REF: Full pp. 258–259 | Seagull pp. 267–270   MSC: Understanding   OBJ: 3

41. Which right was heavily influenced by the American Revolutionary period?
    a. free speech
    b. freedom from excessive bail
    c. free press
    d. freedom of religion
    e. freedom from cruel and unusual punishment

    ANS: E   TOP: Constitutional history | The Bill of Rights   DIF: Difficult   REF: Full p. 259 | Seagull p. 270   MSC: Understanding   OBJ: 3

42. In *The History of the American Revolution,* David Ramsay:
    a. argued that the Constitution represented a repudiation of the Revolution.
    b. urged southern states to demand greater protection for slavery before ratifying the Constitution.
    c. praised American state constitutions for allowing future amendments.
    d. took issue with James Madison's vision of "extending the sphere."
    e. took the British side when explaining why the Revolution occurred.

    ANS: C   TOP: Primary document analysis | Voices of Freedom   DIF: Difficult   REF: Full p. 260 | Seagull p. 268   MSC: Remembering   OBJ: 3

43. The Anti-Federalist James Winthrop argued that a bill of rights was necessary in the Constitution because:
    a. the English had one, so America ought to mirror that example.
    b. the right to bear arms for the militia should be guarded by law.
    c. using the examples of Wilkes and Zenger, the protection of speech and press was essential.
    d. it would secure the minority against the usurpation and tyranny of the majority.
    e. ratification of the Constitution was in doubt without the inclusion of the Bill of Rights.

    ANS: D   TOP: Primary document analysis | Voices of Freedom   DIF: Moderate   REF: Full p. 261 | Seagull p. 269   MSC: Understanding   OBJ: 3

44. Envisioning the nation as a community open to all those devoted to its political institutions and social values is what?
    a. ethnic nationalism
    b. federalism
    c. separation of powers
    d. religious toleration
    e. civic nationalism

    ANS: E   TOP: Constitutional history | National Identity
    DIF: Difficult   REF: Full p. 263 | Seagull p. 272
    MSC: Understanding   OBJ: 3

45. Which of the following is true of American national identity as envisioned by the Constitution of 1787?
    a. The document distinguished only between those defined as American citizens, who were entitled to constitutionally protected rights, and aliens, who were not so entitled.
    b. The Constitution clearly states that persons of African descent could not be U.S. citizens, but that anyone of European or Asian descent could be.
    c. The "people" were free Americans; Native Americans and "other persons," meaning African-American slaves, were not considered part of the political nation.
    d. The Constitution expressly stated that only white men were entitled to the rights it delineated.
    e. The Constitution made clear that only civic nationalism, not ethnic nationalism, defined American national identity.

    ANS: C   TOP: Constitutional history | Ethnicity | Social history | National Identity   DIF: Difficult
    REF: Full p. 263 | Seagull p. 272
    MSC: Understanding   OBJ: 4

46. Which of the following is true of how the U.S. government in the 1790s dealt with Native Americans?
    a. Because the Constitution counted all Indians toward representation in Congress, Indians received all rights and privileges that other Americans did.
    b. Because the Constitution stated Indian tribes were "domestic dependent nations," the government treated them just as it treated nations like Great Britain and France.
    c. Henry Knox, the first secretary of war, pursued policies designed to exterminate Native Americans.
    d. The U.S. government made treaties with them mainly to transfer land to itself or to the states.
    e. No American leaders believed that Native Americans could assimilate into American society, so the government largely ignored Indians.

    ANS: D   TOP: Ethnicity | Indians in the New Nation
    DIF: Easy   REF: Full p. 265 | Seagull p. 272
    MSC: Remembering   OBJ: 4

47. Who was defeated at the Battle of Fallen Timbers in 1794?
    a. Arthur St. Clair
    b. Henry Knox
    c. Little Turtle
    d. Tecumseh
    e. Anthony Wayne

    ANS: C   TOP: Ethnicity | Military history | Indians in the New Nation   DIF: Difficult   REF: Full p. 265 | Seagull p. 274   MSC: Remembering   OBJ: 4

48. Under the Treaty of Greenville of 1795:
    a. Great Britain agreed to remove its remaining forts from U.S. soil.
    b. twelve Indian tribes ceded most of Ohio and Indiana to the federal government.
    c. the U.S. government allowed Indians to petition for citizenship.
    d. the federal government forbade American settlement west of the Mississippi.
    e. the U.S. recognized Great Britain's claim to what is now Ontario.

    ANS: B   TOP: Ethnicity | Indians in the New Nation
    DIF: Difficult   REF: Full p. 265 | Seagull p. 274
    MSC: Remembering   OBJ: 4

49. What was the annuity system involving the U.S. government and certain Indian tribes?
    a. a system under which the Indians ceded land to the United States annually
    b. a system under which the federal government gave annual monetary grants to Indians
    c. a system that placed Indians on reservations
    d. a system that allowed a percentage of Indians each year to attend American schools
    e. a system where the states paid each local tribe an annual fee for their land

    ANS: B   TOP: Ethnicity | Indians in the New Nation
    DIF: Moderate   REF: Full pp. 265–266 | Seagull p. 274   MSC: Remembering   OBJ: 4

50. Hector St. John Crèvecoeur's *Letters from an American Farmer*:
    a. popularized the idea of the United States as a melting pot of ethnicities.
    b. was a thinly disguised allegory explaining the need for the Constitution.
    c. made the author so unpopular in the United States that he was forced to return to France.
    d. argued that America should reject manufacturing and remain an agrarian nation.
    e. made the case that free African Americans were "citizens of color" deserving of full legal rights.

ANS: A   TOP: Ethnicity | Blacks and the Republic
DIF: Moderate   REF: Full p. 267 | Seagull p. 276
MSC: Remembering   OBJ: 4

51. During the early years of the republic,
African-Americans:
   a. were far fewer in number than Native Americans, so
      ignoring them was easy for the founders and early
      leaders.
   b. enjoyed none of the rights whites enjoyed.
   c. made up about 20 percent of the total population.
   d. were all held as slaves except for a few free blacks
      in Massachusetts.
   e. found a champion for the cause of emancipation in
      Hector St. John Crèvecoeur.

   ANS: C   TOP: Social history | Blacks and the Republic
   DIF: Moderate   REF: Full p. 267 | Seagull p. 276
   MSC: Remembering   OBJ: 4

52. The Naturalization Act of 1790 allowed:
   a. all immigrants to become citizens.
   b. only Irish, English, and German immigrants to
      become citizens.
   c. everyone except blacks to become citizens.
   d. only free white persons to become citizens.
   e. only white men to become citizens.

   ANS: D   TOP: Ethnicity | Blacks and the Republic
   DIF: Moderate   REF: Full p. 267 | Seagull p. 276
   MSC: Remembering   OBJ: 4

53. Who wrote *Notes on the State of Virginia*?
   a. James Madison
   b. George Mason
   c. George Washington
   d. St. George Tucker
   e. Thomas Jefferson

   ANS: E   TOP: Social history | Jefferson, Slavery, and
   Race   DIF: Moderate   REF: Full p. 268 | Seagull
   p. 277   MSC: Remembering   OBJ: 4

54. Thomas Jefferson believed that African-Americans:
   a. should eventually be able to enjoy their natural
      rights, but they would have to leave the United
      States to do so.
   b. who were held in slavery should be emancipated
      immediately and that every former slave family should
      be given a forty-acre farm in a western territory.
   c. should, if legally free, be allowed to marry white
      persons.
   d. like Indians, were naturally as intelligent as
      whites.
   e. should all be held in slavery because, like Indians,
      they were clearly inferior to persons of European
      descent.

ANS: A   TOP: Civil rights | Jefferson, Slavery, and
Race   DIF: Moderate   REF: Full pp. 268–269 |
Seagull p. 278   MSC: Remembering   OBJ: 4

55. By the 1790s, the phrase "we the people" had come to
mean what?
   a. The lower classes of society would share in the
      economic growth.
   b. The president would be elected directly by the
      people.
   c. Voting rights should increase for both men and
      women.
   d. America should remain a nation of farmers.
   e. Rights were increasing for white Americans.

   ANS: E   TOP: Civil rights | Constitutional history |
   Principles of Freedom   DIF: Moderate   REF: Full
   p. 270 | Seagull p. 279   MSC: Understanding
   OBJ: 4

True or False

1. At the time of independence, the nation was largely
   urban, with most of its population residing in the large
   seacoast cities.

   ANS: F   TOP: Geographic issues | Introduction
   DIF: Easy   REF: Full p. 239 | Seagull p. 248
   MSC: Remembering   OBJ: 1

2. The U.S. Constitution of 1787 was America's first
   written constitution.

   ANS: F   TOP: Constitutional history | The Articles of
   Confederation   DIF: Easy   REF: Full p. 240 |
   Seagull p. 249   MSC: Remembering   OBJ: 1

3. In the immediate aftermath of independence, Congress
   took the position that by aiding the British, Indians had
   forfeited the right to their lands.

   ANS: T   TOP: Ethnicity | Geographic issues | Con-
   gress and the West   DIF: Easy   REF: Full p. 242 |
   Seagull p. 250   MSC: Remembering   OBJ: 4

4. Congress nearly passed a clause in the Ordinance of
   1784 that would have prohibited slavery throughout the
   West.

   ANS: T   TOP: Civil rights | Geographic issues | The
   Land Ordinances   DIF: Moderate   REF: Full p. 243 |
   Seagull p. 252   MSC: Remembering   OBJ: 1

5. The Northwest Ordinance of 1787 did not acknowledge
   that the Indians owned their land.

   ANS: F   TOP: Ethnicity | Geographic issues | The
   Land Ordinances   DIF: Moderate   REF: Full p. 245
   | Seagull p. 254   MSC: Remembering   OBJ: 1

6. Shays's Rebellion demonstrated to many leading Americans the need for a more central government to ensure private liberty.

   ANS: T   TOP: Social history | Shays's Rebellion
   DIF: Easy   REF: Full p. 246 | Seagull p. 255
   MSC: Remembering   OBJ: 1

7. The Constitutional delegates who met in Philadelphia represented all of American society, as they were a mix of laborers, farmers, merchants, and politicians.

   ANS: F   TOP: Constitutional history | A New Constitution   DIF: Easy   REF: Full pp. 247–248 | Seagull p. 257   MSC: Remembering   OBJ: 2

8. Alexander Hamilton proposed in the Constitutional Convention that the president and senators serve life terms.

   ANS: T   TOP: Constitutional history | The Structure of Government   DIF: Moderate   REF: Full p. 248 | Seagull p. 258   MSC: Remembering   OBJ: 2

9. The New Jersey Plan proposed a single-house legislature, which gave each state one vote.

   ANS: T   TOP: Constitutional history | The Structure of Government   DIF: Moderate   REF: Full pp. 248–249 | Seagull p. 258   MSC: Remembering OBJ: 2

10. The U.S. Constitution of 1787 defined who could and could not vote.

    ANS: F   TOP: Constitutional history | The Limits of Democracy   DIF: Moderate   REF: Full p. 249 | Seagull p. 258   MSC: Remembering   OBJ: 2

11. "Separation of powers" refers to the relationship between the national government and the states.

    ANS: F   TOP: Constitutional history | The Division and Separation of Powers   DIF: Moderate REF: Full p. 250 | Seagull p. 260   MSC: Remembering OBJ: 2

12. The Constitution is a lengthy, wordy document that outlines the structure of government in great detail.

    ANS: F   TOP: Constitutional history | The Division and Separation of Powers   DIF: Moderate REF: Full p. 250 | Seagull p. 259   MSC: Remembering OBJ: 2

13. The U.S. Constitution as written in 1787 does not use the words "slave" or "slavery."

    ANS: T   TOP: Constitutional history | The Debate over Slavery   DIF: Moderate   REF: Full p. 251 | Seagull p. 260   MSC: Remembering   OBJ: 2

14. In the U.S. Constitution, the fugitive slave clause kept the condition of bondage for a slave even if he or she escaped to a free state.

    ANS: T   TOP: Constitutional history | The Debate over Slavery   DIF: Moderate   REF: Full p. 252 | Seagull pp. 260–261   MSC: Understanding OBJ: 2

15. James Madison argued in *The Federalist* that the large size and diversity of the United States was a source of political stability, not a weakness.

    ANS: T   TOP: Constitutional history | "Extend the Sphere"   DIF: Moderate   REF: Full p. 255 | Seagull p. 265   MSC: Remembering   OBJ: 3

16. Anti-Federalists were concerned that the Constitution severely limited liberty.

    ANS: T   TOP: Constitutional history | The Anti-Federalists   DIF: Easy   REF: Full p. 256 | Seagull p. 265   MSC: Remembering   OBJ: 3

17. Two of the original thirteen states initially refused to ratify the Constitution, but ultimately they did ratify it.

    ANS: T   TOP: Constitutional history | The Anti-Federalists   DIF: Difficult   REF: Full p. 257 | Seagull p. 266   MSC: Remembering   OBJ: 3

18. So adamant was he about separating church and state, James Madison opposed the appointment of chaplains to serve Congress and the military.

    ANS: T   TOP: Constitutional history | The Bill of Rights   DIF: Difficult   REF: Full p. 259 | Seagull p. 270   MSC: Remembering   OBJ: 3

19. Not until the twentieth century did the Bill of Rights become revered.

    ANS: T   TOP: Constitutional history | The Bill of Rights   DIF: Difficult   REF: Full p. 259 | Seagull p. 270   MSC: Understanding   OBJ: 3

20. In the 1780s, "We the people" meant a melting pot of all peoples.

    ANS: F   TOP: Ethnicity | National Identity
    DIF: Easy   REF: Full p. 263 | Seagull p. 272
    MSC: Understanding   OBJ: 4

21. Battles over Indian territory continued after ratification of the Constitution.

    ANS: T   TOP: Ethnicity | Geographic issues | Indians in the New Nation   DIF: Easy   REF: Full p. 265 | Seagull p. 272   MSC: Remembering   OBJ: 4

22. In the Constitution, Native Americans were granted citizenship.

ANS: F   TOP: Ethnicity | Indians in the New Nation
DIF: Easy   REF: Full p. 265 | Seagull p. 272
MSC: Remembering   OBJ: 4

23. The U.S. Constitution of 1787 provided a clear
definition of U.S. citizenship that excluded blacks.

ANS: F   TOP: Constitutional history | Blacks and
the Republic   DIF: Moderate   REF: Full
pp. 266–267 | Seagull p. 274   MSC: Remembering
OBJ: 4

24. Crèvecoeur's *Letters from an American Farmer*
described America as a melting pot of Europeans.

ANS: T   TOP: Ethnicity | Blacks and the Republic
DIF: Moderate   REF: Full p. 267 | Seagull p. 276
MSC: Remembering   OBJ: 4

25. Jefferson was unsure whether African-Americans were
fixed permanently in a status of inferiority.

ANS: F   TOP: Social history | Jefferson, Slavery, and
Race   DIF: Moderate   REF: Full p. 268 | Seagull
p. 274   MSC: Understanding   OBJ: 4

26. George Washington made a significant statement about
slavery when he freed his slaves before taking the
presidential office.

ANS: F   TOP: Social history | Jefferson, Slavery, and
Race   DIF: Moderate   REF: Full p. 269 | Seagull
p. 279   MSC: Understanding   OBJ: 4

Short Answer

Identify and give the historical significance of each of the
following terms, events, and people in a paragraph or two.

1. Shays's Rebellion
2. Bill of Rights
3. Naturalization Act of 1790
4. Treaty of Greenville
5. James Madison
6. *Letters from an American Farmer*
7. Articles of Confederation
8. Northwest Ordinance of 1787
9. *The Federalist*
10. slave compromises
11. Anti-Federalists
12. Constitutional Convention

Essay Questions

1. Compare the Articles of Confederation to the Constitution. Which document did a better job of protecting liberties? Running a government? Explain your answer
with specific examples.

ANS: Answers will vary   TOP: Constitutional history
| Political history, changes | The Articles of Confed-
eration | The Confederation's Weaknesses | A New
Constitution | The Structure of Government
DIF: Moderate   MSC: Analyzing   OBJ: 1 / 2

2. How did the framers of the Constitution balance the
competing claims of local self-government, sectional
interests, and national authority?

ANS: Answers will vary   TOP: Constitutional history
| A New Constitution | The Limits of Democracy |
The Division and Separation of Powers
DIF: Moderate   MSC: Understanding   OBJ: 2 / 3

3. Who became full-fledged members of the American
political community under the U.S. Constitution? Fully
explain what criteria were used and who was excluded
from membership.

ANS: Answers will vary   TOP: Civil rights | Constitu-
tional history | Ethnicity | Blacks and the Republic |
Indians in the New Nation | Slavery in the Constitution
DIF: Moderate   MSC: Understanding   OBJ: 4

4. James Madison declared, "Liberty may be endangered by
the abuses of liberty as well as the abuses of power." This
statement reflected a concern that public liberty might
endanger private liberty. Carefully analyze this concern.
Why might some Americans take this view? Which liberty was more valued? How did the final Constitution
reflect this concern?

ANS: Answers will vary   TOP: Constitutional history |
Political history, changes | The Bill of Rights | The
Anti-Federalists   DIF: Moderate   MSC: Analyzing
OBJ: 2 / 3

5. Identify the three major ways that the U.S. Constitution
addressed the institution of slavery. Would you say the
Constitution was a proslavery or an antislavery document? Explain your answer.

ANS: Answers will vary   TOP: Civil rights | Constitu-
tional history | Social history | Slavery in the Constitu-
tion   DIF: Moderate   MSC: Evaluating   OBJ: 2 / 4

6. Explain the arguments of the Anti-Federalists. How did
they define liberty and what role did they see government having in protecting that liberty?

ANS: Answers will vary   TOP: Constitutional history |
The Anti-Federalists   DIF: Moderate
MSC: Understanding   OBJ: 3

7. What do you see as the chief contributions of the Bill of
Rights to American life today?

ANS: Answers will vary   TOP: Constitutional history |
Social history | The Bill of Rights   DIF: Difficult
MSC: Evaluating   OBJ: 3

8. Using *Letters from an American Farmer* and *Notes on the State of Virginia,* discuss the reach of American citizenship. What did it take to be free and to have liberties in the new nation? According to Crèvecoeur and Jefferson, would there ever be a time when America might be a melting pot of more than just white Europeans?

   ANS: Answers will vary   TOP: Civil Rights | Ethnicity | Social history | National Identity | Indians in the New Nation | Blacks and the Republic | Jefferson, Slavery, and Race   DIF: Difficult
   MSC: Analyzing   OBJ: 4

9. As Benjamin Franklin left the room in which the Constitutional Convention was held, supposedly a woman asked him, "What have you men given us in there?" He replied, "A republic, if you can keep it." What do you think Franklin meant by that statement? Certainly think back to the idea of a virtuous citizenry that all the founding fathers believed was essential. Your response should pull from the writings of *The Federalist* as well.

   ANS: Answers will vary   TOP: Constitutional history | *The Federalist* | The Anti-Federalists   DIF: Difficult
   MSC: Evaluating   OBJ: 3

10. Under President Washington, Secretary of War Henry Knox had hoped to pursue a more peaceful policy with the Indians. How did U.S. policy concerning the Indians unfold in the 1790s?

    Answers will vary   TOP: Ethnicity | Political history, changes | Indians in the New Nation   DIF: Moderate
    MSC: Understanding   OBJ: 4

CHAPTER 8 | Securing the Republic, 1790–1815

This chapter concentrates on the political history of the new nation as it enlarged its boundaries and solidified its independence. Starting with George Washington's inauguration, the chapter explains how the founding fathers believed that the preservation of liberty and freedom for the republic relied on the success of the American experiment in self-government. Contrasting views as to how America should develop economically and how its government should operate emerged with the formation of America's first political parties in the early 1790s. Federalists supported Alexander Hamilton's program for economic growth while Republicans embraced Thomas Jefferson's vision of an agrarian republic. These different points of view fostered political debates that enlarged the public sphere. An excerpt from one political society, the Democratic-Republican Society of Pennsylvania, is included in "Voices of Freedom." The chapter also explores the rights of women as a way of illustrating expanding ideas about who should enjoy freedom of expression. "Voices of Freedom" highlights a piece by Judith Sargent Murray, an advocate of increased rights for women. The chapter then examines the presidency of John Adams, highlighting the restrictions placed on liberties through the Alien and Sedition Acts and the Republican response in the Virginia and Kentucky resolutions. Further restrictions to freedom are explored when discussing slavery and politics and the attempted slave rebellion led by Gabriel. The chapter also examines the "Revolution of 1800" and Thomas Jefferson's administration. Jefferson's support for territorial expansion is exemplified by the Louisiana Purchase, which allowed for economic freedom for white farmers as well as the eventual expansion of the Cotton Kingdom and slavery. European infringements on American rights at sea jeopardized free trade, which Republicans considered essential to American freedom. The failures of embargoes as economic weapons against Great Britain and France led to economic crises at home and a cry for war from the War Hawks. In addi-tion, British support for the activities of Tecumseh, a Shawnee urging a pan-Indian response to white American encroachment on Indian lands, alarmed War Hawks. President James Madison, Jefferson's immediate successor, declared war against Great Britain in 1812, and although the war ended by establishing the status quo, it did solidify American independence and freedom from Britain for good.

CHAPTER OUTLINE

I. Introduction: George Washington's Inauguration

II. Politics in an Age of Passion
   A. Hamilton's Program
      1. As secretary of the treasury, Alexander Hamilton's long-range goal was to make the United States a major commercial and military power.
      2. His program had five parts:
         a. Create creditworthiness by assuming state debts
         b. Create a new national debt
         c. Create a bank of the United States modeled after the Bank of England
         d. Tax producers of whiskey
         e. Impose tariffs and provide government subsidies to industries
      3. He also proposed creation of a national army to deal with uprisings like Shays's Rebellion.
   B. The Emergence of Opposition
      1. Opposition to Hamilton's plan was voiced by James Madison and Thomas Jefferson.
         a. Hamilton's plan depended on a close relationship with Britain.

b. Opponents believed the United States' future lay westward, not with Britain.

c. Opponents feared threats to freedom and corruption.

C. The Jefferson-Hamilton Bargain

1. At first, opposition to Hamilton's program arose almost entirely from the South.

2. Hamilton argued the "general welfare" clause of the Constitution justified his program.

3. Jefferson insisted on "strict construction" of the Constitution, which meant the federal government could only exercise powers specifically listed in that document.

4. Jefferson agreed southerners would accept Hamilton's plan in exchange for placing the national capital on the Potomac River between Maryland and Virginia.

D. The Impact of the French Revolution

1. The French Revolution became very radical by 1793, and France went to war with Britain.

2. Despite its radicalism, Jefferson and his followers wanted to support France's attempt at self-government.

3. Washington, Hamilton, and their followers feared anarchy and gravitated toward England.

4. George Washington declared American neutrality.

5. Jay's Treaty did not address the issues with Britain on the high seas, but positioned the United States closer to Britain and abandoned the American alliance with France.

E. Political Parties

1. The Federalist Party supported Washington's and Hamilton's economic plan and close ties with Britain.

a. Freedom rested on deference to authority.

F. The Whiskey Rebellion

1. Whiskey Rebellion of 1794 proved to Federalists that democracy in the hands of ordinary citizens was dangerous.

2. Washington dispatched 13,000 troops to western Pennsylvania to put down the rebellion.

a. He accompanied them part of the way.

G. The Republican Party

1. Republicans were more sympathetic to France and had more faith in democratic self-government.

a. Led by Jefferson and Madison

2. Political language became more and more heated.

a. Each charged the other with betraying the principles of the American Revolution.

H. An Expanding Public Sphere

1. The political debates of the 1790s expanded the public sphere.

2. Newspapers and pamphlets were a primary vehicle for political debate.

a. William Manning's *The Key of Liberty*

I. The Democratic-Republican Societies

1. Supporters of the French Revolution and critics of the Washington administration formed nearly fifty Democratic-Republican Societies in 1793–1794.

2. The societies argued that political liberty meant not simply voting at elections but also constant involvement in public affairs.

3. Societies disappeared by 1795, but their outlook and organization was absorbed into the Republican Party.

4. The Republican Party gained support from political dissenters emigrating from the British Isles.

J. The Rights of Women

1. The expansion of the public sphere offered women an opportunity to take part in political discussions, read newspapers, and hear orations.

2. Mary Wollstonecraft's *A Vindication of the Rights of Woman*

3. Sarah W. Morton wrote poem about slavery.

4. Judith Sargent Murray

a. Well educated as a child, but not permitted to attend college.

b. Essay "On the Equality of the Sexes" insisted that women should be able to exercise their talents.

5. A common call was for greater educational opportunities.

K. Women and the Republic

1. Although politics was a realm for men, the American Revolution had deepened the democratization of public life.

III. The Adams Presidency

A. The Election of 1796

1. Adams won with seventy-one electoral votes, and Jefferson, with sixty-eight electoral votes, became vice president.

2. His presidency was beset by crises.

a. "XYZ affair"

b. Quasi-war with France ended with peace treaty in 1800

c. Fries's Rebellion

B. The "Reign of Witches"

1. The Alien and Sedition Acts limited civil liberties.

2. The main target was the Republican press.
   a. Ten convicted, including a Congressman and several newspaper editors

C. The Virginia and Kentucky Resolutions
  1. The Sedition Act thrust freedom of expression to the center of discussions of American liberty.
    a. Virginia and Kentucky resolutions written by Madison and Jefferson
    b. Focused on federal government, not the states

D. The "Revolution of 1800"
  1. Jefferson defeated Adams in the 1800 presidential campaign.
  2. A constitutional crisis emerged with the election.
    a. Jefferson and Burr finished tied with seventy-three electoral votes.
    b. House decided election with Hamilton swinging votes to Jefferson.
  3. Twelfth Amendment
  4. Hamilton-Burr duel
  5. Adams's acceptance of defeat established the vital precedent of a peaceful transfer of power from a defeated party to its successor.

E. Slavery and Politics
  1. Jefferson's election as president was aided by the three-fifths clause, which gave a disproportionate number of electoral votes to southern states.
  2. The first Congress received petitions calling for emancipation, which set off a long sectional debate in that body.
  3. In 1793, Congress adopted a law to enforce the Constitution's fugitive slave clause.

F. The Haitian Revolution
  1. Events during the 1790s underscored how powerfully slavery defined and distorted American freedom.
  2. A successful slave uprising led by Toussaint L'Ouverture established Haiti as an independent nation in 1804.
    a. Adams, hoping to gain Haiti's sugar trade, supported the revolution.
    b. Jefferson, however, sought to quarantine and destroy Haiti.

G. Gabriel's Rebellion
  1. A slave rebellion was attempted in Virginia in 1800.
  2. The conspiracy was rooted in Richmond's black community.
  3. Gabriel spoke the language of liberty forged in the American Revolution and reinvigorated during the 1790s.

  4. Gabriel and twenty-five others executed before rebellion started.
  5. Virginia's slave laws became stricter.

IV. Jefferson in Power
  1. Jefferson's inaugural address was conciliatory toward his opponents.
  2. However, he hoped to dismantle as much of the Federalist system as possible.

A. Judicial Review
  1. John Marshall, strong believer in national supremacy, was Chief Justice of Supreme Court.
  2. *Marbury v. Madison* (1803) established the precedent of the Court's power of judicial review relative to federal laws.
  3. *Fletcher v. Peck* (1810) extended judicial review to state laws.

B. The Louisiana Purchase
  1. To purchase Louisiana, Jefferson had to abandon his conviction that the federal government was limited to powers specifically mentioned in the Constitution.
  2. Jefferson's concern with the territory was over trade through New Orleans.
  3. Jefferson asserted that the additional territory would allow the republic to remain agrarian and therefore virtuous; he believed that justified his abandonment of "strict construction" principles.

C. Lewis and Clark
  1. Lewis and Clark's objective was both scientific and commercial.
  2. Their journey from 1804 to 1806 brought invaluable information and paved the way for a transcontinental country.

D. Incorporating Louisiana
  1. In 1803, New Orleans was the only part of the Louisiana Purchase territory with a significant non-Indian population.
  2. Louisiana's slaves had enjoyed far more freedom under the rule of Spain than they would as part of the liberty-loving United States.

E. The Barbary Wars
  1. European wars directly influenced the livelihood of American farmers, merchants, and artisans.
    a. Jefferson hoped to avoid foreign entanglements.
  2. Barbary pirates from North Africa demanded bribes from American ships.
  3. Because Jefferson refused to increase payments to the pirates, the United States and

Tripoli engaged in a naval conflict that ended with American victory in 1804.
   a. This was United States' first encounter with the Islamic world.

F. The Embargo
1. War between France and Great Britain hurt American trade.
   a. Britain resumed impressment.
2. Embargo Act resulted in a crippled U.S. economy.
   a. Replaced with Non-Intercourse Act

G. Madison and Pressure for War
1. Macon's Bill no. 2 allowed trade to resume.
2. War Hawks called for war against Britain.
   a. Wished to annex Canada and some southern War Hawks wanted Florida.

V. The Second War for Independence
A. The Indian Response
1. Jefferson hoped to move Indians west of the Mississippi River.
2. By 1800 nearly 400,000 Americans lived west of the Appalachian Mountains.
3. The period from 1800 to 1812 was an "age of prophecy" among Indians as they sought to regain their autonomy.

B. Tecumseh's Vision
1. Tecumseh and Tenskwatawa tried to revive a pan-Indian movement and unite against white Americans.
2. William Henry Harrison destroyed Prophetstown at the Battle of Tippecanoe (1811).

C. The War of 1812
1. Madison asked for war for the sake of national pride.
2. The government found it difficult to finance the war.
3. Americans enjoyed few military successes.
   a. British invaded Washington, D.C. and burned the White House.
   b. Indian tribes siding with British were defeated in Midwest and South.
   c. Jackson achieved the war's greatest victory for the United States at New Orleans in January 1815.
   d. Peace officially came with the Treaty of Ghent in December 1814, although news of it did not arrive until after the Battle of New Orleans.
   e. Thousands of slaves escaped to the British side, most of whom settled in Nova Scotia.
4. Eventually British compensated millions of dollars for loss of slave property.

D. The War's Aftermath
1. The war confirmed the ability of a republican government to conduct a war without surrendering its institutions.
2. The war also strengthened a growing sense of nationalism in Canada.

E. The End of the Federalist Party
1. Hartford Convention was meeting of disgruntled Federalists.
2. Asked for:
   a. amending three-fifths clause
   b. declaration of war vote to be two-thirds
   c. right of state to "interpose" its authority with regard to federal law it saw as unconstitutional
3. Jackson's victory at New Orleans overshadowed Federalist demands.
   a. Within a few years the party disappeared.
4. Federalists raised an issue—southern domination of government—that long outlived their party.

SUGGESTED DISCUSSION QUESTIONS

- Describe how and why political parties arose.
- Explain why Thomas Jefferson thought Alexander Hamilton's economic system "flowed from principles adverse to liberty, and was calculated to undermine and demolish the republic."
- Who did Gabriel think might support his rebellion and why? How was the language of liberty and freedom invoked by Gabriel?
- Why was Napoleon willing to sell the Louisiana territory to the United States?
- Describe the ironies of the Jefferson administration. Compare his views toward a strong central government and his actions as president.
- The War of 1812 is sometimes referred to as the Second War for Independence. Do you think that this is an appropriate title? Why, or why not?
- Reflect back to James Madison's arguments in *The Federalist* that diversity and debate would strengthen the republic, rather than weaken it. Did the events of the 1790 to 1815 period prove Madison right or wrong?
- Discuss the views of Alexander Hamilton and Thomas Jefferson with regard to their interpretations of the Constitution, whether the national government was supreme and their visions of the future America.
- It is 1800. Have the students divide into two groups and organize a political campaign—one side for John Adams, the other for Thomas Jefferson. Have each side nominate one student to represent Adams or Jefferson, while the other students help to write newspaper ads, speeches, policy agendas, and so forth.

SUPPLEMENTAL WEB AND VISUAL RESOURCES

Alexander Hamilton

http://xroads.virginia.edu/~CAP/ham/hamilton.html
This site is a useful resource for exploring Hamilton's political battles as a constitutional reformer. It also includes his background and his changing image through time.

George Washington

http://rotunda.upress.virginia.edu/founders/GEWN
With this digital edition of *The Papers of George Washington*, you may browse, and even do word searches, in the diaries and correspondence of the first president of the United States.

James Madison

http://millercenter.org/president/madison
The Miller Center is part of the University of Virginia. This website page contains links to essays on Madison, including his presidency. There is also a fact sheet about his presidency.

John and Abigail Adams

www.pbs.org/wgbh/amex/adams
American Experience has a special called *John & Abigail Adams*. The subtitle, *Meet the Original Power Couple*, captures the flavor of this dynamic story.

Lewis and Clark

www.pbs.org/lewisandclark/
This website contains numerous links related to the 1997 documentary about Lewis and Clark produced by Ken Burns.

www.mnh.si.edu/lewisandclark/index.html?loc=/lewisandclark/home.html
From the Smithsonian Institution's National Museum of Natural History, this site has an interactive map of Lewis and Clark's trail and explores the flora and fauna they discovered.

Madison and His Time Period
Tecumseh and Tenskwatawa
www.pbs.org/wgbh/amex/weshallremain/the_films/episode_2_about
From the PBS series American Experience, this film examines the pan-Indian movement of the Shawnee brothers, Tecumseh and Tenskwatawa.

The Price of Freedom: Americans at War

americanhistory.si.edu/militaryhistory/exhibition/flash.html
From the Smithsonian Institution's National Museum of American History, select a war (War of 1812) and enter an exhibit that includes a movie, learning resources, statistics, printable exhibition, maps, and time lines.

Thomas Paine

www.infidels.org/library/historical/thomas_paine/index.shtml
This site has a large collection of articles written by Thomas Paine. Included are *The Age of Reason* and *The Rights of Man*.

SUPPLEMENTAL PRINT RESOURCES

Ambrose, Stephen. *Undaunted Courage: Meriwether Lewis, Thomas Jefferson, and the Opening of the American West*. New York: Simon and Schuster, 1997.

Appleby, Joyce. *Inheriting the Revolution: The First Generation of Americans*. Cambridge, MA: Harvard University Press, 2000.

Balieck, Barry. "When the Ends Justify the Means: Thomas Jefferson and the Louisiana Purchase." *Presidential Studies Quarterly* 22, no. 4 (1992): 679–696.

Bolster, W. Jeffrey. *Black Jacks: African American Seamen in the Age of Sail*. Cambridge, MA: Harvard University Press, 1997.

Cornell, Saul. *The Other Founders: Anti-Federalism and the Dissenting Tradition in America, 1788–1828*. Chapel Hill, NC: University of North Carolina Press, 1999.

Dowd, Gregory. *A Spirited Resistance: The North American Indian Struggle for Unity, 1745–1815*. Baltimore, MD: The Johns Hopkins University Press, 1993.

Edmunds, R. David. *Tecumseh and the Quest for Indian Leadership*, 2nd edition. White Plains, NY: Pearson Longman, 2007.

Elkins, Stanley, and Eric McKitrick. *The Age of Federalism: The Early American Republic, 1788–1800*. New York: Oxford University Press, 1993.

Ferling, John. *Adams vs. Jefferson: The Tumultuous Election of 1800*. New York: Oxford University Press, 2004.

Freeman, Joanne. *Affairs of Honor: National Politics in the New Republic*. New Haven, CT: Yale University Press, 2001.

Knott, Stephen. *Alexander Hamilton and the Persistence of Myth*. Lawrence, KS: University Press of Kansas, 2002.

McCullough, David. *John Adams*. New York: Simon and Schuster, 2001.

Read, James. *Power Versus Liberty: Madison, Hamilton, Wilson, and Jefferson*. Charlottesville, VA: University of Virginia Press, 2000.

Skeen, C. Edward. *Citizen Soldiers in the War of 1812*. Lexington, KY: University of Kentucky Press, 1999.

Thomas, Ray. " 'Not One Cent for Tribute': The Public Addresses and American Popular Reaction to the XYZ Affair." *Journal of the Early American Republic* 34, no. 3 (1983): 389–412.

Tise, Larry. *The American Counter-Revolution: A Retreat from Liberty, 1783–1800*. Mechanicsburg, PA: Stackpole Books, 1999.

Tucker, Robert, and David Hendrickson. *Empire of Liberty: The Statecraft of Thomas Jefferson*. New York: Oxford University Press, 1990.

Wallace, Anthony. *Jefferson and the Indians: The Tragic Fate of the First Americans*. Cambridge, MA: Harvard University Press, 1999.

Wood, Gordon S. *Empire of Liberty: A History of the Early Republic, 1789–1815*. New York: Oxford University Press, 2009.

TEST BANK

Matching

TEST I

____ 1. Gabriel

____ 2. Tecumseh

___ 3. John Marshall
___ 4. John Fries
___ 5. Matthew Lyon
___ 6. Mary Wollstonecraft
___ 7. Benjamin Franklin
___ 8. Toussaint L'Ouverture
___ 9. Henry Clay
___ 10. Aaron Burr
___ 11. Sarah Morton
___ 12. Judith Sargent Murray

a. accused under the Sedition Act
b. chief justice of the Supreme Court
c. Haitian slave revolutionary
d. organizer of a slave rebellion in America
e. Pennsylvania militia leader tried for treason
f. president of the Pennsylvania Abolition Society
g. shot Alexander Hamilton in a duel
h. wrote *A Vindication of the Rights of Woman*
i. wrote *The African Chief*
j. War Hawk
k. argued for equal educational opportunities for women
l. pan-Indian movement

Answer Key: d, l, b, e, a, h, f, c, j, g, i, k

TEST 2

___ 1. strict constructionist
___ 2. Jay's Treaty
___ 3. Fries's Rebellion
___ 4. Louisiana territory
___ 5. War Hawks
___ 6. *Marbury v. Madison*
___ 7. Virginia resolution
___ 8. impressments
___ 9. Sedition Act
___ 10. quasi-war
___ 11. Hartford Convention
___ 12. XYZ affair

a. judicial review
b. bribery scandal
c. attacked the Sedition Act as unconstitutional
d. Pennsylvanian farmer uprising
e. unofficial conflict with France
f. forced American sailors into the British navy
g. restrictions placed on freedom of the press
h. ended the Federalist Party
i. called for war against Britain
j. government could only do exactly what the Constitution stated
k. negotiated with Britain
l. bought for $15 million

Answer Key: j, k, d, l, i, a, c, f, g, e, h, b

Learning Objectives

1. Identify the issues that made the politics of the 1790s so divisive.
2. Explain how the competing views of freedom and global events promoted the political divisions of the 1790s.
3. Identify the achievements and failures of Jefferson's presidency.
4. Explain the causes and significant results of the War of 1812.

Multiple Choice

1. When George Washington took office as the first president of the United States, American leaders believed that the new nation's success depended on:
   a. creating political parties as a means of channeling the people's passions.
   b. maintaining political harmony.
   c. protecting all forms of freedom.
   d. Washington's willingness to serve until he died.
   e. coining money.

   ANS: B   TOP: Political history, changes | Introduction: George Washington's Inauguration
   DIF: Moderate   REF: Full p. 273 | Seagull p. 283
   MSC: Remembering   OBJ: 1

2. All of the following men held a high executive or judicial office during George Washington's presidency EXCEPT:
   a. John Adams.
   b. Thomas Jefferson.
   c. James Madison.
   d. Alexander Hamilton.
   e. John Jay.

   ANS: C   TOP: Political history, changes | Politics in an Age of Passion   DIF : Difficult
   REF: Full pp. 273–274 | Seagull p. 283
   MSC: Remembering   OBJ: 1

3. Alexander Hamilton's long-term goal was to:
   a. build up the Republican Party's political power.
   b. assure that the United States would be a primarily agrarian nation.
   c. promote the power of state governments.
   d. make the United States a major commercial and military power.
   e. succeed George Washington as president.

   ANS: D   TOP: Economic development | Hamilton's Program   DIF: Easy   REF: Full p. 274 | Seagull pp. 283–284   MSC: Remembering   OBJ: 1

4. Which of the following was NOT part of Alexander Hamilton's financial program?

a. creating a new national debt, thereby giving bondholders a stake in the nation's future
b. the Bank of the United States, modeled on the Bank of England
c. a tax on whiskey producers as a means of raising revenue
d. taxes and subsidies to promote American manufacturing
e. a national capital city with experimental manufacturing

ANS: E   TOP: Economic development | Hamilton's Program   DIF: Moderate   REF: Full p. 274 | Seagull p. 284   MSC: Remembering   OBJ: 1

5. Which of the following was NOT an objection raised by critics of Hamilton's proposals?
a. Creating a standing army would threaten individual liberty.
b. A whiskey tax would unfairly target backcountry farmers used to distilling their grain.
c. Hamilton's program would create a corrupt alliance between government and large commercial interests.
d. The proposals would prevent the development of manufacturing, and manufacturing was vital to America's future.
e. Hamilton's plan for new government bonds would unfairly reward speculators.

ANS: D   TOP: Political history, changes | The Emergence of Opposition   DIF: Easy   REF: Full p. 275 | Seagull pp. 285–286   MSC: Understanding   OBJ: 1

6. Opponents of Hamilton's economic plan:
a. included George Washington.
b. were mostly northerners who had supported ratification of the Constitution.
c. believed future growth was to be found through close ties with Britain.
d. agreed to a compromise that included placing the national capital in the South.
e. were simply jealous of Hamilton's close relationship with Washington.

ANS: D   TOP: Political history, changes | The Jefferson-Hamilton Bargain   DIF: Moderate   REF: Full p. 275 | Seagull p. 286   MSC: Remembering   OBJ: 1

7. "Strict constructionists" believed:
a. Jay's Treaty should be construed or interpreted to put more restrictions on Indians.
b. freedom of speech and of the press should be restricted if the president believed that to be necessary.
c. the federal government could only exercise powers specifically listed in the Constitution.

d. the "general welfare" clause of the Constitution gave the federal government power to create a national bank.
e. the creation of new western settlements should be strictly limited in order to avoid Indian wars.

ANS: C   TOP: Constitutional history | The Jefferson-Hamilton Bargain   DIF: Moderate   REF: Full p. 275 | Seagull p. 286   MSC: Remembering   OBJ: 1

8. Pierre Charles L'Enfant is well known for:
a. leading a slave rebellion in Saint Domingue.
b. designing Washington, D.C.
c. masterminding the XYZ affair.
d. negotiating the Louisiana Purchase.
e. writing *Letters from an American Farmer*.

ANS: B   TOP: Cultural history | The Jefferson-Hamilton Bargain   DIF: Moderate   REF: Full p. 275 | Seagull p. 286   MSC: Remembering   OBJ: 1

9. Benjamin Banneker was:
a. a scientist who helped survey the new national capital.
b. congressional leader of the opposition to Hamilton in the early 1790s.
c. the secretary of war who publicly disagreed with Washington over Indian policy.
d. an African-American slave whose capture inspired the Fugitive Slave Law.
e. the first black person elected to Congress when he won election in the "Revolution of 1800."

ANS: A   TOP: Cultural history | The Jefferson-Hamilton Bargain   DIF: Moderate   REF: Full pp. 275–276 | Seagull p. 286   MSC: Remembering   OBJ: 1

10. How did Americans respond to the French Revolution?
a. Almost everyone supported it at first, because the French seemed to be following in Americans' footsteps.
b. Hamilton supported the creation of a standing army to prepare the nation should French radicalism spread across the Atlantic.
c. Opponents of the French Revolution formed the Republican Party, headed by Thomas Jefferson.
d. They blocked passage of Jay's Treaty, which showed preference for Great Britain.
e. President Washington immediately spoke out against French radicals and dispatched American warships to assist England.

ANS: A   TOP: Global awareness | The Impact of the French Revolution   DIF: Moderate   REF: Full p. 276 | Seagull p. 287   MSC: Understanding   OBJ: 1

11. What happened to King Louis XVI during the French Revolution?
    a. He abdicated the throne and moved to Switzerland.
    b. He successfully fled to Austria with his wife.
    c. He ruled as a less powerful constitutional monarch after the Revolution.
    d. He was executed.
    e. He was rescued from French imprisonment by British spies.

    ANS: D   TOP: Global awareness | The Impact of the French Revolution   DIF: Easy   REF: Full p. 276 | Seagull p. 287   MSC: Remembering   OBJ: 2

12. Which international partner did Alexander Hamilton think most important for the survival and prosperity of the United States?
    a. the Indians
    b. the Spanish
    c. the French
    d. the West Indians
    e. the British

    ANS: E   TOP: Global awareness | The Impact of the French Revolution   DIF: Moderate   REF: Full p. 276 | Seagull p. 287   MSC: Remembering OBJ: 2

13. Edmond Genet was a French diplomat who:
    a. was also a British spy, which led to his arrest in the United States.
    b. commissioned American ships to fight the British.
    c. sought refuge in America as soon as the French Revolution began in 1789.
    d. became a key adviser to President Washington on European affairs.
    e. sought unsuccessfully to convince the Democratic-Republican Societies to support the French Revolution.

    ANS: B   TOP: Global awareness | The Impact of the French Revolution   DIF : Difficult   REF: Full p. 277 | Seagull p. 287   MSC: Remembering   OBJ: 1

14. Which of the following led directly to the formation of an organized political party opposed to the Federalist Party?
    a. Hamilton-Burr duel
    b. election of 1800
    c. Shays's Rebellion
    d. Virginia and Kentucky Resolutions
    e. Jay's Treaty

    ANS: E   TOP: Political history, changes | The Impact of the French Revolution   DIF: Moderate REF: Full p. 277 | Seagull pp. 287–288 MSC: Remembering   OBJ: 1

15. Which of the following is true of the Whiskey Rebellion of 1794?
    a. The "rebels" largely blamed the Republican Party for their troubles.
    b. The Rebellion ended after a battle in which the "rebel" leader, Rufus King, was killed.
    c. It represented the first major challenge to the administration of President John Adams.
    d. It was the only time in U.S. history that the president commanded an army in the field.
    e. The Rebellion demonstrated that North-South divisions over slavery could turn violent.

    ANS: D   TOP: Political history, changes | The Whiskey Rebellion   DIF: Moderate   REF: Full pp. 278–279 | Seagull p. 288   MSC: Remembering   OBJ: 1

16. The French Revolution:
    a. was very conservative compared to the American Revolution.
    b. reinforced the Republicans' sympathy toward the French.
    c. brought American troops to France to fight for liberty.
    d. had very little impact on american foreign policy.
    e. had the support of the American Federalist Party.

    ANS: B   TOP: Global awareness | The Republican Party   DIF: Moderate   REF: Full p. 279 | Seagull p. 289   MSC: Remembering   OBJ: 2

17. The Democratic-Republican Societies of the 1790s:
    a. criticized the Washington administration.
    b. spoke out against the French Revolution.
    c. formed only about a dozen chapters in various cities.
    d. strongly supported Hamilton's economic program.
    e. broke up and created the Democratic and Republican parties by 1797.

    ANS: A   TOP: Political history, changes | The Democratic-Republican Societies   DIF: Moderate REF: Full p. 280 | Seagull p. 290 MSC: Remembering   OBJ: 1

18. Mary Wollstonecraft's *A Vindication of the Rights of Woman*:
    a. was the first pamphlet published in the United States by an American woman.
    b. was inspired by Thomas Paine's *Rights of Man*.
    c. won strong support from the Federalist Party.
    d. strongly challenged traditional gender roles.
    e. was based on her experiences as a cross-dressing soldier during the Revolutionary War.

    ANS: B   TOP: Social history | The Rights of Women DIF: Moderate   REF: Full p. 281 | Seagull p. 291 MSC: Remembering   OBJ: 1

19. Which of the following is true of women and political life in the new republic of the 1790s?
    a. The use of the word "male" in various provisions of the Constitution of 1787 excluded women from any role in politics.
    b. Women, unlike white men and male African-American slaves, were specifically not counted in determining congressional representation.
    c. Some women contributed to a growing democratization of political life by arguing for increased rights for their sex.
    d. By 1799, women actually gained the right to vote, but not the right to hold office, in four New England states and in Pennsylvania.
    e. The prevailing view of women as intellectually inferior to men meant that women's involvement in politics never was considered.

    ANS: C   TOP: Social history | The Rights of Women
    DIF: Difficult   REF: Full p. 281 | Seagull pp. 291, 294
    MSC: Remembering   OBJ: 1

20. Judith Sargent Murray argued that women's apparent mental inferiority to men simply reflected the fact that women had been denied:
    a. educational opportunities.
    b. the right to vote.
    c. the right to own private property.
    d. enough leisure time.
    e. the ability to earn a living wage.

    ANS: A   TOP: Social history | The Rights of Women
    DIF: Easy   REF: Full p. 281 | Seagull p. 294
    MSC: Remembering   OBJ: 1

21. The 1796 election pitted John Adams and Thomas Pinckney against:
    a. James Madison and John Marshall.
    b. Thomas Jefferson and Aaron Burr.
    c. Aaron Burr and John Jay.
    d. Thomas Jefferson and James Madison.
    e. Alexander Hamilton and Aaron Burr.

    ANS: B   TOP: Political history, changes | The Election of 1796   DIF: Difficult   REF: Full p. 284 | Seagull p. 295   MSC: Remembering   OBJ: 1

22. Which of the following was NOT true of the United States in 1797?
    a. The two political parties not only demonstrated divisions in the nation, but were divided within themselves.
    b. John Adams, the new president, was brilliant but austere and stubborn.
    c. American neutrality in the European war was not working; both England and France were seizing American ships with impunity.

    d. The United States already was divided along sectional lines, with Federalists strong in New England and Republicans strong in the South.
    e. Believing that political parties were wrong, Adams included Jefferson and Hamilton in his government, and they did not get along.

    ANS: E   TOP: Political history, changes | The Election of 1796   DIF: Difficult   REF: Full pp. 284–285 | Seagull p. 296   MSC: Understanding   OBJ: 1

23. The "quasi-war" was a war of the United States against:
    a. England.
    b. Spain.
    c. the Netherlands.
    d. France.
    e. Canada.

    ANS: D   TOP: Global awareness | Military history | The Election of 1796   DIF: Moderate   REF: Full p. 285 | Seagull p. 296   MSC: Remembering   OBJ: 2

24. Fries's Rebellion:
    a. was an uprising in Massachusetts.
    b. was provoked because of heavy taxes on whiskey.
    c. resulted in over 300 deaths and much property destruction.
    d. resulted in the execution of John Fries for treason.
    e. resulted in a loss of support for Federalists in southeastern Pennsylvania.

    ANS: E   TOP: Political history, changes | The Election of 1796   DIF: Difficult   REF: Full p. 285 | Seagull p. 296   MSC: Remembering   OBJ: 1

25. The Sedition Act targeted:
    a. Alexander Hamilton's economic ideas.
    b. Federalists.
    c. the Republican press.
    d. illegal immigrants.
    e. British sympathizers.

    ANS: C   TOP: Political history, changes | The "Reign of Witches"   DIF: Moderate   REF: Full p. 286 | Seagull p. 297   MSC: Remembering   OBJ: 2

26. The Virginia and Kentucky resolutions were a response to:
    a. the election of 1800.
    b. Hamilton's economic plan.
    c. the Alien and Sedition Acts.
    d. Fries's Rebellion.
    e. impressments of American sailors.

    ANS: C   TOP: Political history, changes | The Virginia and Kentucky Resolutions   DIF: Moderate   REF: Full p. 286 | Seagull p. 297   MSC: Remembering   OBJ: 2

27. The Kentucky resolution originally stated that:
    a. states could nullify laws of Congress.
    b. militia could be called on to put down rebellion with force.
    c. freedom of the press could be suspended in time of war.
    d. access to the Mississippi River was reserved only for American citizens.
    e. the United States should go to war in 1812 for conquest of Canada.

    ANS: A   TOP: Political history, changes | The Virginia and Kentucky Resolutions   DIF: Moderate
    REF: Full p. 286 | Seagull p. 297   MSC: Remembering
    OBJ: 2

28. The Sedition Act of 1798:
    a. targeted recent arrivals to the United States.
    b. led to the jailing of Federalist editors.
    c. was more stringent and oppressive than similar laws in Europe.
    d. led Jefferson to argue that states, not the federal government, could punish seditious speech.
    e. was declared unconstitutional by the U.S. Supreme Court two years later.

    ANS: D   TOP: Political history, changes | The Virginia and Kentucky Resolutions   DIF: Moderate
    REF: Full pp. 286–287 | Seagull p. 298
    MSC: Remembering   OBJ: 2

29. Which of the following is NOT true of the presidential election of 1800?
    a. John Adams's acceptance of defeat established the precedent of the peaceful transfer of power in the United States.
    b. The importance of slavery and the three-fifths compromise was demonstrated: without slaves counted as part of the South's population, Thomas Jefferson would have lost.
    c. The election demonstrated the importance of mobilizing large numbers of voters with more modern campaign techniques, which the Republicans effectively employed.
    d. The controversy surrounding who would be president led to the passage of the Twelfth Amendment, which changed the operation of the electoral college.
    e. Thomas Jefferson's victory in the New England states proved to be key to his election.

    ANS: E   TOP: Political history, changes | The "Revolution of 1800" | Slavery and Politics
    DIF: Difficult   REF: Full pp. 287–288 | Seagull pp. 298–300   MSC: Understanding   OBJ: 1

30. Who wrote a petition to Congress as the president of the Pennsylvania Abolition Society, calling for the end of slavery?
    a. Mathew Lyon
    b. Patrick Henry
    c. Sarah Morton
    d. Mary Wollstonecraft
    e. Benjamin Franklin

    ANS: E   TOP: Political history, changes | Slavery and Politics   DIF: Moderate   REF: Full p. 288 |
    Seagull p. 300   MSC: Remembering
    OBJ: 2

31. Which of the following is true of the American response to Toussaint L'Ouverture's slave uprising, which led to the establishment of Haiti as an independent nation in 1804?
    a. John Adams opposed it because it was a threat to the established order.
    b. Thomas Jefferson welcomed Haitian independence as another example of what he had advocated in the Declaration of Independence.
    c. Most white Americans were glad to see France, which had turned politically radical, suffer the loss of Haiti.
    d. Most enslaved Americans opposed L'Ouverture's success because they believed it might inspire a white crackdown on their behavior.
    e. Many white Americans considered L'Ouverture's uprising to be evidence of blacks' unfitness for republican freedom.

    ANS: E   TOP: Global awareness | The Haitian Revolution   DIF: Difficult   REF: Full p. 289 |
    Seagull p. 301   MSC: Understanding
    OBJ: 1

32. Gabriel's Rebellion:
    a. was doomed to fail because the African-American population of Richmond was so small.
    b. demonstrated that the slaves were as aware of the idea of liberty as anyone else.
    c. inspired Virginia to adopt a gradual emancipation law in 1803.
    d. failed partly because its leaders were plantation slaves, who had less contact with the outside world and were unaware of how little support they enjoyed.
    e. prompted several states to pass laws requiring slaves to be educated about the Constitution and the importance of obeying the law.

    ANS: B   TOP: Civil rights | Gabriel's Rebellion
    DIF: Difficult   REF: Full p. 290 | Seagull p. 302
    MSC: Understanding   OBJ: 2

33. After becoming president, how did Thomas Jefferson deal with the Federalists?
    a. He followed through on his inauguration speech's statement ("We are all Republicans, we are all Federalists") and treated them as equals.
    b. He courted their support because he knew that he could never win approval for his policies without them.
    c. He tried to roll back almost everything they had done by cutting taxes and the size of government.
    d. Until just before leaving office, he used the Sedition Act to shut down Federalist newspapers critical of his administration.
    e. He led a successful effort to impeach and remove from office all Federalist judges, whom he then replaced with Republicans.

    ANS: C   TOP: Political history, changes | Jefferson in Power   DIF: Difficult   REF: Full p. 290 | Seagull p. 303   MSC: Understanding   OBJ: 3

34. What was the significance of the case of *Marbury v. Madison*?
    a. It was John Marshall's first case as chief justice.
    b. The Supreme Court asserted the power of judicial review.
    c. The Supreme Court declared that presidential power was greater than congressional power.
    d. The decision gave states important new powers to block a too-powerful federal government.
    e. Marbury's win meant that he became the new chief justice, a post he held for twenty-one years.

    ANS: B   TOP: Constitutional history | Judicial Review   DIF: Moderate   REF: Full pp. 291–292 | Seagull p. 303   MSC: Remembering   OBJ: 3

35. In its decision in the case of *Fletcher v. Peck,* the U.S. Supreme Court:
    a. exercised the authority to overturn a state law that the Court considered in violation of the U.S. Constitution.
    b. declared that corruption involved in the making of a law automatically invalidated that law.
    c. held that slaves who ran away from their masters had to be returned to them, even if the slaves had gone to a free state.
    d. asserted that political parties were constitutional even though they were not mentioned in the 1787 document.
    e. said that the purchase of land from a foreign power, as in the case of Louisiana, was constitutional.

    ANS: A   TOP: Constitutional history | Judicial Review   DIF: Difficult   REF: Full p. 292 | Seagull pp. 303–304   MSC: Remembering   OBJ: 3

36. The land involved in the Louisiana Purchase:
    a. had been claimed by France from the 1600s until the United States acquired it.
    b. included all of what is now Texas and the American Southwest.
    c. was considered by Jefferson to be practically worthless, yet he did not want it to fall into British hands.
    d. stretched from the Gulf of Mexico to Canada and from the Mississippi River to the Rocky Mountains.
    e. consisted only of what is today the state of Louisiana and the southern half of Arkansas.

    ANS: D   TOP: Geographic issues | The Louisiana Purchase   DIF: Difficult   REF: Full p. 292 | Seagull p. 304   MSC: Remembering   OBJ: 3

37. Which of the following is true of the Louisiana Purchase?
    a. The slave rebellion in Haiti almost persuaded Napoleon to keep Louisiana as a base from which to attack the island if necessary.
    b. France had guaranteed the United States commercial access to New Orleans, but Jefferson feared that a British victory over France would deprive the United States of that access.
    c. Jefferson believed that the Constitution explicitly and fully authorized this land deal.
    d. Jefferson expected the land acquisition to make possible the spread of agrarian republicanism.
    e. Ironically, a majority of Republican congressmen opposed the Purchase, so Federalist votes ultimately made its approval possible.

    ANS: D   TOP: Geographic issues | The Louisiana Purchase   DIF: Difficult   REF: Full p. 294 | Seagull p. 306   MSC: Remembering   OBJ: 3

38. Which of the following is NOT true about the expedition of Meriwether Lewis and William Clark?
    a. They never reached the Pacific coast.
    b. They found that the regions west of the Mississippi were already engaging in global trade.
    c. It took them two years to complete their journey.
    d. They brought back numerous plant and animal specimens.
    e. They were seeking a water route to the Pacific Ocean.

    ANS: A   TOP: Geographic issues | Lewis and Clark   DIF: Moderate   REF: Full p. 294 | Seagull p. 306   MSC: Remembering   OBJ: 3

39. Sacajawea was:
    a. an elderly Indian woman whom Lewis and Clark enslaved during their journey.
    b. born to a French-Canadian fur trapper and his native wife during Lewis and Clark's journey.

c. a guide and interpreter for the Lewis and Clark expedition.

d. the only member of the Lewis and Clark expedition to return safely to St. Louis.

e. the young Shoshone woman whom William Clark married during his winter in North Dakota.

ANS: C   TOP: Ethnicity | Geographic issues | Lewis and Clark   DIF: Moderate   REF: Full p. 294 | Seagull p. 306   MSC: Remembering OBJ: 3

40. Which of the following statements is true of New Orleans under Spanish rule?
    a. Men and women enjoyed complete legal equality, which was unheard of in the United States.
    b. Slavery was illegal.
    c. Slave women had the right to go to court for protection against cruelty or rape by their owners.
    d. An owner could not free his or her slaves without special permission from the Spanish monarch.
    e. Native Americans had been considered full citizens, with all of the rights and privileges associated with that status.

ANS: C   TOP: Civil rights | Incorporating Louisiana DIF: Difficult   REF: Full p. 294 | Seagull p. 307 MSC: Remembering   OBJ: 3

41. Why did Jefferson use the U.S. navy against North African states?
    a. The Barbary pirates held American merchant ships hostage and Jefferson sent in the navy rather than pay the ransom.
    b. Jefferson wanted to disarm the pasha of Tripoli, who had gathered weapons he planned to use against the United States.
    c. Plantation owners wanted to import more Africans before the international slave trade became illegal in 1808, and they needed American firepower to help them do it.
    d. Jefferson had tried to cut the naval budget, and Federalists had accused him of being wishy-washy; Jefferson wanted to show that he could be tough.
    e. Tripoli had declared war on the United States after Jefferson had refused demands for increased payments to the Barbary pirates.

ANS: E   TOP: Global awareness | Military history | The Barbary Wars   DIF: Difficult   REF: Full p. 296 | Seagull p. 308   MSC: Remembering   OBJ: 3

42. What was unusual about the Embargo Act of 1807?
    a. It was in response to a British embargo imposed after a British ship sank an American ship—an odd set of circumstances, to say the least.

b. The Republican majority in Congress passed it and Jefferson vetoed it, but he was overridden for the only time in his presidency.

c. It stopped all American vessels from sailing to foreign ports—an amazing use of federal power, especially by a president supposedly dedicated to a weak central government.

d. It would hurt France more than Great Britain, and Jefferson was ardently pro-French.

e. It persuaded the British to agree to American terms, even though Great Britain had not been a target of the Embargo Act.

ANS: C   TOP: Political history, changes | The Embargo   DIF: Moderate   REF: Full p. 296 | Seagull p. 309   MSC: Understanding   OBJ: 3

43. Jefferson's Embargo Act:
    a. was successful in restoring freedom of the seas.
    b. stopped the policy of impressment.
    c. severely hurt the economies of France and England.
    d. provoked war with France.
    e. caused economic depression within the United States.

ANS: E   TOP: Economic development | The Embargo DIF: Moderate   REF: Full pp. 296–297 | Seagull p. 309   MSC: Remembering   OBJ: 3

44. Which of the following contributed to the United States going to war in 1812?
    a. Madison's refusal to support Macon's Bill no. 2
    b. Great Britain's announcement that it would end the impressment of American sailors
    c. congressional War Hawks who pressed for territorial expansion into Florida and Canada
    d. Tecumseh's victory at the Battle of Tippecanoe
    e. the Republican insistence on high tariffs

ANS: C   TOP: Political history, changes | Madison and Pressure for War   DIF: Moderate   REF: Full p. 297 | Seagull p. 310   MSC: Remembering   OBJ: 4

45. The War Hawks in Congress included:
    a. Henry Clay and John C. Calhoun.
    b. John Randolph and Rufus King.
    c. Oliver Perry and Francis Scott Key.
    d. Andrew Jackson and William H. Harrison.
    e. Carter Glass and Ernest Hollings.

ANS: A   TOP: Political history, changes | Madison and Pressure for War   DIF: Difficult   REF: Full p. 297 | Seagull p. 310   MSC: Remembering   OBJ: 4

46. Who wrote that he hoped that the purchase of Louisiana would lead to the transplanting of all the Indians from east of the Mississippi to west of the Mississippi?
    a. Andrew Jackson

b. Thomas Jefferson
c. George Washington
d. William Henry Harrison
e. James Monroe

ANS: B   TOP: Ethnicity | The Second War for
Independence   DIF: Moderate   REF: Full
pp. 297–298 | Seagull p. 310   MSC: Remembering
OBJ: 4

47. Tecumseh and Tenskwatawa were brothers who:
a. preached a militant message to Native Americans early in the nineteenth century.
b. were chiefs of adjacent tribes, the Shawnee and the Seneca.
c. fought beside Andrew Jackson at the Battle of New Orleans.
d. both died at the Battle of Tippecanoe.
e. differed on whether Indians or whites were more at fault for Native American problems.

ANS: A   TOP: Ethnicity | Tecumseh's Vision
DIF: Moderate   REF: Full p. 298 | Seagull p. 311
MSC: Remembering   OBJ: 4

48. Which of the following contributed to the poor American performance in the War of 1812?
a. The nation was deeply divided about whether to go to war.
b. The renewal of the charter of the Bank of the United States in 1811 prompted other banks to refuse to help the government to fund the war.
c. The war in Europe had ended before the War of 1812 began, and the British were able to pay more attention to the war.
d. Because Jefferson had dismantled the entire U.S. navy, Madison found himself without any ability to fight at sea.
e. The United States fought a two-front war: against the British in Canada and against the Spanish in Florida.

ANS: A   TOP: Political history, changes | The War of
1812   DIF: Moderate   REF: Full p. 299 | Seagull
p. 312   MSC: Remembering   OBJ: 4

49. When Andrew Jackson had the chance to obtain African-American help to fight the British in the Battle of New Orleans, he:
a. refused on the grounds that, as a slaveholder, he could not accept their aid.
b. discovered that all the blacks in New Orleans had left the city to support the British.
c. recruited free men of color and promised them the same pay that white recruits received.
d. accepted only enslaved men, to whom he offered freedom as a form of payment.

e. accepted, but that so angered the white recruits that he later dismissed all the black soldiers.

ANS: C   TOP: Social history | The War of 1812
DIF: Difficult   REF: Full p. 300 | Seagull p. 314
MSC: Remembering   OBJ: 4

50. The treaty that ended the War of 1812:
a. gave the United States large tracts of land in the West.
b. gave Canada the option of joining the United States.
c. was a humiliating treaty for Britain.
d. restored the prewar status quo.
e. resulted in the United States losing land to Canada.

ANS: D   TOP: Global awareness | The War of 1812
DIF: Moderate   REF: Full p. 300 | Seagull p. 314
MSC: Remembering   OBJ: 4

51. After the War of 1812, Americans were compensated for lost slaves:
a. by an international arbitration agreement decided by the Russian czar.
b. by the Treaty of Ghent.
c. by Canadian towns buying the slaves' freedom.
d. by the slaves purchasing their freedom.
e. by forcing France to pay Britain's debts.

ANS: A   TOP: Global awareness | The War of 1812
DIF: Moderate   REF: Full p. 302 | Seagull p. 314
MSC: Remembering   OBJ: 4

52. Which of the following was NOT a result of the War of 1812?
a. The Federalist Party disappeared as a significant political entity.
b. Andrew Jackson became a national hero as an example of how virtuous citizens could defeat forces of a "despotic" Europe.
c. Native Americans lost much of their remaining land and power in the Old Northwest and the South, which eased white settlement.
d. Americans felt increasingly separate from Europe.
e. The United States gained land in what is now Maine, Vermont, Michigan, and Minnesota, as well as all of modern Florida.

ANS: E   TOP: Global awareness | Political history,
changes | The War's Aftermath | The End of the
Federalist Party.   DIF: Difficult
REF: Full pp. 302, 303 | Seagull pp. 314–316
MSC: Understanding   OBJ: 4

53. Why did the United States become a one-party nation following the War of 1812?
a. The Republicans were blamed for the British victory in Washington, D.C., and therefore lost power.

b. The Hartford Convention's allegedly treasonous activities fatally damaged the Federalist Party's reputation.

c. Under the Alien and Sedition Acts, Madison was able to silence all opposition.

d. James Monroe's universal popularity as a hero of the War of 1812 made his Republican Party unbeatable.

e. The Federalists were so pleased with the war's outcome that they endorsed a union with the Republicans at their 1816 convention in Hartford.

ANS: B   TOP: Political history, changes | The End of the Federalist Party   DIF: Moderate   REF: Full p. 303 | Seagull p. 316   MSC: Understanding   OBJ: 4

True or False

1. George Washington wore the finest English clothes at his first inauguration.

ANS: F   TOP: Social history | Introduction: George Washington's Inauguration   DIF: Moderate REF: Full p. 273 | Seagull p. 282 MSC: Remembering   OBJ: 1

2. Most of the public government buildings constructed around 1800 in Washington, D.C., were built by using slave labor.

ANS: T   TOP: Social history | The Jefferson-Hamilton Bargain   DIF: Easy   REF: Full p. 276 | Seagull p. 286   MSC: Remembering   OBJ: 1

3. Jay's Treaty abandoned any american alliance with Britain by positioning the United States close to France.

ANS: F   TOP: Global awareness | The Impact of the French Revolution   DIF: Moderate   REF: Full p. 277 | Seagull pp. 287–288   MSC: Remembering   OBJ: 2

4. The Whiskey Rebellion of 1794 proved to Federalists that democracy in the hands of the ordinary citizenry was dangerous.

ANS: T   TOP: Social history | The Whiskey Rebellion   DIF: Moderate   REF: Full p. 278 | Seagull p. 288   MSC: Understanding   OBJ: 1

5. The Republican Party of today started in the 1790s.

ANS: F   TOP: Political history, changes | Political Parties   DIF: Moderate   REF: Full pp. 277–278 | Seagull p. 288   MSC: Remembering   OBJ: 1

6. The Jacobin clubs of Paris were an inspiration for the Democratic-Republican societies.

ANS: T   TOP: Social history | The Democratic-Republican Societies   DIF: Moderate   REF: Full p. 280 | Seagull p. 290   MSC: Remembering   OBJ: 2

7. Newspapers and pamphlets were a primary vehicle for political debate in the early republic.

ANS: T   TOP: Political history, changes | An Expanding Public Sphere   DIF: Easy   REF: Full pp. 280–281 | Seagull p. 289   MSC: Remembering OBJ: 1

8. Women were counted fully in determining representation in Congress, and there was nothing specifically limiting women's rights in the Constitution.

ANS: T   TOP: Political history, changes | Women and the Republic   DIF: Difficult   REF: Full p. 281 | Seagull p. 294   MSC: Remembering   OBJ: 1

9. The Twelfth Amendment required electors to cast separate votes for president and vice president.

ANS: T   TOP: Political history, changes | The "Revolution of 1800"   DIF: Difficult   REF: Full p. 287 | Seagull p. 299   MSC: Remembering   OBJ: 1

10. Most states in the Union supported the Virginia and Kentucky resolutions.

ANS: F   TOP: Political history, changes | The Virginia and Kentucky Resolutions   DIF: Moderate REF: Full p. 287 | Seagull p. 298 MSC: Remembering   OBJ: 2

11. John Adams's acceptance of defeat in 1800 established the vital precedent of a peaceful transfer of power from a defeated party to its successor.

ANS: T   TOP: Political history, changes | The "Revolution of 1800"   DIF: Moderate   REF: Full p. 288 | Seagull p. 299   MSC: Remembering   OBJ: 2

12. The Revolution of 1800 was quite violent.

ANS: F   TOP: Political history, changes | The "Revolution of 1800"   DIF: Moderate   REF: Full p. 288 | Seagull p. 299   MSC: Remembering   OBJ: 3

13. Seeing the events as an extension of their own progress of liberty, white Americans supported the Haitian Revolution and the establishment of Haiti as an independent nation in 1804.

ANS: F   TOP: Global awareness | The Haitian Revolution   DIF: Easy   REF: Full pp. 288–289 | Seagull p. 300   MSC: Remembering   OBJ: 2

14. Slave artisans played a prominent role in Gabriel's Rebellion.

ANS: T   TOP: Social history | Gabriel's Rebellion DIF: Moderate   REF: Full p. 289 | Seagull p. 302 MSC: Remembering   OBJ: 2

15. When Thomas Jefferson became president, he was not interested in dismantling the policies that the Federalists had established.

    ANS: F   TOP: Political history, changes | Jefferson in Power   DIF: Easy   REF: Full p. 290 | Seagull p. 303   MSC: Remembering   OBJ: 3

16. Jefferson was interested in the Louisiana Territory because he wanted to secure permanent access to the port of New Orleans.

    ANS: T   TOP: Geographic issues | The Louisiana Purchase   DIF: Moderate   REF: Full pp. 292–293 | Seagull p. 304   MSC: Remembering   OBJ: 3

17. Acre for acre, the Louisiana Purchase was not a bargain.

    ANS: F   TOP: Geographic issues | The Louisiana Purchase   DIF: Easy   REF: Full p. 293 | Seagull p. 304   MSC: Remembering   OBJ: 3

18. The journey from 1804 to 1806 of Lewis and Clark did not produce much valuable information.

    ANS: F   TOP: Geographic issues | Lewis and Clark   DIF: Easy   REF: Full p. 294 | Seagull p. 306   MSC: Remembering   OBJ: 3

19. Pocahontas served as Lewis and Clark's interpreter.

    ANS: F   TOP: Ethnicity | Lewis and Clark   DIF: Easy   REF: Full p. 294 | Seagull p. 306   MSC: Remembering   OBJ: 3

20. Louisiana's slaves enjoyed far more freedom under the liberty-loving United States than under the rule of tyrannical Spain.

    ANS: F   TOP: Civil rights | Incorporating Louisiana   DIF: Moderate   REF: Full pp. 294–295 | Seagull pp. 306–307   MSC: Remembering   OBJ: 3

21. Free trade and sailors' rights were the two issues that drew the United States into the War of 1812.

    ANS: T   TOP: Global awareness | Madison and Pressure for War   DIF: Easy   REF: Full p. 297 | Seagull pp. 309–310   MSC: Remembering   OBJ: 4

22. The Embargo Act was devastating to the British and French.

    ANS: F   TOP: Economic development | The Embargo   DIF: Moderate   REF: Full p. 297 | Seagull p. 309   MSC: Remembering   OBJ: 3

23. By the early 1800s some members of the Creek and Cherokee tribes were living like white Americans as traders and slaveholders.

ANS: T   TOP: Ethnicity | The Indian Response   DIF: Moderate   REF: Full p. 298 | Seagull pp. 310–311   MSC: Remembering   OBJ: 4

24. Tecumseh and Tenskwatawa tried to revive a pan-Indian movement and unite against the white man.

    ANS: T   TOP: Ethnicity | Tecumseh's Vision   DIF: Moderate   REF: Full p. 298 | Seagull p. 311   MSC: Remembering   OBJ: 4

25. The U.S. military was well prepared for the War of 1812.

    ANS: F   TOP: Military history | Political history, changes | The War of 1812   DIF: Easy   REF: Full p. 299 | Seagull p. 312   MSC: Remembering   OBJ: 4

26. Canadians tried to rebel against Britain during the War of 1812.

    ANS: F   TOP: Global awareness | The War of 1812   DIF: Moderate   REF: Full p. 300 | Seagull p. 312   MSC: Remembering   OBJ: 4

27. The Battle of Washington, D.C., valiantly fought by the Americans, was a much needed victory.

    ANS: F   TOP: Military history | Political history, changes | The War of 1812   DIF: Moderate   REF: Full p. 300 | Seagull p. 312   MSC: Remembering   OBJ: 4

28. The aftermath of the War of 1812 confirmed the ability of a republican government to conduct a war without surrendering its institutions.

    ANS: T   TOP: Political history, changes | The War's Aftermath   DIF: Moderate   REF: Full p. 302 | Seagull p. 314   MSC: Remembering   OBJ: 4

Short Answer

Identify and give the historical significance of each of the following terms, events, and people in a paragraph or two.

1. French Revolution
2. Lewis and Clark
3. War Hawks
4. Whiskey Rebellion
5. John Marshall
6. Democratic-Republican societies
7. Alien and Sedition Acts
8. Gabriel's Rebellion
9. Embargo Act
10. War of 1812
11. Alexander Hamilton
12. Virginia and Kentucky resolutions

Essay Questions

1. George Washington stated that "the preservation of the sacred fire of liberty and the destiny of the republican model of government" depended on the success of the American experiment in self-government. What does this statement mean? How and why did Americans come to see that freedom was the special genius of American institutions?

   ANS: Answers will vary   TOP: Constitutional history | Political history, changes | Introduction: George Washington's Inauguration   DIF: Moderate   MSC: Understanding   OBJ: 1 / 2

2. Alexander Hamilton's plan called for commercial industrialization, which many Americans viewed positively. Explain why some Americans opposed Hamilton's position. What were some of the alternative plans for development?

   ANS: Answers will vary   TOP: Economic development | Political history, changes | Hamilton's Program | The Emergence of Opposition | The Jefferson-Hamilton Bargain   DIF: Moderate   MSC: Understanding   OBJ: 1 / 3

3. The men who wrote the Constitution did not envision the active and continuing involvement of ordinary citizens in affairs of state. Describe the various ways in which ordinary citizens became involved in political concerns. Be sure to include how the concepts of liberty and freedom were used (refer to "Voices of Freedom") and explain who was excluded from political discourse in the period from 1790 to 1815.

   ANS: Answers will vary   TOP: Constitutional history | Political history, changes | Primary document analysis | Social history | The Impact of the French Revolution | The Democratic-Republican Societies   DIF: Moderate   MSC: Understanding   OBJ: 1 / 2 / 3

4. Women were increasingly coming to believe that they too had the right to knowledge, education, public discourse, and employment. Discuss the various arguments being made in the late eighteenth and early nineteenth centuries by women regarding their changing roles in the new republic.

   ANS: Answers will vary   TOP: Political history, changes | Social history | The Rights of Women   DIF: Moderate   MSC: Understanding   OBJ: 1

5. "The Sedition Act thrust freedom of expression to the center of discussions of American liberty." Defend this statement. Be sure to include in your response a discussion of the Virginia and Kentucky resolutions.

   ANS: Answers will vary   TOP: Constitutional history | Political history, changes | The Virginia and Kentucky Resolutions | The "Reign of Witches"   DIF: Moderate   MSC: Evaluating   OBJ: 2

6. In what ways can Thomas Jefferson's presidency be considered a revolution? Did his presidency deliver an Empire of Liberty as he envisioned? Why or why not?

   ANS: Answers will vary   TOP: Geographic issues | Political history, changes | Social history | The "Revolution of 1800" | Jefferson in Power | The Louisiana Purchase   DIF: Moderate   MSC: Evaluating   OBJ: 3

7. What liberties and freedoms of Americans were being violated by European powers prior to the War of 1812? How did Jefferson and Madison view liberty in terms of British and French behavior on the seas? How did the War Hawks view liberty? Was war the only answer by 1812?

   ANS: Answers will vary   TOP: Geographic issues | Global awareness | Political history, changes | The Embargo | Madison and Pressure for War   DIF: Moderate   MSC: Analyzing   OBJ: 3 / 4

8. Did the United States really win the War of 1812? Examine the terms of the peace settlement. What was gained? What was the greater victory for America?

   ANS: Answers will vary   TOP: Geographic issues | Global awareness | Military history | Political history, changes | Social history | The War of 1812 | The War's Aftermath   DIF: Moderate   MSC: Evaluating   OBJ: 4

CHAPTER 9

The Market Revolution, 1800–1840

This chapter concentrates on two of the three historical processes unleashed by the Revolution and accelerated after the War of 1812—the spread of market relations and the westward movement of the population. Americans' understanding of freedom was changing to include economic opportunity, physical mobility, and participation in the democratic system. The chapter chronicles the important advancements made in transportation and communication, the growth of western cities, and the expansion of the Cotton Kingdom and slavery. The chapter then explores the market society through early industrialization. First, in discussing agriculture, the chapter illustrates how commercial farmers began replacing self-sufficient farmers. Then, turning to manufacturing, it explores how factory workers were replacing skilled artisans. Most of the early New England textile workers were women, and a "Voices of Freedom" selection highlights the plight of one of these "operatives." With early industrialization came the growth of immigration, particularly from Ireland and Germany, and the prejudices that came along with it in the form of nativism. The materialism of the market society and loss of the self-sufficient farmer and artisan are in stark contrast in the next section, titled "The Free Individual," which explores the growth of the transcendentalist movement, with its emphasis on individualism, and the religious ferment of the Second Great Awakening. One of America's most prominent intellectuals, Ralph Waldo Emerson, speaks to individualism in "Voices of Freedom." The Second Great Awakening also promoted religious pluralism with new denominations like the Mormons springing up. Next, the chapter looks at the limits of prosperity, noting that women and blacks were excluded from the fruits of the market revolution. As liberty became increasingly identified with economic independence, free blacks were left to the lowest jobs and working women were left with few opportunities. A cult of domesticity was created by middle-class women; for them, the ultimate badge of freedom was to be free from work. Labor organizations were also established and the workers demanded more rights and liberties. The chapter concludes with the observation that the market revolution opened opportunities for some but led others to believe their traditional economic independence was eroding.

CHAPTER OUTLINE

I. Introduction: The Marquis de Lafayette

II. A New Economy
   1. In the first half of the nineteenth century the market revolution changed the United States.
   2. The market revolution represented an acceleration of developments already started during colonial times.
   A. Roads and Steamboats
      1. Improvements in transportation lowered costs and linked farmers to markets.
      2. Toll roads did little to help the economy.
      3. Improved water transportation most dramatically increased the speed and lowered the expense of commerce.
         a. In 1807, Robert Fulton showed the steamboat's technological and commercial feasibility.
         b. In 1811, the first steamboat was used on the Mississippi River.
   B. The Erie Canal
      1. The canal was completed in 1825 and made New York City a major trade port.
      2. The state-funded canal typified funding for internal improvements.

3. By 1837, 3,000 miles of canals had been built.

C. Railroads and the Telegraph
   1. Railroads opened the frontier to settlement and linked markets.
   2. The telegraph introduced a communication revolution.
      a. Samuel F. B. Morse
      b. By 1860, 50,000 miles of telegraph existed.

D. The Rise of the West
   1. Improvements in transportation and communication made possible the rise of the West as a powerful, self-conscious region of the new nation.
   2. People traveled in groups and cooperated with each other to clear land, build houses and barns, and establish communities.
   3. Squatters set up farms on unoccupied land.
   4. Many Americans settled without regard to national boundaries.
      a. Florida fell into the hands of Americans despite Indian resistance and Spain's initial refusal to sell.
      b. Adams-Onís Treaty led to the United States gaining East Florida from Spain and unifying it with the previous annexed West Florida.
   5. By 1840, 7 million Americans lived west of the Appalachian Mountains, with Ohio being the third most populous state.

E. The Cotton Kingdom
   1. The market revolution and westward expansion heightened the nation's sectional divisions.
   2. The rise of cotton production came with Eli Whitney's cotton gin.
   3. The cotton gin revolutionized American slavery.
   4. After 1812, southerners, many with slaves, poured into the territory west and south of the Appalachian Mountains.

F. The Unfree Westward Movement
   1. Historians estimate that between 1800 and 1860 around 1 million slaves were shifted from the older slave states to the Deep South.
   2. Slave trading became a well-organized business.
      a. Slave coffles
   3. Cotton became the nation's most important export, producing 170 million pounds in 1820.

III. Market Society
   A. Commercial Farmers
      1. The North became a region with an integrated economy of commercial farms and manufacturing cities.
      2. Farmers grew crops and raised livestock for sale.
      3. The East provided a source of credit and a market.

      4. Between 1840 and 1860, America's output of wheat nearly tripled.
         a. John Deere's steel plow
         b. Cyrus McCormick's reaper

   B. The Growth of Cities
      1. Cities formed part of the western frontier.
         a. Cincinnati
         b. Chicago became the greatest of all western cities thanks to the railroad.
      2. The nature of work shifted from that of the skilled artisan to that of the factory worker.

   C. The Factory System
      1. Samuel Slater established America's first factory in 1790.
         a. It was based on an outwork system.
      2. The first large-scale American factory was constructed in 1814 at Waltham, Massachusetts.
         a. By 1850, Lowell had fifty-two mills with 10,000 workers.
      3. The American System of manufactures relied on the mass production of interchangeable parts that could be rapidly assembled into standardized, finished products.
      4. The South lagged in factory production.

   D. The Industrial Worker
      1. Americans became more aware of clock time.
      2. Working for an hourly or daily wage seemed to violate the independence Americans considered an essential element of freedom.
         a. Few native-born American men were interested in factory jobs.

   E. The "Mill Girls"
      1. Early New England textile mills largely relied on female and child labor.
      2. Mills had strict rules for young unmarried women.

   F. The Growth of Immigration
      1. Economic expansion fueled a demand for labor, which was met, in part, by increased immigration from abroad.
         a. Ireland and Germany
         b. Settled in the northern states
      2. Numerous factors inspired this massive flow of population across the Atlantic.
         a. European economic conditions
         b. Introduction of the ocean-going steamship

   G. Irish and German Newcomers
      1. American religious and political freedoms also attracted many Europeans fleeing from the failed revolutions of 1848.
      2. The Irish were refugees from disaster, fleeing the Irish potato famine.
         a. They filled many low-wage unskilled jobs in America.

3. German immigrants included a considerably larger number of skilled craftsmen as compared to Irish immigrants.
4. Whereas most Irish immigrants remained in the Northeast, many Germans established themselves in the West, including Cincinnati, St. Louis, and Milwaukee.

H. The Rise of Nativism
1. The influx of Irish elevated the presence of the Catholic Church in America, which many native-born Americans viewed with great suspicion.
2. Those who feared the impact of immigration on American political and social life were called nativists. They blamed immigrants for:
    a. Urban crime
    b. Political corruption
    c. Alcohol abuses
    d. Undercutting wages

I. The Transformation of Law
1. The corporate form of business organization became central to the new market economy.
    a. It enjoyed special privileges and powers granted in a charter.
2. Many Americans distrusted corporate charters as a form of government-granted special privilege.
3. The Supreme Court ruled on many aspects of corporations and employer/employee rights.
    a. Courts upheld right of competition.
    b. *Gibbons v. Ogden*
    c. Charles River Bridge case

IV. The Free Individual
1. Westward migration and urban development created a mobile population.

A. The West and Freedom
1. American freedom had long been linked to the availability of land in the West.
    a. Manifest Destiny
2. In national myth and ideology the West would long remain "the last home of the freeborn American."
    a. The West was vital for economic independence, the social condition of freedom.

B. The Transcendentalists
1. Ralph Waldo Emerson believed that freedom was an open-ended process of self-realization by which individuals could remake themselves and their own lives.
2. Henry David Thoreau echoed his call for individual self-reliance.

C. Individualism
1. Americans came to understand that no one person or government had the right to interfere with the realm of the self.
2. Thoreau worried that the market revolution actually stifled individual judgment; genuine freedom lay within the individual.
    a. Retreated to Walden Pond for two years.
    b. Turned it into *Walden*, a critique of the market revolution.

D. The Second Great Awakening
1. The Second Great Awakening added a religious underpinning to the celebration of personal self-improvement, self-reliance, and self-determination.
2. The Reverend Charles Grandison Finney became a national celebrity for his preaching in upstate New York.
3. The Second Great Awakening democratized American Christianity.
    a. Proliferation of ministers
    b. Evangelical denominations (e.g., Methodists and Baptists) grew tremendously.

E. The Awakening's Impact
1. Promoted the doctrine of human free will
2. Revivalist ministers seized the opportunities offered by the market revolution to spread their message.
3. But many ministers criticized greed.

F. The Emergence of Mormonism
1. Competition among religious groups kept religion vibrant and promoted the emergence of new denominations.
2. Joseph Smith founded the Mormons in the 1820s.
    a. Claimed to have been led by an angel to plates that had writing on them.
3. Smith translated and published the plates as *The Book of Mormon*.
    a. Seen as holy book or work of literature.
    b. Native Americans evolved from three families from Middle East.
    c. Second coming of Christ would take place in New World with Smith as God's prophet.

V. The Limits of Prosperity
A. Liberty and Prosperity
1. Official imagery linked the goddess of liberty ever more closely to emblems of material wealth.
2. Opportunities for the self-made man abounded.
    a. John Jacob Astor made great wealth from fur trade.
3. The market revolution produced a new middle class.

B. Race and Opportunity
  1. Free blacks were excluded from the new economic opportunities.
  2. Barred from schools and other public facilities, free blacks laboriously constructed their own institutional life.
     a. African Methodist Episcopal Church
  3. Free blacks were confined to the lowest ranks of the labor market.
  4. Free blacks were not allowed access to public land in the West.
C. The Cult of Domesticity
  1. Women closed off from most market revolution opportunities.
  2. A new definition of femininity emerged based on values like love, friendship, and mutual obligation.
  3. Virtue came to be redefined as a personal moral quality associated more and more closely with women.
  4. Women were to find freedom in fulfilling their duties within their sphere.
D. Women and Work
  1. Only low-paying jobs were available to women.
     a. Domestic servants, factory workers, and seamstresses
  2. Not working outside the home became a badge of respectability for women.
     a. Freedom was freedom from labor.
  3. Although middle-class women did not work outside the home, they did much work as wives and mothers.
  4. Men wanted a "family wage," which was seen as a form of social justice.
E. The Early Labor Movement
  1. Some felt the market revolution reduced their freedom.
     a. Economic swings widened the gap between classes.
  2. The first Workingman's Parties were established in the 1820s.
     a. By the 1830s strikes had become commonplace.
F. The "Liberty of Living"
  1. Wage workers evoked "liberty" when calling for improvements in the workplace.
  2. Some described wage labor as the very essence of slavery.
     a. Economic security formed an essential part of American freedom.
  3. "Wealth and labor" were at war, according to Orestes Brownson.
     a. Workers' problems were institutional not individual.

SUGGESTED DISCUSSION QUESTIONS

- Discuss how Americans' understandings of freedom were changing to include economic opportunity, physical mobility, and participation in the democratic system.
- Discuss transcendentalism and its impact on defining freedom. Who were the major transcendentalists?
- Compare the experiences of the Irish and German immigrants. What was nativism? Why were many Americans so suspicious of newcomers?
- What were the major aspects of the market revolution?
- Explain how the ideology of individualism encouraged political movements.
- What were the key religious ideas and practices associated with the Second Great Awakening? Which denominations grew as a result of the Second Great Awakening? How did the Awakening take advantage of the market revolution? How did it criticize it?
- Women's experiences in the market revolution were varied. Some women viewed working in the mills as freedom, while others viewed not working as a badge of freedom. Explain this apparent irony.
- Have the students make something at home (a paper airplane, a paper fan, etc.). There should be no real instructions with that assignment. Have them bring it to class. Then have the class organize into a factory setting and have them make your airplane (or fan, or whatever the assignment was), with each student making one part (or "fold" of the plane). Afterward, you can discuss the different experiences of being an artisan in your own home (being creative, working your own hours, controlling quality, having to know how to build the entire unit) versus being a wage earner (no creativity, poor working conditions, no quality control, not having to have a skill, etc.).

SUPPLEMENTAL WEB AND VISUAL RESOURCES

Catholicism, Irish, and Nativism
www.nhc.rtp.nc.us/tserve/nineteen/nkeyinfo/nromcath.htm
Also from the National Humanities Center. Teacher Serve: An Interactive Curriculum Enrichment Service for Teachers. This page takes you to the section on Roman Catholics in the nineteenth century.

Second Great Awakening
http://nationalhumanitiescenter.org/tserve/divam.htm
The National Humanities Center. Teacher Serve: An Interactive Curriculum Enrichment Service for Teachers. This section called "Divining America" has numerous links and essays on religion in American history.

www.nhc.rtp.nc.us/tserve/nineteen/nkeyinfo/nevanrev.htm
This page contains a lengthy essay on the Second Great Awakening.

http://nationalhumanitiescenter.org/pds/tblibrary.htm
Toolbox Library offers a plethora of primary sources, discussion questions, additional online sources, and talking points.

The Erie Canal
www.eriecanal.org/maps.html
This website has historic maps of the New York canal system, sheet music about the canal, stories and images, and links to today's official New York State canal system.

The Lowell Offering
http://library.uml.edu/clh/Off.htm
Two periodicals produced by female workers in the Lowell mills—*The Lowell Offering,* and its successor publication, *The New England Offering*—are available on this website maintained by the library of the University of Massachusetts, Lowell.

Transcendentalism
www.pbs.org/wnet/ihas/icon/transcend.html
PBS affiliate, WNET, has a user-friendly site with a useful matrix of major figures, dates and their significance, and major works, as well as other links to related topics.

Transportation
www.mises.org/journals/scholar/Internal.pdf
This site leads you to a useful essay written by a professor of economics from Loyola College, dealing with the debate over internal improvements at the beginning of the nineteenth century.

SUPPLEMENTAL PRINT RESOURCES

Bernstein, Peter. *Wedding of the Waters: The Erie Canal and the Making of a Great Nation.* New York: W. W. Norton & Company, 2005.

Eisler, Benita, ed. *The Lowell Offering: Writings by New England Mill Women (1840–1845).* New York: W. W. Norton & Company, 1997.

Field, Peter. *Ralph Waldo Emerson: The Making of a Democratic Intellectual.* Lanham, MD: Rowman and Littlefield, 2002.

Hankin, Barry. *The Second Great Awakening and the Transcendentalists.* Santa Barbara, CA: Greenwood Press, 2004.

Horton, James Oliver, and Lois Horton. *In Hope of Liberty: Culture, Community, and Protest Among Northern Free Blacks, 1700–1860.* New York: Oxford University Press, 1997.

Packer, Barbara L. *The Transcendentalists.* Athens, GA: University of Georgia Press, 2007.

Roediger, David. *The Wages of Whiteness: Race and the Making of the American Working Class.* Brooklyn, NY: Verso Books, 1991.

Sheriff, Carol. *The Artificial River: The Erie Canal and the Paradox of Progress, 1817–1862.* New York: Hill and Wang, 1996.

Thornton, Tamara Plakins. "'A Great Machine' or a 'Beast of Prey': A Boston Corporation and Its Rural Debtors in an Age of Capitalist Transformation." *Journal of the Early Republic* 27 (2007): 567–597.

Whitten, David O. "The Depression of 1837: Incorporating New Ideas into Economic History Instruction: A Survey." *Essays in Business and Economic History* 13 (1995): 27–40.

TEST BANK

Matching

TEST 1

____ 1. Robert Fulton
____ 2. Richard Allen
____ 3. Lydia Maria Child
____ 4. Roger Taney
____ 5. John O'Sullivan
____ 6. Charles G. Finney
____ 7. John Jacob Astor
____ 8. Cyrus McCormick
____ 9. Ralph Waldo Emerson
___ 10. Samuel Slater
___ 11. Orestes Brownson
___ 12. John Deere

a. Supreme Court chief justice
b. transcendentalist
c. coined the term "manifest destiny"
d. established America's first factory
e. steamboat innovator
f. African Methodist Episcopal Church
g. steel plow
h. self-made millionaire
i. preacher in New York
j. reaper
k. the *Frugal Housewife*
l. called for a radical change in the wage labor system

Answer Key: e, f, k, a, c, i, h, j, b, d, l, g

TEST 2

____ 1. Second Great Awakening
____ 2. cult of domesticity
____ 3. corporation
____ 4. transcendentalism
____ 5. slave coffles
____ 6. *Commonwealth v. Hunt*
____ 7. cotton gin
____ 8. American System
____ 9. manifest destiny
___ 10. virtue
___ 11. Erie Canal
___ 12. nativism

a. a celebration of the home
b. revolutionized American slavery

c. mass production of interchangeable parts
d. a personal moral quality associated with women
e. a belief that American expansion was divinely appointed
f. religious revival
g. a decree that labor organization was legal
h. a literary and philosophical movement
i. groups chained together while migrating to the Deep South
j. a charted entity that has rights and liabilities distinct from those of its members
k. prejudice against immigrants
l. waterway linking New York City to the Great Lakes

Answer Key: f, a, j, h, i, g, b, c, e, d, l, k

Learning Objectives

1. Identify the main elements of the market revolution.
2. Explain how the market revolution sparked social change.
3. Explain how the meanings of American freedom changed in this period.
4. Describe how the market revolution affected the lives of workers, women, and African-Americans.

Multiple Choice

1. Which of the following is true of Lafayette's 1824 visit to the United States?
   a. He made a series of speeches supporting the emancipation of slaves.
   b. Federalists strongly protested the visit because of Lafayette's connections with the French Revolution.
   c. Southern states banned "persons of color" from ceremonies honoring him.
   d. He negotiated a trade agreement that demonstrated the rising economic influence of the United States.
   e. He came to attend the funeral of his good friend, Thomas Jefferson.

   ANS: C   TOP: Civil rights | Introduction
   DIF: Moderate   REF: Full p. 308 | Seagull p. 319
   MSC: Remembering   OBJ: 4

2. The catalyst for the market revolution was a series of innovations in:
   a. manufacturing.
   b. agriculture.
   c. banking and financing.
   d. labor contracts.
   e. transportation and communication.

   ANS: E   TOP: Economic development | A New Economy   DIF: Moderate   REF: Full p. 308 | Seagull p. 320   MSC: Remembering   OBJ: 1

3. Which improvement most dramatically increased the speed and lowered the expense of commerce in the first half of the nineteenth century?
   a. the transcontinental railroad
   b. canals and steamboats
   c. the factory system
   d. a system of federally financed roads
   e. the establishment of an efficient postal system

   ANS: B   TOP: Economic development | Roads and Steamboats   DIF: Easy   REF: Full p. 309 | Seagull p. 321   MSC: Remembering   OBJ: 1

4. What was the significance of Robert Fulton?
   a. He was responsible for the construction of the Erie Canal.
   b. His work in designing steamboats made upstream commerce possible.
   c. His innovations led to the revolution in turnpike construction in the early nineteenth century.
   d. As mayor of New York City, he worked to make that city a commercial center.
   e. He sponsored congressional legislation that authorized building of the National Road.

   ANS: B   TOP: Economic development | Roads and Steamboats   DIF: Moderate   REF: Full p. 309 | Seagull p. 322   MSC: Remembering   OBJ: 1

5. The Erie Canal gave which city primacy over competing ports in accessing trade with the Northwest?
   a. Baltimore
   b. Philadelphia
   c. Boston
   d. New York
   e. Chicago

   ANS: D   TOP: Economic development | The Erie Canal   DIF: Easy   REF: Full p. 309 | Seagull p. 322   MSC: Remembering   OBJ: 1

6. The Erie Canal:
   a. was far longer than any other canal in the United States at that time.
   b. attracted an influx of farmers migrating from Virginia and the Carolinas to the Northwest.
   c. was strongly opposed by residents of Buffalo and Rochester, who feared their cities would lose business.
   d. was championed by Pennsylvania governor William Findlay.
   e. proved economically unviable and was abandoned within a decade of its opening.

   ANS: A   TOP: Economic development | The Erie Canal   DIF: Moderate   REF: Full p. 309 | Seagull p. 322   MSC: Remembering   OBJ: 1

7. America's first commercial railroad was the:
   a. Pennsylvania Railroad
   b. Union Pacific Railroad
   c. Reading Railroad
   d. Baltimore and Ohio Railroad
   e. South Carolina Railroad

   ANS: D   TOP: Economic development | Railroads and the Telegraph   DIF: Difficult   REF: Full p. 311 | Seagull p. 323   MSC: Remembering   OBJ: 1

8. The American railroad industry in the first half of the nineteenth century:
   a. was exclusively in the North.
   b. stimulated the coal mining industry.
   c. was smaller in terms of total miles of track than the European rail system.
   d. mainly connected one waterway to another waterway.
   e. encouraged entrepreneurs to begin building extensive canal systems for the first time.

   ANS: B   TOP: Economic development | Railroads and the Telegraph   DIF: Moderate   REF: Full p. 311 | Seagull p. 323   MSC: Remembering   OBJ: 1

9. Most of the states that joined the Union in the six years immediately following the War of 1812 were located:
   a. west of the Mississippi River.
   b. in the Old Northwest.
   c. south of the Mason-Dixon Line.
   d. in the Louisiana Purchase territory.
   e. west of the Appalachian Mountains.

   ANS: E   TOP: Geographic issues | The Rise of the West   DIF: Moderate   REF: Full p. 312 | Seagull pp. 324–325   MSC: Understanding   OBJ: 1

10. Which statement about the western settlements is FALSE?
    a. Settlers often set up farms on land to which they did not have legal title.
    b. People cooperated with each other to clear land and build shelters.
    c. The government discouraged western settlement at every turn.
    d. Americans settled without regard to national boundaries.
    e. Improvements in transportation and communication accelerated western settlement.

    ANS: C   TOP: Geographic issues | The Rise of the West   DIF: Moderate   REF: Full p. 312 | Seagull pp. 324–325   MSC: Understanding   OBJ: 1

11. Squatters:
    a. set up farms on unoccupied land.
    b. were corporate charters issued by states as contracts.
    c. strung telegraph lines between poles.
    d. set the dynamite as part of railroad construction crews.
    e. is a derogatory name for the girls who worked in the mill factories.

    ANS: A   TOP: Geographic issues | The Rise of the West   DIF: Easy   REF: Full p. 312 | Seagull p. 325   MSC: Remembering   OBJ: 1

12. Which of the following was not a factor in the nation's acquisition of Florida from Spain?
    a. Andrew Jackson's invasion of the area, during which his men killed British agents and Indian chiefs
    b. the American seizure of Baton Rouge
    c. the desire of Georgia and Alabama planters to eliminate a refuge for fugitive slaves
    d. Spain's loss of Haiti in a slave rebellion, which rendered Florida imperially unimportant
    e. Spain's realization that it was unable to defend the area

    ANS: D   TOP: Geographic issues | The Rise of the West   DIF: Difficult   REF: Full p. 314 | Seagull p. 325   MSC: Understanding   OBJ: 1

13. The first industry to be shaped by the large factory system was:
    a. textiles.
    b. guns.
    c. ironworks.
    d. pottery.
    e. shoemaking.

    ANS: A   TOP: Economic development | The Cotton Kingdom   DIF: Moderate   REF: Full p. 315 | Seagull p. 327   MSC: Remembering   OBJ: 1

14. Which problem with cotton did Eli Whitney solve by inventing the cotton gin?
    a. Whitney figured out how to remove the cotton-destroying boll weevil and thereby save the cotton crop.
    b. Removing seeds from the cotton was a slow and painstaking task, but Whitney made it much easier and less labor-intensive.
    c. Processing cotton required too many different pieces of equipment, but Whitney figured out how to change the equipment more easily and quickly, saving time and money.
    d. Planting the cotton took too many hours to make its growth very profitable, but Whitney enabled planters to use a machine to speed the planting.
    e. The production of southern whiskey required the use of cotton in purifying the liquor, but the cotton absorbed too much liquid; Whitney's machine changed that.

ANS: B   TOP: Economic development | The Cotton Kingdom   DIF: Moderate   REF: Full p. 315 | Seagull p. 327   MSC: Understanding   OBJ: 1

15. Which of the following is NOT an example of the significance of Eli Whitney's cotton gin?
    a. Cotton production increased dramatically in about a quarter of a century.
    b. The Atlantic slave trade to the United States expanded in its last few years of existence.
    c. The federal government moved to consolidate American control of the Deep South by driving out Native Americans and acquiring Florida.
    d. The domestic slave trade grew.
    e. The completion of the Erie Canal allowed the transportation of thousands of pounds of cotton per day.

    ANS: E   TOP: Economic development | The Cotton Kingdom   DIF: Moderate   REF: Full p. 317 | Seagull p. 327   MSC: Understanding   OBJ: 1

16. What was the most important export from the United States by the mid-nineteenth century?
    a. tobacco
    b. coal
    c. timber
    d. cotton
    e. wheat

    ANS: D   TOP: Economic development | The Unfree Westward Movement   DIF: Easy   REF: Full pp. 317–318 | Seagull p. 329   MSC: Remembering   OBJ: 1

17. Which of the following was NOT a way in which westward movement affected the South?
    a. It led to the increased breaking up of slave families and communities.
    b. The plantation economy expanded beyond the coastal regions.
    c. Transportation and banking remained adjuncts of the plantation system.
    d. The South had to develop a highly effective railroad system to transport goods from west to east.
    e. The South's agrarian, slave-based social order reproduced itself as settlers went west.

    ANS: D   TOP: Geographic issues | The Unfree Westward Movement | Market Society   DIF: Difficult   REF: Full pp. 317–318 | Seagull pp. 327–329   MSC: Understanding   OBJ: 1

18. Which of the following was NOT a way that the market revolution changed western farming?
    a. As the West became more settled, western farmers found that they could cater to the market and grow crops they could sell.

    b. John Deere's steel plow made it easier to till larger quantities of soil.
    c. Cyrus McCormick's reaper made it quicker and easier for them to harvest wheat.
    d. Eastern banks and insurance companies financed the acquisitions of supplies needed to expand farmland.
    e. Farmers in the Old Northwest used slave labor to expand their production.

    ANS: E   TOP: Economic development | Commercial Farmers   DIF: Easy   REF: Full p. 319 | Seagull p. 330   MSC: Understanding   OBJ: 1

19. How many cities in 1850 had a population of more than 5,000?
    a. 50
    b. 100
    c. 150
    d. 200
    e. 250

    ANS: C   TOP: Geographic issues | The Growth of Cities   DIF: Difficult   REF: Full p. 319 | Seagull p. 330   MSC: Remembering   OBJ: 2

20. Samuel Slater:
    a. developed stone-crushing technology useful for road building.
    b. established America's first factory.
    c. invented the cotton gin.
    d. established the Erie Canal.
    e. was a steamboat innovator.

    ANS: B   TOP: Economic development | The Factory System   DIF: Moderate   REF: Full p. 319 | Seagull p. 331   MSC: Remembering   OBJ: 2

21. How did the market revolution affect the lives of artisans?
    a. Their lives changed little, because the economy allowed for plenty of room for specialized craftsmen.
    b. New competition created opportunities for the specialized skills of artisans, so their numbers expanded.
    c. Gathered in factories, they faced constant supervision and the breakdown of craftsmanship into specialized tasks.
    d. They began working in factories, which they preferred to enduring years of apprenticeship under the old system.
    e. Most artisans became factory owners and prospered as never before.

    ANS: C   TOP: Social history | The Growth of Cities   DIF: Difficult   REF: Full p. 319 | Seagull p. 331   MSC: Understanding   OBJ: 2

22. Which of the following was responsible for the first large-scale American factory, which was built in Massachusetts?
    a. Henry Clay, whose sponsorship of a protective tariff made the factory economically viable
    b. the cutoff of British imports because of the Embargo of 1807 and the War of 1812
    c. Cyrus McCormick, who built it to produce his reaper
    d. the American victory in the War of 1812, which made the United States economically dominant in the Atlantic world
    e. Samuel F. B. Morse, who became better known for inventing the telegraph

    ANS: B TOP: Economic development | The Factory System DIF: Moderate REF: Full p. 321 | Seagull p. 331 MSC: Remembering OBJ: 2

23. What encouraged the building of factories in coastal towns such as New Bedford and even large inland cities such as Chicago by the 1840s?
    a. Such places generally had cheaper labor (usually consisting of African Americans) than existed in the earlier, highly unionized factory towns such as Lowell and Pawtucket.
    b. Under Henry Clay's American System, federal and state governments subsidized factories in those locations.
    c. Steam power meant factories no longer had to be near waterfalls and rapids to generate the power.
    d. Factory owners were attracted by the highly skilled labor pool of German immigrants who settled in those areas.
    e. The U.S. Supreme Court's decision in *Gibbons v. Ogden* removed obstacles to the placement of factories in densely populated areas.

    ANS: C TOP: Economic development | The Factory System DIF: Difficult REF: Full p. 322 | Seagull p. 332 MSC: Remembering OBJ: 2

24. The "American System of manufactures":
    a. owed a great deal to Eli Terry's development of interchangeable parts in clockmaking.
    b. originated among entrepreneurs in the Old Northwest before spreading to New England.
    c. referred to the production of specialty handmade goods by highly skilled artisans.
    d. was centered entirely on agricultural machinery.
    e. was nearly derailed by Chief Justice John Marshall's hostility to economic development.

    ANS: A TOP: Economic development | The Factory System DIF: Moderate REF: Full p. 322 | Seagull p. 332 MSC: Remembering OBJ: 2

25. How did the market revolution change the way Americans conceived of time?
    a. It led Congress to create time zones in 1823.
    b. Clocks increasingly regulated the separation of work and leisure time.
    c. Artisans began spending their lunch hours in political discussions, rather than just taking breaks as they worked throughout the day.
    d. It lengthened life expectancy because Americans no longer had to work from sunrise to sunset as they had on farms.
    e. It enhanced the individual American's sense of independence to be able to walk away from work at a certain time.

    ANS: B TOP: Social history | The Industrial Worker DIF: Difficult REF: Full p. 323 | Seagull p. 332 MSC: Remembering OBJ: 2

26. Women who worked at the Lowell mills:
    a. never had time to make friends.
    b. commuted daily to work from their family farms.
    c. quickly organized a union to strike for higher wages.
    d. held management positions.
    e. lived in closely supervised boardinghouses.

    ANS: E TOP: Social history | The "Mill Girls" DIF: Moderate REF: Full p. 323 | Seagull p. 333 MSC: Remembering OBJ: 2

27. At the Lowell textile mills:
    a. southern-born women dominated the workforce, because of their superior knowledge of cotton.
    b. the lack of supervision showed that the female workers were capable of managing their own lives, which inspired the women's rights movement.
    c. most women worked once their children were old enough to take care of themselves.
    d. the owners established lecture halls and churches.
    e. immigrant women dominated the workforce in the 1820s.

    ANS: D TOP: Social history | The "Mill Girls" DIF: Moderate REF: Full p. 323 | Seagull p. 333 MSC: Remembering OBJ: 2

28. The majority of the nearly 4 million immigrants that entered the United States between 1840 and 1860 were from:
    a. England and Germany.
    b. Germany and Ireland.
    c. China and Ireland.
    d. Mexico and England.
    e. Germany and China.

    ANS: B TOP: Ethnicity | The Growth of Immigration DIF: Easy REF: Full p. 324 | Seagull p. 334 MSC: Remembering OBJ: 2

29. The "German triangle" in the mid-nineteenth century referred to:
    a. a Baltimore neighborhood with a large German immigrant population.
    b. the identifying patch German immigrants were forced to wear in some American cities.
    c. Cincinnati, St. Louis, and Milwaukee—cities with large German populations.
    d. the special kind of ballot Democrats gave German-speaking voters.
    e. the superior plow that German immigrant Thomas Mannheim introduced to the United States.

    ANS: C   TOP: Ethnicity | Irish and German New-comers   DIF: Moderate   REF: Full p. 325 | Seagull p. 335   MSC: Remembering   OBJ: 2

30. For which of the following did nativists NOT blame immigrants in the 1840s?
    a. urban crime
    b. increased Protestantism
    c. alcohol abuses
    d. undercutting wages
    e. political corruption

    ANS: B   TOP: Ethnicity | The Rise of Nativism
    DIF: Easy   REF: Full p. 326 | Seagull p. 337
    MSC: Understanding   OBJ: 2

31. Which of the following helped to increase the visibility and power of the Catholic Church in America in the mid-nineteenth century?
    a. The fact that President Jackson was Catholic.
    b. The number of Italian Catholic immigrants grew dramatically.
    c. Congressional passage of an Act of Religious Toleration that gave Catholics political rights.
    d. The number of Irish Catholic immigrants grew dramatically.
    e. Archbishop John Hughes's wave of revivals that converted thousands to Catholicism.

    ANS: D   TOP: Ethnicity | The Rise of Nativism
    DIF: Easy   REF: Full p. 326 | Seagull p. 336
    MSC: Remembering   OBJ: 2

32. Which statement about corporations is FALSE?
    a. A corporation could fail without ruining its directors and stockholders.
    b. The corporation was not a vital component in the new market economy.
    c. A corporation enjoyed special privileges and powers granted in a charter from the government.
    d. Corporations were able to raise far more capital than the traditional forms of enterprise.
    e. Many Americans distrusted corporate charters as a form of government granted special privilege.

    ANS: B   TOP: Economic development | The Transformation of Law   DIF: Moderate   REF: Full p. 328 | Seagull p. 337   MSC: Understanding   OBJ: 2

33. In *Gibbons v. Ogden*, the U.S. Supreme Court ruled that:
    a. the Louisiana Purchase was unconstitutional.
    b. Congress had the authority to create the Bank of the United States.
    c. New York could not grant a monopoly on steamboat navigation between New York and New Jersey.
    d. corporations were illegal because their potential to become monopolistic posed a threat to individual free enterprise.
    e. railroad workers had no right to strike since it interfered with national commerce.

    ANS: C   TOP: Constitutional history | The Transformation of Law   DIF: Difficult   REF: Full p. 328 | Seagull p. 338   MSC: Remembering   OBJ: 2

34. In an 1837 case involving the Charles River in Massachusetts, Chief Justice Roger Taney:
    a. declared the community had a legitimate interest in promoting transportation and prosperity.
    b. held that adding a second bridge over the river violated the charter rights of the company that built the first bridge.
    c. granted Robert Fulton's steamboat company a monopoly in the ferry business on the river.
    d. issued an opinion in which the U.S. Supreme Court, for the first time, overturned a state law.
    e. officially declared that capitalism was the economic system of the United States.

    ANS: A   TOP: Constitutional history | The Transformation of Law   DIF: Difficult   REF: Full p. 328 | Seagull p. 338   MSC: Remembering   OBJ: 2

35. In response to the market revolution:
    a. the legal system worked with local governments to find better ways to regulate entrepreneurs.
    b. Chief Justice John Marshall ruled that legislatures could not alter or rescind charters and contracts that previous legislatures had created.
    c. local judges protected businessmen from paying property damages associated with factory construction and from workers seeking to unionize.
    d. Massachusetts Chief Justice Lemuel Shaw held in *Commonwealth v. Hunt* that workers had no right to organize.
    e. corporations proved less able to raise capital than chartered companies did.

    ANS: C   TOP: Social history | The Transformation of Law   DIF: Difficult   REF: Full p. 328 | Seagull p. 338   MSC: Understanding   OBJ: 2

36. According to John O'Sullivan, the "manifest destiny" of the United States to occupy North America could be traced to:
    a. the Treaty of Paris of 1783.
    b. a divine mission.
    c. the Adams-Onis Treaty.
    d. the Bible.
    e. federal treaties with Indian nations.

    ANS: B   TOP: Social history | The West and Freedom
    DIF: Moderate   REF: Full p. 329 | Seagull p. 339
    MSC: Remembering   OBJ: 2

37. The transcendentalist movement:
    a. emphasized individual judgment, not tradition.
    b. is also known as the Second Great Awakening.
    c. stressed teamwork in order to industrialize.
    d. was largely based in the South.
    e. celebrated the economic developments of the market revolution.

    ANS: A   TOP: Cultural history | The Transcen-
        dentalists   DIF: Moderate   REF: Full p. 330 |
        Seagull p. 340   MSC: Understanding   OBJ: 3

38. Who believed that freedom was an open-ended process of self-realization by which individuals could remake themselves and their own lives?
    a. Eli Whitney
    b. Ralph Waldo Emerson
    c. Thomas Jefferson
    d. John O'Sullivan
    e. Andrew Jackson

    ANS: B   TOP: Cultural history | The Transcen-
        dentalists   DIF: Moderate   REF: Full p. 330 |
        Seagull p. 340   MSC: Remembering   OBJ: 3

39. During the first half of the nineteenth century, individualism:
    a. came under attack from Henry David Thoreau.
    b. was defined in a way that distinguished it completely from the idea of privacy.
    c. hampered efforts to spread democracy because it reduced interest in suffrage.
    d. was rooted in the idea of self-sufficiency.
    e. was a subject on which all transcendentalists agreed.

    ANS: D   TOP: Social history | Individualism
    DIF: Moderate   REF: Full p. 330 | Seagull p. 340
    MSC: Understanding   OBJ: 3

40. Henry David Thoreau believed that:
    a. economic independence was essential for freedom.
    b. genuine freedom lay within the individual.
    c. the market revolution brought freedom to many.
    d. true freedom was not obtainable.
    e. government was the ultimate expression of freedom.

    ANS: B   TOP: Social history | Individualism
    DIF: Moderate   REF: Full p. 331 | Seagull p. 341
    MSC: Remembering   OBJ: 3

41. Which of the following statements related to the Second Great Awakening is FALSE?
    a. The Second Great Awakening added a religious underpinning to the celebration of personal self-improvement, self-reliance, and self-determination.
    b. Charles Grandison Finney became a national celebrity for his preaching in upstate New York.
    c. The Second Great Awakening popularized Deism.
    d. The Second Great Awakening made American Christianity a mass enterprise.
    e. Revivalist ministers seized the opportunities offered by the market revolution to spread their message.

    ANS: C   TOP: Cultural history | The Second Great
        Awakening   DIF: Moderate   REF: Full p. 335 |
        Seagull p. 344   MSC: Understanding   OBJ: 3

42. Which denomination enjoyed the largest membership in the United States by the 1840s?
    a. Methodist
    b. Roman Catholic
    c. Quaker
    d. Presbyterian
    e. Episcopal

    ANS: A   TOP: Social history | The Second Great
        Awakening   DIF: Moderate   REF: Full p. 335 |
        Seagull p. 344   MSC: Remembering   OBJ: 3

43. *The Book of Mormon* states:
    a. Joseph Smith was divine.
    b. the second coming of Christ would occur in Europe.
    c. Native Americans were descended from people from the Middle East.
    d. Joseph Smith's visions were untrue.
    e. the market revolution needed more infrastructure to be successful.

    ANS: C   TOP: Cultural history | The Emergence of
        Mormonism   DIF: Difficult   REF: Full p. 336 |
        Seagull p. 346   MISC: Remembering   OBJ: 3

44. According to the Mormons, who was God's prophet?
    a. Richard Allen
    b. Charles Grandison Finney
    c. John Jacob Astor
    d. Orestes Brownson
    e. Joseph Smith

    ANS: E   TOP: Cultural history | The Emergence of
        Mormonism   DIF: Easy   REF: Full p. 336 |
        Seagull p. 346   MISC: Remembering   OBJ: 3

45. The official seals of New Jersey (1821) and Arkansas (1836) both reflect the widespread identification of freedom with:

a. technological progress and material prosperity.
b. women's rights and virtuous citizenry.
c. expanded democracy and technological progress.
d. growing infrastructure and individualism.
e. material prosperity and individualism.

ANS: A   TOP: Social history | Liberty and Prosperity
DIF: Difficult   REF: Full pp. 337–338 | Seagull
p. 347   MSC: Remembering   OBJ: 4

46. John Jacob Astor, who seemed to exemplify the "self-made man":
a. turned out to be a fraud, for it was discovered he counterfeited much of his fortune.
b. used his great wealth to finance the North during the Civil War.
c. made huge profits from distributing the machines built by Thomas Rodgers.
d. began his economic ascent through the purchase of Philadelphia real estate.
e. became wealthy trading goods between the United States and China.

ANS: E   TOP: Economic development | Liberty and Prosperity   DIF: Difficult   REF: Full p. 338 | Seagull p. 347   MSC: Remembering   OBJ: 3

47. What helped to encourage Richard Allen to establish the African Methodist Episcopal Church?
a. Refused admission to Princeton Seminary because of his color, he decided to set up his own religious organization.
b. He was forcibly removed from praying at the altar rail at his former place of worship.
c. He wanted to see an integrated church that combined the elements he admired most in the Methodist and Episcopal denominations.
d. Fredrick Douglass gave him a generous grant to establish a new church.
e. Charles G. Finney persuaded Allen to build a black church since Finney believed worship should be segregated.

ANS: B   TOP: Civil rights | Race and Opportunity
DIF: Moderate   REF: Full p. 339 | Seagull p. 348
MSC: Remembering   OBJ: 4

48. During the first half of the nineteenth century, free black Americans:
a. could not, under federal law, obtain public land.
b. found, as whites did, that the West offered the best opportunities for economic advancement.
c. rose in economic status, but more slowly than whites.
d. joined with white artisans in biracial unions that successfully struck for higher wages.
e. formed predominantly upper-middle-class communities in the North.

ANS: A   TOP: Civil rights | Race and Opportunity
DIF: Moderate   REF: Full p. 339 | Seagull p. 349
MSC: Remembering   OBJ: 4

49. The cult of domesticity:
a. received very little support, which is why people referred to it as a cult, or a small fringe group.
b. represented a significant break with the idea of republican motherhood.
c. was based on the idea that women should be less dependent upon men.
d. led to a decline in birthrates.
e. meant that women would concede their household duties to domestic servants.

ANS: D   TOP: Social history | The Cult of Domesticity
DIF: Difficult   REF: Full p. 340 | Seagull p. 350
MSC: Remembering   OBJ: 4

50. What came to be redefined as a personal moral quality associated more and more closely with women?
a. freedom
b. liberty
c. virtue
d. family
e. temperance

ANS: C   TOP: Social history | The Cult of Domesticity
DIF: Easy   REF: Full p. 340 | Seagull p. 349
MSC: Remembering   OBJ: 4

51. In 1829, Lydia Maria Child wrote a popular book called:
a. *A Housewife No More.*
b. *The Feminine Mystique.*
c. *National Mother, Virtuous Wife.*
d. *Save a Penny for the Family.*
e. *The Frugal Housewife.*

ANS: E   TOP: Social history | Women and Work
DIF: Difficult   REF: Full p. 341 | Seagull p. 351
MSC: Remembering   OBJ: 4

52. The role of a white middle-class woman in antebellum America was primarily to:
a. pursue a college education.
b. take a job outside the home to supplement the family's disposable income.
c. have as large a family as possible.
d. focus her energies on the home and children.
e. produce the daily foodstuffs and necessities that her household required.

ANS: D   TOP: Social history | Women and Work
DIF: Easy   REF: Full pp. 341–341 | Seagull p. 350
MSC: Remembering   OBJ: 4

53. The women who protested during the Shoemakers' Strike in Lynn compared their condition to that of:

a. indentured servants.
b. slaves.
c. Irish immigrants.
d. religious dissenters.
e. Indians.

ANS: B   TOP: Primary document analysis | The Early Labor Movement   DIF: Moderate
REF: Full p. 343 | Seagull p. 352
MSC: Remembering   OBJ: 4

54. What did Noah Webster's *American Dictionary* define as "a state of exemption from the power or control of another"?
a. masculinity
b. individualism
c. artisanship
d. freedom
e. weakness

ANS: D   TOP: Cultural history | The "Liberty of Living"   DIF: Moderate   REF: Full p. 343 | Seagull p. 352   MSC: Remembering   OBJ: 4

55. In his essay "The Laboring Classes," Orestes Brownson argued that:
a. wealth and labor were at war.
b. each worker's problems had to be understood individually.
c. government was the cause of workers' problems.
d. workers were lazy and easily tempted by alcohol.
e. workers had achieved true freedom thanks to free enterprise.

ANS: A   TOP: Social history | The "Liberty of Living"   DIF: Difficult   REF: Full p. 343 | Seagull p. 352   MSC: Remembering   OBJ: 4

True or False

1. The catalyst for the market revolution was a series of innovations in transportation and communication.

ANS: T   TOP: Economic development | A New Economy   DIF: Moderate   REF: Full p. 308 | Seagull p. 320   MSC: Understanding   OBJ: 1

2. Toll roads did much to help the economy.

ANS: F   TOP: Economic development | Roads and Steamboats   DIF: Moderate   REF: Full p. 309 | Seagull p. 321   MSC: Remembering   OBJ: 1

3. In order to satisfy the need for slave labor in the Cotton Kingdom, an estimated 1 million slaves were relocated to the Deep South from the older slave states between 1800 and 1860.

ANS: T   TOP: Geographic issues | The Unfree Westward Movement   DIF: Moderate   REF: Full p. 317 | Seagull p. 327   MSC: Remembering   OBJ: 1

4. After 1814, commercial farmers began replacing the self-sufficient farmer, while factory workers began replacing the skilled artisan.

ANS: T   TOP: Economic development | Commercial Farmers | The Growth of Cities   DIF: Moderate
REF: Full pp. 318–319 | Seagull pp. 330–331
MSC: Remembering   OBJ: 2

5. Because an English law forbade the export of machinery blueprints, Samuel Slater memorized the plans for the power-driven spinning jenny before immigrating to America.

ANS: T   TOP: Global awareness | The Factory System   DIF: Moderate   REF: Full p. 319 | Seagull p. 331   MSC: Remembering   OBJ: 2

6. By the 1850s, Massachusetts had become the second most industrialized region of the world, after Great Britain.

ANS: T   TOP: Global awareness | The Factory System   DIF: Moderate   REF: Full p. 322 | Seagull p. 332   MSC: Remembering   OBJ: 2

7. The early industrial revolution in America was largely confined to New England and a few cities outside it.

ANS: T   TOP: Economic development | The Factory System   DIF: Easy   REF: Full p. 322 | Seagull p. 332   MSC: Remembering   OBJ: 2

8. Even though the days were long at New England textile factories, the girls were still allowed significant autonomy as to when they took their breaks and how long they took for lunch and dinner.

ANS: F   TOP: Social history | The "Mill Girls"
DIF: Moderate   REF: Full p. 323 | Seagull pp. 333–334   MSC: Remembering   OBJ: 2

9. Irish immigrants tended to be more skilled than the German immigrants arriving around the same time.

ANS: F   TOP: Ethnicity | Irish and German Newcomers   DIF: Moderate   REF: Full p. 325 | Seagull p. 335   MSC: Understanding   OBJ: 2

10. The growth in the number of Irish immigrants led to increased anti-Catholicism in the United States.

ANS: T   TOP: Ethnicity | The Rise of Nativism
DIF: Easy   REF: Full p. 326 | Seagull p. 336
MSC: Remembering   OBJ: 2

11. National boundaries made westward expansion difficult as they erected a barrier to settlement.

ANS: F   TOP: Geographic issues | The West and Freedom   DIF: Moderate   REF: Full p. 329 | Seagull p. 339   MSC: Understanding   OBJ: 3

12. John O'Sullivan coined the term "manifest destiny" to describe America's divinely appointed mission to settle all of North America.

    ANS: T   TOP: Geographic issues | The West and Freedom   DIF: Easy   REF: Full p. 329 | Seagull p. 339   MSC: Remembering   OBJ: 3

13. Henry David Thoreau celebrated the innovation of the market revolution.

    ANS: F   TOP: Social history | Individualism   DIF: Moderate   REF: Full p. 331 | Seagull p. 341   MSC: Remembering   OBJ: 3

14. The religious revivals of the early nineteenth century were originally organized by established religious leaders alarmed by the low levels of church attendance in the young republic.

    ANS: T   TOP: Cultural history | The Second Great Awakening   DIF: Moderate   REF: Full p. 334 | Seagull p. 341   MSC: Remembering   OBJ: 3

15. The Second Great Awakening both took advantage of the market revolution and criticized its excesses.

    ANS: T   TOP: Social history | The Awakening's Impact   DIF: Moderate   REF: Full p. 336 | Seagull p. 345   MSC: Remembering   OBJ: 3

16. The founder of the Mormon faith was Joseph Smith.

    ANS: T   TOP: Cultural history | The Emergence of Mormonism   DIF: Easy   REF: Full p. 336 | Seagull p. 345   MSC: Remembering   OBJ: 3

17. The market revolution produced a new middle class.

    ANS: T   TOP: Social history | Liberty and Prosperity   DIF: Easy   REF: Full p. 338 | Seagull p. 348   MSC: Remembering   OBJ: 4

18. The African Methodist Episcopal Church allowed women to preach.

    ANS: T   TOP: Social history | Liberty and Prosperity   DIF: Moderate   REF: Full p. 338 | Seagull p. 348   MSC: Remembering   OBJ: 4

19. Women and blacks fully enjoyed the fruits of the market revolution.

    ANS: F   TOP: Social history | Race and Opportunity | The Cult of Domesticity   DIF: Easy   REF: Full pp. 338, 339 | Seagull pp. 348–349   MSC: Remembering   OBJ: 4

20. One significant way that blacks were able to enjoy economic independence was by settling in the West on federally provided public land.

    ANS: F   TOP: Geographic issues | Race and Opportunity   DIF: Easy   REF: Full p. 339 | Seagull p. 349   MSC: Remembering   OBJ: 4

21. Under the dictates of the cult of domesticity, women were to find freedom in fulfilling their duties within their "sphere."

    ANS: T   TOP: Social history | The Cult of Domesticity   DIF: Easy   REF: Full p. 340 | Seagull p. 350   MSC: Remembering   OBJ: 4

22. There was a significant increase in the American birthrate during the nineteenth century.

    ANS: F   TOP: Social history | The Cult of Domesticity   DIF: Moderate   REF: Full p. 340 | Seagull p. 350   MSC: Remembering   OBJ: 4

23. For middle-class women in the nineteenth century, not working was viewed as a badge of freedom.

    ANS: T   TOP: Social history | Women and Work   DIF: Moderate   REF: Full pp. 340–341 | Seagull p. 350   MSC: Remembering   OBJ: 4

24. During the market revolution, the separation of classes shrunk as wealth was more evenly distributed.

    ANS: F   TOP: Social history | The Early Labor Movement   DIF: Easy   REF: Full p. 341 | Seagull p. 351   MSC: Understanding   OBJ: 4

25. Despite the fact that the first workingman's parties had been established by the 1820s, strikes were still very uncommon in the 1830s.

    ANS: F   TOP: Social history | The Early Labor Movement   DIF: Moderate   REF: Full p. 342 | Seagull p. 352   MSC: Remembering   OBJ: 4

26. As the market revolution took on steam, some critics described wage labor as the very essence of slavery.

    ANS: T   TOP: Social history | The "Liberty of Living"   DIF: Moderate   REF: Full p. 343 | Seagull p. 352   MSC: Remembering   OBJ: 4

Short Answer

Identify and give the historical significance of each of the following terms, events, and people in a paragraph or two.

1. factory system
2. individualism
3. corporations
4. transcendentalism
5. rise of the West
6. nativism

7. Erie Canal
8. Charles G. Finney
9. cult of domesticity
10. free blacks
11. Second Great Awakening
12. wage earners

Essay Questions

1. The Marquis de Lafayette, who fought for American independence and revisited the United States fifty years later, wrote that "I would never have drawn my sword in the cause of America if I could have conceived that thereby I was founding a land of slavery." What might Lafayette have seen in 1824 America that would impel him to make such a statement? How had slavery evolved? Was it expanding? How entrenched in American life was it at this time?

ANS: Answers will vary   TOP: Civil rights | Economic development | Geographic issues | Social history | The Cotton Kingdom | The Unfree Westward Movement | Race and Opportunity   DIF: Moderate
MSC: Applying   OBJ: 1

2. Explain how improvements in transportation and communication made possible the rise of the West as a powerful, self-conscious region of the new nation.

ANS: Answers will vary   TOP: Economic development | Geographic issues | A New Economy | Roads and Steamboats | Railroads and the Telegraph
DIF: Moderate   MSC: Applying   OBJ: 1

3. Discuss the impact of the market revolution on women and African-Americans (both free and slave).

ANS: Answers will vary   TOP: Civil rights | Economic development | Social history | Race and Opportunity | The "Mill Girls" | Women and Work | The "Liberty of Living"   DIF: Difficult
MSC: Understanding   OBJ: 4

4. Explain the shift from artisan to factory worker, and discuss the factory system. What were the advantages and disadvantages? Who was left out? Who benefited? What were some ways workers responded?

ANS: Answers will vary   TOP: Economic development | Social history | The Factory System | The Industrial Worker | The Growth of Cities | The "Liberty of Living"   DIF: Moderate   MSC: Analyzing
OBJ: 2 / 4

5. Thoroughly describe the arguments made that linked American freedom to westward expansion. Who or what were obstacles to freedom in the pursuit of expansion? How did Americans deal with those obstacles?

ANS: Answers will vary   TOP: Economic development | Geographic issues | Political history, changes | The West and Freedom   DIF: Moderate
MSC: Analyzing   OBJ: 3 / 4

6. Explain how transcendentalism and the Second Great Awakening affected the definitions of freedom. How were both movements a response to the market revolution?

ANS: Answers will vary   TOP: Cultural history | Economic development | Social history | The Second Great Awakening | The Awakening's Impact | Liberty and Prosperity | The Transcendentalists
DIF: Moderate   MSC: Analyzing   OBJ: 3

7. What do historians mean when they assert that the Second Great Awakening "democratized" American Christianity? What are the strengths and weaknesses of that assertion?

ANS: Answers will vary   TOP: Cultural history | Economic development | Social history | The Second Great Awakening | The Awakening's Impact
DIF: Difficult   MSC: Analyzing   OBJ: 3

8. Comment on what Alexis de Tocqueville meant when he said that Americans "combine the notions of Christianity and of liberty so intimately in their minds that it is impossible to make them conceive the one without the other." How accurate do you think that observation was?

ANS: Answers will vary   TOP: Cultural history | Economic development | Political history, changes | Social history | The Second Great Awakening | The Awakening's Impact   DIF: Moderate
MSC: Evaluating   OBJ: 3

9. Some women worked in the mills, relishing the freedom and independence they felt away from the farm for the first time, while others developed a cult of domesticity, thinking themselves free to not have to work outside the home. Compare the meaning of freedom for these two groups of women. Think back to previous chapters and compare the role of women during the market revolution with the "republican motherhood" role of women during the American Revolution.

ANS: Answers will vary   TOP: Economic development | Social history | The Cult of Domesticity | Women and Work   DIF: Moderate
MSC: Analyzing   OBJ: 3

10. One German newcomer wrote that "there aren't any masters [in America], here everyone is a free agent." How accurate a statement was that? Why would a German

immigrant view America as free? Do you think an Irish immigrant would feel the same way about America? Why or why not?

ANS: Answers will vary   TOP: Economic development | Ethnicity | Social history | Irish and German Newcomers | The Rise of Nativism   DIF: Moderate
MSC: Evaluating   OBJ: 2

11. During the Revolutionary period, virtue was considered an essential component of a male's character for the survival of the republic. The founding fathers often spoke of a virtuous citizenry as the key to liberty and freedom taking hold. Fifty years later, however, virtue had shifted to become a character sought after in women. Describe why this shift occurred and its consequences.

ANS: Answers will vary   TOP: Social history | The Cult of Domesticity   DIF: Moderate
MSC: Analyzing   OBJ: 4

CHAPTER 10 | Democracy in America, 1815–1840

This chapter concentrates on the last of the three historical processes unleashed by the Revolution that accelerated after the War of 1812—the rise of a vigorous political democracy. Democracy increased as the electorate enlarged with the abolition of property requirements for suffrage in most states. However, women and free blacks were largely excluded from political democracy. Much of the political debate during the period involved economic issues raised by the market revolution spurred by the War of 1812. Some national leaders argued that the federal government had a responsibility to ensure American economic development. They favored the "American System," a political program for economic development that included a high protective tariff, public-financed transportation improvements, and a national bank. Others, such as those injured by the Panic of 1819, viewed government involvement in the economy negatively. Differences also emerged over whether to admit Missouri as a slave state; the two compromises (1820 and 1821) Congress hammered out to address that issue revealed sectional divisions over slavery. Also, under President Monroe (1817–1825), the United States recognized newly independent Latin American nations and asserted that the Americas were off-limits for further European colonization (see Monroe's "Voices of Freedom" excerpt). The chapter highlights the emergence of new political parties from the one-party era of the Monroe presidency (the so-called "Era of Good Feelings," when the Federalist Party disintegrated). Opponents of President John Quincy Adams's vision of vigorous national power, guided by Martin Van Buren's idea that competing political parties were healthy for the nation, coalesced into the Democratic Party that succeeded in electing Andrew Jackson to the presidency in 1828. The new party system took shape during Jackson's two terms when nullification, Indian removal, and a "war" over national banking policy helped to divide the nation into Democrats (Jackson's supporters) and Whigs (his opponents). The sec-

ond "Voices of Freedom" excerpt highlights ideas of John C. Calhoun, a key Jackson opponent, on protecting the power of the South as a minority in a Democratic era. Democrats exploited popular themes to win elections, but the Panic of 1837 and subsequent depression allowed the Whigs to take the White House in 1840. They did so, in part, by using techniques pioneered by the Democrats. Appropriately enough for a more democratic age, the Whigs portrayed their presidential candidate, William Henry Harrison, as a common man.

CHAPTER OUTLINE

I. Introduction: Andrew Jackson
  A. Jackson embodies the major developments of the era.
    1. Market revolution
    2. Westward movement
    3. Expansion of slavery
    4. Growth of democracy
  B. Background
    1. As a boy served as courier in American Revolution
    2. As a young man moved to Tennessee, where he studied law
    3. He owned large plantation with slaves.
  C. America's claim to being oldest democracy

II. The Triumph of Democracy
  A. Property and Democracy
    1. With regard to freedom, political democracy was intimately connected with the market revolution and territorial expansion.
    2. By 1860, all but one state had eliminated property requirements for voting.

B. The Dorr War
 1. Rhode Island had property qualifications for voting in 1841.
 2. Because propertyless wage earners (e.g., factory workers) could not vote, the state's labor movement pushed for reform at the People's Convention (October 1841).
   a. This extralegal convention adopted a new state constitution that enfranchised all white men.
   b. Reformers inaugurated Thomas Dorr as governor.
   c. President Tyler sent in federal troops and the Dorr movement collapsed.
   d. The legislature soon removed the property qualifications for all native-born men, including blacks.
C. Tocqueville on Democracy
 1. By 1840, more than 90 percent of adult white men were eligible to vote.
 2. Democratic political institutions came to define the nation's sense of its own identity.
 3. Tocqueville identified democracy as an essential attribute of American freedom.
 4. Since ancient Greece, a fear existed that democracy could turn into anarchy or tyranny.
 5. The term "citizen" in America had become synonymous with the right to vote.
D. The Information Revolution
 1. Market revolution and political democracy produced an expansion in public sphere and explosion in printing.
   a. Penny press emphasized sensationalism, crime stories, and exposés.
   b. Newspapers had far reach due to low postal rates.
   c. Organized political parties led to more newspapers.
   d. Reduction in printing costs made possible "alternative" papers started by blacks, labor, and abolitionists.
 2. New generation of women writers resulted from this democratization.
   a. Lydia Child
   b. Catherine Maria Sedgwick
   c. Catharine Beecher
E. The Limits of Democracy
 1. As with the market revolution, women and blacks were barred from full democracy.
   a. They were denied on the basis of their alleged natural incapacity.
   b. Democracy absorbed poor white men and immigrants.

 2. Freedom in the public realm in no way implied freedom in private life.
F. A Racial Democracy
 1. Despite increased democracy in America, blacks were seen as a group apart with regard to equality.
 2. Blacks were often portrayed as stereotypes.
 3. Blacks were not allowed to vote in most states.
G. Race and Class
 1. By 1860, blacks could vote in the same way as whites in only five New England states.
 2. No state accorded free blacks full equality before the law.
 3. In effect, race had replaced class as the boundary that separated those American men who were entitled to enjoy political freedom from those who were not.

III. Nationalism and Its Discontents
 A. The American System
 1. Fighting to a draw in the War of 1812 led to a burst of national pride.
 2. A new manufacturing sector emerged from the War of 1812, and many believed that it was a necessary complement to the agricultural sector for national growth.
 3. In 1815, President James Madison put forward a blueprint for government-promoted economic development that came to be known as the American System.
   a. New national bank
   b. Tariffs
   c. Federal financing for better roads and canals ("internal improvements")
 4. President Madison came to believe that a constitutional amendment was necessary for the government to build roads and canals and vetoed the "internal improvements."
 B. Banks and Money
 1. The Second Bank of the United States was a profit-making corporation that served the government.
 2. Local banks promoted economic growth.
 3. Local banks printed money.
   a. The value of paper currency fluctuated wildly.
   b. The Bank of the United States was supposed to prevent the overissuance of money.
   c. The BUS could demand payment in gold and silver from a local bank.
 C. The Panic of 1819
 1. The Bank of the United States participated in a speculative fever that swept the country after the War of 1812 ended.

2. Early in 1819, as European demand for American farm products returned to normal levels, the economic bubble burst.
   a. Demand for land and prices fell.
   b. BUS and state banks quickly called in loans.
D. The Politics of the Panic
   1. The Panic of 1819 disrupted the political harmony of the previous years.
      a. Americans continued to distrust banks.
   2. The Supreme Court ruled in *McCulloch v. Maryland* that the Bank of the United States was constitutional.
      a. Constitutional due to "general welfare clause"
      b. Maryland could not tax the bank.
E. The Missouri Controversy
   1. James Monroe's two terms as president were characterized by the absence of two-party competition ("The Era of Good Feelings").
   2. The absence of political party disputes was replaced by sectional disputes.
   3. Missouri petitioned for statehood in 1819.
      a. Debate arose over slavery.
   4. The Missouri Compromise was adopted by Congress in 1820.
      a. Missouri was admitted to the Union as a slave state and, to maintain sectional balance, Maine was admitted as a free state.
      b. Congress prohibited slavery north of the 36° 30' latitude in remaining Louisiana Purchase territory.
   5. Henry Clay engineered a second Missouri Compromise to deal with Missouri's barring of free blacks (1821), which the state largely ignored.
F. The Slavery Question
   1. Northern Republicans did not want slavery to expand for political reasons.
      a. New York believed the South, especially Virginia, had too much power.
   2. The Missouri debate highlighted that the westward expansion of slavery was a passionate topic that eventually proved to be hazardous to national unity.

IV. Nation, Section, and Party
   A. The United States and the Latin American Wars of Independence
      1. Between 1810 and 1822, Spain's Latin American colonies rose in rebellion and established a series of independent nations.
         a. Unlike the United States, seventeen different nations were created.
         b. Lack of printing presses made communication difficult.
      2. In 1822, the Monroe administration became the first government to extend diplomatic recognition to the new Latin American republics.
      3. In some ways, Latin American constitutions were more democratic than the U.S. Constitution.
         a. Allowed Indians and free blacks to vote
      4. These wars of independence lasted longer and were more destructive.
         a. Difficult to achieve economic development
   B. The Monroe Doctrine
      1. Fearing that Spain would try to regain its colonies, Secretary of State John Quincy Adams drafted the Monroe Doctrine.
         a. No new European colonization of the New World
         b. The United States would abstain from European wars
         c. Europeans should not interfere with new Latin American republics.
   C. The Election of 1824
      1. Andrew Jackson was the only candidate in the 1824 election to have national appeal.
      2. None of the four candidates received a majority of the electoral votes.
         a. The election fell to the House of Representatives.
         b. Henry Clay, out of the running, supported John Quincy Adams.
      3. Clay's "corrupt bargain" gave Adams the White House.
   D. The Nationalism of John Quincy Adams
      1. John Quincy Adams enjoyed one of the most distinguished pre-presidential careers of any American president.
      2. Adams had a clear vision of national greatness.
         a. Supported the American system
         b. Wished to enhance American influence in the Western Hemisphere
   E. "Liberty Is Power"
      1. Adams held a view of federal power far more expansive than most of his contemporaries.
         a. Stated that "liberty is power"
      2. His plans alarmed many, and his vision would not be fulfilled until the twentieth century.
   F. Martin Van Buren and the Democratic Party
      1. Adams's political rivals emphasized:
         a. Individual liberty
         b. States' rights
         c. Limited government
      2. Martin Van Buren viewed political party competition as a necessary and positive influence to achieve national unity.

3. He hoped to reconstruct the Jeffersonian political alliance.

G. The Election of 1828
  1. By 1828, Van Buren had established the political apparatus of the Democratic Party.
  2. Andrew Jackson ran against John Quincy Adams in 1828's scurrilous campaign.
  3. A far higher percentage of the eligible electorate voted in 1828 than before, and Jackson won a resounding victory.

V. The Age of Jackson
  A. The Party System
    1. Jackson was a man of many contradictions.
    2. Politics had become a spectacle.
    3. Party machines emerged.
      a. Spoils system
    4. National conventions chose candidates.
    5. Jackson's Kitchen Cabinet was an informal group of advisers.
      a. Most were newspaper editors.
  B. Democrats and Whigs
    1. Democrats and Whigs differed on issues that emerged from the market revolution and tension between national and sectional loyalties.
    2. Democrats were alarmed by widening gap between social classes.
      a. Democrats favored no government intervention in the economy.
    3. Whigs supported government promotion of economic development through the American System.
  C. Public and Private Freedom
    1. The party battles of the Jacksonian era reflected the clash between public and private definitions of American freedom and their relationship to governmental power.
    2. Democrats supported a weak federal government, championing individual and states' rights.
      a. Reduced expenditures
      b. Reduced tariffs
      c. Abolished the national bank
  D. Politics and Morality
    1. Democrats opposed attempts to impose a unified moral vision on society.
    2. Whigs believed that a strong federal government was necessary to promote liberty.
    3. Whigs argued that government should promote morality to foster the welfare of the people.
  E. South Carolina and Nullification
    1. Jackson's first term was dominated by a battle to uphold the supremacy of federal over state law.
      a. Tariff of 1828

2. South Carolina led the charge for a weakened federal government in part from fear that a strong federal government might act against slavery.

F. Calhoun's Political Theory
  1. John C. Calhoun emerged as the leading theorist of nullification.
    a. *Exposition and Protest*
      i. Influenced by the Virginia and Kentucky Resolutions
      ii. Because states created the Constitution, each one could prevent the enforcement within its borders of federal laws that exceeded powers specifically spelled out in the Constitution.
  2. Daniel Webster argued that the people, not the states, created the Constitution.
    a. Nullification was illegal, unconstitutional, and treasonous.

G. The Nullification Crisis
  1. Calhoun denied that nullification led to disunion.
    a. Concurrent majority
  2. Jackson considered nullification an act of disunion.
  3. When South Carolina nullified the tariff in 1832, Jackson responded with the Force Act.
  4. A compromise tariff (1833) resolved the crisis.
  5. Calhoun left the Democratic Party for the Whigs.

H. Indian Removal
  1. The expansion of cotton and slavery led to forced relocation of Indians.
    a. Indian Removal Act of 1830
    b. Five Civilized Tribes
    c. Cherokees took lead with development of written language, schools, and written laws.
  2. The law marked a repudiation of the Jeffersonian idea that civilized Indians could be assimilated into the American population.

I. The Supreme Court and the Indians
  1. The Cherokees went to court to protect their rights.
    a. *Cherokee Nation v. Georgia*
      i. Indians were wards of federal government.
    b. *Worcester v. Georgia*
      i. Georgia's actions violated Cherokee treaties with federal government.
  2. John Ross led Cherokee resistance.
    a. Trail of Tears
  3. The Seminoles in Florida fought a war against removal (1835–1842).
    a. Three thousand forced to move and a small amount remained.

4. William Apess appealed for harmony between white Americans and Indians.

VI. The Bank War and After
  A. Biddle's Bank
    1. The Bank of the United States symbolized the hopes and fears inspired by the market revolution.
      a. Central political struggle of Age of Jackson
    2. Jackson distrusted bankers as "nonproducers."
    3. The Bank, under its president, Nicholas Biddle, wielded great power.
    4. Using language resonating with popular values, Jackson vetoed a bill to renew the Bank's charter.
    5. Jackson enhanced the role of the presidency as he claimed to be representing the people.
  B. The Pet Banks and the Economy
    1. Both soft-money advocates (associated with state banks) and hard-money advocates supported Jackson's veto.
    2. Jackson authorized the removal of federal funds from the vaults of the national bank and their deposit to state or "pet" banks.
    3. Partly because the Bank of the United States had lost the ability to regulate the currency effectively, prices rose dramatically while real wages declined.
  C. The Panic of 1837
    1. By 1836, the American government for land purchases and the Bank of England for American creditors required gold or silver for payments.
    2. With cotton exports declining, the United States suffered a panic in 1837 and a depression until 1843.
    3. States amended their constitutions prohibiting legislatures from borrowing money, issuing corporate charters, and buying stock in private enterprises.
      a. For a time, Jacksonians had separated both federal and state governments from being involved in the economy.
  D. Van Buren in Office
    1. Martin Van Buren approved the Independent Treasury to deal with the crisis.
    2. The Independent Treasury split the Democratic party.
      a. Calhoun went back to the Democrats.
  E. The Election of 1840
    1. The Whigs nominated William Henry Harrison in 1840.
    2. Harrison was promoted as the "log cabin" candidate.
      a. Running mate was John Tyler
    3. Selling candidates in campaigns was as important as the platform for which they stood.
  F. His Accidency
    1. Harrison died a month after taking office.
    2. Tyler vetoed measures to enact the American System.

SUGGESTED DISCUSSION QUESTIONS

- Discuss how, during the Age of Jackson, politics became a spectacle.
- Describe how Andrew Jackson embodied the prevailing mood of America. What did Americans see in his life and character that made him so popular?
- Discuss the ways liberty and freedom were used to justify the removal of the Indians in the 1830s. How did opponents of Indian removal use liberty and freedom?
- How did the nullification crisis illustrate the divide between North and South? Compare the significance of the nullification crisis with the Missouri Compromise.
- How were "liberty" and "freedom" used by various sides of the debate over the Bank War?
- Women and blacks were left out of the political democracy. These two groups were also left out of the market revolution. Was it inevitable that their exclusion from one would lead to their exclusion from the other? What determined their exclusion?
- Discuss why property ownership was so easily excluded as a voting requirement by the 1840s, when ownership of property had been so vital to defining freedom in the eighteenth century.
- What were the key arguments made in the debate about the removal of Indians from the southeastern states to what is now Oklahoma?

SUPPLEMENTAL WEB AND VISUAL RESOURCES

Andrew Jackson
  http://www.pbs.org/kcet/andrewjackson/
  This is the companion site for the PBS documentary—Andrew Jackson: Good, Evil & The Presidency. The "Themes" and "Special Features" links have essays and interactive activities on Jackson and the time period.

Eastern Indian Wars
  http://americanhistory.si.edu/militaryhistory/exhibition/flash .html

From the Smithsonian Institution's National Museum of American History, select a war (Eastern Indian Wars, 1813–1838) and enter an exhibit which includes a movie, learning resources, statistics, printable exhibition, maps, and time lines.

Indian Removal

http://www.nhc.rtp.nc.us/tserve/nattrans/ntecoindian/essays /indianremoval.htm

Part of the National Humanities Center, this website deals with the effects of removal of Indian tribes east of the Mississippi. Useful resources for teachers, such as discussion guidelines, documents, maps, and time lines.

Missouri Compromise

http://www.loc.gov/rr/program/bib/ourdocs/Missouri.html

The Library of Congress website offers primary documents and background information about the compromise.

The Panic of 1819

www.ohiohistorycentral.org/entry.php?rec=535

From Ohio History Central, this website gives an overview of the Panic, but also offers useful links to related topics, including Andrew Jackson, the banking crisis, and early industrialization.

Trail of Tears

http://www.pbs.org/weta/thewest/program/episodes/two/trail tears.htm

From the PBS series *The West* by Ken Burns, volume 2, "Trail of Tears," concentrates on the Indian Removal Act of 1830.

VOTE: The Machinery of Democracy

http://americanhistory.si.edu/vote/

This Flash Interactive Exhibition from the Smithsonian Institution's National Museum of American History explores how ballots and voting systems have evolved over the years.

SUPPLEMENTAL PRINT RESOURCES

Anderson, Gary Clayton. *The Conquest of Texas: Ethnic Cleansing in the Promised Land, 1820–1875*. Norman, OK: University of Oklahoma Press, 2005.

Brands, H. W. *The Money Men: Capitalism, Democracy, and the Hundred Years' War over the American Dollar*. New York: W. W. Norton & Company, 2006.

Ellis, Richard E. *The Union at Risk: Jacksonian Democracy, States' Rights and the Nullification Crisis*. New York: Oxford University Press, 1987.

Feller, Daniel. "Politics and Society: Toward a Jacksonian Synthesis." *Journal of the Early Republic* 10, no. 2 (1990): 135–161.

———. *The Jacksonian Promise: America, 1815–1840*. Baltimore, MD: Johns Hopkins University Press, 1995.

Forbes, Robert Pierce. *The Missouri Compromise and Its Aftermath: Slavery and the Meaning of America*. Chapel Hill, NC: University of North Carolina Press, 2007.

Holt, Michael F. *The Rise and Fall of the American Whig Party: Jacksonian Politics and the Onset of the Civil War*. New York: Oxford University Press, 1999.

Lewis, James E., Jr. *John Quincy Adams: Policymaker for the Union*. Wilmington, DE: Scholarly Resources, 2001.

Perdue, Theda. *Cherokee Women: Gender and Culture Change, 1700–1835*. Lincoln, NE: University of Nebraska Press, 1998.

Remini, Robert. *Henry Clay: Statesman for the Union*. New York: W. W. Norton & Company, 1991.

Reynolds, David S. *Waking Giant: America in the Age of Jackson*. New York: HarperCollins Publishers, 2008.

Silbey, Joel. *Martin Van Buren and the Emergence of American Popular Politics*. Lanham, MD: Rowman and Littlefield, 2002.

Watson, Harry. *Andrew Jackson vs. Henry Clay: Democracy and Development in Antebellum America*. New York: Bedford/St. Martin's, 1998.

Weeks, William Earl. *John Quincy Adams and American Global Empire*. Lexington, KY: University Press of Kentucky, 1992.

TEST BANK

Matching

TEST I

____ 1. Thomas Dorr
____ 2. Henry Clay
____ 3. John Calhoun
____ 4. Albert Gallatin
____ 5. James Tallmadge
____ 6. John Ross
____ 7. Daniel Webster
____ 8. John Quincy Adams
____ 9. Martin Van Buren
____ 10. Nicholas Biddle
____ 11. William Apess
____ 12. William Henry Harrison

a. his proposal sparked Missouri controversy
b. Second Bank of the United States
c. *A Son of the Forest*
d. temporary Rhode Island governor
e. log cabin candidate
f. theorist behind nullification
g. advocated a powerful federal government as president
h. Jefferson's treasury secretary
i. accused of making a "corrupt bargain"
j. founder of the Democratic Party
k. senator who denounced nullification as treasonous
l. Cherokee resistance leader

Answer Key: d, i, f, h, a, l, k, g, j, b, c, e

TEST 2

____ 1. Missouri Compromise
____ 2. "corrupt bargain"
____ 3. *McCulloch v. Maryland*
____ 4. minstrels

___ 5. Whig Party
___ 6. American System
___ 7. Monroe Doctrine
___ 8. nonfreeholder
___ 9. penny press
___ 10. spoils system
___ 11. *Cherokee Nation v. Georgia*
___ 12. Trail of Tears

a. held Bank of the United States was constitutional
b. America's diplomatic declaration of independence
c. opposed Andrew Jackson
d. election of 1824
e. performers in racist theatrical shows
f. inexpensive newspapers
g. getting a job based on party loyalty, not on merit
h. called Indians "wards" of the federal government
i. political program for economic development
j. men who did not own enough property to vote
k. Cherokee trek to Oklahoma
l. maintained the balance of power between slave and free states

Answer Key: l, d, a, e, c, i, b, j, f, g, h, k

Learning Objectives

1. Identify the social bases for the flourishing democracy of the early mid-nineteenth century.
2. Describe the efforts made in this period to strengthen the economic integration of the nation, and identify the major crises that hindered these efforts.
3. Identify the major areas of conflict between nationalism and sectionalism.
4. Describe the ways Andrew Jackson embodied the contradictions of democratic nationalism.
5. Explain how the Bank War influenced the economy and party competition.

Multiple Choice

1. Andrew Jackson's inauguration was:
   a. small and dignified.
   b. much like the previous presidential inaugurations.
   c. limited to only the upper crust of society.
   d. a large, rowdy event.
   e. a disastrous affair, since Jackson's opponents protested outside the White House.

   ANS: D   TOP: Political history, changes | Introduction: Andrew Jackson   DIF: Easy   REF: Full p. 347 | Seagull p. 355   MSC: Remembering   OBJ: 4

2. In the early to mid-nineteenth century, property qualifications for voting:
   a. continued in Virginia because large slaveholders dominated the state's politics.
   b. survived in all of the slave states, but in none of the free states.
   c. died out entirely, allowing all whites to vote in every state.
   d. were more popular in newer states than in the original thirteen.
   e. disappeared because of the Voting Rights Act championed by President Andrew Jackson.

   ANS: A   TOP: Political history, changes | Property and Democracy   DIF: Moderate   REF: Full p. 348 | Seagull p. 357   MSC: Understanding   OBJ: 1

3. The Dorr War:
   a. stemmed from a disagreement between John Quincy Adams and Andrew Jackson over internal improvements.
   b. refers to fighting that broke out between whites and Cherokees in Georgia.
   c. demonstrated the contentiousness of the national bank debate.
   d. divided Rhode Islanders over the issue of expanding voting rights for white men.
   e. resulted from the nullification crisis.

   ANS: D   TOP: Political history, changes | The Dorr War   DIF: Moderate   REF: Full pp. 348–349 | Seagull pp. 357–358   MSC: Remembering   OBJ: 1

4. The key insight of Alexis de Tocqueville's *Tocqueville on Democracy* was that:
   a. the most important thing about American democracy was that the majority of men could vote.
   b. American democracy was really a sham.
   c. American democracy really represented an important cultural shift.
   d. the ideology of the Whig Party was actually more democratic than that of the Democratic Party.
   e. American democracy could not exist without strong presidential leadership.

   ANS: C   TOP: Cultural history | Tocqueville on Democracy   DIF: Difficult   REF: Full p. 349 | Seagull p. 359   MSC: Understanding   OBJ: 1

5. By 1840, approximately _____ percent of adult white men were eligible to vote.
   a. 40
   b. 55
   c. 65
   d. 75
   e. 90

   ANS: E   TOP: Social history | Tocqueville on Democracy   DIF: Moderate   REF: Full p. 349 | Seagull p. 358   MSC: Remembering   OBJ: 1

6. By the 1830s, the term "citizen" in America had become synonymous with the right to:
   a. accumulate wealth.
   b. vote.
   c. own property.
   d. own slaves.
   e. publicly criticize the government.

   ANS: B   TOP: Social history | Tocqueville on Democracy   DIF: Easy   REF: Full p. 350 | Seagull p. 359   MSC: Understanding   OBJ: 1

7. Women writers benefited from:
   a. men accepting the idea that they had the right to express their political views, just not vote on them.
   b. the increasing popularity of fiction about women workers, based on the Lowell girls.
   c. the Lydia Maria Child Publishing House, which emphasized women's literature.
   d. the growth of the reading public, part of the democratization of American life.
   e. the need for books to explain how women could play a role in the political sphere.

   ANS: D   TOP: Social history | The Information Revolution   DIF: Difficult   REF: Full p. 351 | Seagull p. 360   MSC: Remembering   OBJ: 1

8. A primary reason that both women and blacks were largely excluded from the expansion of democracy was:
   a. the argument that, since they did not have the vote in England, they ought not to have the vote in America.
   b. that they were not citizens, so they could not vote.
   c. that both groups were viewed as being naturally incapable and thus unfit for suffrage.
   d. that members of neither group had asked to be included in politics.
   e. that both groups were largely illiterate, and literacy was a necessary skill for political participation.

   ANS: C   TOP: Social history | The Limits of Democracy   DIF: Moderate   REF: Full pp. 351–352 | Seagull pp. 361–362   MSC: Remembering   OBJ: 1

9. By 1860, free black men could vote on the same basis as whites only in:
   a. Virginia and Maryland.
   b. New York and Pennsylvania.
   c. the Upper Northwest (Michigan, Wisconsin, and Minnesota).
   d. four states in the Lower South.
   e. five New England states.

   ANS: E   TOP: Social history | Race and Class   DIF: Difficult   REF: Full p. 353 | Seagull p. 363   MSC: Remembering   OBJ: 1

10. In the wake of the War of 1812, younger Republicans like Henry Clay and John Calhoun:
    a. continued to support agrarianism, but believed that the nation's economic independence required a manufacturing sector.
    b. demanded that the United States scale back its international involvement and depend exclusively on agriculture for its prosperity.
    c. believed in the need for national economic development, but thought that the federal government should stay out of it and let the states do it.
    d. decided that Jeffersonianism was hopelessly out of date when President James Madison opposed their efforts, and they decided to form their own political party.
    e. threw their support to Andrew Jackson because they realized that their plans were too grandiose to win popular support without a hero as their standard-bearer.

    ANS: A   TOP: Economic development | The American System   DIF: Difficult   REF: Full p. 354 | Seagull p. 364   MSC: Understanding   OBJ: 2

11. In response to the demand for internal improvements, President James Madison:
    a. spoke out vigorously against what Henry Clay called the "American System."
    b. approved a law that created the interstate highway system that we have today.
    c. called for a constitutional amendment to empower the federal government to build roads and canals.
    d. signed into law John Calhoun's bill for federally financed internal improvements.
    e. created a government-funded steamboat company that revolutionized river transportation.

    ANS: C   TOP: Economic development | The American System   DIF: Moderate   REF: Full p. 354 | Seagull p. 365   MSC: Remembering   OBJ: 2

12. The Second Bank of the United States was created:
    a. by Congress in 1816, with the support of President Madison.
    b. to counterbalance the power of the First Bank of the United States.
    c. by President Monroe's executive order in 1820.
    d. by a group of New York bankers after the First Bank of the United States failed.
    e. by Congress in 1832, with the support of President Jackson.

    ANS: A   TOP: Economic development | The American System   DIF: Difficult   REF: Full p. 355 | Seagull p. 365   MSC: Remembering   OBJ: 2

13. In the first half of the nineteenth century, paper money:
   a. could be issued only by the Second Bank of the United States.
   b. was illegal.
   c. promised to pay the bearer on demand a specific amount of gold or silver.
   d. never changed its value because of U.S. government guarantees.
   e. never exceeded the amount of money that the bank printing it held in its vault.

   ANS: C   TOP: Economic development | Banks and Money   DIF: Difficult   REF: Full p. 355 | Seagull p. 366   MSC: Remembering   OBJ: 2

14. The Panic of 1819:
   a. resulted partly from an upsurge in European demand for American farm products that the United States was unprepared to meet.
   b. led to impossibly high prices for western lands.
   c. enhanced trust in banks because they did such a good job of weathering the economic storm.
   d. prompted some states to suspend debt collections, which helped debtors but hurt creditors.
   e. inspired John Marshall's decision against the banking power in *Gibbons v. Ogden.*

   ANS: D   TOP: Economic development | The Politics of the Panic   DIF: Difficult   REF: Full p. 356 | Seagull p. 367   MSC: Understanding   OBJ: 2

15. In its decision in *McCulloch v. Maryland,* the U.S. Supreme Court ruled that:
   a. the Indians were not allowed to sue the federal government.
   b. the Second Bank of the United States was constitutional.
   c. Catholics could not be barred from political office.
   d. the American System was unconstitutional.
   e. states could nullify federal laws with congressional permission.

   ANS: B   TOP: Constitutional history | The Politics of the Panic   DIF: Difficult   REF: Full p. 356 | Seagull p. 367   MSC: Remembering   OBJ: 2

16. The term "Era of Good Feelings" refers to the period of American history when:
   a. the Federalist Party was at its strongest.
   b. there seemed to be political harmony during the Monroe administration.
   c. Americans united across party lines to declare war on Great Britain in the War of 1812.
   d. slavery was gradually abolished in all the states.
   e. Democrats and Whigs cooperated to solve the nation's financial crisis.

   ANS: B   TOP: Political history, changes | The Missouri Controversy   DIF: Moderate   REF: Full p. 357 | Seagull p. 367   MSC: Remembering   OBJ: 2

17. Under the Missouri Compromise of 1820:
   a. the remaining Louisiana Purchase territory was divided into slave and free zones.
   b. Congress banned slavery in any new territory that might ever be added to the United States.
   c. Missouri agreed to gradual emancipation of slavery in exchange for admission to the Union.
   d. Ohio became a free state to balance the admission of Missouri as a slave state.
   e. slave states gained a two-seat advantage in the U.S. Senate.

   ANS: A   TOP: Political history, changes | The Missouri Controversy   DIF: Moderate   REF: Full pp. 358–359 | Seagull p. 368   MSC: Remembering   OBJ: 2

18. Why was a second Missouri Compromise necessary?
   a. Maine's state constitution allowed slavery to continue until 1840.
   b. Missouri's state constitution barred free blacks from entering the state.
   c. Henry Clay refused to vote for the first Missouri Compromise.
   d. Texas wished to enter the Union as a slave state at the same time.
   e. Missouri's state constitution prohibited wage labor.

   ANS: B   TOP: Political history, changes | The Missouri Controversy   DIF: Difficult   REF: Full p. 358 | Seagull p. 369   MSC: Remembering   OBJ: 2

19. Both Thomas Jefferson and John Quincy Adams suggested that the Missouri controversy of 1820–1821:
   a. demonstrated the wisdom of the founding fathers in adopting the three-fifths clause.
   b. should have been solved by adoption of the Tallmadge Amendment.
   c. was not as dangerous as President Monroe made it out to be.
   d. resulted from overly ambitious proslavery politicians seeking to score political points.
   e. revealed a sectional divide that potentially threatened the Union.

   ANS: E   TOP: Political history, changes | The Slavery Question   DIF: Moderate   REF: Full p. 358 | Seagull p. 369   MSC: Remembering   OBJ: 2

20. The independence movements in Latin America between 1810 and 1822:
   a. led Spain to crack down and succeed in consolidating its power in the Americas.

b. gained very little sympathy in the United States because of atrocities committed by revolutionaries.

c. created seventeen different nations, each headed by a person of Indian ancestry.

d. paralleled in some ways the independence movement that created the United States.

e. created new nations that economically developed at a very fast rate.

ANS: D   TOP: Global awareness | The United States and the Latin American Wars of Independence
DIF: Moderate   REF: Full p. 359 | Seagull p. 370
MSC: Understanding   OBJ: 3

21. The Monroe Doctrine:
    a. was the idea that all white men should have voting rights.
    b. secured Florida from Spain.
    c. declared the Americas off-limits for further European colonization.
    d. stated that the United States would be neutral in all international conflicts.
    e. settled the nullification crisis favorably for South Carolina.

    ANS: C   TOP: Global awareness | The Monroe Doctrine   DIF: Moderate   REF: Full p. 361 | Seagull p. 372   MSC: Remembering   OBJ: 3

22. In the presidential election of 1824, who received the most votes but failed to win a majority of either the popular or electoral votes (requiring the House of Representatives to select a president)?
    a. Andrew Jackson
    b. Henry Clay
    c. John Quincy Adams
    d. James Monroe
    e. Nicholas Biddle

    ANS: A   TOP: Political history, changes | The Election of 1824   DIF: Moderate   REF: Full p. 364 | Seagull pp. 372–373   MSC: Remembering   OBJ: 3

23. Henry Clay was charged with orchestrating a "corrupt bargain" during the 1824 election so that he could become:
    a. president.
    b. vice president.
    c. secretary of state.
    d. ambassador to England.
    e. chief justice.

    ANS: C   TOP: Political history, changes | The Election of 1824   DIF: Moderate   REF: Full p. 364 | Seagull p. 373   MSC: Remembering   OBJ: 3

24. John Quincy Adams's vision included all of the following EXCEPT:
    a. territorial expansion.
    b. states' rights.

c. nationalism.

d. a national bank.

e. an expanding market economy.

ANS: B   TOP: Political history, changes | The Nationalism of John Quincy Adams   DIF: Moderate
REF: Full pp. 364–365 | Seagull p. 376
MSC: Understanding   OBJ: 3

25. Which of the following is NOT true of John Quincy Adams?
    a. He enjoyed one of the most distinguished diplomatic careers in American history.
    b. He had a far more expansive view of national power than many of his contemporaries.
    c. He was a firm believer in strict construction of the Constitution.
    d. He was the only member of Monroe's cabinet to oppose reprimanding Andrew Jackson for invading Spanish Florida.
    e. Although a Federalist senator at the time, he had supported Jefferson's embargo policy.

    ANS: C   TOP: Political history changes | The Nationalism of John Quincy Adams | "Liberty Is Power"
    DIF: Moderate   REF: Full p. 365 | Seagull pp. 373, 376
    MSC: Understanding   OBJ: 3

26. As president, John Quincy Adams proposed a comprehensive plan for an activist state, which called for all of the following EXCEPT:
    a. free homesteads for settlers on western public lands.
    b. the establishment of a national university.
    c. creating a naval academy.
    d. building a national astronomical observatory.
    e. legislation promoting agriculture, commerce, and manufacturing.

    ANS: A   TOP: Political history, changes | "Liberty Is Power"   DIF: Difficult   REF: Full p. 365 | Seagull pp. 376–377   MSC: Remembering   OBJ: 3

27. Which of the following statements about Martin Van Buren is FALSE?
    a. By 1828, he had established the political apparatus of the Democratic Party.
    b. Son of a tavern keeper, his principal talent was as a party manager.
    c. A graduate of Harvard, he was known for his sterling intellectual accomplishments.
    d. He believed party discipline could help overcome sectional feelings.
    e. The forcible removal of the Cherokee tribe, known as the Trail of Tears, occurred during his presidency.

    ANS: C   TOP: Political history, changes | Martin Van Buren and the Democratic Party   DIF: Difficult

REF: Full p. 365 | Seagull p. 377   MSC: Understanding   OBJ: 3

28. Which of the following did NOT happen during the election of 1828?
    a. Andrew Jackson challenged Henry Clay to a duel for having engineered his defeat in the "corrupt bargain" of 1824.
    b. John Quincy Adams's supporters accused Andrew Jackson of murder.
    c. Adams's supporters questioned the morality of Andrew Jackson's wife because she married Jackson while she was still married to another man.
    d. Jackson's supporters claimed that Adams had engaged in objectionable sexual practices while serving as a diplomat abroad.
    e. Adams kept in office federal employees who openly campaigned for his opponent.

    ANS: A   TOP: Political history, changes | The Election of 1828   DIF: Difficult   REF: Full p. 366 | Seagull pp. 377–378   MSC: Understanding   OBJ: 4

29. By the time of Jackson's presidency, politics:
    a. remained very much the province of the elite.
    b. was centered on the congressional elections held every other year.
    c. focused on organization, with the public refusing to tolerate showmanship or flowery oratory.
    d. often emphasized individual politicians with mass followings and popular nicknames.
    e. was completely under the control of Martin Van Buren.

    ANS: D   TOP: Political history, changes | The Party System   DIF: Moderate   REF: Full p. 367 | Seagull p. 379   MSC: Remembering   OBJ: 4

30. The practice of giving a political office to someone based on party loyalty is called:
    a. a meritocracy.
    b. the spoils system.
    c. paternalism.
    d. the party system.
    e. nepotism.

    ANS: B   TOP: Political history, changes | The Party System   DIF: Moderate   REF: Full p. 368 | Seagull p. 380   MSC: Remembering   OBJ: 4

31. Many of the members of Jackson's Kitchen Cabinet, as his group of close advisers was known, were:
    a. bankers.
    b. newspaper editors.
    c. women, including Peggy Eaton and Floride Calhoun.
    d. military officers.
    e. Protestant ministers.

    ANS: B   TOP: Political history, changes | The Party System   DIF: Moderate   REF: Full p. 368 | Seagull p. 380   MSC: Remembering   OBJ: 4

32. The national political parties of the second American party system were:
    a. Democrats and Whigs.
    b. Republicans and Democrats.
    c. Whigs and Know-Nothings.
    d. Republicans and Whigs.
    e. Democrats and Federalists.

    ANS: A   TOP: Political history, changes | Democrats and Whigs   DIF: Easy   REF: Full pp. 368–369 | Seagull pp. 380–381   MSC: Remembering   OBJ: 5

33. Democrats in the 1830s generally believed that:
    a. the federal government should be more powerful than state governments.
    b. new corporate enterprises were suspicious.
    c. only government could protect against social inequality.
    d. government should exercise its power to try to improve private morality.
    e. restraining individual competition was a good thing.

    ANS: B   TOP: Political history, changes | Democrats and Whigs   DIF: Difficult   REF: Full p. 369 | Seagull pp. 380–381   MSC: Remembering   OBJ: 4

34. Which is NOT true about the Whigs?
    a. They argued that the role of government was to promote the welfare of the people.
    b. They supported government promotion of the economy.
    c. The Whigs believed that a strong federal government was necessary to promote liberty.
    d. The Whigs united behind the American System.
    e. Their strongest support came from the lower Northwest and the southern backcountry.

    ANS: E   TOP: Political history, changes | Democrats and Whigs   DIF: Moderate   REF: Full p. 369 | Seagull p. 381   MSC: Understanding   OBJ: 5

35. During Jackson's presidency, most Democrats did all of the following EXCEPT:
    a. support reducing federal expenditures.
    b. call for lowering the tariff.
    c. oppose the Second Bank of the United States.
    d. approve of the Indian Removal Act.
    e. speak out against presidential use of the veto.

    ANS: E   TOP: Political history, changes | Public and Private Freedom   DIF: Moderate   REF: Full pp. 369–370 | Seagull p. 381   MSC: Understanding   OBJ: 4

36. Whigs wanted the government involved in all of the following EXCEPT:
    a. restricting alcohol production.
    b. legislating morality.
    c. prohibiting entertainment on Sundays.
    d. restricting corporations.
    e. banning prostitution.

    ANS: D TOP: Political history, changes | Social history | Politics and Morality DIF: Moderate
    REF: Full pp. 369–370 | Seagull p. 382
    MSC: Understanding OBJ: 5

37. The nullification crisis:
    a. involved the fears of some slaveholders that the federal government might take action against slavery.
    b. was based on southern concerns that tariffs were preventing the South from industrializing as fast as the North.
    c. largely concerned the opposition of Southwestern planters to federally financed internal improvements.
    d. brought Andrew Jackson and John C. Calhoun closer together politically.
    e. attracted support from Whigs like Daniel Webster, who saw it as an opportunity to embarrass and annoy Jackson.

    ANS: A TOP: Political history, changes | South Carolina and Nullification DIF: Moderate
    REF: Full p. 371 | Seagull p. 383 MSC: Understanding
    OBJ: 3

38. Who wrote *Exposition and Protest* and emerged by the early 1830s as the most prominent spokesman for the right of nullification?
    a. John C. Calhoun
    b. Henry Clay
    c. Andrew Jackson
    d. John Quincy Adams
    e. Daniel Webster

    ANS: A TOP: Political history, changes | Calhoun's Political Theory DIF: Moderate REF: Full pp. 371–372 | Seagull p. 383 MSC: Remembering
    OBJ: 3

39. The controversy over Peggy Eaton:
    a. led to her divorce from her husband, the secretary of war.
    b. ended when Floride Calhoun came to Eaton's defense.
    c. helped to enhance Martin Van Buren's influence during the Jackson administration.
    d. began when Andrew Jackson accused her of improper sexual advances.
    e. aided Andrew Jackson in winning the presidency in 1828.

    ANS: C TOP: Political history, changes | Calhoun's Political Theory DIF: Moderate REF: Full p. 372 | Seagull pp. 383–384 MSC: Understanding OBJ: 4

40. Who argued in a famous debate with South Carolina's Robert Hayne that the people, not the states, created the Constitution?
    a. John C. Calhoun
    b. John Quincy Adams
    c. Henry Clay
    d. Daniel Webster
    e. Martin Van Buren

    ANS: D TOP: Political history, changes | Calhoun's Political Theory DIF: Moderate REF: Full p. 372 | Seagull p. 384 MSC: Remembering OBJ: 3

41. The Force Act of 1833:
    a. created a standing federal army to deal with threats to national security.
    b. provided for a police force for the District of Columbia.
    c. gave the president authority to use military personnel to collect tariffs.
    d. became law at the insistence of nullification supporters.
    e. was declared unconstitutional by Chief Justice Roger Taney in 1838.

    ANS: C TOP: Political history, changes | The Nullification Crisis DIF: Moderate REF: Full p. 373 | Seagull p. 384 MSC: Remembering OBJ: 3

42. The nullification crisis ended:
    a. in the so-called Dorr War.
    b. with North Carolina's threat to secede in 1832.
    c. with the Supreme Court's opinion in *Hamilton v. Jackson*.
    d. with a compromise tariff.
    e. with Daniel Webster's powerful pro-nullification speech to the Senate.

    ANS: D TOP: Political history, changes | The Nullification Crisis DIF: Moderate REF: Full p. 373 | Seagull pp. 384–385 MSC: Remembering OBJ: 3

43. In his *Cherokee Nation v. Georgia* opinion, Chief Justice John Marshall stated that:
    a. Georgia had to respect Indian title to their lands.
    b. Indians were wards of the federal government.
    c. the Cherokee had to move to the Indian Territory.
    d. President Jackson had full authority over Indian affairs.
    e. Indians were U.S. citizens, with all attendant rights and responsibilities.

    ANS: B TOP: Constitutional history | Ethnicity | The Supreme Court and the Indians DIF: Difficult
    REF: Full p. 374 | Seagull p. 386
    MSC: Remembering OBJ: 3

44. The U.S. Supreme Court's 1832 *Worcester v. Georgia* decision:
    a. supported the right of the Cherokee people to maintain a separate political identity.
    b. approved Georgia's plans to confiscate Cherokee land and move the people to reservations.
    c. struck down Georgia's anti-tariff Nullification Ordinance.
    d. was fully supported by President Andrew Jackson.
    e. was strongly opposed by Whigs.

    ANS: A   TOP: Constitutional history | Ethnicity | The Supreme Court and the Indians   DIF: Difficult   REF: Full p. 375 | Seagull p. 386   MSC: Remembering   OBJ: 3

45. Which Indian nation fought a war with the U.S. army from 1835 to 1842 to resist removal to the West?
    a. Cherokee
    b. Chickasaw
    c. Creek
    d. Seminole
    e. Choctaw

    ANS: D   TOP: Ethnicity | The Supreme Court and the Indians   DIF: Difficult   REF: Full p. 376 | Seagull p. 387   MSC: Remembering   OBJ: 3

46. In the 1830s, Andrew Jackson believed all of the following about the Second Bank of the United States EXCEPT that:
    a. the Bank did not allow for the issuance of enough paper money to meet national demand.
    b. bankers in general were "nonproducers" who merely profited from the labor of others.
    c. the Bank received exclusive privileges that widened the gap between the wealthy and the humble.
    d. the Bank was a "monster" that illegitimately combined political and economic power.
    e. the Bank was engaging in a form of political blackmail against Jackson.

    ANS: A   TOP: Economic development | Biddle's Bank   DIF: Difficult   REF: Full p. 378 | Seagull p. 388   MSC: Understanding   OBJ: 5

47. Who was the president of the Second Bank of the United States in 1832?
    a. Langdon Cheves
    b. Paul Volcker
    c. Henry Clay
    d. Nicholas Biddle
    e. Charles Winchester

    ANS: D   TOP: Economic development | Biddle's Bank   DIF: Moderate   REF: Full p. 378 | Seagull p. 389   MSC: Remembering   OBJ: 5

48. How does the Bank War demonstrate that Andrew Jackson enhanced the power of the presidency?
    a. He became the first president ever to veto a bill passed by Congress.
    b. By removing federal funds from the Bank even after Congress overrode his veto, he showed strong leadership.
    c. He identified himself as the symbolic representative of all the people with his veto message that appealed directly to the public.
    d. Because Jackson forced the Bank to issue more paper money to end a depression, Americans increasingly looked to the White House for economic leadership.
    e. Because Jackson's actions led to an economic decline, he did not enhance the power of the presidency.

    ANS: C   TOP: Political history, changes | Biddle's Bank   DIF: Moderate   REF: Full p. 378 | Seagull p. 389   MSC: Understanding   OBJ: 5

49. "Hard money" in the 1830s referred to:
    a. gold and silver, also called "specie."
    b. wages paid to manual laborers.
    c. money backed by government guarantees.
    d. any money issued by a bank.
    e. highly inflated currency after the Panic of 1837.

    ANS: A   TOP: Economic development | Biddle's Bank   DIF: Moderate   REF: Full p. 378 | Seagull p. 388   MSC: Remembering   OBJ: 5

50. The Panic of 1837:
    a. inspired a more vigorous labor movement in the decade that followed.
    b. led to a relatively mild economic downturn that resolved itself by 1839.
    c. can only be blamed on Andrew Jackson's veto of the bill to recharter the Second Bank of the United States.
    d. was caused, in part, by a decline in British demand for American cotton.
    e. helped farmers, because the cost of transporting goods to markets fell.

    ANS: D   TOP: Economic development | The Panic of 1837   DIF: Difficult   REF: Full p. 380 | Seagull p. 390   MSC: Understanding   OBJ: 5

51. What was President Martin Van Buren's new solution to the problem of what to do about the federal government's relationship to banking?
    a. He called for federal money to be deposited in state-chartered banks known as "pets."
    b. He proposed the creation of the Federal Reserve Bank, with branches in key cities.

c. He created the Third Bank of the United States, but this time headed by a reliable Democrat.

d. He set up a program of federal insurance on individual bank accounts to protect them in times of panic.

e. He proposed that federal funds be controlled by government officials rather than by bankers.

ANS: E   TOP: Political history, changes | Van Buren in Office   DIF: Difficult   REF: Full p. 381 | Seagull p. 391   MSC: Remembering   OBJ: 5

52. In the presidential election of 1840:
a. the Whigs employed political tactics pioneered by Democrats.
b. voter turnout dropped dramatically because no popular candidate like Jackson ran.
c. the Democrats nominated three regional candidates, hoping to throw the election into the House of Representatives.
d. the Democrats and Whigs both produced platforms that clearly laid out the parties' positions on major public issues.
e. the Whigs again nominated Henry Clay.

ANS: A   TOP: Political history, changes | The Election of 1840   DIF: Difficult   REF: Full pp. 381–382 | Seagull p. 392   MSC: Understanding OBJ: 5

53. Whose 1840 presidential campaign portrayed him as a common man who was born in a log cabin and liked to drink hard cider?
a. Andrew Jackson
b. William Henry Harrison
c. Martin Van Buren
d. John Quincy Adams
e. Henry Clay

ANS: B   TOP: Political history, changes | The Election of 1840   DIF: Moderate   REF: Full p. 382 | Seagull p. 392   MSC: Remembering   OBJ: 5

54. As president, John Tyler:
a. worked hard to enact the Whig economic program.
b. proved so popular that he easily won the 1844 presidential election.
c. vetoed a bill to create a new national bank, thus angering Whigs.
d. engaged in a public feud with his vice president that led to the latter's resignation.
e. appointed Roger Taney to the office of chief justice of the U.S. Supreme Court.

ANS: C   TOP: Political history, changes | His Accidency   DIF: Moderate   REF: Full p. 382 | Seagull p. 393   MSC: Remembering   OBJ: 5

True or False

1. The French writer Alexis de Tocqueville identified democracy as an essential attribute of American freedom.

ANS: T   TOP: Political history, changes | Tocqueville on Democracy   DIF: Easy   REF: Full p. 349 | Seagull p. 359   MSC: Remembering   OBJ: 1

2. Steam power helped the proliferation of the penny press.

ANS: T   TOP: Economic development | The Information Revolution   DIF: Moderate   REF: Full p. 350 | Seagull p. 359   MSC: Understanding   OBJ: 1

3. By the early nineteenth century, the term "citizen" had become synonymous with the right to vote.

ANS: T   TOP: Political history, changes | Tocqueville on Democracy   DIF: Easy   REF: Full p. 350 | Seagull p. 359   MSC: Understanding   OBJ: 1

4. Women enjoyed an expansion of democracy for themselves during the 1830s and 1840s, as they were welcomed into the public sphere.

ANS: F   TOP: Social history | The Limits of Democracy   DIF: Easy   REF: Full p. 352 | Seagull pp. 361–362   MSC: Understanding   OBJ: 1

5. Since President Madison believed that a constitutional amendment was necessary for the government to build roads and canals, the Twelfth Amendment was passed by Congress and ratified in 1816.

ANS: F   TOP: Constitutional history | The American System   DIF: Moderate   REF: Full p. 355 | Seagull pp. 364–365   MSC: Understanding   OBJ: 2

6. Since the Bank of the United States handled the Panic of 1819 so efficiently, public support for the banking system increased dramatically.

ANS: F   TOP: Economic development | The Politics of the Panic   DIF: Moderate   REF: Full p. 356 | Seagull p. 367   MSC: Understanding   OBJ: 2

7. James Monroe's two terms as president were characterized by the absence of two-party competition.

ANS: T   TOP: Political history, changes | The Missouri Controversy   DIF: Moderate   REF: Full p. 357 | Seagull p. 367   MSC: Remembering   OBJ: 2

8. The Missouri Compromise debate illustrated that northern Republicans did not want slavery to expand for primarily moral reasons.

ANS: F   TOP: Civil rights | The Slavery Question DIF: Difficult   REF: Full p. 358 | Seagull p. 369 MSC: Understanding   OBJ: 2

9. The Monroe Doctrine was a forceful statement that declared that westward expansion for the United States could not be prevented on any account since its destiny was divinely appointed.

    ANS: F   TOP: Global awareness | The Monroe Doctrine   DIF: Moderate   REF: Full p. 361 | Seagull p. 372   MSC: Remembering   OBJ: 3

10. Andrew Jackson was the only candidate in the 1824 election to have national appeal.

    ANS: T   TOP: Political history, changes | The Election of 1824   DIF: Difficult   REF: Full p. 361 | Seagull p. 372   MSC: Remembering   OBJ: 4

11. John C. Calhoun's "corrupt bargain" gave John Quincy Adams the White House in 1824.

    ANS: F   TOP: Political history, changes | The Election of 1824   DIF: Difficult   REF: Full p. 364 | Seagull p. 373   MSC: Remembering   OBJ: 3

12. Martin Van Buren believed that party politics was an important component in ensuring liberty for the American people.

    ANS: T   TOP: Political history, changes | Martin Van Buren and the Democratic Party   DIF: Moderate REF: Full pp. 365–366 | Seagull p. 377 MSC: Understanding   OBJ: 3

13. The election of 1828 witnessed a campaign that compared John Quincy Adams's education to Andrew Jackson's military career.

    ANS: T   TOP: Political history, changes | The Election of 1828   DIF: Moderate   REF: Full p. 366 | Seagull p. 378   MSC: Understanding   OBJ: 4

14. By 1828, Andrew Jackson had established the political apparatus of the Democratic Party.

    ANS: F   TOP: Political history, changes | The Election of 1828   DIF: Difficult   REF: Full p. 366 | Seagull p. 377   MSC: Remembering   OBJ: 4

15. Andrew Jackson's vision of democracy excluded blacks, but included Indians.

    ANS: F   TOP: Social history | The Age of Jackson DIF: Easy   REF: Full p. 367 | Seagull p. 379 MSC: Understanding   OBJ: 4

16. Andrew Jackson was born into a wealthy and prominent family, but was able to portray himself to the American people as a common man.

    ANS: F   TOP: Social history | The Age of Jackson DIF: Moderate   REF: Full p. 367 | Seagull p. 379 MSC: Understanding   OBJ: 4

17. The Kitchen Cabinet was an informal group of advisers who helped to write speeches for Andrew Jackson.

    ANS: T   TOP: Political history, changes | The Party System   DIF: Moderate   REF: Full p. 368 | Seagull p. 380   MSC: Remembering   OBJ: 4

18. The party battles of the Jacksonian era reflected the clash between public and private definitions of American freedom and their relationship to government power.

    ANS: T   TOP: Political history, changes | Public and Private Freedom   DIF: Moderate   REF: Full p. 369 | Seagull p. 381   MSC: Understanding   OBJ: 4

19. Andrew Jackson's policies resulted in a higher national debt.

    ANS: F   TOP: Political history, changes | Public and Private Freedom   DIF: Moderate   REF: Full p. 370 | Seagull p. 381   MSC: Understanding OBJ: 4

20. Whigs believed that the federal government was responsible for promoting the welfare of the people and securing liberty.

    ANS: T   TOP: Political history, changes | Politics and Morality   DIF: Moderate   REF: Full p. 371 | Seagull p. 382   MSC: Understanding   OBJ: 5

21. Supporters of nullification claimed that the federal government was overstepping its rights and infringing on states' rights.

    ANS: T   TOP: Political history, changes | Calhoun's Political Theory   DIF: Easy   REF: Full p. 372 | Seagull p. 384   MSC: Remembering   OBJ: 3

22. Daniel Webster insisted that the national government had been created by an agreement between sovereign states, each of which retained the right to prevent the enforcement within its borders of acts of Congress that exceeded the powers specifically spelled out in the document.

    ANS: F   TOP: Political history, changes | Calhoun's Political Theory   DIF: Moderate   REF: Full p. 372 | Seagull p. 384   MSC: Understanding   OBJ: 3

23. The Trail of Tears refers specifically to the removal of the Seminole Indians from Florida to present-day Oklahoma.

    ANS: F   TOP: Ethnicity | The Supreme Court and the Indians   DIF: Moderate   REF: Full pp. 375–376 | Seagull pp. 386–387   MSC: Remembering   OBJ: 3

24. The Independent Treasury completely separated the federal government from the nation's banking system.

ANS: T   TOP: Political history, changes | Van Buren in Office   DIF: Difficult   REF: Full p. 381 | Seagull pp. 391–392   MSC: Understanding   OBJ: 5

25. John Tyler's presidency proved very popular with Whigs.

ANS: F   TOP: Political history, changes | His Accidency   DIF: Moderate   REF: Full p. 382 | Seagull p. 393   MSC: Remembering   OBJ: 5

Short Answer

Identify and give the historical significance of each of the following terms, events, and people in a paragraph or two.

1. growth of democracy
2. American System
3. Whig Party
4. Democratic Party
5. John Quincy Adams
6. penny press
7. Missouri Compromise
8. nullification crisis
9. Indian Removal Act
10. Bank War
11. Daniel Webster
12. "King Andrew I"

Essay Questions

1. A delegate to the 1837 Pennsylvania convention remarked that the political community was based on white persons. In this age of expanding political participation, analyze how and why some segments of the population were able to achieve greater liberties, while others were excluded. What arguments did each group make for a greater political voice?

ANS: Answers will vary   TOP: Political history, changes | Social history | Race and Class | The Limits of Democracy | The Information Revolution | Property and Democracy | A Racial Democracy DIF: Moderate   MSC: Analyzing   OBJ: 1

2. Describe John Quincy Adams's dream for the United States when he was secretary of state and when he was president. What role did he want the federal government to play? How did his vision for America expand liberties or freedom? How did it restrict liberties or freedom?

ANS: Answers will vary   TOP: Political history, changes | Social history | The Nationalism of John Quincy Adams | "Liberty Is Power" DIF: Moderate   MSC: Understanding   OBJ: 1 / 2

3. The admittance of Missouri to the Union sparked a national crisis. Describe the debates that led up to the final compromise. How does the Missouri Compromise illustrate that sectional issues would surely arise again?

ANS: Answers will vary   TOP: Political history, changes | The Missouri Controversy   DIF: Moderate MSC: Understanding   OBJ: 3

4. Andrew Jackson, one historian has written, was the "symbol for an age." How might Jackson be considered symbolic of certain ideas and trends in the early nineteenth century? Can you think of other appropriate symbolic figures for that period?

ANS: Answers will vary   TOP: Political history, changes | Social history | The Age of Jackson DIF: Moderate   MSC: Applying   OBJ: 3 / 4

5. Explain how Democrats and Whigs viewed liberty and the role of government in securing liberty.

ANS: Answers will vary   TOP: Political history, changes | Democrats and Whigs | Public and Private Freedom   DIF: Moderate   MSC: Understanding OBJ: 1 / 3 / 5

6. Analyze the arguments that were presented during the nullification crisis. Be sure to comment on how Daniel Webster and John C. Calhoun interpreted the Constitution differently and how each defined the rights of states. Finally, speak to how the crisis illustrated the growing sectional differences in America.

ANS: Answers will vary   TOP: Political history, changes | Calhoun's Political Theory | The Nullification Crisis   DIF: Moderate MSC: Analyzing   OBJ: 3

7. Thinking back to previous chapters, analyze America's policies toward Indians from the Washington administration through the removal of Indians from the southeastern states in the 1830s and early 1840s. What ideas and policies about Indians remained the same? Which changed? Why?

ANS: Answers will vary   TOP: Ethnicity | Political history, changes | Indian Removal | The Supreme Court and the Indians   DIF: Difficult   MSC: Analyzing   OBJ: 4

8. Compare the economic policies of the American System with those of Alexander Hamilton. What was similar? What was different? How do you think Hamilton would have rated presidents like John Quincy Adams and Andrew Jackson?

ANS: Answers will vary   TOP: Economic development | Political history, changes | The American System DIF: Difficult   MSC: Analyzing   OBJ: 1 / 2

CHAPTER 11

The Peculiar Institution

This chapter concentrates on the history of slavery in the Old South, roughly between 1800 and 1860. The chapter begins by discussing the economic dominance of cotton in the South and how the northern and international textile industry depended on the raw material. As the North industrialized, the South's economy rested overwhelmingly on the cash crop of cotton. Next, the chapter describes different classes of southern whites and seeks to explain why non-slaveholding whites supported the institution of slavery. The various proslavery arguments are explained, illustrating how the definition of freedom was bent to justify the "peculiar institution." One of the "Voices of Freedom" pieces focuses on how the Bible sanctions slavery. Slave masters had a variety of tools from which to pick in order to maintain order with the slaves. Physical violence was the most dramatic way of disciplining slaves, but the threat of sale was the most effective. The chapter next considers slave society and culture, with emphasis on slaves' efforts to maintain some form of autonomy via family life, folklore, and religion. Slave culture also cultivated a strong will for freedom. This section also examines free blacks in the slave South. The chapter concludes with a look at various forms of slave resistance, from silent sabotage to full-scale rebellions. One form of resistance, running away, is highlighted in the "Voices of Freedom" piece by Joseph Taper, who escaped from Virginia to Canada.

CHAPTER OUTLINE

I. Introduction: Frederick Douglass
   A. Slave childhood
   B. Leader of abolitionist movement, publishing his autobiography that condemned slavery and racism

II. The Old South
   A. Cotton Is King
      1. Cotton replaced sugar as the world's major crop produced by slave labor in the nineteenth century.
      2. The strength of American slavery rested on cotton.
      3. Cotton industry
         a. Three-fourths of the world's cotton supply came from the southern United States.
         b. Cotton supplied textile mills in the North and in Great Britain.
         c. As early as 1803, cotton represented America's most important export, and by 1860 it represented well over half the total value of exports.
   B. The Second Middle Passage
      1. Although the African slave trade was prohibited, the sale and trade of slaves within the United States flourished.
         a. More than 2 million slaves sold from 1820–1860
      2. The main business districts of southern cities contained the offices of slave traders, and auctions took place at public slave markets.
   C. Slavery and the Nation
      1. The North was not immune to slavery.
         a. Slavery shaped the lives of all Americans.
         b. Northern merchants and manufacturers participated in the slave economy and shared in its profits.
            i. Ships, banks, insurers, and factories
   D. The Southern Economy
      1. Southern economic growth was different from northern.

a. There were few large cities in the South.

b. The cities were mainly centers for gathering and shipping cotton.

2. New Orleans was the only city of significant size in the South.

a. New Orleans had a large immigrant culture.

b. With its French and Caribbean heritage, it had a distinctive culture.

3. The region produced less than 10 percent of the nation's manufactured goods.

4. Slavery proved very profitable for most owners.

E. Plain Folk of the Old South

1. Three-fourths of white southerners did not own slaves.

2. Most white southerners lived on self-sufficient farms.

a. They were not integrated into the market economy.

b. Main reason why the South did not develop much industry

3. Most whites supported slavery.

a. A few, like Andrew Johnson and Joseph Brown, spoke out against the planter elite.

b. Most white southerners supported the planter elite and slavery because of shared bonds of regional loyalty, racism, and kinship ties.

F. The Planter Class

1. In 1850, the majority of slaveholding families owned five or fewer slaves.

2. Fewer than 2,000 families owned 100 slaves or more.

3. Ownership of slaves provided the route to wealth, status, and influence.

4. Slavery was a profit-making system.

a. Men watched the world market for cotton, invested in infrastructure, and carefully managed every detail of their plantations.

b. Plantation mistresses cared for sick slaves, oversaw the domestic servants, and supervised the plantation when the master was away.

5. Southern slave owners spent much of their money on material goods.

a. Wealthiest spent money on lavish entertainment, vacations, and elegant mansions.

G. The Paternalist Ethos

1. Southern slaveowners were committed to a hierarchical, agrarian society.

2. Paternalism was ingrained in slave society and enabled slaveowners to think of themselves as kind, responsible masters even as they bought and sold their human property.

a. Reverend Charles C. Jones

H. The Code of Honor

1. Southern men sometimes dueled as part of a code of honor.

2. Southern women were often trapped in a "domestic circle" of loneliness.

I. The Proslavery Argument

1. By the 1830s, fewer southerners believed that slavery was a necessary evil; instead, they claimed it as the basis for free institutions.

2. Proslavery argument rested on a number of pillars, including a commitment to white supremacy, biblical sanction of slavery, and the historical precedent that slavery was essential to human progress.

3. Another proslavery argument held that slavery guaranteed equality for whites.

J. Abolition in the Americas

1. Between 1800 and 1840, slavery was abolished in most of Spanish America and the British empire.

2. Abolition in the Americas influenced debates over slavery in the United States.

a. Proslavery advocates used post-emancipation decline in sugar and in other cash crops as evidence of British abolitionism's failure.

b. Abolitionists argued that the former slaves' rising living standards (and similar improvements) showed that emancipation had succeeded.

3. By mid-century, New World slavery remained only in Cuba, Puerto Rico, Brazil, and the United States.

K. Slavery and Liberty

1. White southerners declared themselves the true heirs of the American Revolution.

2. Proslavery arguments began to repudiate the ideas in the Declaration of Independence that equality and freedom were universal entitlements.

a. John C. Calhoun believed that the language in the Declaration of Independence was indeed dangerous.

3. Southern clergymen argued that submission of inferior to superior was a "fundamental law."

L. Slavery and Civilization

1. George Fitzhugh, a Virginia writer, argued that "universal liberty" was the exception, not the rule, and that slaves, because they were not burdened with financial concerns, were the happiest and freest people in the world.

2. Abraham Lincoln observed that the proslavery arguments were only functioning to serve the

interests of slave owners, who reaped the greatest benefit from the institution.

    3. By 1830, southerners defended slavery in terms of liberty and freedom; without slavery, freedom was not possible.

III. Life under Slavery

    A. Slaves and the Law

        1. Slaves were considered property and had few legal rights.

        2. Slaves were not allowed to testify against a white person, carry a firearm, leave the plantation without permission, learn how to read or write, or gather in a group without a white person present, although some of these laws were not always vigorously enforced.

        3. Masters also controlled whether slaves married and how they spent their free time.

        4. Trial of Celia: Celia killed her master while resisting a sexual assault.

            a. Celia was charged with murder and sentenced to die, but she was pregnant and her execution was delayed until she gave birth, so as not to deny the current master his property right.

    B. Conditions of Life

        1. Some laws protected slaves against mistreatment.

            a. American slaves as compared to their counterparts in the West Indies and in Brazil enjoyed better diets, lower infant mortality, and longer life expectancies.

            b. Reasons for the above include the paternalistic ethos of the South, the lack of malaria and yellow fever in the South, and the high costs of slaves.

        2. Improvements in the slaves' living conditions were meant to strengthen slavery, not undermine it.

        3. Few slave societies in history have so systematically closed off all avenues to freedom as the Old South.

    C. Free Blacks in the Old South

        1. By 1860, there were nearly half a million free blacks in the United States and most of them lived in the South.

        2. Free blacks were not all that free.

            a. Free blacks were allowed by law to own property and marry and could not be bought or sold.

            b. Free blacks were not allowed by law to own a firearm, dogs, or liquor. They could not testify in court or serve on a jury. They could not strike a white person, even in self-defense.

        3. Unlike in Brazil or in the West Indies, there was little room for a mulatto group in the United States; the result was that free blacks in the Old South enjoyed little respect or prosperity, with few exceptions.

    D. The Upper and Lower South

        1. The majority of free blacks who lived in the Lower South resided in cities like New Orleans and Charleston.

            a. Some of mixed-race heritage became wealthy and owned slaves.

        2. The majority of free blacks lived in the Upper South.

            a. They were in rural areas, working for wages as farm laborers.

            b. The few blacks who owned slaves were free men who had purchased their slave wives and children.

                i. They could not liberate them because any slave who became free had to leave the state.

    E. Slave Labor

        1. Labor occupied most of a slave's daily existence.

        2. There were many types of jobs a slave might perform: cutting wood for fuel for steamboats, working in mines, working on docks in seaports, laying railroad track, repairing bridges or roads, or working as skilled artisans.

    F. Gang Labor and Task Labor

        1. Most slaves worked in the fields.

            a. It is estimated that 75 percent of the women and 90 percent of the men worked as field hands.

        2. On large plantations they worked in gangs under the direction of the overseer, a man who was generally considered cruel by the slaves.

            a. Some of the harshest conditions were in Louisiana sugar fields.

            b. Rice plantations of South Carolina and Georgia still used colonial era task system.

                i. Whites feared malaria-infested swamps.

    G. Slavery in the Cities

        1. Most city slaves were servants, cooks, and other domestics.

        2. Some city slaves were skilled artisans and occasionally lived on their own.

    H. Maintaining Order

        1. The system of maintaining order rested on force.

        2. There were many tools a master had to maintain order, including whipping, exploiting divisions among slaves, incentives, and the threat of sale.

IV. Slave Culture
   A. The Slave Family
      1. Slaves never abandoned their desire for freedom or determination to resist their bondage.
      2. Slave culture was a new creation, shaped by African traditions and American values and experiences.
      3. Despite the threat of sale and the fact that marriage between slaves was illegal, many slaves did marry and create families.
         a. Slaves frequently named children after other family members to retain family continuity.
         b. The slave community had a significantly higher number of female-headed households as compared to the white community.
   B. The Threat of Sale
      1. One slave marriage in three in some states was broken by sale.
      2. Many children were separated from their families by sale.
         a. Ten percent of the teenage slaves in the Upper South were sold in the interstate slave trade.
      3. Slave traders paid little attention to preserving family ties.
   C. Gender Roles among Slaves
      1. Traditional gender roles were not followed in the fields, but during their own time, slaves did fall back on traditional gender roles.
      2. The family was vital to passing traditions from parent to child.
   D. Slave Religion
      1. Black Christianity was distinctive and offered hope to the slaves.
         a. Almost every plantation had its own black preacher.
         b. Slaves worshiped in biracial churches.
         c. Free blacks established their own churches.
      2. Some masters required services with white ministers who emphasized obedience.
   E. The Gospel of Freedom
      1. Slaves transformed Christianity, turning it to their own purposes.
         a. Mixture of African traditions and Christian beliefs
         b. Practiced in secret
      2. Many biblical stories offered hope and solace to slaves, including Exodus, David and Goliath, and Jonah and the whale.
   F. The Desire for Liberty
      1. Slave culture rested on a sense of the injustice of bondage and the desire for freedom.
      2. Slave folklore glorified the weak over the strong and their spirituals emphasized eventual liberation.
      3. All slaves saw the injustice of slavery; the hypocrisy of the Declaration of Independence and rhetoric of freedom heard around them only strengthened their desire for freedom.
      4. Slaves used networking and thus knew about political events and activities of abolitionists.

V. Resistance to Slavery
      1. Because slaves were outnumbered, slave rebellions were rare, but many other forms of resistance existed.
   A. Forms of Resistance
      1. The most common form of resistance was silent sabotage—the breaking of tools, feigning illness, doing poor work.
      2. Less common, but more serious forms of resistance included poisoning the master, arson, and armed assaults.
   B. Fugitive Slaves
      1. Slaves had to follow the North Star as their guide.
      2. Of the estimated 1,000 slaves a year to escape, most escaped from the Upper South.
      3. In the Deep South, fugitive slaves often escaped to the southern cities, to blend in with the free black population.
      4. The Underground Railroad was a loose organization of abolitionists who helped slaves to escape.
         a. Harriet Tubman was an escaped slave who in the 1850s rescued about 75 others from slavery.
   C. The *Amistad*
      1. In 1839, a group of slaves collectively seized their freedom while on board the *Amistad*.
      2. The U.S. Supreme Court accepted John Quincy Adams's argument that the slaves had been illegally seized in Africa and should be freed.
   D. Slave Revolts
      1. In 1811, an uprising on sugar plantations in Louisiana saw slaves marching toward New Orleans before the militia captured them.
      2. In 1822, Denmark Vesey was charged with conspiracy and executed in South Carolina.
         a. Vesey was a religious man who believed the Bible condemned slavery and he saw the hypocrisy of the Declaration of Independence.
         b. The conspiracy was uncovered before Vesey could act.
   E. Nat Turner's Rebellion
      1. Nat Turner was a slave preacher and religious mystic.
         a. He believed God had chosen him to lead an uprising.

2. In 1831, Nat Turner and his followers marched through Virginia, attacking white farm families.
   a. Eighty slaves had joined Turner and sixty whites had been killed (mostly women and children) before the militia put down the rebellion.
   b. Turner was captured and executed.
3. Turner's was the last large-scale rebellion in the South.
4. Turner's rebellion sent shock waves through the South.
   a. The Virginia legislature debated plans for gradual emancipation of the state's slaves, but voted not to take that step.
   b. Instead, Virginia tightened its grip on slavery through new laws further limiting slaves' rights.
5. The year 1831 marked a turning point for the Old South as white southerners closed ranks and defended slavery more strongly than ever.

SUGGESTED DISCUSSION QUESTIONS

• How did the North and South differ from each other? How was slavery the fundamental reason for these differences? How did each region benefit from the other?
• What can the story of Celia tell us about attitudes held by white southerners toward property? Compare that attitude with the idea and practice of paternalism.
• What roles did families and religion play in the lives of slaves? What were some ways slaves were able to maintain their families, even with the constant threat of being separated for life? How were slave families able to maintain traditional gender roles?
• Although slave culture grew from a need to survive in the face of bondage, it continued after emancipation. Explain why this was.
• Think back to previous discussions about the Declaration of Independence and the writing of the Constitution. Compare the meaning the founding fathers gave to "freedom" with the meaning proslavery advocates of the Old South gave to the word. What changed?
• Slaves did not just capitulate to their situation. What were some ways slaves resisted? How did they demonstrate a sense of semi-independence or self-worth? Why did masters allow some of this behavior?
• Why was it so important for the slaveowning southerners to persuade non-slaveowners that the institution of slavery benefited them as well?
• White society reacted strongly toward Nat Turner's Rebellion. What were their reactions, and what can those

reactions tell us about the stability of the peculiar institution in the South?
• Have the students write a debate between John C. Calhoun, who argues that freedom in the United States cannot exist without slavery, and Frederick Douglass, who argues that freedom can never exist in the United States as long as slavery exists.

SUPPLEMENTAL WEB AND VISUAL RESOURCES

African-American Religion
www.nhc.rtp.nc.us/index.htm
The National Humanities Center. Teacher Serve offers essays on religion and the national culture, the environment, and African-American literature and history. The Toolbox Library offers a plethora of primary sources, discussion questions, additional online sources, and talking points.

www.nhc.rtp.nc.us/tserve/nineteen/nkeyinfo/aareligion.htm
This site takes you to African-American Christianity, Part I: To the Civil War.

http://nationalhumanitiescenter.org/tserve/freedom/1609-1865/essays/aafamilies.htm
This page looks at how slavery affected African-American families.

Africans in America
www.pbs.org/wgbh/aia/home.html
Africans in America is a four-part PBS video about America's journey through slavery. Part IV is "Judgment Day, 1831–1865."

Amistad
www.archives.gov/education/lessons/amistad
This National Archives site has links to digitized primary documents involved in the legal proceedings of the *Amistad* prisoners and also includes suggestions for classroom activities.

Anacostia Community Museum
anacostia.si.edu/
Home page for the Center for African-American History and Culture of the Smithsonian Institution.

Gilder Lehrman Center for the Study of Slavery, Resistance, and Abolition
www.yale.edu/glc/
An invaluable site that offers information for classroom activities/events and resources for historians.

Harriet Tubman
www.harriettubmanstudy.org/
National Park Service's Harriet Tubman Special Resource Study has many links and valuable biographical and chronological information.

North American Slave Narratives

docsouth.unc.edu/neh
 This University of North Carolina at Chapel Hill website offers all known published slave narratives up to 1920.

SUPPLEMENTAL PRINT RESOURCES

Bethel, Elizabeth Rauh. *The Roots of African-American Identity: Memory and History in Free Antebellum Communities.* New York: Bedford/St. Martin's, 1997.

Camp, Stephanie M. H. *Closer to Freedom: Enslaved Women and Everyday Resistance in the Plantation South.* Chapel Hill, NC: University of North Carolina Press, 2004.

Cecelski, David. *The Waterman's Song: Slavery and Freedom in Maritime North Carolina.* Chapel Hill, NC: University of North Carolina Press, 2001.

Clarke, Erskine. "Communities in Revolt: A Symposium on Nat Turner's Rebellion." *Journal of the Early Republic* 27 (2007): 655–728.

———. *Dwelling Place: A Plantation Epic.* New Haven, CT: Yale University Press, 2005

Faust, Drew Gilpin. *James Henry Hammond and the Old South: A Design for Mastery.* Baton Rouge, LA: Louisiana State University Press, 1985.

Finkelman, Paul. *Defending Slavery: Proslavery Thought in the Old South, A Brief History with Documents.* New York: Bedford/St. Martin's, 2003.

Fogel, Robert, and Stanley Engerman. *Time on the Cross: The Economics of American Negro Slavery.* New York: W. W. Norton & Company, 1989.

Ford, Lacy K. *Deliver Us from Evil: The Slavery Question in the Old South.* New York: Oxford University Press, 2009.

Harris, J. William. *Plain Folk and Gentry in a Slave Society: White Liberty and Black Slavery in Augusta's Hinterlands.* Middletown, CT: Wesleyan University Press, 1985.

Johnson, Michael P. "Denmark Vesey and His Co-Conspirators." *William and Mary Quarterly*, 3rd series, 63 (2001): 915–976.

Kaye, Anthony E. *Joining Places: Slave Neighborhoods in the Old South.* Chapel Hill, NC: University of North Carolina Press, 2007.

Kolchin, Peter. *American Slavery: 1619–1877,* revised ed. New York: Hill and Wang, 2003.

Larson, Kate Clifford. *Bound for the Promised Land: Harriet Tubman, Portrait of an American Hero.* New York: Ballantine Books, 2003.

Levine, Lawrence. *Black Culture and Black Consciousness: Afro-American Folk Thought from Slavery to Freedom.* New York: Oxford University Press, 1977.

Lichtenstein, Alex. "Coercion Had Its Limits." *Reviews in American History* 23, no. 1 (1995): 20–25.

McLaurin, Melton. *Celia: A Slave.* Athens, GA: University of Georgia Press, 1991.

Penningroth, Dylan C. *The Claims of Kinfolk: African American Property and Community in the Nineteenth-Century South.* Chapel Hill, NC: University of North Carolina Press, 2003.

Williams, Heather Andrea. *Self-Taught: African American Education in Slavery and Freedom.* Chapel Hill, NC: University of North Carolina Press, 2007.

TEST BANK

Matching

TEST 1

___ 1. Frederick Douglass
___ 2. Andrew Johnson
___ 3. Celia
___ 4. Nat Turner
___ 5. John C. Calhoun
___ 6. Harriet Tubman
___ 7. John Quincy Adams
___ 8. Martin Van Buren
___ 9. George Fitzhugh
__ 10. Denmark Vesey
__ 11. Solomon Northup
__ 12. J. D. B. DeBow

a. southern politician who spoke against the slavocracy
b. led a "successful" slave rebellion in Virginia
c. favored returning the slaves of the *Amistad* to Cuba
d. favored returning the slaves of the *Amistad* to Africa
e. escaped slave who led abolitionist movement
f. slave executed for conspiracy
g. defended slavery as a natural part of hierarchical society
h. outspoken proslavery politician
i. part of an organization helping slaves escape to the North
j. slave executed for killing her master
k. southern editor
l. *Twelve Years a Slave*

Answer Key: e, a, j, b, h, i, d, c, g, f, k, l

TEST 2

___ 1. white gold
___ 2. overseer
___ 3. Underground Railroad
___ 4. Brer Rabbit
___ 5. Yeoman farmers
___ 6. Mason-Dixon Line
___ 7. silent sabotage
___ 8. peculiar institution
___ 9. paternalism
__ 10. gang labor
__ 11. Israel Hill
__ 12. Second Middle Passage

a. system to help slaves escape to the North
b. slave trade within the United States
c. poor work and breakage of tools
d. slavery
e. managed slaves in the field
f. community of freed Virginian slaves

g. treating slaves in a fatherly manner
h. working in the fields side-by-side
i. had one or two, if any, slaves
j. boundary line between Pennsylvania and Maryland
k. cotton
l. trickster tale

Answer Key: k, e, a, l, i, j, c, d, g, h, f, b

Learning Objectives

1. Explain how slavery shaped social and economic relations in the Old South.
2. Identify the legal and material constraints on slaves' lives and work.
3. Explain how family, gender, religion, and values combined to create distinct slave cultures in the Old South.
4. Describe the major forms of resistance to slavery.

Multiple Choice

1. Frederick Douglass argued that:
   a. slaves were truer to the principles of the Declaration of Independence than were most white Americans.
   b. the United States should adopt a gradual emancipation plan that would eliminate slavery within forty years.
   c. free blacks would be better off if they moved to Liberia, where a colony of former American slaves had been founded.
   d. blacks should not serve in the U.S. army during the Civil War because of the racial discrimination they faced.
   e. free African Americans should "let down their buckets where they were" and accept inequality, at least for a period of time.

   ANS: A   TOP: Civil rights | Introduction: Frederick Douglass   DIF: Moderate   REF: Full p. 389 | Seagull p. 396   MSC: Remembering   OBJ: 2

2. The U.S. slave population by 1860 was approximately:
   a. 1 million.
   b. 2 million.
   c. 3 million.
   d. 4 million.
   e. 5 million.

   ANS: D   TOP: Geographic issues | The Old South   DIF: Difficult   REF: Full p. 390 | Seagull p. 397   MSC: Remembering   OBJ: 1

3. Which of the following was NOT true of the South and slavery in nineteenth-century America?
   a. The Old South had developed into the largest and most powerful slave society the modern world has known.
   b. The rate of natural increase in the slave population had more than made up for the ban on the international slave trade that was enacted in 1808.
   c. In the South as a whole, slaves made up only 10 percent of the population.
   d. The amount of money invested in or represented by slavery in the United States exceeded that of the nation's factories, banks, and railroads combined.
   e. The Industrial Revolution promoted slavery because it required intensive production of cotton.

   ANS: C   TOP: Social history | The Old South   DIF: Difficult   REF: Full p. 390 | Seagull p. 397   MSC: Understanding   OBJ: 1

4. In the nineteenth century, which product was the world's major crop produced by slave labor?
   a. tobacco
   b. indigo
   c. sorghum
   d. cotton
   e. rice

   ANS: D   TOP: Economic development | Cotton Is King   DIF: Easy   REF: Full p. 390 | Seagull p. 398   MSC: Remembering   OBJ: 1

5. On the eve of the Civil War, approximately how much of the world's cotton supply came from the southern United States?
   a. 90 percent
   b. 75 percent
   c. 50 percent
   d. 33 percent
   e. 25 percent

   ANS: B   TOP: Economic development | Cotton Is King   DIF: Difficult   REF: Full p. 390 | Seagull p. 398   MSC: Remembering   OBJ: 1

6. The internal slave trade in the United States involved the movement of hundreds of thousands of enslaved persons from:
   a. older states like Virginia to the Lower South.
   b. Texas, Louisiana, and Mississippi to Kentucky, Virginia, and Maryland.
   c. the West Indies to the Mississippi River Valley.
   d. the Lower South to the Upper South.
   e. the lower Mississippi River Valley to the upper Mississippi River Valley.

   ANS: A   TOP: Civil rights | Social history | The Second Middle Passage   DIF: Moderate   REF: Full p. 391 | Seagull pp. 398–399   MSC: Remembering   OBJ: 1

7. What economic effect did southern slavery have on the North?
   a. It was minimal, which explains why northerners opposed slavery.

b. Many northerners profited from investing in real-estate partnerships that controlled southern plantations.

c. A few New York shipping companies benefited from slavery, but the institution had little effect otherwise.

d. Southern slavery helped finance industrialization and internal improvements in the North.

e. Southern slavery drained resources from the North and helped keep the whole nation in a depression during the 1850s.

ANS: D   TOP: Economic development | Slavery and the Nation   DIF: Moderate   REF: Full p. 392 | Seagull p. 400   MSC: Understanding   OBJ: 1

8. The term "Lords of the Loom" refers to:
a. early New England factory owners.
b. preachers who wove heart-wrenching stories of slave suffering into their sermons.
c. planters who established textile operations on their plantations.
d. master artisans who produced cloth in the South.
e. an influential 1840s novel about slavery.

ANS: A   TOP: Economic development | Slavery and the Nation   DIF: Moderate   REF: Full p. 392 | Seagull p. 400   MSC: Remembering   OBJ: 1

9. Which of the following is a true statement relative to the Upper South and the Deep South?
a. Committed to slavery, all states in both the Upper South and Deep South seceded from the Union.
b. The Upper South was less economically diversified than the Deep South.
c. Several Upper South states did not join the Confederacy at the time of the Civil War.
d. Neither the Upper South nor the Deep South had major industrial centers.
e. Richmond, Virginia, is considered to be the heart of the Deep South.

ANS: C   TOP: Political history, changes | The Southern Economy   DIF: Moderate   REF: Full p. 393 | Seagull p. 401   MSC: Understanding   OBJ: 1

10. Which of the following is NOT true of the South and its economy in the period from 1800 to 1860?
a. Southern cities, like New Orleans and Baltimore, lay mainly on the periphery of the South.
b. The South produced nearly two-fifths of the nation's manufactured goods, especially cotton textiles.
c. Slavery helped to discourage the immigration of white workers to the South, with such notable exceptions as New Orleans.
d. Slavery proved very profitable for most slave owners.
e. Southern banks existed mainly to finance plantations.

ANS: B   TOP: Economic development | The Southern Economy   DIF: Easy   REF: Full p. 393 | Seagull p. 401   MSC: Understanding   OBJ: 1

11. In 1860, what percentage of southern white families were in the slaveowning class?
a. 10 percent
b. 25 percent
c. 40 percent
d. 55 percent
e. 75 percent

ANS: B   TOP: Social history | Plain Folk of the Old South   DIF: Difficult   REF: Full p. 394 | Seagull p. 402   MSC: Remembering   OBJ: 1

12. Southern farmers in the backcountry:
a. generally worked the land using family labor.
b. were all directly involved in the market economy from the start of the nineteenth century.
c. owned a substantial number of slaves.
d. were highly self-sufficient but still bought most of their supplies from stores.
e. were fortunate that their land was far better for farming than that owned by planters.

ANS: A   TOP: Social history | Plain Folk of the Old South   DIF: Moderate   REF: Full p. 394 | Seagull p. 402   MSC: Remembering   OBJ: 1

13. The relationship between rich southern planters and poor southern farmers:
a. led to numerous violent uprisings in the southern hill country.
b. was complicated by the strong antislavery movement among poor farmers in the 1850s.
c. was strained by planters' insistence that farmers participate in the slave patrols.
d. showed itself in politics, as most poor farmers became Whigs and most wealthy planters became Democrats.
e. benefited in part from a sense of unity bred by criticism from outsiders.

ANS: E   TOP: Social history | Plain Folk of the Old South   DIF: Difficult   REF: Full p. 394 | Seagull p. 403   MSC: Understanding   OBJ: 1

14. Andrew Johnson of Tennessee and Joseph Brown of Georgia rose to political power:
a. because of their membership in and identification with the planter class.
b. in the 1850s, as members of the small but influential southern Republican Party.
c. as self-proclaimed spokesmen of the common man against the great planters.

d. as proponents of gradual emancipation plans in order to destroy the "slavocracy."

e. after gaining popularity for creating public education systems in their states.

ANS: C   TOP: Social history | Plain Folk of the Old South   DIF: Moderate   REF: Full p. 394 | Seagull p. 403   MSC: Remembering   OBJ: 1

15. In 1850, a majority of southern slaveholders owned how many slaves?
   a. 1 to 5
   b. 6 to 10
   c. 15 to 20
   d. 25 to 30
   e. at least 35

ANS: A   TOP: Social history | The Planter Class DIF: Difficult   REF: Full p. 395 | Seagull p. 403 MSC: Remembering   OBJ: 1

16. To qualify as a member of the planter class, a person had to be engaged in southern agriculture and:
   a. own at least ten slaves.
   b. grow specifically cotton or sugarcane.
   c. own at least twenty slaves.
   d. live in a large mansion.
   e. own at least fifty slaves.

ANS: C   TOP: Social history | The Planter Class DIF: Difficult   REF: Full p. 395 | Seagull p. 403 MSC: Remembering   OBJ: 1

17. From 1840 to 1860, the price of a "prime field hand":
   a. rose about 80 percent, which made it harder for southern whites to enter the slaveholding class.
   b. rose less than 10 percent, which kept the size of the planter class about the same.
   c. declined about 15 percent as the supply of slaves in the internal slave trade increased.
   d. became so inexpensive that the slaveholding class grew to include nearly two-thirds of southern whites.
   e. declined because labor-intensive agricultural work became less popular in the South.

ANS: A   TOP: Economic development | Social history | The Planter Class   DIF: Difficult   REF: Full p. 395 | Seagull p. 403   MSC: Understanding OBJ: 1

18. Which event is credited with helping to ingrain the paternalist ethos more deeply into the lives of southern slaveholders?
   a. Nat Turner's Rebellion
   b. the nullification crisis
   c. the development of domestic ideology
   d. the closing of the African slave trade
   e. the secession crisis

ANS: D   TOP: Social history | The Paternalist Ethos DIF: Moderate   REF: Full p. 396 | Seagull p. 404 MSC: Remembering   OBJ: 1

19. In the South, the paternalist ethos:
   a. reflected the hierarchical society in which the planter took responsibility for the lives of those around him.
   b. declined after the War of 1812, as southern society became more centered on market relations rather than on personal relations.
   c. suffered because southern slaveholders lived among their slaves, so that the groups' constant exposure to each other made southern slavery more openly violent than elsewhere.
   d. brought southern society closer to northern ideals.
   e. encouraged southern women to become more active and better educated so that they could help their husbands in their paternal roles.

ANS: A   TOP: Social history | The Paternalist Ethos DIF: Moderate   REF: Full p. 396 | Seagull p. 404 MSC: Remembering   OBJ: 1

20. What did the Reverend Charles C. Jones of Georgia NOT do?
   a. help improve slave housing
   b. help discourage severe punishments for slaves
   c. urge an end to slavery
   d. organize religious instruction of slaves
   e. help improve slave medical care

ANS: C   TOP: Civil rights | The Paternalist Ethos DIF: Moderate   REF: Full p. 396 | Seagull p. 405 MSC: Understanding   OBJ: 1

21. While the North emphasized egalitarianism, the South stressed:
   a. unions.
   b. communal living.
   c. a code of honor.
   d. competition.
   e. social mobility.

ANS: C   TOP: Cultural history | The Code of Honor DIF: Moderate   REF: Full pp. 396–397 | Seagull p. 405   MSC: Understanding   OBJ: 1

22. John C. Calhoun and George Fitzhugh:
   a. agreed that slavery was not a necessary evil but something actually positive and good.
   b. fought a famous duel that demonstrated the southern commitment to the idea of defending one's honor.
   c. competed for power in Andrew Jackson's administration.

d. were known as two of the most vicious slaveholders, who regularly whipped their slaves.

e. agreed on the need for slavery but disagreed as to whether it actually was beneficial to society.

ANS: A   TOP: Civil rights | The Proslavery Argument | Slavery and Civilization   DIF: Moderate
REF: Full pp. 398, 400 | Seagull pp. 406, 408
MSC: Understanding   OBJ: 1

23. By the late 1830s, the South's proslavery argument:
a. rested on the premise that slavery was a necessary evil.
b. was based entirely on secular evidence.
c. had not yet been accepted by major southern political figures.
d. claimed that slavery was essential to human economic and cultural progress.
e. was roundly criticized by southern newspaper editors, ministers, and academics.

ANS: D   TOP: Civil rights | The Proslavery Argument   DIF: Easy   REF: Full pp. 398–399 | Seagull p. 406   MSC: Remembering   OBJ: 1

24. Defenders of American slavery claimed that British emancipation in the 1830s had been a failure because:
a. many newly freed slaves moved to West Africa where they became reenslaved later.
b. of the violence it spawned in the West Indies during the 1840s.
c. many of those freed had moved to the United States where they could obtain only menial jobs.
d. the freed slaves grew less sugarcane, which hurt the economy of the Caribbean.
e. the freed slaves could not take care of themselves and many begged their ex-masters to support them.

ANS: D   TOP: Civil rights | Abolition in the Americas
DIF: Moderate   REF: Full p. 399 | Seagull p. 407
MSC: Understanding   OBJ: 1

25. The end of slavery in most Latin American nations:
a. resulted from violent slave revolts that rocked Latin America from 1822 to 1855.
b. involved gradual emancipation accompanied by recognition of owners' legal rights to slave property.
c. was inspired by the emancipation of slaves that occurred as a result of the American Civil War.
d. followed a pattern very different from that established in the northern United States.
e. did not happen until the United States made emancipation an aim of the Spanish-American War.

ANS: B   TOP: Civil rights | Global awareness | Abolition in the Americas   DIF: Moderate   REF: Full p. 399 | Seagull pp. 406–407   MSC: Remembering   OBJ: 1

26. Who said that the language in the Declaration of Independence—that all men were created equal and entitled to liberty—was "the most false and dangerous of all political errors"?
a. James Madison
b. James G. Birney
c. John C. Calhoun
d. Denmark Vesey
e. Solomon Northup

ANS: C   TOP: Civil rights | Slavery and Liberty
DIF: Difficult   REF: Full p. 400 | Seagull p. 407
MSC: Remembering   OBJ: 1

27. Which of the following statements about slavery and the law is true?
a. Because slaves were property, a master could kill any of his slaves for any reason.
b. Slaves were legally permitted to possess guns if guns were necessary for their work (tasks such as scaring birds away from rice fields, for example).
c. Laws specifically provided for a slave to be taught to read and write if the master so chose.
d. A slave could, with permission from his or her master, testify against a white person in court.
e. Slaves accused of serious crimes were entitled to their day in court, although they faced all-white judges and juries.

ANS: E   TOP: Civil rights | Slaves and the Law
DIF: Difficult   REF: Full p. 401 | Seagull p. 409
MSC: Understanding   OBJ: 2

28. Celia was:
a. the pen name of Floride Calhoun, who secretly criticized her husband, John's, views on slavery.
b. a slave tried for killing her master while resisting a sexual assault.
c. the name used to signify a southern plantation mistress in writings about the institution.
d. a slave who became famous for helping other slaves escape via the Underground Railroad.
e. a character in *Uncle Tom's Cabin*.

ANS: B   TOP: Civil rights | Slaves and the Law
DIF: Moderate   REF: Full p. 402 | Seagull p. 410
MSC: Remembering   OBJ: 2

29. Why did southern slaves live in better conditions by the mid-nineteenth century than those in the Caribbean and South America?
a. They did not; slaves led vastly healthier lives in regions other than the American South.
b. Southern Protestant churches encouraged better treatment of southern slaves than the Roman

Catholic Church did with slaves in the Caribbean and South America.

c. The rising value of slaves made it profitable for slaveowners to take better care of them.

d. Laws in the South were far more protective of slaves than were laws concerning slaves elsewhere.

e. Southern slaves had a greater likelihood of becoming free than did other New World slaves.

ANS: C   TOP: Economic development | Civil rights | Conditions of Life   DIF: Moderate   REF: Full p. 402 | Seagull p. 410   MSC: Remembering OBJ: 2

30. Free blacks in the South were allowed to:
a. own property.
b. be bought and sold.
c. carry a firearm.
d. testify in court.
e. vote.

ANS: A   TOP: Civil rights | Free Blacks in the Old South   DIF: Moderate   REF: Full p. 403 | Seagull p. 411   MSC: Remembering   OBJ: 2

31. In an 1840 letter written from Canada, fugitive slave Joseph Taper asked for divine blessings upon:
a. the writer Harriet Beecher Stowe.
b. his former master.
c. President Martin Van Buren.
d. abolitionist William Lloyd Garrison.
e. Queen Victoria.

ANS: E   TOP: Global awareness | Primary document analysis | Voices of Freedom   DIF: Moderate REF: Full p. 404 | Seagull p. 412   MSC: Remembering OBJ: 2

32. What was the name of the vibrant community of former slaves freed by Virginian Richard Randolph?
a. Sea Island
b. Mount Vernon
c. Israel Hill
d. Sherman's Land
e. Promised Land

ANS: C   TOP: Social history | Free Blacks in the Old South   DIF: Difficult   REF: Full p. 407 | Seagull p. 414   MSC: Remembering   OBJ: 2

33. Free blacks in the United States:
a. had the same rights as whites in the North but faced far more restrictions on their freedom in the South.
b. tended to live in rural areas if they lived in the Lower South.
c. sometimes became wealthy enough to own slaves.
d. made up nearly one-third of the African-American population in the South.

e. could testify in court and vote in most states, but could carry firearms only with the approval of the local sheriff.

ANS: C   TOP: Economic development | Social history | Free Blacks in the Old South   DIF: Moderate REF: Full p. 407 | Seagull p. 414   MSC: Remembering OBJ: 2

34. Which state had the least amount of free blacks?
a. Mississippi
b. Louisiana
c. South Carolina
d. Virginia
e. Maryland

ANS: A   TOP: Civil rights | Free Blacks in the Old South   DIF: Difficult   REF: Full p. 407 | Seagull p. 414   MSC: Understanding   OBJ: 2

35. All of the following statements are true of the work done by southern slaves EXCEPT:
a. by 1860, some 200,000 worked in factories.
b. slaves sometimes were allowed to supervise other laborers, including white workers.
c. masters rented out slaves to do a variety of jobs.
d. the federal government used slaves to build forts and other public buildings in the South.
e. slaves worked exclusively as agricultural field hands and house servants.

ANS: E   TOP: Social history | Slave Labor DIF: Moderate   REF: Full p. 408 | Seagull p. 415 MSC: Understanding   OBJ: 2

36. On the plantation, the white employee in charge of ensuring a profitable crop for the plantation master was called the:
a. journeyman.
b. slave driver.
c. chain gang.
d. overseer.
e. deputy master.

ANS: D   TOP: Economic development | Social history | Gang Labor and Task Labor   DIF: Easy REF: Full p. 409 | Seagull p. 417   MSC: Remembering OBJ: 1

37. Task labor:
a. got its name for tasking the abilities of slaves; it was very difficult, complicated work.
b. was an acronym for Take All Southerners' Knives, a secret organization of slaves planning an insurrection.
c. always was controlled by an overseer.
d. allowed slaves to take on daily jobs, set their own pace, and work on their own when they were done.

e. was the most common form of slave labor organization in the South.

ANS: D   TOP: Social history | Gang Labor and Task Labor   DIF: Moderate   REF: Full pp. 409–410 | Seagull p. 417   MSC: Remembering   OBJ: 1

38. Urban slaves:
    a. most often were domestic servants.
    b. was a term coined by southerners to describe northern factory workers.
    c. had less autonomy than plantation slaves because there were more authorities to watch them.
    d. could work on their own and always kept the majority of their earnings.
    e. increasingly replaced skilled white laborers as the Civil War approached.

ANS: A   TOP: Social history | Slavery in the Cities   DIF: Moderate   REF: Full p. 410 | Seagull p. 417   MSC: Remembering   OBJ: 1

39. The plantation masters had many means to maintain order among their slaves. According to the text, what was the most powerful weapon the plantation masters had?
    a. requiring slaves to attend church
    b. the threat of sale
    c. exploiting the divisions among slaves
    d. withholding food
    e. denying a marriage between two slaves

ANS: B   TOP: Civil rights | Social history | Maintaining Order   DIF: Easy   REF: Full p. 411 | Seagull p. 418   MSC: Understanding   OBJ: 2

40. Slave families:
    a. were rare because there were too few female slaves.
    b. were more common in the West Indies, where living conditions favored their formation and survival.
    c. were headed by women more frequently than were white families.
    d. usually were able to stay together because most slaveowners were paternalistic.
    e. avoided naming children for family members because children so often were sold, and it was better not to build strong kinship ties.

ANS: C   TOP: Social history | The Slave Family   DIF: Moderate   REF: Full p. 412 | Seagull p. 419   MSC: Remembering   OBJ: 3

41. Jumping over a broomstick was a ceremony celebrating:
    a. a fugitive slave arriving in a free state.
    b. a slave marriage.
    c. the birth of a slave baby.
    d. surviving the Middle Passage.

e. a slave's promotion from field hand to domestic servant.

ANS: B   TOP: Cultural history | The Slave Family   DIF: Moderate   REF: Full p. 412 | Seagull p. 419   MSC: Remembering   OBJ: 3

42. Gender roles under slavery:
    a. were the same as those that existed in white society.
    b. differed from those of white society because men and women alike suffered a sense of powerlessness.
    c. greatly differed from those of whites when slaves were able to work on their own; the men took on more women's work and vice versa.
    d. meant that slave husbands refused to let their wives work in the fields.
    e. were unaffected by the ability of masters to take advantage of female slaves sexually.

ANS: B   TOP: Civil rights | Social history | Gender Roles among Slaves   DIF: Difficult   REF: Full p. 413 | Seagull p. 421   MSC: Understanding   OBJ: 3

43. Slave religion:
    a. was based entirely on what slaves learned and heard from white ministers.
    b. existed without approval from masters, who thought that letting slaves learn about religion might weaken their control.
    c. benefited from masters assigning a member of each slave quarters to serve as a slave chaplain.
    d. combined African traditions and Christian beliefs.
    e. died out by the early 1820s because of strong opposition from whites.

ANS: D   TOP: Cultural history | The Gospel of Freedom   DIF: Moderate   REF: Full p. 414 | Seagull p. 422   MSC: Remembering   OBJ: 3

44. Which of the following statements about religious life among African-Americans in southern cities is true?
    a. Blacks usually worshipped in churches where they sat side-by-side with whites.
    b. Urban free blacks sometimes formed their own churches.
    c. African-Americans, free and slave, were banned from religious services.
    d. Free blacks could worship publicly, but slaves were not permitted to do so.
    e. The formation of the Afro-Catholic Church in 1844 was a major development in black Christianity.

ANS: B   TOP: Social history | Slave Religion   DIF: Moderate   REF: Full p. 414 | Seagull p. 422   MSC: Remembering   OBJ: 3

45. Which of the following stories did NOT play a central role in black Christianity?

a. Moses and the exodus from Egypt
b. Noah and the ark
c. David and Goliath
d. Jonah and the whale
e. Daniel and the lion's den

ANS: B   TOP: Cultural history | The Gospel of Free-
   dom   DIF: Moderate   REF: Full p. 414 | Seagull
   p. 422   MSC: Understanding   OBJ: 3

46. The Brer Rabbit stories of slave folklore:
   a. celebrated how the weak could outsmart the more
      powerful.
   b. borrowed heavily from English folktales but did add
      some African elements.
   c. formed the basis of *Uncle Tom's Cabin.*
   d. introduced the character Paul Bunyan to American
      culture.
   e. were largely unknown until the making of a series
      of animated films in the twentieth century.

   ANS: A   TOP: Cultural history | The Desire for
      Liberty   DIF: Moderate   REF: Full p. 415 |
      Seagull p. 423   MSC: Remembering   OBJ: 3

47. Compared to slave revolts in Brazil and in the West
   Indies, slave revolts in the United States were:
   a. larger in scale but less frequent.
   b. smaller in scale but more frequent.
   c. larger in scale and more frequent.
   d. smaller in scale and less frequent.
   e. bloodier and more successful.

   ANS: D   TOP: Civil rights | Global awareness |
      Resistance to Slavery   DIF: Moderate   REF: Full
      p. 416 | Seagull p. 424   MSC: Analyzing   OBJ: 4

48. "Silent sabotage" can be defined as when slaves:
   a. ran away.
   b. did poor work and broke tools.
   c. learned how to read and write.
   d. secretly met to worship.
   e. named their children after kin.

   ANS: B   TOP: Civil rights | Forms of Resistance
   DIF: Easy   REF: Full p. 416 | Seagull p. 424
   MSC: Remembering   OBJ: 4

49. Fugitive slaves:
   a. generally understood that the North Star led to
      freedom.
   b. were more likely to be women than men, because
      they were trying to escape sexual assault.
   c. succeeded in escaping more frequently from the
      Deep South because they had access to ships
      leaving ports like New Orleans and Charleston.
   d. benefited from the refusal of non-slaveowners to
      participate in patrols that looked for fugitives.

e. who escaped to Canada were routinely returned to
   slavery by the British authorities.

ANS: A   TOP: Civil rights | Fugitive Slaves
DIF: Moderate   REF: Full p. 418 | Seagull p. 425
MSC: Remembering   OBJ: 4

50. Historians estimate that approximately _____
   slaves per year escaped to the North or Canada.
   a. 500
   b. 1,000
   c. 2,000
   d. 5,000
   e. 10,000

   ANS: B   TOP: Civil rights | Fugitive Slaves
   DIF: Difficult   REF: Full p. 418 | Seagull p. 425
   MSC: Remembering   OBJ: 4

51. Harriet Tubman:
   a. was a mythical character about whom runaway
      slaves told many stories.
   b. led a slave rebellion in Maryland in 1849 that
      resulted in two dozen deaths.
   c. although born free in New York, was kidnapped
      and made a slave in Louisiana.
   d. cleverly escaped from slavery by pretending to be
      a sickly male slaveowner.
   e. was a fugitive slave who risked her life many times
      to bring others out of slavery.

   ANS: E   TOP: Civil rights | Fugitive Slaves
   DIF: Moderate   REF: Full p. 418 | Seagull p. 425
   MSC: Remembering   OBJ: 4

52. The slave rebellion aboard the *Amistad*:
   a. nearly captured a fort in Charleston, South Carolina.
   b. led to a Supreme Court decision freeing the slaves.
   c. inspired the gag rule.
   d. took place off the coast of Virginia.
   e. helped establish the Republic of Haiti.

   ANS: B   TOP: Civil rights | Global awareness | The
      Amistad   DIF: Moderate   REF: Full p. 419 | Seagull
      pp. 425–427   MSC: Remembering   OBJ: 4

53. Denmark Vesey's conspiracy:
   a. reflected a combination of American and African
      influences.
   b. took place in 1831 and was a success.
   c. reflected the belief of the conspirators that the Bible
      endorsed slavery.
   d. was discovered, but Vesey escaped North to freedom.
   e. resulted in over twenty deaths of white men,
      women, and children.

   ANS: A   TOP: Civil rights | Global awareness | Slave
      Revolts   DIF: Difficult   REF: Full p. 420 | Seagull
      p. 427   MSC: Remembering   OBJ: 4

54. Which statement about Nat Turner's Rebellion is true?
    a. Turner and his followers assaulted mostly men.
    b. Fewer than twenty whites were killed during the rebellion.
    c. Turner escaped capture.
    d. Many southern whites were in a panic after the rebellion.
    e. It occurred in Georgia.

    ANS: D   TOP: Civil rights | Global awareness | Nat Turner's Rebellion   DIF: Moderate   REF: Full p. 421 | Seagull p. 429   MSC: Understanding   OBJ: 4

55. After an 1831 slave rebellion, which state's legislature debated, but did not approve, a plan for gradual emancipation of slaves in that state?
    a. Virginia
    b. South Carolina
    c. Maryland
    d. North Carolina
    e. Louisiana

    ANS: A   TOP: Civil rights | Global awareness | Nat Turner's Rebellion   DIF: Moderate   REF: Full p. 421 | Seagull p. 429   MSC: Remembering   OBJ: 4

True or False

1. By 1860, the economic investment represented by the slave population exceeded the value of the nation's factories, railroads, and banks combined.

   ANS: T   TOP: Economic development | Cotton Is King   DIF: Moderate   REF: Full p. 391 | Seagull p. 398   MSC: Remembering   OBJ: 1

2. Slavery did not affect northern merchants and manufacturers.

   ANS: F   TOP: Economic development | Slavery and the Nation   DIF: Easy   REF: Full p. 391 | Seagull p. 400   MSC: Understanding   OBJ: 1

3. Although the importation of slaves from Africa was prohibited beginning in 1808, the sale and trade of slaves within the United States flourished in later years.

   ANS: T   TOP: Economic development | The Second Middle Passage   DIF: Easy   REF: Full p. 391 | Seagull pp. 398–399   MSC: Remembering   OBJ: 1

4. Although New Orleans was the only city of significant size in the South, it did not have a rich immigrant culture.

   ANS: F   TOP: Ethnicity | The Southern Economy   DIF: Easy   REF: Full p. 393 | Seagull p. 401   MSC: Remembering   OBJ: 1

5. Most white southerner families owned at least one slave.

   ANS: F   TOP: Social history | Plain Folk of the Old South   DIF: Moderate   REF: Full p. 394 | Seagull pp. 401–402   MSC: Remembering   OBJ: 1

6. In the southern slave society, white women on plantations were seen as weak and helpless.

   ANS: T   TOP: Social history | The Code of Honor   DIF: Moderate   REF: Full p. 397 | Seagull p. 405   MSC: Remembering   OBJ: 1

7. John C. Calhoun's key contribution to the proslavery argument was the claim that slavery was a necessary evil.

   ANS: F   TOP: Civil rights | The Proslavery Argument   DIF: Moderate   REF: Full p. 398 | Seagull p. 406   MSC: Remembering   OBJ: 1

8. George Fitzhugh, a Virginia writer, believed slaves in the American South were not only very happy but also, to some degree, the freest people in the world.

   ANS: T   TOP: Civil rights | Slavery and Civilization   DIF: Moderate   REF: Full p. 400 | Seagull p. 408   MSC: Remembering   OBJ: 1

9. Slaves had a few legal rights, but they were not well enforced.

   ANS: T   TOP: Civil rights | Slaves and the Law   DIF: Moderate   REF: Full p. 401 | Seagull p. 409   MSC: Remembering   OBJ: 2

10. By the 1830s, it was illegal to teach a slave to read or write.

    ANS: T   TOP: Civil rights | Slaves and the Law   DIF: Easy   REF: Full p. 401 | Seagull p. 409   MSC: Remembering   OBJ: 2

11. Free blacks in the South could testify in court and serve on juries.

    ANS: F   TOP: Civil rights | Slaves and the Law   DIF: Easy   REF: Full p. 401 | Seagull p. 409   MSC: Remembering   OBJ: 2

12. Unlike in Brazil or the West Indies, there was little room for a mulatto group in the United States.

    ANS: T   TOP: Global awareness | Social history | Free Blacks in the Old South   DIF: Moderate   REF: Full p. 407 | Seagull p. 414   MSC: Understanding   OBJ: 2

13. Slaves working in the fields generally viewed the overseer as a cruel and heartless man.

ANS: T   TOP: Civil rights | Social history | Gang Labor and Task Labor   DIF: Easy   REF: Full p. 409 | Seagull p. 417   MSC: Remembering   OBJ: 2

14. Overall, slaves did not think much about freedom. They were content with their situation as long as their master was kind.

ANS: F   TOP: Civil rights | Slave Culture DIF: Easy   REF: Full p. 411 | Seagull p. 418 MSC: Remembering   OBJ: 3

15. Despite being forbidden by law to marry, many slaves were able to create a family life on the plantation.

ANS: T   TOP: Civil rights | Social history | The Slave Family   DIF: Moderate   REF: Full p. 412 | Seagull p. 419   MSC: Remembering   OBJ: 3

16. Slave traders tried hard to keep slave families together.

ANS: F   TOP: Civil rights | Social history | The Threat of Sale   DIF: Easy   REF: Full p. 412 | Seagull p. 420   MSC: Remembering   OBJ: 3

17. Slaves frequently named children after other family members to retain family continuity.

ANS: T   TOP: Civil rights | Social history | The Slave Family   DIF: Moderate   REF: Full p. 412 | Seagull p. 419   MSC: Remembering   OBJ: 3

18. When not in the field, slaves observed more traditional gender roles.

ANS: T   TOP: Civil rights | Social history | Gender Roles among Slaves   DIF: Moderate   REF: Full p. 413 | Seagull p. 421   MSC: Remembering   OBJ: 3

19. As a general rule, slave owners never allowed their slaves to listen to a white preacher in church.

ANS: F   TOP: Civil rights | Cultural history | Slave Religion   DIF: Easy   REF: Full pp. 413–414 | Seagull p. 422   MSC: Remembering   OBJ: 3

20. Black Christianity is best described as a blend between African traditions and Christian beliefs.

ANS: T   TOP: Cultural history | The Gospel of Freedom   DIF: Easy   REF: Full p. 414 | Seagull p. 422 MSC: Understanding   OBJ: 3

21. By 1860 the South's most populous city was New Orleans.

ANS: T   TOP: Geographic issues | The Old South DIF: Easy   REF: Full p. 417 | Seagull p. 429 MSC: Remembering   OBJ: 1

22. The Underground Railroad used a system of railways to transport slaves.

ANS: F   TOP: Civil rights | Fugitive Slaves DIF: Easy   REF: Full p. 418 | Seagull p. 425 MSC: Remembering   OBJ: 4

23. Denmark Vesey's 1822 slave rebellion resulted in the deaths of more than thirty whites in Charleston.

ANS: F   TOP: Civil rights | Slave Revolts DIF: Moderate   REF: Full p. 420 | Seagull p. 427 MSC: Remembering   OBJ: 4

24. Nat Turner was not a particularly religious man.

ANS: F   TOP: Civil rights | Nat Turner's Rebellion DIF: Moderate   REF: Full p. 420 | Seagull p. 428 MSC: Remembering   OBJ: 4

25. After Nat Turner's Rebellion, the Virginia legislature discussed ending slavery in that state.

ANS: T   TOP: Civil rights | Nat Turner's Rebellion DIF: Moderate   REF: Full p. 421 | Seagull p. 429 MSC: Remembering   OBJ: 4

Short Answer

Identify and give the historical significance of each of the following terms, events, and people in a paragraph or two.

1. fugitive slaves
2. plain folk
3. the *Amistad*
4. free blacks
5. paternalism
6. Second Middle Passage
7. the slave family
8. Nat Turner's Rebellion
9. cotton
10. Frederick Douglass
11. Celia
12. slave resistance

Essay Questions

1. One historian has observed of southern slavery that "nothing escaped, nothing and no one." What do you think that historian meant by that statement? What evidence can you provide to support that observation?

ANS: Answers will vary   TOP: Political history, changes | Social history | Slavery and the Nation DIF: Difficult   MSC: Evaluating   OBJ: 1 / 2 / 3 / 4

2. Despite unimaginable hardships, slaves were able to maintain a sense of identity and a determination to attain freedom. Describe how slave culture aided those endeavors and drove slaves' desire for freedom. Be sure

to consider African heritage, slave family life, folklore, and religious life in your response.

ANS: Answers will vary   TOP: Civil rights | Cultural history | Political history, changes | Social history | Slave Culture | The Slave Family | Gender Roles among Slaves | Slave Religion | The Gospel of Freedom | The Desire for Liberty   DIF: Moderate
MSC: Understanding   OBJ: 3

3. What made slavery "peculiar" in the United States?

ANS: Answers will vary   TOP: Civil rights | Cultural History | Economic development | Global Awareness | Political history, changes | Social history | Slavery and Liberty | Slavery and Civilization
DIF: Moderate   MSC: Evaluating   OBJ: 1 / 2 / 3 / 4

4. For the most part, white southerners defended the "peculiar institution" whether or not they had slaves, whether they were rich or poor, and whether they lived on large plantations or small farms. Why was this the case?

ANS: Answers will vary   TOP: Civil rights | Economic development | Global Awareness | Political history, changes | Social history | The Proslavery Argument | Plain Folk of the Old South | Slavery and Liberty | Slavery and Civilization   DIF: Moderate
MSC: Analyzing   OBJ: 1 / 2 / 3 / 4

5. Discuss the relationship between masters and slaves in the American South. Did masters have all the power in this relationship, or did the enslaved exert some power? Points to consider include paternalism, the size of slaveholdings, slavery and the law, forms of slave resistance, and labor organization (task and gang systems).

ANS: Answers will vary   TOP: Civil rights | Economic development | Political history, changes | Social history | The Paternalist Ethos | Slave Labor | Gang Labor and Task Labor | Maintaining Order | Slaves and the Law | The Threat of Sale | Forms of Resistance | Fugitive Slaves   DIF: Difficult   MSC: Analyzing   OBJ: 1 / 2 / 3 / 4

6. Slave rebellions were rare but important. Compare the slave rebellions (merely planned or actually carried out) of Denmark Vesey and Nat Turner. What did Vesey attempt to do? What did Turner attempt to do? How were these men similar? How did they view slavery and freedom? How did white society react to them, and why?

ANS: Answers will vary   TOP: Civil rights | Political history, changes | Social history | Slave Revolts | Nat Turner's Rebellion   DIF: Moderate
MSC: Analyzing   OBJ: 3 / 4

CHAPTER 12 | An Age of Reform, 1820–1840

This chapter concentrates on the history of reform, including various communal endeavors, public institutions, abolitionism, and feminism. The chapter begins with the story of abolitionist and women's rights advocate Abby Kelley. The reform impulse is explored by looking at examples of the nearly 100 utopian communities, almost all of which set out to reorganize society on a cooperative basis. As the reform movements took on more radical issues like temperance, abolition, and pacifism, many Americans saw the reform impulse as an attack on their own freedom. The era also saw an increase in institution building, which was inspired by the conviction that those who passed through their doors could eventually be released to become productive, self-disciplined citizens. The chapter then examines the crusade against slavery from colonization to immediate abolition. The antislavery movement sought to reinvigorate the idea of freedom as a truly universal entitlement, and at every opportunity, black abolitionists rejected the nation's pretensions as a land of liberty. Perhaps no one expressed this better than Frederick Douglass in his speech about the meaning of Independence Day, featured in "Voices of Freedom." The chapter also explores nineteenth-century feminism, which emerged from the abolitionist movement. Comparing the condition of women with that of slavery was a powerful rhetorical tool, as is illustrated by Angelina Grimké's letter to *The Liberator* in "Voices of Freedom." The chapter concludes with the Seneca Falls Convention and with the split of the organized abolitionist movement into two wings in 1840 (because of disputes over the proper role of women in antislavery work).

CHAPTER OUTLINE

I. Introduction: Abby Kelley
   A. Kelley was one of the first women's abolitionists.

B. She also was an active pacifist and pioneer for women's rights.
C. She gave more speeches than any other female orator.

II. The Reform Impulse
   1. Numerous voluntary associations participated in reforms.
   2. Reformers adopted a wide variety of tactics to bring about social change.
   A. Utopian Communities
     1. About 100 reform communities were established in the decades before the Civil War.
     2. Nearly all the communities set out to reorganize society on a cooperative basis, hoping both to restore social harmony to a world of excessive individualism and also to narrow the widening gap between rich and poor.
       a. Socialism and communism entered the language.
       b. Most tried to find substitutes for conventional gender relations and marriage patterns.
   B. The Shakers
     1. The Shakers were the most successful of the religious communities and had a significant impact on the outside world.
       a. Founder Mother Ann Lee was from England.
     2. Shakers believed men and women were spiritually equal.
     3. They abandoned private property and traditional family life.
       a. Celibacy

4. Economically successful with vegetables, herbs, cattle breeding, and furniture making

C. Oneida
   1. The founder of Oneida, John Noyes, preached that he and his followers had become so perfect that they had achieved a state of complete "purity of heart," or sinlessness.
      a. Started in Vermont
   2. Noyes and his followers abandoned private property and traditional family life.
      a. Complex marriage and adultery charges
      b. Relocation to Oneida, New York
   3. Oneida was an extremely dictatorial environment.
      a. Practiced early form of "eugenics"

D. Worldly Communities
   1. New England transcendentalists established Brook Farm to demonstrate that manual and intellectual labor could coexist harmoniously.
      a. Influenced by French social reformer Charles Fourier
   2. Although it was an exciting miniature university, Brook Farm failed in part because many intellectuals disliked farm labor.

E. The Owenites
   1. The most important secular communitarian was Robert Owen.
   2. Owen promoted communitarianism as a peaceful means of ensuring that workers received the full value of their labor.
   3. At New Harmony, Owen championed women's rights and education.
      a. Failed after a few years due to squabbling
      b. Influenced labor movement, education reform, and women's rights
   4. Other short-lived secular communities included those established by Joseph Warren.

F. Religion and Reform
   1. Some reform movements drew their inspiration from the religious revivalism of the Second Great Awakening.
   2. The revivals popularized the outlook known as perfectionism, which saw both individuals and society at large as capable of indefinite improvement.
   3. Under the impact of the revivals, older reform efforts moved in a new, radical direction.
      a. Prohibition, pacifism, and abolition

G. The Temperance Movement
   1. To members of the North's emerging middle-class culture, reform became a badge of respectability.
   2. The American Temperance Society directed its efforts at both the drunkards and the occasional drinker.
   3. The temperance crusade and other reforms aroused hostility.

H. Critics of Reform
   1. Many Americans saw the reform impulse as an attack on their own freedom.
      a. Catholics rallied against the temperance movement.
         i. Number growing from Irish and German immigration

I. Reformers and Freedom
   1. The vision of freedom expressed by the reform movements was liberating and controlling at the same time.
   2. Many religious groups in the East formed reform groups promoting religious virtue.
      a. They formed the American Tract Society and American Bible Society.

J. The Invention of the Asylum
   1. Americans embarked on a program of institution building.
      a. Jails
      b. Poorhouses
      c. Asylums
      d. Orphanages
   2. These institutions were inspired by the conviction that those who passed through their doors could eventually be released to become productive, self-disciplined citizens.

K. The Common School
   1. A tax-supported state public school system was widely adopted in the North.
   2. Horace Mann was the era's leading educational reformer.
   3. Mann believed that education would "equalize the conditions of men."
      a. Avenue for social advancement
      b. But also prepared them for work in new industrial economy
   4. Common schools provided career opportunities for women, who came to be most of the teachers.
   5. Lack of public education in South widened the divide between North and South.

III. The Crusade against Slavery
   A. Colonization
      1. The American Colonization Society (ACS), founded in 1816, promoted the gradual abolition of slavery and the settlement of black Americans in Africa.
         a. The ACS founded Liberia as its colony in West Africa.
         b. Harriet Martineau's *Society in America* (1837) criticized colonization as impractical.

2. Many prominent political leaders supported the ACS.
3. Like Indian removal, colonization rested on the premise that America is fundamentally a white society.

B. Blacks and Colonization
1. Several thousand blacks emigrated to Liberia with help of American Colonization Society.
2. Most African-Americans adamantly opposed the idea of colonization.
   a. They insisted that blacks were Americans, entitled to the same rights enjoyed by whites.
   b. In 1817, free blacks assembled in Philadelphia for the first national black convention and condemned colonization.

C. Militant Abolitionism
1. A new generation of reformers demanded immediate abolition.
   a. They believed that slavery was both sinful and a violation of the Declaration of Independence.
2. David Walker's *An Appeal to the Coloured Citizens of the World* was a passionate indictment of slavery and racial prejudice.
   a. He used both secular and religious language.

D. The Emergence of Garrison
1. The appearance in 1831 of *The Liberator,* William Lloyd Garrison's weekly journal published in Boston, gave the new breed of abolitionism a permanent voice.
2. Some of Garrison's ideas appeared too radical, but his call for immediate abolition was echoed by many.
   a. Garrison rejected colonization, and *The Liberator* remained the preeminent abolitionist journal.

E. Spreading the Abolitionist Message
1. Abolitionists recognized the democratic potential in the production of printed material.
2. Theodore Weld helped to create the abolitionists' mass constituency by using methods of religious revivals.
3. Identifying slavery as a sin was essential to replacing the traditional strategies of gradual emancipation and colonization with immediate abolition.

F. Slavery and Moral Suasion
1. Nearly all abolitionists, despite their militant language, rejected violence as a means of ending slavery.
2. Many abolitionists were pacifists, and they attempted to convince the slaveholder of his sinful ways.

3. Outside of established institutions, abolitionists adopted the role of radical social critics.

G. Abolitionists and the Idea of Freedom
1. Abolitionists repudiated the idea of wage slavery popularized by the era's labor movement.
   a. Only slavery deprived human beings of their "grand central right—the inherent right of self-ownership."
2. Slavery was so deeply embedded in American society that its destruction would require fundamental changes in the North and South.

H. A New Vision of America
1. The antislavery movement sought to reinvigorate the idea of freedom as a truly universal entitlement.
   a. Abolitionists, not the founders, saw America unbounded by race.
2. They insisted that blacks were fellow countrymen, not foreigners or a permanently inferior caste.
   a. Being born in America should determine citizenship, not race.
3. Abolitionists disagreed over the usefulness of the Constitution.
   a. Garrison burned it.
   b. Frederick Douglass believed Constitution did not protect slavery.
4. Abolitionists consciously identified their movement with the revolutionary heritage.
   a. The Liberty Bell

IV. Black and White Abolitionism
A. Black Abolitionists
1. From its inception, blacks played a leading role in the antislavery movement.
   a. Frederick Douglass and other ex-slaves published accounts of their bondage.
2. Stowe's *Uncle Tom's Cabin* gave the abolitionist message a powerful human appeal as it was modeled on the autobiography of fugitive slave Josiah Henson.
   a. Sold more than a million copies by 1854
   b. Inspired numerous stage versions

B. Abolitionism and Race
1. Although the movement was racially integrated, whites relegated blacks to secondary positions.
2. Abolitionists launched legal and political battles against racial discrimination in the North.
   a. Ended school segregation in Massachusetts in 1855
3. Black abolitionists developed an understanding of freedom that went well beyond that of most of their white contemporaries.

a. Attacked the intellectual foundations of racism
C. Slavery and American Freedom
1. At every opportunity, black abolitionists rejected the nation's pretensions as a land of liberty.
2. Black abolitionists articulated the ideal of color-blind citizenship.
3. Frederick Douglass famously questioned the meaning of the Fourth of July.
D. Gentlemen of Property and Standing
1. Abolitionism aroused violent hostility from northerners who feared that the movement threatened to disrupt the Union, interfere with profits wrested from slave labor, and overturn white supremacy.
2. Editor Elijah Lovejoy was killed by a mob while defending his press.
3. Southerners removed abolitionist literature from the mail and burned it.
4. Abolitionist petitions calling for end to slavery resulted in the "gag rule" in the House, preventing consideration of the petitions.
E. Slavery and Civil Liberties
1. Mob attacks and attempts to limit abolitionists' freedom of speech convinced many northerners that slavery was incompatible with the democratic liberties of white Americans.
2. The fight for the right to debate slavery openly and without reprisal led abolitionists to elevate free opinion to a central place in what Garrison called the gospel of freedom.

V. The Origins of Feminism
A. The Rise of the Public Woman
1. Women were instrumental in the abolition movement.
2. The public sphere was open to women in ways government and party politics were not.
a. Circulated petitions, attended mass meetings, marched in political parades, delivered public lectures, and raised money for political causes
B. Women and Free Speech
1. Participation in abolitionism inspired the early movement for women's rights.
2. Women lectured in public about abolition.
a. Grimké sisters
b. Frances Wright
c. Maria Stewart
3. The Grimké sisters argued against the idea that taking part in assemblies, demonstrations, and lectures was unfeminine.

a. *Letters on the Equality of the Sexes* (1838)
i. Critique of separate sphere for women
ii. Equal pay for equal work
C. Women's Rights
1. Elizabeth Cady Stanton and Lucretia Mott organized the Seneca Falls Convention of 1848.
a. Raised the issue of woman suffrage
2. The Declaration of Sentiments condemned the entire structure of inequality.
D. Feminism and Freedom
1. Lacking broad backing at home, early feminists found allies abroad.
2. Women deserved the range of individual choices, the possibility of self-realization, that constituted the essence of freedom.
3. Margaret Fuller sought to apply to women the transcendentalist idea that freedom meant a quest for personal development.
a. Served as editor of *The Dial* and literary editor of *New York Tribune*.
E. Women and Work
1. Sojourner Truth insisted movement devote attention to the poor and working-class women.
2. The participants at Seneca Falls rejected the identification of the home as women's "sphere."
a. The "bloomer" costume
3. The movement posed a fundamental challenge to some of society's central beliefs.
F. The Slavery of Sex
1. The concept of the "slavery of sex" empowered the women's movement to develop an all-encompassing critique of male authority and their own subordination.
2. Marriage and slavery became powerful rhetorical tools for feminists.
G. Social Freedom
1. The demand that women should enjoy the rights to regulate their own sexual activity and procreation and to be protected by the state against violence at the hands of their husbands challenged the notion that claims for justice, freedom, and individual rights should stop at the household's door.
2. The issue of women's private freedom revealed underlying differences within the movement for women's rights.
H. The Abolitionist Schism
1. When organized abolitionism split into two wings in 1840, the immediate cause was a dispute over the proper role of women in antislavery work.
a. American Anti-Slavery Society (favored women in leadership positions)

b. American and Foreign Anti-Slavery Society (opposed women in leadership positions)
2. The Liberty Party was established in hopes of making abolitionism a political movement.

SUGGESTED DISCUSSION QUESTIONS

- To what were the newly established communal and utopian communities reacting? What was it about society that made these group members attempt to create alternative lifestyles?
- Discuss how the vision of freedom expressed by the reform movements was liberating and controlling at the same time.
- Explain how public school was supposed to "equalize the conditions of men."
- How does the life of Abby Kelley reflect the many reform impulses of antebellum America?
- Discuss what role blacks played in the abolition movement. How did their view of freedom differ from that of the white abolitionists? Why were they so opposed to the colonization movement? Consider Frederick Douglass's speech excerpted in "Voices of Freedom."
- Compare slavery with the condition of women in antebellum America. Was it fair that feminists used slavery as a rhetorical tool for their cause? Be sure to look at Angelina Grimké's piece in the *Voices of Freedom* reader.
- Discuss the early feminist movement and the Seneca Falls Convention. Be sure to consider the activities and views of Angelina and Sarah Grimké, Margaret Fuller, Abby Kelley, Elizabeth Cady Stanton, and Lydia Maria Child. What does each of these women have to say about the role of women in American society?
- Have the students draft a plan for their own utopian community. Ask them to share with the class what their community will look like—its name, structure, rules, gender roles, and so forth.

SUPPLEMENTAL WEB AND VISUAL RESOURCES

David Walker
www.pbs.org/wgbh/aia/part4/4p2930.html
PBS has a special online resource called Africans in America, with an excerpt on David Walker, one of the proponents of abolitionism.

Seneca Falls
www.nps.gov/wori/
The National Parks Service website for Seneca Falls, New York, includes a photo gallery, historical background, classroom ideas, and more.

The Burned-Over District
www.crookedlakereview.com/books/saints_sinners/martin1.html
This is an essay on the famed burned-over district of western New York titled "Saints, Sinners and Reformers."

The Shakers
http://www.pbs.org/kenburns/shakers/
This website is the companion site for the Ken Burns documentary.

http://ecssba.rutgers.edu/
This Rutgers University site contains select papers of Elizabeth Cady Stanton and Susan B. Anthony.

SUPPLEMENTAL PRINT RESOURCES

Boydston, Jeanne, Mary Kelley, and Anne Margolis, eds. *The Limits of Sisterhood: The Beecher Sisters on Women's Rights and Woman's Sphere.* Chapel Hill, NC: University of North Carolina Press, 1988.

Cain, William E., ed. *William Lloyd Garrison and the Fight against Slavery: Selections from The Liberator.* New York: Bedford/St. Martin's, 1995.

DeLombard, Jeannine Marie. *Slavery on Trial: Law, Abolitionism, and Print Culture.* Chapel Hill, NC: University of North Carolina Press, 2007.

Ginzberg, Lori. *Women in Antebellum Reform.* Wheeling, IL: Harlan Davidson, Inc., 2000.

Hamm, Thomas. *God's Government Begun: The Society for Universal Inquiry and Reform, 1842–1846.* Bloomington, IN: Indiana University Press, 1996.

Horton, James Oliver, and Lois Horton. *In Hope of Liberty: Culture, Community, and Protest Among Northern Free Blacks, 1700–1860.* New York: Oxford University Press, 1997.

Jeffrey, Julie Roy. *The Great Silent Army of Abolitionism: Ordinary Women in the Antislavery Movement.* Chapel Hill, NC: University of North Carolina Press, 1998.

Matteson, John. *The Lives of Margaret Fuller: A Biography.* New York: W.W. Norton, 2012.

Mayer, Henry. *All on Fire: William Lloyd Garrison and the Abolition of Slavery.* New York: St. Martin's Press, 1998.

Newman, Richard S. *The Transformation of American Abolitionism: Fighting Slavery in the Early Republic.* Chapel Hill, NC: University of North Carolina Press, 2002.

Rorabaugh, W. J. *The Alcoholic Republic: An American Tradition.* New York: Oxford University Press, 1979.

Varon, Elizabeth R. *We Mean to Be Counted: White Women and Politics in Antebellum Virginia.* Chapel Hill, NC: University of North Carolina Press, 1998.

Wellman, Judith. "The Seneca Falls Women's Rights Convention: A Study of Social Networks." *Journal of Women's History* 3, no. 1 (1991): 9–37.

TEST BANK

Matching

TEST 1

___ 1. Dorothea Dix
___ 2. Sarah Grimké
___ 3. William Lloyd Garrison
___ 4. Elijah Lovejoy
___ 5. Horace Mann
___ 6. David Walker
___ 7. Elizabeth Cady Stanton
___ 8. Theodore Weld
___ 9. Robert Owen
___ 10. Harriet Beecher Stowe
___ 11. Margaret Fuller
___ 12. Harriet Martineau

a. equated slavery with sin
b. *The Liberator*
c. *Uncle Tom's Cabin*
d. *Society in America*
e. organized the Seneca Falls Convention
f. advocate for the mentally ill
g. leading educational reformer
h. *An Appeal to the Coloured Citizens of the World*
i. editor and martyr of the abolitionist movement
j. *Letters on the Equality of the Sexes*
k. New Harmony
l. *Woman in the Nineteenth Century*

Answer Key: f, j, b, i, g, h, e, a, k, c, l, d

TEST 2

___ 1. burned-over districts
___ 2. gag rule
___ 3. common schools
___ 4. temperance
___ 5. the Liberty Party
___ 6. Brook Farm
___ 7. Declaration of Sentiments
___ 8. "bloomer" costume
___ 9. American Colonization Society
___ 10. Washingtonian Society
___ 11. utopian
___ 12. *Freedom's Journal*

a. made abolition a political movement
b. group of reformed drinkers
c. Seneca Falls Convention
d. New England transcendentalists
e. advocated blacks returning to Africa
f. tax-supported public schools
g. a vision for a perfect society
h. area of intensive revivals in New York and Ohio
i. preventing antislavery petitions to be heard in Congress
j. feminist style of dress
k. first U.S. black newspaper
l. movement against alcohol

Answer Key: h, i, f, l, a, d, c, j, e, b, g, k

Learning Objectives

1. Identify the major movements and goals of antebellum reform.
2. Describe the different varieties of abolitionism.
3. Explain how abolitionism challenged barriers to racial equality and free speech.
4. Identify the diverse sources of the antebellum women's rights movement and explain its significance.

Multiple Choice

1. Abby Kelley:
   a. was one of the only female voices in the abolitionist movement.
   b. demonstrated the interconnectedness of nineteenth-century reform movements.
   c. was the first American woman to speak in public.
   d. married a leading temperance advocate.
   e. quit speaking publicly against slavery after her child was born.

   ANS: B   TOP: Social history | Introduction: Abby Kelley   DIF: Moderate   REF: Full p. 425 | Seagull p. 432   MSC: Remembering   OBJ: 4

2. According to Alexis de Tocqueville, what were the most important institutions for organizing Americans?
   a. state and federal governments
   b. schools
   c. political parties
   d. voluntary associations
   e. churches

   ANS: D   TOP: Social history | The Reform Impulse   DIF: Moderate   REF: Full p. 425 | Seagull p. 433   MSC: Understanding   OBJ: 1

3. About _____ reform communities, often called utopian communities, were established in the United States during the first half of the nineteenth century.
   a. 20
   b. 50
   c. 100
   d. 200
   e. 500

ANS: C   TOP: Social history | Utopian Communities
DIF: Difficult   REF: Full p. 426 | Seagull p. 434
MSC: Remembering   OBJ: 1

4. The reform communities established in the years before the Civil War:
   a. followed all of the laws but simply banned ownership of private property.
   b. usually followed standard gender and marital relations.
   c. made no effort to combat the growing disparity between rich and poor.
   d. called themselves utopian because they knew that their efforts were likely to fail.
   e. set out to reorganize society on a cooperative basis.

ANS: E   TOP: Social history | Utopian Communities
DIF: Moderate   REF: Full p. 426 | Seagull p. 435
MSC: Remembering   OBJ: 1

5. Who founded the Shakers?
   a. Joseph Smith
   b. Ann Lee
   c. Aimee McPherson
   d. Louisa Alcott
   e. Robert Matthews

ANS: B   TOP: Cultural history | The Shakers
DIF: Moderate   REF: Full pp. 426–427 |
    Seagull p. 434   MSC: Remembering   OBJ: 1

6. Which statement about Shakers is FALSE?
   a. They practiced "complex marriage" and publicly recorded sexual relations.
   b. Their numbers grew through conversions and the adoption of orphans.
   c. They bred cattle for profit and made furniture.
   d. They believed that men and women were spiritually equal.
   e. They abandoned private property and traditional family life.

ANS: A   TOP: Cultural history | Social history | The
    Shakers   DIF: Moderate   REF: Full p. 427 |
    Seagull p. 436   MSC: Understanding   OBJ: 1

7. The Oneida community:
   a. allowed each member an equal vote in governing the community.
   b. permitted all of its members to own private property.
   c. banished any member who divulged any information about the community's sexual practices.
   d. invented the concept of birth control in America.
   e. controlled which of its members would be allowed to reproduce.

ANS: E   TOP: Social history | Oneida
DIF: Moderate   REF: Full p. 428 | Seagull p. 438
MSC: Understanding   OBJ: 1

8. Brook Farm:
   a. kept manual and intellectual labor strictly separate.
   b. was modeled on the ideas of British reformer Robert Dale Owen.
   c. showed that the Shaker philosophy worked as well in America as in Britain.
   d. was founded by New England transcendentalists.
   e. received favorable publicity from a Nathaniel Hawthorne novel.

ANS: D   TOP: Social history | Worldly Communities
DIF: Moderate   REF: Full p. 429 | Seagull p. 438
MSC: Remembering   OBJ: 1

9. Which of the following correctly pairs the reform community with the state in which it was located?
   a. Brook Farm: Virginia
   b. Oneida: Massachusetts
   c. Zoar: Maine
   d. New Harmony: Indiana
   e. Modern Times: Tennessee

ANS: D   TOP: Social history | The Owenites
DIF: Difficult   REF: Full p. 429 | Seagull p. 439
MSC: Remembering   OBJ: 1

10. Although it only lasted a few years, the New Harmony community:
    a. demonstrated that workers could function without discipline.
    b. influenced education reformers and women's rights advocates.
    c. popularized the abolitionist movement.
    d. allowed Josiah Warren to prove his point about absolute individual freedom.
    e. inspired the formation of more than a dozen offshoot communities by 1850.

ANS: B   TOP: Social history | The Owenites
DIF: Difficult   REF: Full p. 429 | Seagull p. 439
MSC: Remembering   OBJ: 1

11. Utopian communities were unlikely to attract much support because most Americans:
    a. saw property ownership as key to economic independence, but nearly all the utopian communities insisted members give up their property.
    b. feared the Communist Party that endorsed and, in some cases, sponsored these communities.
    c. were Protestants, but all utopian communities required members to deny religious beliefs.
    d. supported the industrial revolution, but most utopian communities turned away from industry in favor of an agrarian lifestyle.

e. considered the utopian communities to be too materialistic and selfish.

ANS: A   TOP: Social history | Religion and Reform DIF: Moderate   REF: Full p. 430 | Seagull p. 439 MSC: Understanding   OBJ: 1

12. How did reformers reconcile their desire to create moral order with their quest to enhance personal freedom?
    a. They did not even try, because they had no intention of enhancing personal freedom.
    b. They claimed that genuine liberty meant allowing others to eliminate those problems that might threaten that liberty.
    c. They argued that too many people were "slaves" to various sins and that freeing them from this enslavement would enable them to compete economically.
    d. They contended that self-discipline was so rare, someone had to step in and make sure that Americans could enjoy the fruits of their labor.
    e. They felt that eliminating temptations would lead to the natural liberty that Protestants had long considered crucial to maintaining a good society.

ANS: C   TOP: Social history | Religion and Reform DIF: Difficult   REF: Full pp. 430–431 | Seagull p. 440 MSC: Analyzing   OBJ: 1

13. Burned-over districts were:
    a. areas in New York City where slaves had set fires.
    b. in Louisiana, where slaves had burned cotton fields as a form of resistance.
    c. regions where few evangelical Protestants lived (as though they had been burned out).
    d. in Kansas and Nebraska, where fighting broke out over issues of slavery.
    e. in New York and Ohio, where intense revivals occurred.

ANS: E   TOP: Cultural history | Social history | Religion and Reform   DIF: Moderate   REF: Full p. 431 | Seagull p. 440   MSC: Remembering OBJ: 1

14. By 1840, the temperance movement in the United States had:
    a. united Americans of all classes and religions in a "war" against alcohol.
    b. virtually disappeared.
    c. convinced Congress to pass a national prohibition law.
    d. made no measurable impact on Americans' drinking habits.
    e. encouraged a substantial decrease in the consumption of alcohol.

ANS: E   TOP: Social history | The Temperance Movement   DIF: Moderate   REF: Full p. 431 | Seagull p. 440   MSC: Remembering   OBJ: 1

15. Members of which of the following groups were generally opposed to the temperance movement?
    a. Catholics
    b. Protestants
    c. women
    d. perfectionists
    e. northern middle class

ANS: A   TOP: Social history | Critics of Reform DIF: Easy   REF: Full p. 432 | Seagull p. 441 MSC: Understanding   OBJ: 1

16. The American Tract Society was focused on:
    a. slavery.
    b. drinking.
    c. feminism.
    d. suffrage.
    e. religion.

ANS: E   TOP: Cultural history | Social history | Reformers and Freedom   DIF: Moderate REF: Full p. 432 | Seagull p. 442   MSC: Remembering OBJ: 1

17. What did reformers commonly believe about prisons and asylums?
    a. That the persons entering these institutions would likely never leave them.
    b. That they were not widely needed and not many were built.
    c. That they would be excellent holding centers for society's undesirables.
    d. That the persons in the facilities could be used as forced labor in factories.
    e. That they could rehabilitate individuals and then release them back into society.

ANS: E   TOP: Social history | The Invention of the Asylum   DIF: Difficult   REF: Full p. 433 | Seagull p. 442   MSC: Understanding   OBJ: 1

18. The proliferation of new institutions such as poorhouses and asylums for the insane during the antebellum era demonstrated the:
    a. lengths to which the federal government would go to provide for the general well-being of its citizens.
    b. power of the Democratic Party.
    c. tension between liberation and control in the era's reform movements.
    d. expansion of liberty for those members of society who could not take care of themselves.
    e. general economic prosperity of the nation.

ANS: C TOP: Social history | The Invention of the Asylum DIF: Moderate REF: Full p. 433 | Seagull p. 442 MSC: Understanding OBJ: 1

19. Horace Mann believed that public schools would do all of the following EXCEPT:
    a. "equalize the conditions of men."
    b. provide an avenue for social advancement.
    c. restore a fractured society.
    d. reinforce social stability.
    e. help eliminate racial discrimination.

    ANS: E TOP: Social history | The Common School DIF: Easy REF: Full p. 434 | Seagull p. 443 MSC: Understanding OBJ: 1

20. Common schools:
    a. had no connection to the emerging industrial economy.
    b. were based on the idea that the elite should be educated in their own schools.
    c. suffered from the opposition of labor unions that wanted children available to work.
    d. existed in every northern state by the time of the Civil War.
    e. proved to be as popular in the North as they were in the South.

    ANS: D TOP: Social history | The Common School DIF: Moderate REF: Full p. 434 | Seagull p. 443 MSC: Remembering OBJ: 1

21. Like Indian removal, the colonization of former slaves rested on the premise that America:
    a. was fundamentally a white society.
    b. wanted what was in the best interest of all the people.
    c. was not financially able to support all who lived there.
    d. provided opportunity for new land to those who desired it.
    e. was a land of diversity and equality.

    ANS: A TOP: Civil rights | Colonization DIF: Easy REF: Full p. 435 | Seagull p. 444 MSC: Understanding OBJ: 2

22. The colonization of freed U.S. slaves to Africa:
    a. received no support from southern slaveholders.
    b. was strongly endorsed by William Lloyd Garrison throughout his career.
    c. led to the creation of the free African nation of Ghana in 1835.
    d. was praised by the English writer Harriet Martineau.
    e. prompted the adamant opposition of most free African-Americans.

ANS: E TOP: Civil rights | Blacks and Colonization DIF: Moderate REF: Full p. 436 | Seagull p. 444 MSC: Remembering OBJ: 2

23. How did the abolitionist movement that arose in the 1830s differ from earlier antislavery efforts?
    a. Actually, the two movements were quite similar in every way; the later one was simply more well-known because more people were literate by the 1830s.
    b. The later movement drew much more on the religious conviction that slavery was an unparalleled sin and needed to be destroyed immediately.
    c. Earlier opponents of slavery had called for immediate emancipation, but the later group devised a plan for gradual emancipation that won broader support.
    d. The later movement banned participation by African-Americans, because they feared that their involvement would cause a backlash.
    e. The movement of the 1830s introduced the idea of colonizing freed slaves outside the United States, which proved immensely popular with southern whites.

    ANS: B TOP: Civil rights | Militant Abolitionism DIF: Moderate REF: Full p. 436 | Seagull p. 445 MSC: Analyzing OBJ: 2

24. The North Carolina–born free black whose *An Appeal to the Coloured Citizens of the World* won widespread attention was:
    a. David Walker.
    b. William Lloyd Garrison.
    c. Lewis Tappan.
    d. Wendell Phillips.
    e. Theodore Weld.

    ANS: A TOP: Civil rights | Militant Abolitionism DIF: Moderate REF: Full p. 436 | Seagull p. 445 MSC: Remembering OBJ: 2

25. The frontispiece of the 1848 edition of David Walker's book depicts a black figure receiving "liberty" and "justice" from:
    a. the Declaration of Independence.
    b. a slave master.
    c. the Constitution.
    d. the Underground Railroad.
    e. heaven.

    ANS: E TOP: Civil rights | Cultural history | Militant Abolitionism DIF: Moderate REF: Full p. 436 | Seagull p. 445 MSC: Understanding OBJ: 3

26. William Lloyd Garrison:
    a. secretly financed Nat Turner's Rebellion.

b. began publishing his newspaper in Richmond, Virginia, in 1831, but moved it to friendlier territory two years later.

c. attracted little support from fellow abolitionists, but historians have discovered his importance.

d. suggested that the North dissolve the Union to free itself of any connection to slavery.

e. published *American Slavery As It Is*, an influential pamphlet.

ANS: D   TOP: Social history | The Emergence of Garrison   DIF: Moderate   REF: Full p. 437 | Seagull p. 446   MSC: Remembering OBJ: 2

27. William Lloyd Garrison published an abolitionist newspaper called:
    a. *Free Press.*
    b. *The Liberator.*
    c. *The Pursuit of Happiness.*
    d. *The North Star.*
    e. *Gideon's Trumpet.*

    ANS: B   TOP: Civil rights | The Emergence of Garrison   DIF: Difficult   REF: Full p. 437 | Seagull p. 446   MSC: Remembering   OBJ: 2

28. William Lloyd Garrison argued in *Thoughts on African Colonization* that:
    a. blacks could never fully achieve equality in America and would be happier in Africa.
    b. because slaves were uneducated, it was necessary to educate them in America before sending them to Africa.
    c. blacks were not "strangers" in America to be shipped abroad, but should be recognized as a permanent part of American society.
    d. colonization should be subsidized through a tax on cotton.
    e. because blacks had no political experience, Garrison himself ought to be appointed governor of the African colony.

    ANS: C   TOP: Civil rights | The Emergence of Garrison   DIF: Moderate   REF: Full p. 437 | Seagull p. 446   MSC: Remembering   OBJ: 2

29. A young minister converted by the evangelical preacher Charles G. Finney, _____ helped to create a mass constituency for abolitionism by training speakers and publishing pamphlets.
    a. David Walker
    b. Theodore Weld
    c. Abby Kelley
    d. Lewis Tappan
    e. Lydia Maria Child

    ANS: B   TOP: Cultural history | Social history | Spreading the Abolitionist Message

DIF: Moderate   REF: Full p. 438 | Seagull p. 446
MSC: Remembering   OBJ: 2

30. How did the abolitionists link themselves to the nation's Revolutionary heritage?
    a. They seized on the preamble to the Declaration of Independence as an attack against slavery.
    b. They cracked the Liberty Bell to signify that the bonds of liberty were breaking under the weight of slavery.
    c. They used mob action, just as the revolutionaries had when they attacked such disagreeable measures as the Stamp Act.
    d. They reminded audiences constantly that the main issue the Sons of Liberty and similar groups had invoked was liberty.
    e. They made a heroic figure of Crispus Attucks, the African-American who died at the Boston Massacre.

    ANS: A   TOP: Civil rights | A New Vision of America   DIF: Easy   REF: Full p. 441 | Seagull p. 450   MSC: Understanding   OBJ: 3

31. The role of African-Americans in the abolitionist movement:
    a. was limited to the writings and speeches of Frederick Douglass.
    b. included helping to finance William Lloyd Garrison's newspaper.
    c. showed that the movement was free from the racism that characterized American society.
    d. was limited because the American Anti-Slavery Society banned them from its board of directors.
    e. grew over time until, by the 1850s, the movement was dominated by blacks.

    ANS: B   TOP: Civil rights | Black Abolitionists   DIF: Moderate   REF: Full p. 441 | Seagull p. 450   MSC: Remembering   OBJ: 3

32. Before the Civil War, who came to believe that the U.S. Constitution did not provide national protection to the institution of slavery?
    a. Frederick Douglass
    b. William Lloyd Garrison
    c. David Walker
    d. John C. Calhoun
    e. Jennings Randolph

    ANS: A   TOP: Civil rights | Constitutional history | A New Vision of America   DIF: Difficult   REF: Full p. 441 | Seagull p. 449   MSC: Remembering   OBJ: 3

33. Abolitionists challenged stereotypes about African-Americans by:
    a. countering the pseudoscientific claim that they formed a separate species.

b. presenting the compositions of Henry Highland Garnet to disprove the belief that African culture was inferior because it produced no classical music composers.

c. pointing to Haiti, the scene of the famous slave revolts of the 1790s and 1800s, as a model of civilization.

d. making January 1, the anniversary of the end of the international slave trade, a holiday throughout the North until the end of the Civil War.

e. nominating Frederick Douglass for president in 1852 and winning him Vermont's electoral votes.

ANS: A   TOP: Civil rights | Social history | Abolitionism and Race   DIF: Moderate   REF: Full p. 442 | Seagull p. 452   MSC: Understanding OBJ: 3

34. Which book was to some extent modeled on the autobiography of fugitive slave Josiah Henson?
   a. *An Appeal to Reason*
   b. *Society in America*
   c. *Twelve Years a Slave*
   d. *Uncle Tom's Cabin*
   e. *Slavery As It Is*

ANS: D   TOP: Civil rights | Cultural history | Black Abolitionists   DIF: Easy   REF: Full p. 442 | Seagull p. 450   MSC: Remembering OBJ: 3

35. According to the mid-nineteenth-century physicians and racial theorists Josiah Nott and George Gliddon:
   a. there were no separate species of races.
   b. blacks and chimpanzees were the same.
   c. skull sizes were the same for all races, but intelligence differed.
   d. there was a hierarchy of races, with blacks forming a separate species between whites and chimpanzees.
   e. there was not yet enough scientific data to prove either the southern or the abolitionist points of view.

ANS: D   TOP: Social history | Abolitionism and Race DIF: Difficult   REF: Full p. 442 | Seagull p. 452 MSC: Analyzing   OBJ: 3

36. *Freedom's Journal*:
   a. was the autobiography of Joseph Taper, a fugitive slave.
   b. published Harriet Beecher Stowe's *Uncle Tom's Cabin*.
   c. was the newspaper of the Owenite community at New Harmony.
   d. was established by Abby Kelley.
   e. was the first black-run newspaper in the United States.

ANS: E   TOP: Civil rights | Slavery and American Freedom   DIF: Moderate   REF: Full p. 443 | Seagull p. 452   MSC: Remembering   OBJ: 3

37. What did the Fourth of July represent to Frederick Douglass?
   a. the hypocrisy of a nation that proclaimed liberty but sanctioned slavery
   b. the ultimate celebration of freedom
   c. a beacon of hope that someday America would honor the claim that "all men are created equal"
   d. an opportunity for slaves to join in a mass rebellion against their masters
   e. the anniversary of the day he ran away from his master and claimed freedom

ANS: A   TOP: Primary document analysis | Slavery and American Freedom   DIF: Easy   REF: Full p. 443 | Seagull p. 452   MSC: Understanding   OBJ: 3

38. The gag rule:
   a. stated that newspapers could not print antislavery materials.
   b. prevented Congress from hearing antislavery petitions.
   c. denied women the right to speak in mixed-sex public gatherings.
   d. prevented Congregational ministers from preaching against Catholics.
   e. was adopted at the Seneca Falls Convention to symbolize that women did not have a voice in politics.

ANS: B   TOP: Political history, changes | Gentlemen of Property and Standing   DIF: Moderate REF: Full p. 444 | Seagull p. 454   MSC: Remembering OBJ: 3

39. The death of Elijah Lovejoy in 1837:
   a. convinced many northerners that slavery was incompatible with white Americans' liberties.
   b. resulted from his leading an anti-abolitionist mob that attacked William Lloyd Garrison.
   c. demonstrated that fugitive slaves like Lovejoy faced great dangers while escaping from "slave catchers."
   d. was played up by temperance pamphleteers to show the hazards of alcoholism.
   e. led Congress to adopt the gag rule in order to prevent the sort of heated arguments that caused his death.

ANS: A   TOP: Civil rights | Slavery and Civil Liberties   DIF: Moderate   REF: Full p. 445 | Seagull p. 454   MSC: Understanding   OBJ: 3

40. Frederick Douglass wrote, "When the true history of the antislavery cause shall be written, _____ will occupy a large space in its pages."

a. newspaper editors
b. black abolitionists
c. freed slaves
d. white abolitionists
e. women

ANS: E   TOP: Social history | The Rise of the Public
   Woman   DIF: Moderate   REF: Full p. 446 |
   Seagull p. 455   MSC: Remembering   OBJ: 4

41. Dorothea Dix devoted much time to the crusade for the:
    a. immediate abolition of slavery.
    b. establishment of common schools in the South.
    c. better treatment for convicted criminals in jail.
    d. construction of humane mental hospitals for the insane.
    e. right for women to vote in local school elections.

ANS: D   TOP: Social history | The Rise of the Public
   Woman   DIF: Moderate   REF: Full p. 447 |
   Seagull pp. 455–456   MSC: Remembering   OBJ: 4

42. Which of the following was NOT a reform movement in which women played a prominent role during the early to mid-nineteenth century?
    a. abolitionism
    b. mental health treatment
    c. the anti-Mexican-War movement
    d. redemption of prostitutes
    e. temperance

ANS: C   TOP: Social history | The Rise of the Public
   Woman   DIF: Easy   REF: Full p. 447 | Seagull
   pp. 455–456   MSC: Analyzing   OBJ: 4

43. Angelina and Sarah Grimké:
    a. supported Catharine Beecher's efforts to expand political and social rights for women.
    b. critiqued the prevailing notion of separate spheres for men and women.
    c. were Pennsylvania-born Quakers whose religion compelled them to oppose slavery.
    d. publicly defended the virtues of southern paternalism in lectures to southern women.
    e. delivered many public lectures in which they detailed their escape from slavery.

ANS: B   TOP: Social history | Women and Free
   Speech   DIF: Moderate   REF: Full pp. 447–478 |
   Seagull p. 457   MSC: Understanding   OBJ: 4

44. The first to apply the abolitionist doctrine of universal freedom and equality to the status of women:
    a. were the Grimké sisters.
    b. was Frederick Douglass.
    c. was Susan B. Anthony.
    d. were Henry Stanton and Elizabeth Cady Stanton.
    e. was James G. Birney.

ANS: A   TOP: Civil rights | Social history | Women's
   Rights   DIF: Difficult   REF: Full p. 448 | Seagull
   p. 457   MSC: Understanding   OBJ: 4

45. The Seneca Falls Convention's Declaration of Sentiments was modeled after the
    a. Declaration of Independence.
    b. U.S. Constitution.
    c. *Woman of the Nineteenth Century.*
    d. *A Vindication of the Rights of Woman.*
    e. *Letters on the Equality of the Sexes.*

ANS: A   TOP: Social history | Women's Rights
DIF: Moderate   REF: Full pp. 448–449 |
   Seagull p. 457   MSC: Understanding
OBJ: 4

46. The Seneca Falls Convention's Declaration of Sentiments:
    a. did not demand voting rights for women because the participants were so divided on that issue.
    b. was modeled on the Bill of Rights in the U.S. Constitution.
    c. was written primarily by the Grimké sisters.
    d. condemned the entire structure of inequality between men and women.
    e. inspired Lucretia Mott and Elizabeth Cady Stanton to become abolitionists.

ANS: D   TOP: Social history | Women's Rights
DIF: Moderate   REF: Full p. 449 | Seagull
   pp. 457–458   MSC: Remembering
OBJ: 4

47. All of the following are true of Margaret Fuller EXCEPT:
    a. she was the first feminist leader educated at a major college.
    b. her father was a member of Congress.
    c. she was the first female literary editor of the *New York Tribune.*
    d. she was a leading transcendentalist.
    e. she believed marrying an American would mean subordinating herself to male dictation.

ANS: A   TOP: Social history | Feminism and
   Freedom   DIF: Moderate   REF: Full p. 449 |
   Seagull p. 458   MSC: Analyzing   OBJ: 4

48. What was a "bloomer" in the 1850s?
    a. a utopian society
    b. a new supporter of abolition
    c. a feminist style of dress
    d. an agricultural reformer
    e. an advocate of free speech

ANS: C   TOP: Cultural history | Social history | Women and Work   DIF: Easy   REF: Full p. 452 | Seagull p. 459   MSC: Remembering   OBJ: 4

49. Which state enacted a far-reaching law allowing married women to sign contracts and buy and sell property?
   a. New Jersey
   b. Massachusetts
   c. Vermont
   d. Pennsylvania
   e. New York

   ANS: E   TOP: Political history, changes | Social history | The Slavery of Sex   DIF: Difficult REF: Full p. 453 | Seagull p. 462   MSC: Remembering OBJ: 4

50. The organized abolitionist movement split into two wings in 1840, largely over:
   a. whether to nominate William Lloyd Garrison or James G. Birney as the antislavery presidential candidate.
   b. the question of abolitionists' taking a public stand on the controversial gag rule.
   c. whether African-Americans should be allowed to speak at mixed-race public events.
   d. a dispute concerning the proper role of women in antislavery work.
   e. disagreements concerning the endorsement of colonization.

   ANS: D   TOP: Social history | The Abolitionist Schism   DIF: Moderate   REF: Full p. 454 | Seagull p. 463   MSC: Understanding OBJ: 4

51. The antislavery poet John Greenleaf Whittier compared reformer Abby Kelley to:
   a. Helen of Troy, who sowed the seeds of male destruction.
   b. an Amazon, a mighty female warrior of Greek mythology.
   c. Queen Elizabeth, who had ruled the British empire with such skill.
   d. Molly Pitcher, the patriotic heroine of the American Revolution.
   e. Joan of Arc, who led the armies of France into battle.

   ANS: A   TOP: Social history | The Abolitionist Schism   DIF: Moderate   REF: Full p. 454 | Seagull p. 464   MSC: Remembering   OBJ: 4

52. The _____ was established in hopes of making abolitionism a political movement.
   a. Liberty Party
   b. Whig Party
   c. North Star Party
   d. Republican Party
   e. Afro-American Party

   ANS: A   TOP: Political history, changes | The Abolitionist Schism   DIF: Difficult   REF: Full p. 455 | Seagull p. 464   MSC: Remembering OBJ: 4

True or False

1. The Shakers believed God had a dual personality, both male and female.

   ANS: T   TOP: Cultural history | The Shakers DIF: Moderate   REF: Full p. 427 | Seagull p. 436 MSC: Remembering   OBJ: 1

2. The antebellum utopian communities were largely located in the Upper South.

   ANS: F   TOP: Geographic issues | Social history | Oneida   DIF: Easy   REF: Full p. 428 | Seagull p. 437   MSC: Remembering   OBJ: 1

3. Although it was an exciting miniature university, the transcendentalists' Brook Farm community failed in part because many of the intellectuals who participated disliked farm labor.

   ANS: T   TOP: Social history | Worldly Communities DIF: Moderate   REF: Full p. 429 | Seagull p. 438 MSC: Remembering   OBJ: 1

4. The American Temperance Society directed its efforts at the drunkards, but not the occasional drinker.

   ANS: F   TOP: Social history | The Temperance Movement   DIF: Moderate   REF: Full p. 431 | Seagull p. 440   MSC: Understanding OBJ: 1

5. To members of the North's emerging middle-class culture, reform became a badge of respectability.

   ANS: T   TOP: Social history | The Temperance Movement   DIF: Easy   REF: Full p. 431 | Seagull p. 440   MSC: Remembering   OBJ: 1

6. In general, Catholics supported the temperance movement.

   ANS: F   TOP: Social history | Critics of Reform DIF: Easy   REF: Full p. 432 | Seagull p. 441 MSC: Understanding   OBJ: 1

7. Institutions like jails, mental hospitals, and public schools were inspired by the conviction that those who passed through their doors could eventually be

released to become productive, self-disciplined citizens.

ANS: T   TOP: Social history | The Invention of the Asylum   DIF: Moderate   REF: Full p. 433 | Seagull p. 442   MSC: Remembering OBJ: 1

8. By 1860, all but two states had established tax-supported school systems for their children.

ANS: F   TOP: Social history | The Common School DIF: Difficult   REF: Full p. 434 | Seagull p. 443 MSC: Remembering   OBJ: 1

9. Most African-Americans enthusiastically favored the colonization idea and moving to Africa.

ANS: F   TOP: Civil rights | Blacks and Colonization DIF: Moderate   REF: Full p. 436 | Seagull p. 444 MSC: Remembering   OBJ: 2

10. In 1817, free blacks assembled in Philadelphia for the first national black convention.

ANS: T   TOP: Civil rights | Blacks and Colonization DIF: Difficult   REF: Full p. 436 | Seagull p. 444 MSC: Remembering   OBJ: 2

11. With his abolitionist writings, David Walker employed both secular and religious language.

ANS: T   TOP: Civil rights | Militant Abolitionism DIF: Moderate   REF: Full p. 436 | Seagull p. 445 MSC: Remembering   OBJ: 2

12. Nearly all abolitionists, despite their militant language, rejected violence as a means of ending slavery.

ANS: T   TOP: Civil rights | Slavery and Moral Suasion   DIF: Moderate   REF: Full p. 439 | Seagull pp. 447–448   MSC: Remembering OBJ: 2

13. Abolitionists were among the first to appreciate the key role of public opinion in a mass democracy, focusing their efforts on awakening the nation to the moral evil of slavery.

ANS: T   TOP: Civil rights | Slavery and Moral Suasion   DIF: Moderate   REF: Full p. 439 | Seagull p. 448   MSC: Understanding   OBJ: 2

14. Many abolitionists were fairly violent, and they attempted to aggressively convince the slaveholder of his sinful ways.

ANS: F   TOP: Civil rights | Slavery and Moral Suasion   DIF: Moderate   REF: Full p. 439 | Seagull p. 448   MSC: Remembering   OBJ: 2

15. Abolitionists agreed with the labor movement's argument that workers were subjugated to "wage slavery."

ANS: F   TOP: Civil rights | Social history | Abolitionists and the Idea of Freedom   DIF: Difficult REF: Full p. 439 | Seagull p. 448   MSC: Understanding OBJ: 2

16. Abolitionists consciously identified their movement with the heritage of the American Revolution.

ANS: T   TOP: Civil rights | A New Vision of America DIF: Easy   REF: Full p. 440 | Seagull p. 450 MSC: Understanding   OBJ: 3

17. Harriet Beecher Stowe's *Uncle Tom's Cabin* gave the abolitionist message a powerful human appeal as it was based on the life of the fugitive slave Josiah Henson.

ANS: T   TOP: Civil rights | Cultural history | Black Abolitionists   DIF: Easy   REF: Full p. 442 | Seagull p. 450   MSC: Remembering   OBJ: 3

18. Black abolitionists developed an understanding of freedom that went well beyond that of most of their white contemporaries.

ANS: T   TOP: Civil rights | Abolitionism and Race DIF: Easy   REF: Full p. 442 | Seagull p. 452 MSC: Understanding   OBJ: 3

19. Mob attacks and attempts to limit abolitionists' freedom of speech convinced many northerners that slavery was incompatible with the democratic liberties of white Americans.

ANS: T   TOP: Civil rights | Slavery and Civil Liberties   DIF: Easy   REF: Full p. 445 | Seagull p. 454   MSC: Remembering   OBJ: 3

20. The fight for the right to debate slavery openly and without reprisal led abolitionists to elevate "free opinion" to a central place in what William Lloyd Garrison called the "gospel of freedom."

ANS: T   TOP: Civil rights | Slavery and Civil Liberties   DIF: Moderate   REF: Full pp. 445–446 | Seagull p. 455   MSC: Understanding   OBJ: 3

21. As women began to take an active role in abolition, public speaking for women became socially acceptable to most Americans.

ANS: F   TOP: Civil rights | Social history | Women and Free Speech   DIF: Moderate   REF: Full p. 447 | Seagull p. 456   MSC: Remembering   OBJ: 4

22. Dorothea Dix devoted her life to the cause of temperance, founding the American Temperance Organization.

ANS: F   TOP: Social history | The Rise of the Public Woman   DIF: Moderate   REF: Full p. 447 | Seagull pp. 455–456   MSC: Remembering   OBJ: 4

23. The Beecher sisters helped organize a movement against Indian removal.

ANS: T   TOP: Social history | The Rise of the Public Woman   DIF: Moderate   REF: Full p. 447 | Seagull p. 455   MSC: Remembering   OBJ: 4

24. The participants at Seneca Falls embraced the identification of the home as the women's "sphere."

ANS: F   TOP: Social history | Women's Rights DIF: Moderate   REF: Full p. 449 | Seagull pp. 457–458   MSC: Remembering   OBJ: 4

25. The demand that women should enjoy the rights to regulate their own sexual activity and procreation and to be protected by the state against violence at the hands of their husbands challenged the notion that claims for justice, freedom, and individual rights should stop at the household's door.

ANS: T   TOP: Social history | Social Freedom DIF: Easy   REF: Full p. 454 | Seagull p. 463 MSC: Understanding   OBJ: 4

26. The abolitionist movement split in two in part because Abby Kelley had been appointed to an office within the American Anti-Slavery Society, which angered some men who believed it was wrong for women to occupy such a prominent position.

ANS: T   TOP: Civil rights | Social history | The Abolitionist Schism   DIF: Moderate   REF: Full p. 454 | Seagull p. 463   MSC: Understanding OBJ: 4

Short Answer

Identify and give the historical significance of each of the following terms, events, and people in a paragraph or two.

1. Abby Kelley
2. William Lloyd Garrison
3. institution building
4. Shakers
5. Oneida
6. freedom celebrations
7. common schools
8. American Colonization Society
9. Grimké sisters
10. Declaration of Sentiments
11. Elijah Lovejoy
12. burned-over districts

Essay Questions

1. The various reform communities that sprang up throughout America during the first part of the nineteenth century typically understood the meaning of freedom differently from mainstream Americans. Analyze the various meanings these groups gave to the word "freedom," and compare those meanings with the ones given by mainstream America. Your essay ought to give the reader a sense of what these communities were rejecting about mainstream society.

ANS: Answers will vary   TOP: Political history, changes | Social history | Utopian Communities | The Shakers | Oneida | Worldly Communities | The Owenites | Religion and Reform   DIF: Moderate MSC: Analyzing   OBJ: 1

2. The abolitionists' greatest achievement lay in shattering the conspiracy of silence that had sought to preserve national unity by suppressing public debate over slavery. Explain how the abolitionists achieved this, and comment on how successful the movement was or was not.

ANS: Answers will vary   TOP: Civil rights | Political history, changes | Social history | Spreading the Abolitionist Message | Gentlemen of Property and Standing | The Emergence of Garrison | Black Abolitionists | Slavery and Civil Liberties DIF: Moderate   MSC: Evaluating   OBJ: 2 / 3

3. Explain how the religious revivals of the Second Great Awakening popularized the outlook known as perfectionism, which held that both individuals and society at large were capable of indefinite improvement. How did this idea of perfectionism relate to the various reform movements that arose in the antebellum period?

ANS: Answers will vary   TOP: Cultural history | Social history | Religion and Reform | The Temperance Movement | The Invention of the Asylum | The Common School | Spreading the Abolitionist Message | Slavery and Moral Suasion   DIF: Moderate MSC: Understanding   OBJ: 2 / 3

4. One person's reform in some cases may be considered an attack on another person's vital interests. Describe how the antebellum reform movements—particularly temperance, colonization, abolition, and women's rights—involved conflict between different sets of ideas and interests.

ANS: Answers will vary   TOP: Civil rights | Social history | Religion and Reform | The Temperance Movement | Critics of Reform | Reformers and Freedom | Colonization | Blacks and Colonization | Spreading the Abolitionist Message | Slavery and

Moral Suasion | Gentlemen of Property and Standing | Women's Rights | Feminism and Freedom
DIF: Difficult   MSC: Analyzing   OBJ: 2 / 3 / 4

5. To what extent was Theodore Weld's argument about the sinfulness of slavery not only radical but also necessary for the popularization of immediate abolition?

ANS: Answers will vary   TOP: Civil rights | Social history | Spreading the Abolitionist Message
DIF: Moderate   MSC: Analyzing   OBJ: 2

6. One of the debates within the antislavery crusade was colonization of African-Americans to Africa. Explain the various arguments for and against colonization.

ANS: Answers will vary   TOP: Civil rights | Global awareness | Colonization | Blacks and Colonization
DIF: Moderate   MSC: Analyzing   OBJ: 2

7. Do you agree with the assertion that blacks viewed freedom in a different way than did whites? Defend or reject this idea using examples from the text.

ANS: Answers will vary   TOP: Civil rights | Social history | Slavery and American Freedom | Blacks and Colonization | Abolitionism and Race | A New Vision of America | Black Abolitionists   DIF: Difficult
MSC: Evaluating   OBJ: 3

8. Abolitionists fought for the right to debate slavery openly and without reprisal. Analyze what led them to elevate "free opinion" to a central place in what William Lloyd Garrison called the "gospel of freedom."

ANS: Answers will vary   TOP: Civil rights | Social history | Spreading the Abolitionist Message | Abolitionists and the Idea of Freedom | Slavery and

Civil Liberties | Slavery and American Freedom | Gentlemen of Property and Standing
DIF: Difficult   MSC: Analyzing   OBJ: 3

9. Frederick Douglass wrote, "When the true history of the antislavery cause shall be written women will occupy a large space in its pages." Was Douglass correct? Explain the role women played in the abolitionist movement. Then analyze how that experience influenced the feminist movement.

ANS: Answers will vary   TOP: Civil rights | Social history | The Rise of the Public Woman | The Abolitionist Schism   DIF: Moderate   MSC: Analyzing
OBJ: 2 / 3 / 4

10. What were the women at Seneca Falls advocating? Be sure to explain how they understood freedom and liberty. What methods were the feminists using to promote their cause?

ANS: Answers will vary   TOP: Civil rights | Political history, changes | Primary document analysis | The Rise of the Public Woman | Women's Rights | Social Freedom | Women and Free Speech | Feminism and Freedom   DIF: Moderate   MSC: Understanding
OBJ: 4

11. Write an essay on what the Fourth of July meant to Frederick Douglass, and compare that to what the Fourth of July meant to the founding fathers in 1776 and to what it means to you today.

ANS: Answers will vary   TOP: Civil rights | Political history, changes | Primary document analysis | Slavery and American Freedom   DIF: Moderate
MSC: Evaluating   OBJ: 3

CHAPTER 13 | A House Divided, 1840–1861

This chapter concentrates on the events that led to the Civil War. It opens with a vignette demonstrating the touchiness of southerners about slavery by the 1850s. Mississippi's Jefferson Davis objected to placing a "liberty cap" atop the statue planned for the U.S. Capitol's dome, because of the association of such caps with ancient Roman slaves' yearning for freedom. The main reason slavery had assumed a central role in the nation's debate by the 1850s was territorial expansion— what many Americans called their "manifest destiny" to control the continent, a topic the chapter explores through coverage of Texas independence and annexation, the settlement of Oregon and California, and finally the Mexican War. The war with Mexico, begun in 1846 by President James Polk in an effort to acquire California, was relatively short but controversial because many believed the war would encourage slavery's expansion. Opponents included Henry David Thoreau and Abraham Lincoln. The ultimate acquisition of California and most of the rest of the present American Southwest (the Mexican Cession) formally occurred with the 1848 Treaty of Guadalupe Hidalgo, which ended the war. Soon thousands of Americans and others flocked to California because of the discovery of gold there in early 1848. This gold rush created wealth as well as ethnic conflict. Also, even before the treaty transferred land to the United States, Representative David Wilmot (D-Pennsylvania) proposed banning slavery from territory that might be taken from Mexico. This Wilmot Proviso gave rise to the Free Soil Party, which spread antislavery's appeal far beyond abolitionists, and intensified sectional debate.

The Compromise of 1850 solved the issue of the status of slavery within the Mexican Cession, but created new controversy with a stronger Fugitive Slave Act. The Kansas-Nebraska Act (1854) reopened the sectional divide over slavery in the territories by overturning the Missouri Compromise's prohibition on slavery in what were now Kansas

and Nebraska territories. The consequences of the Act included political realignment with the collapse of the Whigs, a brief nativist Know-Nothing movement, and the rise in the North of the Republican Party, based on free labor ideology. In addition, a short civil war broke out between freesoil and proslavery factions in Kansas. The attempt of the U.S. Supreme Court to settle the slavery controversy resulted in the *Dred Scott* decision (1857). Chief Justice Roger Taney's ruling that blacks could not be U.S. citizens and that Congress could not ban slavery from territories pleased most southern whites but angered many northerners. That the Court did not solve the issue is clear when reading this chapter's "Voices of Freedom," a selection from one of the debates in the 1858 U.S. Senate race between Stephen Douglas and Abraham Lincoln. Another election, that for president in 1860, took place amid mounting sectional tension due to John Brown's raid on Harpers Ferry and the division of the Democratic Party over whether to protect slavery in territories. The Republican Lincoln won this highly sectional election, which led to the secession of seven slave states and the formation of the Confederate States of America before his inauguration. The chapter ends with the April 1861 Fort Sumter crisis, which kicked off the Civil War.

CHAPTER OUTLINE

I. Introduction: Statue of Freedom
    1. Jefferson Davis opposed plans to erect a Capitol dome statue wearing a liberty cap because it could be seen as symbolic of slaves seeking freedom.

II. Fruits of Manifest Destiny
    A. Continental Expansion

1. In the 1840s, slavery moved to the center stage of American politics because of territorial expansion.
2. Americans settled in Oregon (administered by both England and the United States) and Utah (part of Mexico).
   a. Many believed God wanted United States to expand to the Pacific Ocean.

B. The Mexican Frontier: New Mexico and California
1. Mexico won its independence from Spain in 1821.
   a. The northern frontier of Mexico was California, New Mexico, and Texas.
2. California's non-Indian population in 1821 was vastly outnumbered by Indians.
   a. Mexican government dissolved the great mission landholdings.
   b. Californios, a new class of Mexican cattle ranchers, arose in the 1830s.
   c. By 1840, through New England ships, California was linked commercially to the United States.

C. The Texas Revolt
1. The first part of Mexico to be settled by significant numbers of Americans was Texas.
   a. Moses Austin made agreement with Spanish government.
2. Alarmed that its grip on the area was weakening, the Mexican government in 1830 annulled existing land contracts and barred future emigration from the United States.
   a. Stephen Austin led the call from American settlers demanding greater autonomy within Mexico.
3. General Antonio López de Santa Anna sent an army in 1835 to impose central authority.
4. Rebels formed a provisional government that soon called for Texan independence.
   a. The Alamo
   b. Sam Houston routed Santa Anna's army at San Jacinto, winning Texas independence.
5. Texas desired annexation by the United States, but neither Jackson nor Van Buren acted on that because of political concerns regarding adding another slave state.

D. The Election of 1844
1. The issue of Texas annexation was linked to slavery and affected the nominations of presidential candidates.
   a. Clay and Van Buren agreed to keep Texas out of the presidential campaign.
2. James Polk, a Tennessee slaveholder and friend of Jackson, received the Democratic nomination instead of Van Buren.

   a. Supported Texas annexation
   b. Supported "reoccupation" of all of Oregon
3. Dark horse Polk defeated Clay in close election.
   a. Texas came into union just before Polk took office.

E. The Road to War
1. Polk had four clearly defined goals:
   a. Reduce the tariff
   b. Reestablish the Independent Treasury system
   c. Settle the Oregon dispute
   d. Bring California into the Union
2. Polk initiated war with Mexico to get California.
   a. Fighting started in Texas' disputed border area.

F. The War and Its Critics
1. Although the majority of Americans (inspired by manifest destiny) supported the war, a vocal minority feared the only aim of the war was to acquire new land for the expansion of slavery.
   a. Henry David Thoreau wrote *On Civil Disobedience.*
   b. Abraham Lincoln questioned Polk's right to declare war by introducing a resolution in Congress requesting the president to specify the precise spot where blood had first been shed.

G. Combat in Mexico
1. Combat took place on three fronts.
   a. California and the "Bear Flag Republic"
   b. General Stephen Kearney and Santa Fe
   c. Winfield Scott and Central Mexico
2. Treaty of Guadalupe Hidalgo, 1848
   a. United States gained California and present-day New Mexico, Arizona, Nevada, and Utah.
   b. United States paid Mexico $15 million.
3. War seen by Mexicans to this day as central event in their history and source of resentment.

H. Race and Manifest Destiny
1. A region (northern Mexico) that for centuries had been united was suddenly split in two, dividing families and severing trade routes.
   a. "Male citizens" were guaranteed American rights.
   b. Indians were described as "savage tribes."
2. The spirit of manifest destiny gave a new stridency to ideas about racial superiority.
3. Race in the mid-nineteenth century was an amorphous notion involving color, culture, national origin, class, and religion.

a. Anglo-Saxon Protestants were innately liberty-loving; blacks, Indians, Hispanics, and Catholics were not.

I. Redefining Race
  1. Mexico had abolished slavery and declared persons of Spanish, Indian, and African origin equal before the law.
  2. The Texas constitution adopted after independence not only included protections for slavery but denied civil rights to Indians and persons of African origin.

J. Gold Rush California
  1. Non-Indian population was 15,000 in 1848, but climbed to 360,000 by 1860.
  2. California's gold-rush population was incredibly diverse.
    a. Latinos
    b. Europeans
    c. Chinese

K. California and the Boundaries of Freedom
  1. White miners expelled foreign miners from prospecting areas.
  2. The boundaries of freedom in California were tightly drawn.
    a. Indians, Asians, and blacks were all prohibited basic rights.
    b. Thousands of Indian children, declared orphans, were bought and sold as slaves.

L. The Other Gold Rush
  1. Gold was discovered in Victoria, one of the British colonies that then made up Australia, in 1851.
  2. Like California, Victoria attracted gold-seekers from afar and its population grew quickly.
  3. Like San Francisco, the city of Melbourne rose to prominence based on its proximity to the gold fields.
  4. Also as in California, certain ethnic groups suffered during the gold rush.
    a. The population of native Australians, known as aboriginals, declined dramatically.
    b. Australians patterned anti-Chinese laws on measures passed in California.

M. Opening Japan
  1. U.S. navy's Commodore Matthew Perry sailed warships into Tokyo Harbor and demanded that Japan negotiate a trade treaty with the United States (1853–1854).
  2. Japan opened two ports to U.S. merchant ships in 1854; later in the decade, it established full diplomatic relations with the United States.
  3. The United States was interested in Japan primarily as a refueling stop on the way to China.

III. A Dose of Arsenic
  A. The Wilmot Proviso
    1. Territory from Mexico fraying bonds of union.
      a. Methodist and Baptist churches split along sectional lines and issue of slavery.
    2. In 1846, Congressman David Wilmot of Pennsylvania proposed a resolution prohibiting slavery from all territory acquired from Mexico.
    3. In 1848, opponents of slavery's expansion organized the Free Soil Party.
      a. The party nominated Martin Van Buren for president.
      b. Whig candidate Zachary Taylor, war hero and slaveholder, won election.
  B. The Free Soil Appeal
    1. The free soil position had a popular appeal in the North because it would limit southern power in the federal government.
    2. Wage earners of the North also favored the Free Soil movement.
    3. The Free Soil platform of 1848 called both for barring slavery from western territories and for the federal government providing homesteads to settlers without cost.
    4. Many southerners considered singling out slavery as the one form of property barred from the West to be an affront to them and their distinctive way of life.
    5. The admission of new free states would overturn the delicate political balance between the sections and make the South a permanent minority.
  C. Crisis and Compromise
    1. The year 1848 brought revolution in Europe, only to be suppressed by counterrevolution.
    2. With the slavery issue appearing more and more ominous, established party leaders moved to resolve differences between the sections.
      a. The Compromise of 1850 included:
        i. Admission of California as a free state
        ii. Abolition of the slave trade (not slavery itself) in the District of Columbia
        iii. Stronger Fugitive Slave law
        iv. Mexican Cession territories would determine the status of slavery there.
  D. The Great Debate
    1. Powerful leaders spoke for and against the Compromise:
      a. Daniel Webster (for the Compromise)
      b. John C. Calhoun (against the Compromise)
      c. William Seward (against the Compromise)

2. President Taylor, Compromise opponent, died in office, and the new president, Millard Fillmore, secured the adoption of the Compromise.

E. The Fugitive Slave Issue
1. The Fugitive Slave Act allowed special federal commissioners to determine the fate of alleged fugitives without benefit of a jury trial or even testimony by the accused individual.
   a. Ironically, the South, which mostly favored states' rights, supported an Act that gave the Federal government great power to recover escaped slaves.
2. In a series of dramatic confrontations, fugitives, aided by abolitionist allies, violently resisted capture.
3. The fugitive slave law also led several thousand northern blacks to flee to safety in Canada.

F. Douglas and Popular Sovereignty
1. Franklin Pierce won the 1852 presidential election.
2. Stephen Douglas saw himself as the new leader of the Senate after the deaths of Calhoun, Clay, and Webster.
3. Douglas introduced a bill to establish territorial governments for Nebraska and Kansas so that a transcontinental railroad could be constructed.
   a. Slavery would be settled by popular sovereignty (territorial voters, not Congress, would decide).

G. The Kansas-Nebraska Act
1. Under the Missouri Compromise, slavery had been prohibited in the Kansas-Nebraska area.
2. The *Appeal of the Independent Democrats* was issued by antislavery congressmen opposed to the Kansas-Nebraska bill because it would potentially open the area to slavery.
3. The Kansas-Nebraska bill became law.
   a. Democrats no longer unified as many northern Democrats opposed the bill.
   b. The Whig Party collapsed.
   c. The South became solidly Democratic.
   d. The Republican Party emerged in the North to prevent the further expansion of slavery.

IV. The Rise of the Republican Party
A. The Northern Economy
1. The rise of the Republican Party reflected underlying economic and social changes.
   a. Railroad network grew from 5,000 miles to 30,000 by 1860.
2. By 1860, the North had become a complex, integrated economy.

3. Two great areas of industrial production had arisen:
   a. Northeastern seaboard
   b. Great Lakes region

B. The Rise and Fall of the Know-Nothings
1. In 1854, the American, or Know-Nothing, Party emerged as a political party appealing to anti-Catholic and anti-immigrant and, in the North, antislavery sentiments.
2. In many states, however, these white European immigrants could vote even before becoming citizens.
   a. But non-whites whose ancestors lived in the country for centuries could not vote.

C. The Free Labor Ideology
1. Republicans managed to convince most northerners (antislavery Democrats, Whigs, Free Soilers, and Know-Nothings) that the "Slave Power" posed a more immediate threat to their liberties and aspirations than did "popery" (Catholicism) or immigration.
   a. This appeal rested on the idea of free labor.
2. Free labor could not compete with slave labor, and so slavery's expansion had to be halted to ensure freedom for the white laborer.
3. Republicans cried "freedom national," meaning not abolition but ending the federal government's support of slavery.
   a. Republicans as a whole were not abolitionists.

D. Bleeding Kansas and the Election of 1856
1. Bleeding Kansas seemed to discredit Douglas's policy of leaving the decision of slavery up to the local population—thus, aiding the Republicans.
   a. Civil war within Kansas
   b. Bloodshed in Congress as Senator Charles Sumner was beaten with a cane by representative Preston Brooks
2. The election of 1856 demonstrated that parties had reoriented themselves along sectional lines.

V. The Emergence of Lincoln
A. The *Dred Scott* Decision
1. After having lived in free territories, the slave Dred Scott sued for his freedom.
2. The Supreme Court justices addressed three questions:
   a. Could a black person be a citizen and therefore sue in federal court?
   b. Did residence in a free state make Scott free?
   c. Did Congress possess the power to prohibit slavery in a territory?

3. Speaking for the majority, Chief Justice Roger A. Taney declared that only white persons could be citizens of the United States.
4. Scott remained a slave as Illinois law had no effect on him.
5. Taney ruled that Congress possessed no power under the Constitution to bar slavery from a territory, so Scott was still a slave.
   a. The decision in effect declared unconstitutional the Republican platform of restricting slavery's expansion.

B. The Decision's Aftermath
1. Rather than abandoning their opposition to the expansion of slavery, Republicans now viewed the Court as controlled by the Slave Power.
2. Buchanan administration tried to admit Kansas as a slave state under Lecompton Constitution.
   a. Stephen Douglas united with Republicans to block Kansas' admittance.

C. Lincoln and Slavery
1. In seeking reelection, Douglas faced an unexpectedly strong challenge from Abraham Lincoln.
2. Although Lincoln hated slavery, he was willing to compromise with the South to preserve the Union.
3. Lincoln's speeches combined the moral fervor of the abolitionists with the respect for order and the Constitution of more conservative northerners.

D. The Lincoln-Douglas Campaign
1. Lincoln campaigned against Douglas for Illinois's senate seat.
2. The Lincoln-Douglas debates remain classics of American political oratory.
   a. To Lincoln, freedom meant opposition to slavery.
   b. Douglas argued that the essence of freedom lay in local self-government and individual self-determination.
   c. Douglas asserted at the Freeport debate that popular sovereignty was compatible with the *Dred Scott* decision.
3. Lincoln shared many of the racial prejudices of his day.
   a. He did not want to give blacks the right to vote.
   b. But he did not exclude blacks from the human family.
4. Douglas was reelected by a narrow margin.

E. John Brown at Harpers Ferry
1. An armed assault by the abolitionist John Brown on the federal arsenal at Harpers Ferry, Virginia, further heightened sectional tensions.

a. Brown had a long career of involvement in antislavery activities.
2. Placed on trial for treason to the state of Virginia, Brown's execution turned him into a martyr to much of the North.
3. South did not like adulation of Brown in the North.

F. The Rise of Southern Nationalism
1. More and more southerners were speaking openly of southward expansion.
   a. Ostend Manifesto
   b. William Walker and filibustering in Mexico and Nicaragua
2. By the late 1850s, southern leaders were bending every effort to strengthen the bonds of slavery.

G. The Democratic Split
1. At the 1860 convention the Democratic Party reaffirmed the doctrine of popular sovereignty with its platform.
   a. Delegates from seven Lower South states left the convention.
2. This split led to two separate conventions six weeks later.
   a. Northerners nominated Douglas.
   b. Southerners nominated John Breckinridge.
3. The Democratic Party, last great bond of national unity, had been shattered.

H. The Nomination of Lincoln
1. Republicans nominated Lincoln over William Seward, who had reputation for radicalism.
2. Lincoln's devotion to the Union appealed to many voters.
3. The party platform:
   a. Denied the validity of the *Dred Scott* decision
   b. Opposed slavery's expansion
   c. Added economic initiatives

I. The Election of 1860
1. In effect, two presidential campaigns took place in 1860.
   a. Lincoln vs. Douglas in North
   b. Douglas vs. Breckinridge and John Bell in South
      i. Bell was leader of Constitutional Unionists, who wanted to preserve the Constitution and union.
2. The most striking thing about the election returns was their sectional character.
3. Without a single vote in ten southern states, Lincoln was elected the nation's sixteenth president.

VI. The Impending Crisis
   A. The Secession Movement
      1. Rather than accept permanent minority status in a nation governed by their opponents, Deep South political leaders boldly struck for their region's independence.
      2. In the months that followed Lincoln's election, seven states, stretching from South Carolina to Texas, seceded from the Union.
   B. The Secession Crisis
      1. President Buchanan denied that a state could secede, but also insisted that the federal government had no right to use force against it.
      2. The Crittenden plan proposed the protection of slavery where it existed and extension of Missouri Compromise line to the Pacific Ocean.
         a. Lincoln rejected the plan because it allowed for the expansion of slavery.
      3. The Confederate States of America was formed before Lincoln's inauguration by the seven states that had seceded.
         a. Jefferson Davis as president
         b. Confederate Constitution explicitly guaranteed slavery
   C. And the War Came
      1. In time, Lincoln believed, secession might collapse from within.
      2. Lincoln also issued a veiled warning: "In your hands, my dissatisfied fellow countrymen, and not in mine, is the momentous issue of civil war."
      3. Lincoln made sure the North did not fire the first shot.
      4. After the Confederates began the Civil War by firing on Fort Sumter on April 12, 1861, Lincoln called for 75,000 troops to suppress the insurrection.
      5. Four Upper South states (Arkansas, North Carolina, Tennessee, and Virginia) seceded and joined the Confederacy rather than aid Lincoln in suppressing the rebellion.

SUGGESTED DISCUSSION QUESTIONS

- Discuss the controversy over Thomas Crawford's *Statue of Freedom.*
- Discuss manifest destiny. Was westward expansion across the continent inevitable? How was the language of freedom used to justify expansion?
- Discuss how westward expansion and the Mexican War affected California.
- What were the promises and realities of free labor? Why didn't proponents of free labor also take on the issue of abolition?
- What destroyed the second American party system, and how was the electorate realigned?
- Why is it ironic that the South supported the Fugitive Slave Act?
- How did the events of the 1850s lead to the collapse of the Union in 1861?
- Who was responsible for the coming of the Civil War? Was it the South's fault? The North's? Were strong personalities important? Was the war inevitable?
- Have the students familiarize themselves with the Lincoln-Douglas debates and then have them role-play the debates, taking turns being Lincoln or Douglas. Have topics in a hat for them to pull out to debate for a set period of time.

SUPPLEMENTAL WEB AND VISUAL RESOURCES

John Brown
   www.pbs.org/wgbh/aia/part4/4p1550.html
   From PBS's *Africans in America,* this site chronicles John Brown's life.

Lincoln
   http://millercenter.org/president/lincoln
   The Miller Center at the University of Virginia has an extensive website about the presidents and their administrations. This takes you to the page on Lincoln.

Lincoln-Douglas Debates
   http://www.nps.gov/liho/historyculture/debates.htm
   From the National Park Service, this site has a map of the locations of the debates, as well as a transcript of each debate.

Manifest Destiny
   www.historytools.org/sources/manifest_destiny.pdf
   This PDF file reproduces the 1845 article where John O'Sullivan coins the term "manifest destiny."

Sectionalism and Politics in the 1850s
   http://history.furman.edu/editorials/see.py
   Furman University's Secession Era Editorials Project contains numerous editorials from newspapers around the United States commenting on the Kansas-Nebraska Act, the caning of Charles Sumner, the *Dred Scott* case, and the Harpers Ferry raid.

The Mexican War
   http://americanhistory.si.edu/militaryhistory/exhibition/flash.html
   From the Smithsonian Institution's National Museum of American History, select a war (Mexican War) and enter an exhibit that includes a movie, learning resources, statistics, printable exhibition, maps, and time lines.

www.loc.gov/rr/hispanic/ghtreaty/
From the Library of Congress, the Treaty of Guadalupe Hidalgo can be viewed.

SUPPLEMENTAL PRINT RESOURCES

Chaffin, Tom. *Pathfinder: John Charles Frémont and the Cause of American Empire*. New York: Hill and Wang, 2002.

Fehrenbacher, Don E. *Slavery, Law, and Politics: The Dred Scott Case in Historical Perspective*. New York: Oxford University Press, 1981.

Freehling, William W. *The Road to Disunion, Volume II: Secessionists Triumphant, 1854–1861*. New York: Oxford University Press, 2007.

Gienapp, William. "Nativism and the Creating of a Republican Majority in the North before the Civil War." *Journal of American History* 72, no. 3 (1985): 529–559.

Goldfield, David. America Aflame: How the Civil War Created a Nation. New York: Bloomsbury Press, 2011.

Grimsted, David. *American Mobbing, 1828–1861: Toward Civil War*. New York: Oxford University Press, 1998.

Holt, Michael. *The Rise and Fall of the American Whig Party: Jacksonian Politics and the Onset of the Civil War*. New York: Oxford University Press, 1999.

Karsten, Peter. "Labor's Sorrow? Workers, Bosses, and the Courts in Antebellum America." *Reviews in American History* 21, no. 2 (1993): 447–453.

Majewski, John. *A House Dividing: Economic Development in Pennsylvania and Virginia Before the Civil War*. New York: Cambridge University Press, 2000.

Morrison, Michael. *Slavery and the American West: The Eclipse of Manifest Destiny and the Coming of the Civil War*. Chapel Hill, NC: University of North Carolina Press, 1997.

Oakes, James. *The Radical and the Republican: Frederick Douglas, Abraham Lincoln, and the Triumph of Antislavery*. New York: W. W. Norton & Company, 2006.

Peterson, Merrill. *John Brown: The Legend Revisited*. Charlottesville, VA: University of Virginia Press, 2002.

Roberts, Brian. *American Alchemy: The California Gold Rush and Middle-Class Culture*. Chapel Hill, NC: University of North Carolina Press, 2000.

Weeks, William Earl. *Building the Continental Empire: American Expansion from the Revolution to the Civil War*. Lanham, MD: Ivan R. Dee, Publisher, 1996.

Winders, Richard Bruce. *Mr. Polk's Army: The American Military Experience in the Mexican War*. College Station, TX: Texas A&M University Press, 1997.

TEST BANK

Matching

TEST I

___ 1. Dred Scott
___ 2. Abraham Lincoln
___ 3. John Frémont
___ 4. Martin Van Buren
___ 5. John Brown
___ 6. William Walker
___ 7. Henry David Thoreau
___ 8. John Breckinridge
___ 9. Stephen Douglas
___ 10. Henry Clay
___ 11. Preston Brooks
___ 12. David Wilmot

a. *On Civil Disobedience*
b. 1848 Free Soil presidential candidate
c. author of the Kansas-Nebraska Act
d. tried to attach bill to war declaration to ban slavery
e. author of the Compromise of 1850
f. caned Charles Sumner
g. a slave who sued for his freedom
h. led a raid on Harpers Ferry
i. 1860 Republican presidential candidate
j. 1860 southern Democratic presidential candidate
k. 1856 Republican presidential candidate
l. filibustering

Answer Key: g, i, k, b, h, l, a, j, c, e, f, d

TEST 2

___ 1. manifest destiny
___ 2. Wilmot Proviso
___ 3. Kansas-Nebraska Act
___ 4. Fugitive Slave Act
___ 5. Ostend Manifesto
___ 6. Free Soil Party
___ 7. Compromise of 1850
___ 8. Know-Nothing Party
___ 9. Californios
___ 10. appeal of the Independent Democrats
___ 11. filibustering
___ 12. gold rush

a. issued by antislavery congressmen
b. suggested the United States buy or seize Cuba
c. returned runaway slaves to their master
d. America's mission to settle the West
e. Mexican cattle ranchers
f. sudden increase in California's population
g. voided the Missouri Compromise
h. no slavery in land acquired by Mexico
i. expedition to Central America
j. opponents to the expansion of slavery
k. anti-immigrant political party
l. California's entry into the Union as a free state

Answer Key: d, h, g, c, b, j, l, k, e, a, i, f

Learning Objectives

1. Identify the major factors contributing to U.S. territorial expansion in the 1840s.
2. Explain why the expansion of slavery became the most divisive political issue in the 1840s and 1850s.
3. Identify the combination of issues and events that fueled the creation of the Republican Party in the 1850s.
4. Explain what enabled Lincoln to emerge as president from the divisive party politics of the 1850s.
5. Describe the final steps on the road to secession.

Multiple Choice

1. Why did Mississippi politician Jefferson Davis object in the 1850s to the original design of the *Statue of Freedom* that now adorns the U.S. Capitol dome?
   a. He disliked the fact that the sculptor was a former slave who had won acclaim for his talent, thus suggesting blacks were as gifted as whites.
   b. The use of a soldier as the key figure made the nation appear too militaristic.
   c. It portrayed "Freedom" as a nude woman, which he saw as inappropriate.
   d. Its use of an ancient Roman liberty cap on "Freedom" raised a touchy matter about slaves' longing for freedom.
   e. He believed using "freedom" in the statue's name was a subtle attack on slave states, so he preferred using "justice" instead.

   ANS: D   TOP: Political history, changes | Introduction: Statue of Freedom   DIF: Moderate
   REF: Full p. 459 | Seagull p. 466   MSC: Understanding   OBJ: 2

2. Why did slavery become more central to American politics in the 1840s?
   a. The Methodist Church, the nation's largest denomination, called on all its members to free their slaves.
   b. Territorial expansion raised the question of whether new lands should be free or slave.
   c. Members of the abolitionist Republican Party, formed in 1844, insisted on debating slavery.
   d. President John Tyler's antislavery policies caused a major proslavery backlash led by John C. Calhoun.
   e. As the 1848 constitutional deadline for ending the African slave trade drew near, Americans became obsessed with slavery.

   ANS: B   TOP: Geographic issues | Political history, changes | Continental Expansion   DIF: Easy
   REF: Full p. 459 | Seagull p. 467
   MSC: Remembering   OBJ: 1

3. When Mexico won its independence from Spain in 1821:
   a. it was much smaller in area than the United States at the time.
   b. California became a major American trading partner within half a decade.
   c. its Indian population was relatively large compared to its non-Indian population.
   d. its leaders founded new missions in California to assure continued Catholic power.
   e. Americans immediately began settling in California in large numbers.

   ANS: C   TOP: Ethnicity | Global awareness | The Mexican Frontier: New Mexico and California
   DIF: Difficult   REF: Full p. 460 | Seagull pp. 467–468
   MSC: Remembering   OBJ: 1

4. In 1821, the opening of the Santa Fe Trail between Santa Fe and _____ led to a reorientation of New Mexico's commerce from the rest of Mexico to the United States.
   a. Houston, Texas,
   b. San Diego, California,
   c. New Orleans, Louisiana,
   d. Omaha, Nebraska,
   e. Independence, Missouri,

   ANS: E   TOP: Economic development | Geographic issues | The Mexican Frontier: New Mexico and California   DIF: Difficult   REF: Full p. 460 | Seagull p. 468   MSC: Remembering   OBJ: 1

5. The term "Californios" referred in the 1830s and 1840s to _____ in California.
   a. Mexican cattle ranchers
   b. the Indian inhabitants
   c. U.S.-born immigrants
   d. any individual
   e. American merchants

   ANS: A   TOP: Ethnicity | The Mexican Frontier: New Mexico and California   DIF: Moderate   REF: Full p. 460 | Seagull p. 469   MSC: Remembering   OBJ: 1

6. American settlement in Texas in the 1820s and 1830s:
   a. took place without approval from the Mexican government.
   b. did not exceed the Mexican population there until the United States annexed Texas in 1845.
   c. led Stephen Austin to demand more autonomy from Mexican officials.
   d. included no slaves, because Mexico had banned slavery in its territory.
   e. was in communities whose American-born residents were called Tejanos by their Mexican neighbors.

ANS: C   TOP: Geographic issues | Global awareness | The Texas Revolt   DIF: Moderate   REF: Full pp. 460–461 | Seagull p. 471   MSC: Remembering OBJ: 1

7. Presidents Andrew Jackson and Martin Van Buren rejected adding Texas to the United States because:
   a. the Texas Republic's congress opposed joining the United States, preferring to stay independent.
   b. the Mexican army's resounding victory at the Alamo made them fearful of antagonizing a powerful government.
   c. the population of Texas was too small to justify it.
   d. Henry Clay wanted to add it and, as the Whig leader, he was their sworn enemy.
   e. the presence of slaves there would reignite the issue of slavery, and they preferred to avoid it.

   ANS: E   TOP: Political history, changes | The Texas Revolt   DIF: Moderate   REF: Full p. 462 | Seagull p. 472   MSC: Remembering   OBJ: 1

8. Which two political figures agreed to keep the issue of annexing Texas out of the 1844 presidential campaign if possible?
   a. John Tyler and John C. Calhoun
   b. Henry Clay and Daniel Webster
   c. Henry Clay and Martin Van Buren
   d. Henry Clay and James Polk
   e. Andrew Jackson and John Quincy Adams

   ANS: C   TOP: Political history, changes | The Election of 1844   DIF: Difficult   REF: Full p. 463 | Seagull p. 472   MSC: Remembering   OBJ: 1

9. When Democrats demanded the "reannexation" of Texas in 1844, they:
   a. implied that Texas had once been part of the United States through the Louisiana Purchase.
   b. were consciously appealing to northern Whigs.
   c. were seeking to take the slavery issue out of the presidential campaign.
   d. neglected to say anything about the status of Oregon.
   e. realized their stand would not be very popular in the South.

   ANS: A   TOP: Geographic issues | Political history, changes | The Election of 1844   DIF: Easy   REF: Full p. 464 | Seagull p. 472   MSC: Understanding   OBJ: 1

10. "Fifty-four forty or fight" referred to demands for American control of:
   a. Texas.
   b. Oregon.
   c. California.
   d. Mexico.
   e. Kansas and Nebraska.

   ANS: B   TOP: Geographic issues | Political history, changes | The Election of 1844   DIF: Moderate   REF: Full p. 464 | Seagull p. 472   MSC: Remembering   OBJ: 1

11. James Polk had four clearly defined goals when he entered the White House. Which was NOT one of his goals?
   a. Reduce the tariff.
   b. Settle the slavery dispute.
   c. Settle the Oregon dispute.
   d. Bring California into the Union.
   e. Reestablish the Independent Treasury system.

   ANS: B   TOP: Economic development | Geographic issues | The Road to War   DIF: Moderate   REF: Full p. 464 | Seagull p. 473   MSC: Understanding   OBJ: 1

12. During the Mexican War:
   a. Mexican troops occupied much of Texas after winning at the Alamo.
   b. the bulk of the fighting occurred in California.
   c. for the first time, the U.S. troops occupied a foreign capital.
   d. an American revolt in California led briefly to a monarchy.
   e. Whigs strongly supported Polk's policies.

   ANS: C   TOP: Global awareness | The War and Its Critics   DIF: Moderate   REF: Full p. 465 | Seagull p. 473   MSC: Remembering   OBJ: 1

13. Who questioned President Polk's right to declare war by introducing a resolution to Congress requesting that the president specify the precise spot where blood had first been shed?
   a. Daniel Webster
   b. John C. Calhoun
   c. Stephen Douglas
   d. Abraham Lincoln
   e. Charles Sumner

   ANS: D   TOP: Geographic issues | The War and Its Critics   DIF: Moderate   REF: Full p. 466 | Seagull p. 474   MSC: Remembering   OBJ: 1

14. Who wrote *On Civil Disobedience* as a response to the U.S. war with Mexico?
   a. Abraham Lincoln
   b. Ralph Waldo Emerson
   c. David Walker
   d. David Wilmot
   e. Henry David Thoreau

ANS: E   TOP: Cultural history | Political history, changes | The War and Its Critics   DIF: Moderate   REF: Full p. 466 | Seagull p. 474   MSC: Remembering   OBJ: 1

15. The Treaty of Guadalupe Hidalgo of 1848 provided for all of the following EXCEPT:
    a. the transfer of California to the United States.
    b. guaranteeing to male citizens in the Mexican Cession "their liberty and property."
    c. payment of $15 million to Mexico by the United States.
    d. U.S. control of all of the Oregon Country.
    e. confirmation of the U.S. annexation of Texas.

    ANS: D   TOP: Geographic issues | Global awareness | Combat in Mexico   DIF: Moderate   REF: Full p. 467 | Seagull pp. 474–475   MSC: Understanding   OBJ: 1

16. With the exception of Alaska, what was the last piece of territory acquired by the United States toward the solidification of its present boundaries in North America?
    a. The Mexican Cession
    b. California
    c. Oregon
    d. The Gadsden Purchase
    e. Texas

    ANS: D   TOP: Geographic issues | Combat in Mexico   DIF: Difficult   REF: Full p. 467 | Seagull p. 475   MSC: Remembering   OBJ: 1

17. According to John L. O'Sullivan's *Democratic Review,* what was the key to the history of nations and the rise and fall of empires?
    a. race
    b. democracy
    c. economic freedom
    d. slavery
    e. printing

    ANS: A   TOP: Social history | Race and Manifest Destiny   DIF: Moderate   REF: Full p. 469 | Seagull p. 476   MSC: Remembering   OBJ: 1

18. All of the following took place under the constitution and state laws of independent Texas EXCEPT:
    a. protect slavery.
    b. deny free blacks entrance to Texas.
    c. deny civil rights to people of African heritage.
    d. allow Native Americans equal rights.
    e. allow the purchase of land by only whites.

    ANS: D   TOP: Civil rights | Political history, changes | Redefining Race   DIF: Moderate   REF: Full p. 469 | Seagull pp. 476–477   MSC: Understanding   OBJ: 1

19. The California gold rush turned _____ into perhaps the world's most diverse city.
    a. San Diego
    b. Los Angeles
    c. Malibu
    d. Sacramento
    e. San Francisco

    ANS: E   TOP: Ethnicity | Geographic issues | Gold Rush California   REF: Full p. 470 | Seagull p. 478   MSC: Remembering   OBJ: 1

20. The California gold rush:
    a. actually had only a small impact on California's population because its rich farmlands already attracted thousands of new settlers each year.
    b. attracted almost equal numbers of men and women.
    c. resulted in laws that discriminated against "foreign miners."
    d. made considerable wealth for average miners because gold mining demanded no real investment of capital.
    e. hurt the development of San Francisco because gold discoveries shifted interest to areas outside of town.

    ANS: C   TOP: Ethnicity | Geographic issues | California and the Boundaries of Freedom   DIF: Moderate   REF: Full p. 470 | Seagull p. 478   MSC: Remembering   OBJ: 1

21. Which of the following statements related to ethnicity was true in California in the 1850s?
    a. Thousands of Indian children were declared orphans and treated as slaves.
    b. The state recognized more than 15,000 African-Americans as slaves of whites who had moved there.
    c. Men of all backgrounds, except those from China, were allowed to vote and serve on juries.
    d. Indian communities prospered by renting land and selling supplies to gold miners.
    e. Wealthy Mexican landowners dominated the new state government and would do so until the 1880s.

    ANS: A   TOP: Ethnicity | California and the Boundaries of Freedom   DIF: Difficult   REF: Full p. 470 | Seagull p. 479   MSC: Understanding   OBJ: 1

22. During the 1850s, 80 percent of the world's gold came from two places that experienced gold rushes at about the same time, California and:
    a. Canada.
    b. Argentina.
    c. South Africa.
    d. Australia.
    e. Congo.

ANS: D   TOP: Economic development | Global awareness | The Other Gold Rush   DIF: Moderate   REF: Full p. 471 | Seagull p. 479   MSC: Remembering   OBJ: 1

23. Which American naval officer negotiated a treaty that opened two Japanese ports to U.S. ships in 1854?
    a. Oliver H. Perry
    b. John Paul Jones
    c. Alfred Mahan
    d. Chester Nimitz
    e. Matthew Perry

    ANS: E   TOP: Global awareness | Opening Japan   DIF: Moderate   REF: Full p. 472 | Seagull p. 479   MSC: Remembering   OBJ: 1

24. In 1846, Congressman David Wilmot proposed to:
    a. prohibit slavery from all territory acquired from Mexico.
    b. allow voters to decide the status of slavery in new territories.
    c. divide the Oregon Country between Great Britain and the United States.
    d. annex Cuba in order to avoid southern secession.
    e. allow slavery to expand into California and New Mexico.

    ANS: A   TOP: Civil rights | Geographic issues | The Wilmot Proviso   DIF: Moderate   REF: Full p. 473 | Seagull p. 481   MSC: Remembering   OBJ: 2

25. The Free Soil Party:
    a. demonstrated that antislavery sentiment had spread far beyond abolitionist ranks.
    b. cost Henry Clay the presidency by siphoning off votes from him in New York.
    c. was powerful enough to convince James Polk not to seek reelection.
    d. strongly opposed the Wilmot Proviso but agreed to let it pass as part of a compromise.
    e. nominated Zachary Taylor for president.

    ANS: A   TOP: Political history, changes | The Wilmot Proviso   DIF: Moderate   REF: Full p. 473 | Seagull p. 481   MSC: Understanding   OBJ: 2

26. Which of the following countries did NOT go through some kind of popular upheaval in 1848?
    a. Hungary
    b. Great Britain
    c. France
    d. Russia
    e. Italy

    ANS: D   TOP: Global awareness | Crisis and Compromise   DIF: Difficult   REF: Full pp. 474–475 | Seagull p. 483   MSC: Understanding   OBJ: 2

27. Which of the following was NOT a provision of the Compromise of 1850?
    a. California would enter the Union as a free state.
    b. The slave trade would be abolished in Washington, D.C.
    c. The Oregon Territory would be created.
    d. A tougher fugitive slave law would be enacted.
    e. Territories created from the Mexican Cession would vote on whether to allow slavery.

    ANS: C   TOP: Civil rights | Geographic issues | Crisis and Compromise   DIF: Moderate   REF: Full p. 475 | Seagull p. 484   MSC: Understanding   OBJ: 2

28. The opponents of the Compromise of 1850:
    a. included key Whig leaders Henry Clay and Daniel Webster.
    b. received a boost from President Zachary Taylor.
    c. were surprised when John C. Calhoun spoke in favor of the Compromise.
    d. argued that California must become a free state, which the Compromise did not allow.
    e. were thrilled to have the support of influential Vice President Millard Fillmore.

    ANS: B   TOP: Political history, changes | The Great Debate   DIF: Difficult   REF: Full p. 475 | Seagull p. 484   MSC: Understanding   OBJ: 2

29. The Fugitive Slave Act of 1850:
    a. won the grudging support of Ralph Waldo Emerson as a necessary compromise.
    b. gave new powers to federal officers to override local law enforcement.
    c. was declared unconstitutional in the *Dred Scott* case.
    d. angered southerners by weakening an earlier law on fugitive slaves.
    e. convinced Abraham Lincoln to retire briefly from political life.

    ANS: B   TOP: Civil rights | Political history, changes | The Fugitive Slave Issue   DIF: Moderate   REF: Full pp. 475–476 | Seagull p. 485   MSC: Remembering   OBJ: 2

30. Stephen Douglas's motivation for introducing the Kansas-Nebraska Act was to:
    a. boost efforts to build a transcontinental railroad.
    b. spread slavery.
    c. win the position of speaker of the House of Representatives.
    d. pacify southerners who strongly supported the idea of popular sovereignty.
    e. help Franklin Pierce win a second term as president.

ANS: A   TOP: Economic development | Geographic issues | Douglas and Popular Sovereignty
DIF: Moderate   REF: Full p. 477 | Seagull p. 486
MSC: Understanding   OBJ: 2

31. Which of the following is an example of the political impact of the Kansas-Nebraska Act?
    a. A strong, united Whig Party won the White House in the next presidential election.
    b. Nearly half of northern Democrats joined the patriotic American Party.
    c. The Whig Party collapsed, and many disgruntled northerners joined the new Republican Party.
    d. Stephen Douglas and Abraham Lincoln decided to become running mates for the presidential election of 1856.
    e. The new Free Soil Party strongly endorsed the Act and won new congressional seats in several Upper South districts.

    ANS: C   TOP: Political history, changes | The Kansas-Nebraska Act   DIF: Moderate   REF: Full pp. 478–479 | Seagull p. 487   MSC: Understanding OBJ: 2

32. The controversy over the arrest of Anthony Burns in 1854 shows:
    a. the problematic nature of the *Dred Scott* decision.
    b. that abolitionists were definitely declining in influence.
    c. the unpopularity of the Fugitive Slave Act in parts of the North.
    d. the popularity of the Whig Party in the South.
    e. that the gag rule had serious consequences well into the 1850s.

    ANS: C   TOP: Civil rights | Social history | The Fugitive Slave Issue   DIF: Moderate   REF: Full p. 479 | Seagull p. 489   MSC: Remembering OBJ: 2

33. From 1848 to 1860, most of the railroad construction was in which region?
    a. Northeast
    b. Southeast
    c. Southwest
    d. Midwest
    e. West Coast

    ANS: D   TOP: Economic development | The Northern Economy   DIF: Easy   REF: Full p. 479 | Seagull p. 489   MSC: Remembering   OBJ: 3

34. What attracted voters to the Know-Nothing Party?
    a. its desire to dissolve the Missouri Compromise
    b. its move to annex Cuba for the expansion of American slavery

    c. its call for immediate emancipation of all slaves
    d. its opposition to the *Dred Scott* decision
    e. its denunciation of Roman Catholic immigrants

    ANS: E   TOP: Ethnicity | Political history, changes | The Rise and Fall of the Know-Nothings
    DIF: Easy   REF: Full p. 481 | Seagull p. 490
    MSC: Remembering   OBJ: 3

35. In 1854, the Know-Nothings won all the congressional races as well as the governorship in:
    a. Louisiana.
    b. South Carolina.
    c. Ohio.
    d. Massachusetts.
    e. Georgia.

    ANS: D   TOP: Ethnicity | Political history, changes | The Rise and Fall of the Know-Nothings
    DIF: Moderate   REF: Full p. 481 | Seagull p. 490
    MSC: Remembering   OBJ: 3

36. By 1856, the Republican Party included individuals who had been, until rather recently, members of each of the following political groups EXCEPT:
    a. northern Whigs.
    b. Free Soilers.
    c. Know-Nothings.
    d. antislavery Democrats.
    e. Federalists.

    ANS: E   TOP: Political history, changes | The Free Labor Ideology   DIF: Easy   REF: Full p. 483 | Seagull p. 490   MSC: Understanding   OBJ: 3

37. The Republican Party founded in the 1850s strongly endorsed the same policy about slavery in the territories that _____ had begun advocating in 1846.
    a. David Wilmot
    b. Stephen Douglas
    c. John C. Calhoun
    d. Roger Taney
    e. Henry Clay

    ANS: A   TOP: Geographic issues | Political history, changes | The Free Labor Ideology   DIF: Difficult
    REF: Full p. 483 | Seagull p. 490
    MSC: Understanding   OBJ: 3

38. The Republican free labor ideology:
    a. convinced northerners that Catholic immigrants posed a more significant threat than the southern slave power.
    b. won Republicans significant support from non-slaveholders in the South in 1856.
    c. owed its origins to Abraham Lincoln's reemergence in the wake of the Kansas-Nebraska Act.
    d. accepted southerners' point that slavery protected their liberty, but explained that the economic

benefits of free labor would outweigh the damage abolition would do to southern liberty.

e. led to the argument by Abraham Lincoln and William Seward that free labor and slave labor were essentially incompatible.

ANS: E   TOP: Political history, changes | Social history | The Free Labor Ideology   DIF: Moderate
REF: Full p. 484 | Seagull p. 491
MSC: Understanding   OBJ: 3

39. The caning of Charles Sumner by Preston Brooks:
   a. showed the extreme violence of which northern abolitionists were capable.
   b. actually helped the new Republican Party.
   c. was denounced by most southerners as barbaric.
   d. occurred because Sumner praised the attack on Lawrence, Kansas.
   e. was unusual because both men were proslavery Democrats.

ANS: B   TOP: Political history, changes | Social history | Bleeding Kansas and the Election of 1856
DIF: Moderate   REF: Full p. 484 | Seagull p. 492
MSC: Understanding   OBJ: 3

40. The Republican presidential candidate in 1856 was:
   a. John Breckinridge.
   b. Abraham Lincoln.
   c. Charles Sumner.
   d. John Frémont.
   e. James Buchanan.

ANS: D   TOP: Political history, changes | Bleeding Kansas and the Election of 1856   DIF: Difficult
REF: Full p. 485 | Seagull p. 492
MSC: Remembering   OBJ: 3

41. The *Dred Scott* decision of the U.S. Supreme Court:
   a. declared Congress could not ban slavery from territories.
   b. endorsed the "free soil" policy of the Republicans.
   c. backed the idea of "popular sovereignty."
   d. freed Dred and Harriet Scott.
   e. extended the Missouri Compromise line to California.

ANS: A   TOP: Civil rights | Constitutional history | The *Dred Scott* Decision   DIF: Difficult
REF: Full p. 486 | Seagull p. 493   MSC: Understanding
OBJ: 4

42. On matters related to citizenship, the U.S. Supreme Court declared in *Dred Scott* that:
   a. free African-Americans could vote.
   b. anyone that a state considered to be a citizen was a U.S. citizen.

c. free-born blacks were U.S. citizens, but those born into slavery and later freed could not be citizens.
d. citizenship was limited to males.
e. only white persons could be U.S. citizens.

ANS: E   TOP: Civil rights | Constitutional history | The *Dred Scott* Decision   DIF: Difficult
REF: Full p. 486 | Seagull p. 493
MSC: Remembering   OBJ: 4

43. The Lecompton Constitution was the:
   a. antislavery constitution adopted in Nebraska.
   b. proslavery constitution proposed for Kansas.
   c. pro-secession constitution of North Carolina.
   d. Missouri constitution preferred by Abraham Lincoln.
   e. compromise offered in 1861 to end the secession crisis.

ANS: B   TOP: Civil rights | Constitutional history | The Decision's Aftermath   DIF: Moderate
REF: Full p. 486 | Seagull p. 494   OBJ: 4

44. Which event sparked Abraham Lincoln to reenter politics?
   a. Compromise of 1850
   b. Mexican-American War
   c. *Dred Scott* decision
   d. Raid on Harpers Ferry
   e. Kansas-Nebraska Act

ANS: E   TOP: Political history, changes | Lincoln and Slavery   DIF: Moderate   REF: Full p. 487 |
Seagull p. 495   MSC: Remembering   OBJ: 4

45. The famous Lincoln-Douglas debates took place during the campaign for:
   a. U.S. president in 1856.
   b. U.S. president in 1860.
   c. governor of Illinois in 1858.
   d. a congressional seat from Illinois in 1856.
   e. U.S. senator from Illinois in 1858.

ANS: E   TOP: Political history, changes | The Lincoln-Douglas Campaign   DIF: Difficult
REF: Full pp. 487–488 | Seagull p. 496
MSC: Remembering   OBJ: 4

46. During his debate with Abraham Lincoln in Freeport, Illinois, Stephen Douglas:
   a. called for the free soil principle to determine the status of slavery in the West.
   b. denounced popular sovereignty as a fraud.
   c. praised the temperance movement and other key social reforms.
   d. insisted that popular sovereignty was compatible with the *Dred Scott* decision.

e. argued that slaveholders had a constitutional right to take their slaves anywhere.

ANS: D   TOP: Constitutional history | Political history, changes | The Lincoln-Douglas Campaign   DIF: Difficult   REF: Full p. 488 | Seagull p. 496   MSC: Understanding   OBJ: 4

47. Who was responsible for the 1856 Pottawatomie Creek Massacre in Kansas and led the raid on the federal arsenal at Harpers Ferry, Virginia, in 1859?
   a. Frederick Douglass
   b. Joseph Lane
   c. Robert E. Lee
   d. Henry Ward Beecher
   e. John Brown

ANS: E   TOP: Social history | John Brown at Harpers Ferry   DIF: Easy   REF: Full p. 489 | Seagull p. 497   MSC: Remembering   OBJ: 4

48. Which 1854 document called for the United States to seize Cuba?
   a. The Monroe Doctrine
   b. The Ostend Manifesto
   c. The Wilmot Proviso
   d. The Webster-Ashburton Treaty
   e. The Frémont Manifesto

ANS: B   TOP: Global awareness | The Rise of Southern Nationalism   DIF: Moderate   REF: Full pp. 492–493 | Seagull p. 500   MSC: Remembering   OBJ: 4

49. In the 1850s, Tennessee-born William Walker became famous for:
   a. creating a utopian community in northern California.
   b. his proslavery novels that heightened sectionalism.
   c. breeding the "Tennessee Walker," a horse prominent in westward expansion.
   d. seeking to establish himself as ruler of a slaveholding Nicaragua.
   e. defying fellow whites in his native region and becoming a prominent abolitionist.

ANS: D   TOP: Global awareness | The Rise of Southern Nationalism   DIF: Moderate   REF: Full p. 493 | Seagull p. 501   MSC: Remembering   OBJ: 4

50. The Democratic Party split in 1860 over the question of whether to:
   a. renominate President James Buchanan for a second term.
   b. protect slavery in the territories or allow popular sovereignty in them.

c. impeach Chief Justice Roger Taney for the *Dred Scott* decision.
   d. endorse the acquisition of Cuba by the United States, thus increasing slave territory.
   e. immediately bring Kansas and Nebraska into the Union as slave states.

ANS: B   TOP: Civil rights | Political history, changes | The Democratic Split   DIF: Moderate   REF: Full pp. 493–494 | Seagull pp. 501–502   MSC: Remembering   OBJ: 4

51. The 1860 Republican platform stated all of the following EXCEPT that:
   a. the *Dred Scott* decision was invalid.
   b. slavery should be abolished in the nation's capital.
   c. slavery should not be allowed to expand.
   d. the government should help build a transcontinental railroad.
   e. the government should grant free homesteads in the West.

ANS: B   TOP: Civil rights | Constitutional history | Economic development | Geographic issues | The Nomination of Lincoln   DIF: Difficult   REF: Full p. 494 | Seagull p. 502   MSC: Understanding   OBJ: 4

52. In the 1860 election, how many different presidential candidates won electoral votes?
   a. two
   b. three
   c. four
   d. five
   e. none, because the electoral college was suspended for that election.

ANS: C   TOP: Political history, changes | The Election of 1860   DIF: Difficult   REF: Full p. 494 | Seagull p. 503   MSC: Remembering   OBJ: 4

53. In the presidential election of 1860, the two candidates who received the most votes in the southern states were:
   a. John Breckinridge and John Bell.
   b. Abraham Lincoln and Stephen Douglas.
   c. Abraham Lincoln and John Breckinridge.
   d. William Seward and John Bell.
   e. Roger Taney and Stephen Douglas.

ANS: A   TOP: Political history, changes | The Election of 1860   DIF: Difficult   REF: Full p. 495 | Seagull p. 503   MSC: Remembering   OBJ: 4

54. Which of the following puts these events in the proper chronological order, from first to last?

I. Virginia seceded from the Union.

II. Abraham Lincoln was elected president.

III. Confederate States of America formed.

IV. South Carolina seceded from the Union.
   a. IV, I, III, II
   b. III, I, IV, II
   c. II, I, III, IV
   d. I, II, III, IV
   e. II, IV, III, I

ANS: E TOP: Chronology | The Secession Movement | The Secession Crisis | And the War Came DIF: Difficult REF: Full pp. 495–498 | Seagull pp. 503–506 MSC: Remembering OBJ: 5

55. In 1860, which state became the first to pass an ordinance of secession and declare itself separated from the Union?
   a. Virginia
   b. Kentucky
   c. Georgia
   d. South Carolina
   e. Tennessee

ANS: D TOP: Political history, changes | The Secession Movement DIF: Easy REF: Full p. 496 | Seagull p. 504 MSC: Remembering OBJ: 5

56. During the secession winter of 1860–1861, who offered the most widely supported compromise plan in Congress, which allowed the westward extension of the Missouri Compromise line?
   a. Abraham Lincoln
   b. John Crittenden
   c. Jefferson Davis
   d. Zachary Taylor
   e. Andrew Johnson

ANS: B TOP: Political history, changes | The Secession Crisis DIF: Moderate REF: Full p. 496 | Seagull p. 504 MSC: Understanding OBJ: 5

57. The American Civil War began in April 1861, when:
   a. Confederate forces fired upon and captured Fort Sumter.
   b. U.S. naval vessels bombarded the city of Wilmington, North Carolina.
   c. Confederate and Union cavalry clashed in disputed territory in Texas.
   d. General William Sherman led Union soldiers on a devastating march through Georgia.
   e. Confederate infantry attacked Gettysburg, Pennsylvania.

ANS: A TOP: Political history, changes | And the War Came DIF: Moderate REF: Full p. 498 | Seagull p. 506 MSC: Remembering OBJ: 5

True or False

1. In spite of the controversy over the *Statute of Freedom*, Thomas Crawford refused to change his original design of the statue.

ANS: F TOP: Cultural history | Introduction DIF: Moderate REF: Full p. 459 | Seagull p. 467 MSC: Remembering OBJ: 2

2. The Texas independence movement was sparked in part because the Mexican government, alarmed that its grip on the area was weakening, annulled existing land contracts and barred future emigration from the United States in 1830.

ANS: T TOP: Global awareness | The Texas Revolt DIF: Moderate REF: Full pp. 460–461 | Seagull pp. 470–471 MSC: Remembering OBJ: 1

3. Unlike most previous presidents, James Polk was not a slaveholder.

ANS: F TOP: Political history, changes | The Election of 1844 DIF: Moderate REF: Full p. 463 | Seagull p. 472 MSC: Remembering OBJ: 1

4. The issue of Texas annexation was hotly linked to slavery and affected the nominations of presidential candidates in the 1840s.

ANS: T TOP: Civil rights | Political history, changes | The Election of 1844 DIF: Easy REF: Full pp. 463–464 | Seagull pp. 472–473 MSC: Understanding OBJ: 1

5. Abraham Lincoln fully supported President Polk's justification for declaring war against Mexico in 1846.

ANS: F TOP: Political history, changes | The War and Its Critics DIF: Moderate REF: Full p. 466 | Seagull p. 474 MSC: Remembering OBJ: 1

6. In California after the Mexican-American War, landowners of Spanish heritage had to adjust to a new identity as if they were immigrants.

ANS: T TOP: Ethnicity | Political history, changes | Race and Manifest Destiny DIF: Moderate REF: Full p. 468 | Seagull p. 476 MSC: Understanding OBJ: 1

7. The explosive population growth and competition for gold brought cooperation among California's many racial and ethnic groups as they worked together for wealth.

ANS: F TOP: Ethnicity | Geographic issues | California and the Boundaries of Freedom DIF: Moderate REF: Full p. 470 | Seagull p. 478 MSC: Understanding OBJ: 1

8. The city of Melbourne in Australia prospered because of a gold rush, much as San Francisco did, and at about the same time.

    ANS: T   TOP: Global awareness | The Other Gold Rush   DIF: Moderate   REF: Full p. 471 | Seagull p. 479   MSC: Remembering   OBJ: 1

9. Matthew Perry led the contingent of U.S. warships that helped to open Japan to American trade in 1854.

    ANS: T   TOP: Global awareness | Opening Japan DIF: Moderate   REF: Full p. 472 | Seagull p. 479 MSC: Remembering   OBJ: 1

10. As it divided over the issue of slavery, the Catholic Church broke into a northern and southern branch.

    ANS: F   TOP: Civil rights | Cultural history | A Dose of Arsenic   DIF: Moderate REF: Full p. 473 | Seagull p. 480 MSC: Remembering   OBJ: 2

11. The Wilmot Proviso was an attempt to annex Cuba.

    ANS: F   TOP: Geographic issues | Political history, changes | The Wilmot Proviso   DIF: Moderate REF: Full p. 473 | Seagull p. 481 MSC: Remembering   OBJ: 2

12. The Free Soil idea in the West appealed to racist northerners who worried about competing against black laborers.

    ANS: T   TOP: Civil rights | Geographic issues | The Free Soil Appeal   DIF: Moderate REF: Full p. 474 | Seagull p. 483 MSC: Understanding   OBJ: 2

13. It is ironic that the South supported the Fugitive Slave Act because that law gave enormous power to the federal government to override local authorities, which is something that the South had traditionally opposed.

    ANS: T   TOP: Civil rights | Political history, changes | The Fugitive Slave Issue   DIF: Moderate REF: Full p. 476 | Seagull p. 485 MSC: Understanding   OBJ: 2

14. The Fugitive Slave Act provided for the return of runaway slaves to their owners.

    ANS: T   TOP: Civil rights | Political history, changes | The Fugitive Slave Issue   DIF: Easy REF: Full p. 476 | Seagull p. 485 MSC: Remembering   OBJ: 2

15. Many free blacks in the North that had escaped slavery by running away fled to Canada to avoid being caught and brought back to the South under the Fugitive Slave Act.

    ANS: T   TOP: Civil rights | Political history, changes | The Fugitive Slave Issue   DIF: Moderate REF: Full p. 477 | Seagull p. 486 MSC: Understanding   OBJ: 2

16. The *Appeal of the Independent Democrats* was not a very effective piece of political persuasion.

    ANS: F   TOP: Political history, changes | The Kansas-Nebraska Act   DIF: Moderate REF: Full p. 478 | Seagull p. 487 MSC: Remembering   OBJ: 2

17. The development of railroads and economic integration of the Northeast and Northwest created the groundwork for the political unification of the Republican Party.

    ANS: T   TOP: Economic development | Political history, changes | The Northern Economy DIF: Moderate   REF: Full p. 479 | Seagull p. 489 MSC: Understanding   OBJ: 3

18. Nativism emerged as a major political movement in 1854, with the sudden appearance of the Liberty Party.

    ANS: F   TOP: Ethnicity | Political history, changes | The Rise and Fall of the Know-Nothings DIF: Easy   REF: Full p. 481 | Seagull pp. 489–490 MSC: Remembering   OBJ: 3

19. The free labor ideology was based on the assumption that free labor could not compete with slave labor and so slavery's expansion had to be halted to ensure freedom for the white laborer.

    ANS: T   TOP: Civil rights | Social history | The Free Labor Ideology   DIF: Difficult   REF: Full p. 483 | Seagull p. 491   MSC: Understanding   OBJ: 3

20. Prior to becoming president in 1857, James Buchanan did not have much political experience.

    ANS: F   TOP: Political history, changes | Bleeding Kansas and the Election of 1856   DIF: Moderate REF: Full p. 485 | Seagull p. 492 MSC: Remembering   OBJ: 3

21. Moderate Republicans like Abraham Lincoln supported the *Dred Scott* decision.

    ANS: F   TOP: Political history, changes | The Decision's Aftermath   DIF: Moderate   REF: Full p. 486 | Seagull p. 494   MSC: Remembering OBJ: 4

22. Abraham Lincoln opposed increasing economic opportunities for free blacks.

    ANS: F   TOP: Civil rights | Political history, changes | Lincoln and Slavery   DIF: Moderate

REF: Full p. 487 | Seagull p. 495
MSC: Remembering   OBJ: 4

23. Stephen Douglas said during the Lincoln-Douglas debates, "A house divided against itself cannot stand. I believe this government cannot endure, permanently half slave and half free."

ANS: F   TOP: Political history, changes | The Lincoln-Douglas Campaign   DIF: Easy
REF: Full p. 487 | Seagull p. 496
MSC: Remembering   OBJ: 4

24. The Lincoln-Douglas debates were relatively insignificant in American political history and of little consequence to the outcome of the U.S. senate race.

ANS: F   TOP: Political history, changes | The Lincoln-Douglas Campaign   DIF: Easy
REF: Full p. 488 | Seagull p. 496
MSC: Remembering   OBJ: 4

25. John Brown was one of the most infamous black abolitionists, after Frederick Douglass.

ANS: F   TOP: Social history | John Brown at Harpers Ferry   DIF: Moderate   REF: Full p. 489 | Seagull p. 500   MSC: Remembering   OBJ: 4

26. The Ostend Manifesto suggested seizing all of Mexico, rather than just the Mexican Cession, during the Mexican War.

ANS: F   TOP: Global awareness | The Rise of Southern Nationalism   DIF: Moderate
REF: Full p. 493 | Seagull p. 500
MSC: Remembering   OBJ: 4

27. The Republican Party under Lincoln promised free homesteads in the West, a protective tariff, and government aid in building a transcontinental railroad.

ANS: T   TOP: Economic development | Geographic issues | The Nomination of Lincoln   DIF: Moderate
REF: Full p. 494 | Seagull p. 502
MSC: Remembering   OBJ: 4

28. Abraham Lincoln won the 1860 presidential election without a single vote in ten southern states.

ANS: T   TOP: Political history, changes | The Election of 1860   DIF: Moderate   REF: Full p. 495 | Seagull p. 503   MSC: Remembering   OBJ: 4

29. By the time Lincoln actually took the oath of office, seven states had already seceded from the Union.

ANS: T   TOP: Political history, changes | The Secession Movement   DIF: Easy   REF: Full p. 497 | Seagull p. 504   MSC: Remembering   OBJ: 5

Short Answer

Identify and give the historical significance of each of the following terms, events, and people in a paragraph or two.

1. Californios
2. "free labor" ideology
3. Republican Party
4. Free Soil
5. John Brown
6. Mexican Cession
7. Bleeding Kansas
8. Lincoln-Douglas debates
9. filibustering
10. *Dred Scott* decision
11. Compromise of 1850
12. Wilmot Proviso

Essay Questions

1. Did morality or economics dominate the debates over slavery in the 1850s? Explain the various arguments made for and against the expansion of slavery. Who, if anyone, was arguing for abolition?

ANS: Answers will vary   TOP: Civil rights | Constitutional history | Economic Development | Political history, changes | Social history | The Wilmot Proviso | The Free Soil Appeal | Crisis and Compromise | The Great Debate | Douglas and Popular Sovereignty | The Free Labor Ideology   DIF: Moderate
MSC: Evaluating   OBJ: 1 / 2 / 3 / 4

2. John O'Sullivan declared that race was the key to the history of nations and the rise and fall of empires. How accurate do you think that statement was? Why?

ANS: Answers will vary   TOP: Civil rights | Social history | Race and Manifest Destiny | Redefining Race   DIF: Moderate   MSC: Evaluating   OBJ: 1 / 2

3. What did Emerson mean by "Mexico will poison us"? Was he right? Why or why not?

ANS: Answers will vary   TOP: Civil rights | Geographic issues | Global awareness | Political history, changes | The Wilmot Proviso | The Free Soil Appeal | Crisis and Compromise   DIF: Difficult   MSC: Evaluating   OBJ: 1 / 2

4. Many Americans and immigrants from other lands believed California presented a magnificent opportunity for economic freedom once gold was discovered. However, the boundaries of freedom were tightly drawn in California. Explain the expansions and limitations of freedom there.

ANS: Answers will vary   TOP: Ethnicity | Geographic issues | Global awareness | Political history, changes | Gold Rush California | California and the Boundaries of Freedom   DIF: Moderate   MSC: Evaluating   OBJ: 1 / 2

5. Analyze the arguments of the Free Soil Party. How did its members understand freedom? How did slavery fit into their platform?

ANS: Answers will vary   TOP: Civil rights | Political history, changes | The Free Soil Appeal   DIF: Easy   MSC: Analyzing   OBJ: 2

6. Thinking back to previous chapters, fully explain how the forces of the market revolution heightened the tension between freedom and slavery.

ANS: Answers will vary   TOP: Civil rights | Economic development | Political history, changes | Social history | The Northern Economy | The Rise of Southern Nationalism   DIF: Difficult   MSC: Analyzing   OBJ: 2 / 3

7. Explain how the various parties reacted to the Kansas-Nebraska Act. Be sure to discuss why the Whig Party failed, why the Democratic Party split, and why the Republican Party unified. How did each party view slavery and define freedom?

ANS: Answers will vary   TOP: Civil rights | Economic development | Political history, changes | The Northern Economy | The Free Labor Ideology | The Rise of Southern Nationalism | The Democratic Split | The Free Labor Ideology   DIF: Difficult   MSC: Analyzing   OBJ: 2 / 3

8. Using the Lincoln-Douglas debates, explore how each man viewed freedom. What can their political debates tell us about American society on the eve of the Civil War?

ANS: Answers will vary   TOP: Civil rights | Political history, changes | Social history | Primary document analysis | The Lincoln-Douglas Campaign | Voices of Freedom   DIF: Moderate   MSC: Analyzing   OBJ: 4 / 5

9. Analyze Roger Taney's decision in the *Dred Scott* case. How did the ruling mirror the sectional debates that had been occurring in Congress? What consequences did the decision have on the liberties and freedoms of blacks in America?

ANS: Answers will vary   TOP: Civil rights | Constitutional history | Political history, changes | The *Dred Scott* Decision | The Decision's Aftermath   DIF: Moderate   MSC: Analyzing   OBJ: 4

10. Examine the aftermath of the Mexican War and its consequences for Indians, slaves, and free blacks in the newly acquired areas. Think back to Thomas Jefferson's idea of an Empire of Liberty. Did the newly acquired land from the Mexican War promote Jefferson's idea, or as with the Louisiana Purchase, was it an empire of liberty for only a few?

ANS: Answers will vary   TOP: Civil rights | Economic development | Ethnicity | Political history, changes | Social history | Race and Manifest Destiny | Redefining Race | Gold Rush California | California and the Boundaries of Freedom | The Free Soil Appeal | Crisis and Compromise   DIF: Difficulty   MSC: Evaluating   OBJ: 1 / 2

11. How do you explain why and when certain slave states seceded from the Union? Why did some slave states—Delaware, Kentucky, Maryland, and Missouri—not secede from the Union?

ANS: Answers will vary   TOP: Political history, changes | The Secession Movement | The Secession Crisis   DIF: Moderate   MSC: Analyzing   OBJ: 5

CHAPTER 14

A New Birth of Freedom: The Civil War, 1861–1865

This chapter concentrates on the history of the American Civil War, touching on some major battles, the coming of emancipation, and early experiments with Reconstruction. The chapter begins with a compelling story of a German immigrant who volunteered in the Union army. His story illustrates how many northerners changed their view of the war from seeing it as a war fought to defend the Union to a war fought to end slavery. The chapter examines how the war was both a modern war and a total war and the relative advantages that the North had over the South. After a series of Union defeats, Abraham Lincoln began a fundamental shift in his thinking and issued the Emancipation Proclamation. Afterward, blacks fought valiantly for the Union. The chapter then looks at the Civil War as a second American Revolution, exploring the vision Lincoln had for universal political democracy and human liberty. Lincoln's views are explored in detail in "Voices of Freedom." The northern economy benefited greatly from the war, while the South suffered economic crisis. The chapter then turns to the Confederate Nation. Also included in "Voices of Freedom" is a letter by South Carolina plantation owner Thomas Drayton expressing fears that the Union wants to enslave white southerners. The chapter also looks at southern unionists, women, and the question of black soldiers for the Confederacy. Victories at Gettysburg and Vicksburg turned the tide for a Union victory, which was finally achieved when Confederate General Robert E. Lee surrendered to Union General Ulysses S. Grant at Appomattox in April 1865. Meanwhile, experiments on the Sea Islands and Grant's "negro paradise" served as illustrations of what Reconstruction might look like. Lincoln also had a plan, but was assassinated days after Lee's surrender.

CHAPTER OUTLINE

I. Introduction: Marcus Spiegel

II. The First Modern War
   A. The Two Combatants
      1. The Union had many advantages (e.g., manufacturing, railroad mileage, and financial resources), but it would need to conquer an area larger than western Europe to win.
      2. Confederate soldiers were highly motivated fighters.
      3. On both sides, the outbreak of war stirred powerful feelings of patriotism.
      4. Recruits were not ready for regimentation.
      5. One estimate had the Army of the Potomac only fighting thirty days in the first two years of the war.
   B. The Technology of War
      1. Railroads were vital to the war effort.
      2. Ironclads were superior to wooden ships and revolutionized naval warfare.
      3. Introduction of the rifle changed the nature of combat.
         a. Most recent estimate has 750,000 soldiers killed.
      4. Modern warfare included POW camps and disease.
      5. Wars in other countries in same general time period were deadly, too.
         a. China lost 23 million in Taiping Rebellion (1850–1864).
         b. Paraguay lost more than 250,000 in war against Brazil, Argentina, and Uruguay.

C. The Public and the War
1. Both sides were assisted by a vast propaganda effort to mobilize public opinion.
2. The war was brought to the people via newspapers and photographs.
   a. Matthew Brady
   b. Civil War was turning point for photography as an art and business.
D. Mobilizing Resources
1. The outbreak of the war found both sides unprepared.
2. Feeding and supplying armies was a challenge for both sides.
3. Despite the North's advantages, victory on the battlefield was elusive.
E. Military Strategies
1. The Confederacy adopted a defensive strategy.
2. Lincoln's early generals did not successfully use the North's advantages in manpower and technology.
3. Lincoln realized that his armies had to defeat the Confederacy's armies and dismantle slavery.
F. The War Begins
1. In the East, most of the war's fighting took place in a narrow corridor between Washington and Richmond.
2. The first Battle of Bull Run, a Confederate victory, shattered any illusions that war was romantic.
3. After the First Bull Run, George McClellan assumed command of the Union army of the Potomac.
G. The War in the East in 1862
1. General Lee blunted McClellan's attacks in Virginia and forced him to withdraw back to the vicinity of Washington.
2. Successful on the defensive, Lee now launched an invasion of the North.
3. McClellan's Army of the Potomac stopped Lee at the Battle of Antietam (Maryland), the single bloodiest day in U.S. history (September 17, 1862).
4. Ambrose Burnside replaced McClellan after Antietam.
5. Burnside's assault on Lee at Fredericksburg, Virginia, resulted in a disastrous Union defeat (December 1862).
H. The War in the West
1. Ulysses S. Grant was the architect of early success in the West.
2. In February 1862, Grant won the Union's first significant victory when he captured Fort Henry and Fort Donelson in Tennessee.

3. Grant withstood a surprise Confederate attack at the Battle of Shiloh (Tennessee).

III. The Coming of Emancipation
A. Slavery and the War
1. In numbers, scale, and the economic power of the institution of slavery, American emancipation dwarfed that of any other country.
2. At the outset of the war, Lincoln invoked time-honored northern values to mobilize public support.
3. Lincoln initially insisted that slavery was irrelevant to the conflict.
   a. Feared four border states would leave the Union
B. The Unraveling of Slavery
1. Early in the war, Congress adopted a resolution proposed by Senator John J. Crittenden of Kentucky, which affirmed that the Union had no intention of interfering with slavery.
2. The policy of ignoring slavery unraveled and, by the end of 1861, the military began treating escaped blacks as contraband of war (property of military value subject to confiscation).
3. Blacks called the conflict a "freedom war."
C. Steps toward Emancipation
1. Since slavery stood at the foundation of the Southern economy, antislavery northerners insisted that emancipation was necessary to weaken the South's ability to sustain the war.
2. Throughout 1861 and 1862, Lincoln struggled to retain control of the emancipation issue.
   a. Union General John C. Frémont issued a proclamation freeing slaves in Missouri (August 1861).
   b. Fearing the negative impact on loyal border states, Lincoln rescinded Frémont's order.
   c. Lincoln proposed gradual emancipation and colonization for border-state slaves.
D. Lincoln's Decision
1. During the summer of 1862, Lincoln concluded that emancipation had become a political and military necessity.
2. Upon Secretary of State William Seward's advice, he delayed announcing emancipation until a Union victory.
3. On September 22, 1862, five days after Antietam, Lincoln issued the Preliminary Emancipation Proclamation.
4. The initial northern reaction was not encouraging, with important Democratic wins in the fall elections.

E. The Emancipation Proclamation
1. Lincoln signed the Emancipation Proclamation on January 1, 1863, which declared slaves in Confederate-held territory to be free.
2. Despite its limitations, the proclamation set off scenes of jubilation among free blacks and abolitionists in the North and "contrabands" and slaves in the South.
3. The Emancipation Proclamation not only altered the nature of the Civil War and the course of American history but also represented a turning point in Lincoln's own thinking.

F. Enlisting Black Troops
1. Of the proclamation's provisions, few were more radical in their implications than the enrollment of blacks into military service.
2. Initially not done as Union army feared white soldiers would not fight alongside blacks and border states would be alienated.
3. By the end of the war, over 180,000 black men had served in the Union army and 24,000 in the navy.
4. Most black soldiers were emancipated slaves who joined the army in the South.

G. The Black Soldier
1. For black soldiers, military service proved to be a liberating experience.
   a. At least 130 former soldiers served in political office after the Civil War.
2. The Union navy treated black sailors much the same as white sailors.
3. Within the army, black soldiers did not receive equal treatment to white soldiers.
4. Black soldiers played a crucial role not only in winning the Civil War but also in defining the war's consequences.
5. Service of black soldiers affected Lincoln's own outlook.
   a. Must be treated the same as whites when captured
   b. Must be part of prisoner exchanges

IV. The Second American Revolution
A. Liberty and Union
1. The Union's triumph consolidated the northern understanding of freedom as the national norm.
2. Emancipation offered proof of the progressive nature and global significance of the country's history.

B. Lincoln's Vision
1. The U.S. Civil War took place as modern states around the world consolidated their power and reduced local autonomy.

a. Japan
b. Argentina
c. Italy
d. Germany
2. To Lincoln, the American nation embodied a set of universal ideas, centered on political democracy and human liberty.
3. The Gettysburg Address identified the nation's mission with the principle that "all men are created equal."

C. From Union to Nation
1. The war forged a new national self-consciousness, reflected in the increasing use of the word "nation"—a unified political entity—in place of the older "Union" of separate states.

D. The War and American Religion
1. Northern Protestantism combined Christianity and patriotism in a civic religion that saw the war as transforming the United States into a true land of freedom.
2. Lincoln shrewdly used religious symbolism to generate public support.
3. Southern clergy preached about the Confederate cause as being God's will.
4. Religion helped Americans to cope with unprecedented mass death.
   a. "Transformation of heaven": equated heaven with family gatherings in middle-class living rooms
   b. Heightened popularity of spiritualism (communication with the dead)
5. New government action to deal with death
   a. Systems for recording deaths and other casualties
   b. National military cemeteries were only for Union soldiers not Confederates.

E. Liberty in Wartime
1. Republicans saw criticism of the war effort or Lincoln's policies as equivalent to treason.
2. Lincoln consolidated executive power and twice suspended the writ of habeas corpus throughout the entire Union for those accused of "disloyal activities."
3. After the war, the Court made it clear that the Constitution was not suspended in wartime (*Ex parte Milligan,* 1866).
4. Lincoln was not a despot, but the Civil War showed that civil liberties were curbed with demands for patriotism and national unity.

F. The North's Transformation
1. The rising class of capitalist entrepreneurs gained power.

2. The North experienced the war as a time of prosperity.
   a. Industry benefited from inflation and government contracts.

G. Government and the Economy
   1. Congress adopted policies that promoted economic growth and permanently altered the nation's financial system.
      a. The Homestead Act
      b. The Land-Grant College Act

H. Building the Transcontinental Railroad
   1. Congress passed land grants for railroads.
   2. The transcontinental railroad was completed in 1869.
      a. Labor force included thousands of Chinese
      b. National markets were expanded.

I. The War and Native Americans
   1. Withdrawal of troops from the West increased conflict between Indians and white settlers.
      a. Sioux attack in Minnesota
      b. Chivington's massacre of Cheyenne and Arapaho at Sand Creek, Colorado
   2. Union campaign against Navajo led to the tribe's Long Walk, or removal to a reservation.
   3. Confederates treated Indians better than did the United States.
      a. Confederate Constitution allowed Indian tribes to elect congressional representatives.
      b. Slave-owning tribes, such as Cherokee, sided with the Confederacy.

J. A New Financial System
   1. The need to pay for the war produced dramatic changes in U.S. financial policy:
      a. Increased tariff
      b. New taxes on goods
      c. First income tax
      d. Bonds
   2. Wartime economic policies greatly benefited northern manufacturers, railroad men, and financiers.
   3. Taken together, the Union's economic policies vastly increased the power and size of the federal government.

K. Women and the War
   1. Women stepped into the workforce as nurses, factory workers, and government clerks.
   2. Hundreds of thousands of northern women took part in humanitarian organizations.
      a. Women played leading role in organizing Sanitary Fairs.
   3. Northern women were brought into the public sphere, and the war work offered them a taste of independence.

      a. Clara Barton, president of the American National Red Cross, lobbied for the United States to endorse the First Geneva Convention of 1864.

L. The Divided North
   1. Republicans labeled those opposed to the war "Copperheads."
   2. The war heightened existing social tensions and created new ones.
      a. New York City draft riot killed more than 100 people.
      b. Irish immigrants led the angry mob.
      c. Targets were draft offices; wealthy, industrial sites; and blacks.

V. The Confederate Nation
A. Leadership and Government
   1. Jefferson Davis proved unable to communicate the war's meaning effectively to ordinary men and women.
   2. Under Davis, the Confederate nation became far more centralized than the Old South had been.
      a. Confederate government controlled railroads
      b. Confederate government built factories
   3. King Cotton diplomacy sought to pressure Europeans to side with the Confederacy, but this failed.
   4. Davis did not deal effectively with obstructionist governors.

B. The Inner Civil War
   1. Social change and internal turmoil engulfed much of the Confederacy.
   2. The draft encouraged class divisions among whites.
      a. Wealthy slave owners received draft exemptions for having twenty or more slaves.
      b. Many southern yeomen started to see the conflict as "a rich man's war and poor man's fight."

C. Economic Problems
   1. The South's economy, unlike the North's, was in crisis during the war.
   2. Numerous yeoman families, many of whom had gone to war to preserve their economic independence, sank into poverty and debt.
      a. Food riots occurred in many places.
   3. By the war's end, over 100,000 southern men had deserted.

D. Southern Unionists
   1. Southerners loyal to the Union made a significant contribution to Union victory.

a. At least 50,000 southern white men fought for the Union.

2. Virginian Elizabeth Van Lew provided vital information to Union forces.

E. Women and the Confederacy

1. Even more than in the North, the war placed unprecedented burdens on southern white women.

a. Rose Greenhow served as a Confederate spy.

2. The war led to the first political mobilization of non-slaveholding white women.

3. The growing disaffection of southern white women contributed to the decline in home-front morale and encouraged desertion from the army.

F. Black Soldiers for the Confederacy

1. A shortage of manpower led the Confederate Congress in March 1865 to authorize the arming of slaves.

2. War ended before substantial recruitment of blacks as Confederate soldiers.

a. Only two companies reached the front in Richmond, but war ended several days later.

3. South's decision to use black troops undermined proslavery ideology.

VI. Turning Points

A. Gettysburg and Vicksburg

1. Lee advanced onto northern soil in Pennsylvania, but was held back by Union forces under the command of General George Meade at the Battle of Gettysburg (July 1863).

a. Pickett's Charge failed and was Lee's greatest blunder.

2. General Grant secured a Union victory at Vicksburg, Mississippi (July 1863).

B. 1864

1. Grant, in 1864, began a war of attrition against Lee's army in Virginia.

2. At the end of six weeks of fighting, Grant's casualties stood at 60,000—almost the size of Lee's entire army—while Lee had lost 30,000 men.

a. Fall of 1864: Grant begins siege of Lee at Petersburg.

3. General William T. Sherman entered Atlanta, seizing Georgia's main railroad center.

4. Some Radical Republicans nominated John C. Frémont on a platform calling for a constitutional amendment to abolish slavery, federal protection of the freed people's rights, and confiscation of the land of leading Confederates.

5. The Democratic candidate for president was General George B. McClellan.

6. Lincoln won, aided by Frémont's withdrawal and Sherman's capture of Atlanta.

VII. Rehearsals for Reconstruction and the End of the War

A. The Sea Island Experiment

1. The Union occupied the Sea Islands (off South Carolina's coast) in November 1861.

2. Women took the lead as teachers in educating the freed slaves of the islands.

a. Charlotte Forten and Laura Towne

3. By 1865, black families were working for wages, acquiring education, and enjoying better shelter and clothing and a more varied diet than under slavery.

a. Introduced contentious issue of whether land ownership should be part of black freedom

B. Wartime Reconstruction in the West

1. After the capture of Vicksburg, the Union army established regulations for plantation labor.

a. Freed people signed labor contracts and were paid wages.

2. Neither side was satisfied with the new labor system.

3. At Davis Bend, Grant established a "negro paradise."

C. The Politics of Wartime Reconstruction

1. In 1863, Lincoln announced his Ten-Percent Plan of Reconstruction.

a. No role for blacks

b. Leniency toward the South

2. Free blacks in New Orleans complained about the Ten-Percent Plan and found sympathy from Radical Republicans.

3. Wade-Davis Bill offered as an alternative plan.

a. Required a majority of a state's voters to pledge loyalty

b. Lincoln pocket-vetoed the plan.

D. Victory at Last

1. Sherman marched from Atlanta to the sea in November–December 1864, and then headed into South Carolina, bringing even greater destruction.

2. The Thirteenth Amendment was approved on January 31, 1865.

3. On April 3, 1865, Grant took Richmond.

4. Lee surrendered to Grant at Appomattox Court House, Virginia, on April 9.

5. Lincoln was shot on April 14 and died the next morning.

E. The War and the World

1. Grant's post-presidential world tour illustrates how non-Americans saw the war.

a. England's Duke of Wellington hailed Grant as a military genius.

b. English workers saw war as having saved the leading experiment in democracy and vindicated free labor principles.

c. German Chancellor Bismarck saw nation-building as war's central achievement.

i. Grant told Bismarck that war was also "to destroy slavery."

F. The War in American History

1. The Civil War laid the foundation for modern America.

2. Both sides lost something they had gone to war to defend.

a. Confederacy lost slavery.

b. The war hastened the transformation of Lincoln's America of free labor, small shops, and independent farmers into an industrial giant.

3. The work of achieving equality for blacks remained to be done.

SUGGESTED DISCUSSION QUESTIONS

- Describe why the Civil War was both a modern war and a total war.

- Why wasn't the Union more successful early in the war when it had clear advantages over the Confederacy? Why was a strategy of merely capturing the Confederate capital of Richmond not enough to win the war?

- Describe the various ways blacks, both in and out of the military, aided in the war and also defined its consequences.

- Over time, Lincoln switched from using the term "Union" to using the term "nation." Discuss the significance of this shift in thinking.

- How does the Gettysburg Address express ideas of freedom and liberty? What purpose did Lincoln give the Civil War in that address?

- In the face of a significant manpower shortage, why was the Confederacy still so hesitant to use slaves as soldiers?

- Was Lincoln's Reconstruction Plan suitable considering the massive toll the Civil War took on American society?

- Have students imagine themselves as Civil War soldiers, either for the Union or the Confederacy. Have each student decide his or her own fictional background. Maybe some are women hiding their gender, maybe some have brothers fighting for the Confederacy, maybe some are immigrants, and maybe others are from a long line of military veterans. Have each student write a letter home discussing the war and his or her feelings about it.

SUPPLEMENTAL WEB AND VISUAL RESOURCES

Black Civil War Soldier
www.npr.org/templates/story/story.php?storyId=6417951&ft=1&f=498668
This November 1, 2006, story from NPR's "All Things Considered" tells of a black veteran of the 54th Massachusetts Regiment, receiving overdue honors.

Binding a Nation
www.postalmuseum.si.edu/exhibits/2a6_anationdivided.html
From the Smithsonian Institution's National Postal Museum, this exhibit depicts the efforts to keep communication alive during the war through soldiers' letters, efforts by family members to get around the blockades, and patriotic envelopes colorfully decorated with symbols of the writer's cause.

Jefferson Davis
www.civilwarhome.com/jdavisbio.htm
The extensive material on this website covers the role of Jefferson Davis during the war.

Robert E. Lee
www.civilwarhome.com/leebio.htm
This site highlights General Lee's contributions to the Civil War. More information can be found on other aspects of the Civil War as well.

Shenandoah Valley Communities
http://valley.vcdh.virginia.edu/
This University of Virginia's Virginia Center for Digital History website compares two counties in the Shenandoah Valley during the Civil War. The site offers maps, diaries, newspapers, public records, time lines, and a wealth of other material.

The Civil War
www.pbs.org/civilwar/film/episode5.html
Documentary by Ken Burns, Episode 5, "The Universe of Battle (1863)," covers the battles of Gettysburg and Vicksburg and discusses the wartime participation of women and African-Americans.

americanhistory.si.edu/militaryhistory/exhibition/flash.html
From the Smithsonian Institution's National Museum of American History, select a war (Civil War) and enter an exhibit that includes a movie, learning resources, statistics, printable exhibition, maps, and time lines.

The Emancipation Proclamation
http://www.scribd.com/doc/117165086/The-Meaning-and-Making-of-Emancipation
This links to a 200-plus page e-book called *The Meaning and Making of Emancipation*. Besides information on the Emancipation Proclamation, there is analysis of earlier attempts to emancipate slaves and examination of events that led to the Civil War. This National Archive book is free and can be down-

loaded as a PDF file. At the back of the book, there are two pages of sources, many of which are available online.

Ulysses S. Grant
www.mscomm.com/~ulysses/page152.html
This site solely concentrates on Ulysses S. Grant. Many links are also available for further research.

SUPPLEMENTAL PRINT RESOURCES

Bailey, Anne. "A Texas Cavalry Raid: Reaction to Black Soldiers and Contrabands." *Civil War History* 35, no. 2 (1989): 138–152.

Blight, David. *Race and Reunion: The Civil War in American Memory.* Cambridge, MA: Harvard University Press, 2001.

Brands, H. W. *The Man Who Saved the Union: Ulysses Grant in War and Peace.* New York: Doubleday, 2012.

Cashin, Joan E. *First Lady of the Confederacy: Varina Davis's Civil War.* Cambridge, MA: Harvard University Press, 2006.

Cimbala, Paul, and Randall Miller, eds. *An Uncommon Time: The Civil War and the Northern Home Front.* Bronx, NY: Fordham University Press, 2002.

Faust, Drew Gilpin. *Mothers of Invention: Women of the Slaveholding South in the American Civil War.* Chapel Hill, NC: University of North Carolina Press, 1996.

Foner, Eric. *The Fiery Trial: Abraham Lincoln and American Slavery.* New York: W. W. Norton, 2011.

Goldfield, David. *America Aflame: How the Civil War Created a Nation.* New York: Bloomsbury Press, 2011.

Harris, William H. *With Charity for All: Lincoln and the Restoration of the Union.* Lexington, KY: University of Kentucky Press, 1997.

Inscoe, John C., and Robert C. Kenzer, eds. *Enemies of the Country: New Perspectives on Unionists in the Civil War South.* Athens, GA: University of Georgia Press, 2001.

Manning, Chandra. *What This Cruel War Was Over: Soldiers, Slavery, and the Civil War.* New York: Knopf, 2007.

Nelson, Scott, and Carol Sheriff. *A People at War: Civilians and Soldiers in America's Civil War, 1854–1877.* New York: Oxford University Press, 2008.

Rable, George. *The Confederate Republic: A Revolution against Politics.* Chapel Hill, NC: University of North Carolina Press, 2007.

Reardon, Carol. *Pickett's Charge in History and Memory.* Chapel Hill, NC: University of North Carolina Press, 1997.

TEST BANK

Matching

TEST I

___ 1. Ulysses S. Grant
___ 2. Jefferson Davis
___ 3. Thaddeus Stevens
___ 4. George McClellan
___ 5. Robert E. Lee
___ 6. Abraham Lincoln
___ 7. Elizabeth Van Lew
___ 8. John Frémont
___ 9. Laura Towne
___ 10. William T. Sherman
___ 11. Clara Barton
___ 12. Alexander Stephens

a. 1864 Democratic presidential candidate
b. challenged Lincoln for the 1864 Republican nomination
c. vice president of the Confederacy
d. American National Red Cross
e. southern spy for the Union
f. president of the Confederacy
g. Radical Republican from Pennsylvania
h. practiced a war of attrition
i. surrendered to General Grant
j. favored a Ten-Percent Plan of Reconstruction
k. teacher on the Sea Islands
l. marched through the South

Answer Key: h, f, g, a, i, j, e, b, k, l, d, c

TEST 2

___ 1. Anaconda Plan
___ 2. Bull Run
___ 3. Copperheads
___ 4. King Cotton diplomacy
___ 5. Antietam
___ 6. Emancipation Proclamation
___ 7. contrabands
___ 8. Appomattox
___ 9. Pickett's Charge
___ 10. Confederate capital
___ 11. Crittenden Compromise
___ 12. "Negro paradise"

a. escaped slaves
b. deadliest battle of the war
c. Richmond
d. Union not to interfere with slavery
e. surrender of the Confederacy
f. relied on British support
g. Gettysburg
h. a naval blockade
i. freed slaves
j. spectators came with picnic baskets to watch
k. opponents of the war
l. established by Grant

Answer Key: h, j, k, f, b, i, a, e, g, c, d, l

Learning Objectives

1. Explain why the Civil War is considered the first modern war.
2. Describe how a war to preserve the Union became a war to end slavery.
3. Explain how the Civil War transformed the national economy and created a stronger nation-state.
4. Explain how the war effort and leadership problems affected the society and economy of the confederacy.
5. Identify the military and political turning points of the war.
6. Identify the most important wartime "rehearsals" for Reconstruction.

Multiple Choice

1. The example of German immigrant Marcus Spiegel demonstrated that:
   a. freedom motivated the immigration of Irish immigrants, but German immigrants of the mid-nineteenth century came to the United States in pursuit of economic success.
   b. the significant Jewish population in the United States was ambivalent about the issues that caused the Civil War.
   c. the views of average Americans evolved considerably during the course of the Civil War.
   d. Democrats were unwilling to go to war with a Republican president in the White House.
   e. while Jews were few in number, their role at the Battle of Gettysburg made military heroes of many of them.

   ANS: C   TOP: Ethnicity | Introduction: Marcus Spiegel   DIF: Moderate   REF: Full p. 503 | Seagull p. 511   MSC: Applying   OBJ: 2

2. Among the Confederacy's advantages during the Civil War was:
   a. that its rail network was more advanced than the Union's.
   b. its large size, which made it more difficult for the Union to conquer.
   c. that the Lower South had long had significant manufacturing facilities.
   d. its military-aged white male population was slightly higher than the Union's.
   e. that so many of its men volunteered to fight that it never resorted to a draft.

   ANS: B   TOP: Military history | The Two Combatants   DIF: Moderate   REF: Full p. 504 | Seagull p. 511   MSC: Understanding   OBJ: 1

3. *Monitor* and *Merrimac* were:
   a. ironclad ships.
   b. steam locomotives.
   c. battle sites in Virginia.
   d. nicknames of Generals Grant and Lee.
   e. names of rifles.

   ANS: A   TOP: Military history | The Technology of War   DIF: Easy   REF: Full p. 504 | Seagull p. 513   MSC: Remembering   OBJ: 1

4. All of the following are examples of technological changes that helped to make the Civil War a modern war EXCEPT for the:
   a. rifle.
   b. ironclad ship.
   c. observation balloon.
   d. primitive hand grenade.
   e. field telephone.

   ANS: E   TOP: Military history | The Technology of War   DIF: Easy   REF: Full pp. 504–505 | Seagull p. 513   MSC: Understanding   OBJ: 1

5. Approximately how many Union and Confederate soldiers died during the Civil War?
   a. 110,000
   b. 245,000
   c. 440,000
   d. 750,000
   e. 988,000

   ANS: D   TOP: Military history | The Technology of War   DIF: Moderate   REF: Full p. 505 | Seagull p. 514   MSC: Understanding   OBJ: 1

6. At the first Battle of Bull Run:
   a. spectators from the city came with picnic baskets to watch.
   b. the Union won a smashing victory.
   c. both sides suffered more casualties than they did in any other single day during the war.
   d. the Confederates swept northward and briefly captured Washington, D.C.
   e. General Grant made a name for himself.

   ANS: A   TOP: Military history | Social history | The War Begins   DIF: Moderate   REF: Full p. 509 | Seagull p. 516   MSC: Remembering   OBJ: 1

7. Which of the following puts these Civil War battles in the proper chronological order, from first to last?
   I. Antietam
   II. First Bull Run
   III. Spotsylvania and Cold Harbor
   IV. Gettysburg

a. I, III, II, IV
b. II, III, I, IV
c. II, I, IV, III
d. III, IV, I, II
e. IV, II, III, I

ANS: C   TOP: Chronology | The War Begins | The War in the East in 1862 | Gettysburg and Vicksburg | 1864   DIF: Difficult   REF: Full pp. 509, 510, 537 | Seagull pp. 516, 518, 545   MSC: Remembering OBJ: 1

8. Who was offered a command in the Union army, but declined because of his devotion to his native state?
   a. Alexander Stephens
   b. Thomas "Stonewall" Jackson
   c. Jefferson Davis
   d. Robert E. Lee
   e. George Thomas

ANS: D   TOP: Military history | Political history, changes | The War in the East in 1862   DIF: Moderate   REF: Full p. 509 | Seagull p. 518 MSC: Remembering   OBJ: 1

9. The major Confederate army in the East, commanded by Robert E. Lee, was called the Army of:
   a. the Rappahannock.
   b. the Blue Ridge.
   c. Southern Maryland.
   d. the Chesapeake.
   e. Northern Virginia.

ANS: E   TOP: Military history | The War in the East in 1862   DIF: Moderate   REF: Full p. 509 | Seagull p. 550   MSC: Remembering   OBJ: 1

10. At Antietam:
    a. General Lee was successful and pushed north into Pennsylvania.
    b. General McClellan surrendered his troops.
    c. the nation suffered more casualties than on any other day in its history.
    d. the Union's river fleet proved crucial to the outcome.
    e. Lincoln announced the Thirteenth Amendment.

ANS: C   TOP: Military history | The War in the East in 1862   DIF: Moderate   REF: Full p. 510 | Seagull p. 518   MSC: Remembering   OBJ: 1

11. During the first two years of the war, Union forces were generally:
    a. more successful in the West than in the East.
    b. ill-trained, which changed when General McClellan took over in 1863.
    c. successful in all regions in which the war took place.

d. unable to take any territory held by the Confederates.
e. more successful in the East than in the West.

ANS: A   TOP: Military history | The War in the West DIF: Difficult   REF: Full p. 511 | Seagull p. 518 MSC: Understanding   OBJ: 1

12. General George McClellan did all of the following EXCEPT:
    a. mold the Army of the Potomac into an effective fighting machine.
    b. win major victories at Fort Henry and Fort Donelson in Tennessee.
    c. run for president as a Democrat in 1864.
    d. tend to overestimate the size of enemy forces.
    e. command Union forces at the pivotal Battle of Antietam.

ANS: B   TOP: Military history | Political history, changes | The War in the West   DIF: Difficult REF: Full p. 511 | Seagull p. 518 MSC: Understanding   OBJ: 1

13. When did Great Britain abolish slavery in its empire?
    a. 1790s
    b. 1810s
    c. 1830s
    d. 1850s
    e. 1870s

ANS: C   TOP: Chronology | Slavery and the War DIF: Difficult   REF: Full p. 511 | Seagull p. 520 MSC: Remembering   OBJ: 2

14. The last nation in the Western Hemisphere to abolish slavery was:
    a. the United States.
    b. Cuba.
    c. Brazil.
    d. Haiti.
    e. Jamaica.

ANS: C   TOP: Civil rights | Slavery and the War DIF: Difficult   REF: Full p. 511 | Seagull p. 520 MSC: Remembering   OBJ: 2

15. In what year did slavery officially end in the Western Hemisphere?
    a. 1863
    b. 1865
    c. 1874
    d. 1880
    e. 1888

ANS: E   TOP: Chronology | Slavery and the War DIF: Difficult   REF: Full p. 511 | Seagull p. 520 MSC: Remembering   OBJ: 2

16. During the early days of the war, the U.S. Congress adopted a resolution proposed by Senator John Crittenden of Kentucky that:
    a. drafted men into the Union army, the first such draft in U.S. history.
    b. called for the gradual emancipation of slaves throughout the nation.
    c. criticized the civil liberties policies of the Lincoln administration.
    d. affirmed that the Union had no intention of interfering with slavery.
    e. extended the Missouri Compromise line to the eastern border of California.

    ANS: D   TOP: Political history, changes | The Unraveling of Slavery   DIF: Difficult   REF: Full p. 513 | Seagull p. 520   MSC: Remembering
    OBJ: 2

17. Lincoln was hesitant to support abolition early in the war because he:
    a. did not believe slaves could be productive American citizens.
    b. owned slaves himself.
    c. feared losing the support of the slaveholding border states within the Union.
    d. did not want to support the policies of the Radical Republicans.
    e. promised during his 1860 campaign that he was against abolition.

    ANS: C   TOP: Civil rights | Political history, changes | Slavery and the War   DIF: Moderate   REF: Full p. 513 | Seagull p. 520   MSC: Remembering
    OBJ: 2

18. During the Civil War, the term "contraband camps" referred to:
    a. camps in which materials such as rifles and gunpowder were kept.
    b. camps of southern slaves who had escaped from their masters and entered Union lines.
    c. training grounds for the youthful musicians who played to raise the morale of the troops.
    d. holding areas for items seized by customs agents for failure to pay tariffs.
    e. places near battlefields where the Union army temporarily kept Confederate prisoners.

    ANS: B   TOP: Civil rights | Military history | The Unraveling of Slavery   DIF: Moderate   REF: Full p. 513 | Seagull p. 520   MSC: Remembering
    OBJ: 2

19. Which Union general in Missouri decreed freedom to that state's slaves in 1861, a year before Lincoln issued the Emancipation Proclamation?

    a. George McClellan
    b. John Frémont
    c. Phil Sheridan
    d. William Sherman
    e. Ulysses S. Grant

    ANS: B   TOP: Civil rights | Military history | Steps toward Emancipation   DIF: Difficult   REF: Full p. 514 | Seagull p. 521   MSC: Remembering
    OBJ: 2

20. Which of the following is NOT true of Abraham Lincoln's slavery policy during the first two years of the war?
    a. He initially insisted that slavery was irrelevant to the Civil War.
    b. He supported the colonization of freed slaves on an island near Haiti.
    c. He rescinded an emancipation order by a Union general in Missouri.
    d. He proposed gradual, compensated emancipation in the border states.
    e. He proposed a constitutional amendment to abolish slavery immediately.

    ANS: E   TOP: Civil rights | Military history | Steps toward Emancipation   DIF: Difficult   REF: Full p. 514 | Seagull pp. 521–522   MSC: Understanding
    OBJ: 2

21. Lincoln's issuance of an emancipation proclamation:
    a. was delayed on the advice of General George McClellan.
    b. won universal support throughout the North.
    c. led to a strong Republican showing in the congressional and state elections of 1862.
    d. followed the narrow Union victory in the Battle of Antietam.
    e. led Great Britain to recognize the independence of the Confederate States of America.

    ANS: D   TOP: Civil rights | Military history | Lincoln's Decision   DIF: Moderate   REF: Full p. 515 | Seagull pp. 522–523   MSC: Remembering
    OBJ: 2

22. The Emancipation Proclamation of January 1, 1863:
    a. was declared unconstitutional by the U.S. Supreme Court later that year.
    b. did not apply to the border slave states that had not seceded.
    c. freed slaves throughout the United States.
    d. was very popular with voters associated with the Democratic Party.
    e. was cited by Tennessee as the reason it rejoined the Union in 1864.

ANS: B   TOP: Civil rights | Political history, changes | The Emancipation Proclamation
DIF: Moderate   REF: Full p. 516 | Seagull p. 523
MSC: Remembering   OBJ: 2

23. The 54th Massachusetts Volunteer Regiment is best known as:
a. a regiment of free blacks who charged Fort Wagner, South Carolina.
b. the "Irish Brigade," because its members were born in Ireland.
c. the regiment that forced Richmond's surrender.
d. a regiment that was fully integrated, with noncommissioned black and white soldiers fighting side-by-side.
e. the first regiment to see battle in the war.

ANS: A   TOP: Civil rights | Military history | Enlisting Black Troops   DIF: Moderate
REF: Full p. 518 | Seagull p. 526
MSC: Remembering   OBJ: 2

24. During the Civil War, black soldiers:
a. did nothing to dispel racial prejudice with their performance.
b. were mostly northern-born free blacks.
c. performed the same duties as white soldiers from the outset, but at lower pay.
d. helped inspire Republicans to believe that emancipation also demanded equal rights before the law.
e. were allowed into the Union army only in the last year of the war.

ANS: D   TOP: Civil rights | Military history | Political history, changes | The Black Soldier
DIF: Difficult   REF: Full p. 519 | Seagull p. 527
MSC: Understanding   OBJ: 2

25. Beginning in 1863, what did Frederick Douglass urge northern blacks to do?
a. enlist in the Union army
b. embark to Liberia
c. head north to Canada
d. demand voting rights as a condition of supporting the war
e. protest the war until Lincoln promised to end slavery

ANS: A   TOP: Civil rights | Military history | The Black Soldier   DIF: Moderate   REF: Full p. 519 | Seagull p. 527   MSC: Remembering
OBJ: 2

26. Lincoln's vision during the Civil War:
a. was to build a nation-state similar to what Otto von Bismarck was building in Germany and to what Guiseppe Mazzini was building in Italy.
b. was that the American nation embodied a set of universal ideals rooted in political democracy and human freedom.
c. was essentially that of the Democratic Party: an activist federal government building up American industry.
d. allowed for African-Americans to achieve freedom because they already lived in the United States, but did not extend to immigrants.
e. was best expressed in his words, "As He died to make men holy, let us die to make men free."

ANS: B   TOP: Civil rights | Political history, changes | Lincoln's Vision   DIF: Difficult   REF: Full p. 520 | Seagull p. 529   MSC: Understanding   OBJ: 3

27. Lincoln spoke of "a new birth of freedom" for the nation in his:
a. first inaugural address.
b. second inaugural address.
c. preliminary Emancipation Proclamation.
d. Sanitary Commission speech.
e. Gettysburg Address.

ANS: E   TOP: Civil rights | Political history, changes | Lincoln's Vision   DIF: Moderate
REF: Full p. 521 | Seagull p. 529
MSC: Remembering   OBJ: 3

28. During the Civil War, northern Protestant ministers:
a. usually preached sermons that emphasized the needlessness of the war.
b. organized a major pacifist campaign to end the war by Christmas 1862.
c. helped create a civic religion combining Christianity and patriotism.
d. were generally opposed to the goals of the Lincoln administration.
e. raised hundreds of thousands of dollars to assist Confederates in order to show they loved their enemies.

ANS: C   TOP: Political history, changes | Social history | The War and American Religion
DIF: Moderate   REF: Full p. 522 | Seagull p. 530
MSC: Understanding   OBJ: 3

29. With regard to civil liberties during the Civil War, President Lincoln:
a. always let courts and judges have the final say.
b. suspended the writ of habeas corpus.
c. ordered most Democratic newspapers shut down.
d. urged the impeachment of federal judges who opposed him.
e. strictly followed the *Ex parte Milligan* decision rendered in 1866.

ANS: B   TOP: Political history, changes | Liberty in Wartime   DIF: Difficult   REF: Full p. 523 | Seagull p. 532   MSC: Remembering   OBJ: 3

30. In the *Ex parte Milligan* case, the U.S. Supreme Court stated that:
    a. Milligan should be hanged for writing pro-Confederate editorials during the Civil War.
    b. secession was unconstitutional.
    c. accused persons must be tried before civil courts where there were open rather than military tribunals.
    d. a president could order the jailing of civilians for any reason whatsoever during wartime.
    e. Congress, not the president, has the power to suspend the writ of habeas corpus.

ANS: C   TOP: Constitutional history | Military history | Liberty in Wartime   DIF: Difficult   REF: Full p. 523 | Seagull p. 532   MSC: Remembering   OBJ: 3

31. Clement Vallandigham was:
    a. hanged for treason on orders of President Lincoln.
    b. the Confederate general who won the Battle of Chancellorsville against great odds.
    c. the Union general who turned back a Confederate invasion at Gettysburg.
    d. Lincoln's first vice president.
    e. a northern politician banished to the Confederacy.

ANS: E   TOP: Political history, changes | Liberty in Wartime   DIF: Difficult   REF: Full p. 523 | Seagull p. 532   MSC: Remembering   OBJ: 3

32. Economically, the Civil War led to:
    a. a decline in prosperity for North and South alike.
    b. the emergence of a nation-state committed to national economic development.
    c. a tariff reduction to attract foreign goods to make up for the decline in domestic production.
    d. the creation of the Third Bank of the United States, despite opposition from old Jacksonian Democrats.
    e. the building of a transcontinental railroad, completely through private financing.

ANS: B   TOP: Economic development | Government and the Economy   DIF: Moderate   REF: Full p. 524 | Seagull p. 533   MSC: Remembering   OBJ: 3

33. Colonel John Chivington is remembered for:
    a. becoming a martyr when tortured and killed by Sioux warriors.
    b. leading the cavalry charge that turned back a Confederate assault at Shiloh.
    c. his refusal to surrender his Confederate troops until weeks after Lee's final surrender.
    d. organizing a band of pro-Union Creek Indians who fought bravely at Vicksburg.

    e. leading an attack that killed perhaps 400 Indian men, women, and children.

ANS: E   TOP: Ethnicity | Military history | The War and Native Americans   DIF: Difficult   REF: Full p. 525 | Seagull p. 536   MSC: Remembering   OBJ: 3

34. Captains of industry like steel magnate Andrew Carnegie and oil man John D. Rockefeller:
    a. began creating or consolidating their fortunes during the Civil War.
    b. benefited after the war from the respect their military service earned for them.
    c. became important advisers to President Lincoln.
    d. voluntarily provided important resources to the war effort.
    e. made millions bilking southerners who were buying war bonds.

ANS: A   TOP: Economic development | A New Financial System   DIF: Moderate   REF: Full p. 528 | Seagull p. 537   MSC: Remembering   OBJ: 3

35. Which of the following is true of the Confederacy and Native Americans?
    a. Indians were united in their opposition to the Confederacy because of its white supremacist policies.
    b. The Davis administration ordered the Navajo to leave their ancestral territory.
    c. Slaveowning Indians generally supported the Confederacy.
    d. Treating Indian tribes as fully independent nations, the Confederacy sent ambassadors to the Five Civilized Tribes.
    e. Confederate troops massacred Indians on several occasions, most notably at Sand Creek, Texas.

ANS: C   TOP: Ethnicity | Political history, changes | The War and Native Americans   DIF: Moderate REF: Full p. 528 | Seagull p. 536 MSC: Remembering   OBJ: 3

36. "Greenback" was a Civil War-era nickname for:
    a. sailors.
    b. draft dodgers.
    c. members of the Irish Brigade.
    d. paper money.
    e. any Confederate soldier.

ANS: D   TOP: Economic development | A New Financial System   DIF: Moderate   REF: Full p. 528 | Seagull p. 536   MSC: Remembering   OBJ: 3

37. The U.S. Sanitary Commission:
    a. was the first major organization to be run entirely by women.

b. raised money for the families of soldiers on both sides.

c. coordinated war donations on the northern home front.

d. was the nation's first garbage collection agency.

e. introduced the idea of germ theory to Civil War hospitals.

ANS: C   TOP: Social history | Women and the War
DIF: Moderate   REF: Full p. 529 | Seagull p. 537
MSC: Remembering   OBJ: 3

38. During the Civil War, northern white women:

a. staged "bread riots" in major cities to protest food shortages.

b. began obtaining jobs as government clerks.

c. were recruited to sell war bonds door-to-door.

d. were allowed to accompany their husbands into battle if they did not have children.

e. demonstrated outside the White House in favor of the Emancipation Proclamation.

ANS: B   TOP: Social history | Women and the War
DIF: Moderate   REF: Full p. 529 | Seagull p. 537
MSC: Remembering   OBJ: 3

39. Who lobbied for the United States to endorse the First Geneva Convention of 1864?

a. Clara Barton

b. Elizabeth Van Lew

c. Zebulon Vance

d. Bret Harte

e. Harriet Beecher Stowe

ANS: A   TOP: Global awareness | Political history, changes | Social history | Women and the War
DIF: Moderate   REF: Full p. 530 | Seagull pp. 538–539
MSC: Remembering   OBJ: 3

40. Copperheads were:

a. what Republicans called northern opponents of the war.

b. supporters of minting more copper coins to inflate the currency.

c. advocates of creating the Third Bank of the United States.

d. southern whites who opposed the Confederacy.

e. the strongest supporters of emancipation.

ANS: A   TOP: Political history, changes | The Divided North   DIF: Moderate   REF: Full p. 530 | Seagull p. 539   MSC: Remembering   OBJ: 3

41. Which of the following is NOT true of the New York City riots of 1863?

a. They were mostly the doing of Irish immigrants.

b. The introduction of the draft sparked them.

c. Union troops ultimately ended them.

d. Rioters targeted the wealthy and African-Americans.

e. They convinced Lincoln to delay issuing the Emancipation Proclamation.

ANS: E   TOP: Military history | Social history | The Divided North   DIF: Moderate   REF: Full p. 531 | Seagull p. 539   MSC: Understanding   OBJ: 3

42. Which of the following is true of Jefferson Davis and his governing?

a. Although Davis had a poor prewar reputation as an orator, his speechmaking rose to new heights as the Confederacy's president.

b. His administration actually suffered from the Confederacy's lack of political parties.

c. He had Lincoln's common touch, but the lack of newspapers in the South reduced his ability to communicate it.

d. He strongly opposed centralizing authority in the Confederacy's Richmond government.

e. On more than one occasion, Davis, a West Point alumnus, led Confederate troops into battle.

ANS: B   TOP: Political history, changes | Leadership and Government   DIF: Difficult   REF: Full p. 531 | Seagull p. 540   MSC: Understanding OBJ: 4

43. "King Cotton diplomacy" led Great Britain to:

a. find new supplies of cotton outside the South.

b. recognize the independence of the Confederate States of America.

c. repudiate the Emancipation Proclamation.

d. use its warships to break the Union blockade.

e. stage multiple raids from Canada into the Upper Northwest.

ANS: A   TOP: Global awareness | Leadership and Government   DIF: Moderate   REF: Full pp. 531–532 | Seagull p. 540   MSC: Remembering OBJ: 4

44. Which of the following did NOT cause divisions within the Confederacy?

a. the draft, which allowed southerners to be exempt if they owned a certain number of slaves

b. food shortages, especially as the Union tightened its blockade

c. the heavy taxes on planters, who resented paying the majority of the war's costs

d. the decision of the Confederate Congress to issue paper money

e. the impressment, or seizure, of farm produce to feed soldiers

ANS: C   TOP: Economic development | Military history | Economic Problems   DIF: Difficult
REF: Full p. 533 | Seagull p. 541
MSC: Understanding   OBJ: 4

45. Rose Greenhow:
    a. was president of the American National Red Cross.
    b. worked as a nurse in the Union army.
    c. was a Confederate spy in Washington, D.C.
    d. was a Union soldier who hid her gender from the troops.
    e. was a slave under the Emancipation Proclamation.

    ANS: C   TOP: Social history | Women and the Confederacy   DIF: Difficult   REF: Full p. 535 | Seagull p. 542   MSC: Remembering   OBJ: 4

46. Which statement about the Confederacy is FALSE?
    a. Its citizens were not wholly united behind the cause of its independence.
    b. The Confederate nation became far more centralized than the Old South had been.
    c. Social change and internal turmoil engulfed much of the Confederacy.
    d. Its economy was in crisis, and many families fell into poverty and debt.
    e. From the beginning of the war it recruited and deployed thousands of black soldiers.

    ANS: E   TOP: Economic development | Political history, changes | Social history | Black Soldiers for the Confederacy   DIF: Easy   REF: Full p. 535 | Seagull p. 543   MSC: Understanding   OBJ: 4

47. In July 1863, the Union won two key victories that are often identified as turning points in the war. These victories occurred at:
    a. Wilmington, North Carolina, and New Orleans, Louisiana.
    b. Gettysburg, Pennsylvania, and Vicksburg, Mississippi.
    c. Lexington, Kentucky, and Charleston, South Carolina.
    d. Antietam Creek, Maryland, and Appomattox Court House, Virginia.
    e. Fort Donelson, Tennessee, and Cold Harbor, Virginia.

    ANS: B   TOP: Military history | Gettysburg and Vicksburg   DIF: Moderate   REF: Full p. 537 | Seagull pp. 544–545   MSC: Remembering   OBJ: 5

48. The Union's manpower advantage over the Confederacy:
    a. was short-lived once the Confederacy began using slaves as soldiers.
    b. proved essential for the success of Grant's attrition strategy.
    c. was rather slight.
    d. although substantial, did not matter in determining the war's outcome.
    e. existed only because the Union had lower draft requirements than the Confederacy.

    ANS: B   TOP: Military history | 1864   DIF: Easy   REF: Full p. 537 | Seagull pp. 545–546   MSC: Understanding   OBJ: 5

49. In the May and June 1864 battles in Virginia (between the armies of Grant and Lee):
    a. the Union army was forced to retreat down the peninsula in defeat.
    b. Lee's brutality earned him the nickname "the Butcher."
    c. the Confederates launched the heroic but unsuccessful Pickett's Charge.
    d. the Union army, despite high casualties, pressed forward in its campaign.
    e. Grant's men decisively defeated Lee's army, which forced the evacuation of Richmond.

    ANS: D   TOP: Military history | 1864   DIF: Difficult   REF: Full pp. 537–538 | Seagull p. 545   MSC: Understanding   OBJ: 5

50. Which September 1864 event helped Lincoln win reelection as president that November?
    a. Lee's surrender at Appomattox Court House
    b. the Confederate surrender of Savannah
    c. Grant's victory at Vicksburg
    d. McClellan's rout of the Confederates at Seven Pines
    e. Sherman's capture of Atlanta

    ANS: E   TOP: Military history | Political history, changes | 1864   DIF: Difficult   REF: Full pp. 538–539 | Seagull p. 546   MSC: Remembering   OBJ: 5

51. The "Sea Island Experiment" refers to:
    a. northern reformers' efforts to assist former slaves with the transition to freedom.
    b. the Confederacy's trial use of slaves as soldiers along the South Carolina coast.
    c. a U.S. government plan to introduce advanced technology to southern farming in order to decrease the need for slaves.
    d. the unsuccessful effort of General Ulysses Grant to allow former slaves to run their own farms in Mississippi.
    e. the code name for the Confederate navy's submarine-building program.

    ANS: A   TOP: Civil rights | The Sea Island Experiment   DIF: Moderate   REF: Full pp. 539–540 | Seagull p. 546   MSC: Remembering   OBJ: 6

52. Rehearsals for reconstruction during the Civil War demonstrated that:
    a. African-Americans were so used to slavery, they would work only when forced to do so.
    b. the main aspiration of former slaves was the ownership of their own land.
    c. African-Americans were willing to sign contracts forcing them to labor if they were treated more fairly than they had been under slavery.

d. former slaves would not work for wages, only for land.

e. African-Americans had no interest in their political future, only in their economic well-being.

ANS: B   TOP: Civil rights | The Sea Island Experiment   DIF: Moderate   REF: Full p. 540 | Seagull p. 547   MSC: Applying   OBJ: 6

53. The Wade-Davis Bill in 1864:
a. received strong support from congressional Democrats but not from Republicans.
b. called for at least two-thirds of a southern state's voters to take a loyalty oath.
c. showed Radical Republicans' frustration with Lincoln's Reconstruction plan.
d. was the model for Lincoln's later Ten-Percent Plan.
e. failed to receive sufficient votes in the Senate and therefore died.

ANS: C   TOP: Political history, changes | The Politics of Wartime Reconstruction   DIF: Difficult REF: Full p. 541 | Seagull p. 548   MSC: Applying OBJ: 6

54. General Sherman marched from Atlanta to the sea in order to:
a. link up with Grant's army.
b. engage Lee in battle.
c. demoralize the South's civilian population.
d. secure Richmond for the Union.
e. free Union prisoners at Andersonville.

ANS: C   TOP: Military history | Victory at Last DIF: Moderate   REF: Full p. 541 | Seagull pp. 548–549   MSC: Remembering   OBJ: 6

55. The Thirteenth Amendment:
a. abolished slavery throughout the United States.
b. was strongly supported by Democrats in 1864.
c. set up a gradual plan of emancipation.
d. defined U.S. citizenship to include African-Americans.
e. specifically gave black men the right to vote.

ANS: A   TOP: Constitutional history | Victory at Last DIF: Moderate   REF: Full p. 541 | Seagull p. 549 MSC: Remembering   OBJ: 6

56. Lincoln's second inaugural address:
a. blamed the South for the war.
b. described the Civil War as divine punishment.
c. blamed the North for the war.
d. proved to be his final speech.
e. called for black suffrage.

ANS: B   TOP: Political history, changes | Victory at Last   DIF: Difficult   REF: Full pp. 541, 513 | Seagull p. 549   MSC: Understanding   OBJ: 6

57. A major part of the Anaconda Plan was:
a. a naval blockade of the South.
b. the storming of Richmond early in the war.
c. Lee's decision to move his forces north in 1862.
d. to assassinate Lincoln.
e. Sherman's march to the sea.

ANS: A   TOP: Military history | Mobilizing Resources   DIF: Moderate   REF: Full p. 543 | Seagull p. 551   MSC: Understanding   OBJ: 1

58. In his last speech, Lincoln said what regarding postwar policy?
a. Democracy demanded that African-Americans should play leading roles in southern politics.
b. Southern whites would never concede defeat, so Reconstruction must be mild.
c. He would defer to Radical Republicans in Congress.
d. There should be at least limited black suffrage.
e. Large southern planters should be made to pay dearly for having caused the war.

ANS: D   TOP: Political history, changes | Victory at Last   DIF: Moderate   REF: Full p. 543 | Seagull p. 550   MSC: Understanding   OBJ: 6

59. How was Ulysses Grant received in Europe during his tour in the 1870s?
a. He was regarded as a mediocre military leader.
b. He was praised as a "Hero of Freedom."
c. He was heralded as greater than Lincoln.
d. He was criticized widely for his "war of attrition."
e. He was booed by workers as a capitalist tool.

ANS: B   TOP: Global awareness | The War and the World   DIF: Moderate   REF: Full pp. 543–544 | Seagull p. 551   MSC: Understanding   OBJ: 2

60. Which of the following was NOT an effect of the Civil War?
a. It shifted national power from southern slaveholders to northern capitalists.
b. It dramatically increased the power of the federal government.
c. It placed the challenge of protecting and defending African-American freedom on the national agenda.
d. It greatly expanded the powers of the presidency and reduced the influence of Congress.
e. It hastened the destruction of Lincoln's America—of the small farmer and independent producer—in favor of the industrial giant.

ANS: D   TOP: Political history, changes | The War in American History   DIF: Difficult   REF: Full p. 544 | Seagull p. 551   MSC: Understanding OBJ: 6

61. Frederick Douglass viewed the abolition of slavery as:
    a. not the end of the nation's work, but the beginning of a new phase of it.
    b. the crowning achievement of his life.
    c. proof that the nation really did not suffer from racial prejudice.
    d. confirmation that Lincoln deserved to be remembered as a Christ-like martyr.
    e. an important step that must be followed by the colonization of freed slaves outside the United States.

    ANS: A   TOP: Civil rights | The War in American History   DIF: Moderate   REF: Full p. 545 | Seagull p. 552   MSC: Understanding   OBJ: 6

True or False

1. On both sides, the outbreak of war stirred powerful feelings of patriotism.

   ANS: T   TOP: Social history | The Two Combatants DIF: Easy   REF: Full p. 504 | Seagull p. 511 MSC: Understanding   OBJ: 1

2. Overall, the number of soldiers who died in the Civil War was approximately equivalent to the number of American soldiers who died during World War II.

   ANS: F   TOP: Military history | The Technology of War   DIF: Moderate   REF: Full p. 506 | Seagull p. 514   MSC: Understanding   OBJ: 1

3. Medical knowledge had made great strides in the first half of the nineteenth century; thus few soldiers died from wounds, infections, or diseases during the Civil War.

   ANS: F   TOP: Military history | The Technology of War   DIF: Easy   REF: Full p. 506 | Seagull p. 514 MSC: Understanding   OBJ: 1

4. The Union naval blockade was very effective early in the war.

   ANS: F   TOP: Military history | Mobilizing Resources   DIF: Moderate   REF: Full p. 508 | Seagull p. 515   MSC: Remembering   OBJ: 1

5. Abraham Lincoln realized that his armies had to capture the Confederate capital, Richmond, in order to win the war.

   ANS: F   TOP: Military history | Military Strategies DIF: Moderate   REF: Full p. 508 | Seagull p. 516 MSC: Understanding   OBJ: 1

6. Lincoln's primary purpose in raising troops in 1861 to put down the southern rebellion was to restore the Union.

   ANS: T   TOP: Military history | Political history, changes | Slavery and the War   DIF: Easy   REF: Full p. 513 | Seagull p. 520   MSC: Remembering   OBJ: 2

7. It was clear to most people from the beginning of the war that the war meant the end of slavery.

   ANS: F   TOP: Civil rights | The Unraveling of Slavery   DIF: Moderate   REF: Full p. 513 | Seagull p. 520   MSC: Understanding   OBJ: 2

8. In the early days of the war, northern military commanders returned fugitive slaves to their owners.

   ANS: T   TOP: Civil rights | Military history | The Unraveling of Slavery   DIF: Moderate REF: Full p. 513 | Seagull p. 520 MSC: Remembering   OBJ: 2

9. Due to Lincoln's announcement of the Emancipation Proclamation, Republicans suffered reverses in the 1862 mid-term elections.

   ANS: T   TOP: Political history, changes | Lincoln's Decision   DIF: Moderate   REF: Full p. 515 | Seagull p. 523   MSC: Remembering   OBJ: 2

10. The Emancipation Proclamation represented a turning point in Lincoln's own thinking.

    ANS: T   TOP: Civil rights | Political history, changes | The Emancipation Proclamation   DIF: Moderate REF: Full p. 517 | Seagull p. 523 MSC: Understanding   OBJ: 2

11. Fewer than 50,000 blacks served in the Union army during the war.

    ANS: F   TOP: Military history | Enlisting Black Troops   DIF: Moderate   REF: Full p. 518 | Seagull p. 525   MSC: Remembering   OBJ: 2

12. Black Union soldiers captured by the Confederates faced sale into slavery or immediate execution.

    ANS: T   TOP: Civil rights | Military history | The Black Soldier   DIF: Moderate   REF: Full p. 519 | Seagull p. 527   MSC: Remembering   OBJ: 2

13. Both the Confederacy and the Union violated their citizens' civil liberties during the war.

    ANS: T   TOP: Political history, changes | Liberty in Wartime   DIF: Easy   REF: Full p. 523 | Seagull pp. 531–532   MSC: Understanding   OBJ: 3

14. In a letter to his brother, South Carolina plantation owner Thomas Drayton feared whites in the South were going to be enslaved.

    ANS: T   TOP: Primary document analysis | Voices of Freedom   DIF: Moderate   REF: Full p. 526 | Seagull p. 534   MSC: Understanding   OBJ: 4

15. Lincoln raised the money to pay for the war mostly through an income tax.

ANS: F TOP: Economic development | A New Financial System DIF: Difficult REF: Full p. 528 | Seagull p. 536 MSC: Remembering OBJ: 3

16. Women took to factory jobs and nursing during the war.

ANS: T TOP: Social history | Women and the War DIF: Easy REF: Full pp. 528–529 | Seagull p. 537 MSC: Remembering OBJ: 3

17. The New York City draft riots, begun as an attempt to resist the draft, turned into an assault on the city's black population.

ANS: T TOP: Civil rights | Social history | The Divided North DIF: Moderate REF: Full p. 531 | Seagull p. 539 MSC: Understanding OBJ: 3

18. The provision of the draft law allowing individuals to provide a substitute or buy their way out of the army caused widespread indignation.

ANS: T TOP: Social history | The Divided North DIF: Easy REF: Full p. 531 | Seagull p. 539 MSC: Understanding OBJ: 3

19. King Cotton diplomacy was intended to promote economic self-sufficiency in the South and force Spain to intervene on the side of the Confederacy.

ANS: F TOP: Economic development | Global awareness | Leadership and Government DIF: Easy REF: Full p. 531 | Seagull p. 540 MSC: Understanding OBJ: 4

20. Desertion was not a major problem in the Confederate army as it was in the Union army.

ANS: F TOP: Military history | Economic Problems DIF: Easy REF: Full pp. 533–534 | Seagull pp. 541–542 MSC: Understanding OBJ: 4

21. Major General George Pickett led a charge, aptly known as Pickett's Charge, during the Second Battle at Bull Run.

ANS: F TOP: Military history | Gettysburg and Vicksburg DIF: Moderate REF: Full p. 537 | Seagull pp. 544–545 MSC: Remembering OBJ: 5

22. Backed by many Radical Republicans for a time in 1864, presidential hopeful John Frémont ran on a campaign that called for the confiscation of the land of leading Confederates.

ANS: T TOP: Political history, changes | 1864 DIF: Moderate REF: Full p. 539 | Seagull p. 546 MSC: Understanding OBJ: 5

23. The Sea Islands experiment demonstrated how ex-slaves could be gainfully employed, educated, and well provided for.

ANS: T TOP: Civil rights | The Sea Island Experiment DIF: Moderate REF: Full pp. 539–540 | Seagull p. 547 MSC: Applying OBJ: 6

24. In Lincoln's Ten-Percent Plan, blacks played a predominant role in Reconstruction.

ANS: F TOP: Civil rights | Political history, changes | The Politics of Wartime Reconstruction DIF: Moderate REF: Full p. 541 | Seagull p. 548 MSC: Remembering OBJ: 6

25. The Wade-Davis Bill was the Democrats' proposed Reconstruction plan.

ANS: F TOP: Political history, changes | The Politics of Wartime Reconstruction DIF: Moderate REF: Full p. 541 | Seagull p. 548 MSC: Remembering OBJ: 6

26. The Thirteenth Amendment, like the rest of the Constitution to that point, never mentioned the words "slave" or "slavery."

ANS: F TOP: Constitutional history | Victory at Last DIF: Moderate REF: Full p. 541 | Seagull p. 549 MSC: Remembering OBJ: 6

Short Answer

Identify and give the historical significance of each of the following terms, events, and people in a paragraph or two.

1. King Cotton diplomacy
2. black soldiers
3. Copperheads
4. Homestead Act
5. Gettysburg Address
6. transcontinental railroad
7. Emancipation Proclamation
8. First Bull Run
9. New York draft riots
10. Sea Island experiment
11. Reconstruction plans
12. women and the Confederacy

Essay Questions

1. What did the Union soldiers believe they were fighting for? What did the Confederate soldiers believe they were fighting for?

ANS: Answers will vary TOP: Military history | Political history, changes | The Two Combatants | The Public and the War | The Inner Civil War DIF: Moderate MSC: Understanding OBJ: 2 / 3 / 4

2. What was the basic premise of the Confederate government? What advantages did the Confederacy have, and why did its leaders think victory would be theirs?

   ANS: Answers will vary   TOP: Military history | Political history, changes | Leadership and Government | The Inner Civil War | Military Strategies | The Technology of War | Mobilizing Resources
   DIF: Moderate   MSC: Understanding   OBJ: 1 / 4

3. Compare and contrast the leadership abilities of wartime presidents Abraham Lincoln and Jefferson Davis. How significant was each man's leadership to the course of the war?

   ANS: Answers will vary   TOP: Military history | Political history, changes | Leadership and Government | Lincoln's Vision | Liberty in Wartime | The Emancipation Proclamation   DIF: Moderate
   MSC: Analyzing   OBJ: 2 / 3 / 4

4. How did the war affect the economies of the North and of the South?

   ANS: Answers will vary   TOP: Economic development | Military history | The North's Transformation | Government and the Economy | Economic Problems   DIF: Moderate   MSC: Analyzing
   OBJ: 3 / 4

5. What strategy did General Grant ultimately adopt to achieve victory for the Union, and why did he do so? Why was his strategy criticized?

   ANS: Answers will vary   TOP: Military history | Political history, changes | 1864   DIF: Moderate
   MSC: Understanding   OBJ: 1 / 5

6. Describe the changes in Lincoln's thinking that led to the Civil War being waged as a total war.

   ANS: Answers will vary   TOP: Military history | Political history, changes | Military Strategies
   DIF: Moderate   MSC: Understanding   OBJ: 1 / 2 / 3 / 5

7. Using Lincoln's speech at Sanitary Fair in 1864 (excerpted in "Voices of Freedom"), explain how Lincoln defined liberty. How does this speech reflect a change in his thinking from 1861? Why do you think Lincoln had to change his thinking in order to achieve victory in this war?

   ANS: Answers will vary   TOP: Civil rights | Military history | Political history, changes | Primary document analysis | Voices of Freedom | Lincoln's Decision | Liberty and Union   DIF: Moderate
   MSC: Analyzing   OBJ: 1 / 2 / 3 / 5

8. Blacks eagerly signed up for service in the army and navy after the Emancipation Proclamation was issued. Describe the life of a black soldier. How did it differ from the experiences of black sailors? Overall, how important were black servicemen in the outcome of the war? Finally, discuss what fighting in the war meant to these men.

   ANS: Answers will vary   TOP: Civil rights | Military history | Political history, changes | Enlisting Black Troops | The Black Soldier   DIF: Moderate
   MSC: Analyzing   OBJ: 2 / 6

9. Frederick Douglass declared, "The work does not *end* with the abolition of slavery, but only *begins*." In a thoughtful essay, discuss what you foresee as the work that will need to be done to secure freedom and liberty to the ex-slaves. Is emancipation enough? Why or why not?

   ANS: Answers will vary   TOP: Civil rights | Political history, changes | Social history | The Sea Island Experiment | Wartime Reconstruction in the West | The Politics of Wartime Reconstruction | The Divided North   DIF: Difficult   MSC: Creating
   OBJ: 2 / 6

10. Lincoln observed in 1864 that "we all declare for liberty but in using the same *word* we do not all mean the same *thing*." He continued to explain what the North meant and what the South meant, and how victory meant a national norm as defined by the North. Illustrate how liberty would come to be understood for the nation after the Civil War and analyze whether the abolishment of slavery was enough to propel the United States to finally exist as its founding documents suggested it should.

    ANS: Answers will vary   TOP: Civil rights | Political history, changes | Social history | Primary document analysis | Liberty and Union | Lincoln's Vision | Voices of Freedom | The Politics of Wartime Reconstruction | The Sea Island Experiment | Wartime Reconstruction in the West | The Divided North
    DIF: Difficult   MSC: Analyzing   OBJ: 2 / 6

11. Discuss and compare the dress rehearsals for Reconstruction in South Carolina, Louisiana, and Mississippi from a civil rights and economic perspective. Analyze Lincoln's initial plans for restoring the Union.

    ANS: Answers will vary   TOP: Civil rights | Economic development | Political history, changes | Social history | The Sea Island Experiment | Wartime Reconstruction in the West | The Politics of Wartime Reconstruction   DIF: Moderate
    MSC: Analyzing   OBJ: 6

CHAPTER 15

"What Is Freedom?": Reconstruction, 1865–1877

This chapter concentrates on the history of Reconstruction. Opening with an explanation of the origins of General William T. Sherman's Special Field Order 15, which set aside forty-acre plots of land for former slave families, the chapter explores what freedom meant to newly free African-Americans and how white American society responded to emancipation. There were many meanings of freedom for blacks, and they relished various opportunities to express their liberation from slavery. Land ownership became a contentious issue as blacks were ultimately denied free access to land. One of the "Voices of Freedom" selections highlights this controversy with a petition from freedmen to President Andrew Johnson. The devastation of the Civil War also caused many white farmers to face poverty as tenant farmers and sharecroppers. The chapter discusses the national political developments that led from President Johnson's lenient plan to the Radical Reconstruction designed by congressional Republicans. In response to Johnson's many presidential pardons of ex-Confederates and to the South's implementation of Black Codes, Republicans in Congress fought back with the Civil Rights Act of 1866, the Fourteenth Amendment, and the Reconstruction Act. Johnson resisted and was impeached by the House, but avoided being removed from office by the Senate. The Fifteenth Amendment finished the Radical Republicans' Reconstruction agenda, but it split the feminist movement because it failed to give the vote to women. The chapter's second "Voices of Freedom" piece touches on the frustrations of feminist Elizabeth Cady Stanton with her fellow abolitionist Gerrit Smith's stand on woman suffrage. The chapter then looks at how Reconstruction shaped southern politics—and at how southern politics shaped Reconstruction. Once Radical Reconstruction accorded suffrage rights to southern black men, African-Americans voted and ran for office. Blacks held over 2,000 public offices during Reconstruction, and there were four-

teen black members of the U.S. House and two black U.S. senators. Many white southerners, however, felt threatened by black political power, and the Ku Klux Klan began a campaign of terror and violence that sought to intimidate Republican voters, white and black. After the Klan was abolished through the efforts of President Ulysses Grant, white Democrats continued efforts to "redeem" the South from perceived corruption, misgovernment, and northern and black control. Reconstruction ended in 1877 after a compromise was made between the Republicans and Democrats over the disputed 1876 presidential election.

CHAPTER OUTLINE

I. Introduction: Sherman Land

II. The Meaning of Freedom
    A. Blacks and the Meaning of Freedom
        1. The destruction of slavery made freedom the central question on the nation's agenda.
        2. African-Americans' understanding of freedom was shaped by their experience as slaves and observation of the free society around them.
        3. Blacks relished the opportunity to demonstrate their liberation from the regulations (significant and trivial) associated with slavery.
           a. Many moved to southern cities and towns as they seemed to have more freedoms.
    B. Families in Freedom
        1. The family was central to the postemancipation black community.
           a. Widows of black soldiers successfully collected pensions.
        2. Freedom subtly altered relationships within the family.

a. Emancipation increased the power of black men within the family.

b. Black women withdrew from work as field laborers and house servants to the domestic sphere.

   i. Eventually many black women would go to work because of dire poverty.

C. Church and School

1. The rise of the independent black church, with Methodists and Baptists commanding the largest followings, redrew the religious map of the South.

   a. Black ministers came to play a major role in politics.

2. Blacks of all ages flocked to the schools established by northern missionary societies, the Freedmen's Bureau, and groups of ex-slaves.

   a. Education also took place outside the classroom.

   b. Black colleges such as Fisk, Hampton, and Howard started.

D. Political Freedom

1. The right to vote inevitably became central to the former slaves' desire for empowerment and equality.

   a. Being denied suffrage meant "the stigma of inferiority."

2. To demonstrate their patriotism, blacks throughout the South organized Fourth of July celebrations.

   a. For years, many white southerners would remain indoors on this holiday.

E. Land, Labor, and Freedom

1. Former slaves' ideas of freedom were directly related to land ownership.

   a. Many former slaves insisted that through their unpaid labor, they had acquired a right to the land.

2. Ex-slaves' definition of freedom resembled whites'.

   a. Self-ownership

   b. Family stability

   c. Religious liberty

   d. Political participation

   e. Economic autonomy

F. Masters without Slaves

1. The South's defeat was complete and demoralizing.

   a. Planter families faced profound changes.

2. Most planters defined black freedom in the narrowest manner, as a privilege, not as a right.

   a. Whites felt the slave was "free, but free only to labor."

G. The Free Labor Vision

1. The victorious Republican North tried to implement its own vision of freedom.

   a. Free labor would result in the ex-slaves being more productive.

2. The Freedmen's Bureau was to establish a working free labor system.

H. The Freedmen's Bureau

1. The task of the Bureau—establishing schools, providing aid to the poor and aged, settling disputes, etc.—was daunting, especially since it had fewer than 1,000 agents.

   a. Direction of O. O. Howard

   b. Experiment in government social policy that seems more comfortable as part of twentieth century's New Deal or Great Society

2. The Bureau's achievements in some areas, notably education and health care, were striking.

   a. Nearly 3,000 schools reported to the Bureau.

I. The Failure of Land Reform

1. Blacks wanted land of their own, not jobs on plantations.

2. President Andrew Johnson ordered nearly all land in federal hands returned to its former owners.

3. Because no land distribution took place, the vast majority of rural freedpeople remained poor and without property during Reconstruction.

   a. Many worked on white-owned plantations, often for their former owners.

J. Toward a New South

1. Sharecropping came to dominate the cotton South and much of the tobacco belt.

2. Sharecropping initially arose as a compromise between blacks' desire for land and planters' desire for labor discipline.

   a. For blacks it was preferable to gang labor, but over time sharecropping became oppressive.

K. The White Farmer

1. The aftermath of the war hurt small white farmers.

   a. Crop-lien system (use of crop as collateral for loans from merchants for supplies)

   b. White farmers increased cotton cultivation, cotton prices plummeted, and they found themselves unable to pay back loans.

2. Both black and white farmers found themselves caught in the sharecropping and crop-lien systems.

   a. A far higher percentage of black farmers than white farmers rented land.

      b. Every census from 1880 to 1940 counted more white than black sharecroppers.

  L. The Urban South

    1. Southern cities experienced remarkable growth after the Civil War.

      a. Rise of a new middle class

  M. Aftermaths of Slavery

    1. The Reconstruction-era debates over transitioning from slavery to freedom had parallels in other Western Hemisphere countries where emancipation occurred in the nineteenth century.

      a. Generally, planters encouraged or required former slaves to work on plantations, while former slaves sought to assert independence in their daily lives.

      b. Planters sought other laborers to replace their slave forces (British Caribbean planters brought workers from India, while southern U.S. planters recruited some workers from China).

    2. Only in the United States did former slaves gain political rights quickly.

      a. Right to vote

III. The Making of Radical Reconstruction

  A. Andrew Johnson

    1. Johnson identified himself as the champion of the "honest yeomen" and a foe of large planters.

    2. Johnson lacked Lincoln's political skills and keen sense of public opinion.

    3. Johnson believed that African-Americans had no role to play in Reconstruction.

  B. The Failure of Presidential Reconstruction

    1. Johnson's plan for Reconstruction offered pardons to the white southern elite.

    2. Johnson's plan allowed the new state governments a free hand in managing local affairs.

    3. At first many northerners were willing to give Johnson's plan a chance.

      a. But conduct of white southerners turned the Republican North against the plan.

  C. The Black Codes

    1. Southern governments began passing new laws that restricted the freedom of blacks.

    2. These new laws violated free labor principles and called forth a vigorous response from the Republican North.

      a. Few groups of rebels in history have been treated more leniently than the defeated Confederates.

      b. North was not motivated by a desire to "punish," but to ensure emancipation of slaves.

  D. The Radical Republicans

    1. Radical Republicans called for the dissolution of Johnson's state governments and then new ones established that did not have "rebels" in power, and which gave blacks the right to vote.

    2. The Radicals fully embraced the expanded powers of the federal government born of the Civil War.

      a. Charles Summer

      b. Thaddeus Stevens

    3. Thaddeus Stevens's most cherished aim was to confiscate the land of disloyal planters and divide it among former slaves and northern migrants to the South.

      a. His plan was too radical for most others in Congress.

  E. The Origins of Civil Rights

    1. Most Republicans were moderates, not radicals.

    2. Senator Lyman Trumbull of Illinois proposed two bills to modify Johnson's policy:

      a. Extend the life of the Freedmen's Bureau

      b. Civil Rights Bill (equality before the law was central; it sought to overturn Black Codes)

    3. Johnson vetoed both bills.

      a. It would centralize power in national government and deprive states the ability to regulate themselves.

      b. It discriminated "against the white race."

    4. Congress passed the Civil Rights Bill over his veto and later extended the life of the Freedmen's Bureau.

  F. The Fourteenth Amendment

    1. It placed in the Constitution the principle of citizenship for all persons born in the United States and empowered the federal government to protect the rights of all Americans.

      a. It did not provide for black suffrage.

    2. The Fourteenth Amendment produced an intense division between the parties (Democrats unanimously opposed it, most Republicans were for it).

  G. The Reconstruction Act

    1. Johnson campaigned against the Fourteenth Amendment in the 1866 midterm elections.

    2. All southern states except for Tennessee refused to ratify the Fourteenth Amendment.

    3. In March 1867, over Johnson's veto, Congress adopted the Reconstruction Act, which:

      a. Divided the South into five military districts

      b. Called for creation of new southern state governments, with black men given the vote

4. The Reconstruction Act thus began Radical Reconstruction, which lasted until 1877.

H. Impeachment and the Election of Grant

   1. To demonstrate his dislike for the Tenure of Office Act, Johnson removed the secretary of war from office in 1868.

   2. Johnson was impeached and the Senate fell one vote short from removing him from office.

     a. Some Republicans voted to keep Johnson based on his promise not to interfere anymore with Republican policies.

I. The Fifteenth Amendment

   1. Republican Ulysses S. Grant won the 1868 presidential election.

   2. Congress approved the Fifteenth Amendment in 1869.

   3. It provided for black suffrage.

     a. Had many loopholes (states could discriminate on bases other than race: illiteracy, inability to pay a tax, etc.)

     b. Did not extend suffrage to women

J. The Great Constitutional Revolution

   1. The laws and amendments of Reconstruction reflected the intersection of two products of the Civil War era—a newly empowered national state and the idea of a national citizenry enjoying equality before the law.

   2. Before the Civil War, American citizenship had been closely linked to race.

     a. Naturalization Act of 1790 had limited naturalization process to whites.

     b. *Dred Scott* decision of 1857 had denied blacks U.S. citizenship.

   3. The new amendments also transformed the relationship between the federal government and the states.

   4. In twentieth century, Fourteenth Amendment played key role in many Supreme Court decisions that expanded rights of American citizens.

K. Boundaries of Freedom

   1. That the United States was a "white man's government" had been a widespread belief before the Civil War.

   2. Reconstruction Republicans' belief in universal rights also had its limits.

     a. Asian immigrants were still excluded from the naturalization process.

L. The Rights of Women

   1. The destruction of slavery led feminists to search for ways to make the promise of free labor real for women.

   2. Other feminists debated how to achieve "liberty for married women."

M. Feminists and Radicals

   1. Talk of woman suffrage and redesigning marriage found few sympathetic male listeners.

   2. Some feminists (Elizabeth Cady Stanton, Susan B. Anthony) opposed the Fifteenth Amendment because it did not enfranchise women; other feminists (Abby Kelley and Lucy Stone) supported the Amendment as a step toward woman suffrage.

   3. The divisions among feminists led to the creation of two hostile women's rights organizations that would not reunite until the 1890s.

     a. National Woman Suffrage Association (led by Stanton)

     b. American Woman Suffrage Association (led by Stone)

   4. Despite their limitations, the Fourteenth and Fifteenth Amendments and the Reconstruction Act of 1867 marked a radical departure in American and world history.

IV. Radical Reconstruction in the South

A. The Tocsin of Freedom

   1. Among the former slaves, the passage of the Reconstruction Act inspired an outburst of political organization.

   2. Blacks used direct action to remedy long-standing grievances.

     a. Sit-ins, strikes and speaking tours

   3. The Union League aided blacks in the public sphere.

   4. By 1870, the Union had been restored and southern states had Republican majorities.

B. The Black Officeholder

   1. Two thousand African-Americans occupied public offices during Reconstruction.

     a. Fourteen elected to U.S. House of Representatives

     b. Two elected to U.S. Senate

   2. The presence of black officeholders and their white allies made a real difference in southern life.

     a. Blacks received fair trials.

     b. More fairness in local governing

   3. Majority of state and local black officeholders were former slaves.

C. Carpetbaggers and Scalawags

   1. Carpetbaggers were northern-born white Republicans who often held political office in the South.

   2. Scalawags were southern-born white Republicans.

     a. Some were wealthy (e.g., James Alcorn, a Mississippi planter).

  b. Most had been up-country non-slaveholders before the Civil War and some had been Unionists during the war.
  3. Small group of Scalawags helped swing some state and local elections for Republicans.
D. Southern Republicans in Power
  1. Southern Republican governments established the South's first state-supported public schools.
  2. The new governments also pioneered civil rights legislation.
  3. Republican governments took steps to strengthen the position of rural laborers and to promote the South's economic recovery.
E. The Quest for Prosperity
  1. During Reconstruction, every state helped to finance railroad construction.
    a. Saw this as key to economic development in the region
    b. But economic development was weak.
  2. Investment opportunities in the West lured more northern investors than southern investors, and economic development remained weak in the South.
  3. More success was found with local biracial governing.

V. The Overthrow of Reconstruction
A. Reconstruction's Opponents
  1. Corruption did exist during Reconstruction, but it was not confined to a race, region, or party.
  2. Opponents could not accept the idea of former slaves voting, holding office, and enjoying equality before the law.
B. "A Reign of Terror"
  1. Republican presence in South led to more organized opposition and violence, by 1868.
  2. Secret societies sprang up in the South with the aim of preventing blacks from voting and destroying the organization of the Republican Party.
  3. The Ku Klux Klan was organized in 1866.
    a. It launched what one victim called a "reign of terror" against Republican leaders, black and white.
    b. Example: Colfax, Louisiana, massacre (1873)
  4. Congress and President Grant, with the passage of three Enforcement Acts in 1870 and 1871, put an end to the Ku Klux Klan by 1872.
C. The Liberal Republicans
  1. The North's commitment to Reconstruction waned during the 1870s.

  2. Some Republicans, alienated from Grant by corruption in his administration, formed the Liberal Republican Party.
    a. Horace Greeley
  3. Liberal Republicans believed that power in the South should be returned to the region's "natural leaders."
  4. Grant easily defeated Greeley, the Liberal Republican and Democratic Party candidate, to win reelection in 1782.
D. The North's Retreat
  1. The Liberal attack on Reconstruction contributed to a resurgence of racism in the North.
    a. *The Prostrate State* depicted corruption in South Carolina and blamed African-American politicians.
  2. The 1873 depression also distracted the North from Reconstruction.
  3. The Supreme Court whittled away at Congress's guarantees of black rights.
    a. *Slaughterhouse Cases* (1873)
    b. *United States v. Cruikshank* (1876)
E. The Triumph of the Redeemers
  1. Redeemers claimed to have "redeemed" the white South from corruption, misgovernment, and northern and black control.
    a. Violence occurred in broad daylight.
    b. Grant refused to provide federal help to stop violence.
F. The Disputed Election and Bargain of 1877
  1. The election between Rutherford B. Hayes (Republican) and Samuel Tilden (Democrat) was very close, with disputed electoral votes from Florida, Louisiana, and South Carolina.
  2. Congress set up a special Electoral Commission to determine winner of disputed votes.
  3. Behind the scenes, Hayes made a bargain to allow southern white Democrats to control the South if his election was accepted.
  4. The compromise led to Hayes's election and the Democrats' having a free hand in the South.
G. The End of Reconstruction
  1. Reconstruction ended in 1877, but in some states blacks continued to vote and hold office until the 1890s.
  2. Even while it lasted, however, Reconstruction revealed some tensions inherent in the nineteenth-century discussions of freedom.

SUGGESTED DISCUSSION QUESTIONS

- There were many proposals for land reform. Describe the various plans, why they did not work, and the consequences of their failure. Discuss the petition to Andrew Johnson in "Voices of Freedom."

- What course did Presidential Reconstruction take? How did the South respond?

- What did freedom mean to the blacks? How did they express their newfound freedom?

- What made the Radical Republicans "radical"?

- Discuss Charles Sumner's remark that rather than being a threat to liberty, the federal government had become "the custodian of freedom."

- Discuss why the Fifteenth Amendment did not include a reference to sex or race. What were Elizabeth Cady Stanton's frustrations as indicated in "Voices of Freedom"?

- Why did Reconstruction come to end in 1877?

- It is early 1866 and congressional Republicans are already strongly criticizing Andrew Johnson's plan of Reconstruction. Have the students form small groups and draft their own plans for Reconstruction. Have each student present his or her plan to the class and explain the proposed objectives, outcomes, and perceived advantages over Johnson's plan.

SUPPLEMENTAL WEB AND VISUAL RESOURCES

Andrew Johnson

www.millercenter.virginia.edu/academic/americanpresident/johnson

The Miller Center of Public Affairs from the University of Virginia has an extensive site about Johnson and his administration.

Freedmen's Bureau

freedmensbureau.com/

A dot-com site filled with useful information and helpful links. The website has the bureau's records, as well as articles and genealogical information.

Ku Klux Klan

www.pbs.org/wnet/jimcrow/stories_org_kkk.html

This is the PBS site for the program *The Rise and Fall of Jim Crow.*

Reconstruction

www.pbs.org/wgbh/amex/reconstruction/

PBS's American Experience website for *Reconstruction: The Second Civil War* offers information on the video as well as related classroom material, documents, background, and so forth.

SUPPLEMENTAL PRINT RESOURCES

Abbott, Richard H. *For Free Press and Equal Rights: Republican Newspapers in the Reconstruction South.* Athens, GA: University of Georgia Press, 2004.

Ash, Stephen V. *A Year in the South, 1865: The True Story of Four Ordinary People Who Lived Through the Most Tumultuous Twelve Months in American History.* Hampshire, UK: Palgrave Macmillan, 2002.

Bigham, Darrel E. *On Jordan's Banks: Emancipation and Its Aftermath in the Ohio River Valley.* Lexington, KY: University Press of Kentucky, 2005.

Bond, James. *No Easy Walk to Freedom: Reconstruction and the Ratification of the Fourteenth Amendment.* Westport, CT: Greenwood Publishing, 1997.

Brown, Elsa Barkley. "Negotiating and Transforming the Public Sphere: African American Political Life in the Transition from Slavery to Freedom." *Public Culture* 7 (1994): 107–146.

Cimbala, Paul. *Under the Guardianship of the Nation: The Freedmen's Bureau and the Reconstruction of Georgia, 1865–1870.* Athens, GA: University of Georgia Press, 1997.

Duncan, Russell. *Freedom's Shore: Tunis Campbell and the Georgia Freedmen.* Athens, GA: University of Georgia Press, 1987.

Foner, Eric. *Nothing But Freedom: Emancipation and Its Legacy.* Baton Rouge, LA: Louisiana State University Press, 1983.

Lane, Charles. *The Day Freedom Died: The Colfax Massacre, the Supreme Court, and the Betrayal of Reconstruction.* New York: Henry Holt, 2008.

McPherson, James. *Abraham Lincoln and the Second American Revolution.* New York: Oxford University Press, 1991.

Nelson, William E. *The Fourteenth Amendment: From Political Principle to Judicial Doctrine.* Cambridge, MA: Harvard University Press, 1988.

O'Donovan, Susan Eva. *Becoming Free in the Cotton South.* Cambridge, MA: Harvard University Press, 2007.

Quigley, David. *Second Founding: New York City, Reconstruction, and the Making of American Democracy.* New York: Hill and Wang, 2003.

Ross, Michael A. "Justice Miller's Reconstruction: The Slaughter-House Cases, Health Codes, and Civil Rights in New Orleans, 1861–1873." *Journal of Southern History* 64 (1998): 649–676.

TEST BANK

Matching

TEST I

___ 1. Thaddeus Stevens

___ 2. Andrew Johnson

___ 3. Charles Sumner

___ 4. Rutherford B. Hayes

___ 5. Edwin Stanton

___ 6. Elizabeth Cady Stanton

___ 7. Lyman Trumbull

___ 8. Hiram Revels

___ 9. Ulysses S. Grant
___ 10. Horace Greeley
___ 11. Blanche Bruce
___ 12. James Pike

a. second black U.S. senator
b. proposed the Civil Rights Bill of 1866
c. Presidential Reconstruction
d. Liberal Republican's presidential candidate
e. *The Prostrate State*
f. Radical Republican congressman from Pennsylvania
g. Whiskey Ring
h. ended Reconstruction
i. National Woman Suffrage Association
j. Radical Republican senator from Massachusetts
k. first black U.S. senator
l. secretary of war

Answer Key: f, c, j, h, l, i, b, k, g, d, a, e

TEST 2

___ 1. Special Field Order 15
___ 2. carpetbaggers
___ 3. Howard University
___ 4. scalawag
___ 5. Black Codes
___ 6. Enforcement Acts
___ 7. Redeemers
___ 8. Compromise of 1877
___ 9. Freedmen's Bureau
___ 10. Ku Klux Klan
___ 11. Whiskey Ring
___ 12. impeachment

a. restrictions placed on freed blacks in South
b. scandal in the Grant administration
c. origin of "40 acres and a mule"
d. northern-born Republicans in the South during Reconstruction
e. ended Reconstruction
f. government agency that helped blacks in South
g. black school in Washington, D.C.
h. public official charged with wrongdoing
i. southern-born white Republican
j. targeted Ku Klux Klan
k. Democrats who took control in South during 1870s
l. terrorist organization

Answer Key: c, d, g, i, a, j, k, e, f, l, b, h

Learning Objectives

1. Identify the visions of freedom the former slaves and slaveholders pursued in the postwar South.

2. Describe the sources, goals and compelling visions for Reconstruction.

3. Describe the social and political effects of Radical Reconstruction in the South.

4. Explain the main factors in both the North and South for the overthrow of Reconstruction.

Multiple Choice

1. General William T. Sherman's Special Field Order 15:
   a. gave freed slaves the right to find family members who had been sold.
   b. set aside the Sea Islands and forty-acre tracts of land in South Carolina and Georgia for black families.
   c. gave forty acres and a mule to blacks who wished to move to the unsettled American Southwest.
   d. gave his men instructions to burn their way through the southern interior to the Atlantic coast.
   e. established the Freedmen's Bureau to help blacks make the transition from slavery to freedom.

   ANS: B   TOP: Civil rights | Economic development | Introduction: Sherman Land   DIF: Moderate
   REF: Full p. 549 | Seagull p. 555
   MSC: Remembering   OBJ: 1

2. Which of the following best describes the black response to the ending of the Civil War and the coming of freedom?
   a. Sensing the continued hatred of whites toward them, most blacks wished to move back to Africa.
   b. Most blacks stayed with their old masters because they were not familiar with any other opportunities.
   c. Blacks adopted different ways of testing their freedom, including moving about, seeking kin, and rejecting older forms of deferential behavior.
   d. Desiring better wages, most blacks moved to the northern cities to seek factory work.
   e. Most blacks were content working for wages and not owning their own land because they believed that they had not earned the right to just be given land from the government.

   ANS: C   TOP: Civil rights | Social history | Blacks and the Meaning of Freedom   DIF: Easy
   REF: Full p. 550 | Seagull p. 557
   MSC: Understanding   OBJ: 1

3. How did emancipation affect the structure of the black family?
   a. Men and women maintained equality within the household, making black families far more matrilineal than white families.
   b. Men often remained at home while women went out and labored—a major shift from their roles while in slavery.

c. Black women adopted the domestic roles that white women had long had, but retained their duties in the fields and in the workplace.

d. The black family became more like the typical white family, with men as the breadwinners and women as the homemakers.

e. Emancipation did not lead to any changes in the black family's structure.

ANS: D   TOP: Civil rights | Social history | Families in Freedom   DIF: Difficult   REF: Full p. 551 | Seagull pp. 557–558   MSC: Understanding   OBJ: 1

4. During Reconstruction, the role of the church in the black community:

a. declined because ex-slaves realized they owed their freedom to fellow human beings, not to God.

b. changed as African-Americans joined white churches rather than worshipping separately.

c. declined as other black-run institutions became more central in African-American life.

d. was central, as African-Americans formed their own churches.

e. became less important, as northern white churches moved into the South and took in most blacks.

ANS: D   TOP: Civil rights | Cultural history | Social history | Church and School   DIF: Easy   REF: Full p. 551 | Seagull p. 558   MSC: Remembering   OBJ: 1

5. Which denominations had the largest followings among blacks after the Civil War?

a. Anglican and Catholic

b. Congregational and Presbyterian

c. Methodist and Baptist

d. Lutheran and Methodist

e. Episcopal and Baptist

ANS: C   TOP: Cultural history | Church and School DIF: Moderate   REF: Full p. 551 | Seagull p. 558 MSC: Remembering   OBJ: 1

6. Howard University is well known as:

a. the first medical school to admit women.

b. the first black university in Mississippi.

c. the oldest university in New England.

d. a black university in Washington, D.C.

e. the law school where Abraham Lincoln earned his degree.

ANS: D   TOP: Cultural history | Church and School DIF: Moderate   REF: Full p. 551 | Seagull p. 558 MSC: Remembering   OBJ: 1

7. Anything less than _____ would betray the Civil War's meaning, black spokesmen insisted.

a. new southern railroads

b. full citizenship

c. woman suffrage

d. farming jobs

e. due process

ANS: B   TOP: Political history, changes | Political Freedom   DIF: Moderate   REF: Full p. 552 | Seagull p. 559   MSC: Understanding   OBJ: 1

8. For most former slaves, freedom first and foremost meant:

a. railroading building.

b. jobs.

c. land ownership.

d. voting.

e. jury duty.

ANS: C   TOP: Economic development | Political history, changes | Masters without Slaves
DIF: Difficult   REF: Full p. 552 | Seagull p. 559
MSC: Understanding   OBJ: 1

9. How did the Civil War affect planter families?

a. For the first time, some of them had to do physical labor.

b. They lost their slaves but were otherwise unaffected.

c. Few lost loved ones because they were able to avoid military service.

d. They endured immediate problems, but their economic revival was quick.

e. Since they defined freedom broadly, they got along well with their ex-slaves.

ANS: A   TOP: Social history | Masters without Slaves
DIF: Moderate   REF: Full p. 554 | Seagull pp. 560–561   MSC: Understanding   OBJ: 1

10. The northern vision of the Reconstruction-era southern economy included all of the following EXCEPT:

a. emancipated African-Americans would labor more intensively than ever because they had the same opportunities for advancement that northern whites had long enjoyed.

b. northern capital and migrants would energize the southern economy.

c. the Freedmen's Bureau would establish a workable labor system.

d. the labor system would be as close to slavery as possible, thereby assuring high productivity.

e. the South would eventually resemble the North.

ANS: D   TOP: Economic development | The Free Labor Vision   DIF: Easy   REF: Full p. 554 | Seagull p. 561   MSC: Understanding   OBJ: 1

11. The Freedmen's Bureau:

a. was badly administered because director O. O. Howard lacked military experience.

b. won much southern white support because it consistently supported the planters in disputes with former slaves.

c. made notable achievements in improving African-American education and health care.

d. carried out a successful program of distributing land to every former slave family.

e. enjoyed the strong support of President Andrew Johnson in its work on behalf of civil rights.

ANS: C TOP: Civil rights | Social history | The Freedmen's Bureau   DIF: Moderate   REF: Full p. 555 | Seagull p. 562   MSC: Understanding   OBJ: 1

12. Sharecropping:
   a. meant that African-Americans were paid their share daily for doing specific tasks.
   b. was a compromise between African-Americans' desire for discipline and planters' desire to learn to do physical labor.
   c. was most popular in the old rice-plantation areas of South Carolina and Georgia.
   d. became more popular because of rising farm prices that brought increased prosperity.
   e. was preferred by African-Americans to gang labor (because they were less subject to supervision).

ANS: E TOP: Economic development | Social history | Toward a New South   DIF: Moderate   REF: Full p. 557 | Seagull p. 564   MSC: Understanding OBJ: 1

13. The crop-lien system:
   a. applied only to African-American farmers.
   b. became better as farm prices increased in the 1870s.
   c. enabled yeoman farmers to continue to function under the same system as before the Civil War.
   d. annoyed bankers and merchants who resented how it made them dependent on farmers.
   e. kept many sharecroppers in a state of constant debt and poverty.

ANS: E TOP: Economic development | Social history | The White Farmer   DIF: Difficult   REF: Full p. 558 | Seagull p. 564   MSC: Understanding   OBJ: 1

14. White farmers in the late nineteenth-century South:
   a. by and large owned their own land.
   b. included many sharecroppers involved in the crop-lien system.
   c. refused to grow cotton because it had been a "slave crop."
   d. were all enormously prosperous following the end of the Civil War.
   e. saw their debts decrease as crop prices went up from 1870 to 1900.

ANS: B TOP: Economic development | Social history | The White Farmer   DIF: Easy   REF: Full p. 558 | Seagull p. 564   MSC: Understanding   OBJ: 1

15. During Reconstruction, southern cities:
   a. enjoyed newfound prosperity as merchants traded more frequently with the North.
   b. were as poverty-stricken as rural southern areas.
   c. benefited from the building of a transcontinental railroad from Washington, D.C., to Los Angeles.
   d. benefited as rice and tobacco production markedly grew.
   e. experienced major population losses as blacks trekked north in the Great Migration.

ANS: A TOP: Economic development | The Urban South   DIF: Difficult   REF: Full p. 558 | Seagull p. 565   MSC: Remembering   OBJ: 1

16. What did the freedmen request in their "Petition of Committee on Behalf of the Freedmen to Andrew Johnson" in 1865?
   a. the right to purchase a homestead
   b. an opportunity to attend a black college
   c. the purchase of some mules
   d. help reuniting their family that had been sold
   e. the right to vote

ANS: A TOP: Primary document analysis | Voices of Freedom   DIF: Moderate   REF: Full p. 560 | Seagull p. 566   MSC: Understanding   OBJ: 1

17. With the end of slavery in the British Caribbean, more than 100,000 laborers came from where to fill the labor shortage?
   a. South Carolina
   b. Canada
   c. Mexico
   d. Australia
   e. India

ANS: E TOP: Economic development | Aftermaths of Slavery   DIF: Difficult   REF: Full p. 562 | Seagull p. 565   MSC: Remembering   OBJ: 1

18. Which of the following is NOT true about Andrew Johnson?
   a. Born into poverty, as a youth he worked as a tailor's apprentice.
   b. Through hard work, he rose into the planter class and then became a successful politician.
   c. He was the only senator from a seceded state to refuse to leave the U.S. Senate.
   d. Lincoln's party nominated him for vice president in 1864 in hopes of extending its organization into the South.
   e. He identified as the champion of the "honest yeomen."

ANS: B TOP: Political history, changes | Andrew Johnson   DIF: Difficult   REF: Full p. 562 | Seagull pp. 568–569   MSC: Understanding   OBJ: 2

19. Andrew Johnson:
    a. simply continued Lincoln's Reconstruction policies.
    b. agreed with Lincoln that some African-Americans should be allowed suffrage rights.
    c. won the Democratic presidential nomination in 1868, but narrowly lost the election.
    d. lacked Lincoln's political skills and keen sense of public opinion.
    e. displayed a great ability to compromise, very much like Lincoln.

    ANS: D   TOP: Political history, changes | Andrew Johnson   DIF: Easy   REF: Full p. 562 | Seagull p. 569   MSC: Understanding   OBJ: 2

20. The southern Black Codes:
    a. allowed the arrest on vagrancy charges of former slaves who failed to sign yearly labor contracts.
    b. allowed former slaves to testify in court against whites and to serve on juries.
    c. were some of the first laws adopted as part of Radical Reconstruction in 1867.
    d. were denounced by President Johnson and declared unconstitutional by the Supreme Court.
    e. pleased northerners because they saw that the rule of law was returning to the South.

    ANS: A   TOP: Civil rights | The Black Codes
    DIF: Moderate   REF: Full p. 563 | Seagull p. 570
    MSC: Remembering   OBJ: 2

21. Radical Republicans:
    a. tended to come from the border states that had seen most of the vicious fighting during the Civil War.
    b. wanted legitimate democracy in the South, with power to be shared by planters and freed slaves.
    c. fought Andrew Johnson from the day he entered the White House.
    d. fully embraced the expanded powers of the federal government born during the Civil War.
    e. agreed on the need to end slavery but disagreed with one another over whether the freed slaves were entitled to civil rights.

    ANS: D   TOP: Political history, changes | The Radical Republicans   DIF: Moderate   REF: Full p. 564 | Seagull p. 571   MSC: Remembering   OBJ: 1

22. Which of the following is NOT true of Thaddeus Stevens?
    a. He was an outspoken opponent of slavery before the Civil War.
    b. During the Civil War, he called for arming African-Americans.
    c. He proposed confiscating land from disloyal planters and dividing it among former slaves.
    d. He represented Massachusetts in the U.S. Senate.
    e. He was a strong supporter of racial equality during Reconstruction.

    ANS: D   TOP: Civil rights | Political history, changes | The Radical Republicans   DIF: Difficult
    REF: Full p. 564 | Seagull p. 571
    MSC: Understanding   OBJ: 2

23. The most ambitious, but least successful, of the Radical Republicans' aims was:
    a. land reform.
    b. black suffrage.
    c. federal protection of civil rights.
    d. public education.
    e. reunification of the Union.

    ANS: A   TOP: Political history, changes | The Radical Republicans   DIF: Easy   REF: Full p. 565 | Seagull p. 571   MSC: Understanding   OBJ: 1

24. The Civil Rights Bill of 1866:
    a. was proposed by border-state Democrats.
    b. provided African-Americans with the right to vote.
    c. defined the rights of American citizens without regard to race.
    d. allowed states to determine essential citizenship standards.
    e. won the support of President Andrew Johnson.

    ANS: C   TOP: Civil rights | Political history, changes | The Origins of Civil Rights
    DIF: Moderate   REF: Full p. 565 | Seagull p. 572
    MSC: Remembering   OBJ: 2

25. When Congress sent Andrew Johnson the Civil Rights Bill of 1866, he:
    a. signed it, creating an irreparable breach between himself and the Republicans.
    b. argued that it discriminated against whites.
    c. contended that it gave too much authority to the states.
    d. won widespread public approval for his response.
    e. suggested that it did not go far enough to secure racial equality.

    ANS: B   TOP: Civil rights | Political history, changes | The Origins of Civil Rights
    DIF: Moderate   REF: Full p. 565 | Seagull p. 572
    MSC: Understanding   OBJ: 2

26. The Fourteenth Amendment:
    a. passed despite the opposition of Charles Sumner.
    b. specifically defined suffrage as one of the civil rights to which freedpeople were entitled.
    c. represented a compromise between the moderate and conservative positions on race.
    d. marked the most important change in the U.S. Constitution since the Bill of Rights.
    e. placed into the U.S. Constitution an essential holding of the *Dred Scott* decision.

ANS: D   TOP: Civil rights | Constitutional history | The Fourteenth Amendment   DIF: Moderate   REF: Full p. 566 | Seagull p. 573   MSC: Understanding   OBJ: 2

27. In March 1867, Congress began Radical Reconstruction by adopting the _____, which created new state governments and provided for black male suffrage in the South.
   a. Fourteenth Amendment
   b. Fifteenth Amendment
   c. Civil Rights Act of 1867
   d. Sumner-Stevens Act
   e. Reconstruction Act

   ANS: E   TOP: Political history, changes | The Reconstruction Act   DIF: Difficult   REF: Full p. 567 | Seagull p. 573   MSC: Remembering   OBJ: 2

28. What early 1868 action by Andrew Johnson sparked his impeachment by the U.S. House of Representatives?
   a. He fired Secretary of State William Seward, an ally of Radical Republicans.
   b. He vetoed a bill to extend the life of the Freedmen's Bureau.
   c. He bribed a Republican senator to support his Reconstruction policies.
   d. He defiantly released a letter showing he had given support to the Confederacy in 1863.
   e. He allegedly violated the Tenure of Office Act.

   ANS: E   TOP: Political history, changes | Impeachment and the Election of Grant   DIF: Difficult   REF: Full p. 567 | Seagull p. 574   MSC: Remembering   OBJ: 2

29. Why was Andrew Johnson acquitted on charges of impeachment?
   a. Johnson's lawyers assured moderate Republicans that he would behave for the rest of his term, so several voted to acquit him.
   b. No one would testify against him.
   c. Leading Radical Republican Benjamin Wade brilliantly managed the president's defense.
   d. Ulysses Grant urged Republicans to acquit Johnson because convicting him might hurt Grant's chances in the presidential election.
   e. Many feared a constitutional crisis because, without a vice president in office, no one knew who would succeed Johnson as president.

   ANS: A   TOP: Political history, changes | Impeachment and the Election of Grant   DIF: Moderate   REF: Full p. 567 | Seagull p. 574   MSC: Remembering   OBJ: 2

30. "Waving the bloody shirt" referred to:
   a. a powerful symbol of Ku Klux Klan violence against African-Americans.
   b. a Democratic campaign prop that reminded voters that Republicans had been responsible for the Civil War.
   c. a Republican attempt to associate Democrats with secession and treason.
   d. a sign of surrender that southern whites used to signify their loss of power.
   e. Andrew Johnson's use of Abraham Lincoln's death for political purposes.

   ANS: C   TOP: Political history, changes | Impeachment and the Election of Grant   DIF: Moderate   REF: Full p. 567 | Seagull p. 574   MSC: Remembering   OBJ: 2

31. For the 1868 Democratic presidential ticket, Horatio Seymour and Francis Blair Jr. had a campaign motto of:
   a. Liberty, Equality, and the Southern Way.
   b. Forgive and Heal. White and Black Men Should Work Together.
   c. Civil Rights for All.
   d. This Is a White Man's Country. Let White Men Rule.
   e. I "See More" Peace and Prosperity Ahead with Real Reconstruction.

   ANS: D   TOP: Civil rights | Political history, changes | Impeachment and the Election of Grant   DIF: Difficult   REF: Full p. 567 | Seagull p. 574   MSC: Remembering   OBJ: 2

32. All of the following are true of passage of the Fifteenth Amendment EXCEPT:
   a. it split the feminist movement into two major organizations.
   b. the Democratic Party bitterly opposed it.
   c. it led the American Anti-Slavery Society to disband.
   d. it opened the door to voting restrictions not based on race.
   e. it aided the election of Ulysses Grant to the presidency in 1868.

   ANS: E   TOP: Constitutional history | The Fifteenth Amendment   DIF: Difficult   REF: Full p. 568 | Seagull p. 575   MSC: Understanding   OBJ: 2

33. The Fifteenth Amendment:
   a. sought to guarantee that one could not be denied suffrage rights based on race.
   b. made states responsible for determining all voter qualifications.
   c. granted women the right to vote in federal but not state elections.
   d. was endorsed by President Andrew Johnson.
   e. was drafted by Susan B. Anthony.

   ANS: A   TOP: Constitutional history | The Fifteenth Amendment   DIF: Moderate   REF: Full p. 568 | Seagull p. 575   MSC: Remembering   OBJ: 2

34. During Reconstruction, those like Elizabeth Cady Stanton and Lucy Stone who supported a woman's right to vote:
    a. all endorsed the Fifteenth Amendment even though it did not guarantee female suffrage.
    b. all opposed the Fifteenth Amendment because it did not guarantee female suffrage.
    c. found themselves divided over whether or not to support the Fifteenth Amendment.
    d. strongly supported the Fifteenth Amendment because it did guarantee female suffrage.
    e. refused to take a position on the Fifteenth Amendment because it did not define citizenship.

    ANS: C   TOP: Constitutional history | Social history | Feminists and Radicals   DIF: Difficult   REF: Full p. 571 | Seagull p. 578   MSC: Understanding OBJ: 2

35. The U.S. Supreme Court's decision in the 1873 case in which Myra Bradwell challenged an Illinois statute excluding women from practicing law:
    a. was the first time the Court interpreted the Fourteenth Amendment as establishing gender equality.
    b. was a severe blow to the idea of "separate spheres" for men and women.
    c. resulted the following year in congressional passage of the groundbreaking Legal Practice Act.
    d. demonstrates that, while racial definitions of freedom were changing, gendered ones still existed.
    e. was praised by Bradwell, who went on to become the first woman on the Illinois Supreme Court.

    ANS: D   TOP: Constitutional history | Social history | Feminists and Radicals   DIF: Difficult   REF: Full pp. 571–572 | Seagull p. 578   MSC: Understanding OBJ: 2

36. With the beginning of Radical Reconstruction, southern African-Americans in the late 1860s and early 1870s took direct action to remedy long-standing grievances. These actions included:
    a. sit-ins that helped to integrate horse-drawn streetcars in southern cities.
    b. protest marches that desegregated public school systems in all the Upper South states.
    c. violent attacks to intimidate Democratic voters from participating in politics.
    d. the creation for the first time of all-black churches.
    e. a series of lawsuits that resulted in the U.S. Supreme Court's declaring segregation unconstitutional.

    ANS: A   TOP: Civil rights | The Tocsin of Freedom DIF: Difficult   REF: Full p. 572 | Seagull p. 579 MSC: Understanding   OBJ: 3

37. Hiram Revels and Blanche Bruce were the first two black:
    a. members of the U.S. House of Representatives.
    b. governors.
    c. mayors of southern towns.
    d. U.S. senators.
    e. federal judges.

    ANS: D   TOP: Political history, changes | The Black Officeholder   DIF: Moderate   REF: Full p. 573 | Seagull p. 580   MSC: Remembering   OBJ: 3

38. Black officeholders during Reconstruction:
    a. were extremely rare.
    b. were entirely carpetbaggers and scalawags.
    c. helped ensure a degree of fairness in treatment of African-American citizens.
    d. were limited to local offices.
    e. demonstrated that whites had lost all of their political power in the South.

    ANS: C   TOP: Civil rights | The Black Officeholder DIF: Moderate   REF: Full p. 574 | Seagull p. 581 MSC: Understanding   OBJ: 3

39. During Reconstruction, southern state governments helped to finance:
    a. railroads.
    b. canals.
    c. telegraph lines.
    d. interstate roads.
    e. colonization of freedmen and freedwomen.

    ANS: A   TOP: Political history, changes | The Quest for Prosperity   DIF: Easy   REF: Full p. 574 | Seagull p. 583   MSC: Remembering   OBJ: 3

40. Most of those termed "scalawags" during Reconstruction had been:
    a. owners of large southern plantations before the Civil War.
    b. non-slaveholding white farmers from the southern up-country prior to the Civil War.
    c. enslaved African-Americans before emancipation.
    d. Union soldiers during the war, but then they decided to stay in the South.
    e. Confederate officers and Confederate government officials during the Civil War.

    ANS: B   TOP: Political history, changes | Carpetbaggers and Scalawags   DIF: Moderate REF: Full p. 575 | Seagull p. 581   MSC: Remembering OBJ: 3

41. Southern Republicans during Reconstruction:
    a. excluded former Confederates from their ranks.
    b. established the South's first state-supported schools.

c. redistributed most former plantation lands to freedmen and poor whites.

d. helped elect African-American governors in four states.

e. ran the most corrupt governments in American history.

ANS: B   TOP: Political history, changes | Southern Republicans in Power   DIF: Difficult   REF: Full p. 575 | Seagull p. 582   MSC: Remembering OBJ: 3

42. Which of the following was NOT an accomplishment of southern governments run by Republicans during Reconstruction?

a. state-supported public schools

b. widespread transformation of plantations into black-owned farms

c. pioneering civil rights legislation

d. finance of railroad construction in the region

e. tax incentives to attract northern manufacturers to invest in the region

ANS: B   TOP: Political history, changes | Southern Republicans in Power | The Quest for Prosperity DIF: Difficult   REF: Full pp. 575, 576 | Seagull pp. 582–583   MSC: Remembering   OBJ: 3

43. The Whiskey Ring scandal took place during the administration of:

a. Abraham Lincoln.

b. Andrew Johnson.

c. Ulysses Grant.

d. Rutherford Hayes.

e. Chester Arthur.

ANS: C   TOP: Political history, changes | Reconstruction's Opponents   DIF: Moderate REF: Full p. 577 | Seagull p. 583 MSC: Remembering   OBJ: 4

44. The bloodiest act of violence during Reconstruction took place in _____ in 1873, where armed whites killed hundreds of former slaves, including fifty militia members who had surrendered.

a. York County, South Carolina,

b. Marietta, Georgia,

c. Lynchburg, Virginia,

d. Colfax, Louisiana,

e. Guilford County, North Carolina,

ANS: D   TOP: Civil rights | "A Reign of Terror" DIF: Difficult   REF: Full p. 578 | Seagull p. 585 MSC: Remembering   OBJ: 4

45. The Enforcement Acts, passed by Congress in 1870 and 1871, were designed to:

a. end Reconstruction by allowing state governments to oversee citizenship rights.

b. stop the activities of terrorist groups such as the Ku Klux Klan.

c. enforce the Emancipation Proclamation in the Confederate states.

d. increase the authority of the Freedmen's Bureau.

e. eliminate racial discrimination in public spaces such as hotels and theaters.

ANS: B   TOP: Civil rights | Political history, changes | "A Reign of Terror"   DIF: Moderate REF: Full p. 578 | Seagull p. 585 MSC: Remembering   OBJ: 4

46. The Liberal Republican movement in 1872:

a. sought stronger action to assure the political and social rights of African-Americans in the South.

b. was led by President Grant as a way of countering a Democratic resurgence in the southern states.

c. was successful in electing Rutherford B. Hayes president of the United States that year.

d. initially had little to do with Reconstruction but encouraged opposition to Grant's policies in the South.

e. drew most of its strength from southern black leaders such as James S. Pike and Albion Tourgée.

ANS: D   TOP: Political history, changes | The Liberal Republicans   DIF: Difficult   REF: Full p. 579 | Seagull p. 586   MSC: Understanding   OBJ: 4

47. *The Prostrate State* depicts:

a. an ailing slave who is unable to live long enough to see emancipation.

b. South Carolina under allegedly corrupt Negro rule during Reconstruction.

c. an economically weak South unable to contribute to the national economy.

d. a terrorized black community during the reign of the Ku Klux Klan.

e. an apathetic Congress that has given up on Reconstruction after 1870.

ANS: B   TOP: Political history, changes | The North's Retreat   DIF: Difficult   REF: Full p. 580 | Seagull p. 586   MSC: Understanding   OBJ: 4

48. The U.S. Supreme Court ruled in the Slaughterhouse Cases that:

a. most rights of citizens are under the control of state governments rather than the federal government.

b. states cannot interfere with vigorous federal enforcement of a broad array of civil rights guaranteed by the Fourteenth Amendment.

c. the federal government has sole authority under the Commerce Clause to regulate the meatpacking industry.

d. voting rights of African-Americans under the Fifteenth Amendment cannot be abridged or denied by any state.

e. Reconstruction had progressed too far and was now officially ended.

ANS: A   TOP: Constitutional history | The North's Retreat   DIF: Difficult   REF: Full pp. 581–582 | Seagull p. 587   MSC: Understanding   OBJ: 4

49. In 1875, when Mississippi governor Adelbert Ames asked President Grant for help because white rifle clubs had openly assaulted and murdered Republicans, Grant:
    a. immediately sent troops to assist the governor.
    b. arrested the white men responsible for the terror.
    c. commended Ames for his swift actions.
    d. accused Ames of falsifying reports in order to harm Democrats.
    e. told Ames that the northern public was "tired out" with southern problems.

    ANS: E   TOP: Political history, changes | The Triumph of the Redeemers   DIF: Moderate   REF: Full p. 582 | Seagull p. 588   MSC: Remembering   OBJ: 4

50. In the 1870s, who claimed to have saved the white South from the corruption and misgovernment of northern and black officials?
    a. Republicans
    b. Carpetbaggers
    c. Redeemers
    d. Scalawags
    e. Ulysses Grant

    ANS: C   TOP: Political history, changes | The Triumph of the Redeemers   DIF: Moderate   REF: Full p. 582 | Seagull p. 587   MSC: Remembering   OBJ: 4

51. The election of 1876:
    a. was won by Rutherford B. Hayes, by a landslide.
    b. was finally decided by the Supreme Court.
    c. marked the final stage of Reconstruction, which ended in 1880.
    d. was tainted by claims of fraud in Florida, South Carolina, and Louisiana.
    e. was won by Ulysses S. Grant, by a narrow count.

    ANS: D   TOP: Political history, changes | The Disputed Election and Bargain of 1877   DIF: Difficult   REF: Full p. 583 | Seagull pp. 588–589   MSC: Remembering   OBJ: 4

52. The Bargain of 1877:
    a. allowed Samuel Tilden to become president.
    b. led to the appointment of a southerner as postmaster general.

c. marked a compromise between Radical and Liberal Republicans.
d. called for the passage of the Fifteenth Amendment.
e. was made by Grant to prevent his impeachment over the Whiskey Ring.

ANS: B   TOP: Political history, changes | The Disputed Election and Bargain of 1877   DIF: Difficult   REF: Full p. 583 | Seagull p. 589   MSC: Remembering   OBJ: 4

53. The civil rights era of the 1950s and 1960s is sometimes called the:
    a. Equality Era.
    b. Gilded Age.
    c. Socialist Era.
    d. Information Age.
    e. Second Reconstruction.

    ANS: E   TOP: Civil rights | The End of Reconstruction   DIF: Moderate   REF: Full p. 583 | Seagull p. 590   MSC: Remembering   OBJ: 4

54. The two maps of the Barrow Plantation demonstrate:
    a. that little changed in the South after the Civil War.
    b. the African-American commitment to education.
    c. that slaves tried to move as far away as possible from their old masters.
    d. that African-Americans had no interest in building their own churches.
    e. that African-Americans were content to live in their old slave quarters.

    ANS: B   TOP: Primary document analysis | Church and School   DIF: Moderate   REF: Full p. 589 | Seagull p. 596   MSC: Understanding   OBJ: 1

True or False

1. Black ministers during Reconstruction played a major role in politics, holding some 250 public offices.

   ANS: T   TOP: Cultural history | Political history, changes | Church and School   DIF: Moderate   REF: Full p. 551 | Seagull p. 558   MSC: Remembering   OBJ: 1

2. The Civil War was devastating to the South, which lost nearly one-fifth of its white adult male population.

   ANS: T   TOP: Military history | Social history | Masters without Slaves   DIF: Easy   REF: Full p. 553 | Seagull p. 560   MSC: Remembering   OBJ: 1

3. Because of land redistribution, the vast majority of rural freedmen and freedwomen prospered during Reconstruction.

ANS: F   TOP: Economic development | Social history | The Failure of Land Reform   DIF: Easy
REF: Full p. 556 | Seagull p. 563
MSC: Understanding   OBJ: 1

4. By the mid-1870s, white farmers were cultivating as much as 80 percent of the region's cotton crop.

ANS: F   TOP: Economic development | Social history | The White Farmer   DIF: Moderate   REF: Full p. 558 | Seagull p. 564   MSC: Remembering   OBJ: 1

5. By and large, white voters in the South returned prominent Confederates and members of the old elite to power during Presidential Reconstruction.

ANS: T   TOP: Political history, changes | The Failure of Presidential Reconstruction   DIF: Moderate
REF: Full p. 563 | Seagull p. 569   MSC: Understanding
OBJ: 2

6. Compared to rebels in the rest of world history, the rebels of the defeated Confederacy were treated very harshly.

ANS: F   TOP: Social history | The Black Codes
DIF: Easy   REF: Full p. 563 | Seagull p. 570
MSC: Remembering   OBJ: 2

7. Thaddeus Stevens's most cherished aim was to confiscate the land of disloyal planters and divide it among former slaves and northern migrants to the South.

ANS: T   TOP: Political history, changes | Social history | The Radical Republicans   DIF: Moderate
REF: Full p. 565 | Seagull p. 571   MSC: Remembering
OBJ: 2

8. The Civil Rights Act of 1866 became the first major law in American history to be passed over a presidential veto.

ANS: T   TOP: Civil rights | Political history, changes | The Origins of Civil Rights   DIF: Moderate
REF: Full p. 566 | Seagull p. 572   MSC: Remembering
OBJ: 2

9. With the passage of the Fourteenth Amendment, all people born in the United States were automatically citizens.

ANS: T   TOP: Constitutional history | The Fourteenth Amendment   DIF: Moderate   REF: Full p. 566 | Seagull p. 572   MSC: Remembering   OBJ: 2

10. The Senate, following the House's impeachment vote, removed Andrew Johnson from office.

ANS: F   TOP: Political history, changes | Impeachment and the Election of Grant   DIF: Easy
REF: Full p. 567 | Seagull p. 574   MSC: Remembering
OBJ: 2

11. The 1868 presidential campaign did not appeal to racism but only to economic concerns.

ANS: F   TOP: Civil rights | Impeachment and the Election of Grant   DIF: Moderate   REF: Full pp. 567–568 | Seagull pp. 574–575   MSC: Understanding   OBJ: 2

12. Lucy Stone favored the Fifteenth Amendment and established the American Woman Suffrage Association.

ANS: T   TOP: Constitutional history | Social history | Feminists and Radicals   DIF: Moderate
REF: Full p. 571 | Seagull p. 578
MSC: Remembering   OBJ: 2

13. When the Union was restored by 1870, the southern states had Democratic majorities.

ANS: F   TOP: Political history, changes | "The Tocsin of Freedom"   DIF: Moderate   REF: Full p. 573 | Seagull p. 580   MSC: Remembering   OBJ: 3

14. Black suffrage made little difference in the South as very few blacks voted or ran for public office during Reconstruction.

ANS: F   TOP: Civil rights | Political history, changes | The Black Officeholder   DIF: Easy   REF: Full p. 573 | Seagull p. 580   MSC: Understanding
OBJ: 3

15. In 1870, Hiram Revels became the first black U.S. senator in American history.

ANS: T   TOP: Political history, changes | The Black Officeholder   DIF: Difficult   REF: Full p. 573 | Seagull p. 580   MSC: Remembering   OBJ: 3

16. White southern Democrats considered scalawags traitors to both their party and their race.

ANS: T   TOP: Political history, changes | Carpetbaggers and Scalawags   DIF: Easy   REF: Full p. 575 | Seagull p. 581   MSC: Understanding   OBJ: 3

17. While Republicans were in power in the South, they established the region's first state-supported public schools.

ANS: T   TOP: Political history, changes | Southern Republicans in Power   DIF: Moderate   REF: Full p. 575 | Seagull p. 582   MSC: Remembering
OBJ: 3

18. Investment opportunities in the West lured more northern investors than in the South, and economic development in the South remained weak.

    ANS: T   TOP: Economic development | Geographic issues | The Quest for Prosperity   DIF: Difficult REF: Full p. 576 | Seagull p. 583 MSC: Understanding   OBJ: 3

19. Opponents of Radical Reconstruction could not accept the idea of former slaves voting, holding office, and enjoying equality before the law.

    ANS: T   TOP: Civil rights | Reconstruction's Opponents   DIF: Easy   REF: Full p. 577 | Seagull p. 584   MSC: Understanding   OBJ: 4

20. The Ku Klux Klan was an organization of the lower classes of the South—those who felt left out of white society.

    ANS: F   TOP: Civil rights | "A Reign of Terror" DIF: Moderate   REF: Full p. 578 | Seagull p. 585 MSC: Remembering   OBJ: 4

21. James Pike's *The Prostrate State* was in support of the black Republican governments in the South during Reconstruction.

    ANS: F   TOP: Civil rights | The North's Retreat DIF: Moderate   REF: Full p. 580 | Seagull pp. 586–587   MSC: Remembering   OBJ: 4

22. The 1873 depression strengthened the North's resolve to ensure the success of Reconstruction since the depression really hurt the South's farmers, highlighting the need for reform in the region.

    ANS: F   TOP: Economic development | Political history, changes | The North's Retreat   DIF: Moderate REF: Full p. 581 | Seagull p. 587 MSC: Understanding   OBJ: 4

23. The *Slaughterhouse Cases* are an example of the Supreme Court whittling away at the freedoms gained by the blacks during Reconstruction.

    ANS: T   TOP: Civil rights | Constitutional history | The North's Retreat   DIF: Moderate   REF: Full p. 581 | Seagull p. 589   MSC: Understanding OBJ: 4

24. In Mississippi in 1875, white rifle clubs drilled in public and openly assaulted and murdered Republicans.

    ANS: T   TOP: Social history | The Triumph of the Redeemers   DIF: Moderate   REF: Full p. 582 | Seagull p. 588   MSC: Remembering   OBJ: 4

25. As part of the Bargain of 1877, President Grant appointed a southerner to his cabinet.

ANS: F   TOP: Political history, changes | The Disputed Election and Bargain of 1877   DIF: Moderate REF: Full p. 583 | Seagull p. 589 MSC: Remembering   OBJ: 4

Short Answer

Identify and give the historical significance of each of the following terms, events, and people in a paragraph or two.

1. Fourteenth Amendment
2. Ku Klux Klan
3. Liberal Republicans
4. Andrew Johnson
5. sharecropping
6. black officeholders
7. Radical Republicans
8. Black Codes
9. Freedmen's Bureau
10. Fifteenth Amendment
11. Redeemers
12. feminists

Essay Questions

1. What did freedom mean for the ex-slaves? Be sure to address economic opportunities, gender roles, religious independence, and family security.

   ANS: Answers will vary   TOP: Civil rights | Economic development | Political history, changes | Social history | Blacks and the Meaning of Freedom | Families in Freedom | Church and School | Political Freedom   DIF: Moderate   MSC: Applying   OBJ: 1

2. Why did Radical Republicans believe that Andrew Johnson would support their agenda? Why was Johnson ultimately unable to lend his support to the Civil Rights Act of 1866 or to the Fourteenth Amendment?

   ANS: Answers will vary   TOP: Civil rights | Constitutional history | Political history, changes | Social history | The Radical Republicans | The Origins of Civil Rights | Andrew Johnson   DIF: Moderate MSC: Analyzing   OBJ: 2

3. For whites, freedom, no matter how defined, was a given, a birthright to be defended. For African-Americans, it was an open-ended process, a transformation of every aspect of their lives and of the society and culture that had sustained slavery in the first place. Defend this statement.

   ANS: Answers will vary   TOP: Civil rights | Economic development | Political history, changes | Social history | Blacks and the Meaning of Freedom

| Families in Freedom | Church and School | Political Freedom   DIF: Difficult   MSC: Evaluating   OBJ: 1

4. Explain how wartime devastation set in motion a train of events that permanently altered the white yeomanry's independent way of life, leading to what they considered a loss of freedom.

ANS: Answers will vary   TOP: Economic development | Political history, changes | Social history | The White Farmer   DIF: Moderate   MSC: Analyzing   OBJ: 1

5. Reconstruction witnessed profound changes in the lives of southerners, black and white, rich and poor. Explain the various ways that the lives of these groups changed. Were the changes for the better or worse?

ANS: Answers will vary   TOP: Civil rights | Economic development | Political history, changes | Social history | Toward a New South | Blacks and the Meaning of Freedom | Masters without Slaves | The White Farmer | Families in Freedom | Church and School | Political Freedom   DIF: Difficult   MSC: Evaluating   OBJ: 1 / 2 / 3

6. Stating that he "lived among men, not among angels," Thaddeus Stevens recognized that the Fourteenth Amendment was not perfect. Explain the strengths and weaknesses of the Fourteenth Amendment. What liberties and freedoms did it extend in the nineteenth century—and to whom? How did it alter the relationship between the federal government and the states?

ANS: Answers will vary.   TOP: Civil rights | Constitutional history | Economic development | Political history, changes | Social history | The Fourteenth Amendment | The Radical Republicans   DIF: Moderate   MSC: Evaluating   OBJ: 2

7. What faults did the Republicans see with Presidential Reconstruction? How did they propose to rectify those deficiencies? Be sure to distinguish moderate Republicans from Radical Republicans in your answer.

ANS: Answers will vary   TOP: Civil rights | Economic development | Political history, changes | Social history | The Failure of Presidential Reconstruction   DIF: Moderate   MSC: Analyzing   OBJ: 2 / 3

8. Who were the Redeemers, what did they want, and what were their methods? How did the Redeemers feel that their freedom was being threatened by Radical Reconstruction? Conclude your essay with a comment on how you think the federal government should have responded to the Redeemers.

ANS: Answers will vary   TOP: Civil rights | Political history, changes | Social history | The Triumph of the Redeemers   DIF: Moderate   MSC: Analyzing   OBJ: 3 / 4

9. Do you think the permanent distribution of land to former slaves would have made a difference in the outcome of Reconstruction? Why or why not?

ANS: Answers will vary   TOP: Civil rights | Economic development | Political history, changes | Social history | The Failure of Land Reform   DIF: Moderate   MSC: Evaluating   OBJ: 1 / 4

10. Was Reconstruction a success or a failure? Or was it something in between? In your response, consider land policy, key legislation during Presidential and Radical Reconstruction, southern politics, racial and political violence, and northern "fatigue" with Reconstruction. Be sure to make clear what you mean by success and failure.

ANS: Answers will vary   TOP: Civil rights | Constitutional history | Economic development | Political history, changes | Social history | The Reconstruction Act | The Failure of Presidential Reconstruction | The North's Retreat | The Failure of Land Reform | "A Reign of Terror" | The Tocsin of Freedom | Toward a New South | The Black Codes   DIF: Difficult   MSC: Evaluating   OBJ: 1 / 2 / 3 / 4

11. The debate surrounding the creation and ratification of the Fifteenth Amendment divided one-time political allies over the matter of women's suffrage. What were the arguments for and against including a woman's right to vote in the Fifteenth Amendment? What did this debate say about the boundaries of freedom defined by Reconstruction?

ANS: Answers will vary   TOP: Civil rights | Constitutional history | Political history, changes | Social history | The Fifteenth Amendment   DIF: Moderate   MSC: Analyzing   OBJ: 2

Appendix: Sample Final Exam

Multiple Choice

1. In the pre-Columbia Americas, some of the societies grandest in scale and organization were in present-day:
   a. Canada.
   b. Cuba and Puerto Rico.
   c. United States.
   d. Mexico and Central America.
   e. Brazil.

   ANS: D   TOP: Global awareness | Indian Societies of the Americas   DIF: Easy   MSC: Remembering

2. Europeans concluded that Indians were barbaric because they were:
   a. too free.
   b. good hunters.
   c. poor farmers.
   d. too accepting of Christianity.
   e. unwilling to trade.

   ANS: A   TOP: Ethnicity | Indian Freedom | European Freedom   DIF: Moderate   MSC: Understanding

3. In which country's colonies did the women have the most rights and independence?
   a. England
   b. France
   c. the Netherlands
   d. Spain
   e. Portugal

   ANS: C   TOP: Global awareness | Freedom in New Netherland   DIF: Moderate   MSC: Remembering

4. In the sixteenth century if a person was struggling economically in England, what might happen to him?
   a. He ended up living in a Church of England monastery.
   b. He was encouraged to leave for the New World.
   c. He was impressed into the navy.
   d. He was sent to Spain.
   e. He was given land in northern England.

   ANS: B   TOP: Global awareness | The Social Crisis   DIF: Difficult   MSC: Understanding

5. The early English southern colonies developed differently from the northern ones due to:
   a. seaports.
   b. Native Americans.
   c. language.
   d. cash crops.
   e. their varied terrain.

   ANS: D   TOP: Economic development | Geographic issues | Settling the Chesapeake | The New England Way   DIF: Difficult   MSC: Understanding

6. Which event set the stage for the absorption of Plymouth into Massachusetts?
   a. Salem Witch Trial
   b. Leisler's Rebellion
   c. King Philip's War
   d. Toleration Act
   e. Dominion of New England

   ANS: E   TOP: Political history, changes | Changes in New England   DIF: Moderate   MSC: Remembering

7. All of the following attracted settlers to the thirteen colonies EXCEPT:
   a. availability of land.
   b. lack of a military draft.

c. absence of restraints on economic opportunity.

d. less restrictions on religion.

e. trade alliances with Native Americans.

ANS: E   TOP: Political history, changes | Religious Diversity   DIF: Moderate   MSC: Remembering

8. The most common bond among Africans in America in the seventeenth century was:

a. kinship.

b. language.

c. race.

d. music.

e. slavery.

ANS: E   TOP: Civil rights | Cultural history | Becoming African-American   DIF: Moderate
MSC: Understanding

9. The middle ground that Native Americans faced in the Ohio River Valley was:

a. a passage to slavery.

b. a line preventing the English from settling in the West.

c. the best hunting grounds.

d. an area between European empires and Indian sovereignty.

e. the process of being converted to Christianity.

ANS: D   TOP: Ethnicity | Geographic issues | Religious Diversity   DIF: Moderate
MSC: Remembering

10. The final event in the Revolutionary period that culminated in the Continental Congress was the:

a. Intolerable Acts.

b. Boston Massacre.

c. Sugar Act.

d. Townshend Duties.

e. Stamp Act.

ANS: A   TOP: Political history, changes | The Continental Congress   DIF: Difficult
MSC: Understanding

11. In contrast to political writings in the 1760s, Thomas Paine's *Common Sense* in 1776:

a. broke the colonists' connection with their king.

b. stated that taxes were wrong

c. discussed reconciliation with Parliament.

d. focused on colonial slavery.

e. criticized trade regulations.

ANS: A   TOP: Political history, changes | *Common Sense*   DIF: Difficult   MSC: Understanding

12. George Washington's strategy in fighting the American Revolution was:

a. to focus on the South to protect slavery.

b. to keep his army together as long as possible.

c. not to let the French aid the colonies.

d. to repeatedly attack the British forces.

e. to hold onto Philadelphia, where the Continental Congress resided.

ANS: B   TOP: Military history | The First Years of the War   DIF: Difficult   MSC: Understanding

13. The American Revolution and then the War of 1812 saw the Native Americans in the Ohio River Valley _____ land.

a. mostly gain

b. mostly lose

c. flee from all of their

d. retain their

e. sell all of their

ANS: B   TOP: Ethnicity | Geographic issues | The Indians' Revolution | The War's Aftermath
DIF: Moderate   MSC: Remembering

14. Which war sparked the process of abolition of slaves in the North?

a. Civil War

b. War of 1812

c. American Revolution

d. Mexican-American War

e. French and Indian War

ANS: C   TOP: Civil rights | Abolition in the North
DIF: Easy   MSC: Remembering

15. A difference between Shays's Rebellion when compared to the Whiskey Rebellion was:

a. Shays's Rebellion involved taxes while the Whiskey Rebellion did not.

b. The Whiskey Rebellion was an urban conflict, but Shays's Rebellion was in the countryside.

c. The Whiskey Rebellion destroyed the public's confidence in the national government while Shays's Rebellion added to government support.

d. A state government stopped Shays's Rebellion while the national government put down the Whiskey Rebellion.

e. Shays's Rebellion occurred during the American Revolution and the Whiskey Rebellion was after it.

ANS: D   TOP: Political history, changes | Shays's Rebellion | The Whiskey Rebellion   DIF: Difficult
MSC: Understanding

16. Which document was the first constitution of the United States?

a. Magna Carta

b. Bill of Rights

c. Articles of Confederation

d. Declaration of Independence

e. Constitution

ANS: C   DIF: Easy   TOP: Constitutional history | The Articles of Confederation   MSC: Remembering

17. What happened during Washington's first term?
    a. The president came close to being impeached.
    b. Washington actively pursued a monarchy.
    c. His cabinet disagreed on how to interpret the Constitution.
    d. The government collapsed.
    e. He worked with Thomas Jefferson to give more rights to the states.

    ANS: C   DIF: Moderate   TOP: Constitutional history | Political history, changes | The Emergence of Opposition   MSC: Remembering

18. In the late eighteenth century, what did female writers emphasize with regard to women's rights?
    a. education
    b. voting
    c. free speech
    d. divorce rights
    e. property rights

    ANS: A   DIF: Moderate   TOP: Social history | The Rights of Women   MSC: Remembering

19. How were political parties different in the 1790s when compared to the 1830s?
    a. In the 1830s, they were societies that discussed political issues.
    b. By the 1830s, they were weaker and more ineffectual than the 1790s.
    c. By the 1830s, they had grown to avert sectionalism and held national conventions.
    d. In the 1830s, they only served ceremonial purposes and held toasts.
    e. In the 1790s, they used newspapers more for promoting their ideas and candidates.

    ANS: C   TOP: Political history, changes |Political Parties | Martin Van Buren and the Democratic Party | The Party System   DIF: Difficult   MSC: Understanding

20. The various push-pull factors forcing people to leave Europe and come to the United States included all of the following EXCEPT:
    a. potato famine.
    b. cotton farming.
    c. failed political revolutions.
    d. promise of jobs.
    e. family already living in the United States.

    ANS: B   TOP: Ethnicity | Geographic issues | Irish and German Newcomers   DIF: Moderate   MSC: Understanding

21. All of the following cities were frequent destinations for German immigrants in the nineteenth century EXCEPT:

    a. Atlanta.
    b. New York.
    c. St. Louis.
    d. Milwaukee.
    e. Cincinnati.

    ANS: A   TOP: Ethnicity | Geographic issues | Irish and German Newcomers   DIF: Moderate   MSC: Remembering

22. When comparing the eighteenth century Great Awakening to the Second Great Awakening:
    a. the earlier one led to more abolitionism.
    b. the later one did not focus on alcohol.
    c. both did not increase church attendance.
    d. the later one stressed more the idea of personal choice in spiritual matters.
    e. the earlier one did not have revivals.

    ANS: D   TOP: Cultural history | The Awakening's Impact   DIF: Moderate   MSC: Understanding

23. Compared to the "cult of domesticity," the earlier "republican motherhood" had emphasized women:
    a. doing more housework.
    b. having fewer children.
    c. doing factory work.
    d. being more virtuous.
    e. playing a small public role.

    ANS: E   TOP: Social history | The Cult of Domesticity   DIF: Moderate   MSC: Understanding

24. The Whigs most resembled which other political party?
    a. the Whigs from England because they stood for the average citizen rather than an aristocracy
    b. the Federalists because of their support for wealthy businessmen
    c. Jeffersonian Republicans who advocated for an agrarian nation
    d. the Democrats of the 1850s who advocated for states' rights
    e. the Free Soil Party, which focused on the extension of slavery as the primary component of their platform

    ANS: B   TOP: Political history, changes | Political Parties | Democrats and Whigs   DIF: Difficult   MSC: Understanding

25. Which of the following politicians was never elected president in the nineteenth century?
    a. Henry Clay
    b. James Monroe
    c. Franklin Pierce
    d. Martin Van Buren
    e. Zachary Taylor

ANS: A   TOP: Political history, changes | The
    Election of 1824   DIF: Moderate
MSC: Understanding

26. The Washington administration encouraged Indians to
    _____ while the Jackson administration
    promoted a policy of _____ for the Indians.
    a. assimilate . . . genocide
    b. go west . . . cultural autonomy
    c. assimilate . . . removal
    d. fight each other . . . removal
    e. go west . . . assimilation

    ANS: C   TOP: Ethnicity | Political history, changes |
        Indians in the New Nation | Indian Removal
    DIF: Difficult   MSC: Understanding

27. All of the following events deal with the role of
    government EXCEPT:
    a. Bacon's Rebellion.
    b. the Great Awakening.
    c. the Albany Plan.
    d. the nullification crisis.
    e. the Hartford Convention.

    ANS: B   TOP: Political history, changes | Bacon's
        Rebellion: Land and Labor in Virginia | The Great
        Awakening | Colonial Identities | The End of the
        Federalist Party | The Nullification Crisis
    DIF: Difficult   MSC: Understanding

28. All of the following events focused on the expansion of
    slavery EXCEPT:
    a. the Missouri Compromise.
    b. the aftermath of Georgia becoming a royal
       colony.
    c. the opening up of Japan.
    d. the Northwest Ordinance of 1787.
    e. the Compromise of 1850.

    ANS: B   TOP: Political history, changes | The
        Georgia Experiment | The Land Ordinances | The
        Missouri Controversy | Opening Japan | Crisis and
        Compromise   DIF: Difficult   MSC: Understanding

29. All of the following were grand statements supporting
    states' rights EXCEPT:
    a. the Hartford Convention.
    b. *Exposition and Protest.*
    c. the Kentucky resolution.
    d. the Virginia resolution.
    e. *Federalist* no. 10.

    ANS: E   TOP: Constitutional history | Political his-
        tory, changes | "Extend the Sphere" | The Virginia
        and Kentucky Resolutions | The End of the Federal-
        ist Party | Calhoun's Political Theory
    DIF: Difficult   MSC: Understanding

30. In the mid-nineteenth century, what did many
    slaveowners such as John Calhoun say about the
    Declaration of Independence?
    a. It must be adhered to at all costs.
    b. Jefferson was a slave owner so slavery was justified.
    c. Not all men were created equal.
    d. There was no happiness to pursue.
    e. Jefferson's statement criticizing slavery should be
       restored to the document.

    ANS: C   TOP: Civil rights | The Proslavery Argument
        DIF: Difficult   MSC: Understanding

31. When compared to their counterparts in the West
    Indies and Brazil, American slaves experienced all of
    the following EXCEPT:
    a. malaria.
    b. better diets.
    c. paternalism.
    d. longer life expectancy.
    e. lower infant mortality.

    ANS: A   TOP: Civil rights | Social history | The Pro-
        slavery Argument   DIF: Difficult
    MSC: Understanding

32. In the nineteenth century, most of the slaves who
    escaped permanently were from:
    a. Virginia and Maryland.
    b. Mississippi.
    c. Alabama.
    d. Georgia and Florida.
    e. North Carolina and South Carolina.

    ANS: A   TOP: Civil rights | Social history | Fugitive
        Slaves   DIF: Easy   MSC: Remembering

33. What happened in the wake of both the Stono
    Rebellion and Nat Turner's Rebellion?
    a. Slavery was abolished in South Carolina and
       Virginia, respectively.
    b. The importation of slaves ended.
    c. Slaves were no longer taught Christianity.
    d. Since it was seen to anger slaves, the breaking up of
       slaves through sales was prohibited.
    e. Slave codes and laws became more restrictive.

    ANS: E   TOP: Civil rights | Social history | The Crisis
        of 1739–1741 | Nat Turner's Rebellion
    DIF: Easy   MSC: Remembering

34. The year 1831 marked a turning point for the Old
    South as white southerners closed ranks and defended
    slavery more strongly than ever because of which two
    events?
    a. slave trade embargo and the *Amistad* rebellion
    b. start of the Underground Railroad and
       abolitionism

c. Gold was discovered in Georgia and the Vesey rebellion plot was uncovered.

d. start of *The Liberator* and Nat Turner's Rebellion

e. Frederick Douglass escaped the gag rule established in Congress.

ANS: D   TOP: Civil rights | Nat Turner's Rebellion | The Emergence of Garrison   DIF: Moderate   MSC: Remembering

35. All of the following were examples of Utopian societies EXCEPT:
a. New Harmony.
b. Know-Nothings.
c. Shakers.
d. Oneida.
e. Owenites.

ANS: B   TOP: Social history | The Shakers | Oneida | The Owenites   DIF: Moderate   MSC: Remembering

36. By 1860, the only professional job where women were the majority of workers involved:
a. law.
b. religion.
c. factories.
d. communications.
e. education.

ANS: E   TOP: Social history | The Common School   DIF: Moderate   MSC: Remembering

37. Frederick Douglass and other abolitionists in the 1840s and 1850s disagreed with the idea of colonization with regard to ex-slaves primarily because:
a. to them slaves were just as American as whites.
b. of the monetary cost involved.
c. of the long voyage to Africa.
d. no ex-slaves were interested in missionary work.
e. they did not want to be later colonizers.

ANS: A   TOP: Social history | Blacks and Colonization   DIF: Moderate   MSC: Understanding

38. By the middle of the nineteenth century, what was the best way for women to participate in the political process?
a. vote in a presidential election
b. be an active member of a political party
c. lecture in public about an issue
d. run for political office
e. serve as an editor of a major daily city newspaper

ANS: C   TOP: Social history | The Rise of the Public Woman   DIF: Moderate   MSC: Understanding

39. The Missouri Compromise, Compromise of 1850, and Kansas-Nebraska Act focused primarily on which issue?
a. tariffs
b. abolition
c. extension of slavery
d. railroad building
e. Native American rights

ANS: C   TOP: Geographic issues | Political history, changes | The Missouri Controversy | Crisis and Compromise | The Kansas-Nebraska Act   DIF: Difficult   MSC: Understanding

40. All of the following were part of Lincoln's views on slavery EXCEPT:
a. he disliked how critics called the United States a nation of hypocrites because of slavery.
b. he felt the idea of enslaving people was an injustice.
c. he wanted to stop the extension of slavery.
d. he saw blacks as fully equal.
e. he wanted labor—black or white—to be free.

ANS: D   TOP: Civil rights | Political history, changes | Lincoln and Slavery   DIF: Difficult   MSC: Understanding

41. How did President Buchanan react when seven southern states seceded?
a. He denied that a state could secede, but also insisted that the federal government could not use force.
b. He sent troops to South Carolina to try to end secession, but the Union troops fired the first shot at Fort Sumter.
c. He accepted secession and began diplomacy with the Confederate states.
d. He promised the South that he would restore slavery in northern states like Massachusetts.
e. He acted as a forceful president, but this course of action did not work.

ANS: A   TOP: Political history, changes | The Secession Crisis   DIF: Difficult   MSC: Understanding

42. At the start of the Civil War, the Union army had the following advantages over the Confederates EXCEPT:
a. more guns.
b. the ability to fight a defensive war.
c. more manpower.
d. a larger navy.
e. more textiles.

ANS: B   TOP: Military history | Mobilizing Resources   DIF: Easy   MSC: Remembering

43. The two Union generals who were able to successfully carry out the strategy of a war of attrition were:
    a. Pickett and Stuart.
    b. Meade and Sickles.
    c. Burnside and McClellan.
    d. Hooker and Farragut.
    e. Grant and Sherman.

    ANS: E TOP: Military history | 1864 | Victory at Last DIF: Moderate MSC: Remembering

44. An advantage Lincoln had over Confederate President Jefferson Davis was that the Union president:
    a. was a bigger physical presence.
    b. did not gain England as an ally.
    c. had better generals.
    d. was better at communicating the war's importance.
    e. had no political parties to help organize the war effort.

    ANS: D TOP: Political history, changes | Leadership and Government DIF: Moderate MSC: Understanding

45. Ironically, (the) _____ freed virtually no slaves at the beginning of 1863.
    a. *Exposition and Protest*
    b. *The Liberator*
    c. Emancipation Proclamation
    d. Gettysburg Address
    e. second inaugural address of Abraham Lincoln

    ANS: C TOP: Political history, changes | The Emancipation Proclamation DIF: Moderate MSC: Understanding

46. An institution black southerners started to control during Reconstruction was:
    a. manufacturing.
    b. the post office.
    c. the patent office.
    d. churches.
    e. the military.

    ANS: D TOP: Social history | Church and School DIF: Moderate MSC: Remembering

47. What made the Declaration of Independence more of a reality for African Americans?
    a. celebrating July 4
    b. passage of the Thirteenth and Fourteenth Amendments
    c. rewriting the document to reflect race
    d. giving them their former slaveowners' land
    e. condemning Thomas Jefferson as a slaveowner

    ANS: B TOP: Political history, changes | The Great Constitutional Revolution DIF: Moderate MSC: Remembering

48. The biggest failure during the Reconstruction period was:
    a. not using legal and military means to stop the Ku Klux Klan in the South.
    b. not allowing African-Americans to serve in the House of Representatives and Senate.
    c. not providing an amendment to protect the right to vote for black men.
    d. that African-Americans were not declared citizens.
    e. that no help was given to African-Americans to achieve land ownership in the South.

    ANS: E TOP: Political history, changes | The Radical Republicans DIF: Difficult MSC: Understanding

49. What was NOT a factor in helping to bring about an end to Reconstruction?
    a. The Supreme Court asserted that most rights of citizens are under the control of state governments rather than the federal government.
    b. An economic depression drew northern attention away from issues in the South.
    c. Racism in the North increased, leading some to see blacks as unfit to lead.
    d. The Redeemers used the Ku Klux Klan and violence to regain control of state governments.
    e. Northern politicians grew tired of hearing about perceived corruption in the South.

    ANS: A TOP: Political history, changes | The North's Retreat DIF: Difficult MSC: Understanding

50. With the close of Reconstruction, the United States in 1877 had achieved all of the following EXCEPT:
    a. extended railroad lines across the continent.
    b. removal of most of the Indians from the eastern United States.
    c. giving women the right to vote through a national amendment.
    d. establishing the idea of government-run schools in many states.
    e. creating a factory system for the mass manufacturing of textile goods.

    ANS: C TOP: Economic development | Ethnicity | Political history, changes | Social history | The Factory System | The Supreme Court and the Indians | The Common School | Building the Transcontinental Railroad | Feminists and Radicals DIF: Easy MSC: Remembering

True or False

1. If Johannes Gutenberg's invention had not been part of fifteenth-century Europe, then it might have taken longer to spread information about Columbus's voyages.

   ANS: T   TOP: Global awareness | Social history | Exploration and Conquest   DIF: Moderate
   MSC: Understanding

2. The Catholic Church did not play a significant role in the administration of Spanish colonies.

   ANS: F   TOP: Global awareness | Political history, changes | Governing Spanish America
   DIF: Moderate   MSC: Understanding

3. In the seventeenth century, it was more common for an African slave in the South to gain his freedom than it was in the eighteenth century.

   ANS: T   TOP: Civil rights | Slavery and the Law
   DIF: Moderate   MSC: Understanding

4. When compared to the Spanish and French colonies, the English colonies sent more families as permanent settlers.

   ANS: T   TOP: Geographic issues | A Diverse Population   DIF: Moderate
   MSC: Understanding

5. Slave labor was not connected to the growth and prosperity of all thirteen British colonies.

   ANS: F   TOP: Economic development | Geographic issues | Atlantic Trade   DIF: Moderate
   MSC: Understanding

6. Before 1763, Parliament had never taxed or regulated the thirteen colonies.

   ANS: F   TOP: Political history, changes | Taxing the Colonies   DIF: Moderate   MSC: Remembering

7. By the 1790s, the Declaration of Independence's idea of "all men are created equal" had become a reality for all males in the United States.

   ANS: F   TOP: Civil rights | The Global Declaration of Independence   DIF: Moderate
   MSC: Remembering

8. With regard to religion, the founders of the nation who were Deists deemphasized religious biblical doctrine, but valued the morals that organized religion taught.

   ANS: T   TOP: Cultural history | The Founders and Religion | Christian Republicanism   DIF: Moderate
   MSC: Remembering

9. As a result of the American Revolution, the majority of women began to participate directly in the political process.

   ANS: F   TOP: Social history | Gender and Politics
   DIF: Moderate   MSC: Remembering

10. Slave rebellions were much more common in the nineteenth century than in the colonial period.

    ANS: F   TOP: Civil rights | The Crisis of 1739–1741 | Nat Turner's Rebellion   DIF: Moderate
    MSC: Remembering

11. Neither the Constitution nor the Declaration of Independence ended slavery.

    ANS: T   TOP: Primary document analysis | The Declaration of Independence | Slavery in the Constitution   DIF: Moderate   MSC: Remembering

12. During the debate over ratification of the Constitution, the Anti-Federalists had more control over city and town newspapers.

    ANS: F   TOP: Constitutional history | The Anti-Federalists   DIF: Moderate
    MSC: Remembering

13. Two presidents who opposed the idea of a national banking system were Thomas Jefferson and Andrew Jackson.

    ANS: T   TOP: Economic development | Political history, changes | The Jefferson-Hamilton Bargain | Biddle's Bank   DIF: Moderate
    MSC: Remembering

14. Thomas Jefferson contradicted his ideals on a limited role for the national government by orchestrating the Louisiana Purchase.

    ANS: T   TOP: Geographic issues | Political history, changes | The Louisiana Purchase   DIF: Moderate
    MSC: Understanding

15. In the North, the market revolution and westward expansion transformed the region into an integrated economy of subsistence farms connected to manufacturing cities.

    ANS: F   TOP: Economic development | Geographic issues | Commercial Farmers   DIF: Difficult
    MSC: Understanding

16. Immigrants went in bigger numbers to the South than the North because there was a higher demand for labor.

    ANS: F   TOP: Ethnicity | Geographic issues | The Growth of Immigration   DIF: Moderate
    MSC: Understanding

17. Some of the harshest conditions American slaves faced were in Louisiana sugar fields.

    ANS: T   TOP: Civil rights | Social history | Gang Labor and Task Labor   DIF: Moderate   MSC: Remembering

18. In the nineteenth century, more slaves were Christian than in the colonial period.

    ANS: T   TOP: Civil rights | Cultural history | Slave Religion   DIF: Moderate   MSC: Remembering

19. Lack of public education in the North widened the divide between North and South.

    ANS: T   TOP: Social history | The Common School   DIF: Moderate   MSC: Remembering

20. Abolitionists such as William Lloyd Garrison and Frederick Douglass played a bigger role in ending slavery than abolitionists who wanted to use the colonization method.

    ANS: T   TOP: Civil rights | Social history | Colonization | Militant Abolitionism   DIF: Moderate   MSC: Understanding

21. In the 1840s and 1850s, William Lloyd Garrison saw more potential with the Constitution ending slavery than Frederick Douglass did.

    ANS: F   TOP: Civil rights | Social history | A New Vision of America   DIF: Moderate   MSC: Understanding

22. At the Seneca Falls Convention of 1848, woman's suffrage was not part of the Declaration of Sentiments.

    ANS: F   TOP: Social history | Women's Rights   DIF: Moderate   MSC: Remembering

23. Leaders such as Frederick Douglass and Elizabeth Cady Stanton were trying to make the ideals of the Declaration of Independence a reality for all Americans regardless of race or gender.

    ANS: T   TOP: Civil rights | Social history | Slavery and American Freedom | Women's Rights   DIF: Easy   MSC: Remembering

24. Republicans were not abolitionists, but wanted to stop the extension of slavery into new territory.

    ANS: T   TOP: Political history, changes | The Free Labor Ideology   DIF: Moderate   MSC: Remembering

25. Rather than accept permanent minority status in a nation governed by their opponents, Deep South political leaders boldly pushed for secession.

    ANS: T   TOP: Political history, changes | The Secession Crisis   DIF: Moderate   MSC: Understanding

26. Unlike the patriots in the American Revolution, the Confederates were willing to employ primarily a defensive strategy during the Civil War.

    ANS: F   TOP: Military history | The First Years of the War | Military Strategies   DIF: Moderate   MSC: Understanding

27. Few groups of rebels in history have been treated more leniently than the defeated Confederates of the Civil War.

    ANS: T   TOP: Political history, changes | The Black Codes   DIF: Moderate   MSC: Understanding

Short Answer

Identify and give the historical significance of each of the following terms, events, and people in a paragraph or two.

1. Indian concepts of freedom and views on the land
2. Spanish colonization in North America
3. English Civil War and Glorious Revolution
4. indentured servants
5. colonial slavery
6. Great Awakening
7. Thomas Paine
8. religious freedom and toleration in late eighteenth century
9. creating and ratifying the Constitution
10. Alexander Hamilton
11. market economy
12. Andrew Jackson as president
13. life under slavery in the antebellum South
14. abolitionism
15. women's rights movement
16. Kansas-Nebraska Act
17. Abraham Lincoln as president
18. Robert E. Lee
19. Emancipation Proclamation
20. Radical Republican Reconstruction

Essay Questions

1. Compare how the Spanish, French, Dutch, and English established and governed their colonies in North America. How did each of these European groups relate to the Indians? What were the reasons behind the culture clash between Europeans and Native Americans?

   ANS: Answers will vary   TOP: Ethnicity | Geographic issues | Global awareness | Political history, changes | Social history | Indian Freedom | European

Freedom | The Spanish Empire | The French and Dutch Empires | The Coming of the English | Settling the Chesapeake | The New England Way | Global Competition and the Expansion of England's Empire   DIF: Moderate   MSC: Understanding

2. Compare the American Revolution to the Civil War with regard to sovereignty. Did the northern role in the government resemble the British in the Revolutionary period? Ultimately, was the South fighting a second War for Independence?

   ANS: Answers will vary   TOP: Political history, changes | Social history | The Crisis Begins | The Road to Revolution | The Coming of Independence | A Dose of Arsenic | The Rise of the Republican Party | The Impending Crisis | The Coming of Emancipation | The Second American Revolution
   DIF: Moderate   MSC: Analyzing

3. In the Civil War, did Robert E. Lee follow similar military strategies as George Washington in the American Revolution? Which general had a more difficult task? Why were the colonists able to win their fight for independence, but not the Confederates?

   ANS: Answers will vary   TOP: Military history | Securing Independence | The First Modern War | Turning Points   DIF: Moderate   MSC: Analyzing

4. Discuss the evolution of slavery in the United States. Compare colonial slavery to antebellum with regard to resistance and the role of religion. Did slave culture change over time? What were the owners like in the colonial era? What about the antebellum? What shaped the methods of control in each period?

   ANS: Answers will vary   TOP: Civil rights | Cultural history | Social history | Origins of American Slavery | Slavery and Empire | Slave Culture and Slave Resistance | An Empire of Freedom | The Old South | Life under Slavery | Slave Culture | Resistance to Slavery   DIF: Difficult   MSC: Understanding

5. Compare the first Great Awakening to the Second Great Awakening. Discuss how each Awakening changed American society. Which played a more prominent role in influencing American society?

   ANS: Answers will vary   TOP: Cultural history | Social history | The Great Awakening | The Second Great Awakening | Religion and Reform
   DIF: Moderate   MSC: Evaluating

6. Analyze the role of women in American society from 1607–1877. How did European/American women compare to their counterparts in Native American societies?

In what century did American women have the most say in shaping and influencing society? Was the influence more from the public or private sphere?

   ANS: Answers will vary   TOP: Political history, changes | Social history | Indian Gender Relations | European Views of the Indians | Powhatan and Pocahontas | Women and the Family | The Puritan Family | The Trials of Anne Hutchinson | Women and the Household Economy | Daughters of Liberty | The Rights of Women | Women and the Republic | The Origins of Feminism | The Fifteenth Amendment | The Rights of Women | Feminists and Radicals   DIF: Moderate
   MSC: Analyzing

7. Examine the migrations to the thirteen colonies of various groups from Europe and analyze the diversity of colonial society. How did this diversity compare to the nineteenth century when immigrants arrived by the millions in the United States? Analyze how the native-born Americans reacted to these foreigners. What role did being of English heritage and Protestant play?

   ANS: Answers will vary   TOP: Ethnicity | Social history | The Coming of the English | Settling the Chesapeake | The New England Way | Global Competition and the Expansion of England's Empire | The Growth of Colonial America | Market Society | The Rise and Fall of the Know-Nothings
   DIF: Moderate   MSC: Analyzing

8. Discuss Hamilton and Jefferson's interpretations of the Constitution, the role of the national government, and visions for what American society should be. By 1877, evaluate whose ideas on governing and visions had become more realized.

   ANS: Answers will vary   TOP: Constitutional history | Political history, changes | Social history | Politics in an Age of Passion | Jefferson in Power
   DIF: Moderate   MSC: Evaluating

9. By focusing on five key presidents—Washington, Jefferson, Jackson, Lincoln, and Grant—discuss the evolution and role of the presidency from 1789–1877.

   ANS: Answers will vary   TOP: Constitutional history | Political history, changes | Politics in an Age of Passion | Jefferson in Power | The Age of Jackson | The Bank War and After | The Coming of Emancipation | The Second American Revolution | Rehearsals for Reconstruction and the End of the War | The Making of Radical Reconstruction | Radical Reconstruction in the South | The Overthrow of Reconstruction   DIF: Difficult   MSC: Understanding

10. With regard to economics and social aspects, compare the development of the North with the South. How were these regions connected? How did their development into two different societies lead to secession and a Civil War?

    ANS: Answers will vary   TOP: Economic development | Ethnicity | Social history | A New Economy | Market Society | The Free Individual | The Limits of Prosperity | The Old South | Life under Slavery | Slave Culture | Resistance to Slavery
    DIF: Moderate   MSC: Analyzing

11. Was slavery the primary cause of the Civil War? Explain. In any scenario could the Civil War have been avoided?

    ANS: Answers will vary   TOP: Economic development | Ethnicity | Social history | Fruits of Manifest Destiny | A Dose of Arsenic | The Rise of the Republican Party | The Emergence of Lincoln | The Impending Crisis   DIF: Moderate
    MSC: Evaluating

12. Did Reconstruction establish the ideals of the Declaration of Independence? In other words, had "all men are created equal" and "Life, Liberty and the pursuit of Happiness" been realized and achieved both politically and economically?

    ANS: Answers will vary   TOP: Civil rights | Economic development | Political history, changes | Social history | The Meaning of Freedom | The Making of Radical Reconstruction | Radical Reconstruction in the South | The Overthrow of Reconstruction   DIF: Moderate   MSC: Analyzing

13. Discuss the development of freedom, liberty, and equality in colonial America up through 1877. How was the development different for whites, blacks, Native Americans, and women?

    ANS: Answers will vary   TOP: Civil rights | Political history, changes | Social history | Indian Freedom, European Freedom | The Overthrow of Reconstruction   DIF: Difficult   MSC: Understanding